FRIENDLY PRESS

Editor and Designer—Stu Waldman and Marty Goldstein
Publisher—Peggy Flaum
Jacket Photo—Grant Peterson
Editorial Assistants—Robin Wasserman, Kirk Oliphant and Lecia Wood
Production—Sharon Kaplan, Celia Brayley, Meggin Chinkel Siefert,
          Anne Bobinta Rix and Cynthia Rhett

Articles Editor—Brant Mewborn
Photo Editor—Laurie Kratochvil
Photo Research—Valerie Vogel and Margery Goldberg
Copy Editor—Jay Martel
Research Editor—Steve Futterman
Permissions Editor—Mary Astadourian

Special thanks to Sarah Lazin, Carol LeFluffy,
Paul Grushkin at Bill Graham Presents.
And the Grateful Dead for the title.

BOMC offers recordings and compact discs, cassettes
and records. For information and catalog write to
BOMR, Camp Hill, PA 17012.

Published by Friendly Press, Inc.,
401 Park Avenue South, New York City 10016, United States of America.

Typography by Cardinal Type Service, Inc., New York City.

Text films and separations prepared by Dai Nippon Printing Co., Tokyo, Japan.

Printed by R.R. Donnelley and Sons, Co., Willard, Ohio, United States of America.

Library of Congress Cataloging-in-Publication Data

What a Long Strange Trip It's Been.
1. Music, Popular (Songs, etc.)—History and criticism.
2. Rock music—History and criticism. I. Rolling Stone.
ML3470.W48 1987   784.5'4'09047   87-8511
ISBN # 0-914919-10-5

20 YEARS OF

WHAT A LONG, STRANGE TRIP IT'S BEEN

EDITED BY JANN S.WENNER

May you grow up to be righteous,
May you grow up to be true,
May you always know the truth
And see the lights surrounding you.
May you always be courageous,
Stand upright and be strong,
May you stay forever young,

May you stay forever young.
—BOB DYLAN, *"Forever Young"*

This collection is dedicated to:

The people who started ROLLING STONE, particularly my wife, Jane.
And Ralph J. Gleason, and Tess and Arthur Schindelheim, Sim Wenner,
Ed Wenner and Dorothy Wenner, Joan Roos and Bob and Linda Kingsbury.
The people who, understanding what ROLLING STONE was about,
gave their time, energy and faith to publishing ROLLING STONE, running the offices
and running the company, and the writers, editors and artists
who made great personal and professional contributions throughout the years.
With this enormous assembly of talent, ROLLING STONE grew and grew.
And to the musicians and artists whose work inspired us;
to our readers, every one, who have kept ROLLING STONE alive.

Contents

CHAPTER II: 1971-1974

CHAPTER III: 1975-1979

CHAPTER IV: 1980-1987

Introduction

To commemorate the twentieth anniversary of ROLLING STONE, we undertook this book, along with special issues of the magazine, in an effort to understand two decades in the social, cultural and political history of America, which, however provocative and powerful in our imagination, have not yet been thoughtfully—often not even accurately—accounted for.

The pieces in this book form an impressionistic chronology that attempts to suggest some of the ideas and events of the last twenty years and the experiences of a generation. This collection is not meant to be *the* best of ROLLING STONE; many excellent ROLLING STONE writers and articles could not be included. Rather, this anthology is intended to convey the passage of time and a sense of recent history.

For reasons of space and sometimes readability (in-depth reporting beyond the call of duty was an indulgence of our earlier years), the articles that are included in this anthology have been carefully trimmed. We also took advantage of hindsight to correct some factual errors and smooth out the rougher edges of deadline writing and editing. Otherwise, these articles appear the way they were.

From the very outset of the magazine in 1967, we made a point of commissioning serious, comprehensive interviews with musicians and artists, much as *The Paris Review* had done with writers. In 1970, John Lennon was bursting to tell the truth about the Beatles, who had until then been sealed off from the public; he spoke without restraint. It was the agonized, feet-of-clay brilliance of John Lennon; it was history being made. Several years after my interview with Pete Townshend, he told me that it was during the course of our talks that he first fully formulated the concept for *Tommy*.

Jonathan Cott, one of ROLLING STONE's most prolific and catholic interviewers, was on the masthead of our first issue; we knew each other as students in Berkeley. Jonathan did our first interview with Mick Jagger, in 1968, and his interview with Jagger a decade later is perhaps one of the best ever done with rock's most disarming and evasive artist. In 1968 Jonathan also did the first ROLLING STONE interview with John Lennon, and in 1980 he did the last.

Jerry Hopkins was operating a head shop in Los Angeles in 1968, when he saw an ad in ROLLING STONE soliciting new writers. He submitted an article on Jim Morrison and soon became a full-time ROLLING STONE correspondent. Joe Eszterhas was a star reporter for *The Cleveland Plain-Dealer* in 1968, when he first visited the ROLLING STONE offices to buy some back issues. Joe recalls having had the distinct feeling that he was perceived as an undercover narcotics agent by the staff. A few years later, he joined our staff and wrote many reports on undercover narcotics operations.

In 1974 Howard Kohn, a young refugee from a stunning career with *The Detroit Free Press*, was hired by ROLLING STONE editor David Felton to write a series on the Karen Silkwood case. David, another fugitive from big-time daily journalism (at *The Los Angeles Times*), had been hired to cover the Charles Manson case, for which we won our first National Magazine Award. During the course of the Silkwood assignment, Howard developed an inside line on Patty Hearst. The kidnapped heiress had eluded a massive national manhunt, but ROLLING STONE went to press with the exclusive tale of her year on the lam the very week she was caught. Featured as the lead on the three network newscasts and on page one of nearly every newspaper in the United States, it turned out to be the biggest scoop in ROLLING STONE's history.

The first time I met Hunter S. Thompson, he arrived in my office, two hours late, wearing a curly, bubble-style wig and carrying a six-pack of beer in one hand and his leather satchel stuffed with notebooks, newspapers, tape recorders, booze, et cetera, in the other. He was wearing the wig because he had shaved his head during his bid to become sheriff of Pitkin County, Colorado. The story of that campaign, "Freak Power in the Rockies," was his first piece in ROLLING STONE, and we never quite stopped. Hunter began writing *Fear and Loathing in Las Vegas* in the basement of my home in San Francisco. In 1971 he became our full-time correspondent and moved to Washington, D.C., to cover the 1972 presidential election. Hunter's work in ROLLING STONE became legend; it changed things for everyone. Hunter became an extraordinary and celebrated literary figure, ROLLING STONE became a meaningful voice in national affairs, and political reporting and writing were forever restyled and reshaped. It was one of those rare, fated, supercharged collaborations.

In early 1968 Charles Perry became ROLLING STONE's first salaried employee, at twenty-five dollars a week. Charlie, an expert in Near Eastern languages and cuisine, became the unlikely guardian of the spirit of irony and hipness that was the soul of ROLLING STONE. Later on, he was entrusted with the responsibility of telling the story of the Haight-Ashbury. "From Eternity to Here," which Charlie later published as a book (*The Haight-Ashbury: A History*), sprang from an idea suggested to me by Hunter, and it now stands as the truth about those times.

In 1971 we succeeded in enlisting Tom Wolfe to cover the last Apollo flights. His articles appeared in a four-part series titled "Post Orbital Remorse: The Brotherhood of the Right Stuff." ("The Right Stuff" was Tom's phrase; I added "The Brotherhood.") Tom's reports were filed in the then-typical ROLLING STONE style: last-minute deadlines, with manuscripts transmitted by telecopier ("the mojo wire," as Hunter dubbed it). How proud we were: Tom Wolfe in ROLLING STONE. And *The Right Stuff* turned out to be a classic. Twelve years later, we collaborated on another major work, *The Bonfire of the Vanities*, a full-length novel serialized in ROLLING STONE over an entire year.

Annie Leibovitz came to ROLLING STONE in 1969, when she was an art-school student; Bob Kingsbury, the magazine's first great art director, had spotted her. For ten years as our staff photographer, she dominated the look and feel of ROLLING STONE. She was a member of an inner circle of talents at the magazine who found their own identities while shaping ROLLING STONE's. Her last assignment for ROLLING STONE turned out to be the last photo sessions with John Lennon. The power of Annie's gift and John Lennon's statement in those portraits should be compared to the portrait they made a decade earlier, on the first assignment Annie did for ROLLING STONE.

In 1975 I took Annie to lunch with Dick Avedon at his studio in New York. In looking for ideas and directions for Annie and ROLLING STONE, I had been following Avedon's work. Avedon, who I feel is America's greatest living photographer, had also learned and polished his craft at a magazine. Soon after, Dick took our assignment to do portraits of the 1976 presidential candidates and reformulated it into portraits of the entire power structure of America. They were published in a single issue and titled "The Family."

I have shared the editing of ROLLING STONE with many people over the years. (Brant Mewborn, a longtime editor at ROLLING STONE, was my associate on this book. Thanks also to Friendly Press's Stu Waldman and Marty Goldstein.) During the first years in San Francisco, Paul Scanlon, a great editor, was my right arm, sharing the responsibility for all our major feature writers. Running the music coverage during that same period was Ben Fong-Torres. In New York, four very strong editors have played big roles in overseeing some of our best work: Jim Henke, Terry McDonnell, Susan Murcko and Robert Wallace.

No look back at ROLLING STONE would be accurate without remembering Ralph J. Gleason. As a columnist for *The San Francisco Chronicle*, Gleason put his reputation as one of America's premier jazz critics on the line to take a stand on behalf of rock & roll. He was an adviser and mentor to many of the key figures on the budding San Francisco rock-music scene. Among the people he took under his wing was myself, then a nineteen-year-old student at the University of California at Berkeley. The name ROLLING STONE came directly from the essay he wrote titled "Like a Rolling Stone," in *The American Scholar.*

"All the News That Fits" has been ROLLING STONE's slogan throughout the years. It is meant to suggest that ROLLING STONE's mission is defined on its own terms and that those terms are honest and simple. They have to do with always digging for the truth, insisting on accuracy in writing and reporting—in the belief that laziness in executing this duty is the cause for a lack of confidence in the press at large—and above all, not shrinking from saying what we think and telling it like it is.

—J.S.W.
April 1987
New York, New York

I think it's time we stop,
Children, what's that sound
Everybody look what's going down
—STEPHEN STILLS, *"For What It's Worth"*

Prologue: 1965–1967

There's nothing you can do that can't be done
Nothing you can sing that can't be sung
Nothing you can say but you can learn how to play the game
It's easy
—JOHN LENNON, PAUL McCARTNEY, *"All You Need Is Love"*

From Eternity to Here

by Charles Perry   February 1976

The sheriff was there the night the Red Dog opened. Line of duty. Virginia City was something between a sleepy village and a ghost town in 1965, living on memories of Nevada's gold rush and a trickle of tourists. When the town got a nightclub, that was something to check out.

And anyway, some of the citizens were pressing him to go down there, because…because there was something strange about the young people who'd remodeled the Comstock House into the Red Dog Saloon. Their odd doings at 4 a.m. Their extravagant western dress—vests and string ties and six-shooters, as if they really thought they were living on the frontier. And something else, an attitude.…That slavering red dog on the sign out front, for one thing.

But they've done a hell of a job, the sheriff marveled as he mounted the plank sidewalk. All period furnishings, he noted as he opened the doors. Antique brass lamps, yards of velvet drapery. The waitresses all in Miss Kitty costumes, bartender in a striped shirt with sleeve garters.

Touched by the old West nostalgia, the sheriff sidled up to the busy bar, determined to join the spirit of things, to follow the hallowed Code of the West; he'd check his gun at the bar.

"How do, bartender."

"How do, Sheriff." Funny look in his eyes.

"Looks real nice, you've done a fine job."

"Glad you like it, Sheriff."

"Check my gun?"

Without blinking, the bartender lifted the gun out of his hand, executed a practiced glance down the barrel, spun the chambers, cocked the hammer, fired two quick shots into the floor and handed it back.

"Works fine, Sheriff."

★   ★   ★

The San Francisco scene started at the Red Dog Saloon, as much as you can say it started at any one place. Most of the elements were there: rock & roll, a sort of light show, the first psychedelic dance poster, the theatrical life style and acid. Lots of acid. The best LSD in the world, in fact, the genuine Owsley.

When the Red Dog opened on June 29th, 1965, Owsley Stanley had been making LSD for about four months and the Berkeley contingent at the Red Dog knew him. Chandler Laughlin, the saloon's entertainment director and manager of the resident rock band, remembers precisely the first night Owsley's acid was available: March 5th. "It was the second night of the Fuck Rally at Cal," he recalls. "Me and a Hell's Angel named Gypsy and Neal Cassady and his old lady, Ann Murphy and a bunch of other people drove down past the campus, where the students were shouting 'Fuck! Fuck! Fuck!,' out to where Owsley was, picked up the acid and went on down to the Cabale Coffee House to hear the Chambers Brothers rock & roll."

Even before Owsley, acid had been spreading fast in the Bay Area for about two years, though at the time nobody had any idea just how fast. Even though LSD was still legal, the scene seemed to itself a tiny fringe movement, probably not much larger than the circle of acidheads one happened to know. It was a buttoned up sort of psychedelic scene, with self-conscious religious or therapeutic goals.

But already down around Stanford University a novelist named Ken Kesey had a scene where people took LSD for *adventure,* just to see what would happen. And Kesey was pushing the limits of what *could* happen. He had opened his acid parties to the most notorious outlaw motorcycle gang, the Hell's Angels, to whom he had been introduced by a journalist named Hunter S. Thompson. Furthermore, the British-sparked rock & roll revival had been going on for more than a year, and one way or another a lot of people were picking up on the fact that instead of spending your trip on a prayer mat or staring at a Zen rock garden, you could dance.

At the time, anybody would have thought the scene in the Bay Area was Berkeley. The Free Speech Movement the year before had made headlines all over the world and there was still a lot of political ferment there. The *Berkeley Barb,* third oldest of the underground newspapers, was just starting.

But the artistic community was restless, caught between the austere late-Fifties avant-garde tradition, the late beatnik experiments with events and happenings and the pop-art dalliance with simple fun. The directors of Berkeley's Open Theatre were tired of conventional art presentations. At the San Francisco Tape Music Center, where Steve Reich, Terry Riley, Morton Subotnick and others had been putting on New Music concerts for four years, codirector Ramon Sender felt the same way. The improvisational group called the Committee was reorganizing; the Mime Troupe was performing political satires in public parks.

By coincidence, the Tape Center was at the edge of a neglected San Francisco neighborhood known, from its principal intersection, as the Haight-Ashbury district. It was a quiet place, largely made up of retired Russians with a peaceful integration of blacks and Orientals. It happened to have the most convenient cheap housing for

San Francisco State College students. Really cheap—$175 a month would get you two bottom floors of a beautiful Victorian mansion with four fireplaces and leather wallpaper. Like many obscure neighborhoods, it was the location of a discreet sprinkling of gay bars. It had attracted a few settlers from North Beach where media pressure and police harassment had closed down the beat scene a few years before.

"For the most part, we were rejects from other towns," remembers Rock Scully, a State graduate student and integration-march organizer at the time. "We were pretty big swellheads who had stood out like sore thumbs and split. The Haight-Ashbury was a very beautiful place, the houses were nice and lent themselves well to us—the high ceilings, the gas jets that still worked." In a setting of Victorian moldings and scrollwork, in cheap rooms with stained-glass doors and window seats, a hip aesthetic developed around the *art-nouveau* not-quite-antiques that were going cheap at secondhand stores. There were pads in the Haight entirely decorated in Victoriana, with gaslights instead of electric bulbs. In the same area as the Tape Center, on Divisadero Street, a tiny shop that opened in 1964 embodied the style. Magic Theater for Madmen Only was part art gallery, part hip artifact shop, part stash-box market, under surveillance as a dope-dealing operation; it established the pattern for later hip boutiques.

But the Haight was quiet, residential. There was no place to hang out in public but a donut shop or a laundromat—unless you wanted to go to a bar, and the dopers were self-righteous about booze. It was just a neighborhood where rather a lot of people were interested in art and getting high.

One sometime Haight resident was an actor turned folk singer named Marty Balin. Like everybody else in the Haight and Berkeley and Palo Alto he was listening to the Beatles. Like Bob Dylan, like the Los Angeles group that took the name the Byrds, like the New York group the Lovin' Spoonful, he'd started thinking about breaking the first commandment of the folk music movement—thou shalt not go commercial—which above all meant playing rock & roll on electric guitars. Balin was part owner of a folk-music coffeehouse called the Matrix, two and a half miles removed from the Haight on Fillmore Street: the perfect showcase for his idea. There were others going electric besides Balin and his Jefferson Airplane, like the band in Palo Alto that would take the name Grateful Dead and the future Quicksilver Messenger Service in Marin County.

To a psychedelic eye in the sky, the Bay Area would have looked like a maze of tiny puddles of acidheads, each ignorant of the others. The Red Dog Saloon was one place where people could get an inkling—from out in Nevada—of how big it was becoming.

The Red Dog was a sound commercial adventure, with its live entertainment and French cooking; at one time it was drawing fifty cars a night from Reno and Carson City. But the people who ran it were making a style out of it the way the Haight hippies were doing on their turf. "'This is an old Western town,' we'd tell ourselves," says Chan Laughlin. "'And we're more old Western than anybody else. Just remember, when your feet hit the floor in the morning you're in a grade B movie. This *is* that saloon down the street where the manager has his office under the stairs and all the gun hands sit around out front and periodically he comes out and motions a couple of them to ride away and rustle some cows. It's that place, complete with fancy girls going around bending over tables and the music and the people roaring and ordering more drinks and carrying on.'" One day somebody goosed their script along a little further by riding into Red Dog on a horse.

The place had been conceived as a folk-music club, but somebody'd heard of a rock & roll band in the Haight and they seemed pretty wild. The Charlatans, as they called themselves, had been organized as an art statement by an engineer named George Hunter, who was a leading exemplar of the Haight-Ashbury Victorian hip trip, and they included Michael Ferguson, proprietor of Magic Theater for Madmen Only. So they became the Red Dog's house band and moved straight into the Comstock Lode style. At one time they would come onstage carrying matched-caliber Winchester rifles and lean them against the amplifier before picking up their guitars. One week when money was short, the club's owner bought a load of rifles at a discount and paid everybody in Old West hardware. Art is art, sure—but a ripple of apprehension passed through the good burghers of Virginia City when they saw one of those *strange young people* walk down C Street with a double armload of rifles.

It wasn't the only trouble the Red Dog scene was having. There were more and more people doing things like walking around at 4 a.m. giggling at rocks. The envious bartender down the street was spreading incredible rumors about drug use and underage girls. Once in a while some local cowboys would take exception to somebody's Beatles-length hair and things got uncomfortable when some of the local teenagers got turned on to grass. The last straw came September 1st when Laughlin and the Charlatans' guitarist were busted for grass in Rodeo, California. The next day the owner fired the Charlatans; the day after that Ken Kesey showed up with a busful of his Merry Pranksters for a twenty-four-hour party. The day after that, the owner padlocked the club.

It had lasted just over two months, an adventure seemingly outside of time. But some were not reconciled to the end of the adventure—notably a group of people living in a bohemian enclave on Pine Street in San Francisco: Jack Towle, who had the reputation of having established ten dollars as the ceiling price of a lid of grass in San

Francisco; an ex-Red Dog employee named Ellen Harmon; Alton Kelly, a collage artist who had helped build the Red Dog; and Luria Castell, a political activist who had dipped into a number of the local bohemias and the burgeoning Sunset Strip rock scene in L.A. as well.

They were living at a place called the Dog House in a curious no man's land between the Fillmore black ghetto and the wealthy Pacific Heights district. There were half a dozen apartment houses full of heads and dealers in the neighborhood, not to mention the San Francisco Zen Temple. The Dog House apartment manager was Bill Ham, an artist who had been working with moving light projections—a "light box" designed by him had sat on the Red Dog stage behind the Charlatans.

For months Ham had been working on a different technique. He would manipulate liquid pigments in a glass dish over a spotlight, and the moving abstract paintings that resulted would be projected off an overhead mirror onto a screen. The usual evening's entertainment for the half dozen head houses on Pine Street was to go into Ham's basement and watch the light painting in collaboration with a guitarist or flutist. By the end of '65 Ham was doing public shows at the Tape Center.

Like most of the bohemians on Pine Street, like the nascent scene in the Haight, the Dog House was mostly supporting itself by dealing. But the border kept getting hotter and more heads kept getting busted and the Dog House crowd started casting around for alternate employment. Somehow the "dog" part stuck— maybe it was because there were lots of dogs running around the Dog House, maybe it was because Ellen's dog had just got run over, maybe it was because they'd all recently tripped out on the idea of running a pet cemetery as an income scam. Take your pick of stories. They were now the Family Dog and they were going to put on dances.

They borrowed money and looked for a hall. From her days with the Fair Play for Cuba Committee and other radical causes, Luria knew of one called Longshore-men's Hall, a modernistic, dome-shaped union hall near Fisherman's Wharf. Ralph J. Gleason, *The San Francisco Chronicle* jazz columnist who had already gone out on a limb to praise the Beatles, Bob Dylan and the Jefferson Airplane, gave them a mention in his column; a few posters went up in strategic spots around the Bay Area, advertising a Tribute to Dr. Strange for October 16th.

October 16th, 1965, was also the day of the biggest antiwar march to date, from the University of California campus to the Oakland Army Induction Center. It was an impressively large demonstration and it was also the end of a dream. After Ken Kesey had turned the Hell's Angels on to acid, they'd started hanging around Telegraph Avenue. But when the chips were down and Sonny Barger, the president of the large Oakland chapter, decided to oppose the peace marchers, the Angels formed ranks behind him and the imagined shock troops of the revolution forcibly halted the march at the Oakland border. For one day in American history, Stewart Brand observed, nobody knew who the good guys were.

That night hundreds of people—some of them direct from the march and even a few Angels—converged on the peculiar dome-shaped building near Fisherman's Wharf where the city's premiere rock band, Marty Balin's Jefferson Airplane, was sharing the bill with the legendary Charlatans and Bill Ham's exotic show of flowing colored lights. Nobody was quite prepared for it. The people who weren't stoned on acid looked stoned. Allen Ginsberg could be seen wandering around in his white hospital-orderly suit, staring around with a look of amazement. There were *all* these…crazy…people…wearing Haight-Ashbury Victorian clothes, cowboy and Indian costumes, slinky antique gowns, paisley prints, spacesuits, with paint on their faces and feathers in their hair, dancing, dancing.

It was like this. If you thought something interesting might be going on at a rock dance named for a magician in Marvel Comics who could travel between dimensions by mind power, you were liable to find it was just what you'd always wanted but never realized it.

Say no more. A lot of little puddles had started running together.

A week later the Family Dog put on another dance named for a cartoon character, a Tribute to Sparkle Plenty, headlining the Lovin' Spoonful. Word had spread and more people came. The Kesey seance band, for the moment nameless, came in to marvel after an afternoon of tripping; Phil Lesh accosted Luria Castell and confided, "Lady, what this seance needs is us!" The beat poet Michael McClure, who'd been living in the Haight for four years, remembers "this vibrant scene, people really allowing themselves to be themselves—to be Jean Harlow or Billy the Kid or Napoleon or Jesus. I was used to seeing intense self-expression in poetry, or in someone's painting. Here were people acting it out in their bodies—really bright, really real.

"But I didn't see people jumping around aimlessly or pointlessly. I saw the whole thing organized—organized from each individual point. Whitehead said that at every point in the universe, the universe is its own organ of self-experience. I saw these individuals as highly organized points of self-experience, which is the experience of everything."

It seemed to take a historical moment to digest this phenomenon, which was not only an experience of incredible exuberance but a reinforcement of the generation's sense of uniqueness, a more decisive one than even radical politics had been. Two weeks later the Dog put on a Tribute to Ming the Merciless with a crazy musician they'd heard about from the Sunset Strip scene named Frank Zappa. It was their third dance and the Family Dog was not a moneymaking institution; in fact, they were broke. Inexperienced wasn't the word—they'd never gotten a dance permit, hadn't even known they'd needed one.

The same night as Ming the Merciless, November 6th, there had been another show in town that had done quite well. The San Francisco Mime Troupe, recently busted for performing in the park without a permit, had put on a benefit called Appeal I. It featured, along with jazz, folk music and Allen Ginsberg, two of the acts that were playing Longshore that night: the Airplane (the Mime Troupe's loft was the Airplane's rehearsal hall) and Frank Zappa's Mothers. Hundreds of people had to be turned away. The show was put on by the Mime Troupe's business manager, himself an ex-actor, Bill Graham.

The discouraged Dog tried to interest Graham in teaming up with them, but without success. Luria by this time had moved into a place in the Haight, managed by a guy named Danny Rifkin, where Luria's acquaintance Rock Scully was also living. Rock and Danny helped her put on a fourth dance, which actually netted $1500. Meanwhile, on December 10th, Bill Graham had put on Appeal II for the Mime Troupe in a large hall in the Fillmore district, the original Fillmore Auditorium.

With the considerable boost of the public gatherings at these dances, the psychedelic scene—still quite legal—started going more public. On January 3rd, 1966, two brothers named Ron and Jay Thelin opened a shop on Haight Street they called the Psychedelic Shop to sell books, records, roach clips and an ever-shifting variety of things they felt were related to the psychedelic experience. Meanwhile Ken Kesey's Acid Test parties had expanded in successive weeks from wild gatherings with the Angels at Kesey's home in the depths of the San Francisco peninsula to a private home in San Jose, a bar in Palo Alto, the Muir Beach Lodge in Marin County (where the Grateful Dead made the acquaintance of their future patron, the accomplished chemist Owsley Stanley) and to an Acid Test at the Fillmore on January 8th. The Family Dog was throwing a dance at California Hall the same night and there was an attempt to coordinate the two affairs—a single-ticket price that would get you into both places and a bus that ran between the two.

Scully and Rifkin phased out of the Dog and into the Grateful Dead scene at this point, on the introduction of the Dead's new friend, Owsley. The rest of the original Family Dog people split to Mexico in despair and the business was left in the hands of Kelly, who was doing poster art for the shows; George Hunter, founder of the Charlatans; Stanley Mouse (Miller), a "hot-rod surrealist" from Detroit who'd made a name for himself painting monsters on T-shirts at car shows; and Chet Helms, a friend who'd been putting together a band out of public jam sessions at the Albin Brothers' place at 1090 Page Street in the Haight.

Meantime, a really big event was in the works and publicity had already started. On New Year's Eve afternoon there had been a small parade through Montgomery Street, San Francisco's financial district, cheering on the office workers who were following the tradition of throwing their old calendars out of the windows. The parade was Ramon Sender of the Tape Center, Ben and Rain Jacopetti from Open Theater and a biologist who'd gotten interested in Indians, Stewart Brand. "Be aware that you're in a parade," they told everyone they met, "and you'll be as beautiful as what you do."

Ken Kesey had given Brand the idea of putting on a three-day Trips Festival to gather avant-garde and psychedelic arts into a show at Longshoremen's Hall. It would feature Kesey's Acid Test, of course. The Acid Tests were pushing the limit. A week after the Be a Parade parade, Brand ran into Neal Cassady—the legendary beatnik pillhead, nonstop rapper, manic madman of Jack Kerouac novels—at the Fillmore Acid Test, standing in the balcony of the Fillmore Auditorium looking down at the welter of self-interfaced microphones and TV circuits, the Grateful Dead playing at one end of the hall and Kesey's own Psychedelic Symphony playing at the other. Brand had never seen Cassady so serene. "Total chaos going on on the floor, right? People wailing on Ron Boise's thunder sculpture, taking their shoes off and counting their toes, and television cameras pointing at each other and general weirdness. And he's just sort of nodding. Then he says, 'Looks like your publicity for the Trips Festival is going pretty well.'"

The handbill for the Trips Festival tells what people thought was going on: "The general tone of things has moved on from the self-conscious happening to a more JUBILANT occasion where the audience PARTICIPATES because it's more fun to do so than not. Maybe this is the ROCK REVOLUTION. Audience dancing is an assumed part of all the shows, & the audience is invited to wear ECSTATIC DRESS & bring their own GADGETS (a.c. outlets will be provided)." The "trip" had been somewhat slipperily defined as "an electronic experience, a new medium of communication and entertainment."

To handle the nuts and bolts of the operation they asked Bill Graham, whose three Mime Troupe benefits had been models of efficiency compared to anything they knew. Graham for his part wanted to learn what this new scene was all about. He got a lesson during the Saturday-night Acid Test, when he was hurrying around with his efficiency-expert clipboard checking whether everything was going according to schedule. To his horror, he saw a giant of a man—Kesey, whom he hadn't met before—standing at the back door letting in Hell's Angels. He was wearing one of the superhero costumes favored by the principal Merry Pranksters, more or less on the spacesuit model.

"Why are you *doing* this?" Graham pleaded "I'm out there working my *balls* off to make sure this thing runs right, watching the doors, and back here you're—" Kesey closed the mask on his space helmet.

Another novelty for Graham was the division of the spoils. By consensus it was agreed that the Acid Test with the Grateful Dead was the greatest success of the three nights. The Open Theater and America Needs Indians shows were out of scale in the huge hall; the Tape Center acts hadn't caught fire. So after the show the principals decided not to split the profits evenly, but to give Kesey half.

But Graham had not only run the show well, he had carefully observed what got the most response. The artists who'd put the thing together, in the spirit of letting everybody join in, hadn't been willing to sift out the less-successful entertainment. Two weeks after the Trips Festival, Graham put on a dance that was not a benefit, but his first straight commercial dance: Bill Graham Presents the Jefferson Airplane with Sights and Sounds from the Trips Festival. There was music, a light show and an atmosphere tolerant of any amount of bizarre behavior. And Graham added an extra show on Sunday afternoon.

That first Sunday afternoon the saga of Ken Kesey's multiple drug busts took on a new turn. The famous Merry Pranksters bus, with its collages and many layers of psychedelic paint, was found on a deserted beach in Eureka, California, not far from the border of Kesey's home state of Oregon. In it was a rather literary suicide note, containing the lines, "Ocean ocean I'll beat you in the end." It was not a real suicide note, of course, and the planting of the bus near the Oregon border was a false lead too. Kesey had headed in the opposite direction—now with a warrant out for his arrest—to Los Angeles, where the Acid Tests had moved, and from there to Mexico.

★   ★   ★

As the dance scene expanded, so did the Haight. When the original Family Dog people returned from Mexico, they were stunned. There were huge dances every weekend. More shops had started opening during the summer of '66 and more people moved in; the Haight became the central grass-and-psychedelic market for the Bay Area and there was a living to be made for hundreds of dealers. In fact, everybody was a dealer on one level or another, and most of the shops opening up were the product of spare capital in the dope trade. Life was cheap, life was aesthetic, life was stoned—particularly when a new batch of Owsley's acid would hit the market and his lieutenants would walk up and down Haight Street passing out free samples.

Ken Kesey's bus
Photograph
by Gene Anthony

Life was an adventure. There were international adventures in books—yoga, occultism, Wilhelm Reich's sexual liberation theories and Zen were established features of bohemian communities, and the Haight brought in the uniquely psyche-delic elements of American Indian lore, the oracular *I Ching* and texts of Tibetan Buddhism, valued for their descriptions of acidlike visions. There were aesthetic adventures in crafts, folk music, psychedelic painting or just blowing soap bubbles. A stroll through Golden Gate Park might wind you up at the new Avery Brundage Collection of Asian Art. There were emotional adventures in the mercurial social relationships of psychedelic folk. There were existential adventures in the ever-para-noid world of dope dealing.

And always there was the weekly occasion to paint your face, rock out at a dance concert and be reminded of how many people were doing the same thing. The straight world had scarcely begun to notice anything was happening but in the Haight there was a momentum of excitement that was at least cosmic.

The adventure started getting unexpected outside verification. Dylan's *Blonde on Blonde* came out, containing not only "Rainy Day Women #12 & 35," with its refrain "Everybody must get stoned," but desperate psychodramas of unresolved relationships that any acidhead could relate to. And right around the same time that the Board of Permit Appeals was trying to close the Fillmore, the Beatles—those remote objects of adoration—brought out *Yesterday and Today* with an album cover that the record company rejected as being "in poor taste." Everybody had to get a copy and steam off the "tasteful" cover that had been hastily glued over the original one to see the Beatles in butcher coats holding joints of meat and parts of baby dolls. Far out.

But the paranoia potential of the adventure was just about to be given a fateful boost. Already there was a lot of pressure to make LSD illegal. As early as April 1966, the U.S. attorney general had been demanding laws against acid, even in the absence of studies showing it was dangerous. Federal laws against possession of LSD went into effect on October 6th, 1966. The Haight responded with a party—the Lunatic Protest Demonstration, the first big free concert in the Panhandle section of Golden Gate Park, two blocks from Haight Street.

The intellectual adventure had gotten big enough that for six months there had been an attempt to start a newspaper. After an initial faction fight between the acid mystics and the Marxists, which produced one issue with cover stories on masturbation and concentration camps, Ron Thelin of the Psychedelic Shop threw his support to Allen Cohen, a poet who had dealt acid for Owsley and had turned Thelin on to acid in the first place. Named *The City of San Francisco Oracle*, the paper lasted only thirteen issues under Cohen, but by the time he abandoned it in 1967, it was selling over 100,000 copies worldwide.

"Our philosophy at that time was that newspapers are a lie," says Cohen. "We were going to make in the newspaper format a judo that would show everyone that newspapers were destroying sensibilities, causing paranoia and fear. We were going to fill our newspaper with art, philosophy, poetry and attend to this change of consciousness that was happening in the Haight-Ashbury and, we hoped, the world. Though none of us really had a program of exactly what we wanted to do, except that we knew that if we could keep control of quality, we could serve as vehicles for the forces that were emerging."

The early issues retained some of the underground newspaper format: political news, a "What's Happening" entertainment guide and stock low-budget tabloid format. But a new art director named Gabe Katz brought about a decisive change. Instead of setting the text in straight columns of type, he rearranged it in columns of varying width that turned the text into part of the design of the page. Colored patterns were printed over it, sometimes making the text as hard to read as a Fillmore dance poster. In fact, in 1967 the poster artist Mouse designed an issue. Starting with issue six, the *Oracle* started experimenting with split-fountain inking, a technique that washed every page with blending colors. Incredible liberties were taken with magazine design, such as jumping the end of a story to one of six circles on a back page with the words "Continued on p. 21 middle of a circle right center."

★   ★   ★

The older Haight crowd was already at work on another event. It's not clear where the idea came from—it had probably been on a lot of people's minds when they remembered the thrill of the Trips Festival gathering a bigger crowd than any Acid Test or dance. Perhaps it came from Steve Durkee, Richard Alpert's one-time roommate who later went on to found the Lama Foundation commune in New Mexico; he'd had a plan for a huge gathering to be held in the Grand Canyon in the summer of '66. Whatever, the *Oracle* and associates had come up with a plan for a Human Be-In.

It was subtitled "A Gathering of the Tribes." The name signified that it was not simply meant to be a giant Acid Test but a union of acidheads with the Berkeley radicals, who had begun to feel themselves left out of things since the notoriety of the Free Speech Movement had died down. Jerry Rubin, who until recently had been denouncing drugs, along with Jack Weinberg of the FSM, Dick Gregory (who didn't show) and the more political of the beat elder statesmen—Michael McClure, Allen Ginsberg, Gary Snyder—were going to share the stage with the *quite*, apolitical Alpert and Leary and rock & roll: the Dead, Quicksilver, Big Brother and the

Airplane. "A new concept of human relations being developed within the youthful underground," the *Oracle* announced, "must emerge, become conscious and be shared so that a revolution of form can be filled with a Renaissance of compassion, awareness and love in the Revelation of the unity of all mankind."

It took place on January 14th, 1967, an unusually clear day—the day picked by an astrologer—in the Polo Field in Golden Gate Park. Newspaper accounts at the time put the attendance at figures from 10,000 to 20,000. The actual figure scarcely matters (in fact, the event did not entirely fill the Polo Field and a scheduled rugby match took place at the other end of the field at the same time). Even 10,000 was a huge gathering. In the context of a nation insanely embroiled in a war in Vietnam and recently in actual race war on its own soil, the sight of thousands upon thousands of people committed to "peace and love" was overwhelming. (Also overwhelming was Owsley's acid, which was distributed—among other ways—in the free turkey sandwiches the Diggers had made from turkeys Owsley had also donated.)

As for the "union of love and activism previously separated by categorical dogma and label mongering" that, it was promised, would "finally occur ecstatically," little of Jerry Rubin's or anybody else's speeches could be heard outside the immediate vicinity of the loudspeakers. Even there, most people were paying little or no attention, simply walking around and blowing their minds on all the faces assembled.

The Be-In was a great long stare in the mirror for the psychedelic community, both at the event and in the awed coverage given it by the news media—everybody was impressed by the fact that the notorious Hell's Angels had stood guard over the generator for the PA system. The temptation to admire the image in the mirror was great. In the next issue of the *Oracle*, the column titled "Aquarian Beat" revealed that "the scene that's happening now is a double thing. Not only a new earth (Aquarian Age) but also a new man walking it (Sixth Subrace)." (But even nontheosophists were expecting the best from this generation already; two weeks before the Be-In, *Time* had chosen as its Man of the Year "anybody in the world under 25.")

At the end of the Be-In, Allen Ginsberg suggested that the crowd pick up after itself, and the Polo Field was left clean. For a while there was a spate of projects planned to operate on "Be-In energy," like the Haight Street Clean-In a week later. The press ran it for laughs—the "dirty hippies" being "introduced to a broom"—but the sidewalks were swept.

The real invasion was just beginning. The Airplane's second album was climbing the national sales charts, the jubilant and enigmatic Be-In had aroused press attention and now San Francisco newspapers were running story after story about kids—rich kids, from Hillsborough—running off to the Haight, living in bizarre apartments, going shoeless and braless, eating garbage, getting busted for drugs:

the media discovered the "Hippie Haven" in California's biggest tourist town. Between March and September 1967, virtually every major publication and certainly every TV network did at least one story on the "Hashbury." Over and over they showed Hippie Hill in Golden Gate Park, trip parties, dancers and light shows, free concerts in the Panhandle, hippies holding flowers or panhandling, Timothy Leary looking solemn and stupefied or flashing his famous grin.

It was advertising, of a sort, but it advertised what the reporters saw and that was limited by their haste, their prejudices and story instincts, and the Haight community's own fumbling attempt to put its best foot forward. So the stories dwelt on drugs, sex, dirt, insanity and something called "love and flowers." These were all middle-class stereotypes about bohemians, except the love and flowers part, which was novel. The insanity had a novel flavor too, as when a young man in his twenties jumped off a pedestrian overpass onto a six-lane traffic artery because his magic stone told him to.

As a result, they made the Haight a magnet for people who were into drugs, sex, dirt, insanity and love in any combination, and for those who cared to exploit or just gawk. But what was really going on was mostly unreported. How could anyone have kept track? Who noticed Charlie Manson when he lived at 636 Cole Street?

Even for the people who were there, it was going too fast to follow. The drug trade, still the economic base of the community, had reached unbelievable dimensions. Owsley had a widespread distribution network that controlled how fast his LSD reached the market and at what price. He kept ahead of imitators trying to peddle their acid as "Owsley" by maintaining high quality, investing in better pill presses and dyeing his product a different color every batch. By some estimates he made 4 million hits of acid, of which he may have given away as much as he sold—as promotion when a new batch was coming on the street, as subsidy to institutions that interested him such as the Diggers or the Communication Company, as a psychedelic gift to every musician he thought important. He was as much a fixture backstage at the Fillmore and Avalon as he was out on the dance floor.

A dealer named Larry got his first inkling of how big the drug market was one time when Owsley was releasing a new batch. As usual, the price was $4000 a gram (a dollar a hit, wholesale), and as usual Owsley's lieutenants wouldn't take any bills smaller than hundreds. This one month, Larry couldn't find a bank within sixty miles that had any $100 bills to exchange.

With the swiftly increasing number of people on Haight Street, the Psychedelic Shop installed two theater seats in its window for anybody who cared to watch the show. Things started happening faster and faster.

Well we all shine on
Like the moon and the stars and the sun
Well we all shine on
Come on and on and on and on
—JOHN LENNON, *"Instant Karma"*

1967–1970

"There must be some way out of here," said the joker to the thief.
"There's too much confusion, I can't get no relief.
Businessmen, they drink my wine, plowmen dig my earth,
None of them along the line know what any of it is worth."
—BOB DYLAN, *"All Along the Watchtower"*

Voices

What I think society is mad about is they're getting old and very soon they'll be gone, and they wondering what these young people are gonna do with this world, and they're mad because they can't do what they used to do, and they can't dance because they've got arthritis and rheumatism, they can't jump up in the air. It's jealousy against the young race, and it's not fair, because even the Bible said that the young would be weaker but wiser.
—LITTLE RICHARD, *May 1970*

★   ★   ★

What's different about this revolutionary generation is not what the young people want—freedom. Everyone has always wanted that. What's different is the way they go after it. They know what they want, but they don't know exactly how to reach for it.
—MICHELANGELO ANTONIONI, *March 1969*

★   ★   ★

The audiences were hostile to what we did. They gave us a bad time. Now, historically, musicians have felt real hurt if the audience expressed displeasure with their performance. They apologized and tried to make the people love them. We didn't do that. We told the audience to get fucked.
—FRANK ZAPPA, *July 1968*

★   ★   ★

I think music is the main interest of the younger people. It doesn't really matter about the older people now because they're finished anyway. There's still going to be years and years of having all these old fools who are governing us and who are bombing us and doin' all that because, you know, it's always them.

I don't expect to see the world in a perfect state of bliss— you know, like 100 percent. But it doesn't matter. It's on the way now.
—GEORGE HARRISON, *February 1968*

★   ★   ★

I think there should be a national carnival, much the same as Mardi Gras in Rio. There should be a week of national hilarity…a cessation of all work, all business, all discrimination, all authority. A week of total freedom. That'd be a start. Of course, the power structure wouldn't really alter. It would just last for a week and then go back to the way it was. I think we need it.
—JIM MORRISON, *July 1969*

We think that this decade was the beginning of the end and that it was a positive decade, not a depressing one which people have tried to put around. It's the decade of all the music, the generation, and the freedom and the sort of awareness and all the jazz and the moratoriums and the Woodstocks and the Isle of Wights and everything. This is just the beginning. What we've got to do is keep hope alive. Because without it we'll sink.
—JOHN LENNON, *February 1970*

★   ★   ★

Whatever it takes to make it be more than a hate thing, because there's hate and you stack up a bunch of hates and it's hate city, and that ain't no place to live.

Let's burn the White House, but let's build a Green House.
—WAVY GRAVY, *August 1970*

★   ★   ★

On one side you got war, degradation, death, submission, guilt, fear, competition; and on the other hand you got a bunch of people lyin' out on the beach, walking around in the sun, laughin', playin' music, makin' love and gettin' high, singin', dancin', wearin' bright colors, tellin' stories, livin' pretty easy. You offer that alternative to a kid, man, and the kid ain't crazy yet. I think that they've probably lost the majority of their kids by now.
—DAVID CROSBY, *July 1970*

★   ★   ★

I'm certainly not going to be a politician and change it, in or out of the system. I'm going to sing my songs, because that's what I do. Some Oriental philosopher, Tao, once said that people who want to be political leaders are the least qualified to do it, and that's true. The people who really are qualified won't mess with it. So we always get second best.
—LEON RUSSELL, *December 1970*

★   ★   ★

I prefer Abbie Hoffman to Richard Nixon simply because he's more entertaining, more interesting to listen to. I don't care what the two of them are talking about—they could be talking about toothpaste—and Abbie's gonna come out hands down because he's just a more entertaining guy.
—GRACE SLICK, *November 1970*

Pete Townshend: The Rolling Stone Interview

by Jann S. Wenner   September 1968

When did you start smashing guitars?

It happened by complete accident the first night. We were just kicking around in a club that we played every Tuesday, and I was playing the guitar and it hit the ceiling. It broke, and it kind of shocked me 'cause I wasn't ready for it to go. I was expecting everybody to go, "Wow, he's broken his guitar," but nobody did anything, which made me kind of angry and determined to get this precious event noticed by the audience. I proceeded to make a big thing of breaking the guitar. I pounced all over the stage with it, and I threw the bits on the stage, and I picked up my spare guitar and carried on as though I really meant to do it.

Were you happy about it?

Deep inside I was very unhappy because the thing had got broken. It got around, and the next week people came up to me and they said, "Oh, we heard all about it, man; it's 'bout time someone gave it to a guitar," and all this kind of stuff. It kind of grew from there. We'd go to another town, and people would say, "Oh yeah, we heard that you smashed a guitar." It built and built until one day, a very important daily newspaper came to see us and said, "Oh, we hear you're the group that smashes up guitars. Well, we hope you're going to do it tonight, because we're from the *Daily Mail*. If you do, you'll probably make the front pages."

This was only going to be like the second guitar I'd ever broken, seriously. I went to my manager, Kit Lambert, and I said, you know, "Can we afford it? It's for publicity." He said, "Yes, we can afford it, if we can get the *Daily Mail*." I did it, and of course the *Daily Mail* didn't buy the photograph and didn't want to know about the story. After that, I was into it up to my neck and have been doing it since.

Pete Townshend
Photograph by Baron Wolman

What new ideas for albums do you have?

Well, the album concept in general is complex. It's derived as a result of quite a few things. We've been talking about doing an opera, we've been talking about doing albums, we've been talking about a whole lot of things. We've condensed all of these ideas, all this energy and all these gimmicks, and whatever we've decided on for future albums, into one juicy package. The package I hope is going to be called *Deaf, Dumb and Blind Boy*. It's a story about a kid who's born deaf, dumb and blind and what happens to him throughout his life. The deaf, dumb and blind boy is played by the Who, the musical entity. He's represented musically, represented by a theme that we play, which starts off the opera itself, and there's a song describing the deaf, dumb and blind boy. But what it's really all about is the fact that because the boy is D, D and B, he's seeing things basically as vibrations, which we translate as music. That's really what we want to do—create this feeling that when you listen to music you can actually become aware of the boy, and aware of what he is all about, because we are creating him as we play.

The whole album is about his experience?

Yes, it's a pretty far-out thing, actually. Inside, the boy sees things musically and in dreams, and nothing has got any weight at all. He is touched from the outside, and he feels his mother's touch, he feels his father's touch, but he just interprets them as music. His father gets pretty upset that his kid is deaf, dumb and blind. One night he's drunk, and he sits over the kid's bed and starts to talk to him; the kid just smiles up, and his father is trying to get through to him, telling him all about how other dads have a kid they can teach to play football and all this kind of crap, and he starts to say, "Can you hear me?" The kid, of course, can't hear him. He's groovin' in this musical thing, this incredible musical thing.

The kid just smiles. The father starts to hit him, and at this moment the whole thing becomes incredibly realistic. On one side you have the dreamy music of the boy. And on the other you have the reality of the father. You've got blows, you've got communication. Musically, I want the thing to break out, I want to hand it over to Keith [Moon]— "This is your scene, man. Take it from here." And the kid doesn't catch the violence. He just knows that some sensation is happening. He doesn't feel the pain. He just accepts it.

A similar situation happens later in the opera, where the father gets the mother to take the kid away from home to an uncle. The uncle is a bit of a perv. He plays with the kid's body, and the boy experiences sexual vibrations, and again it's just basic music, it's interpreted as music. It's got no association with sleaziness or with any of the things normally associated with sex. None of the romance, none of the visual stimulus, none of the sound stimulus. Just basic touch. It's meaningless. Or not meaningless—you just don't react, you know. Slowly but surely the kid starts to get it together, out of this incredible simplicity in his mind. He starts to realize that he can see and he can hear and he can speak. And that all the time he has been able to hear and see.

The music has got to explain what happens, that the boy elevates and finds something that is incredible. To us, it's nothing to be able to see and hear and speak, but to him it's absolutely overwhelming. This is what we want to do musically. Lyrically, it's quite easy to do it. In fact, I've written it out several times. It makes great poetry, but so much depends on the music, so much.

The main characters are going to be the boy and his musical things. He's got a mother and a father and an uncle. There is a doctor who tries to do some psychiatric treatment on the kid, which is only partly successful. The first two big events are when he sees himself in a mirror, suddenly seeing himself for the first time; he takes an immediate back step, bases his whole life around his own image. The music and the lyrics become introverted, and he starts to talk about himself, starts to talk about his beauty. Not knowing, of course, that what he saw was him, but still regarding it as something that belonged to him, and of course it did all of the time anyway.

It's a very complex thing, and I don't know if I'm getting it across.

You are. This theme, not so dramatically, seems to be repeated in so many songs that you've written and the Who have performed—a young cat, our age, becoming an outcast from a very ordinary sort of circumstances. Not a "Desolation Row" scene, but a very common set of middle-class situations. Why does this repeat itself?

I don't know. I never really thought about that.

You must have thought about where it comes from. If it's not your parents, was it the scene around you when you were young?

One of the things that has impressed me most in life was the mod movement in England, which was an incredible youthful thing. It was a movement of young people, much bigger than the hippie thing, the underground and all these things. It was an army, a powerful aggressive army of teenagers with transport—man, these scooters—and with their own way of dressing. It was acceptable, this was important. Their way of dressing was hip, it was fashionable, it was clean, and it was groovy. You could be a bank clerk, man, it was acceptable. You got them on their own ground. They thought, "Well, there's a smart young lad." And also you were hip. That was the good thing about it. To be a mod, you had to have short hair, money enough to buy a real smart suit, good shoes, good shirts; you had to be able to dance like a madman.

You had to be in possession of plenty of pills all the time and always be pilled up. You had to have a scooter covered in lamps. You had to have like an army anorack to wear on the scooter. That was being a mod, and that was the end of the story.

That's why I dig the mods, man, because we were mods and that's how we happened. That's my generation, that's how the song "My Generation" happened. The mods could appreciate the Beatles' taste. They could appreciate their haircuts, their peculiar kinky things that they had going at the time.

The mods seemed to have graduated from "My Generation" and "The Kids Are Alright" to very ordinary people, with very ordinary problems.

When you look at the people who were mods, they are now ordinary people—and I'm going through the same changes. I'm becoming more and more ordinary as I go along. This is the natural progression of boring maturity and boring spirituality and boring ascendance of the evolutionary path. You become simpler and simpler and more and more down to the simple ways of life to become able to blunder through life without getting anybody uptight at all.

When I write today, I feel that it has to tell a little story. Seriously. And I can't shake this. Like "Odorono," I dug because it was a little story and, although I thought it's a good song, it was about something groovy, like it was about underarm perspiration, I still did make a story out of it, didn't I? It had a beginning and an end, just like it was a literary piece, but there's no need to make "Odorono" a story. There was no need to have any lyric at all, really, other than perhaps some type of Mothers of Invention-type underarm deodorant noises, whatever they might be. "Tattoo" is a story, and "My Generation" is a story; in fact, I'm getting storier and storier until now, as I just told you, the next album is just a huge, complicated story.

We were talking about mods and the army of mods, the rock & roll army. Obviously you've thought about it a lot, and obviously it's connected with music some way. What is the role of rock & roll in this youth movement?

Music was as much a fashion as the fashion it created. It was an incredibly flippant fashion. Music was just a feather. You went from record to record, and you went from group to group, but you always dug the Who.

What would happen is that the phenomena of the Who could invoke action. The sheer fact that four mods could actually form themselves into a group that sounded quite good, considering that most mods were lower-class garbagemen, you know. Nowadays, okay, there are quite a few mod groups. But mods aren't the kind of people that could play the guitar, so it was groovy for them to have a group. Our music at the time was representative of what the mods dug, and it was meaningless rubbish. We used to play, for example, "Heat Wave," a very long version of "Smokestack Lightning," and that song we sang tonight, "Young Man Blues," fairly inconsequential kind of music that they could identify with and perhaps something where you banged your feet or clapped your hands on the fifth beat. I mean they used to like all kinds of things.

We used to make sure that if there was a riot, a mod-rocker riot, we would be playing in the area. That was a place called Brighton. That's where they used to assemble. We'd always be playing there. And we got into the spirit of the whole thing. Of course, the words *rock & roll* wouldn't even be mentioned.

You see, as individuals these people were nothing. They were the lowest, they were England's lowest common denominators. Not only were they young, they were also lower-class young. They had to submit to the middle class's way of dressing and speaking and acting in order to get the jobs that kept them alive. They had to do everything in terms of what existed already around them. That made their way of getting something across that much more latently effective, the fact that they were hip and yet still, as far as granddad was concerned, exactly the same. It made the whole gesture so much more vital. It was incredible. As a force, they were unbelievable. That was the Bulge, that was England's Bulge. All the war babies, all the old soldiers coming back from war and screwing until they were blue in the face—this was the result. Thousands and thousands of kids, too many kids, not enough teachers, not enough parents, not enough pills to go around. Everybody just grooving on being a mod.

It seemed to find its highest form of transcendence in music.

I don't think that's so. I think it found its highest transcendence in the actual event of being a mod. I know where I'm at now, I know what it's like to be a member of a successful group. I know what it's like to be a member of a group that it's difficult to be a member of. It's a great feeling to be in a group that's happening of any kind.

But I also know what it's like to be a mod among 2 million mods, and it's incredible. It's like being the only white man at the Apollo. Someone comes up and touches you, and you become black. It's like that moment, that incredible feeling of being part of something that is much bigger than race and much bigger than—it was impetus. It covered everybody, everybody looked the same, and everybody acted the same, and everybody wanted to be the same.

It was the first move that I have ever seen in the history of youth toward unity—unity of thought, unity of drive and unity of motive. It was the closest to patriotism that I've ever felt.

How do you think that compares with what today is called the American hippie scene?

I think it compares. I think the hippie thing compares favorably, but it's a different motivation. There are beloved figures. There is pot, there is the Maharishi, there is the Beatles, there is being anti-the-U.S.A.—there are a lot of red herrings, which aren't what it's all about. What it is all about is the hippies, you know, the people. Not the actions, not the events, not the tripping out or the latest fad or the latest record. The thing is people.

This is what they seem to overlook. You see this is the thing about the media barrage—you become aware only of the products around you because they're glorified. So when somebody gets stoned, they don't groove to themselves, really; they just sit around and dig everything that's around them. They dig other people, the way the room looks, the way the flowers look, the way the music sounds, the way that the group performs, how good the Beatles are. "How nice that is." They never say, "How fantastic am I." This is the whole thing; they're far too concerned with what is feeding into them and not so much with what they are. This is the difference between the mod thing in England and the hippie thing over here. The hippies are waiting for information. Information is perpetually coming in, and they sit and wait for it.

A lot of people, in a lot of new groups—not necessarily good ones at all—have tried to imbue rock & roll with a tremendous amount of spirituality and deep meaning. What do you think of this tendency?

I don't want that record to dictate to me, to say, well, "This is where your head should be while you're listening to this record; you should be in a spiritual groove." The thing is, you can take anything—you can take "I'm dreaming of a white Christmas" at a spiritual level, if you want to. It is, in effect, a spiritual song. It's effective on every spiritual level, and it's a complete, wonderful musical effort. It's got to be accepted for what it is. It's a piece of pure, wonderful existence. So when it gets down to justifying music or preloading it, saying, "This is going to be a spiritual thing," what you've got to do instead is work from the lowest level and let the spiritual people get the spiritual bag out of what you're doing.

Primarily, by itself, the record's got to entertain. That's the whole thing: it's just a piece of entertainment, like life itself. If life ceases to entertain, what do you want to do? You want to commit suicide. It's got to entertain, whether it be badly or nicely. It shouldn't dictate; it should never dictate.

What do you think are the implications of the so-called rock & roll revival? Are people now fed up with the pretentious phenomena of the last year? Are they getting back to the values of rock & roll?

Let's hope so. To me, what is really happening is that rock & roll is being completely mischanneled. The whole effect of pop music was being followed through. What pop music was doing to people was something incredibly big, and so all the musicians that were creating rock & roll are saying, "Wow, it's doing something incredibly big, we're gonna follow this through." You can't create something as huge as rock & roll and then come along and say, "Well, I'm going to do the follow-up now, which is going to be spirituality." You can't do it. Rock & roll is enormous. It's one of the biggest musical events in history. It's equal to *the* classical music. It's equal and it's transcending slowly but surely because of the impetus, the weight of the feeling.

It's like saying, "Get all the pop music, put it into a cartridge, put the cap on it and fire the gun." You don't care whether those ten or fifteen numbers sound roughly the same. You don't care what periods they were written in, what they mean, what they're all about. It's the bloody explosion that they create when you let the gun off. It's the event. That's what rock & roll is. That is why rock & roll is powerful. It is a single force. It is a single force that threatens a lot of the crap which is around at the moment in the middle class and in the middle-aged politics or philosophy. It blasts it, out of its sheer brashness. It's like suddenly everybody getting hung up on a bum trip: Mother has just fallen down the stairs, Dad's lost all his money at the dog track, the baby's got TB. In comes the kid, man, with his transistor radio, grooving to Chuck Berry. He doesn't give a shit about mom falling down the stairs. He's with rock & roll.

That's what rock & roll says to life: it says, you know, I'm hip, I'm happy, forget your troubles and just enjoy! And, of course, this is the biggest thing it has to offer. At the same time it can have content, if one desires content in something as incredible as it is already. The rock & roll songs I like, of course, are songs like "Summertime Blues"— man, that's beautiful. It says everything: Don't have the blues, it's summertime; you don't get the blues in summertime! There is no such thing. That's why there's no cure for them.

You and the group came out of a rough area, were very restless and had this thing: you were going to show everybody.

When I was in school, the geezers that were snappy dressers and got chicks would always like to talk about my nose. This seemed to be the biggest thing in my life: my fucking nose, man. Whenever my dad got drunk, he'd come up to me and say, "Look, son, you know looks aren't everything," and shit like this. He's getting drunk, and he's ashamed of me because I've got a huge nose, and he's trying to make me feel good. I know it's huge, and of course it became incredible, and I became an enemy of society. I had to get over this thing. I've done it. I do not think about my nose anymore. And if I had said this when I was a kid, if I ever said to myself, "One of these days you'll go through a whole day without once thinking that your nose is the biggest in the world, man"—you know, I'd have laughed.

It was huge. At that time, it was the reason I did everything. It's the reason I played the guitar. The reason I wrote songs. Everything. What I wanted to do was distract attention from my nose to my body and make people look at my body instead of at my face—turn my body into a machine. What is interesting is the fact that it was me versus society, until I could convince them that there was more to me than what they thought.

Now it's incredible to think about it. It's a very funny story, and it always makes me laugh at my parents, my father particularly. He was in a band whose leader was much richer than him, and the leader had shows of his own and a lovely house, and my dad still rents a house, never had a house of his own. They both started together and went to the same school and all this, and he used to say—and this guy, the leader of the band, happened to have a huge nose, absolutely huge— "Look at Ronny, look at Ronny. He's the leader of a famous orchestra. He's got a beautiful wife, a beautiful house, a lovely car. What more can you want? He makes music all his life. He's a respected man. What more can you want in life? He's got a huge nose, Peter."

I mean, I used to be completely speechless—of course, that's what I'm gonna have. I'm gonna have a huge car, a beautiful wife and all these things. And I have! It's so much like a fucking fairy tale in many ways.

What is your life like today?

Mainly laughs, actually, mainly laughs. The Who on tour is a very difficult trip; it's a delicate one, and it could be dangerous. Like one person gets a slight down, and the rest of us get a slight down, and so we have to keep spirits up even if it's false. Playing is enjoyable because we make it enjoyable.

Some people say to be a performer you've got to have that technique of being able to forget all your troubles and go up there and smile. It's a privilege, man, to be able to do that—when you're down, to be able to go onstage and elevate yourself back to what it's all about, to basic simple communication. To not get hung up in your own pathetic little scenes. It is an honor for someone who is on a fucked-up trip to get on a stage and do something simple and basic and honest and good. I think that people who are entertainers or performers are just damn lucky to have the chance. It's a perfect way of enjoying life. When you're on the stage, nothing goes wrong. Life is just heaven on the stage. Life is heaven onstage with the Who—that would be true, actually.

The Woodstock Festival

by Greil Marcus   September 1969

It was Sunday afternoon, Joe Cocker and the Grease Band had finished their powerhouse set, and suddenly the sky turned black and everyone knew it was going to rain again. It did. The ground on which two or three hundred thousand kids were sitting was begging to be turned back into mud, it got its wish—and it couldn't have mattered less to anyone. The wind hit then, too; it seemed to come from some half-forgotten Biblical apocalypse, but no one was ready for the Last Judgment, so we turned calamity into celebration.

"Cut the power, cut the power," they shouted on the stage, and the kids yelled, "Fuck the rain, fuck the rain," but it was really just another chance for a new kind of fun. Odd gifts of the elements, latter-day saints appeared out of nowhere. In front of the bandstand a black boy and a white boy took off their clothes and danced in the mud and the rain, round and round in a circle that grew larger as more joined them.

Moon Fire, a warlock, preached to a small crowd that had gathered under the stage for shelter. A tall man with red-brown hair and shining eyes, barefoot and naked under his robes, he had traveled to the festival with his lover, a sheep ("Call her Sunshine if you're a vegetarian, Chops if you're not," he said). Off in a corner was his staff, topped by a human skull, the pole bearing the message: DON'T EAT ANIMALS, LOVE THEM/THE KILLING OF ANIMALS CREATES THE KILLING OF MEN. He carefully explained how sheep were blessed with the greatest capacity of love of all animals, how a sheep could actually conceive by a man, though, tragically, because of some forgotten curse, the offspring was doomed to die at birth. Albert Grossman, his pigtail soaking wet, was standing nearby, and Moon Fire ambled over to offer his blessing. Grossman grinned. Rain simply meant it was a good time to meet new people.

The rain had been coming down for a long time now, but it seemed safe, and the stage crew put on a record. Creedence Clearwater's "Born On the Bayou" went soaring out of the great sound system and over the enormous crowd, and suddenly the Battle of the Bands of the night before had turned into American Bandstand. Three hundred thousand people jumped out of the mud and started to dance. Bopping their bodies and shaking their hair to the beat, hopping over and into the new puddles of garbage and mud.

The crush of more than a quarter of a million people sitting down had been some sight, but this was almost more than anyone could believe. Frisbees began to sail out of the crowd toward the stage, and the sound men jumped forward to throw them back. Then a football, then oranges, sandwiches, whatever was close at hand and worth throwing to other people.

Country Joe and the Fish had been scheduled to go on next, and Barry Melton cornered the head man and announced that the band wanted to play. "You can't play now. You'll all get electrocuted!" "We wanna play, man, we wanna play now. We don't need electricity." "They want to play," said one staffer to another. "You tell them they can't. Not me." The Fish played. In pouring down rain, good old never-say-die-and-never-down Country Joe and the Fish got up and pantomimed their music for the crowd that had turned them on. Barry grabbed a mike with no cord, Mark Kapner hoisted his little ukelele, and Joe handled the footballs that kept bouncing onto the stage. Greg Dewey, their new drummer, brought out his kit and sat down and pounded out a loud, fast, dancing drum solo. A tall fellow jumped onstage and began to dance across the boards while everyone cheered. Then he flashed and pulled off his pants and danced naked in the rain, grinning wildly, holding out his arms in a big gesture of welcome. Someone passed a bottle of champagne into the audience and then all of the food that could be found onstage. The Fish kept on playing, and Joe kept on smiling. They reminded me of the rodeo clowns that run into the pit when a rider's hurt and the bull's ready to trample him. They came through. But nobody was scared.

★   ★   ★

Friday was the first day of the Woodstock Music and Arts Fair, now moved to White Lake near Bethel, New York, a hundred miles from New York City and fifty miles from Woodstock proper. The intrepid ROLLING STONE crew thought it would be bright to beat the traffic, so we left the city early in the morning and headed up. When we got to Monticello, a little town eight miles from the festival, the traffic was light. Then we hit it. Eight miles of two-lane road jammed with thousands of cars that barely moved. Engines boiling over, people collapsed on the side of the road, everyone smiling in common bewilderment.

Automotive casualties looked like the skeletons of horses that died on the Oregon Trail. People began to improvise, driving on soft shoulders until they hit the few thousand who'd thought of the same thing, then stopping again. Finally the two lanes were transformed into four and still nothing moved. Bulbous vacationers (for this was the Catskills, laden with chopped liver and bad comedians) stared at the cars and the freaks and the nice kids, their stomachs sticking out into the road. Here we were, trying to get to the land of Hendrix and the Grateful Dead, all the while under the beady eyes of Mantovani fans.

There wasn't any traffic control. We sat still in our car and figured out all sorts of brilliant solutions to the transportation problem, everything from one-way roads to hired buses (a plan that failed at the last minute), but we still weren't getting anywhere, and it had been four hours now. This was the road on the map, right? No other way to get there? A lot of kids were pulling over and starting to walk through the fields. We had six miles to go. It was a cosmic traffic jam, where all the cars fall into place like pieces in a jigsaw puzzle and stay there forever.

The police estimated that there were a million people on the road that day trying to get to the festival. A million people; 186,000 tickets had been sold; the promoters figured that maybe 200,000, tops, would show. That seemed outlandish, if believable. But no one was prepared for what happened, and no one could have been.

Perhaps a quarter of a million never made it. They gave up and turned back, or parked on the highway and set up tents on the divider strip and stuck it out. Shit, they'd come to camp out for three days, and they were gonna do it. Many had walked fifteen miles in the rain and the mud, only to give up a mile or so before the festival

and turn back, but they were having fun. Camped on the highway with no idea where White Lake was or what was going on, they were making friends, dancing to car radios and making their own music on their own guitars.

"Isn't it pretty here, all the trees and the meadows? And whenever it gets too hot, it rains and cools everyone off. Wow." "Yeah, but you paid eighteen dollars and drove all the way from Ohio and you can't even get to the festival. Aren't you disappointed? Or pissed off?" "No, man. Everyone is so friendly, it's like being stuck in an elevator with people when the power goes off. But it's much nicer here than in an elevator."

It was an amazing sight, the highway to White Lake: it looked, as someone said, like Napoleon's army retreating from Moscow. It looked like that for three days. Everywhere one looked one saw tents and campfires, cars rolled into ditches, people walking, lying down, drinking, eating, reading, singing. Kids were sleeping, making love, wading in the marshes, trying to milk the local cows and trying to cook the local corn. The army of New York State Quickway 17B was on maneuvers.

★   ★   ★

Thinking back to Saturday, one image sticks in my mind, an image that I doubt is shared by many but one that I will never forget. Friday night, folk music had been played—Joan Baez, Arlo Guthrie, Sweetwater and Ravi Shankar. But by the next morning the future was unclear, and rumors that the area had been declared an official disaster seemed quite credible. Many left Saturday morning, oppressed by water shortages, ninety-degree heat, ninety-nine percent humidity and the crush of bodies.

"I love all these people," said a young girl, "they're all beautiful, and I never thought I'd be hassled by so many beautiful people, but I am, and I'm going home." Faces were drawn and tired, eyes blank, legs moving slowly on blistered and sore feet. The lack of water, food and toilets was becoming difficult, though everyone shared, and many simply roamed the area with provisions with the sole purpose of giving them away. But it got hotter and hotter, and a boy was running toward the lake in a panic, cradling his little puppy in his arms. The dog was unconscious, its tongue out of its mouth but not moving. The boy thought the dog was going to die, and he was scared. He kept running, and I stared after him, and then I left the festival and decided to go home. I couldn't get a plane, and I was lucky to stay, but that scene was real, and it too was part of the festival at White Lake.

★   ★   ★

Everyone in the country has seen pictures of the crowd. Was it bigger than it looked? Whoever saw so many people in the same spot, all with the same idea? Well, Hitler did, and General MacArthur, and Mao, but this was a somewhat better occasion. They came to hear the music, and they stayed to dig the scene and the people and the countryside. Any time, no matter who was playing, one could see thousands moving in every direction and more camped on every hill and all through the woods. The magnificent sound system was clear and audible long past the point at which one could no longer see the bands.

The outstanding thing was the unthinkable weight of the groups that played. Take Saturday night and Sunday morning (the music was scheduled to begin at one in the afternoon and run for twelve hours, but it began at three or four and went until the middle of the next morning). Here's the lineup: Joe Cocker, Country Joe and the Fish, Ten Years After, the Band, Johnny Winter, Blood, Sweat and Tears, Crosby, Stills, Nash and Young, the Paul Butterfield Blues Band, Sha Na Na and Jimi Hendrix. It's like watching God perform the Creation. "And for My next number...."

Sometime around four in the morning the stage crew began to assemble the apparatus for the festival's most unknown quantity, Crosby, Stills, Nash and Young. This was not exactly their debut—they'd played once or twice before—but this was a national audience, both in terms of the composition of the crowd and the press and because of the amazing musical competition with which they were faced.

It took a very long time to get everything ready, and the people onstage crowded around the amplifiers and the nine or ten guitars and the chairs and mikes and organ, more excited in anticipation than they'd been for any other group that night. A large semicircle of equipment protected the musicians from the rest of the people. The band was very nervous. Neil Young was stalking around, kissing his wife, trying to tune his guitar off in a corner, kissing his wife again, staring off away from the crowd. Stills and Nash paced back and forth and tested the organ and the mikes, and drummer Dallas Taylor fiddled with his kit and kept trying to make it more than perfect. Finally, they went on.

They opened with "Suite Judy Blue Eyes," stretching it out for a long time, exploring the figures of the song for the crowd, making their quiet music and flashing grimaces at each other when something went wrong. They strummed and picked their way through other numbers, and then began to shift around, Crosby singing with Stills, then Nash and Crosby, back and forth. They had the crowd all the way. They seemed like several bands rather than one.

Then they hit it. Right into "Long Time Gone," a song for a season if there ever was one: Stills on organ, shouting out the choruses; Neil snapping out lead; Crosby aiming his electric twelve-string out over the edge of the stage, biting off his words and stretching them out—lyrics as strong as any we are likely to hear.

There's something, something, something
Goin' on around here
That surely, surely, surely
Won't stand
The light of day
Ooooooohhh!
And it appears to be a long time...

I have never seen a musician more involved in his music. At one point Crosby nearly fell off the stage in his excitement.

Deep into the New York night they were, early Sunday morning in the dark after three days of chaos and order, and it seemed like the last of a thousand and one American nights. Two hundred thousand people covered the hills of a great natural amphitheater, campfires burning in the distance, the lights shining down from the enormous towers onto the faces of the band. Crosby, Stills, Nash and Young were just one of the many acts at this festival, and perhaps they wouldn't top the bill if paired with Hendrix or the Airplane or Creedence Clearwater or the Who or the Band, but this was their night. Their performance was scary, brilliant proof of the magnificence of music, and I don't believe it could have happened with such power anywhere else. This was a festival that had triumphed over itself, as Crosby and his band led the way toward the end of it.

★   ★   ★

The big cliché of the festival, heard more before than afterward, came down to this: If Monterey was the beginning, Woodstock was the end. Al Aronowitz, writing in the New York Post, spoke for many when he called the festival "a wake." But Woodstock was not a wake. It was a confused, chaotic founding of something new, something our world must now find a way to deal with. The limits have changed now; they've been pushed out. The priorities have been rearranged, and new, "impractical" ideas must be taken seriously. The mind boggles.

The festival constituted the third largest city in the state of New York. To call it over was like saying that the entire population of Minneapolis had to pick up and leave, right now. To convey the meaning of it one must chase after ultimately useless metaphors about stars in the sky or the people in China. Well, if you laid 'em all in a line, they'd reach around the equator five times. Got it? But everyone there was a rock & roll fan and knew how to dance and had a favorite song. People just like those everyone hangs out with, but this time it seemed as if they were all in one place at one time. They weren't though—not yet.

Year of the Fork, Night of the Hunter

by David Felton and David Dalton   June 1970

But the decadence of history is looking for a pawn

To a nightmare of knowledge he opens up the gate

A blinding revelation is served upon his plate

That beneath the greatest love is a hurricane of hate

—PHIL OCHS, *"Crucifixion"*

Three young girls dance down the hallway of the Superior Court Building in Los Angeles, holding hands and singing one of Charlie's songs. They might be on their way to a birthday party in their short, crisp cotton dresses, but actually they are attending a preliminary hearing to a murder trial.

A middle-aged lady in Bel Air wants to "mother" Charlie, and two little girls send a letter to him in jail: "At first we thought you were guilty. But then we read in the papers about these kids who were stabbed to death in the same way as the Sharon Tate murders. We knew you hadn't done it because you were in jail at the time. We knew you hadn't done it anyway when we saw your face in the newspaper …Love,…."

Charlie gets letters from little girls every day. They come from New Hampshire, Minnesota, Los Angeles. A convicted bank robber who met Charlie in jail writes "The Gospel According to Pawnee Fred, the Thief on the Other Cross," in which he asks, "Is Manson Son of Man?"

Thirty miles northwest of the courthouse, seven miles due north of Leonard Nimoy's Pet Pad in Chatsworth (supplies, fish, domestics, exotics), a circle of rustic women at the Spahn Movie Ranch weave their own hair into an elaborate rainbow vest for Charlie. Most of them are early members of Charlie's three-year-old family. There's Lynne Fromme—they call her Squeaky—Sandra Good, Gypsy, Brenda, Sue, Cappy, Jeany.

"We've been working on this vest for two years," says Sandra, "adding things, sewing on patches. It's for Charlie to wear in court." And Squeaky adds, "Wouldn't it be beautiful to have a photograph of Charlie wearing it? And all of us standing around close to him, hugging him like we used to?"

Wouldn't it be beautiful to have the others standing around, too, the rest of the family, the others imprisoned? Tex Watson and Patti Krenwinkel and Linda Kasabian and, oh yeah, the snitch, Sadie Glutz. Her real name is Susan Atkins, but the family calls her Sadie Glutz because that's what Charlie named her.

Meanwhile, Charlie sits blissfully in his cell at the Los Angeles County Jail, composing songs, converting fellow inmates to his gospel of love and Christian submission, and occasionally entertaining a disturbing thought: Why haven't they gotten in touch? A simple phone call would do it. Surely they've received the telegrams, the letters. Surely they realize that he knows, he *understands* their glorious revelation; he understands the whole fucking double album.

> *Everywhere there's lots of piggies*
>
> *Living piggy lives*
>
> *You can see them out for dinner*
>
> *With their piggy wives*
>
> —GEORGE HARRISON, *"Piggies"*

★　　　★　　　★

Ten blocks from the new county jail stands the old County Hall of Justice, a grotesque, brown brick fortress that for decades has guarded the Los Angeles Civic Center from aesthetic inroads. The entire sixth floor belongs to the district attorney and his staff, a member of which, now alone on his lunch hour, unlocks a file cabinet and withdraws several neatly bound, family-type photo albums. Slowly he turns each page, studies each snapshot, each personality:

• Sharon Tate, considered one of Hollywood's prettier, more popular, promising young stars; wife of genius film sorcerer Roman Polanski. After her biggest film, *Valley of the Dolls*, she retreated to private life to enjoy her first pregnancy. The photographs show her in her eight month.

• Jay Sebring, the handsome young hair stylist who revolutionized the fashion industry by introducing hair styling to men, convincing them—despite early masculine scoffs—there was something better looking than a shave, even if you had to pay ten times the price. He once was Miss Tate's fiancé.

• Wojciech Frykowski, Polanski's boyhood pal who came to Hollywood with hopes of directing films himself. His luck at this was dismal, and even Polanski later admitted he had little talent. Instead, he began directing home movies inside his head, investing heavily in many forms of exotic dope.

• Abigail Folger, heiress to the Folgers Coffee millions, an attractive Radcliffe girl considered by neighbors to be the most charming of Polanski's house guests. She met Frykowski in New York and had become his lover.

• Steven Parent, an eighteen-year-old from the Los Angeles suburb of El Monte, a friend of Polanski's caretaker, unknown to the others, a nobody like the rest of us. Had fortune been on his side, he would have so remained.

• Leno LaBianca, owner of a grocery-store chain, and his wife Rosemary, an ordinary couple of the upper middle class, fond of such quiet pleasures as boating, water-skiing and watching late-night television in their pajamas. They knew nothing of Sharon Tate and her friends, living miles away in different neighborhoods and different worlds.

• Gary Hinman, music teacher, bagpipe player and one-time friend of Charlie Manson's. He once, in fact, gave the Manson family his Toyota, although the circumstances surrounding that gift have since come into question.

The snapshots are homey little numbers, color polaroids taken by staff photographers from the county coroner's office and the Los Angeles Police Department. They show all the wounds, the nakedness, the blood. Sometimes the exposure is a little off, but the relevant details are there—shots of the rooms, the bullet holes, the blood on the furniture and floors, the bizarre blood writing on the walls, words like RISE and HELTER SKELTER and PIGGIES.

★   ★   ★

Los Angeles is the third largest city in America, according to population, but easily the largest, according to raw real estate. It is bordered by the Pacific Ocean to the south and southwest, by Ventura County to the west, by the San Gabriel Mountains and fire-prone Angeles National Forest to the north and by scores of cruddy, smoggy little towns and cities to the east. Charles Manson knew his city well. Like many Los Angeles residents, he learned to drive long distances regularly without giving a second thought. During his two years as a free man in Southern California, he frequently "made the rounds," visiting friends, keeping business appointments, preaching to small groups, giving and taking material possessions.

Starting at the Spahn Movie Ranch in the extreme northwestern corner of Los Angeles, drive two miles east on Santa Susana Pass Road to Topanga Canyon itself. It was here that Manson and his family first lived after arriving from Haight-Ashbury in late 1967, and it was here that Manson first met Gary Hinman.

Hinman's house is a little further down the road, almost where Topanga Canyon meets the beach at Pacific Coast Highway.

You can't see into the house now, of course, because the cops boarded it up last July after they found Hinman's body perforated with stab wounds. They say he was tortured for forty-eight hours. On a nearby wall they found the words POLITICAL PIGGIES and a neat little cat's-paw print in blood. Bobby Beausoleil, a guitarist and member of Manson's family, has already been sentenced to death, and Manson and Susan Atkins are awaiting trial in the matter.

After driving onto Pacific Coast Highway, take a left, and after two miles, take another left. Now you're on Sunset Boulevard, winding through wealthy Pacific Palisades where, for a short time in early 1968, the Manson family lived with Beach Boy Dennis Wilson. Wilson moved shortly after Manson allegedly threatened him with a bullet.

Keep driving east on Sunset for another eight or ten miles past Brentwood Heights, past Mandeville Canyon, over the San Diego Freeway, past UCLA and Bel Air and Beverly Glen. And when you reach the center of Beverly Hills, turn left on Canon and head north into Benedict Canyon. Now here you may need a more detailed map because the streets get pretty tricky with all the turns and dead ends. But up in Benedict Canyon there's this little dirt road, Cielo Drive, which dead ends at the old, rambling, hillside house where producer Terry Melcher, Doris Day's son, used to live. Manson paid several business calls on him there, but the business was never completed before Melcher moved out early last summer.

Neighbors hardly had had a chance to meet the new residents when, on the bright Saturday morning of last August 9th, Mrs. Winifred Chapman, a maid, ran screaming from the house, across the huge grounds and parking lot, through the iron gate and down the road: "There's bodies and blood all over the place!"

Not a bad description. Police found Steven Parent just inside the gate, shot five times in his white Rambler, the wheels of the car already turned toward the road in a mad attempt to escape. Wojciech Frykowski's body lay in front of the house, shot and stabbed again and again. Twenty yards down the rolling lawn, underneath a fir tree, they found Abigail Folger dead and curled up in a bloody nightgown.

Inside the house Jay Sebring and Sharon Tate lay stabbed to death near the living-room couch, connected by a single nylon cord wrapped around their necks and thrown over a rafter. Sebring was also shot and his head covered with a pillowcase. On the front door police found the word PIG written in blood with a towel. If the gate's locked, you won't be able to see the house because it's set back some from the road. Anyway, that's where it is.

Now make a U and head back down to Sunset. Continue east for another ten miles, along the famous and more and more plastic Sunset Strip, past the tall, swanky office-building monuments to Hollywood flackery, past the decaying radio empires of the Forties, clear to Western Avenue, where you take a left. A mile north, Western turns right and becomes Los Feliz Boulevard, cutting east through the wealthy, residential Los Feliz District that skirts the foothills of Griffith Park. After about three miles, just before Los Feliz crosses the Golden State Freeway, drive into the winding, hillside streets to your right, where you'll find Waverly Drive.

In August 1968, Manson and his family started visiting Harold True, a UCLA student who lived with some other guys on Waverly. They were all good friends, and the family just liked to go up there and hang around and smoke dope and sing and shoot the shit. True later moved to Van Nuys, where he presently lives with Phil Kaufman, a former member of the family who produced Manson's record.

True's neighbors, incidentally, were Leno and Rosemary LaBianca who, a year later on the morning of August 10th, were found stabbed—or rather carved—to death inside their home. The words DEATH TO PIGS, HELTER SKELTER and RISE were written, again in blood, on the kitchen walls. And someone had etched WAR on Leno LaBianca's stomach with a fork.

Anyway, those are just some of the spots Manson liked to visit on his frequent tours of the big city. Cut back to Los Feliz, head north on the Golden State Freeway for eighteen miles, cut west across the north end of the Valley on Devonshire Street—another ten miles—turn right on Topanga Canyon Boulevard, and you're practically back at the Spahn ranch.

The whole round trip is eighty miles or so. That may seem like a big distance, but actually the roads are good and it shouldn't take longer than two or three hours, especially if you take it on a Sunday afternoon or, say, late at night.

★　　　★　　　★

Perhaps no two recent events have so revealed the cut-rate value of public morality and private life as the killing of Sharon Tate and the arrest of Charles Manson. Many were quick to criticize *The Los Angeles Times* for publishing bright and early one Sunday morning the grisly (and since recanted) confessions of Susan Atkins. Any doubts about Manson's power to cloud men's minds were buried that morning between Dick Tracy and one of the world's great real-estate sections. Sexy Sadie laid it down for all to see.

Critics accused the *Times* of paying a healthy sum to promoter Larry Schiller, who had obtained the confession from Miss Atkins's attorneys in return for a cut of the profits. The *Times* responded publicly with silence, privately with denial. No money was paid, said the editors. Schiller had sold the story to various European

Sunday editions, they said, and an eight-hour time difference allowed the *Times* to pick it up from one of their European correspondents. In other words, "If we hadn't run it here, some other paper would have."

ROLLING STONE has since learned that the *Times* explanation was at least partly correct. No money was paid, that's true, or at least not that much. Because, dig, the *Times* people didn't buy the confession—they wrote it. Word for word. Not only the confession but the book that followed, *The Killing of Sharon Tate,* with "eight pages of photographs," published by New American Library, a *Times-Mirror* subsidiary.

In the volume, Schiller gratefully acknowledges "the invaluable aid of two journalists who worked with the author in preparing this book and the original interviews with Susan Atkins." Those two journalists, it turns out, were Jerry Cohen and Dial Torgerson, both veteran members of the *Times* rewrite crew.

What possible justification could the *Times* editors have had for running the confessions? Can an individual's right to a fair trial be compromised so easily by the fictitious right of the public to be entertained? If Miss Atkins's confession does not constitute damaging pretrial publicity, what does?

Clearly Charles Manson already stands as the villain of our time, the symbol of animalism and evil. He is already so hated by the public that all attempts so far to exploit his reputation have failed miserably. Of the 2000 albums of his music that were pressed, less than 300 have sold. A skin flick based on popular assumptions about Manson and his family, *Love in the Commune,* closed after two days in San Francisco. Even Cohen and Torgerson's book is reportedly in financial trouble.

The most blatant, if less damaging, assault on the concept of pretrial impartiality comes not from the Establishment or the Far Right, but the Far Left, the Weathermen faction of the SDS. According to an item from the *Liberation News Service,* the Weathermen have made Manson a revolutionary hero on the assumption that he is guilty. Praising him for having offed some "rich honky pigs," they offer us a prize example of bumper-sticker mentality: MANSON POWER—THE YEAR OF THE FORK!

The underground press in general has assumed a paranoid-schizo attitude toward Manson, undoubtedly hypersensitive to the relentless gloating of the cops who, after a five-year search, finally found a long-haired devil you could love to hate. Starting in mid-January, the *Los Angeles Free Press* banner-headlined Manson stories for three weeks in a row: MANSON CAN GO FREE! M.D. ON MANSON'S SEX LIFE! MANSON INTERVIEW! EXCLUSIVE! EXCLUSIVE! Later, the *Free Press* began a weekly column by Manson written from jail. About the same time, a rival underground paper, *Tuesday's Child,* ran Manson's picture across the entire front page with the headline MAN OF THE YEAR: CHARLES MANSON. In case you missed the point, in their next issue they covered the front page with a cartoon of Manson on the cross. The plaque nailed above his head read simply HIPPIE.

Of course, not all the stories in the *Free Press* and *Tuesday's Child* were pro-Manson. Some were very lukewarm, others were simply anticop. The question that seemed to split underground editorial minds more than any other was simply: Is Manson a hippie or isn't he?

★   ★   ★

It's hard to imagine a better setting for Manson's vision of the Apocalypse, his black revolution, than Los Angeles, a city so large and cumbersome it defies common senses, defies the absurd. For thousands of amateur prophets it provides a virtual Easter-egg hunt of spooky truths. Its climate and latitude are identical to Jerusalem. It easily leads the country in our race toward ecological doom. It has no sense of the past; the San Andreas Fault separates it from the rest of the continent by a million years.

If Manson's racial views seem incredibly naive, which they are (after preaching against the Black Panthers for two years, he recently asked who Huey Newton was), they are similar to views held by hundreds of thousands of others in that city and by that city's mayor. Citizens there last year returned to office Mayor Sam Yorty, whose administration was riddled with conflicts of interest and bribery convictions, rather than elect a thoughtful, soft-spoken, middle-of-the-road ex-cop who happened to be black. Full-page newspaper ads, sponsored by a police organization, pictured the man as a wild African savage and asked voters, "Will Your Home Be Safe with Bradley as Mayor?"

The Spahn Movie Ranch may seem a miserable place for kids to live, with its filthy, broken-down shacks and stagnant streams filled daily with shoveled horse shit. Life there may seem degenerate, a dozen or more people eating garbage, sleeping, balling and raising babies in a twenty-foot trailer. But for more than two years most of those kids have preferred that way of life—life with Charlie—than living in the homes of their parents. The press likes to put the Manson family in quotation marks—"family." But it's a real family, with real feelings of devotion, loyalty and disappointment. For Manson and all the others, it's the only family they've ever had.

One is tempted to say that Manson spent twenty-two of his thirty-five years in prison, that he is more a product of the penal system than Haight-Ashbury. But it cannot be dismissed that easily. Charles Manson raises some very serious questions about our culture, whether he is entirely part of it or not.

There is no new morality, as *Time* and *Life* would have us believe, but a growing awareness that the old morality has not been practiced for some time. The right to pursue different goals, to be free of social and economic oppression, the right to live in peace and equity with our brothers—this is Founding Fathers stuff. In the meantime, we must suffer the void, waiting for the old, dead, amoral culture to be buried. For the younger among us, the wait is extremely frustrating, even unbearable.

Into this void rode Charlie Manson in the fall of 1967, full of charm and truth and gentle goodness, like Robert Mitchum's psychopathic preacher in *Night of the Hunter* with LOVE and HATE inscribed on opposing hands. This smiling, dancing music man offered a refreshing short cut, a genuine and revolutionary new morality that redefines, or rather eliminates, the historic boundaries between life and death. Behind Manson's attitude toward death is the ancient mystical belief that we are all part of one body—an integral tenet of Hinduism, Buddhism and Christianity, as expressed by Saint Paul in *1 Corinthians*: "For as the body is one and hath many members, and all the members of that one body, being many, are one body; so also is Christ."

But Manson adds a new twist; he wants us to take the idea literally, temporarily. He believes that he, and all human beings—are God and the Devil at the same time, that all human beings are part of each other, that human life has no individual value. If you kill a human being, you're just killing a part of yourself; it has no meaning. "Death is psychosomatic," says Manson.

Thus, the foundation of all historic moral concepts is neatly discarded. Manson's is a morality of amorality. "If God is one, what is bad?" he asks. Manson represents a frightening new phenomenon, the acid-ripped street fighter, erasing the barrier between the two outlaw cultures—the head and the hood—described by Tom Wolfe in *The Electric Kool-Aid Acid Test*:

> The Angels were too freaking real. Outlaws? They were outlaws by choice, from the word go, all the way out in Edge City. Further! The hip world, the vast majority of acid heads, were still playing the eternal charade of the middle-class intellectuals—Behold my wings! Freedom! Flight!—but you don't actually expect me to jump off that cliff, do you?

Perhaps it was inevitable for someone like Manson to come along—someone who would jump off that cliff.

★   ★   ★

Charles Manson
Photograph by UPI/Bettman Newsphotos

THE MOST DANGEROUS MAN IN THE WORLD
An Audience with Charles Manson, a.k.a. Jesus Christ

Moving slowly across the municipal geometry of civic buildings and police officers, a man comes toward us looking directly into the sun, his arms stretched out in supplication, like the Sierra Indian. From a hundred feet away his eyes are flashing, all two-dimensional boundaries gone. A strange place to be tripping, outside the new, all concrete, Los Angeles County Jail.

"You're from ROLLING STONE," *he says.*

"How did you know?"

No answer. He leads us to the steps of the jail's main entrance, pivots and again locks his gaze into the sun.

"Spirals," he whispers. "Spirals coming away…circles curling out of the sun." His fingers weave patterns in the air. A little sun dance.

"A hole in the fourth dimension," we suggest.

His easy reply: "A hole in all dimensions."

This is Clem, an early member of the family called Manson. Inside is another, Squeaky, a friendly girl with short, red hair and freckles. Her eyes, too, are luminous, not tripping, but permanently innocent. Children from the Village of the Damned.

We went to the attorney-room window to fill out forms. Two guards watched from a glass booth above. A surprise: we were not searched. "Step inside the gate," says a disembodied voice. "Keep clear of the gate."

After nearly an hour he comes in. The guards greet him, casual, friendly.

"Hi, Charlie, how are you today?"

"Hi, man, I'm doin' fine," he says, smiling.

He's wearing prison clothes, blue denim jacket and pants. His hair is very long and bushy, he pushes it out of his face nervously. He looks different, older and stranger than in the press photos. His beard has been shaved off recently, and it is growing back black and stubbly. He has a long face with a stubborn jaw, wizened and weathered like the crazy country faces you see in old TVA photographs. A cajun Christ. He moves, springing, light as a coyote.

"Can't shake hands," he explains, jumping back. "Against the rules."

He unfolds casually in the chair. He strokes his chin, like a wizard trapped under a stone for a thousand years.

Are you really happy with your record?

All the good music was stolen. What's there is a couple of years old. I've written hundreds of songs since then. I've been writing a lot while I was in jail.

I never really dug recording, you know, all those things pointing at you. You get into the studio, and it's hard to sing into microphones. [*He clutches his pencil rigidly, like a mike.*] Giant phallic symbols pointing at you. All my latent tendencies …[*He starts laughing and making sucking sounds. He is actually blowing the pencil!*] My relationship to music is completely subliminal, it just flows through me.

"Ego Is a Too Much Thing" is a strange track. What do you mean by ego?

Ego is the man, the male image. [*His face tenses, his eyes dart and threaten. He clenches his fist, bangs it on the table. He gets completely behind it, acting it out, the veins standing out in his neck.*] Ego is the phallic symbol, the helmet, the gun. The man behind the gun, the mind behind the man behind the gun. My philosophy is that ego is the thinking mind. The mind you scheme with, make war with. They shoved all the love in the back, hid it away. Ego is like, "I'm going to war with my ego stick." [*He waves an imaginary rifle around, then sticks it in his crotch.*]

In "Ego" there's this line, "Your heart is a-pumpin', your paranoia's a-jumpin."

Yeah, well, paranoia is just a kind of awareness, and awareness is just a form of love. Paranoia is the other side of love. Once you give in to paranoia, it ceases to exist. That's why I say, submission is a gift, just give in to it, don't resist. It's like saying, "Tie me on the cross!" Here, want me to hold the nail? Everything is beautiful if you want to experience it totally.

How does paranoia become awareness?

It's paranoia…and it's paranoia…and it's paranoia…UNH! [*He mimics terror, total paranoia, scrunching up his body into a ball of vibrating fear that suddenly snaps and slumps back in ecstasy.*] It's like when I went into the court-room. Everybody in the courtroom wanted to kill me. I saw the hatred in their eyes, and I knew they wanted to kill me, and I asked the sheriffs, "Is somebody going to shoot me?" That's why I feel like I'm already dead. I know it's coming. It's the cops who put that feeling into their heads. They don't come in with that.

They whisper, so I can hear it, "Sharon Tate's father is in court." And then they go over and shake him down to see if he has a gun, and they're just putting that idea into his head. He has a nice face. I saw him the first day in court. He doesn't want to kill me. They're putting that into his head. You know, they say things like, "We wouldn't want you to shoot the defendant." And every day I see him in court, his face gets a little harder, and one day he's gonna do it.

And they put the whole thing in his head, feeding him all those negative vibrations. And if you keep doing that, it's got to happen. I know it's coming. They all got their things pointed at me, and they want to use them badly. But actually they can't use them, and that's what makes them so mad. They can't make love with them, they're all suffering from sex paranoia.

They've been following me for three years, trying to find something, and wherever they go there's like thirty women. And that really makes them mad. They can't understand what all these women are doing with one guy.

They're looking for something dirty in everything, and if you're looking for something, you'll find it. You have to put up some kind of face for them, and that's the only face they understand.

The answer is to accept the cross. I've accepted it. I can go up on the cross in my imagination. Oh, ooooooh, aaaah! [*The orgasmic crucifixion! He gives a long sigh of relief.*]

Have you ever seen the coyote in the desert? [*His head prowls back and forth.*] Watching, tuned in, completely aware. Christ on the cross, the coyote in the desert—it's the same thing, man. The coyote is beautiful. You can learn from the coyote just like you can learn from a child. A baby is born into this world in a state of fear. Total paranoia and awareness. He sees the world with eyes not used yet. As he grows up, his parents lay all this stuff on him. They tell him, when they should be letting him tell them. Let the children lead you.

The death trip is something they pick up from their parents, mama and papa. They don't have to die. You can live forever. It's all been put in your head. They program him by withholding love. They make him into a mechanical toy. [*He sings from his album, jerking his arms like a spastic Tin Man.*] "I am a mechanical boy/ I am my mother's toy."

Everything happened perfectly for me in my life. I picked the right mother, and my father, I picked him too. He was a gas, he cut out early in the game. He didn't want me to get hung up. [*Charlie laughs privately at his private joke.*]

Can you tell us what you mean by submission? If we are all one, how can you justify being a leader?

There is only One. I'm the One. Me is first. I don't care about you. I'm not thinking about what other people think, I just do what my soul tells me. People said I was a leader. Here's the kind of leader I was. I made sure the animals were fed. Any sores on the horses? I'd heal them. Anything need fixing? I'd fix it. When it was cold, I was always the last one to get a blanket.

Pretty soon I'd be sitting on the porch, and I'd think, "I'll go and do this or that." And one of the girls would say, "No, let me." You've got to give up, lie down and die for other people, then they'll do anything for you. When you are willing to become a servant for other people, they want to make you a master. In the end, the girls would be just dying to do something for me. I'd ask one of them to make a shirt for me, and she'd be just thrilled because she could do something for me. They'll work twenty-four hours a day if you give them something to do.

I can get along with girls, they give up easier. I can make love to them. Man has this ego thing. [*Charlie stiffens up, holding on to his prick.*] I can't make love to that. Girls break down easier. When you get beyond the ego thing, all you're left with is you; you make love with yourself. With a girl, you can make love with her until she's exhausted. You can make love with her until she gives up her mind, then you can make love with love. [*Charlie starts to run his hands up and down his body, caressing himself like a stripper, his fingers tingling like a faith healer in a trance. They dance all over his body.*] You climax with every move you make, you climax with every step you take. The breath of love you breathe is all you need to believe. [*Charlie pulls a thousand postures from the air. He squirms, stiffens, anguishes with ecstasy.*] Oooooh, aaaaaaaah, uhhhhn! Your beard, it feels sooooo good, mmmmmmmm! [*His fingers, with half-inch-long nails, fondle his own face, his stubbly chin, impersonating the hands of an unseen lover, making love with himself.*] Your beard feels sooo good, mmmmmmmm, yes it does. It all comes from the father into the woman. [*Suddenly he assumes his teaching position.*] See, it's because I am a bastard that I can accept the truth. Hell, I am my father! The Father…the Son…[*He withdraws in mock terror from some imaginary host of accusers, pushing the thought away with extended hands.*] No, no, NO…it's not me…you've got it all wrong. I'm not—you couldn't think that! I don't know what you're talking about. Listen, I'll get a job. [*He continues fighting his phantom, Jacob wrestling with his angel, then giggles.*] See, the cop-out is Christianity. If you believe in Christianity, you don't have to believe in Christ. Get a job and you won't have to think about it at all.

Being in jail protected me in a way from society. I was inside, so I couldn't take part, play the games that society expects you to play. I've been in jail twenty-two years. The most I was out was maybe six months. I just wasn't contaminated, I kept my innocence.

I got so I actually loved solitary. That was supposed to be punishment. I loved it. There is nothing to do in prison anyway, so all they can get you to do is "Get up! Sit down!" So solitary was great. I began to hear music inside my head. I had concerts inside my cell. When the time came for my release, I didn't want to go. Yeah, man, solitary was beautiful.

What do you feel about Judge Keene taking away your pro per privilege?

The judge is just the flip side of the preacher. He took away my *pro per* privilege because they don't want me to speak. They want to shut me up, because they know if I get up on the stand, I am going to blow the whole thing wide open. They don't want to hear it.

Between you and me, if that judge asks for my life, I'm going to give it to him right there in the courtroom. But first of all he is going to have to deal with my music, the music in my fingers and my body. [*Charlie demonstrates. His nails tap out an incredible riff on the table, the chair, the glass of the booth, like the scurrying footsteps of some strung-out rodent.*]

He is going to have to deal with that power. I'm probably one of the most dangerous men in the world if I want to be. But I never wanted to be anything but me. If the judge says death, I am death. I've always been dead. Death is life.

Anything you see in me is in you. If you want to see a vicious killer, that's who you'll see, do you understand that? If you see me as your brother, that's what I'll be. It all depends on how much love you have. I am you, and when you can admit that, you will be free. I am just a mirror.

Did you see what they did to that guy in the Chicago Seven trial? Hoffman saw in those guys what he wanted to see. That's why he found them guilty. The white man is fading, everybody knows that. The black man will take over, they can't stop it. And they won't be able to stop me either unless they gag me.

Why do you think black people will gain power?

They were the first people to have power. The pharaohs were black. The Egyptians took one man and raised him up above the rest. They put him on the throne and they fed all these lines of energy into him. [*He folds his arms across his chest like Tutankhamen, holding his pencil between two fingers like a pharaoh's rod.*] That means power. This represents the penis, the power. They built the pyramids with this energy. Love built the pyramids. Power without love is aggression. There has been no true love since the pharaohs. Except for J.C. He knew what love meant.

Tempt me not. Do you remember the story about Jesus on the hill? You know, the Devil takes Him to the edge of this cliff, [*Charlie leans over the table as if precariously on the edge of the Void*] and he says to Him, "If you're God, prove it by jumping off the edge." And Jesus says, "There ain't nothing to prove, man." When you doubt, your mind is in two parts. It's divided against itself. See, Christ is saying, "Past, get behind me." The Devil is in the past. The Devil is the past. What he is saying is, "Don't think. He who thinks is lost, because if you have to think about something, to doubt it, you're lost already."

My philosophy is: Don't think. I don't believe in the mind that you think with and scheme with. I don't believe in words.

If you don't believe in words, why do you use so many of them?

Words are symbols. All I'm doing is jumbling the symbols in your brain. Everything is symbolic. Symbols are just connections in your brain. Even your body is a symbol.

Can you explain the meaning of Revelations, Chapter 9?

What do you think it means? It's the battle of Armageddon. It's the end of the world. It was the Beatles' "Revolution 9" that turned me on to it. It predicts the overthrow of the Establishment. The pit will be opened, and that's when it will all come down. A third of all mankind will die. The only people who escape will be those who have the seal of God on their foreheads. You know the part, "They will seek death, but they will not find it."

Can you explain the prophecies you found in the Beatles' double album?

[*Charlie starts drawing some lines on the back of a sheet of white paper, three vertical lines and one horizontal line. In the bottom area he writes the word SUB.*] Okay. Give me the names of four songs on the album. [*We chose "Piggies," "Helter Skelter" and "Blackbird," and he adds "Rocky Raccoon." Charlie writes down the titles at the top of each vertical section. Under "Helter Skelter" he draws a zigzag line, under "Blackbird" two strokes, somehow indicating bird sounds. Very strange.*] This bottom part is the subconscious. At the end of each song, there is a little tag piece on it, a couple of notes. Or like in "Piggies," there's "oink, oink, oink." Just these couple of sounds. And all these sounds are repeated in "Revolution 9." Like in "Revolution 9" all these pieces are fitted together and they predict the violent overthrow of the white man. Like you'll hear "oink, oink," and then right after that, machine-gun fire. [*He sprays the room with imaginary slugs.*] AK - AK - AK - AK - AK - AK!

Do you really think the Beatles intended to mean that?

I think it's a subconscious thing. I don't know whether they did it or not. But it's there. It's an association in the subconscious. This music is bringing on the revolution, the unorganized overthrow of the Establishment. The Beatles know in the sense that the subconscious knows.

What does "Rocky Raccoon" mean, then?

Coon. You know that's a word they use for black people. You know the line, "Gideon checked out/And he left it no doubt/To help with good Rocky's revival." Rocky's revival—re-vival. It means coming back to life. The black man is going to come back into power again. "Gideon checks out" means that it's all written out there in the New Testament, in the Book of Revelations.

Do you think you will ever get out of jail?

I don't care. I'm as at home here as anywhere. Anywhere is anywhere you want it to be. It's all the same to me. I'm not afraid of death, so what can they do to me? I don't care what they do. The only thing I care about is my love.

Death is psychosomatic. The gas chamber? [*Charlie laughs.*] My God, are you kidding? It's all verses, all climaxes, all music. Death is permanent solitary confinement, and there is nothing I would like more than that.

★   ★   ★

A bell rings. A deputy comes over to tell us the time is up. The jail is closing for the night. Charlie gives us a song he's composed in jail, "Man Cross Woman," written neatly on lined yellow paper ripped from a legal tablet.

Charlie just stands at the entrance to the attorney room, smiling. Outside, in the distance, Clem and Squeaky wave and smile back ecstatically at their captured kind, their fingers pressed against the glass. The deputies watch Charlie, puzzled, as he flops his head from one side to the other like a clown. They cannot see Clem and Squeaky behind them, imitating his every movement, communicating in a silent animal language.

An Evening with the Grateful Dead

by Michael Lydon   September 1970

Wchange and our changings change, a friend said once. It sounded true, but it seems too that through it all we stay the same. That obscure rumination takes us to, of all places, backstage at the Fillmore West, a spot that has witnessed its share of changes and has gone through some of its own. Backstage used to be a few murky closets with just a few inches and a thin wall separating them from the amps. Now the car dealer on the corner has gone through his changes, and Bill Graham has extra floor space for a dressing room as big as the lobby of a grand hotel.

No palms but a lot of sofas, on one of which sat Jerry Garcia as if he owned the place. It had once been the Carousel, changed from an Irish dance hall to a mad den of psychedelic thieves. Jerry Garcia had played the original Fillmore—he had been a founding member, so to speak. Bill Graham had owned that Fillmore, and now he owned this one. There was a time when Bill Graham was always on hand when the Dead were playing, but this night he was in New York on business (the next night in L.A.), and a second- or third-generation underling, a soft-faced young man named Jerry Pompili, was watching the clock and counting the heads on behalf of Fillmore Inc.

It was just past the 8:30 showtime, and Jerry P. approached Garcia and asked if they were ready to go on. Jerry G. was deep into one of his eyeball-to-glittering-eyeball monologues, but he paused long enough for a glance around that indicated he was the only musician present and accounted for. "The other guys will be here in a minute, man," he said. "Phil's the only one who might be late."

"Well, what happens if Phil is late?" said Pompili allowing into his voice a hint of his hope that the Dead would find a way to start without him, to be nice for once. A hopeless hope.

"Nothing happens," said Jerry G., grinning deep within his hairy tangle. "We'll start whenever Phil arrives."

"Okay," said Pompili, shrinking like a tired balloon, and Jerry geared back up to rapping speed, instantly oblivious to the interruption.

Everything had changed, and nothing too. After over five years of extra-inning play, the celebrated Fillmore (and all of rock & roll showbiz) versus Grateful Dead game was still a nothing-nothing tie. For five of those years the Dead took their lumps, always scraping through but never out of trouble. In the past half year, however, their tenacity has finally begun to pay off (perseverence furthers, says the *Book of Changes*). The years of weathering cosmic crises have given them an unshakeable musical and group foundation (and even an odd sort of financial stability), and on that they are building afresh.

Typically, their luck waited until the last possible moment to change. Nineteen sixty-nine ended with the near disaster of Altamont. The Dead family had been crucial in its organization, and they were as responsible as anyone for the sanctioned presence of the Angels. That day (they did not even get to play in the end) was, says Jerry, "a hard, hard lesson." While they were absorbing it in early 1970, they had an epic management crisis. Their manager, whom they had chosen because of his honesty and earnestness, was irritating some family members who did not trust his ingratiating manner. Weeks of tense encounters led to a showdown, and the manager was let go. Only then did the band discover that he had been bilking them all along; by then he had disappeared, and no one had the time or the heart for a suit.

Then they got busted en masse in New Orleans (their second time, the first was in the fall of '67 in San Francisco). That turned out to be just an inconvenience of time and money, but in March they didn't know that. In the middle of all of this they had to do a record. Something complex was out of the question; Jerry and his writing partner Robert Hunter had some tunes, so they walked into Pacific High Recorders in San Francisco and banged it out in nine days.

The result was *Workingman's Dead*, one of the best of the few good records released this year, their simplest production since the first LP, and their most popular release so far. "It was something," said Jerry. "All this heavy bullshit was flying around us, so we just retreated in there and made music. Only the studio was calm. The record was the only concrete thing happening. The rest was part of that insane legal and financial figment of everybody's imagination, so I guess it came out of a place that was real to all of us. It was good old solid work. T.C. [keyboardist Tom Constanten] had just left to go his own way, and with his influence gone, we got back to being a rock & roll band again, not an experimental-music group. Man, we had been wanting to boogie for a long time.

"We're feeling good," Jerry went on, "really laid back, a little older and groovier, not traveling so much, staying at home and quieting down. We used to push ourselves and get crazy behind it, but now we're all getting more done but not having to work at it so hard."

No one could say when the turn from the old Grateful Dead to the new began, but the key was opening up the band's structure. The Dead's complex personal changes are as legendary as their public ones, and they ended only when they decided that they didn't have to be just the Grateful Dead. They could also be Bobby Ace and the Cards from the Bottom, a country group led by Bob Weir, or Mickey Hart and the Heartbeats, which has performed a lot of golden-oldie rockers. At the same time (spring 1969), Jerry got a pedal-steel guitar to fool around with and ended up commuting down to Palo Alto twice a week to play Nashville style in a little club. That group became the New Riders of the Purple Sage, and other Dead members sat in from time to time.

All that country music got them singing, something for which they had not been noteworthy in the past, and hours of three-part harmony rehearsals got them back to acoustic instruments. Less noise made them less wired. The small quiet groups could and did do club work around the Bay, which meant gigs without touring or equipment hassles. All that ended up with the groove that made *Workingman's Dead* possible and has created a unique musical experience that they call, rather formally, An Evening with the Grateful Dead.

Phil arrived, sweeping in with madman-long strides, a few minutes before nine, and the latest evening began before a happy crowd of old-time heads. They opened with the acoustic part (there's no other name), Jerry and Bob Weir on guitars, Pigpen on piano, Phil on electric bass, and Bill Kreutzmann (who alternates with Mickey Hart) on drums. The first tune was "Truckin'," an easygoing autobiography of a band's life on the road, dotted with busts and bad times and long-gone friends like Sweet Jane, who they've heard is "livin' on reds/ Vitamin C and cocaine/All her friends can say is 'ain't it a shame'." Jerry and Bob shared lead guitar and vocals, Pig doodled around when he wanted—and just sat there when he didn't—and Phil and Bill just kept the beat. David Nelson of the New Riders came in on mandolin about halfway through, Jerry switched to his Fender, and it was all very sweet and funky. They ended with "Swing Low, Sweet Chariot," and believe it or not, the Grateful Dead looked angelic at last.

The New Riders came on after the break—Jerry on pedal steel, Mickey on drums, David Nelson on electric guitar, Marmaduke on lead vocal and acoustic and Dave Torbert on bass. They opened with "Six Days on the Road," and that set the pace for a rolling set of country rock that probably sounded like the Perkins Brothers when Carl was working honky-tonks around Jackson, Tennessee. Except that Carl Perkins never had a drummer as tense as Mickey Hart, and while Jerry most often was tastefully traditional on the steel, he allowed himself some short freakouts, banshee-style, seldom heard below the Mason-Dixon. They ended with "Honky Tonk Women," which was a gas; Keith Richards, from a film clip in the light show, watched them without cracking a smile.

Then it was time for the Grateful Dead, and everyone was on their feet and moving as they began—as they used to begin—with "Dancin' in the Streets" ("It doesn't matter what you wear/Just as long as you are there"). After that came the lovely "Mama Tried," which the Everly Brothers had on their *Roots* album, and then Pigpen took it away with an all-out dramatic rendition of "It's a Man's Man's Man's World." Out of that into "Not Fade Away," and it was past 1:30. Jerry Garcia was still going strong after four hours on three instruments, but the Fillmore floor had gotten to me, and we wandered out with that Bo Diddley-by-way-of-Buddy Holly beat

Next page: The Grateful Dead
Photograph by Annie Leibovitz

on and on and on ("My love is bigger than a Cadillac...").

It wasn't one of those weird nights when, acid-blitzed, they gushed out music as hypnotic energy; it was more legible and, if not as spellbinding, more open music.

Those weird nights are surely not gone forever, but the Dead are a bit more careful these days. "Altamont showed us that we don't want to lead people up that road anymore," Jerry had said before the show. "It taught us to be more cautious, to realize and respect the boundaries of our power and our space." The Dead never called themselves leaders, but they were high-energy promotors of the psychedelic revolution. On one hand they know now that it's not going to come as quickly as they thought; on the other, they know it is already too big for them to direct. They are now just helpers, like the rest of us. "At least the pressure's off," Jerry said.

He is disturbed, however, about what he calls the "political pseudoreality that we find when we go out on tour. Dig: there's a music festival, but because there are people there, radicals say it's a political festival now, not a music festival. I don't want to take over anybody's mind. If a musical experience is forcibly transferred to a political plane, it no longer has the thing that made it attractive. There is something uniquely groovy about the musical experience; it is its own beginning and its own end. It threatens no one.

"The San Francisco energy of a few years back has become air and spread everywhere. It was the energy of becoming free, and so it became free. But the political energy, the Berkeley energy, has assumed a serpentine form, become an armed, burrowing, survival thing. It's even still on the firebrand, 'To the barricades!' trip that I thought we had been through in this country and wouldn't have to will on ourselves again.

"Accentuate the positive, though, that's my motto," he said with a gleam in his eye, "and there are more heads every day. Heads are the only people who have ever come to see us, and it used to be that if we played some places, no one would come out because there weren't any heads in town. Today there is no place without its hippies. No place.

"We realized when we started out," Jerry continued, "that as a group we were an invention, as new as the first chapter of a novel. We started with nothing to lose. Then suddenly there was something, but always with the agreement that we could go back to being nothing if we wanted. So nothing that has ever gone down for the group has ever been real except to the fiction that could be made unreal at any time. A lot of times when we were at that point, we consulted the *I Ching*, and the change we've gotten has always said push on. So we have. There's not much else we can do until the next change."

Freak Power in the Rockies

by Hunter S. Thompson   October 1970

A memoir and rambling discussion (with rude slogans) of Freak Power in the Rockies...on the weird mechanics of running a takeover bid on a small town...and a vulgar argument for seizing political power and using it like a gun ripped away from a cop...with jangled comments on the uncertain role of the Head and the awful Stupor Factor...and other disorganized notes on how to punish the Fatbacks, how to make sure that today's pig is tomorrow's offal...and why this crazed new world can only be dealt with by...a New Posse!

Joe Edwards, a twenty-nine-year-old head, lawyer and bike racer from Texas, looked like he might, in the waning hours of election day in November 1969, be the next mayor of Aspen, Colorado.

The retiring mayor, Dr. Robert "Buggsy" Barnard, had been broadcasting vicious radio warnings for the previous forty-eight hours, raving about long prison terms for vote fraud and threatening violent harassment by "phalanxes of poll watchers" for any strange or freaky-looking scum who might dare to show up at the polls. We checked the laws and found that Barnard's radio warnings were a violation of the "voter intimidation" statutes, so I called the district attorney and tried to have the mayor arrested at once. But the D.A. said, "Leave me out of it; police your own elections."

Which we did, with finely organized teams of poll watchers: two inside each polling place at all times, with six more just outside in vans or trucks full of beef, coffee, propaganda, checklists and bound Xerox copies of all Colorado voting laws.

The idea was to keep massive assistance available, at all times, to our point men inside the official voting places. And the reasoning behind this rather heavy public act was our concern that the mayor and his cops would create some kind of ugly scene and rattle the underground grapevine with fear rumors that would scare off a lot of our voters. Most of our people were fearful of any kind of legal hassle at the polls, regardless of their rights. So it seemed important that we should make it very clear, from the start, that we knew the laws and we weren't going to tolerate any harassment of our people. None.

And since the only person who had actually threatened to intimidate voters was the mayor, we decided to force the confrontation as soon as possible in Ward 1, where Buggsy had announced that he would personally stand the first poll-watching shift for the opposition. If the buggers wanted a confrontation, we decided to give it to them.

The polling place in Ward 1 was a lodge called the Cresthaus, owned by an old and infamous Swiss Nazi who calls himself Guido Meyer. Martin Bormann went to Brazil, but Guido came to Aspen, arriving several years after the Great War. Ever since then he has spent most of his energy (including two complete terms as city magistrate) getting even with this country by milking the tourists and having young (or poor) people arrested.

So Guido was watching eagerly when the mayor arrived in his parking lot at ten minutes to seven, creeping his Porsche through a gauntlet of silent Edwards people. We had mustered a half dozen of the scurviest looking *legal* voters we could find, so when the mayor arrived at the polls these freaks were waiting to vote. Behind them, lounging around a coffee dispenser in an old VW van, were at least a dozen others, most of them large and bearded, and several so eager for violence that they had spent the whole night making chain whips and loading up on speed to stay crazy.

Buggsy looked horrified. It was the first time he had ever laid eyes on a group of nonpassive, superaggressive heads. What had got into them? Why were their eyes so wild? And why were they yelling, "You're fucked, Buggsy....We're going to croak you....Your whole act is doomed....We're going to beat your ass like a gong."

What indeed? He scurried inside to meet Guido, but instead ran into Tom Benton, the hairy artist and known radical. Benton was grinning like a crocodile and waving a small black microphone, saying, "Welcome, Buggsy. You're late. The voters are waiting outside. Yes, did you see them out there? Were they friendly? And if you wonder what I'm doing here, I'm Joe Edwards' poll watcher. The reason I have this little black machine here is that I want to tape every word you say when you start committing felonies by harassing our voters."

The mayor lost his first confrontation almost instantly. One of the first obvious Edwards voters of the day was a blond kid who looked about seventeen. Buggsy began to jabber at him, and Benton moved in with the microphone, ready to intervene. But before Benton could utter a word, the kid began snarling at the mayor, yelling, "Go fuck yourself, Buggsy! *You* figure out how old I am. I know the goddamn law! I don't have to show you proof of anything! You're a *dying man*, Buggsy! Get out of my way. I'm ready to vote!"

After that, we stopped worrying about the mayor. No goons had shown up with blackjacks, no cops were in evidence, and Benton had established full control of his turf around the ballot box. Elsewhere, in Wards 2 and 3, the freak vote was not so heavy and things were going smoothly. In Ward 2, in fact, our official poll watcher (a drug person with a beard about two feet long) had caused a panic by challenging dozens of straight voters. The city attorney called Edwards and complained that some ugly lunatic in Ward 2 was refusing to let a seventy-five-year-old woman cast her ballot until she produced a birth certificate. We were forced to replace the man; his zeal was inspiring, but we feared he might spark a backlash.

This had been a problem all along. We had tried to mobilize a huge underground vote, without frightening the burghers into a counterattack. But it didn't work, primarily because most of our best people were also hairy and very obvious. Our opening shot—the midnight registration campaign—had been ramrodded by bearded heads Mike Solheim and Pierre Landry, who worked the streets and bars for head voters like wild junkies in the face of near-total apathy.

★ ★ ★

Our ten-day registration campaign had focused almost entirely on the head-dropout culture; they wanted no part of activist politics, and it had been a hellish effort to convince them to register at all. Many had lived in Aspen for five or six years, and they weren't at all concerned with being convicted of vote fraud—they simply didn't want to be hassled. Most of us are living here because we like the idea of being able to walk out our front doors and smile at what we see. On my own front porch I have a palm tree growing in a blue toilet bowl, and on occasion I like to wander outside, stark naked, and fire my .44 Magnum at various gongs I've mounted on the nearby hillside. I like to load up on mescaline and turn my amplifier up to 110 decibels for a taste of "White Rabbit" while the sun comes up on the snow peaks along the Continental Divide.

Which is not entirely the point. The world is full of places where a man can run wild on drugs and loud music and firepower—but not for long. I lived a block above Haight Street for two years, but by the end of '66 the whole neighborhood had become a cop magnet and a bad sideshow. Between the narcs and the psychedelic hustlers, there was not much room to live.

What happened in the Haight echoed earlier scenes in North Beach and the Village, and it proved once again the basic futility of seizing turf you can't control. The pattern never varies: a low-rent area suddenly blooms new and loose and human—and then fashionable, which attracts the press and the cops at about the same time. Cop problems attract more publicity, which then attracts fad salesmen and hustlers—which means money, and that attracts junkies and jack-rollers. Their bad action causes publicity and, for some perverse reason, an influx of bored, upwardly mobile types who dig the menace of "white ghetto" life and whose expense-account tastes drive local rents and street prices out of reach of the original settlers, who are forced, once again, to move on.

One of the most hopeful developments of the failed Haight-Ashbury scene was the exodus to rural communes. Most of the communes failed—for reasons that everybody can see now in retrospect (like that scene in *Easy Rider* where all those poor freaks were trying to grow their crops in dry sand)—but the few that succeeded, like the Hog Farm in New Mexico, kept a whole generation of heads believing that the future lay somewhere outside the cities.

In Aspen, hundreds of Haight-Ashbury refugees tried to settle in the wake of that ill-fated Summer of Love in 1967. The summer was a wild and incredible dope orgy here, but when winter came, the crest of that wave broke and drifted on the shoals of local problems, such as jobs, housing and deep snow on the roads to shacks that, a few months earlier, had been easily accessible. Many of the West Coast refugees moved on, but several hundred stayed; they hired on as carpenters, waiters, bartenders, dishwashers. And a year later they were part of the permanent population. By mid-'69 they occupied most of Aspen's so-called low-cost housing—the tiny midtown apartments, outlying shacks and trailer courts.

So most of the freaks felt that voting wasn't worth the kind of bullshit that went with it, and the mayor's illegal threats only reinforced their notion that politics in America was something to be avoided. Getting busted for grass was one thing, because the "crime" was worth the risk, but they saw no sense in going to court for a political technicality, even if they weren't guilty.

This sense of "reality" is a hallmark of the drug culture, which values the Instant Reward—a pleasant four-hour high—over anything involving a time lag between the effort and the end. On this scale of values, politics is too difficult, too complex and too abstract to justify any risk or initial action. It is the flip side of the Good German syndrome.

The idea of asking young heads to go clean never occurred to us. They could go dirty, or even naked, for all we cared...all we asked them to do was first register and then vote. A year earlier these same people had seen no difference between Nixon and Humphrey. They were against the war in Vietnam, but the McCarthy crusade had never reached them. At the grass roots of the dropout culture, the idea of going clean for Gene was a bad joke. Both Dick Gregory and George Wallace drew unnaturally large chunks of the vote in Aspen.

Robert Kennedy would probably have carried the town, if he hadn't been killed, but he wouldn't have won by much. The town is essentially Republican; GOP registration outnumbers Democratic by more than two to one. But the combined total of both major parties just about equals the number of registered independents, most of whom pride themselves on being totally unpredictable. They are a jangled mix of Left Crazies and Birchers, cheap bigots, dope dealers, Nazi ski instructors and spaced-out psychedelic farmers with no politics at all beyond self-preservation.

★   ★   ★

For the past ten years Aspen has been the showpiece and money hub of a gold rush that has made millionaires. In the wake of World War II, they flocked in from Austria and Switzerland (never from Germany, they said) to staff the embryonic nerve-resort centers of a sport that would soon be bigger than golf or bowling. Now, with skiing firmly established in America, the original German hustlers are wealthy burghers. They own restaurants, hotels, ski shops and vast chunks of real estate in places like Aspen.

Our program, basically, was to drive the real-estate goons completely out of the valley; to prevent the state highway department from bringing a four-lane highway into the town and in fact *to ban all auto traffic from every downtown street*. Turn them all into grassy malls where everybody, even freaks, could do whatever's right. The cops would become trash collectors and maintenance men for a fleet of municipal bicycles, for anybody to use. No more huge, space-killing apartment buildings to block the view of anybody who might want to look up from any downtown street and see the mountains. No more land rapes, no more busts for flute playing or blocking the sidewalk...fuck the tourists, dead-end the highway, zone the greedheads out of existence and in general create a town where people could live like human beings, instead of slaves to some bogus sense of Progress that is driving us all mad.

Joe Edwards's platform was against the developers, not the old timers and ranchers, and it was hard to see, from their arguments, how they could disagree in substance with anything we said...unless what they were really worried about was the very good chance that a win by Edwards would put an end to their option of selling out to the highest bidder. With Edwards, they said, would come horrors like zoning and ecology, which would cramp their fine Western style, the buy-low-sell-high ethic—free enterprise, as it were. The few people who bothered to argue with them soon found that their nostalgic talk about "the good old days" and "the tradition of this peaceful valley" was only an awkward cover for their fears about "socialist-thinking newcomers."

Whatever else the Edwards campaign may or may not have accomplished, we had croaked that stupid sentimental garbage about the "land-loving old timers."

As the de facto campaign manager, I felt like a man who had started some kind of bloody gang fight by accident, and as the Edwards campaign grew crazier and more vicious, my only real concern was to save my own ass by warding off a disaster. I didn't know Edwards at all, but by mid-October I felt personally responsible for his future, and his prospects, at that point, were not good. Bill Dunaway, the "liberal" publisher of *The Aspen Times*, told me on the morning of the election that I had "singlehandedly destroyed Joe Edwards's legal career in Aspen" by "forcing him into politics."

This was the liberal myth—that some drug-addled egomaniac writer from Woody Creek had run amok on horse tranquilizers and then laid his bad trip on the local head population, who were normally quite peaceful and harmless, as long as they had enough drugs. But now, for some goddamned reason, they had gone completely wild, and they were dragging poor Edwards down with them.

Right...poor Edwards. He was recently divorced and living with his girl-friend in a local garret, half starving for income in a town full of lame dilettante lawyers, and his name was completely unknown except as "that bastard who sued the city" a year earlier on behalf of two longhairs who claimed the cops were discriminating against them. This was true, and the lawsuit had a terrible effect on the local police. The chief—now a candidate for sheriff—had quit or been fired in a rage, leaving his patrolmen on probation to a federal judge in Denver, who put the suit in limbo while warning the Aspen cops that he would bust the city severely at the first sign of "discriminatory law enforcement" against hippies.

This lawsuit had severe repercussions in Aspen. The mayor was shackled, the city council lost its will to live, the city magistrate, Guido Meyer, was fired instantly—even before the police chief—and the local cops suddenly stopped busting longhairs for things like "blocking the sidewalk," which carried a ninety-day jail sentence that summer, along with a $200 fine.

That bullshit stopped at once, and it has stayed stopped, thanks entirely to Edwards's lawsuit; the local liberals called an ACLU meeting and let it go at that. So only a waterhead could have been surprised when, a year later, a handful of us in search of a mayoral candidate decided to call on Joe Edwards. Why not? It made perfect sense, except to the liberals, who were not quite comfortable with a Freak Power candidate. They didn't mind Edwards, they said, and they even agreed with his platform—which we had carefully carved to their tastes—but there was something very ominous, they felt, about the "rabble" support he was getting. Not the kind of people one really wanted to sip vichyssoise with—wild heads, bikers and anarchists who didn't know Stevenson and hated Hubert Humphrey. Who were these people? What did they want?

What indeed? The local businessmen's bund was not puzzled. Joe Edwards, to them, was the leader of a communist drug plot to destroy their way of life, sell LSD to their children and Spanish Fly to their wives. Never mind that many of their children were already selling LSD to each other and that most of their wives couldn't get humped on a bad night in Juarez…that was all beside the point. The *point* was that a gang of freaks was about to take over the town.

And why not? We had never denied it. Not even in the platform, which was public and quite mild. But somewhere around the middle of the Edwards campaign, even the liberals got a whiff of what his platform really meant. The knew, from long experience, that a word like ecology can mean almost anything—and to most of them it meant spending one day a year with a neighborhood clean-up crew, picking up beer cans and sending them back to Coors for a refund that would be sent, of course, to their favorite charity.

But ecology, to us, meant something else entirely. We had in mind a deluge of brutally restrictive actions that would cripple not only the obvious land rapers but also that quiet cabal of tweedy-liberal speculators who insist on dealing in private, so as not to foul the image. Like Armand Bartos, the New York "art patron" and jet-set fashion pacer often hummed about in *Women's Wear Daily*…who is also the owner, builder and oft-cursed landlord of Aspen's biggest and ugliest trailer court. The place is called Gerbazdale, and some of the tenants insist that Bartos raises the rent every time he decides to buy another pop-art original.

"I'm tired of financing that asshole's art collection," said one tenant. "He's one of the most blatant goddamned slumlords in the Western World. He milks us out here, then gives the money to shitheads like Warhol."

Bartos is in the same league with Wilton "Wink" Jaffee Jr., a New York stockbroker recently suspended for unethical manipulation of the market. Jaffe has taken great pains to cultivate his image in Aspen as that of an arty-progressive Eastern aesthete. But when the SEC zapped him, he responded by quickly leasing a chunk of his vast ranch, between Aspen and Woods Creek, to a high-powered gravel-crushing operation from Grand Junction, which immediately began grinding up the earth and selling it, by the ton, to the state highway department. And now, after destroying the earth and fouling the Roaring Fork River, the swine are demanding a zoning variance so they can build an asphalt plant on the elegant Aspen estate that Wink Jaffee no doubt describes quite often to his progressive friends on Wall Street.

These, and others like them, are the kind of shysters and horsy hypocrites who pass for liberals in Aspen. So we were not surprised when many of them made a point of withdrawing their support about halfway through the Edwards campaign. At first they had liked our words and our fiery underdog stance (fighting the good fight in another hopeless cause, et cetera), but when Edwards began looking like a winner, our liberal allies panicked.

★   ★   ★

After a savage, fire-sucking campaign, we lost by only six votes out of 1200. Actually, we lost by one vote, but five of our absentee ballots didn't get here in time, primarily because they were mailed (to places like Mexico and Nepal and Guatemala) five days before the election.

We came very close to winning control of the town, and that was the crucial difference between our action in Aspen and, say, Norman Mailer's campaign in New York, which was clearly doomed from the start. At the time of Edwards' campaign we were not conscious of any precedent. Even now, in calm retrospect, the only similar effort that comes to mind is Bob Scheer's 1966 run for a U.S. Congress seat in a Berkeley-Oakland district—when he challenged liberal Jeffrey Cohelan and lost by something like two percent of the vote. Other than that, most radical attempts to get into electoral politics have been colorful, foredoomed efforts in the style of the Mailer-Breslin gig.

On the strength of the Edwards showing, I decided to run for sheriff. A preliminary canvass shows me running well ahead of the Democratic incumbent and only slightly behind the Republican challenger. The root point is that Aspen's political situation is so volatile—as a result of the Joe Edwards campaign—that any Freak Power candidate is now a possible winner.

I will have to work very hard—and spew out some really heinous ideas during my campaign—to get *less* than thirty percent of the vote in a three-way race. And an underground candidate who really wanted to win could assume, from the start, a working nut of about forty percent of the electorate, with his chances of victory riding almost entirely on his backlash potential—or how much active fear and loathing his candidacy might provoke among the burghers who have controlled local candidates for so long.

The possibility of victory can be a heavy millstone around the neck of any political candidate who might prefer, in his heart, to spend his main energies on a series of terrifying, whiplash assaults on everything the voters hold dear. There are harsh echoes of *The Magic Christian* in this technique: the candidate first creates an impossible psychic maze, then he drags the voters into it and flails them constantly with gibberish and rude shocks. This was Mailer's technique, and it got him 55,000 votes in a city of 10 million people. But in truth it is more a form of vengeance than electoral politics.

The Magic Christian concept is one of the "new politics" coin. It doesn't work, but it's fun, unlike that coin's other face, which emerged in the presidential campaigns of Gene McCarthy and Bobby Kennedy in 1968. In both cases, we saw establishment candidates claiming conversion to some newer and younger state of mind (or political reality) that would make them more in tune with a newer, younger and weirder electorate that had previously called them both useless. We are talking about political action formats: if *The Magic Christian* concept is one, then the Kennedy-McCarthy format has to qualify as another…particularly since the national Democratic party is already working desperately to make it work again in 1972, when the Democrats' only hope of unseating Nixon will again be some shrewd establishment candidate on the brink of menopause who will suddenly start dropping acid in late '71 and then hit the rock-festival trail in the summer of 1972. He will doff his shirt at every opportunity, and his wife will burn her bra…and millions of the young will vote for him, against Nixon.

Or will they? There is still another format, and this is the one we stumbled on in Aspen. Why not challenge the Establishment with a candidate they've never heard of? Who has never been primed or prepped or greased for public office? And whose lifestyle is already so weird that the idea of "conversion" would never occur to him? In other words, why not run an honest freak and turn him loose, on *their* turf, to show up all the "normal" candidates for the worthless losers they are and always have been? Why defer to the bastards? Why assume they're intelligent? Why believe they won't crack and fold in a crunch?

This is the essence of what some people call "the Aspen technique" in politics: neither opting out of the system, nor working within it…but calling its bluff, by using its strength to turn it back on itself…and by always assuming that the people in power are not smart. By the end of the Edwards campaign, I was convinced, despite my lifelong bias to the contrary, that the Law was actually on our side. Not the cops or the judges or the politicians, but the actual Law itself as printed in the dull and musty lawbooks that we constantly had to consult because we had no other choice.

TENTATIVE PLATFORM
Thompson for Sheriff, Aspen, Colorado, 1970

1. Sod the streets at once. Rip up all the city streets with jackhammers, and use the junk asphalt (after melting) to create a huge parking and auto-storage lot on the outskirts of town, preferably somewhere out of sight. All refuse and garbage could be centralized in this area, in memory of Mrs. Walker Paepke, who sold the land for development. The only automobiles allowed into town would be limited to a network of "delivery alleys," as shown in the very detailed plan drawn by architect-planner Fritz Benedict in 1969. All public movement would be by foot and a fleet of bicycles maintained by the city police force.

2. Change the name Aspen, by public referendum, to Fat City. This would prevent greedheads, land rapers and other human jackals from capitalizing on the name Aspen. Thus, Snowmass-at-Aspen, recently sold to Kaiser-Aetna of Oakland, would become Snowmass-at-Fat-City. All road signs and road maps would have to be changed from Aspen to Fat City. The local post office and chamber of commerce would have to honor the new name. Aspen, Colorado, would no longer exist, and the psychic alterations of this change would be massive in the world of commerce: Fat City Ski Fashions, the Fat City Slalom Cup, Fat City Music Festival, Fat City Institute for Humanistic Studies, et cetera. The main advantage here is that changing the name of the town would have no major effect on the town itself or on those people who came here because it's a good place to *live*. What effect the name change might have on those who came here to buy low, sell high and then move on is fairly obvious... and eminently desirable. These swine should be fucked, broken and driven across the land.

3. Drug sales must be controlled. My first act as sheriff will be to install, on the courthouse lawn, a bastinado platform and a set of stocks, in order to punish dishonest dope dealers in a proper public fashion. Each year these dealers cheat millions of people out of millions of dollars. As a breed, they rank with subdividers and used-car salesmen, and the sheriff's department will gladly hear complaints against dealers at any hour of the day or night, with immunity from prosecution granted to the complaining party—provided the complaint is valid. In the meantime, it will be the general philosophy of the sheriff's office that no drug worth taking should be sold for money. Nonprofit sales will be viewed as borderline cases and judged on their merits. But *all* sales for money profit will be punished severely. This approach, we feel, will establish a unique and very human ambiance in the Aspen, or Fat City, drug culture, which is already so much a part of our local reality that only a Falangist lunatic would talk about trying to eliminate it. The only realistic approach is to make life in this town very ugly for all profiteers—in drugs and all other fields.

4. Hunting and fishing should be forbidden to *all* nonresidents, with the exception of those who can obtain the signed endorsement of a resident. Fines will be heavy, and the general policy will be merciless prosecution for all offenders. But, as in the case of the proposed city name change, this local endorsement plan should have no effect on anyone except greedy, dangerous kill freaks who are a menace wherever they go. By this approach—making hundreds or even thousands of individuals personally responsible for protecting the animals, fish and birds who live here—we would create a sort of de facto game preserve without the harsh restrictions that will necessarily be forced on us if these blood thirsty geeks keep swarming in here each autumn to shoot everything they see.

5. The sheriff and his deputies should *never* be armed in public. Every urban riot, shoot-out and bloodbath (involving guns) in recent memory has been set off by some trigger-happy cop in a fear frenzy. Under normal circumstances, a pistol-grip Macebomb, such as the MK-V made by General Ordnance, is more than enough to quickly wilt any violence problem that is likely to emerge in Aspen. And anything the MK-V can't handle would require reinforcements anyway...in which case the response would be geared at all times to massive retaliation; a brutal attack with guns, bombs, pepper foggers, wolverines and all other weapons deemed necessary to restore the civic peace. The whole notion of disarming the police is to *lower* the level of violence while guaranteeing, at the same time, a terrible punishment to anyone stupid enough to attempt violence on an unarmed cop.

6. It will be the policy of the sheriff's office to savagely harass all those engaged in any form of land rape. This will be done by acting , with utmost dispatch on any and all righteous complaints. My first act in office—after setting up machinery for punishing dope dealers—will be to establish a Research Bureau to provide facts on which any citizen can file a writ of seizure, a writ of stoppage, a writ of fear, of horror...yes...even a writ of assumption...against any greedhead who has managed to get around our antiquated laws and set up a tar vat, scum drain or gravel pit. These writs will be pursued with overweening zeal...and always within the letter of the law. Selah.

Faces: 1967–1970

Clockwise, from left to right:
The Supremes
Stevie Wonder
Grace Slick and Janis Joplin
Little Richard
The Beatles
Oakland draft protest

91

Clockwise, from left to right:
Black students
Frank Zappa
R. Crumb's Mr. Natural
Crosby, Stills, Nash & Young
Jimi Hendrix
Easy Rider
Maharishi Mahesh Yogi
Joni Mitchell

Clockwise, from left to right:
2001: A Space Odyssey
Michael Jackson
Cheech and Chong
John Lennon and Yoko Ono
Rod Stewart
Jackson Browne
Jim Morrison

Mother, mother
There's too many of you crying
Brother, brother, brother
There's far too many of you dying
—MARVIN GAYE, ALFRED CLEVELAND,
  RENALDO BENSON, *"What's Going On"*

1971–1974

If I could stick a knife in my heart
Suicide right on the stage
Would it be enough for your teenage lust
Would it help ease the pain
—MICK JAGGER, KEITH RICHARDS, *"It's Only Rock 'n' Roll"*

Voices

The fact of the matter is that popular music is one of the industries of the country. It's all completely tied up with capitalism. It's stupid to separate it. That's an illusory separation.
—PAUL SIMON, *July 1972*

★   ★   ★

My own conditioning is that one voice says to me, "Carly, you mustn't try to dominate the situation, you mustn't tell everybody what to play, you mustn't expect James to do the dishes." And the other voice is saying, "I want my musicians to play in a slower tempo, and it's James's turn to do the dishes tonight."
—CARLY SIMON, *February 1973*

★   ★   ★

The idea of getting minds together smacks of the Flower Power period to me. The coming together of people I find obscene as a principle. It is not human. It is not a natural thing as some people would have us believe.
—DAVID BOWIE, *February 1974*

★   ★   ★

How many times can you use those words—justice, freedom. It's like margarine, man. You can package it and you can sell that too. In America they have a great talent for doing that.
—KEITH RICHARDS, *August 1971*

★   ★   ★

I'm advocating that you strenuously and with a great deal of hard work and self-discipline and struggle, that you change your own life, that you live according to the way you really believe in....that's the revolution as I see it.
—CHARLES REICH, *February 1971*

The whole thing could happen, but I think the fact that it got desperate—in the sense that the economics started to drive everything out—that it was the drawing-power formula that worked, those kinds of realities, business world realities. And the thing ultimately turned into a merchandising trip, a showbiz trip. That wrecked it. That wrecked it for me, anyway.

—JERRY GARCIA, *January 1972*

★   ★   ★

The dream is over. It's just the same only I'm thirty and a lot of people have got long hair, that's all.

Nothing happening except that we grew up; we did our thing just like they were telling us. Most of the so-called Now Generation are getting jobs and all of that.

—JOHN LENNON, *February 1971*

★   ★   ★

I get accused of being a capitalist bastard, because, you know: "How many cars you got?" "Eight." "Big 'ouse?" "Yes." Well, I love all that; I enjoy it. I have lots of friends over and we sit up, drinking and partying. I need the room to entertain. I enjoy seeing other people enjoy themselves. That's where I get my kicks. I'm kinky that way. I have the amount of cars I do because I smash them up a lot. Six are always in the garage; it's a fact. They're always saying I'm a capitalist pig. I suppose I am. But ah…it ah…it's good for me drumming, I think. Oh-hoooo-ha-haha!

—KEITH MOON, *December 1972*

★   ★   ★

Oh, fuck Jerry Rubin. For chrissake, Jerry and Abbie will probably be doing a vaudeville show ten years from now! Look at those characters in the Conspiracy Seven! They couldn't organize a successful luncheon let alone a social revolution.

—SAUL ALINSKY, *March 1971*

John Lennon: The Rolling Stone Interview

by Jann S. Wenner   January 1971

When did you realize that what you were doing transcended...

People like me are aware of their so-called genius at ten, eight, nine. I always wondered, why has nobody discovered me? In school, didn't they see that I was cleverer than anybody in the school? That the teachers were stupid too? That all they had was information I didn't need? I got fuckin' lost being in high school. I used to say to me auntie, "You throw my fuckin' poetry out and you'll regret it when I'm famous." And she threw the bastard stuff out.

Do you think you're a genius?

Yes, if there is such a thing, I am one.

When did you first realize that?

When I was about twelve. I used to think I must be a genius but nobody's noticed. I used to think, either I'm a genius or I'm mad—which is it? I used to think, well, I can't be mad, because nobody's put me away; therefore, I'm a genius. I mean, genius is a form of madness, and we're all that way. But I used to be a bit coy about it, you know, like me guitar playing. I didn't become something when the Beatles made it or when you heard about me; I've been like this all me life.

But it was obvious to me. Why didn't they put me in art school? Why didn't they train me? Why did they keep forcing me to be a fuckin' cowboy like the rest of them. I was different. I was always different. Why didn't anybody notice me?

A couple of teachers would encourage me to be something or other, to draw or to paint—to express myself. But most of the time they were trying to beat me into being a fuckin' dentist or teacher. And then the fuckin' fans tried to beat me into being a fuckin' Beatle or an Engelbert Humperdinck, and the critics tried to beat me into being Paul McCartney.

The Beatles were always talked about—and the Beatles talked about themselves— as being part of the same person.

Well...yes.

What's happened to those four parts?

They remembered they were four individuals. You see, we believed the Beatles myth, too. We were a band that made it very, very big, that's all.

Why?

Because we were performers, and what we generated was fantastic. When we played straight rock there was nobody to touch us in Britain.

What did being from Liverpool have to do with your art?

It's the second biggest port in England. The north is where the money was made in the 1800s; that was where all the brass and the heavy people were, and that's where the despised people were. We were the ones who were looked down upon as animals by the southerners, the Londoners. In the States, the Northerners think that down South, people are pigs, and the people in New York think West Coast is hick. So we were hicksville.

Liverpool is a very poor city, and tough. But people have a sense of humor because they are in so much pain. So they are always cracking jokes, and they are very witty. It's an Irish place, too; it is where the Irish came when they ran out of potatoes, and it's where black people were left or worked as slaves or whatever.

It is cosmopolitan, and it's where the sailors would come home with blues records from America. Liverpool has the biggest country & western following in England besides London—always besides London because there is more of it there.

I heard country & western music in Liverpool before I heard rock & roll. The people take their country & western music very seriously. I remember the first guitar I ever saw. It belonged to a guy in a cowboy suit and a cowboy hat and a big dobro. They were real cowboys and they took it seriously. There were cowboys long before there was rock & roll.

What was it like in the early days in London?

When we came down, we were treated like real provincials by the Londoners. We were, anyway.

What was it like, say, running around discotheques with the Stones?

Oh, that was a great period. We were like kings of the jungle then, and we were very close to the Stones. I spent a lot of time with Brian [Jones] and Mick [Jagger], and I admired them. I dug them the first time I saw them in whatever that place is they came from—the Crawdaddy in Richmond.

We were all just at the prime, and we all used to just go around London in our cars and meet each other and talk about music with the Animals and Eric [Burdon] and all that. It was a really good time. That was the best period, famewise; we didn't get mobbed so much. I don't know; it was like a men's smoking club, just a very good scene.

We created something, Mick and us, we didn't know what we were doing, but we were all talking, blabbing over coffee, like they must have done in Paris, talking about paintings...me, Burdon and Brian Jones would be up night and day talking about music, playing records and blabbing and arguing and getting drunk. It's beautiful history, and it happened in all these different places. I just miss New York. In New York they have their own cool clique. Yoko came out of that.

This is the first time I'm really seeing it, because I was always too nervous, I was always the famous Beatle. Dylan showed it to me once on sort of a guided tour around the Village, but I never got any feel of it. I just knew Dylan was New York, and I always sort of wished I'd been there for the experience that Bob got from living around here.

What is the nature of your relationship with Bob?

It's sort of an acquaintance, because we were so nervous whenever we used to meet. It was always under the most nerve-wracking circumstances, and I know I was always uptight and I know Bobby was. We were together and we spent some time, but I would always be too aggressive or vice versa and we didn't really speak. But we spent a lot of time together.

He came to me house, which was Kenwood, can you imagine it, and I didn't know where to put him in this sort of bourgeois home life I was living; I didn't know what to do and things like that. I used to go to his hotel rather, and I loved him, you know, because he wrote some beautiful stuff. I used to love that, his so-called protest things. I listen to his words. He used to come with his acetate and say "Listen to this John, and did you hear the words?" I said that doesn't matter, the sound is what counts—the overall thing. I had too many father figures and I liked words, too, so I liked a lot of the stuff he did. You don't have to hear what Bob Dylan's saying, you just have to hear the way he says it.

Do you see him as a great?

No, I see him as another poet, or as competition. You read my books that were written before I heard of Dylan or read Dylan or anybody, it's the same. I didn't come after Elvis and Dylan, I've been around always. But if I see or meet a great artist, I love 'em. I go fanatical about them for a short period, and then I get over it. If they wear green socks I'm liable to wear green socks for a period too.

When was the last time you saw Bob?

He came over to our house with George after the Isle of Wight and when I had written "Cold Turkey." I was just trying to get him to record. We had just put him on piano for "Cold Turkey" to make a rough tape but his wife was pregnant or something and they left. He's calmed down a lot now.

I just remember before that we were both in shades and both on fucking junk, and all these freaks around us and Ginsberg and all those people. I was anxious as shit.

You were in that movie with him that hasn't been released?

I've never seen it but I'd love to see it. I was always so paranoid and Bob said "I want you to be in this film." I thought why? What? He's going to put me down; I went all through this terrible thing.

In the film, I'm just blabbing off and commenting all the time, like you do when you're very high or stoned. I had been up all night. We were being smart alecks, it's terrible. But it was his scene, that was the problem for me. It was his movie. I was on his territory, that's why I was so nervous. I was on his session.

What about the tours?

The Beatles' tours were like *Fellini's Satyricon*. If you could get on our tours, you were in. Wherever we went there was a whole scene going. When we hit town, we hit it, we were not pissing about. You know, there's photographs of me groveling about, crawling about in Amsterdam on my knees, coming out of whorehouses and things like that, and people saying, "Good morning, John," and all of that. And the police escorted me to the places because they never wanted a big scandal. I don't really want to talk about it because it will hurt Yoko, and it's not fair. Suffice it to say, just put it like they were *Satyricon* on tour and that's it, because I don't want to hurt the other people's girls, either, it's just not fair.

YOKO: How did you manage to keep that clean image? It's amazing.

Because everybody wants the image to carry on. The press around with you want you to carry on because they want the free drinks and the free whores and the fun. Everybody wants to keep on the bandwagon. It's *Satyricon*. We were the Caesars. Who was going to knock us when there's a million pounds to be made? All the handouts, the bribery, the police, all the fuckin' hype, you know. Everybody wanted in. I just got meself in a party. I was an emperor. I had millions of chicks, drinks, drugs, power and everybody saying how great I was. It was like being in a fuckin' train. It was fantastic! I came out of the sticks; I hadn't heard about anything —Van Gogh was the most far-out thing I had ever heard of. Even London was something we used to dream of, and London's nothing. I came out of the fuckin' sticks to take over the world, it seemed to me. I was enjoying it, but I was wrapped in it, too. I was hooked.

It just built up, the bigger we got, the more unreality we had to face and the more we were expected to do. They were always threatening what they would tell the press about us, to make bad publicity if we didn't see their bloody daughter with the braces on her teeth. And it was always the police chief's daughter or the lord mayor's daughter—all the most obnoxious kids, because they had the most obnoxious parents. We had these people thrust on us. Like being insulted by these junked-up middle-class bitches and bastards who would be commenting on our working-class-ness and our manners. I would go insane, swearing at them, whatever; I'd always do something. I couldn't take it, it was awful. It was a fuckin' humiliation. One has to completely humiliate oneself to be what the Beatles were, and that's what I resent. It just happens bit by bit, until this complete craziness surrounds you and you're doing exactly what you don't want to do with people you can't stand—the people you hated when you were ten.

Would you take it all back?

If I could be a fuckin' fisherman, I would, you know. If I had the capabilities of being something other than I am, I would. It's no fun being an artist. You know what it's like, writing, it isn't fun, it's torture. I read about Van Gogh, Beethoven, any of them—and I read an article the other day—well, if they'd had psychiatrists we wouldn't have Gauguin's great pictures. And these fuckin' bastards there just sucking us to death, that's about all that we can do, is do it like circus animals. I resent being an artist, in that respect, I resent performing for fucking idiots who don't know anything. They can't feel; I'm the one that's feeling, because I'm the one expressing. They live vicariously through me and other artists. I'd sooner be in the audience, really, but I'm not capable of it. One of my big things is that I wish I was a fisherman. I know it sounds silly, and I'd sooner be rich than poor and all the rest of that shit, but the pain...I wish I was...ignorance is bliss or something. If you don't know, man, there's no pain, probably there is, but that's how I express it.

What do you think the effect of the Beatles was on the history of Britain?

I don't know about the history. The people who are in control and in power and the class system and the whole bullshit bourgeois scene is exactly the same except that there is a lot of middle-class kids with long hair walking around London in trendy clothes and Kenneth Tynan's making a fortune out of the word *fuck*. The same bastards are in control, the same people are runnin' everything, it's exactly the same. They hyped the kids and the generation.

We've grown up a little, all of us, and there has been a change and we are a bit freer and all that, but it's the same game, nothing's really changed. They're doing exactly the same things, selling arms to South Africa, killing blacks on the street, people are living in fucking poverty with rats crawling over them. It's the same. It just makes you puke. And I woke up to that, too. The dream is over. It's just the same only I'm thirty and a lot of people have got long hair, that's all.

Nothing happening except that we grew up; we did our thing just like they were telling us. Most of the so-called Now Generation are getting jobs and all of that. We're a minority, you know, people like us always were, but maybe we are a slightly larger minority because of something or other.

Why do you think the impact of the Beatles was so much bigger in America than it was in England?

For the same reason that American stars are so much bigger in England, I suppose, the grass is greener. And we were really professional by the time we got here: we learned the whole game. When we arrived here we knew how to handle press. The British press are the toughest in the world; we could handle anything. We were all right. I know on the plane over I was thinking, oh, we won't make it, or I said it on a film or something, but that's that side of me. We knew we would wipe 'em out if we could just get a grip on you.

And when we got here you were all walkin' around in fuckin' Bermuda shorts with Boston crew cuts and stuff on your teeth. The chicks looked like 1940s horses. There was no conception of dress or any of that jazz. We just thought what an ugly race, what an ugly race. It looked just disgusting and we thought how hip we were. But of course we weren't, it was just the five of us. Us and the Stones were really the hip ones, the rest of England were just the same as they ever were. You tend to get nationalistic, and we used to really laugh at America, except for its music. And it was black music we dug and over here the blacks were laughin' at people like Chuck Berry and the blues singers. The blacks thought it wasn't sharp to dig the really funky black music, and the whites only listened to Jan and Dean and all that.

We felt that we had…that the message was listen to this music. It was the same in Liverpool, we felt very exclusive and underground in Liverpool listening to all those old-time records. And nobody was listening to any of them except Eric Burdon in Newcastle and Mick Jagger in London. It was that lonely. It was fantastic. We came over here and it was the same: nobody was listening to rock & roll or to black music in America. We were coming to the land of its origin but nobody wanted to know about it.

You always said that the Beatles wanted to be bigger than Elvis.

Yes.

Why?

Because Elvis was the biggest. We wanted to be the biggest. Doesn't everybody?

When did you realize that you were bigger than Elvis?

I don't know. See, it's different once it happens. It's like, when you actually get to number one, or whatever, it's different. It's the going for it that's fun.

How do you rate yourself as a guitarist?

I'm okay. I'm not very good technically, but I can make it fuckin' howl and move. I was rhythm guitarist. It's an important job. I can make a band drive.

How do you rate George?

He's pretty good. Ha, ha. I prefer myself. I have to be honest, you know. I'm really very embarrassed about my guitar playing in one way because it's very poor. I can never move, but I can make a guitar speak, you know. Yoko has made me get very cocky about my guitar. You see, one part of me says, "Yes, of course I can play because I can make a rock move." But the other part of me says, "Well, I wish I could just do it like B.B. King." If you put me with B.B., I would feel silly. I'm an artist and if you give me a tuba I'll bring something out of it. I don't know…ask Eric Clapton, he thinks I can play, ask him. You don't have to…you see a lot of you people…want technical things, then you think that's…it's like wanting technical films. Most critics of rock & roll, and guitarists, are in the stage of the Fifties where they wanted a technically perfect film, finished for them, and they would feel happy. I'm a cinema-verité guitarist. I'm a musician and you have to break down your barriers to be able to hear what I'm playing. There's a nice little bit I played, they had it on the back of *Abbey Road*. There is a little break where Paul plays, George plays and I play. And you listened to it. And there is one bit, one of those where it stops, one of those "Carry That Weight" where it suddenly goes boom, boom on the drums and then we all take it in turns to play. I'm the third one on it. I have a definite style of playing. I've always had. I was overshadowed. They call George the invisible singer, well, I'm the invisible guitarist.

Which songs really stick in your mind as Lennon-McCartney songs?

"I Want to Hold Your Hand," "From Me to You," "She Loves You"…I'd have to have the list, there's so many—trillions of 'em. In a rock band you have to keep writing singles. We both had our fingers in each other's pies.

I remember the simplicity that was evident in "She's So Heavy," which was about Yoko. In fact, a reviewer wrote of "She's So Heavy," he seems to have lost his talent for lyrics, it's so simple and boring. But when it gets down to it, when you're drowning, you don't say, "I would be incredibly pleased if someone would have the foresight to notice me drowning and come and help me," you just scream. And in "She's So Heavy," I just sang, "I want you, I want you so bad, she's so heavy, I want you," like that. I started simplifying my lyrics then, on the double album.

What about on 'Rubber Soul'—"Norwegian Wood"?

I was trying to write about an affair without letting me wife know I was writing about an affair, so it was very gobbledygook. I was sort of writing from my experiences—girls' flats, things like that.

I remember this single coming out: "Day Tripper"/"We Can Work It Out."

That was a drug song, in a way.

"Day Tripper"?

Yes. Because it was a day tripper. I just liked the word.

At some point, right in there between 'Help' and 'A Hard Day's Night,' you got into drugs and got into drug songs.

Help was made on pot, *A Hard Day's Night* I was on pills. That's drugs, that's bigger drugs than pot. I've been on pills since I was fifteen, no, since I was seventeen or nineteen…since I became a musician. The only way to survive in Hamburg to play eight hours a night was to take pills. The waiters gave you them…the pills and drink. I was a fucking dropped-down drunk in art school. *Help* was where we turned on to pot and dropped drink, simple as that. I've always needed a drug to survive. The others too, but I always had more. I always took more pills, more of everything because I'm more crazy, probably.

When did you first start writing message songs, serious songs?

Probably after dinner, I don't know. "Day Tripper" wasn't a serious message song.

I don't mean serious message songs in that sense. I mean there was a big change in your music from "Can't Buy Me Love" to "We Can Work It Out."

I suppose it was pot then. "We Can Work It Out" was…Paul wrote that chorus, I wrote the middle bit about "Life is very short/There is no time for fussing and fighting…" all that bit. I don't remember any changeover. Other than when you take pot you're a little more aggressive than when you take alcohol. When you're on alcohol and pills, you just couldn't remember anything.

How do you think LSD affected your conception of music, in general?

Well, it was only another mirror; it wasn't a miracle. It was more of a visual thing, and a therapy—that "looking at yourself" bit, you know? It did all that. But it didn't write the music. I write the music in the circumstances I'm in, whether it's on acid or in the water. The thing that we forget about the acid is to live now, this moment. Hold on now, we might have a cup of tea, we might get a moment's happiness any minute now. So that's what it's all about, just moment by moment. That's how we're living now, but really living like that and cherishing each day, and dreading it too. It might be your last, I mean it sounds funny, but you might get run over by a car and all that. I'm really beginning to cherish it when I'm cherishing it.

"Happiness Is a Warm Gun" is a nice song.

Oh, I like that, one of my best. I had forgotten about that. Oh, I love it. I think it's a beautiful song. I like all the different things that are happening in it. Like "God," I had put together some three sections of different songs, it was meant to be—it seemed to run through all the different kinds of rock music.

It wasn't about "H" at all. "Lucy in the Sky with Diamonds," which I swear to God, or swear to Mao, or to anybody you like, I had no idea spelled LSD—and "Happiness"—George Martin had a book on guns which he had told me about—I can't remember—or I think he showed me a cover of a magazine that said HAPPINESS IS A WARM GUN. It was a gun magazine, that's it: I read it, thought it was a fantastic, insane thing to say. A warm gun means you just shot something.

When did you realize that LSD were the initials of "Lucy in the Sky with Diamonds"?

Only after I read it or somebody told me. I didn't even see it on the label. I didn't look at the initials. I don't look—I mean I never play things backwards. I listened to it as I made it. Every time after that though I would look at the titles to see what it said, and usually they never said anything.

You said to me 'Sgt. Pepper' is the one. That was the album?

Well, it was a peak. Paul and I were definitely working together, especially on "A Day In The Life" that was a real…the way we wrote a lot of the time: you'd write the good bit, the part that was easy, like "I read the news today" or whatever it was, then when you got stuck or whenever it got hard, instead of carrying on, you just drop it; then we would meet each other, and I would sing half, and he would be inspired to write the next bit and vice versa. He was a bit shy about it because I think he thought it's already a good song. Sometimes we wouldn't let each other interfere with a song either, because you tend to be a bit lax with someone else's stuff, you experiment a bit. So we were doing it in his room with the piano. He said "Should we do this?" "Yeah, let's do that."

I keep saying that I always preferred the double album, because *my* music is better on the double album; I don't care about the whole concept of *Pepper,* it might be better, but the music was better for me on the double album, because I'm being myself on it. I think it's as simple as the new album, like "I'm So Tired" is just the guitar. I felt more at ease with that than the production. I don't like production so much. But *Pepper* was a peak all right.

You say on your record that "Freaks on the phone won't leave me alone/So don't give me that brother, brother…"

Because I'm sick of all these aggressive hippies or whatever they are, the Now Generation, sort of being very uptight with me, you know, either on the street or anywhere, or on the phone, demanding my attention as if I owed them something. I'm not their fucking parents, that's what it is. They come to the door with a fucking peace symbol and expect to just sort of march around the house or something like an old Beatle fan. They're under a delusion of awareness by having long hair and that's what I'm sick of. I'm sick of them, they frighten me, a lot of uptight maniacs going around wearing fuckin' peace symbols.

What did you think of Charles Manson and that thing?

I don't know what I thought when it happened. I just think a lot of the things he says are true, that he is a child of the state, made by us, and he took their children in when nobody else would, is what he did. Of course he's cracked, all right.

How would you trace the breakup of the Beatles?

After Brian [Epstein] died, we collapsed. Paul took over and supposedly led us. But what is leading us when we went round in circles? We broke up then. That was the disintegration.

When did you first feel that the Beatles had broken up? When did that idea first hit you?

I don't remember. I was in my own pain. I wasn't noticing, really. I just did it like a job. We made the double album, the set … it's like if you took each track off and gave it all mine and all George's … it was just me and a backing group, Paul and a backing group. I enjoyed it, but we broke up then.

You said you quit the Beatles first.

Yes.

How?

Well, I said to Paul, "I'm leaving." I knew before we went to Toronto. I told Allen [Klein] I was leaving, I told Eric Clapton and Klaus [Voormann] that I was leaving and that I'd probably like to use them as a group. I hadn't decided how to do it—to have a permanent new group or what. Then later on I thought, fuck, I'm not going to get stuck with another set of people, you know, whoever they are. So I announced it to myself and to the people around me on the way to Toronto. Allen came with me, and I told Allen it was over. When I got back, there were a few meetings, and Allen had said, well, cool it, 'cause there was a lot to do businesswise, you know, and it would not have been suitable at the time. And then we were discussing something in the office with Paul, and I kept saying no, no, no to everything, you see. So it came to a point I had to say something, of course, and Paul asked, "What do you mean?" I said, "I mean the group is over, I'm leaving."

What was Paul's reaction?

Like anybody when you say divorce—you know, their face goes all sorts of colors. It's like he knew, really, that this was the final thing.

How did you meet Yoko?

There was a sort of underground clique in London; John Dunbar, who was married to Marianne Faithfull, had an art gallery in London called Indica, and I'd been going around to galleries a bit on me off days in between records, also to a few exhibitions in different galleries that showed sort of unknown artists or underground artists.

I got the word that this amazing woman was putting on a show the next week, something about people in bags, in black bags, and it was going to be a bit of a happening and all that. So I went to a preview the night before it opened. I went in—she didn't know who I was or anything—and I was wandering around. There were a couple of artsy-type students who had been helping, lying around there in the gallery, and I was looking at it and was astounded. There was an apple on sale there for two hundred quid; I thought it was fantastic—I got the humor in her work immediately. I didn't have to have much knowledge about avant-garde or underground art, the humor got me straightaway. It was two hundred quid to watch the fresh apple decompose.

But it was another piece that really decided me for or against the artist: a ladder that led to a painting, which was hung on the ceiling. It looked like a black canvas with a chain with a spyglass hanging on the end of it. I climbed the ladder, looked through the spyglass, and in tiny little letters it said, YES.

So it was positive. I felt relieved. It's a great relief when you get up the ladder and you look through the spyglass and it doesn't say NO or FUCK YOU or something.

I was very impressed. John Dunbar introduced us—neither of us knew who the hell each other was. She didn't know who I was; she'd only heard of Ringo; I think it means apple in Japanese. And Dunbar had sort of been hustling her, saying, "That's a good patron; you must go and talk to him or do something." Dunbar insisted she say hello to the millionaire—you know what I mean. And she came up and handed me a card that said BREATHE on it—one of her instructions—so I just went [*pants*]. This was our meeting.

When did you realize that you were in love with her?

It was beginning to happen; I would start looking at her book, but I wasn't quite aware what was happening to me. Then she did a thing called Dance Event, where different cards kept coming through the door every day saying BREATHE and DANCE and WATCH ALL THE LIGHTS UNTIL DAWN, and they upset me or made me happy, depending.

I'd get very upset about it being intellectual or all fucking avant-garde, then I'd like it, and then I wouldn't. Then I went to India with the Maharoonie and we corresponded. The letters were still formal, but they just had a little side to them. I nearly took her to India, but I still wasn't sure for what reason; I was still sort of kidding myself, with sort of artistic reasons and all that.

When we got back from India, we were talking to each other on the phone. I called her over; it was the middle of the night and Cynthia [Lennon's first wife] was away, and I thought, well, now's the time if I'm gonna get to know her any more. She came to the house and I didn't know what to do, so we went upstairs to my studio and I played her all the tapes that I'd made, all this far-out stuff, some comedy stuff, and some electronic music. She was suitably impressed, and then she said, "Well, let's make one ourselves." So we made *Two Virgins*. It was midnight when we started; it was dawn when we finished, and then we made love at dawn. It was very beautiful.

What was it like getting married?

It was very romantic. It's all in the song "The Ballad of John and Yoko," if you want to know how it happened. Gibraltar was like a little sunny dream. I couldn't find a white suit—I had sort of off-white corduroy trousers and a white jacket. Yoko had all white on.

What was your first peace event?

The first peace event was the Amsterdam Bed Peace, after we got married.

What was that like? That was your first re-exposure to the public.

It was a nice high. We were in the Hilton, looking over Amsterdam—it was very crazy; the press came, expecting to see us fuckin' in bed. They'd all heard John and Yoko were going to fuck in front of the press for peace. So when they all walked in—about fifty or sixty reporters flew over from London, all sort of very edgy, we were just sitting in pajamas saying, "Peace, brother." That was it.

There was a point at which you decided you and Yoko would give up your private life.

No, we never decided to give up our private life. We decided that if we were going to do anything like get married, or like this film we are going to make now, that we would dedicate it to peace. And during that period, because we are what we are, it evolved that somehow we ended up being responsible to produce peace.

Why can't you be alone without Yoko?

I can be, but I don't wish to be.

There is no reason on earth why I should be without her. There is nothing more important than our relationship, nothing. And we dig being together all the time. And both of us could survive apart, but what for? I'm not going to sacrifice love, real love, for any fuckin' whore, or any friend, or any business because, in the end, you're alone at night. Neither of us wants to be, and you can't fill the bed with groupies; that doesn't work. I don't want to be a swinger. Like I said in the song, I've been through it all, and nothing works better than to have somebody you love hold you.

What about Yoko's art?

We are both showing each other's experience to each other. I had to open up to hear it—I had to get out the concept of what I wanted to hear…I had to allow abstract art or music in. She had to do the same for rock & roll. It was an intellectual exercise, because we're all boxed in. We are all in little boxes, and somebody has to go in and rip your fuckin' head open for you to allow something else in.

What is holding people back from understanding Yoko?

She was doing all right before she met Elvis. Howard Smith announced he was going to play her music on FM and all these idiots rang up and said, "Don't you dare play it, she split the Beatles." She didn't split the Beatles and even if she did, what does that have to do with it or her fucking record? She is a woman and she's Japanese; there is racial prejudice against her and there is female prejudice against her. It's as simple as that.

Her work is far out. Yoko's bottom thing is as important as *Sgt. Pepper.* The real hip people know about it. There are a few people that know; there is a person in Paris who knows about her; a person in Moscow knows about her; there's a person in fucking China that knows about her. But in general, she can't be accepted, because she's too far out. It's hard to take. Her pain is such that she expresses herself in a way that hurts you—you cannot take it. That's why they couldn't take Van Gogh, it's too real, it hurts; that's why they kill you.

What do you think of America?

America is where it's at. I should have been born in New York. I should have been born in the Village; that's where I belong. Why wasn't I born there? Paris was it in the eighteenth century; London, I don't think, has ever been it, except literary-wise, when Wilde and Shaw and all of them were there. New York is it.

I regret profoundly that I was not an American and not born in Greenwich Village. That's where I should have been. It never works that way. Everybody heads toward the center; that's why I'm here now.

Are you pleased with your new album, 'John Lennon/Plastic Ono Band'?

I think it's the best thing I've ever done. I think it's realistic and it's true to me. That has been developing over the years from "In My Life," "I'm a Loser," "Help," "Strawberry Fields." They're all personal records. I always wrote about me when I could. I didn't really enjoy writing third-person songs about people who live in concrete flats and things like that. I like first-person music. But because of my hang-ups and many other things, I would only write specifically about me now and then. Now I write all about me and that's why I like it. It's me! And nobody else.

You said at one point that you have to write songs to justify your existence.

I said a lot of things. I write songs because that's the thing I choose to do, you know, and I can't help writing them; that's a fact. Sometimes…I felt as though you work to justify your existence, but you don't. You work to exist and vice versa, and that's it, really.

What do you think are the best songs that you have written?

Ever?

Ever. What is the best song you have ever written?

The one best song?

Have you ever thought of that?

I don't know. If somebody asked me what is my favorite song, is it "Stardust" or something…I can't…that kind of decision making I can't do. I always liked "Walrus", "Strawberry Fields," "Help," "In My Life." Those are some of my favorites, you know.

Why "Help"?

Because I meant it; it's real. The lyric is as good now as it was then. It's no different, you know, and it makes me feel secure to know that I was that aware of myself then. It was just me singing "help," and I meant it. I don't like the recording that much; we did it too fast, trying to be commercial.

I like "I Want to Hold Your Hand"; we wrote that together, and it's a beautiful melody. I might do "I Want to Hold Your Hand" and "Help" again, because I like them.

Why "Strawberry Fields"? Did you think that was real?

Yeah, it was real for then, and it's...I think it's like talking, you know...it's like that Elton John one where he's singing, oh, I don't know—he talks to himself, sort of singing, which I thought was nice; it reminded me of that.

Songs like "Girl"?

Yeah, I liked that one.

"Run For Your Life"?

"Run for Your Life" I always hated.

Why?

I don't know, it was one of those I knocked off just to write a song, and it was phony. But "Girl" is real. There is no such thing as *the* girl; she was a dream, but the words are all right. It's about "Was she taught when she was young that pain would lead to pleasure/Did she understand it," and all that. They're sort of philosophy quotes. It was reasonable, and I was thinkin' about it when I wrote it; it wasn't just a song, and it was about that girl—which happened to turn out to be Yoko in the end—the one that a lot of us were looking for. There're many songs I forget that I do like. I like "Across the Universe," too.

Why?

Because it's one of the best lyrics I've written. In fact, it could be the best, I don't know. It's one of the best; it's good poetry, or whatever you call it, without chewin' it, it stands. See, the ones I like are the ones that stand as words without melody, that don't have to have any melody. It's a poem, you know; you could read 'em.

What do you think the future of rock & roll is?

Whatever we make it. If we want to go bullshitting off into intellectualism with rock & roll, we are going to get bullshitting rock intellectualism. If we want real rock & roll, it's up to all of us to create it and stop being hyped by, you know, revolutionary image and long hair. We've got to get over that bit. That's what cutting hair is about. Let's own up now and see who's who, who's doing something about what, and who's making music and who's laying down bullshit. Rock & roll will be whatever we make it.

Why do you think it means so much to people?

Because it is primitive enough and has no bullshit, really, the best stuff, and its beat gets through to you. Go to the jungle and they have the rhythm and it goes throughout the world—it's as simple as that. You get the rhythm going, everybody gets into it. I read that Eldridge Cleaver said that blacks gave middle-class whites back their bodies, you know, put their minds and bodies together through the music. It's something like that, it gets through—to me it got through. It was the only thing to get through to me after all the things that were happening when I was fifteen. Rock & roll was real. Everything else was unreal. And the thing about rock & roll—good rock & roll, whatever good means—is that it's real, and realism gets through to you despite yourself. You recognize something in it which is true, like all true art.

What's a rough picture of your immediate future, say the next three months.

I'd like to just vanish just a bit. It wore me out, New York. I love it. I'm just sort of fascinated by it, like a fucking monster. Doing the films was a nice way of meeting a lot of people. I think we've both said and done enough for a few months, especially with this article. I'd like to get out of the way and wait till they all…

Do you have a rough picture of the next few years?

Oh no, I couldn't think of the next few years; it's abysmal thinking of how many years there are to go, millions of them. I just play it by the week. I don't think much ahead of a week.

Do you see a time when you'll retire?

No, I couldn't, you know.

YOKO: He'll probably work until he's eighty or until he dies.

I can't foresee it. Even when you're a cripple you carry on painting. I would paint if I couldn't move.

Do you have a picture of "when I'm sixty-four"?

No, no. I hope we're a nice old couple living off the coast of Ireland or something—looking at our scrapbook of madness.

Ohio Honors Its Dead

by Joe Eszterhas   June 1971

A year ago on the fourth of May—on a windswept sunny day exactly like this one—Dean Kahler, who wanted to be a cop when he was a kid, threw himself onto green grass on the downward slope of Blanket Hill and felt a "bee sting": a steel-jacketed National Guard bullet had entered his lower back and blown apart his spinal cord.

So today he has his chair. Dean Kahler, 21, a friendly redhead in sneakers, sits in the sun on the Kent State University Commons surrounded by 7000 people, grinning, driving the meanest chopped-down, souped-up wheelchair you've ever seen. He guns it up a wooden ramp to the speaker's platform—the way you'd gun a Corvette or Harley down an alley—whirring his tires, showing off.

Exactly one year after the bodies were carted away from Blanket Hill, after the street cleaners came to spray the blood away, after *that*, the horror, the thirteen-second volley of gunfire, the bullet holes in the trees, Dean Kahler reaches up for the mike, pulls it down and says:

"Brothers and sisters, I don't know whether I'm happy to see you again. I can't find the words. It's very hard for me to speak to you. We all have to go out and work against this war and remember that four people died. Things have been happening on this campus oppressive to me. We believe in nonviolence, yeah, but we shouldn't be afraid to practice what we preach. So this afternoon, when we sit-in at the ROTC office, we shouldn't be afraid to get our heads busted for what we believe in."

He finishes and wheels himself back, the only speaker on the university's elaborate and carefully structured memorial who does not play forensic games, the only speaker (this pale guy in the souped-up wheelchair with the shattered spinal cord) to talk about having the guts to get your head busted for something you believe in.

The university president, Robert I. White, who was having a martini when the shots rang out last year, sits a few feet down from the gleaming wheelchair, looking uncomfortable. Four sets of parents, their lifestyles altered, their flag-decal belief in America buried in four separate cemeteries across the land—Allison, Jeff, Sandy and Bill, lives between dashes set on grave markers—are away from the campus today because Robert I. White did not think it would be "beneficial" to invite them to the ceremonies marking the deaths of their children.

At the same time Dean Kahler shows off his wheelchair, the National Guardsmen of the 145th and 107th, the men on the firing line, are drilling, ready to be called again in case of trouble. The former governor, James A. Rhodes, whose use of the guard at Kent State almost elected him to the senate, is in Miami, under a warmer sun.

And the participants of that national tableau, that internationally known front-page picture: the sobbing fourteen-year-old runaway with the burned-out face kneeling over Jeff Miller's bleeding body, and the photographer who made her a tragic superstar—where are they? Mary Vecchio, of Opa Locka, Florida, is in a juvenile home serving a six-month sentence because she tried, once again, to run away. John Filo, the photographer, is there on the commons, corncob pipe in mouth, bending for new angles, accepting congratulations for his borrowed-camera art for which, yesterday, he won a Pulitzer Prize and for which, in those long months afterward, a sweat-shirt manufacturer offered him $10,000.

There is a guy behind the speaker's stand with a KENT STAY UNITED button, the hype slogan cranked out for network consumption. He is cleaning his fingernails with a four-inch blade, his face Appalachian beef-red, wearing the kind of flap-up fur hat first seen in Korea around places like Pork Chop Hill. He is listening to all the words—tragedy, peace, dedication, requiem—and his eyes are beaded on Jesse Jackson, the dynamic black man from Chicago who's trying to blackanize the heartland; he's sitting on the stand. The look is a steal from *In the Heat of the Night*—an Ohio Steiger keeping a good eye, by gawd, on that big buck nigger.

A biology prof, a stereotype of overfed academe, says solemnly that there is "evidence *Eddie* Hoffman is here." ("You mean Abbie Hoffman?" "Yeah, that's him." "Hairless?" "Yeah." "Oh, wow!") Campus security men are perched, binocular-faced, helmet-nosed, on the roof of the new library, which affords a panoramic view of the rolling campus. Word spreads about Minox-wielding "secret police," and on the roofs of all campus buildings, there are three-foot-high bright chartreuse numbers to guide the way for the highway-patrol helicopter hovering overhead.

The "evidence" that outside agitators are present is in the pretty brown eyes of a girl named Nancy Kurshan, who used to be Jerry Rubin's sweetheart and who has now made Kent her home, having achieved the mandatory prestige bust after a few weeks on campus for spray-painting an administration building with antiwar slogans. She says she came to Kent because she likes it, a reasonable proposition, but the administration and security men know better. She came on orders from Rubin, this fatigue-jacketed pony-league Bernardine, to organize the local revolution. So one of the always available eyes is fixed on Nancy Kurshan, a pretty girl, and the campus newspaper runs an interview and calls it "The Portrait of One Outside Agitator."

The town figured it out right after the shooting: outside agitators had planned the whole riot, probably financed by Fidel Castro, which was why they carried around those pictures of that other long-haired commie, "Chee."

Commie is not a hyperbolic term here, for the town newspaper, *The Record Courier* (published by University Board of Trustees president Robert Dix) still uses that word in its headlines. And with that kind of daily insight into the hairy roots of communism, outside agitators are quickly spotted and arrested. Last year, after the shooting, Uncle Sam—a fifty-two-year-old barber from Connellsville, Pennsylvania, also known as Mr. Rainbow, who got to campus three hours after the shooting in his Uncle Sam suit—was arrested. This year Uncle Sam came back with a sign that said, UNCLE SAM BACK AGAIN, KICKED OFF KSU CAMPUS BY NATIONAL GUARD.

You gotta give Uncle Sam credit. It takes balls to visit Armageddon, even in an Uncle Sam suit. The epicenter of Armageddon is the Portage County Courthouse where, the week before the anniversary of the shooting, on court order all visitors had to show a special pass to the deputy sheriff at the door, signing in and out each time they left the building, radicalizing a local housewife *ad extremum,* forcing her to yell, "This place is getting just like Russia!" to the deputy wearing the stars-and-stripes patch at the door.

"Ohia" reaction was par for the course: a group of mayors praised General Del Corso for his "handling" of the riots; an American Independent party candidate got 1000 signatures in a few hours "affirming" the shooting; and Ronald L. Kane, the politically ambiguous county prosecutor, a strict law-and-order man who admits having more respect for his German shepherd than for faculty types, got fan mail from around the country. One letter said: "I would like to tell you how much I appreciate your attitude and what you have done. More power to you and keep your chin up." It came from Paul Newman's mother, Mrs. Martie Newman of Covina, California, confirming that generation gaps haunt even movie families.

Some of the more progressive townspeople, the Kiwanis-Jaycee types, got together and found the best search-and-destroy weapon against the agitators— Jesus—picking as their hired gun the best counteragitprop man in the business, the Reverend Billy Graham, and tried to convince him to douse those longhairs with religion. Billy thought it over and declined.

But if Jesus was looking Kent's way, He must have been struck dumb. In the fall, the university got a $20,000 federal justice study grant for a new law-enforcement center. A few days before the anniversary, the conviction of a kid who had been arrested for trespassing on campus in the hours after the shooting was upheld by the Ohio Supreme Court. And between the cash and the kid's reaffirmed conviction was a void, a graven silence. A year after the shooting, "justice" meant a flat refusal—by the Nixon administration, the Silent Majority, and the Calley brigades—to accept the facts of the shootings and to act on them.

The "facts" in this case were made "crystal clear" by the FBI. But when it came to saying that the shooting was not justified, that the National Guard was not surrounded, their lives not in danger, America refused to listen even to J. Edgar Hoover, preferring, instead, to accept as truth the words of Seabury Ford, a former

National Guardsman and a chief prosecutor of the Portage County Grand Jury.

The Justice Department summary of the FBI report said, "There is some reason to believe that the claim by the National Guard that their lives were endangered by the students was fabricated subsequent to the events." The Portage County Grand Jury report said, "The guardsmen fired their weapons in the honest and sincere belief and under circumstances which would have logically caused them to believe they would suffer serious bodily injury had they not done so." The Justice Department said, "The guardsmen were *not surrounded*. Photographs and television film show that only a very few students were between the guard and the Commons.... Although many claim they were hit by rocks at some time during the confrontation, only one guardsman was injured seriously enough to require medical treatment." The Portage County Grand Jury said, "Photographic evidence has established beyond any doubt that as National Guardsmen approached the top of the hill adjacent to Taylor Hall a large segment of the crowd surged up the hill...there was a constant barrage of rocks and flying objects."

The grand jury, acting on its "evidence", indicted twenty-five persons—students, ex-students and teachers. The federal government, looking at the FBI's findings, did nothing. Although the facts were totally contradictory and although parents of the dead students, along with church groups, launched a massive campaign, the Federal government refused to call a Federal grand jury, knowing:

• That the FBI report was never made available to the Portage County Grand Jury by its prosecutors.

• That Seabury Ford, a chief prosecutor and a man who helped write the report, not only was an ex-member of the guard unit that did the shooting, but also headed the Portage County Republican party. He was quoted as saying, "The whole damn country is not going to quiet down until the police are ordered to shoot to kill."

• That the grand jury never summoned a guardsman who had been on the hill. Captain Raymond pointedly told the FBI, "Our lives were not in danger. It was not a shooting situation."

The federal government preferred, it seemed, to ignore even J. Edgar Hoover's facts when those facts were politically unsavory, even if it meant that twenty-five people who were themselves potential targets in the shooting gallery on Blanket Hill would be judged the criminals. But at the same time—face-saving gesture!—the federal government would pay Kent State $20,000 for a justice study.

To quote a most remarkable part of the grand-jury report: "On Sunday night, October 11th, during the second performance on the Kent State University campus by the musical group known as the Jefferson Airplane, while the Airplane was doing their musical numbers, color slides were projected onto a screen behind the group consisting of psychedelic colors, scenes of the Ohio National Guard on the Kent State campus, and scenes of the shooting of May 4th complete with views of the bodies of the victims....What disturbs me is that such a group of intellectual and social misfits should be afforded the opportunity to disrupt the affairs of a major university...."

Maybe what they were really saying, through calculated innuendo, was that the Airplane were guilty and the guardsmen were not.

★   ★   ★

Bojangles, Barry Levine, 20, an emaciated but charismatic kid from Long Island with Lancelot hair and jingling leather bracelets, was Allison Krause's boyfriend and sat next to her that day in the ambulance, holding her hand as she died on the way to the hospital with a bullet in her side. He went back for a while in the fall, walking the leaf-strewn knolls around Blanket Hill. Then, overcome by a paralyzing visceral sadness, he had to leave.

"I saw a bunch of friends of mine and Allison's," he wrote a friend. "Boy, they miss her! The scene at Kent was pretty sad. I watched meetings of students planning activities for May 4th, and there just didn't seem to be much feeling behind the plans. They seemed to have forgotten what had happened. They were merely filling an *image* this country had built for Kent State University May 4th. It was quite sad. I got kind of sick...."

The year began, really, a few weeks before that long summer ended, when the class of 1970 graduated in June and came back to campus for the first time since the street cleaners had done their job on Blanket Hill. The ceremonial curiosity of death was there, and the students and their parents puffed up Blanket Hill. Mom says, "Donald, let's get a picture of Jimmy here with the Instamatic." A lumpy woman with a new pink dress and humidity stains, she has stopped by the pagoda at the crest of the hill where the guard turned. "It would be nice to show Harry and Sue just where it happened."

The school year began with a rally soaked in lukewarm symbolism. The slogan had been changed to "Power to the Peaceful" while the whole world was watching. A television newsman stood at the crest of the hill, combing his hair and cursing the steady rain that would ruin his film. Robert I. White talked about "the lifeblood flows again," not realizing the funereal import of his words, and *The Phoenix,* a street paper, had some gritty and more relevant advice: "It is now illegal to call a law enforcement officer a pig in the City of Kent."

It was a routine year, if that can be imagined. A campus Ugly Man Contest was held, trivia swept the dorms—"What is General Del Corso's first name? Sylvester, right!"—and visitors, from Nixon speechwriter Patrick Buchanan to Allen Ginsberg, put in speeches. Any notable visitor to Kent this year could guarantee himself good newspaper play just by going there.

By Christmas, student body president Craig Morgan, an ROTC student indicted by the Portage County Grand Jury, was talking about the greatest enemy on campus: apathy. While Kent was something special nationally, Ohio kids very clearly were still Ohio kids.

The apathy extended even to the Medical Fund, organized to help the nine students who were wounded that day, and floundering now because of lack of concern. Senator Ted Kennedy held a cocktail party to raise money, but the event was as much pure cocktail party—a mixer for the beautiful people buzzing around the shooting, a velvet pant-suit affair—as it was a fund-raiser. Mark Harris, the fund's organizer, would say, "Many extremely wealthy persons drank and ate more than they donated."

By Christmas, Barry Levine was long gone, jingling his bracelets in California, still asking about Allison's gravestone and trying to organize a free school. Town and campus officials were reinforcing their bulwark against conspiracies and agitators, saying, at roast-beef luncheons, that if Kent State shut down again it would sound the death knell for higher education in America.

On the morning of January 28th, their worst fears were confirmed. The university, innocent victim of outside influences, shut down. All classes were canceled, campus police worked overtime, and the kids stared out their dormitory windows. Everyone was foot deep in trouble, in twelve inches of... *snow*.

★   ★   ★

In his headlined calls for reason and calm, and in his parenthetical warnings of trouble, university president Robert I. White was saying, What happened is behind us, let us for the greater glory and good of Kent State University look to the future. But if he showed a willingness to look to the future, it was with good reason.

To look at Robert I. White's actions that weekend a year ago is to observe the corporate head of this educational complex, the company president, at his most bureaucratic. Robert I. White, on that fateful weekend, acted more like Columbia's Grayson Kirk than Kirk ever did. The man has always been noted for holding himself aloof, a breathing icon as inaccessible to students as to other university presidents. "A lot of us," said Don Perko, the head of Kent's largest fraternity, "didn't even know what he looked like."

On May 1st, 1970, Robert I. White had a trip planned to Iowa City, Iowa, where he headed the American College Testing Program. He had watched the Nixon announcement of the move into Cambodia the night before and he had thought, "Oh, boy, here we go again," fearing demonstrations. During the day of May 1st, he had watched two student rallies, was aware of the frustrated restlessness of his student body. Yet, knowing these things, he still decided to take his trip to Iowa. Not only did he decide to go, but, aware of at least the possibility of trouble on his campus, he decided to do a little sightseeing. He flew into Mason City so he could enjoy the quiet barren peacefulness of the countryside and drove a rent-a-car the few hundred miles to Iowa City.

Informed by his aides of the rioting in downtown Kent that night, he did not come back. The next day, Saturday, he was informed that the ROTC building had been burned, given the news not by any of his aides but by his housekeeper. He would later claim he tried to come back when he heard the building had been burned and guardsmen were on the campus—hallelujah!—but a fog kept his plane from taking off.

He flew back into Kent Sunday morning and, at the airport, met Governor James A. Rhodes, who informed White that his "intelligence had outside agitators from all over the country on the Kent campus." White knew the university's information had no outside agitators present, yet he made no argument with Rhodes. Nor did he tell him that in his view the presence of National Guardsmen would provide all the outside agitating that a student body, abhorring the latest Indo-Chinese invasion, needed.

He accepted the Rhodes decision and the Rhodes "intelligence," knowing too that Rhodes was two days away from the primary test that would end his political career, desperately riding a last-minute law-and-order campaign train, and that Kent provided the governor with the perfect statewide stage for his table-thumping theatrics. He accepted that highly politically suspect decision and the presence of those guardsmen, red-eyed from road-patrolling a violent teamsters strike, and went back to his presidential mansion overlooking the university Commons, making no effort to communicate with his students. When he was accidentally spotted by a few students that afternoon, he was sarcastically cheered.

Nor did he even bother to check, let alone argue, the interpretation that day of a third-echelon National Guard officer who said that the governor's loosely-flung "state of emergency" meant absolutely no assemblies, peaceful or otherwise, on the Kent State campus, knowing that many of his students would find this interpretation equally abhorrent, that many would view it as the ultimate violation of their civil liberties. And that night, when a group of sit-down demonstrators asked White to address them, the negative reply was sent to the demonstrators within one minute— a few minutes before the guard moved on the sit-downers with tear gas and bayonets.

But Robert White at his bureaucratic worst can be seen Monday, May 4th, the day of the shooting. After word spreads that there will be a rally at noon on the Commons, White meets at the Kent firehouse with town and guard officials. What happens at this meeting is simply incredible. A decision is made to break up that noon rally. Who made the decision and why?

In sworn testimony before the President's Commission on Campus Unrest, Guard Brigadier General Robert Canterbury answered the questions: "President White asked that the noon rally not be permitted. He said it would be highly dangerous." White, in sworn testimony before the same commission, said he had nothing to do with the rally and the decision to break it up was "batted at me from all sides." (Interestingly, the commission never followed up the blatant contradiction. Someone was lying under oath, perjury was in the air.) Even giving White the benefit of a very weighty doubt, no one at the meeting contradicted the Mayor of Kent, LeRoy Satrom, who said, "White spent most of his time doodling."

The meeting ended at eleven o'clock. Everyone who attended knew the rally at noon would be forcibly broken up by the guard. What did White do? At 11:45, knowing armed guardsmen would move on his students in fifteen minutes, Robert I. White went to lunch, where the sound of gunfire interrupted his second martini.

I interviewed White on a Cleveland television news show a few months after the shooting. He brought an aide with him, a glib carotene public-relations specialist who asked all the cameramen to shoot "the president" only in profile. White asked that we discuss only "the future" of Kent State University and not "what has happened." I refused.

Had he been present that weekend, I asked, would he have asked for the guard on campus?

"I want to dispel all doubt on that," he said. "There's been enough said. Had I been there I would have asked for the guard. Period."

"You mean," I asked incredulously, "you would have asked for the guard on your campus knowing they had loaded weapons?"

"Well, ah," he said, "no."

Through the year, White's attitude was clearly felt in the university's preparations for the May 4th anniversary. The administration's policy was that *they* would plan the anniversary program and *they* would invite the speakers and the state trespass law would be invoked against all unauthorized speakers. When the university announced its choice of main speakers, a bill topped by cuddly-puppy poet Rod McKuen, many students felt insulted. Four of the wounded—Dean Kahler, Tom Grace, Alan Canfora, Robby Stamps—condemned the plans, saying, "The presence of individuals such as Rod McKuen will only serve to continue the distortion of truth." Rod, sitting by some seashore, must have picked up the vibrations: the day before the memorial, pleading "prior commitments," he canceled out.

On that sunny day a year after the gunfire, Ken Johnson, an activist, would in a few short sentences come closer to the truth than the thousands of oratorical profundities that were to follow. "The university," he said, "has put forth an incredible proposition: that the less said about the circumstances of the shooting, the better."

Small wonder, then, that as Dean Kahler wheeled his flashy wheelchair up to the speaker's stand, Robert I. White looked not only characteristically pain-faced, but also very uncomfortable.

★   ★   ★

What do you do when four of your brothers and sisters have been shot to death on the hill you use for making out and nobody wants to talk about why they were killed or what for? Well, you blow a few bubbles, maybe, or go fly a kite.

Three days before the anniversary, on a cloudy Saturday afternoon—exactly one year after the ROTC building was burned, while the largest antiwar demonstration in American history was forming in Washington—a rally was being held on the Kent Commons. There was a bubblegum-blowing contest and a soap-blowing contest and frisbee tossers and kite flyers were lining up in cordons, the way the guard had lined up before they swept the Commons on the way to Blanket Hill. A two-year-old, an expert bubble blower, was the final judge. A campus policeman helped a shapely coed fly a kite. A kazoo band played, and a guinea pig named Pershing romped in the grass.

And in Pittsburgh, Arthur Krause, a Westinghouse executive, was at home with his wife Doris, planning a birthday. The tombstone, they had hoped, would arrive before this day, which would have been Allison Krause's twentieth birthday. I called Art Krause, a hard-driving intense man, an ex-marine decorated with the Purple Heart, and his wife, Doris.

"It's so damn senseless," Art said. "They won't even invite us to their observance. They just want to forget. How can I forget?"

"My God," Doris said, "what are they going to do? I saw all those pictures of those kids at the Washington rally, military all over the place, all those guardsmen and helicopters and stuff, and it's like the whole thing is happening again."

"I picked up some kids on the turnpike today, going to D.C.," Art said, "and I told them to cool it. It's a mind-draining thing. They're all going down there because you've got to if you're concerned."

"He picks up hitchhikers all the time now," Doris interrupted.

"I also picked up a kid from West Virginia," Art said, "and he was accusing himself that he didn't go down there. He'd been having some trouble with drugs. I told him that I had some difficulties with my daughter, that she had smoked some pot and stuff. I talked to him straight. I wish I could have talked to Allison like that. God, we've got to make this country work."

"It's too much of a job," Doris said. "When I saw the way they whisked that little girl away [Leslie Bacon] to Seattle, that little girl they're accusing of conspiracy, I thought: we're only a few steps from Nazi Germany."

"You know," Art said, "today they're playing up Law Day, and I listened to all those words. You know they all have double meanings, those words? A year ago I never would have noticed those meanings. What do you do? What do you do?"

"You know what it is with me?" Doris says. "She was my daughter. How can I grieve for her and not work for justice. I know the only thing I can damn well do for her is not to cry, because it's too easy, but to work.

"To work, to work, not to cry," she says, her voice rising, then breaking unevenly over the phone.

★   ★   ★

If the Justice Department is to hear Doris Krause's plea, all they have to do is act on the words of Spiro Agnew. Spiro Agnew talked about the shooting on *The David Frost Show* two weeks afterward and called it "murder...not first degree... but overreaction...." (Right on, Spiro!)

The first federal action after the shooting—besides Richard Nixon's insensitive comment about the shooting being the inevitable result of campus disruptions—was on May 25th, when presidential news aide Herb Klein told CBS that "a high-level commission to get to the bottom of the facts" would be appointed. But that same day, another White House press aide, Gerald Warren, "clarified" Klein and said the purpose of the commission "wouldn't necessarily be to get to the bottom of the facts of the shooting" but that it would be a "broad study." When the commission, headed by the ever-diplomatic William Scranton, former governor of Pennsylvania, finally got together, it soon showed it would be just that: a broad study not interested in the circumstances of the shooting.

It was not interested in—and indeed was never to discover—the cause of the shooting. It did not use its power of subpoena to summon guardsmen who were on the firing line, and its reporting was suspiciously less than accurate— referring once to a girl who was "reportedly" bayonetted when even a cub reporter could easily have learned the girl's name and the exact nature of her wounds. In its report on

Kent, the commission was characteristically two-sided and superficial, once again avoiding the kind of blame-pinning that would have resulted in culpability.

Governor Rhodes, with only a few months left in office, after turning down the commission's invitation to testify, very hurriedly put together a state grand jury chaired by a young, politically ambitious Republican prosecutor from conservative rural Ohio named Robert Balyent. When it was discovered that Mr. Ford, the other prosecutor, was a former guardsman, Attorney General Paul W. Brown called it "irrelevant." The Portage County Grand Jury subsequently issued its famous report —the shot heard around the world— indicting the twenty-five students, ex-students and faculty members, and very nearly indicting the Jefferson Airplane.

Meanwhile, parts of the puzzle that wouldn't fit kept appearing. The Justice Department summary of the FBI report was leaked to the press with its allegations that guardsmen may have trumped up their stories afterward, as well as with specific named references to guardsmen who aimed at students, naming, too, one guardsman who emptied his magazine. Commission member Joseph Rhodes, a young black man from Harvard, said there was also "some evidence" that two of the guardsmen who had been on the firing line had gone to Kent to "kill kids".

The Justice Department, meanwhile, continued the vacillation. Attorney General Mitchell appeared on *The David Frost Show*—to wipe out Spiro's boo-boo? and, in connection with Kent, talked about campus snipers, causing Frost to point out, before a commercial, that the FBI said there were no snipers at Kent. The week of the anniversary, commission member Joe Rhodes said simply that he had learned from reliable sources inside the Justice Department that a federal grand jury was being "personally held back by one man: Richard M. Nixon."

The same Richard Nixon who, on March 11th, addressing the National Conference of the Judiciary, said, "Justice delayed is not only justice denied, it is justice circumvented, justice mocked, and the system of justice undermined."

My friend Mike Roberts, who had covered the war in Vietnam for a while, and I were assigned by *The Cleveland Plain Dealer* to cover the shooting at Kent and, in the days after, when we understood that no newspaper interested in circulation, advertising and public approval was going to print the truth about Kent, we decided we'd try to put it into a book.

We lined up a publisher and, for an amount less than we would have made in our weekly paychecks, took several months' leave to research and write the facts of the shooting. We had no predispositions; if anything, Mike—whose cousin, General Elvy Roberts, was leading the drive into Cambodia that fateful weekend—leaned a bit toward the military. But we soon concluded that what had happened at Kent State was murder—murder in a right-wing context, where highway-patrol investigators were very quick to turn a legal-aid center into a "radical communications center."

There was no conspiracy, we decided, no outside agitation. The demonstrations were the result of the expanded war, and the guard action was senseless overreaction. A free-fire zone had been created for thirteen seconds on a campus, and the circumstances of its creation needed objective legal review.

Enter, at this point, James A. Michener, writer of best-selling fiction. Michener came to Kent for the *Reader's Digest,* accompanied by a research team recruited by that magazine, and was greeted with open arms and open files. Aside from a petty writer's jealousy—I bumped into him in a Kent bar one night as he was being fawned over like a baggy-pantsed Papa Hemingway—we thought he'd write a definitive book and shrugged our shoulders.

But we soon heard disturbing noises from Kent. Michener, appearing as the university's winter graduation speaker, said there was no "desirable" outcome from a federal grand jury. "The only purpose for convening such a jury would be to pin greater blame on the National Guard." A student in the audience, who couldn't listen to that, got up, tried to argue, and was arrested.

When the first installment of the *Reader's Digest* report appeared, we were stunned. There was at Kent, we were led to believe, outright conspiracy—at the Friday night downtown trashing, at the burning of the ROTC building. Michener defended James Rhodes's actions and never mentioned guard bayonetings. Most dismaying was that he offered no evidence, stringing the threat of conspiracy together with anonymous quotes and innuendo. He referred to a mysterious "house on Ash Street" filled with revolutionaries and admitted in his next sentence, "Although there is no such street in Kent, the house is not imaginary."

But we had never heard of real houses that could stand, without crumbling, on imaginary streets, and when the second installment came out, we were appalled. The same anonymous quotes, a sympathetic account of the guard on Blanket Hill suffering rock fire and, once again, the contention that Kent State "harbored revolutionaries."

We were sick but powerless—two reporters in the journalistic wilderness, lining up against Jim Michener, international best-seller, Pulitzer Prize winner, world traveler and Book of the Month Club expert.

Enter, at this point, I.F. Stone, Izzie to his friends, the remarkable Little Big Man of American journalism, a one-man truth squad who looked at Kent, didn't like what he saw, shared our conclusions and wrote a four-part magazine series that became a book called *The Killings at Kent State.*

As Michener's book appeared (impressively bearing the Kent State University emblem), Art Krause, more angered perhaps at Michener's conclusions than the rest of us, called I.F. Stone, who called us. We were collectively pissed off, convinced as Stone said later to Michener's face, that he'd done "a whore's job for the *Reader's*

Digest." It was time to pool our forces.

The opportunity for confrontation came when *The Today Show* invited all four of us to participate, on April 28th, in an hour-long round-table discussion about Kent State. It was very early in the morning, and Izzie, casting suspicious glances at the gun-toting NBC cop, brought his wife. Jim Michener was already in the waiting room, his legs crossed, signing an autograph when we came in. If I remembered him in the Kent bar, he remembered me just as warmly, because the first thing he said was "Where's your beard, *boy?*" It set the tone for hand-to-hand combat.

We began with ninety-second statements, Izzie saying, "If the killings had been in reverse, and if the FBI had turned up evidence that there were some signs of conspiracy to obstruct justice, I am sure that the country would not have let that be pushed under the rug."

Michener said, "Looking at what happened at Kent last year, I felt there was a tendency toward confrontation across the whole country that was to lead to a confrontation. It was *willed by certain people.* They wanted it to happen because they wanted to radicalize the student body."

I'd had about enough. I said that the war had caused the demonstrations and added, "Now to imply in any manner that these disturbances were the result of outside agitation, revolutionary activity or certain people who willed it is to shirk the facts of what happened at Kent State."

Michener let that one zing by and started to talk about a federal grand jury, saying that a grand jury would indict only more "poor students." It set off a knife fight.

ESZTERHAS: I'm a reporter, not a prophet. How can you say what a federal grand jury will or will not do.

MICHENER: I have a keen desire for justice, and I don't want to see more college kids hit over the head by our legal system.

ESZTERHAS: You're being a bit cynical, prejudging a federal grand jury.

STONE: The point is that if we believe in law and order, the law ought to take its course.

MICHENER: But the law doesn't take its course.

ESZTERHAS: Don't you believe in American justice?

MICHENER: I believe fully in American justice.

Hugh Downs, trying to referee all this, interrupted Michener: "Aren't you in effect indicting the American system of justice?"

MICHENER: I am indeed. There is no possibility that the guard in Ohio can be brought to the dock on what happened at Kent.

We had *coldcocked* him then: he was indicting a system of justice that he had just said he fully believed in, saying in effect that it didn't work and he believed in it.

The recent appointee to the United States Information Agency was saying there was no justice in America. Saying there was no justice in America, he wasn't going to try to work for it, resigning himself, instead, to accepting it, saying it would be a "disaster."

Izzie Stone stabbed him a few times about the *Reader's Digest's* right-wing-ism and, as the show ended, was trying to read a statement from the Kent Student Senate that called Michener's book "fiction," while I was trying to make him name the "new cadre of secret leaders" he was talking about. But his hands were shaking now, his voice raised, and he was shouting.

STONE: In justice to the students, may I quote from a statement approved by the Senate of Kent?

MICHENER: Now wait a minute, I know that statement.

STONE: Now let me speak. You smeared those kids.

MICHENER: I won't let you read that.

The show ended with Hugh Downs shaking his head, saying, "They're still at it," amid a cacophony of raised voices.

The shouting continued into the little waiting room. Michener, still shaking, told us the reason he wouldn't let Izzie read the statement was because it was unfair. The kid who signed that statement, Michener said, was one of the revolutionaries he was talking about, certain to be indicted if he publicly mentioned his name.

I wondered if all students who would criticize his facts as fiction would be turned into revolutionaries. But by this time I'd had enough of all this and New York. I was happy to get back to Ohio and the wilderness. Jim Michener was off, too, to Washington, to be officially confirmed by the Senate as a member of the United States Information Agency.

★   ★   ★

The anniversary itself was a bizarre anticlimax. They carried candles around Blanket Hill the night before, confronting their private bogymen of heart and night. The next day, in the wind and sun, they trooped to the Commons—7000 students out of a student body of 20,000—and listened to the victory bell toll again and to the never-ending stream of words…from a rabbi who promised them no pieties and gave them pieties…from Robert I. White, who quoted the Bible…from the Reverend Jesse Jackson, who brought them momentarily to their feet with a chant, "I am! I am! Somebody! Black! Proud! White! Young! Somebody! God's child! I am! I am!"

At one o'clock in the afternoon, at a time when, a year ago, the ambulances still lined the hill, about five of the 7000 crowded across the Commons, across the knolls, to the Rockwell Library, the home of the ROTC office, where the May Day Coalition planned a sit-in and unauthorized off-campus speakers, in violation of White's edict. Inside the building a squad of campus policemen, wearing flack-jackets and riot helmets and carrying tear-gas canisters, waited for the command. The new university police chief, James Fyke, trying hard to "identify the leaders," stood at a window with binoculars, saying, "The only thing that's gonna drive these kids away is snow." He ordered three busloads of his men, ready for action, to wait behind a faraway knoll.

Mark Lane was the main speaker chosen to violate White's rules, and he came dressed for the occasion—new bells, unused engineer boots, a fatigue jacket and a high-priced curved-stem briar pipe. But by the time he spoke, most of the kids, stirred on by the burning of a few draft cards, had placed themselves near the library doors, forgetting about Mark Lane's insistent rhetoric. Dean Kahler, with the shattered spine and the hotshot wheelchair, was blocking an entrance with his paralyzed body, daring anyone to knock that beautiful machine down.

There were about 500 participants in the sit-in, ready to see what would happen, expecting the flack jackets to come streaming over the knolls to distribute busts on the heads, and for a while it looked like they were coming. Robert I. White, outraged that his edicts had been violated, that his deodorized observance was sullied, was going to send his flack jackets charging in half an hour, but a group of faculty members, horrified, haunted by ghosts of an eternity past, stopped him.

The sit-in dragged on. A yippie leader's mother, a suburban matron in Bonwit Teller dress, sat down next to her son. Robert Dix, the trustee chairman and *Record Courier* publisher, appeared in the midst of all that hair, a generational apparition, while his newspaper was hitting the streets, calling the demonstrations in Washington a "national disgrace."

"We're all against the war, but we have to be patient, the university must survive," he said, gradually fading away.... after a student asked him about his holdings in Thailand... after a student asked him why he wore a revolver on his tie clip... after he was offered a joint and the sweet smell of grass was blown into his face.

But the sit-in faded, too. By nightfall there were only fifty there, and the next day at noon only twenty-five. When a spokesman said the university would permit them to go into the classrooms to give antiwar speeches, the remaining dozen grasped at the straw and packed their belongings and ended the anniversary with a few hoarse and tattered chants that sounded more like catcalls.

On the fourth of May, Art Krause, exiled from the campus where his daughter died, visited her grave and looked, once again, at the flower that a stranger had planted on the tiny plot.

He had asked a friend to place, for Allison's friends, an ad in the newspapers of the country, a short and personal note: "This is in memory of Allison, who was shot to death a year ago at Kent State by National Guardsmen."

His friends tried *The Washington Post,* noted for its liberalism, and got a call back the next day from an assistant to executive editor Benjamin Bradlee. The *Post* would not run the ad unless all reference to the National Guard was deleted.

"It is not the policy of the *Post* to publish ads that are defamatory," the aide said.

"Of what?"

"Of the National Guard."

"It has been clearly established that she was shot by the guard," Art's friend said, "established by the FBI, by the president's commission."

"It obviously hasn't been established," the aide said, "because no guardsman has been indicted." Catch-22: The guard is not guilty because the guard has not been indicted.

The St. Louis Post-Dispatch called to apologize. They had agreed to run the ad but, regrettably, "Somebody in the composing room had thrown it out."

So Art Krause came home from the cemetery, thinking about the Purple Heart he had won and the daughter he had lost, and he waited on this day for the cranks to start calling. When the phone rang and he heard a deep Southern voice, he thought, "All right, finally—I've been waiting, you have not disappointed me." But the caller was not a crank.

The caller said that about a year ago he had gotten out of the navy, on his way home from 'Nam. When he heard about Allison, a total stranger, something had snapped inside his mind. He had gone out to the cemetery and planted a flower on her grave. He just wondered how his flower was doing.

Art Krause went to bed and slept as well as he could on this night and opened his mail in the morning, knowing it would be here, knowing someone would have to send one on the anniversary of her death. And there it was, in a plain white envelope stamped with an American flag: "Krause, Your Daughter Was a Foul-mouthed Whore, Which is Bad Enough, but You Are a Dirty Pimp."

Art Krause put the letter away, smiling, and went to work, another routine day at the office.

The Struggle for Sly's Soul at the Garden

by Timothy Crouse   November 1971

I am making a last herculean effort to save his career," boomed David Kapralik, personal manager to Sly Stone. Kapralik is an ex-carnival barker who has been known to resume barking at the click of a reporter's pen, but this time the situation seemed to warrant hyperbole. Sly Stone's career had recently hit rock bottom.

In the past two years, Sly has managed to rack up the most erratic performance record since Judy Garland. According to his agent, he canceled twenty-six of the eighty engagements scheduled for him in 1970—twenty because his stomach was in convulsions and another six because of a clash with Kapralik. He was late for eight shows. This year Sly has canceled twelve shows out of forty—ten because of a legal battle with Kapralik and two because his drummer quit. He has been late for two shows. As the cancellations mounted, Kapralik's slogan, "The Incredible and Unpredictable Sly Stone," gradually lost its bright, euphemistic ring. Several weeks ago Sly found that no promoter in America would touch him. "Except," proclaims Kapralik, "the saint that came along, Ken Roberts." Ken Roberts booked Sly into Madison Square Garden for three successive nights in the first week of September. It was Sly's last chance.

A week before Sly's first concert, Kapralik opened shop on the forty-third floor of the Hilton in a suite so elegant that the bed had canopies. Besides being a barker, Kapralik has been a radio actor; vice-president of Columbia Records in charge of A&R; the manager of Sparrow (who later became Steppenwolf) and of Dino Valente; fired by CBS and later reinstated as head of A&R by Epic. He is a compendium of histrionic gestures; his elastic actor's face begs for a Hirschfeld caricature, the main feature of which would be his dark-circled, hyperthyroid, pinwheel eyes.

He dresses in a modified ringmaster's outfit—lace-embroidered, diaphanous brown shirt and white canvas pants stuffed into high boots. A veteran of Esalin, he makes masterful use of eye contact and disarming candor. He was in New York on two missions: to alert the press to the impending drama of Sly's three concerts and to get Sly back in the good graces of Columbia Records.

Kapralik was fully up to killing two birds with one phone call. When Bob Altshuler, head of publicity for Columbia, rang up, Kapralik glanced at me and said, "Keep your tape running, Timothy." He proceeded to inform both of us of his newest bravura gesture.

"Sly has not rehearsed the band in two years," he said into the receiver, as if the receiver were a packed house. "I gave Sly the message that if I did not have the completed album in my hands today and if he didn't begin rehearsing his group today, then I was on my way to Madrid via TWA flight 904, and Ken Roberts and my staff would take over.

"The album arrived at eight o'clock this morning, and I've just learned that rehearsal is set for this evening, so I may not go to Madrid. But I don't bluff, ya know? Last time he fucked up on the Cavett show, I went to Hawaii for a month. That's how I communicate to him without talking directly, because there are months that go by when Sly doesn't talk to me and I don't talk to him."

The first thing that Kapralik explained to each reporter who came to Room 4329 was the difference between Sylvester Stewart and Sly Stone. Sylvester is creative, rational, responsible "and representative of everything that is life affirming and healthful in our society.

"Okay, that's Sylvester Stewart, he's a poet. And then there's also Sly Stone, the street cat, the hustler, the pimp, the conniver, sly as a fox and cold as stone.... That's the strutter, the street dude who walks up there with that charisma that holds an audience captive, right? Four hundred thousand at Woodstock and 25,000 at Madison Square. He's irresponsible, opportunistic and unethical, and he pimps our minds if we let him."

For the past five years, Kapralik has devoted himself to saving Sylvester Stewart from Sly Stone. The one clear message that emerges even from Kapralik's most overwhelming flights of pea-game hype is that he cares desperately about Sylvester Stewart. At one point, with two Librium trimming his engines to such a low rev that he was actually sitting still, Kapralik leaned back and summed up: "You can take Sly Stone and shove him up the nearest narc's ass. But Sylvester Stewart—I love him. I would give my life for him. I'm crying, man, 'cause I love him so much." And, indeed, a couple of large tears were trickling down Kapralik's cheeks.

According to Kapralik, the last two years have been an extended battle for Sylvester's soul, with the "militants of nihilism" aligned against the "militant of affirmation," Kapralik. In other words, the Panthers were trying hard to enlist Sly's talents and influence for their own purposes. At the same time, certain members of the Stewart family were fighting to maintain their own vested interests in Sly. Both these forces were out to dispose of Kapralik, who had left his executive post at CBS and sold all of his CBS stock in order to invest his money and his time in Sly.

When they first met, says Kapralik, Sly was a cynical twenty-three-year-old disc jockey and street hustler. And Kapralik worked to bring out all that was "beautiful and life affirming" in Sylvester. "Hey, a black man who's bright, who says, 'You can make it if you try'—that's *important!*

"During that period last year, Sylvester Stewart had enormous pressures on him to get rid of me—the whitey Jew manager—and to align himself with the voices of despair and nihilism and parochialism and separatism, and I pulled with all my energy to keep him from becoming a spokesman for those things. And Sylvester stood shoulder to shoulder with me. That poor kid was torn apart. And when you are torn apart, that means a lot of pain. And one of the clinical ways to ease the pain is cocaine."

At times, the struggle generated such bitterness between Sly and Kapralik that Sly refused to work. There were assassination threats against both Sly and Kapralik. Sly developed all the symptoms of a bleeding ulcer, though not the ulcer itself. Kapralik says that he himself got deep into cocaine and attempted suicide three times. Perhaps it was as a result of the feud that Kapralik invented the Sly-Sylvester dichotomy, so that he could vent unlimited spleen against Sly while remaining totally loyal to Sylvester.

Last January, Kapralik sued Sly for $250,000 in loans and back commissions. Faced with the threat of having the box office attached at every concert, Sly declined to perform. The suit was withdrawn when Sly agreed to accept certain changes in his road operation. "It was an idle threat," says Kapralik's attorney, Peter Bennett. "We just used that economic pressure to get Sylvester to cut down on the number of people who were totally valueless to the operation." So Sly dropped what Kapralik calls the "parasites, sycophants and ass kissers." He took on Ira Seidel, a seasoned road manager who has handled the Beatles, the Rolling Stones, the Supremes and Frank Sinatra. "Ira had never seen a road operation so fucked up," says Bennett.

Although Kapralik refused to tolerate chaos on the road, he let Sky take his time in making a new record—two years to be exact. Sly showed up at the studio at all hours of the day and night and slept in a camper parked outside. Sometimes the engineers waited for him, and he never appeared. At other times he sat in the studio and felt around for new tunes on his guitar, at $140 an hour. Columbia finally put Sly on suspension for failing to deliver "product." That meant Sly couldn't collect his back royalties, which were substantial, until he handed over thirty sides worth of material.

"How do you get them to understand what has really been happening for these last two years?" asks an indignant Kapralik. "Because Sylvester Stewart does not create product. Sylvester Stewart is an innovator, he is inventive, he is a seminal source of new sounds, new fusions, new concepts. Ya don't turn them out like you turn out pizzas or you turn out records. They're life statements." He winds up with the zinger. "Two years," he says, "is a *short* time to wait."

Faced with Kapralik's ardent campaign, a sharp lawyer and a completed album, CBS has lifted suspension. And when Kapralik walked to the stereo and put on the acetate of the new album, it became clear that there was truth in his campaign slogan. Intensely autobiographical and disconcertingly original, the album could only have come from long and unrestrained experimentation. It contained a healthy number of hit singles, but it was also threaded with new and complicated rhythms, new textures and new strands of blues and country. Like John Lennon's albums, it was clearly the work of a man "ripping into his soul," to use Kapralik's expression.

After listening to the album, Kapralik spelled out its special significance. "Sly once told me, 'Sometimes a man has got to risk losing everything just to check himself out.' By whatever has gone down in the last two years—missed concerts, late performances, lawsuits, no records out—he has abdicated his having $3 or $4 million. But he checked himself out, and now everything is coming up that life-affirming, humanistic perspective. Everything is coming up Sylvester Stewart!"

Despite these auguries of Sylvester's moral and psychological well-being, the fact remains he is broke. "Sly has lost more money in two years than the average rock group would have earned in that period of time," says Peter Bennett. The legal fees and penalties have added up. Sly has sometimes had to pay inflated penalties to promoters who attached his equipment. And he has spent a good deal of money to maintain his own regal lifestyle.

As a result of his losses, Sly recently found that he couldn't make the mortgage payment on his $250,000 studio-equipped house, which had once belonged to John Phillips. He was evicted. A friend found him an apartment in a plush, high-rise Beverly Hills apartment house. Sly played his tape recorder until five or six in the morning, but no one complained to him. Then, two weeks ago, Sly woke up to the news that the landlord had filed a $3 million lawsuit against him for conspiring to drive all the tenants out of the apartment house. Some of the tenants have since countered with a petition asking Sly to stay, on the grounds that he lends class to the building. But for the moment, Sly is homeless.

For the past six months, Sly's performance record has been relatively spot-less. But just as Sly started to straighten out, his old reputation began to catch up with him. His Madison Square Garden contract, for instance, was ominously studded with penalties—$5000 if he wasn't at the Garden every night by eight o'clock; $20,000 if he had not gone on stage by 10:30.

On Wednesday, the day of the first concert, Sly missed six flights in a row in Los Angeles. By the time Sly arrived at the Garden, just after 8:00 p.m., there were already problems. Ruth Copeland, the first act on the bill, had been prevented from entering the Garden for an hour by security guards because she couldn't prove she was Ruth Copeland. Ruth started late and sang an extra ten minutes. Rare Earth went on and played twenty extra minutes. The stage was finally ready for Sly at 10:50, and he was supposed to have finished his set at eleven. The band filtered out of the dressing room; Sly came last, picking up his knees like a drum majorette and grinning a steely grin. He walked a gauntlet of agents, attorneys, promoters, old-guard members of his retinue, new guard. There was a queasy tension about the whole scene. Kapralik caught up with Sly in the corridor, took him by the biceps, looked him hard in the eye and puffed at him. Sly puffed back. "It's something we do when things are going well," Kapralik explained. "We give each other breath." Sly's girlfriend, a striking black lady with high Indian cheekbones, trailed along behind him and patted his enormous Louis XV bouffant Afro into place. Sly went on to tepid, tired applause.

The set lacked fire. They played most of the greatest hits, wandering off into endless raggedy jams by way of segues. When Sly finally attacked "Higher" with confidence, the crowd used all of its waning energy to stomp.

Sly finished his last encore at twenty past twelve. The delays by the other acts had cost him $7500 in overtime fees. On the ride back to the hotel, Kapralik was unusually quiet.

On Thursday night, Kapralik ushered me into the cinder-block dressing room, which was dark as the Land of the Shades. In one corner, discernible in his white jumpsuit, was Sly. Sly was itching to make a pronouncement, for he didn't like the Sly-Sylvester theory that Kapralik had been purveying. "Right or wrong, good or bad, Sylvester Stewart and Sly Stone are the same person," he said softly. "Sometimes they give you two names, your real one and your also-known-as. But we're the same people—Sly, Sylvester and the whole Family Stone. We're all one, you got that?"

Sly gave the group a pep talk before they went onstage. They went on at the stroke of ten and played a transformed set. No mumbling rap, no jams, just one unbroken, hysterical climb. The group exited at 10:59. As Sly walked down the stage steps to the waiting limo, he was still beating out a riff on his tambourine.

There were delays again on Friday, costing Sly more overtime fees. But by now it was clear that Sly was back in business; he had broken the house record at the Garden, he was going to clear over $100,000 for three nights, and Ken Roberts was planning thirty more dates for him. The show went well until, in the middle of a set, a kid jumped onstage and told a roadie that someone in the audience was aiming a shotgun at Sly. Sly got the word, walked behind the amps and huddled with Kapralik.

KAPRALIK: I'll go on if you don't want to go back on.

SLY: I'll go back on, man. Whatever's going to happen is going to happen.

Sly returned and did a neat bit of crowd engineering. "Look around you," he said, "and make sure the person next to you doesn't have a shotgun. We just want to play for you." With one stroke, Sly had acquired 24,999 bodyguards. (A suspect was seized later by Garden security guards, but no shotgun was discovered.)

But the incident was disturbing. Kapralik may be right about Sly Stone. There is something dangerously, provocatively arrogant about his glorified gang-leader looks. As he walked down Forty-second Street that afternoon on a shopping expedition, one street dude after another had approached him to pick a fight. Now he had whipped into "I Want to Take You Higher," and 25,000 people were grunting "hey, hey, hey," like the Russian Army Chorus. Early on in Sly's career, it became a cliché to say that his concerts looked like Nuremberg rallies; but as every fist in the house began to punch at the air, it was that which came to mind.

Apparently Kapralik was flashing the same idea. "Can you imagine how I felt when the reviewers called him a neofascist after his first New York concerts!" he shouted over the uproar. He gestured at the array of fists. "Thank God it's life affirming, you know what I mean! My life is a small price to pay for that!" His eyes rolled up toward the vaulted Garden roof and beyond. "Thank you, God!" he shouted.

★   ★   ★

The moment I stepped into Sly Stone's room at the New York Hilton, the expression "holed up" sprang to mind. The room had the stagnant, stockpiled look of a fugitive's hideout. It was the middle of the night. The covers and sheets on the oversized double bed were cluttered with signs of a woman's presence—spools of thread and a wheel of contraceptive pills.

Across from the foot of the bed, on top of a cabinet that contained a radio and TV, were stacked turntables, tape decks, speakers and cassette recorders of all brands and sizes—a sound laboratory. On the far side of the bed sat a coffee table with another turntable and more speakers on it. The main door of the room was locked and chained; Sly's aides barked an ominous challenge of "Who is it?" at anyone intrepid enough to knock. In the adjacent living room, the remains of a lobster dinner were congealing. It was as if all of Sly's loot had been hastily collected here, everything he needed to make a last stand, to run his life without recourse to the outside world.

The key men were in attendance, too. There was Richie, a bear of a man, the long-haired former Berkeley music major who had been at work day and night for a week mixing Sly's album. Richie sat in a corner and said little. There was J.R., a heavy-voiced Italian-American who functions as a sort of squire to Sly. "I want to find a quiet room and talk to Sly alone," I said to J.R.

"I'm allowed, aren't I?" J.R. replied.

J.R. was wearing no shirt over his huge barrel-shaped torso and his torpedo biceps. He had slicked-back black hair, a slightly hooked nose and gap teeth. He sat in a chair a couple of feet away from Sly, toweling himself off. He and Sly had just waged a shaving-cream fight that used up the better part of a can of Barbasol, several pots of coffee and a bucket of ice cubes.

Sprawled on the bed, surveying everything and everyone with grand indifference, was Sly. He was clad in white vinyl boots and red leather pants with fringe; his hairdo was several inches high and shaped like a *Guardia Civil* hat. It was astonishing to find Sly in his stage regalia offstage; it was like meeting a circus clown who lounged around the house with the putty still affixed to his nose. Sly extended his hand without raising his body and mumbled several indecipherable sentences. Suddenly he said something distinct. "I got to pee," he said. "Okay if I pee?" Sly and J.R. locked themselves in the bathroom and didn't come out for half an hour.

At the twenty-minute mark, I nearly got up and left. I didn't like the feeling of having entered an untidy, four-suite province in which Sly's whim was law and where everyone seemed to regard the release of Sly's record as a national priority. I was tired of waiting for Sly, something I had been doing on and off for three days.

When Sly finally emerged, he looked strikingly more alert. He moved over to me and assumed the offensive immediately. He had failed to appear the other day because of "valid negligence," he said. I said that valid negligence was a contradiction in terms. Sly bristled, drew himself up and stared at me. "What are you, dense?" he said.

Suddenly he switched to a conciliatory mood, offering me a snort from a tin of something labeled "Ozona Sniffing Powder." It was a tease; the powder happened to look exactly like cocaine. "Don't worry, it's legal," he said mockingly. "I ain't about to hip you to anything." The Ozona was a snuff that smelled faintly of wintergreen. "I give you the first one free. Then I make you pay for the next," said Sly.

I sat down on a stool at the foot of the bed, turned on my tape recorder and began to ask questions. "Wait a moment," said Sly. "Wait just a moment. We want our own copy, to check for accuracy." Richie set up a professional-looking multidialed stereo cassette recorder on the bed. Sly tested it at length, yawned, sighed and then began the interview by asking me whether I would like to look at the instruction booklet for his camper. No? Okay, he would interview me; he would; just wait and see.

One thing was clear. Sly didn't want me to interview him. He was wearing a mask of studied innocence. His eyes were half-shut, hooded with apathy. His lips were curled back, revealing a smile of total ambiguity.

Having been a disc jockey, Sly can speak like Demosthenes if he cares to, but he frequently prefers to mumble ("Thank You Falettinme Be Mice Elf Agin" is a very accurate transcription of Sly's elocution at moments when he doesn't want to be understood). "What was that?" I would say. Sly would lean back on the pillows and quote from one of his new songs. "'I can't say it more than once/'Cause I'm thinkin' twice as fast/Yodal ayee, yodal ayee hoo!' Hey, what's happening?"

I asked whether Kapralik had been right when he said that Sly was really two people. "He's probably either right or wrong," said Sly. "They're so close together, that's all right." Sly hadn't had a chance to read what Kapralik had said. He had been too busy writing songs in his head. He was writing a song in his head right now, but if I wanted to hear it, we'd have to forget about the interview.

"Kapralik said that Sylvester is fantastic, he's responsible, he gets everywhere on time, he's a beautiful cat," I said, trying to bring Sly back to the question.

"Did he say that?" said Sly.

"But Sly on the other hand is not responsible, he's a fuck-up...."

"Did he say that? I'll tell you what is true. David Kapralik tries his best. And I don't think he has any malice in his heart. Whatever he said, he didn't know what he was talking about, I don't think. 'Cause I am who I am when I am it."

What about the bodyguards Sly was rumored to have until recently? What about his German shepherd, named Gun, who is allegedly trained to kill? What was it that Sly had to be protected from?

"I don't know anything about all this," Sly drawled. "My dog's really nice, man. He'd like you. I didn't train my dog to do anything wrong to people. He likes girls, like I do."

"The rumor goes," I said, "that you were going around with three or four bodyguards...."

"Naaaahh."

"...and that you beat up some people in the lobby of a New York motel a while back."

"I'll tell you what happened," Sly volunteered. After meandering off on a minor tangent, he told me. "There were no guards there, I don't think. And I didn't beat anybody up. I just tried to keep from getting beat up. Some guys jumped on Cynthia, and one guy held her down with his knee. There were about six guys jumped on my brother. My dad said, 'Hey, you always take care of your brother.' So I didn't understand anything other than goin' down there and talkin' it over. But they didn't want to talk. So I got afraid. And fear breeds bravery."

"What was the bravery?" I asked.

"The bravery was the result of the fear," said Sly. "I just kinda ran through the lobby." He gave a deep, rumbling laugh, chorused by J.R. "You'da been proud. I was right. I had a peace sign on and a flower and everything."

What about the rumor of assassination threats by the Panthers?

"Panthers are only leopards," Sly said, matter-of-factly. "Leopards are only panthers. I got a lot of Panther padnahs. Is you hip to it?" He closed his eyes, opened his mouth and let loose a guttural, sinister, mind-clearing "Baah!" "I got a lot of Panther brothers," he continued. "They ain't gonna assassinate anybody, 'cause I'm from the ghetto. You know, they'll tell 'em to stop. They'll say, 'Stop'."

How about Kapralik's interpretation of the song "Family Affair"? Kapralik maintained that Sly was being torn apart by two factions—Kapralik on the one hand, certain members of the Stewart family and the Panthers on the other. "Well, I'll tell ya," said Sly. "They may be trying to tear me apart. I don't feel it. I don't feel being torn apart. Song's not about *that*. Song's about *a* family affair, whether it's a result of genetic processes or a situation in the environment."

I paused for a second to consult my notes—for about ten seconds, actually. "Wake up," said Sly and—*thwak*—pegged a wet washcloth square in my face. A wet washcloth in the face is not as bracing as it might sound. It leaves a soggy, heavy sensation—like egg. It makes you feel pretty silly as you sit and wipe off the water. Meanwhile, your mind is groping for a comeback—what would it do to Sly's Sir Fopling hairdo if you poured a pitcher of something over it. Baaah! Summoning up all of my macho, I picked up the washcloth and said, "Wouldn't want to catch *you* nodding off." Sly closed his eyes and thrust his face out. Sly looked big. Sly is big. The air was crackling with a tacit threat of escalation. I longed to throw the washcloth back, but my arm wouldn't budge. A minute passed, Sly relaxed, and then I threw it. J.R. let out a low whistle. Sly mumbled something about "owing me one."

Later, Sly got up to yell at someone who had tried to make an unsanctioned entrance into the room. He came back flipping a screwdriver as if he were going to throw it at me. I flinched. "Only one thing I know how to do with a screwdriver," Sly said innocently. "Screw."

Having gotten the message that Sly didn't approve of the direction the interview was taking, I switched to some technical questions about the recording sessions. Was it true that Sly played many of the instruments himself, overdubbing the parts onto the tape? What did he play on the new record? "I've forgotten, man," Sly just managed to say. "Whatever was left. Clean your nose, Rich. Jesus. All this stuff and shit. You'll never know about the sessions. You gotta be there. If you wanna ask a question, talk into my mike, man."

Maybe Sly would like to talk about Africa. There's a song on the new record called "Africa Talks to You." For instance, why didn't Sly make his planned safari to Kenya? At this question, J.R. doubled over in helpless laughter. "Oh, God, Kenya," he kept repeating, and he stumbled around the room as if he had just walked into a cloud of tear gas. "Hey, J.R.," said Sly, "this washcloth don't have enough water." Turning back to me, he growled, "Can't make all them gigs. I don't wanna shoot any animals. I wrote a song about Africa because in Africa the animals are animals. The tiger is a tiger, the snake is a snake, you know what the hell he's gonna do. Here in New York, the asphalt jungle, a tiger or a snake may come up looking like, uhhh, you."

Sly's eyelids were drooping lower. For the third time he said, "Hey, man, will you get this shit *through*." I didn't bother to remind him that he had wanted the interview. His answers were getting more slurred, and he said he didn't even want to talk about the time the soul DJs boycotted his records in Washington. For a question about the future of a group he was producing—Little Sister—he perked up momentarily. "I'm ready," he said, and then, "I'm through. We got Little Sister material. *They* can't handle it. The record companies are pretty fucked up. And they try to fuck you around, to fuck the kids around. The executives, on higher levels, they don't really associate with, uhhh—you have to live the blues to sing about the blues. And honest to God, Clive Davis hasn't really been livin' a hell of a lot of blues."

Sly declined to get more specific about his problems with the Columbia executives, or theirs with him. He did say that the Family Stone alone had three albums' worth of material ready to master, whenever Richie could get it mixed. And that the band was rehearsing some of the new material to do at concerts. "Hey, we're taking care of business," he said. "You'd be proud of us. The younger generation. Hula hoops and the whole shtick . . . Hey, you gonna write nice things?" I said I hoped I would. Sly closed his eyes and went: "Motha. Motha. Motha. Baaah!"

"Where's that come from?" I asked.

"The heart," said Sly. J.R. applauded.

Sly was growing increasingly restless, lapsing into monosyllables, so I turned off my tape recorder, got up and thanked him.

Sly sat up and shook hands. "It's been a real pleasure," he said. "As far as I can see. To the best of my knowledge." J.R. ushered me toward the door while Sly got up and headed for one of his tape decks.

Just as I started to go out the door, I heard a sodden *thwaak* a couple of inches from my ear. It was the washcloth.

The Banshee Screams in Florida

by Hunter S. Thompson   April 1972

The whistle-stops were uneventful until his noon arrival in Miami, where Yippie activist Jerry Rubin and another man heckled and interrupted him repeatedly. The Senator at one point tried to answer Rubin's charges that he had once been a hawk on (Vietnam) war measures. He acknowledged that he had made a mistake, as did many other senators in those times, but Rubin did not let him finish.

Muskie ultimately wound up scolding Rubin and fellow heckler Peter Sheridan, who had boarded the train in West Palm Beach with press credentials apparently obtained from Rolling Stone's Washington correspondent, Dr. Hunter S. Thompson.

—MIAMI HERALD, *February 20th, 1972*

When Jerry Rubin showed up at the train station that Saturday afternoon to hassle Muskie, the senator from Maine was apparently the only person in the crowd who didn't know who he was. His first response to Rubin was, "Shut up, young man—I'm talking."

"You're not a damn bit different from Nixon," Rubin shouted back.

And it was at this point that Muskie seemed to lose his balance and fall back from the rail. What happened, according to a firsthand account by Monte Chitty of *The University of Florida Alligator,* was that "the Boohoo reached up from the track and got hold of Muskie's pant leg, waving an empty glass through the bars around the caboose platform with his other hand and screaming, 'Get your lying ass back inside and make me another drink, you worthless old fart!'"

"It was really embarrassing," Chitty told me. "The Boohoo kept reaching up and grabbing Muskie's legs, yelling for more gin...Muskie tried to ignore him, but the Boohoo kept after him, and after a while it got so bad that even Rubin backed off. He was acting just like he did the night before, only six times worse."

"The Boohoo," of course, was the same vicious drunkard who had terrorized the Muskie train all the way from Palm Beach, and he was still wearing a press badge that said HUNTER S. THOMPSON—ROLLING STONE.

Chitty and I had met him the night before, about 2:30 a.m., in the lobby of the Ramada Inn, where the press party was quartered. We were heading out to the street to look for a sandwich shop, feeling a trifle bent and very hungry...and as we passed the front desk, here was this huge wild-eyed monster, bellowing at the desk clerk about "All this chickenshit" and "All these pansies around here trying to suck up to Muskie" and "Where the fuck can a man go in this town to have a good time, anyway?"

A scene like that wouldn't normally interest me, but there was something very special about this one, something very familiar about it. I listened for a moment and then recognized the Neal Cassady speed-booze-acid rap—a wild combination of menace, madness, genius and fragmented coherence that wreaks havoc on the mind of any listener. This is not the kind of thing you expect to hear in the lobby of a Ramada Inn, and especially not in West Palm Beach, so I knew we had no choice but to take this man along with us.

"Don't mind if I do," he said. "At this hour of the night I'll fuck around with just about anybody."

He had just got out of jail, he explained. Fifteen days for vagrancy, and when he'd hit the bricks today he just happened to pick up a newspaper and see that Ed Muskie was in town…and since he had this friend who "worked up top," he said, for Big Ed…well, he figured he'd just drift over to the Ramada Inn and say hello.

But he couldn't find his friend. "Just a bunch of pansies from CBS and The New York Times, hanging around the bar," he said. "I took a few bites out of that crowd, and they faded fast—just ran off like curs. But what the shit can you expect from people like that? Just a bunch of lowlife ass-kissers who get paid for hanging around with politicians."

Just for the quick hell of it, I'd like to explain or at least insist—despite massive evidence to the contrary—that this geek was in fact an excellent person, with a rare sense of humor that unfortunately failed to mesh, for various reasons, with the prevailing humors on Muskie's Sunshine Special.

Just how he came to be wearing my press badge is a long and tangled story, but as I recall it had something to do with Sheridan convincing me that he was one of the original ranking Boohoos of the Neo-American Church and also that he was able to rattle off all kinds of obscure and pithy tales about his experiences in places like Milbrook, the Hog Farm, La Honda and Mike's Pool Hall in San Francisco.…

…which would not have meant a hell of a lot if he hadn't also been an obvious aristocrat of the Freak Kingdom. There was no doubt about it. This bastard was a serious, king-hell crazy. He had that rare weird electricity about him—that extremely wild and heavy presence that you only see in a person who has abandoned all hope of ever behaving normally.

Monte Chitty and I spent about five hours with Sheridan that night in West Palm Beach, and every place we went he caused trouble. He terrified the manager of a rock club by merely walking up to the bar and asking if he could check his hat, a mashed-up old Panama. The manager coiled up like a bull snake, recognizing something in Sheridan's tone of voice, or maybe it was just the vibrations that gave him a bad social fear, and I could see in his eyes that he was thinking, "Oh my God—here it comes. Should we Mace him now or later?"

All of which is basic to any understanding of what happened on the Muskie campaign train—and which also explains why his "up top friend" (whom Women's Wear Daily later identified as Ronnie Evans, one of Muskie's chief tacticians) was not immediately available to take care of his old buddy, Pete Sheridan, who was fresh out of jail with no place to sleep and no transportation down to Miami.

"To hell with that," I said. "Take the train with us. It's the presidential express, a straight shot into Miami and all the free booze you can drink. Why not? Any friend of Ronnie's is a friend of Ed's, I guess. But since you can't find Ronnie at this hour of the night, and since the train is leaving in two hours, well, perhaps you should borrow this little orange press ticket, just until you get aboard."

"I think you're right," he said.

"I am," I replied. "And besides, I paid thirty dollars for the goddamn thing, and all it got me was a dozen beers and the dullest day of my life."

"Maybe I can put it to better use," he said.

Which he did—and I was subsequently censured very severely by other members of the campaign press corps for allowing my credentials to fall into foreign hands. There were also ugly rumors to the effect that I had somehow conspired with this monster Sheridan—and also Jerry Rubin—to "sabotage" Muskie's wind-up gig in Miami, and that Sheridan's beastly behavior at the train station was the result of a carefully laid plot by me, Rubin and the International Yippie Braintrust.

★   ★   ★

It never occurred to me that anything could be worse than getting stuck on another Nixon campaign, so it came as a definite shock to find that hanging around Florida with Ed Muskie was even duller and more depressing than traveling with Evil Dick himself.

One of the worst things about the trip was the fact that the candidate spent the whole time sealed off in his private car with a traveling zoo of local party bigwigs. The New Hampshire primary was two weeks off, and Muskie was still greedily pursuing his dead-end strategy of piling up endorsements from "powerful Democrats" in every state he visited—presumably on the theory that once he got the party bosses signed up, they would automatically deliver the votes. By the time the deal went down in New Hampshire, Muskie had signed up just about every Democratic politician in the country whose name was well known by more than 100 people, and it did him about as much good as a notarized endorsement from Martin Bormann. A week later, when he staggered to a fourth place finish in Florida, a fishmonger in Cairo, Illinois, announced that he and U.S. Senator Harold Hughes of Iowa were forming a corporation to market Muskie dartboards. Hughes had planned to be present at the ceremony in Cairo, the man said, but the senator was no longer able to travel from one place to another without the use of custom Weight-Belts.

The New Hampshire results hit the Muskie bandwagon like a front wheel blowout, but Florida blew the transmission. Big Ed will survive Illinois, whatever the outcome. But he still has to go to Wisconsin, where anything but victory will probably finish him off, and his chances of beating Humphrey up there on the Hube's home court are not good. The latest Gallup poll, released on the eve of the Illinois primary but based on a nationwide survey taken prior to the vote in New Hampshire, showed Humphrey ahead of Muskie for the first time.

According to almost every media wizard in the country, Wisconsin is "the crunch," especially for Muskie and New York mayor John Lindsay, who was badly jolted in Florida when his gold-plated media blitz apparently had no effect at all on the voters. Lindsay spent almost a half million dollars in Florida, yet limped home fifth with seven percent of the vote—just a point ahead of McGovern, who spent less than $100,000.

★   ★   ★

One of the biggest losers in Florida was not listed in the election results. He was Robert Squier, whose TV campaign for Muskie was a debacle. Squier's TV spots depicted Muskie as an extremely slow-spoken man who had probably spent half his life overcoming some kind of dreadful speech impediment, only to find himself totally hooked on a bad downer habit or maybe even smack. The first time I heard a Muskie radio spot I was zipping along on the Rickenbacker Causeway, coming in from Key Biscayne, and I thought it was a new Cheech and Chong record. It was the voice of a man who had done about twelve reds on the way to the studio—a very funny ad.

Whatever else the Florida primary might or might not have proved, it put a definite kink in the Media Theory of politics. It may be true that all you have to do to be president of the U.S.A. is look attractive on TV and have enough money to hire a Media Wizard. Only a fool or a linthead would argue with the logic at the root of the theory: if you want to sell yourself to a nation of TV addicts, you obviously can't ignore the medium. But the Florida vote served to remind a lot of people that the medium is only a tool, not a magic eye. If you want to be president, and you're

certified attractive, the only other thing you have to worry about when you lay out all
that money for a Media Wizard is whether or not you're hiring a good one instead of a
bungler…and definitely lay off the reds when you go to the studio.

★   ★   ★

Remember when you go out to vote tomorrow that the eyes of America are upon you, all the live-long day. The eyes of America are upon you, they will not go away.
—SENATOR GEORGE McGOVERN, *at a rally at the University of Miami the night before the Florida primary*

Cazart!…this fantastic rain outside: a sudden cloudburst, drenching everything. The sound of rain smacking down on my concrete patio about ten feet away from the typewriter, rain beating down on the surface of the big, aqua-lighted pool out there across the lawn…rain blowing into the porch and whipping the palm fronds around in the warm night air.

Behind me, on the bed, my waterproof Sony says, "It's 5:28 right now in Miami…." Then Rod Stewart's hoarse screech: *"Mother, don't you recognize your son?…"*

Beyond the rain I can hear the sea rolling on the beach. This atmosphere is getting very high, full of strange memory flashes….

"Mother, don't you recognize me now?…"

Wind, rain, surf. Palm trees leaning in the wind, hard funk-blues on the radio, a flagon of Wild Turkey on the sideboard…are those footsteps outside? High heels running in the rain?

Keep on typing…but my mind is not really on it. I keep expecting to hear the screen door bang open and then turn around to see Sadie Thompson standing behind me, soaked to the skin…smiling, leaning over my shoulder to see what I'm cranking out tonight…then laughing softly, leaning closer; wet nipples against my neck, perfume around my head…and now on the radio: *"Wild Horses…we'll ride them someday…."*

Perfect. Get it on. Don't turn around. Keep this fantasy rolling and try not to notice that the sky is getting light outside. Dawn is coming up, and I have to fly to Mazatlán in five hours to deal with a drug fugitive. Life is getting very complicated. After Mazatlán I have to rush back to San Francisco and get this gibberish ready for the printer….then on to Wisconsin to chronicle the next act in this saga of downers and treachery called "The Campaign Trail."

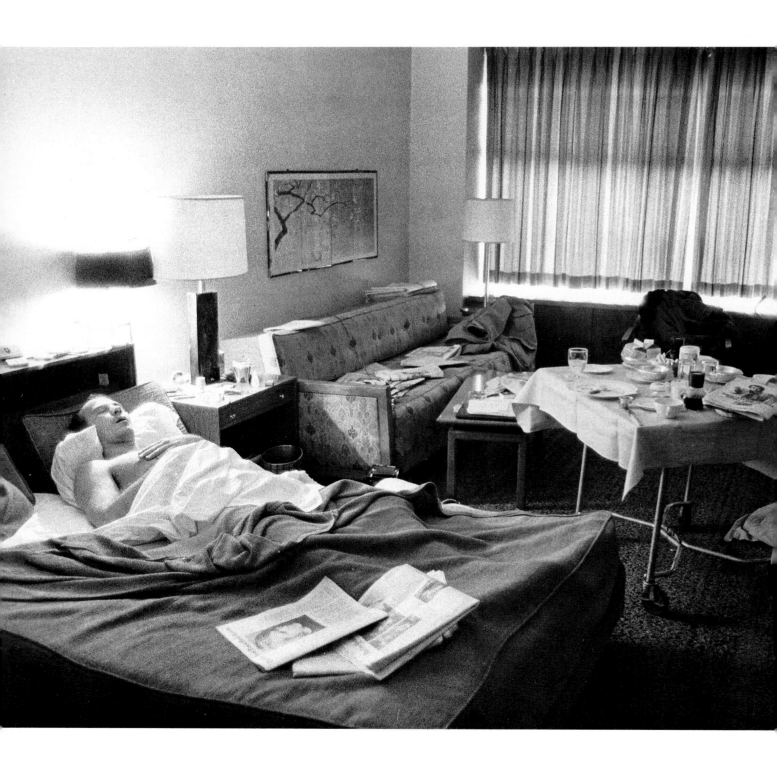

Wisconsin is the site of the next Democratic primary. Six serious candidates in this one—racing around the state in chartered jets, spending ten grand a day for the privilege of laying a series of terrible bummers on the natives. Dull speeches for breakfast, duller speeches for lunch, then bullshit with gravy for dinner.

How long, o Lord...how long? Where will it end? The only possible good that can come of this wretched campaign is the ever-increasing likelihood that it will cause the Democratic party to self-destruct.

A lot of people are seriously worried about this, but I am not one of them. I have never been much of a party man myself....and the more I learn about the realities of national politics, the more I'm convinced that the Democratic party is an atavistic endeavor—more an obstacle than a vehicle—and that there is really no hope of accomplishing anything genuinely new or different in American politics until the Democratic party is done away with. It is a bogus alternative to the politics of Nixon: a gang of senile leeches like George Meany, Hubert Humphrey and Mayor Daley... Scoop Jackson, Ed Muskie and Frank Rizzo, the supercop of Philadelphia.

George McGovern is also a Democrat, and I suppose I have to sympathize in some guilt-stricken way with whatever demented obsession makes him think he can somehow cause this herd of venal pigs to see the light and make him their leader. But after watching McGovern perform in two primaries, I think he should stay in the senate, where his painfully earnest style is not only more appreciated but far more effective than it is on the nationwide stump.

His surprising neovictory in New Hampshire was less a triumph than a spinoff from Muskie's incredible bungling. But up close he is a very likable and convincing person—in total contrast to Ed Muskie, who seems okay on TV or at the other end of a crowded auditorium, but who turns off almost everybody who has the misfortune of having to deal with him personally.

The New Hampshire primary is perhaps the only important national election where a candidate like McGovern can be truly effective. Crowds seem to turn him off instead of on. He lacks that sense of drama, that instinct for timing and orchestration that is the real secret of success in American politics.

The main problem in any democracy is that crowd pleasers are generally brainless swine who can go out on a stage and whup their supporters into an orgiastic frenzy, then go back to the office and sell every one of the poor bastards to the Conglomerate Loan Company for a nickel apiece. Probably the rarest form of life in American politics is the man who can turn on a crowd and still keep his head straight—assuming it was straight in the first place.

Which harks back to McGovern's problem. He is probably the most honest big-time politician in America; Robert Kennedy, several years before he was murdered, called George McGovern "the most decent man in the senate." Which is not quite the same thing as being the best candidate for president of the United States. For that, McGovern would need at least one dark kinky streak of Mick Jagger in his soul.... Not much, and perhaps not even enough so people would notice at lunch in the Capitol Hill Hotel or when he walks down the hallway of the Senate Office Building— but just enough to drift out on the stage in front of a big crowd and let the spectacle turn *him* on.

That may be the handle. Maybe the whole secret of turning a crowd on is getting turned on yourself by the crowd. The only candidate running for the presidency today who seems to understand this is George Wallace...which might partially explain why Bobby Kennedy was the only candidate who could take votes away from Wallace in '68. Kennedy, like Wallace, was able to connect with people on some kind of visceral, instinctive level that is probably both above and below "rational politics." McGovern does not appear to have this instinct. He does not *project* well, and his sense of humor is so dry that a lot of people insist on calling it "withered."

Maybe so—and that may be the root of the reason why I can't feel entirely comfortable around George...and he would probably not agree with my conviction that a sense of humor is the main measure of sanity.

But who can say for sure? Humor is a very private thing. One night about five years ago in Idaho, Mike Solheim and I were sitting in his house talking about Lenny Bruce in a fairly serious vein, when he suddenly got up and put on a record that I still remember as one of the most hysterical classics of satire I'd ever heard in my life. I laughed for twenty minutes. Every line was perfect. "What's the name of this album?" I said. "I thought I'd heard all of his stuff, but this one is incredible."

"You're right," he said, "but it's not Lenny Bruce."

"Bullshit," I said. "Let's see the jacket."

He smiled and tossed it across the room to me. It was General Douglas MacArthur's famous farewell speech to congress in 1952. Remember that one? The "old soldiers never die" number? My friend Raoul Duke calls it "one of the ten best mescaline records ever cut."

I am still a little sick about that episode. Solheim and I are still friends, but not in the same way. That record is not for everybody. I wouldn't recommend it to a general audience. But then, I wouldn't recommend it to George McGovern either.

★　　　　★　　　　★

Jesus! The only small point I meant to make when I jackknifed into this trip was that McGovern is unusual, for a politician, in that he is less impressive on TV than he is in person.

One of Muskie's main problems, thus far, has been that not even his own hired staff really like him. The older ones try to explain this problem away by saying, "Ed's under a lot of pressure these days, but he's really a fine guy, underneath." The younger staffers have apparently never had much contact with "the real Muskie." With very few exceptions, they justify their strained allegiance to the man by saying, "I wouldn't be working for him except that he's the only Democrat who can beat Nixon."

Or at least that's what they said before the polls closed in Florida. After that—when it quickly became apparent that Muskie couldn't even beat Scoop Jackson, much less Hubert Humphrey or George Wallace—he was faced with a virtual election-night mutiny among the younger staff people, and even the veterans were so alarmed that they convened an emergency conference in Muskie headquarters at Miami's Dupont Plaza Hotel and decided that the candidate would have to drastically *change his image.*

For months they'd been trying to sell the Man from Maine as a comfortable, mushmouth, middle-of-the-road compromiser who wouldn't dream of offending anybody—the ideal centrist candidate, who would be all things to all men. But the voters were not quite that stupid. Muskie bombed in New Hampshire, on what even the candidate admitted was his own turf. Then he came down to Florida and got stomped so badly that his campaign staffers were weeping uncontrollably in front of TV cameras in the ballroom that had been advertised all day as the scene of "Muskie's victory party."

I got there just after he had come down from his upstairs hideaway to console the crowd and denounce George Wallace on network TV as "a demagogue of the worst sort" and "a threat to the country's underlying values of humanism, of decency, of progress." This outburst was immediately interpreted by local politicians as a slur on the people of Florida—calling forty-two percent of the electorate dupes and Racist Pigs because they voted for George Wallace.

U.S. Senator Ed Gurney (Republican-Florida) demanded an apology, but Muskie ignored him and went back upstairs to the smoke-filled room where his wizards had already decided that his only hope was a fast turn to the Left. No more of that centrist bullshit. They looked both ways and—seeing the Right very crowded —convinced each other that Muskie's new image would be "The Liberal Alternative to Hubert Humphrey."

Robert Squier, Muskie's national media adviser, emerged from the meeting and said, "We're going to erase that yellow stripe in the middle of the road." Another one of the brain-trusters tried to put a better face on it. "The irony of this defeat," he said, "is that it will make Muskie what we all wanted him to be all along...the only question is whether it's too late." This painful think session was "summed up" for

The New York Times by a nameless "key aide-adviser" who explained, "The reason people didn't vote for Ed Muskie here is that they didn't have any reason to."

Zang! The candidate's reaction to this ultimate nut of wisdom was not recorded, but we can only assume he was pleased to see signs that at least one of his ranking advisers was finally beginning to function well enough on the basic motor-skill and signal-recognition level that he might soon learn to tie his own shoes.

If I were running for the presidency of the United States and heard a thing like that from somebody I was paying a thousand dollars a week, I would have the bastard dropped down an elevator shaft. But Muskie has apparently grown accustomed to this kind of waterhead talk from his staff. They are not an impressive group. One of the first things you notice around any Muskie headquarters, local or national, is that many of the people in charge are extremely fat. Not just chubby or paunchy or flabby, but serious glandular cases. They require assistance getting in and out of elevators.

Under normal circumstances, I wouldn't mention this kind of thing, for all the obvious reasons: general humanity, good taste, relevance, et cetera. But in the context of what has happened to Ed Muskie in the first two primaries, it's hard to avoid the idea that there may be some ominous connection between the total failure of his campaign and the people who are running it.

As late as February 15th, Ed Muskie was generally conceded—even by his political opponents—to be within an eyelash or two of having the Democratic nomination so skillfully locked up that the primaries wouldn't even be necessary. He had the public endorsements of almost every Big Name in the party. Ed Muskie, they all agreed, was the only Democrat who could beat Nixon in November.

The word went out early, and it filtered down to low-level fringe groups like the National Association of Student Governments and other "youth vote" organizers, who were suddenly faced with the choice of either "getting your people behind Muskie" or "crippling the party with another one of those goddamned doomed protest movements that would end up like all the rest and not accomplish anything except to guarantee Nixon's reelection." A lot of people bought this, particularly the "youth leader" types who saw themselves playing key roles in a high-powered, issue-oriented Muskie campaign that would not only dump Nixon but put a certified "good guy" in the White House.

★   ★   ★

In retrospect, the Sunshine Special looks far more like an ill-conceived disaster than it did at the time, when Rubin and the Boohoo made such a shambles of

Muskie's arrival in Miami that the local news media devoted almost as much time and space to the senator's clash with antiwar hecklers at the train station as it did to the whole 400-mile, 36-hour whistle-stop tour, which covered the length of the state and produced what the candidate's headquarters said were "five major statements in five cities."

It probably cost the Muskie campaign around $15,000— slightly over $5000 of that for rental of the five-car train from Amtrak. Staff salaries and special expenses for the trip (a dozen advance men spending four or five days each in towns along the route to make sure Big Ed would draw crowds for the TV cameras; payment to musicians, Rosey Grier, et cetera)...a list of *all* expenses would probably drive the cost of the spectacle up closer to $20,000.

For all this money, time and effort, Muskie's combined whistle-stop crowds totaled less than 3000. In addition, his "major statements" along the way were contemptuously dismissed as "oatmeal" by most of the press. In a word, the Sunshine Special *bombed. The Miami Herald* reported that Muskie's trip into "the politics of the past" was considered a failure even by the senator's own staff.

Meanwhile, in that same issue of the *Herald,* right next to the ugly saga of the Sunshine Special, was a photograph of a grinning George Wallace chatting with national champion stock-car racer Richard Petty at the Daytona 500, where 98,600 racing fans were treated to "a few informal remarks" by Wallace, who said he had only come to watch the races and check up on his old friend Dick Petty.

That appearance at the Daytona 500 didn't cost Wallace a dime, and the AP wirephoto of him and Petty that went to every daily and Sunday newspaper in Florida was worth more to Wallace than his own weight in pure gold....and there was also the weight of the 98,600 racing fans, who figure that any friend of Richard Petty's must sit on both of God's shoulders in his spare time.

★   ★   ★

The Florida primary is over now. George Wallace stomped everybody, with forty-two percent of the vote in a field of eleven. Ed Muskie finished a sick fourth, with only nine percent ... and then he went on all the TV networks to snarl about how this horrible thing would never have happened except that Wallace is a Beast and a Bigot.

Which is at least half true, but it doesn't have much to do with why Muskie got beaten like a gong in Florida. The real reason is that the Man from Maine is running one of the stupidest and most incompetent political campaigns since Tom Dewey took his dive and elected Truman in 1948.

If I had any vested interest in the Democratic party, I would do everything possible to have Muskie committed at once. Another disaster at the polls might put him around the bend.

I am probably not the only person who has already decided to be almost anywhere except in Ed Muskie's headquarters when the polls close on election night. The place will probably be dead empty, and all the windows taped...TV crews hunkered down behind overturned ping-pong tables, hoping to film the ex-front-runner from a safe distance when he comes crashing into the place to blame his sixth-place finish on some kind of unholy alliance between Ti-Grace Atkinson and Judge Crater. Nor is there any reason to believe he will forbear physical violence at that time. With his dream finished and his nerves completely shot, he might start laying hands on people.

Hopefully, some of his friends will be there to restrain the wiggy bastard. All we can be sure of, however, is the list of those who will not be there, under any pretense at all. Senator Harold Hughes will not be there, for instance, and neither will Senator John Tunney. Nor will any of the other senators, governors, mayors, congressmen, labor leaders, liberal pundits, fascist lawyers, fixers from ITT and extremely powerful Democratic national committeewomen who are already on the record as full-bore committed to stand behind Big Ed.

None of those people will be there when Muskie sees the first returns from Wisconsin and feels the first rush of pus into his brain. At that point he will have to depend on his friends, because that suitcase full of endorsements he's been dragging around won't be worth the price of checking it into a bus-station locker.

It is becoming increasingly possible that Hubert Humphrey will be the Democratic presidential nominee this year, which would cause another Nixon-Humphrey campaign. And a thing like that would probably have a serious effect on my nerves. I'd prefer no election at all to another Humphrey nightmare. Six months ago it seemed out of the question. But no longer. Humphrey is the bookies' choice in Wisconsin, which would finish Muskie and make Hubert the high rider all the way to the Oregon and California primaries in early June.

The "other race" in Wisconsin is between McGovern and Lindsay, which might strike a lot more sparks than it has so far if anybody really believed the boneheads who run the Democratic party would conceivably nominate either one of them. But there is a definite possibility that the Democratic convention this year might erupt into something beyond the control of anybody; the new delegate-selection rules make it virtually impossible for old-style bosses like Mayor Daley to treat delegates like sheep hauled in to be dipped.

A candidate like Lindsay or McGovern might be able to raise serious hell in a deadlocked convention, but the odds are better than even that Hubert will peddle his ass to almost anybody who wants a chunk of it, then arrive in Miami with the nomination sewed up and Nixon waiting to pounce on him the instant he comes out of his scumbag.

Another Nixon-Humphrey horror would almost certainly cause a fourth party uprising and guarantee Nixon's reelection, which might bring the hounds of hell down on a lot of people for the next four very long years.

But personally I think I'd be inclined to take that risk. Hubert Humphrey is a treacherous, gutless old ward-heeler who should be put in a goddamned bottle and sent out with the Japanese current. The idea of Humphrey running for president again makes a mockery of a lot of things that it would take me too long to explain or even list here. Hubert Humphrey wouldn't understand what I was talking about anyway. He was a swine in '68, and he's worse now. If the Democratic party nominates Humphrey again in '72, the party will get exactly what it deserves.

Keith Moon: The Rolling Stone Interview

by Jerry Hopkins   December 1972

It is probably fitting that Keith Moon plays the most aggressive instrument, drums, in the most explosive of groups, the Who, for Moon clearly seems more outrageous and more violent than any of his contemporaries. Behind him for a period of ten years, for more than a third of his life, he has left a trail of empty Courvoisier bottles, splintered drum kits, wrecked automobiles and gutted hotel rooms, punctuating every conceivable incident with a bark of total pleasure and amusement.

There are uncounted Keith Moon stories floating around. Keith tells several here. Unfortunately, much is lost in translating Moon to print. His energetic sprints around the room, his dozen or so precise vocal impressions and dialects, the rubbery, gap-toothed face, the singing and dancing, the infectious volleys of laughter—all must be experienced. So must his $150,000 modern house, set on the site of an ancient monastery nearly an hour from London in the green, suburban stockbroker belt. The walls of the bar are painted in a Marvel Comics hero-villain motif, and the ceiling is draped like a sultan's tent. The sitting room is a huge, richly cushioned "conversation pit," with a color television and a stainless-steel fireplace that's never been used. There is almost no furniture. But there is a stuffed albatross, a polar-bear rug, several rifles, an old jukebox and a sound system that will send multidecibel music far beyond the boundaries of his seven-acre estate.

From the outside, the house looks to be a collection of square pyramids painted a glaring white. On one side is a tree so large it had to be lowered in by two helicopters. On the other side workmen are presently excavating a swimming pool that will be lined with marble and will offer the underwater swimmer the latest recorded melodies.

When I arrived, the live-in housekeeper—Moon's mother-in-law—was in Spain on holiday. His long-haired mechanic and driver, Dougal, was working on the engine of the 1936 Chrysler, which was parked between the XKE Jaguar and the Dino Ferrari. The missus, Kim, and the child, Mandy, 6, were out. And the lord of the manor was banging away with a shotgun, firing randomly into the tall, leafy reaches of a horse-chestnut tree.

How did you come to the group to begin with?

First they were called the Detours, then the Who, then the High Numbers, then the Who again. I joined in the second phase, when they were changing from the Detours to the Who. I was in another group on the same pub circuit called the Beachcombers.

Did that mean surfing music?

It did when I joined, yeah. Ah-ha-ha-ha.

So the Beachcombers was a surfing band, sort of?

Sort of. It relied on vocals more than instruments. As I'm a disgusting singer…I mean, the boys don't let me sing. I don't blame them. I sometimes forget meself and join in, and they have to come down on me: "Moon…out!" I mean, I even get sent offstage during "Behind Blue Eyes" just in case I forget meself. It's the only number of the Who's that really requires precise harmony. The rest of it's all "YEEEEAAAHHHH—magic bus!" We shout. It doesn't matter. So they send me off during "Blue Eyes," because either I'm buggering about and I put the boys off or I try to sing and really put them off.

Anyway, I'd decided my talent as a drummer was wasted in a tight-knit harmony group like the Beachcombers, and the only band that I heard of that sounded as loud as I did was the Detours. So when I heard their drummer had left, I had plans to insinuate meself into the group. They were playing at a pub near me, the Oldfield. I went there, and they had a session drummer sitting in with them. I got up onstage and said, "Well, I can do better than him." They said go ahead and got behind this other guy's drums, and I did one song, "Road Runner." I'd had several drinks to get me courage up, and when I got onstage, I went *arrrrrrrrrggggggghhhhhhhhh* on the drums, broke the base-drum pedal and two skins and got off. I figured that was it. I was scared to death.

Afterward, I was sitting at the bar, and Pete came over. He said, "You… come 'ere." I said, mild as you please: "Yesyes?" And Roger, who was the spokesman then, said, "What're you doing next Monday?" I said, "Nothing." I was working during the day, selling plaster. He said, "You'll have to give up work. There's this gig on Monday. If you want to come, we'll pick you up in the van." I said, "Right." They said they'd come by at seven. And that was it. Nobody ever said, "You're in." They just said, "What are you doing Monday?"

The first American tour. Do you remember it with fondness?

For me it was a tour of discovery. It was three months with 'Erman's 'Ermits. Backing up the 'Ermits was ideal. It was a position that suited us. We weren't on the line. If the place sold only a portion of what it could have sold, the disaster was never blamed on us, it was blamed on 'Erman's 'Ermits. We didn't have the responsibility. We had time to discover. We found the good towns.

Which ones are they?

For the Who they're New York, Chicago, Detroit, Los Angeles, San Francisco and Cleveland. They have the best audiences for us.

Was it on this tour you had your infamous birthday party?

Yes. That's how I lost me front tooth. In Flint, Michigan. We had a show that night. We were all around the 'Oliday Inn pool, 'Erman's 'Ermits and meself. I was twenty-one and they started giving me presents. Somebody gave me a portable bar, and somebody else the portable booze. I'd started drinking about ten o'clock in the morning, and I can't remember the show. Then the record companies 'ad booked a big room in the 'otel, one of the conference rooms, for a party. As the hours went on, it got louder and louder, and everybody started getting well out of their minds, well stoned. The pool was the obvious target. Everybody started jumping in the pool with their clothes on.

The Premier Drum Company 'ad given me a 'uge birthday cake, with like five drums stacked up on top of each other. As the party degenerated into a slanging, I picked up the cake, all five tiers, and hurled it at the throng. People started picking up the pieces and 'urling it about. Everybody was covered in marzipan and icing sugar and fruitcake. The manager 'eard the fracas and came in. There it was, his great carpet, stained irrevocably with marzipan and fruitcake trodden in, and everybody dancing about with their trousers off. By the time the sheriff came in, I was standing there in me underpants. I ran out, jumped into the first car I came to, which was a brand-new Lincoln Continental. It was parked on a slight hill, and when I took the hand brake off, it started to roll. It smashed straight through this pool surround [fence], and the whole Lincoln Continental went into the 'Oliday Inn swimming pool, with me in it. Ah-ha-ha-ha!

So there I was, sitting in the eight-foot-six in the driver's seat of a Lincoln Continental, underwater. And the water was pouring in—coming in through the bloody pedal 'oles in the floorboard, you know, squirting in through the windows. In a startling moment of logical, I said, "Well, I can't open the doors until the pressure is the same...." It's amazing 'ow I remembered those things from my physics class! I knew I'd have to wait until the pressure was the same.

So I'm sitting there, thinking about me situation, as the water creeps up me nose. Today I can think of less outrageous ways of going than drowning in a Lincoln Continental in a 'Oliday Inn swimming pool, but at that time I had no thoughts of death whatsoever. There was none of that all-me-life-passing-before-me-eyes-in-a-flash. I was busy planning. I knew if I panicked, I'd 'ave 'ad it. So when there's just enough air in the top of the car to take a gulp, I fill up me lungs, throw open the door and go rising to the top of the pool. I figured there'd be quite a crowd gathered by now. After all, I'd been down there underwater for some time. I figured they'd be so grateful I was alive, they'd overlook the Lincoln Continental. But no. There's only one person standing there, and 'e's the pool cleaner, and 'e's got to have the pool clean in the morning, and he's furious.

So I went back to the party, streaming water, still in me underpants. The first person I see is the sheriff, and 'e's got 'is 'and on 'is gun. Sod this! And I ran, I started to leg it out the door, and I slipped on a piece of marzipan and fell flat on me face and knocked out me tooth. Ah-ha-ha-ha!

I spent the remainder of the night under the custody of the sheriff at a dentist's. The dentist couldn't give me any anesthetic because I was pissed out me mind. So 'e 'ad to rip out what was left of the tooth and put a false one in, and the next day I spent a couple of hours in the nick [jail]. The boys had chartered me a plane because they had to leave on an earlier flight. The sheriff took me out in the law car, and he puts me on the plane and says [*American accent*], "Son, don't ever dock in Flint, Michigan again." I said, "Dear boy, I wouldn't dream of it." And I was lisping around the new tooth. Ah-ha-ha-ha!

By now I'd learned 'ow destructive we'd all been. During the merriment someone 'ad upset all the fire extinguishers and turned them on all the cars in the car park. Six of them 'ad to 'ave new paint jobs; the paint all peeled off. We'd also destroyed a piano. Completely destroyed it. Reduced to kindling. And don't forget the carpet. And the Lincoln Continental in the bottom of the pool. So I got a bill for $24,000. Ah-ha-ha-ha! I wasn't earning 'alf that on the tour, and I'd spent everything by the time I'd got to Flint, Michigan. I was in debt up past me eyebrows before this 'appened. Luckily, 'Erman's 'Ermits and the boys split it up, about thirty of us gave a thousand dollars each. It was like a religious ceremony as we all came up and dropped a thousand dollars into a big 'at and sent it off to the 'Oliday Inn with a small compliments card with BALLS written across it and the words SEE YOU SOON. Ah-ha-ha-ha!

You can't have destroyed as many rooms as legend has it.

You want to bet?

Have there been other times when . . .

Lots. Yes. I get bored, you see. There was a time in Saskatoon, in Canada. It was another 'Oliday Inn, and I was bored. Now, when I get bored, I rebel. I said, *"Fuck it! Fuck the lot of ya!"* And I took out me 'atchet and chopped the 'otel room to bits. The television, the chairs, the dresser, the cupboard doors, the bed—the lot of it. Ah-ha-ha-ha! It happens all the time.

I've always heard it was Pete who started the destruction onstage, but you make it sound as if it might've been your idea. Was it?

The way the story goes, Pete put the neck of his guitar through a low ceiling when he jumped too 'igh, but that's not it. It 'appened when somebody got pissed off with the gig, with the way things were going. When Pete smashed his guitar, it was because 'e was pissed off. When I smashed me drums, it was because I was pissed off. We were frustrated. You're working as hard as you can to get that fucking song across, to get that audience by the balls, to make it an event. When you've done all that, when you've worked your balls off and you've given the audience everything you can give, and they don't give anything back, that's when the fucking instruments go, because, "You fucking bastards! We've worked our fucking balls off! And you've given us nothing back!"

That's one way the instruments got smashed. Another way was if a member of the group was too fuckin' stoned to give it their best. Then he was letting down the other three. In a lot of cases it was me, through drinking too much. You know, just getting out of it at the wrong time. Then Pete or Roger or John says, "You cunt! You fucking let us down! You fucking bastard, if you want to get pissed, why don't you wait until after the show!"

You all seem to be fairly available to the press.

We're doing fuck-all else. Ah-ha-ha-ha! Some people say I'll do anything for the press, it's true…that I make meself too available. I just like to 'ave fun. There was this time Keith Altham and Chris Williams, who look after our PR, phoned me up and said I 'ad to be at their office at three o'clock for an interview. Well, you know, the pubs shut at three, so I was rather delayed, because they don't turn out until ha'past. So it was quarter to four before I eventually started. I was back up in my office at Track [Records] and finally I remembered; I'd forgotten all about it. So, uhhh, "Oh, Christ, they're gonna be angry." Right opposite the office is a chemist's, so I sent Dougal, me driver, over there to pick up some rolls of bandages and plaster, and I did all me leg up, strapped me arms up and purchased a stick, a walking stick. Then I went over to the office: "Sorry I'm late, but the 'ospital delayed me."

I'd called earlier and told them I'd been run over by a bus on Oxford Street. They didn't think that unlikely. I think they've adopted the attitude that anything's likely with Moon, y'see. So I walk into the office…'obble in, actually…and they say, " 'Ow did it 'appen?" I said, "I was just crossing Oxford Street and a Number Eight from Shepherd's Bush 'it me right up the arse and sent me spinning across Oxford

Circus." So Keith and Chris say they'll cancel the interview. I say no, but maybe they'd be so kind as to carry me down the four flights of steps to the street. They thought I'd come up by meself, on me walking stick, y'see.

So they carried me down the stairs, and we're walking along. I'm 'obbling along the street again, and this bloody lorry comes along as I'm crossing the street, and it screams to a 'alt in front of me. I say, " 'Ang on, mate, I can't go fast on these legs," and Keith has a go at the lorry driver: "You 'eartless bastard, can't you see this man's injured! 'Ave you no 'eart, 'ave you no soul, you bastard! Trying to run over a cripple!"

We went on to the interview, and in the middle, after about four brandies, I just ripped off all the plaster and jumped up on the seat and started dancing. Ah-ha-ha-ha!

Have you ever been injured in any of your stunts? Aside from the missing front tooth?

I broke me collarbone once. That was in me own 'otel, the one I own, one Christmas. I collapsed in front of the fire at four o'clock one morning, and some friends of mine decided to put me to bed, and they were in as bad a state as I was, but they were still on their feet. Just about. One of them got 'old of me 'ead, the other got 'old of me feet, and they attempted to drag me up the stairs. They got me up two flights and then promptly dropped me down both of them, breaking me collarbone, y'see. But I didn't know this until I woke up in the morning and tried to put me fucking shirt on. I went through the fuckin' roof.

Now... I was supposed to do a television show, the *Top of the Pops New Year's Eve Special*, and two days before I 'ave me arm all strapped up so I can't drum. I went to me doctor, dear Dr. Robert, and he gave me a shot on the day of the gig so I wouldn't feel anything. I put a shirt over the cast, fastened the drumstick to my wrist with a sticking plaster, sat down behind the drum kit, and got Mr. Vivian Stanshall to tie a rope around me wrist. We then threw the rope over the lighting pipe overhead, the one that holds the floods and all, and I kept an eye on the television monitor. Every time I was on camera, I'd give the signal to Viv, and he'd give a pull on the rope, which caused me right arm to shoot up and then come crashing down on the cymbal. Ah-ha-ha-ha!

These farcical situations... I'm always tied up in them. They're always like Laurel and Hardy sketches. And they always 'appen to me! Ah-ha-ha-ha! I think unconsciously I want them to 'appen, and they do.

Is that the image you have of yourself?

I suppose to most people I'm probably seen as an amiable idiot... a genial twit. I think I must be a victim of circumstance, really. Most of it's me own doing. I'm a victim of me own practical jokes. I suppose that reflects a rather selfish attitude: I like to be the recipient of me own doings. Nine times out of ten I am. I set traps and fall into them. Oh-ha-ha-ha-HA-HA-HA-HA! Of course the biggest danger is becoming a parody.

Your wife, Kim, must be extraordinarily sympathetic and patient.

She is. She sort of takes it in 'er stride.

How did you meet her?

Heh-heh-eh-eh. Ah-ha-ha-ha! I met her in Bournemouth when I was playing a show. She was sixteen and she hung out at the club where we worked, the Disc. Sometime later when I went down to see her, I was on a train, and Rod Stewart was on the train. This was about ten years ago. We got chatting, and we went to the bar car. It was Rod "the Mod" Stewart in those glorious days, and he'd just been working with Long John Baldry. He was playing a lot of small discotheques and pubs, doing the sort of work we were doing. I said to Rod, "Where are you going?" He said, "Bournemouth." "So'm I," I said. "I'm going down there to see my chick." He said, "So'm I." So I showed Rod a picture of Kim, and he said, "Yeah…that's 'er." Ah-ha-ha-ha!

What happened?

I don't remember. We were in the bar car, and we both got paralytic. I only remember the trip back. Oh-hee-ha-ha-ha!

How'd your mother-in-law come to live with you?

She's me 'ousekeeper. And she's a great cook. You see, I was cradle snatching. I snatched her daughter at sixteen, right out of convent school, and she 'adn't learned 'ow to cook yet, so I said, "Get your mother up 'ere." She's been living with us for about a year now. She's not the accepted idea of a mother-in-law. At my 'ouse there's no real accepted idea of anything.

Do you have favorite drummers?

Not many. D.J. Fontana [Elvis' original drummer] is one. Let's see…the drummers I respect are Eric Delany and Bob Henrit [from Argent] and…I got a 'uge list, really, and all for different reasons. Technically, Joe Morello is perfect. I don't really have a favorite drummer. I have favorite drum pieces, and that's it. I would never put on a LP of a drummer and say everything he did I love, because that's not true.

How'd you start on drums?

Jesus Christ, I think I got a free drum kit in a packet of corn flakes. Ah-ha-ha-ha! But no…drum solos are fucking boring. Any kind of solo is. It detracts from the group identity.

How much of a group effort are the songs? How much do you change those demos when you record?

Not a hell of a lot. Because Pete knows. When Pete writes something, it sounds like the Who. The drum phrases are my phrases, even though it's Pete playing drums. He's playing the way I play. He's playing my flourishes. The same thing for the bass part, and the guitar of course is 'is own. Only the vocals change some.

Two years later, how do you look back on 'Tommy'?

With disbelief. Ah-ha-ha-ha! I can't believe we spent six months doing it. It took six months to make. That's studio time, and that's talking about it, discussing it, arranging it, producing it and writing it. Getting it all together. Recording it, and then saying we could do it better and recording it again.

Other than with disbelief, how do you remember it?

Well, it is disbelief. I just can't believe that we did that album. It was an amazing album to do. It was, at the time, very un-Who-like. A lot of the songs were sort of soft. We never played like that. And we didn't have an idea then as to how it was all going to turn out. Here we were, spending all this time on a project that none of us really knew all that much about.

Then came the 'Tommy' tours…

Because we'd been in the studio so long, we immediately went on an American tour. We incorporated a lot of *Tommy*. In fact, the act was mostly *Tommy*. After that, on the opera 'ouse tour, we played just two numbers to warm up—we'd do "Summertime Blues" and "I Can't Explain" or something—and then we'd do the opera. We did about six or seven opera 'ouses. I enjoyed them. Nice sound. But it was a bit strange. It was rather like playing to an oil painting.

The Who's always been a working band, a touring band. Do you still enjoy the road?

[*Using soft voice, as if delivering a eulogy*] I love it. It's my life. If I was to be deprived of touring…I love being responsible for the enjoyment of a packed 'ouse. Knowing the four of us can go onstage and give enjoyment to that many thousand people, that's fucking something, man, that does me right in. If I'm good and the group is good, you can get 14,000…140,000!…get them on their fucking feet. Yeah. That's where it's at. That's what it's all about for me.

Can you tell me what you're worth?

I don't know. Not now. Some time ago me accountant told me I 'ad a lot of money. I said, " 'Ow much?" He said, "Well, you're very well fixed." I said, " 'Ow much? I mean, am I a millionaire?" "Well, technically, yes." So I said, "What should I do about it?" and he said, "Well, obviously if you've got that much money, and you've got these tax bills, it's logical to spend money so that you can claim it against the tax that's owed." "I see…so I should spend money?" "Well, yes, you should." So six weeks later I'd spent it all. Ah-ha-ha-ha! I'd bought four 'ouses, a 'otel, eight cars, a swimming pool, tennis courts, expensive wristwatches that fall apart, a riverside bungalow just five minutes away, furnished in French renay-sance-period furniture. I'd spent it all. It was gone. Ah-ha-ha-ha!

I get accused of being a capitalist bastard, because, you know: "How many cars you got?" "Eight." "Big 'ouse?" "Yes." Well, I love all that; I enjoy it. I have lots of friends over, and we sit up, drinking and partying. I need the room to entertain. I enjoy seeing other people enjoy themselves. That's where I get my kicks. I'm kinky that way. I have the amount of cars I do because I smash them up a lot. Six are always in the garage; it's a fact. They're always saying I'm a capitalist pig. I suppose I am. But, ah…it ah…it's good for me drumming, I think. Oh-ho-ho-ha-ha!

You really do have troubles with cars?

I came off the road in the AC Cobra at one hundred and ten. We flew over a canal and sort of collapsed in a mangled heap in a field about ten foot from a reservoir. The Cobra people were very unhappy when I took the wreckage into their garage. They only made about ninety-eight of them and they're touchy about how they're driven. Ha-ha-ha! I've tried to bump-start the 1936 Chrysler several times, always with disastrous results. Once I tried to bump-start it with my X-type Jag, which is built so low to the ground, it slid under the Chrysler. Another time I tried to bump-start with the Rolls…forgetting there was nobody sitting in the Chrysler. I pushed it right into the fish pond on the front lawn.

When did the group swing away from drugs towards booze?

Ah-ha…a change-of-pace question. Ah-ha-ha-ha! I think we just sort of grew out of drugs. The drugs aren't necessary now. They were then, as a crutch. We went through just about everything. Not Roger so much. He smoked, but that was it. The rest of us went through the same stages everybody goes through—the bloody drug corridor. You know. We were no exception. Eventually we stopped fucking about with the chemicals and started on the grape. Drinking suited the group a lot better. When we started drinking, that's when it all started getting together.

We're all pretty good drinkers. After the show there's always the celebration drink, or the noncelebration drink. Then there's always the clubs. John and I, generally, go clubbing. We just like the social side of drinking. Everybody I know is a drinker. I've met some of my best friends in pubs.

You've been in two films without the others...

Yeah, one was *200 Motels* with Frank Zappa. The other was *Countdown* with Harry Nilsson, both with Ringo.

I was at the Speakeasy with Pete, and Frank 'appened to be at the next table. He overheard some of our conversation and leaned over and said [*American accent*], "How'd you guys like to be in a film?" We said [*English accent*], "Okay, Frank." And he said [*back to American accent*], "Okay, be at the Kensington Palace Hotel at seven o'clock tomorrow morning." I was the one who turned up. Pete was writing and sent his apologies, and I was given the part Mick Jagger was to play—that of a nun. Mick didn't want to do it.

Then there was a bit in one of the local papers that said Ringo was making *Countdown* with Peter Frampton and Harry Nilsson and a lot of others, so I called Ringo up and said, "Is there a part in it for me?" He said yes, and I turned up. I do some drumming.

Was that your first meeting with Nilsson?

Yes. We were supposed to be on the set at six, but it was nine before everyone was there. Then somebody brought out a bottle of brandy. Me, I think. Ah-ha-ha-ha! And Peter Frampton said no, no, too early, and some of the others said no. But 'Arry was standing there with an 'alf-pint mug. I knew at that moment it was destiny put us together. Ah-ha-ha-ha!

So we were drinking brandy at nine and, thanks to Mal Evans, white wine all the rest of the day. Then about six o'clock somebody came round and slipped little envelopes into our hands. It was a pay packet! I 'adn't 'ad a pay packet in ten years. And 'Arry'd never 'ad one. We were pretty well out of it, and we looked at each other and then tore up 170 pounds in one-pound notes, threw it up in the air and danced about, cackling like schoolboys. Ah-ha-ha-ha! Dancing and leaping about, clutching bottles of Blue Nun Liebfraumilch in our hands, singing, "We're millionaires, aren't we?"

Inside Alice

by Harry Swift   May 1973

Alice Cooper's shining F-27 with the black dollar sign emblazoned on its tail is zigzagging without apparent purpose from Pittsburgh to Detroit. The plane is shaking so violently that the stewardess, as she comes staggering out of the pilot's cabin, falls into the lap of a recently hired guitarist who has joined the Alice Cooper Band for the length of this tour. He is clutching the shifting jello-bag chair he is sprawled in and stares in fear out the porthole.

Aynsley Dunbar, veteran British drummer who is accompanying Alice's warm-up act, Flo and Eddie, abruptly ceases gnawing the glitter off his fingernail and screams, "Holy shit! The pilot is going to fuckin' kill us!"

One of the Flo and Eddie roadies leans over to Dunbar. "Don't worry, Aynsley. It's a short flight to Detroit, just a hop, skip and a plunge."

Aynsley whimpers. His head sinks into his studded leather jacket.

Watching the private stewardesses lurch by, Mr. Shep Gordon, the whiskery president of Alive Enterprises, management firm to Alice Cooper, twists his head and sniggers. "They've never flown with us before," he says. "The pilot fired our other two stewardesses; you should have seen them—they were cool. First week on the plane they double-fucked absolutely everybody on the tour."

The interior of the chartered, four-engine F-27 is covered with scrawled drawings, spit-stained posters and mutilated magazine pinups. Some passengers are fear-frozen and strapped into their seats, while others are sprawled out on the cushion-covered floor in a section where seats have been ripped out for purposes of hanging much looser than one usually is permitted on airplanes. With joints being tossed around like spitballs, beer cans rolling up and down the aisles and rock & roll blasting from eight JBL speakers, the forty-eight-passenger bird is a dangerous but stone-carefree flyer.

"Sure, it's expensive," Gordon continues, "but having our own chartered plane is good for everybody's morale. We don't have to fuck around waiting in airports, and we can do what we want once we're on the plane. It's also important for our image; it lends it more magic. We fly into a town in our *own* plane, and it's like the circus is coming.

"My most important function," he confides, "is to keep Alice totally insulated from reality…to see that it never enters his world and disrupts it with the petty daily shit that most of us have to deal with. Alice never has to talk to a waitress in a restaurant. To be an artist is difficult enough. It's a tremendous strain to be as creative and to give as much to an audience as Alice does at every show. That's why he stays drunk most of the time. He has a can of Budweiser at his bedside when he wakes up in the morning. It's simply *necessary* in order to sustain the fantasy, in order to be Alice and to give the performance night after night."

Truly, alcohol is a battle that Alice has to fight on the road every day.

Although he has been drinking only four years now, by his own estimate he finishes a case a day.

Gordon and his partner Joey Podell (who is taking care of business back at the New York office) have been managing Alice Cooper since the late Sixties, back when the group was known only as a rank of transvestites from Van Nuys. Those were the days when even the imprimatur of Frank ("Genius") Zappa could not convince such a small audience that they were anything but a band of no-excuse Queen Geeks.

"I had some money to spend, and I thought it would be fun to somehow get involved in the rock & roll scene, where people at least seemed to get laid a lot," Shep Gordon recalls. "But gradually I saw Alice's real potential and put more and more of myself into it. Even when all my money was gone, I still stuck with him. We used to have to sneak out of six-dollar-a-night motels to beat the bill. Alice's girl, Cindy, used to cook up a big pot of spaghetti or rice on Mondays, and we'd all live on it for the next week."

The tour is pegged to gross in the general neighborhood of $4.5 million. It started on March 5th in Rochester, New York, and will end three months later on June 3rd in Madison Square Garden, after taxiing in and out of fifty-six American metropolises.

Just yesterday, at the plush Knoedler Galleries in New York City, Salvador Dali had unveiled his well-publicized 360-degree hologram of Alice. Cooper and Dali had descended the gallery's nearly airborne marble staircase together to meet an angry, surly Gotham press corps. Dali, flaming in layers of flowing white and gold robes, strode grandly to the microphones as Alice bopped along beside him in a motorcycle jacket slung open at the breasts.

As usual, the fingers of Alice's black-leather elbow-length gloves were wrapped clawlike around the inevitable bottle—Michelob this time instead of the stubby proletarian Bud, perhaps in deference to the moment's pomp. The pair got down to the business at hand. Alice sat bemused, sipping his beer and making coy faces at the press while Dali hovered over him, circling Alice's head in huge gestures with a shining index finger. He trumpeted a booming monologue in his incomprehensible accent about how he, "the Dali," had produced a perfect replica of the brain of "the Alice Cooperpopstar."

One flight up, contained within a cylinder the size and shape of a standard popcorn machine, was an image of Alice performing, behind which could be viewed —from all angles—the image of a human brain inset with Dali's trademark, the limp watch. At the very back of the brain rests a chocolate eclair, which Dali claims, with inarguable logic, is the symbol of Alice's music.

"Has Dali ever heard your music?" someone asked Alice.

"I don't really know," Alice replies. "But that's what I love about Dali—he makes absolutely no sense. He told me the reason he wanted to do the hologram with us was because we were the most confusing people he'd ever met. That's the only thing that we really have in common—confusion. We don't make any sense at all to each other in a conversation. He speaks in five different languages at once, and you're supposed to understand what he's talking about! We just stand there, and then I'll say something that has nothing to do with what he's talking about. And then he'll say something back that has nothing to do with what I was talking about. We just go on like that."

The collaboration makes a lot of sense to Alice, since it points out his own legitimate relationship to the established avant-garde and to surrealism in particular.

"The power of our show," says Alice, "is just the whole idea of bringing back cabaret. We are really doing a Seventies stage thing on decadence. The cabaret was a period in German history when they were interested in decadence. And that's exactly what we're doing. Only we're doing it with rock music instead of the old beer-drinking music. And that's not too far away either—we do beer-drinking music too.

"The whole idea behind the *Billion Dollar Babies* album was exploiting the idea that people do have sick perversions. There are so many sick people today, and they always come off as the business guy who's working at the Holiday Inn in Omaha and can't get off with his wife. But down deep he's got different sexual perversions; maybe the guy does go up in the attic with his daughter. That's what *Billion Dollar Babies* was showing. The whole album is about sexual perversions, American sexual perversions. It's got to be American—we're very nationalistic."

What's your favorite perversion?

"I keep picturing Tuesday Weld—and her bee-stung lips, right? her big lips—in a dirty slip, with a beer can by her side and no shoes on. Heh! And a cigarette. And dirty hair and everything, like a real Tennessee Williams character. And then I rape her.

"I'm not really too much into sadism, except for mass sadism. In other words, I'm not into sadism with a woman, but I love to go on the stage and torture audiences to the point where I *know* that they are all going to scratch and jump on each other just to get a little piece of the poster. I love to watch that and laugh at it. And they know it. The audiences are masochistic."

★   ★   ★

As the ride from the Detroit airport to the Howard Johnson's Motor Lodge proceeds along the cheerless highway, Ashley Pandel, head of Alice Cooper promotion, breaks into the smoky silence to announce that "No More Mr. Nice Guy" was just-next-to-hot on Detroit radio and was being played on *all* the AM rockers. Alice orders the driver to turn on the car radio, and sure enough, there it is, the angry Alice Cooper, easily the most hip of *au courant* primordial voices: "No more Mr. Nice Guy/ No more Mr. Cle-e-e-ean/ They say, 'He's sick, he's obscene.'"

Alice Cooper's combination fuck-off and put-down message to the press is so cosmically timed to this slightly uptight moment that even one of the very culprits to whom the message is addressed can see the clear-cut and unabashed irony of it all as he sits squeezed next to Alice. And on top of that insouciant insult, Alice is actually singing along, just kind of carelessly grooving with himself, but maybe just a hair too carelessly.

The song must have provided Alice with a nice sense of nobility; all at once he assumes the benevolence of a man of significance who knows that he has made his point and made it well. His hand suddenly darts into his carpetbag to tap the last can of Budweiser. Snapping off the pop top and assaying a professional swig, Alice passes it to his early-morning guest.

"I can empathize with anyone who drinks beer in the morning," says Alice in simple tones, edging toward the graciousness that befits a billion-dollar baby. Many other worlds are befitting him these past three years as well, he feels.

"I just bought a house right next door to Barry Goldwater. It was a tax shelter thing where I had to get rid of some money, so I bought a house. Heh! In about five years I'm going to move there. I'm renting it right now to the president of a chemical corporation, and it's a good investment, anyway. He probably knows by now, but what I'm going to do is have a mystery neighbor party, wear a bag over my head and invite all the neighbors. A lot of the Phoenix bigwigs live right in this area, Paradise Valley. When they're all there, I'm gonna take the bag off. The cool thing is my house is bigger than his! And I have more money than him. But Barry Goldwater's really a pretty good guy."

Phoenix is Alice's home town, where he claims he had "a real cool childhood." His return there will no doubt be prodigious, but it will also be only private; the city will not allow him to play any of its concert halls.

"I'm not trying to kill myself," Alice continues, "that's silly. I have a lust for life; I wouldn't be doing this if I didn't really like seeing new places and doing new things. I love the idea of life, yet I have this other self, and he goes up there and makes fun of death.

"Offstage, I'm Ozzie Nelson. I'm gentle. I walk around eating cookies and milk—well, cookies and beer. I work in opposites. Offstage I'm pretty nonviolent. I'm stable. I have a girlfriend, the same girl for five years now, Cindy. She isn't on the tour because she hates us. She hates our music, and she hates our image. She's a gorgeous, beautiful girl, one of the most sought-after ladies in New York. I really like the fact that she hates us.

"I work in opposites. If I'm exposing myself that much onstage—not physically, but mentally exposing all my problems onstage—I would rather not let a lot of people know what I really do."

Press conferences are held in every city. They are, by and large, boisterous and boozy affairs in which the local reporters only rise to the oft-heard straight line.

Midway in each local *Meet the Press,* just when it would begin to appear that Alice might imminently keel with teenage boredom from keeping the *Bulletin,* *Dispatch* and *News-Herald* gnomes and cretins amused as the questions become fewer and duller…midway through each press conference, Mark Volman and Howard Kaylan, who are Flo and Eddie, suddenly heel into the conference room rendering an off-key "Stout Hearted Men." They sit down with Alice to face a nation's free press like the Three Stooges revisited.

Alice still hasn't publicly revealed his real name.

"I told the press today," he reports later, "that I was Jimmy Piersall's illegitimate son. I think that's a great idea. For some reason that really fits my sense of humor. Did you ever see Jimmy Piersall's story, *Fear Strikes Out?* He was totally nuts! He was the Alice Cooper of baseball. He was always hitting people with bats. I decided today that I was going to be his illegitimate son.

"Oh, I love to lie. That's one of my favorite things in the world, coming up to somebody, especially press people, and telling them some enormous lie that couldn't possibly be true. You can throw in anything you want."

Alice chooses to have Flo and Eddie join him at the daily press preliminaries rather than the members of his own band. All four of his own musicians appear, once offstage, to be manic-depressive in varying clinical degrees. They tend to hang together, wary of outsiders. This is due, in some measure, to the years of constantly beating off the attacks Alice provokes in factory town bars, California truck stops and other like-minded hangouts.

"Every once in a while Alice will pop up when I'm not expecting it," Alice explains. "Especially though in bars when I'm real wiped out. Last night, I got carried out of another one. I was saying some awfully bad things about cripples, and I was telling thalidomide jokes. I was just awful. And I was telling Kennedy jokes, too, like how they had to recall all the Kennedy half dollars 'cause they forgot the hole. But then I blurted out about the thalidomide child that could count to eleven on one hand. Helen Keller jokes—I mean these are sick! For some reason, when it's one of those things that you're not supposed to say, it's always a lot funnier. I love sick jokes. We had a Bangla Desh one: 'What's the last thing that they need in Bangla Desh?' 'After-dinner mints.'"

★   ★   ★

Backstage in Detroit, Alice quietly introduces his mother. "Have you met my mom? Isn't she just like Tammy Wynette?"

Now, what can this healthy and genuinely pleasant middle-aged woman, wife to an ordained minister, think of her son? In the first place, why does he call himself Alice? What must "Mrs. Cooper" ponder on while she watches her son greet the demimonde's atavistic backstage set in a moth-eaten dressing room, which, like dressing rooms of most civic auditoriums, favors the brightly lit public-lavatory ambiance. What or who does "Mrs. Cooper" possibly hold responsible for the ugly-duckling son who chose the life of a truly weirded-out, somewhat magical swan? Not to mention, for a moment, his stage costume, the white leotards, torn in spots as though gnawed by rats, conjoined to one of Alice's personally designed pairs of aqua-shaded leopard-skin thigh boots with six-inch platform heels.

It's what you have to do for a living these days, she tells the neighbors, after Alice's occasional family visits. There's a Rolls Royce, a gift from Alice that "Reverend Cooper" drives, which proves there could be worse ways. Indeed, America has approved of Alice with its most glorious honors, and that justifies the private hopes of the "Coopers" that their son was only calculating it for these last seven years and didn't really believe in it as a way of life. It's only that first album cover, *Pretties for You*, which still makes her throat tighten.

"I've been throwing up every single morning on this tour," Alice is telling her, "but it's not from drinking. I've got a real bad head cold, and it's in my chest now. Every morning I wake up and watch all my quiz shows and drink two or three warm beers, 'cause it's good for your stomach in the mornings. Then I get phlegm in my throat and gag. I just throw up water, but then I feel great! It makes you feel so alive. The doctor came over today, and we all got shots, B-12 and things like that. He examined us all and said I'm the healthiest one in the group—as bad as I look."

"Alice has always been unusual," she says. She pulls out the wrinkles of her pants suit, nods her lightly lacquered beehive and, in a brave, matter-of-fact tone, concludes, "Alice has always done exactly what he's wanted to. He's always been Alice to us."

Alice Cooper opens his show with restraint. He stalks across the stage to begin the long-awaited evening's life drama, bathed in a blue spotlight wash as the screams go up in the house. The band, each member in white silk, is locked in cages that hang separately like framed, lost portraits in the surrounding void. In the four-to eight-dollar seats, twelve-to-eighteen-year-old faces strain toward the stage, where a twenty-five-year-old man with a woman's name prowls with a twelve-foot black-leather whip in hand.

Alice, sweating to the navel, is tormented; he skulks across the stage and then retreats to the crackling darkness behind the throbbing 14,000 watts of black amplifiers. Unobserved by the crowd, he swiftly finishes a Bud.

Alice Cooper's is perhaps the most completely realized stage performance of its genre ever presented. Alice welcomes us to a dream without descriptions, only experience. In the second part of the show, Alice quickly assumes an even more sinister character, that of the violent rapist in "Raped and Freezin'." He impales a silver bust on a microphone stand and bashes it with his cane in a screaming rage. And the inchoate, steaming, senseless resentment builds.

The roadies empty onto the stage a rough-hewn wheelbarrow filled with dismembered department store dummies, unattached hands, amputated torsos, wooden legs and limbs ripped from sockets—prosthetic appliances of the most tragic kinds. Through the plagued, dismembered landscape, Alice struts, kicking baby heads into the crowd. Next, brandishing a sword, he impales limbs, smashes bony heads and tender craniums in a frenzied, mad-dog dance.

Alice's finale is a simple, elegant anthem of necrophilia, "I Love the Dead," in which the monster Alice is martyred on a guillotine. The band moves from their pedestals toward center stage to brutally twist the wrist bracelets onto his bleeding arms. Drained and passive, Alice bows his head with one last helpless jerk into the guillotine slot to receive the punishment for his necrophilia.

Silence. *Thunk!* Isolated screams are heard. The hangman pulls the bloody head of Alice Cooper—grisly in its wax-museum reality—out of the basket and twists spastically around the stage with the dripping trophy. A tape loop of "I Love the Dead" blares maddeningly throughout the arena.

Meanwhile, Alice Cooper has crawled unseen behind the dark, towering amplifier banks...and is well into a newly cracked can of Bud. He sits, sweating, and listens for the encore, a recording of Kate Smith singing "God Bless America." Then, reassuringly reheaded, he lifts himself up to join the entire cast onstage—in a salute to the American flag.

★   ★   ★

Back at his hotel, Alice is shirtless, drained and curled into a big soft chair in front of a twenty-four-inch Sylvania color set with a can of the King of Beers in his hand, watching a film starring Omar Sharif. Alice and Omar are good personal friends.

"Omar is a great guy, but this movie sure is a turkey," Alice remarks. "Watching television is the only thing I love to do. It's probably my favorite hobby. The

TV is a vast vault of useless knowledge. And I love it. I just think it's great. I get up in the morning and watch the farm report. It's on at six. I really don't think that there's anything wrong with television. A lot of people think that it could be better. Well, everything could be better."

Alice's hulking bodyguard, Mike Ramsey, formerly an MP, a U.S. Army tournament boxer and now a black belt in karate, is talking in a threatening monotone to someone on the phone who claims to know Alice. "You say you met him when he went to see *Fritz the Cat*? Do you really expect him to remember this insignificant occasion?"

"Ahhh, nasty," purrs Alice, still staring at the screen.

"No, I'm afraid he doesn't remember you. Goodbye." Ramsey sits back down and ponders his gig with Mr. Cooper. "Well, I'll tell ya, lots of people think it's a glamorous job, working as Alice's bodyguard, or should I say, 'traveling companion'…"

"That's sounds kinda fruity to me," Alice says.

"…some people would be damned proud to have an honor and a responsibility like this, but to tell you the truth I don't really give a shit, because as far as I'm concerned *the guy's a fuckin' loser!*"

Alice slides onto the floor, cackling hysterically.

"Hey, *The Creature from the Black Lagoon* is on now," Alice says, flicking the dial to another station. "He is the coolest monster that ever lived. I mean it. I want you to get a look at him when he comes up dripping from the Black Lagoon. There's something almost handsome about this monster."

At Alice's feet is a petite, straight-laced nineteen-year-old college student named Joyce Ciletti, from Wampum, Pennsylvania. She is doing a psychology thesis on Alice Cooper. During the past two years she has distributed several thousand questionnaires in which people are asked to give their responses to the Alice Cooper phenomenon. At the moment, she is deeply engrossed in studying the form that Alice himself just finished filling out for her.

Also in the room is Detroit's only hip rock critic, who met Alice that morning at the airport. He is not interested in *The Creature from the Black Lagoon*. From a couch across the room he beckons Joyce Ciletti over. In one hand he is holding a Budweiser and in the other one of those sturdy little battle-gray Sony cassette recorders.

"It took me a year to write the final questionnaire," she explains. "You have to use certain words so they understand it completely, and it must be set up in a certain fashion, scientifically. I'll be passing them out at probably nine concerts on this tour, about 3000 at each concert.

"The questions about Alice start out asking what part of the concert did they

Alice Cooper
Photograph by Annie Leibovitz

like the most, dislike the most, and what would they do onstage if they were Alice Cooper. The second part is completely empirical. It's a series of statements they respond to on an agree-disagree scale: 'I feel that Alice Cooper is one of the top groups in the country today.' And then it says things like: 'Alice promotes attitudes in favor of violence.' 'Alice promotes attitudes in favor of homosexuality.' 'After seeing Alice's concert, I was more excited than after another concert.' 'Alice's appeal is primarily a sexual one.'

"At this age level, it's a commitment age. The kids are really committed, and they're being very underestimated.

"I see Alice as comprising the elements of temper in this era: confusion, sadism, masochism. With Alice, sex and violence is not completely differentiated. It's a combination. For instance, the hangings that he used to have. You'll find that that sexually arouses an audience. They had to quit having hangings in the 1800s because there was extreme debauchery afterward.

"On death row, for instance, the reporters that are there to see a hanging frequently have an orgasm after the hanging. They stopped having public hangings. But it did sexually arouse the males. We don't know what it does to the females. I don't know exactly how that works for Alice, but a lot of girls I interviewed say, 'Oh, it gave me such supreme satisfaction.' I'm sure they don't know why, but that's the reason. A lot of people have written in and said that's what they liked the most.

"It seems to me that after a concert they are left amazed. They are not left violent, at least from what I see, they aren't. Alice more or less drains them. They're left stunned. Many people say that he's decadent, and that the kids—because they perceive him at a visceral level—aren't getting anything out of it. But some of the comments on the questionnaires are amazing. A typical one would be 'I believe in what Alice is saying in his lyrics, because he's satirizing our society and holding us up to see that he is not the one that's sick but the society's sick.' So on and so forth. Do you mean do I think it causes them to do something violent or sexual?"

"Well, do you think it alters their attitudes?"

"For some people I've talked to, it has a little bit, as far as their attitudes on sex. A lot of them feel different after they see the concert."

"Is it altering attitudes toward bisexuality and homosexuality?"

"No, no. That is the *one* thing that has *not* come up in the preliminary results at all. Uh, there's maybe three people, so far, out of all these results, that have said that."

"Then what's it about?"

"Alice is the picture of the American 1970s. He's definitely middle-class American. There's no doubt about it. It's symbolic from his Budweiser through his whole act. And we are definitely a very violent society. Just watch TV for a while, or go see *The Godfather.* Alice understands this, and exactly what it implies, completely."

"What is his insight?"

"He sees that we're all mad, that there is no truly sharp differentiation between abnormality and normality—it's simply a matter of semantics."

★   ★   ★

After Joyce leaves, in the company of Detroit's only hip rock critic, Alice has a whim to leave a fish head under Mark Volman's door, and within the instant he is tiptoeing barefoot into the hall with his dinner plate in hand. Ten seconds later there is a shattering crash. Mike Ramsey flies from his chair, tearing out the door and down the hall. There, two adolescent girls who've been hanging around the hotel all day have spotted Mr. C.

"Hey Alice," they call, "can we come and talk to you?" Their mother, who just got·off work in the downstairs coffee shop, is with them.

"I want your autograph, honey," the older one demands in the nasal accent of the upper Midwest. And the other one starts whining, too: "Give me your auto…"

Alice is drunk. He sees piranha fish all around him, nipping at him, ready to start tearing his arms. Suddenly, he faces them, spinning toward them on his heels like a gunslinger, and in one flashing instant pulls down his pants and his jockey shorts, swings it right out and wiggles it at them: the flaccid little beetle-nut pecker of the superstar.

Watergate: A Portfolio
by Ralph Steadman

MARCH 1971
(Slimy Enterprise To
Reelect the Pres.).
Night falls and
operation SLEEP
is inaugurated.
Plans are made
by a band of dedicated
fortune hunters
who firmly believe
that if vast quantities
of money
keep pouring in,
it must be right.

President Nixon
is asleep at the time....

MAY 1971 Nixon enjoys gentle support.
Muskie moves ahead
of front-runner Democrats.
Nixon sleeps....

SUMMER 1971 'The Pentagon Papers' published in 'The New York Times.'
Nixon woken for split second by trusted aide John Ehrlichman
(former Seven-Up, Sani-Flush salesman).
Nixon has coughing fit and relapse....

184

JANUARY 1972 Muskie ahead of Nixon in Harris Polls survey.
Shadowy figures work feverishly through the long night to check the rot.
FBI Chief Hoover dies, carrying his secrets to the grave....
(Wait a minute—no, he doesn't!)

FEBRUARY-MARCH 1972 Muskie stomped at New Hampshire.
Democrats get nervous as new man McGovern moves ahead.
Hunter Thompson gets noticed.

MAY 1972 Democratic headquarters
at Watergate hotel bugged.
Conventions, ballyhoo, landslide for Nixon, et cetera.

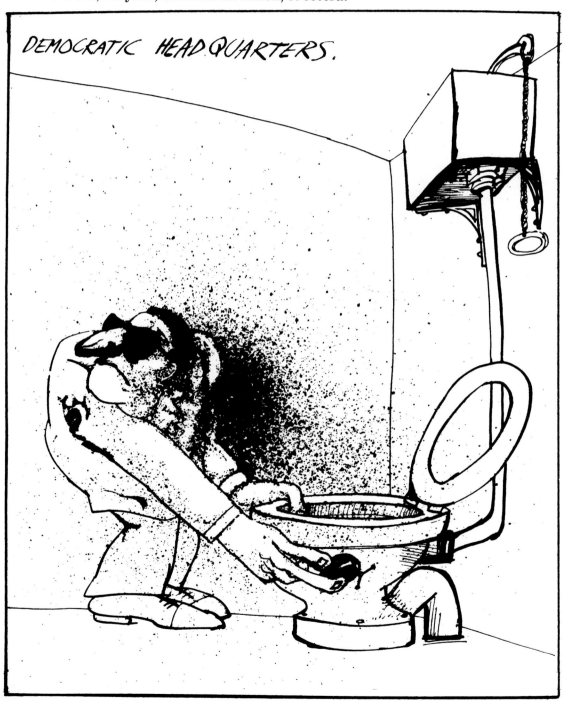

MARCH 1973 Nixon disturbed from sleep
by grumbling murmurs of White House cleaner Martha Mitchell.
Thinks it's time to say "Howdy Folks" to the nation on TV.

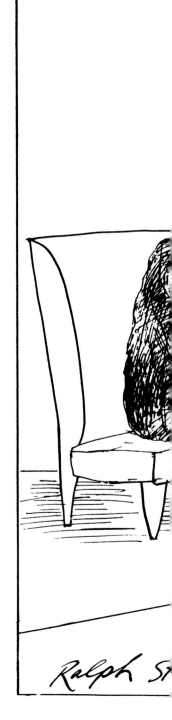

APRIL 1973 Nixon can't sleep.
Complains of domestic upsets. Says "Howdy Folks" on TV.
Consults Doctor, Sam Ervin.

Ask a Marine

by David Harris   July 1973

Ron Kovic was born on the Fourth of July, 1946, and spent much of his youth laying cap-pistol ambushes for the Long Island Railway trains that clanked in and out of Massapequa. In those days, the Fourth of July still meant something in the state of New York. Every year, the American Legion marched, and Ron's birthday shone through it all as a blessing, if not a small miracle, in the family. Being born like that wasn't something the Kovics took lightly. Ron's father had left the family farm to work for A&P, and Ron's Uncle Jim fought all over Korea with the United States Marine Corps. The two of them sat in the kitchen behind beers and talked. Uncle Jim said he'd seen good men splattered for the birthday his nephew had been given as a gift from God. Ron's dad nodded his head.

After overhearing a few of these family discussions, Ron had his heart set. He ran his body until it was a young bunch of ropes. He was Massapequa High's finest wrestler and the American Legion cannon's biggest fan. The sign by the road said, MARINE CORPS BUILDS MEN: BODY, MIND AND SPIRIT, and Ron knew it was true. No one in the neighborhood was surprised when Ron Kovic finished high school and joined up. He was meant for the marines. They were just in his stars.

When Ron signed his life over to the bald eagle, he went to Parris Island with all the others just like himself. His dream commenced with the drill instructor lining all eighty-two up on the parade deck. Their heads were shaved, and they wore their first khaki in wrinkles and lumps. The DI introduced himself and told them they were a bunch of maggots. He would address them as "the herd," and they would respond with "Aye, aye, sir." They would say "Aye, aye, sir" when they opened their mouths and "Aye, aye, sir" before they closed them. If they did everything he said and did it quicker than he could say it, then he would transform them from lowly maggots into something the U.S. Marine Corps could use. That was the DI's first promise. His second promise was to beat their asses if they didn't. Ron listened hard. The walls of

Ron Kovic
Photograph courtesy of Ron Kovic

his stomach grew hair, and he settled into his life. He was going to be a marine. For goddamned sure, he was going to be a marine.

The first thing the Marine Corps taught Ron Kovic was how to take a quick shit. It seemed strange, and Ron had always been a slow one to crap, but he learned like a beaver. He had to. The DI wouldn't have it any other way.

Private Kovic was much better at push-ups. They became his specialty. He was held up to the squad as the supreme push-up body. He did push-ups in his rack at night after the lights were out. It squeaked, and everybody who heard it thought Ron was crazy. Maybe he was. Ron wanted to be a marine bad. He shot expert with his rifle and learned to repeat the chain of command. Recruits were required to, every night before lights out.

"Chain of command," the DI screamed.

"Chain of command," they answered and began, "the President of the United States is Lyndon Baines Johnson…the Secretary of Defense is Robert S.…" The chain dangled down to "my junior drill instructor is" and stopped. The eighty-two shaved heads said it like a prayer to put themselves to sleep at night.

The prayer worked. Ron Kovic became Private Kovic and marched in the graduation parade. The Marine Corps gave him the same dress blue uniform he'd seen on the posters. When he wore it, Ron Kovic was a proud son of a bitch and wanted everybody to see.

After boot camp, Private Kovic was sent to Camp Lejeune and then on to Radio School at Norfolk Marine Barracks. When he was done in Norfolk, the private was a private first class and assigned to the Second Field Artillery. Then he heard about Vietnam. Right away he wanted to go. That's where the marines were fighting, and that's what a marine is supposed to do.

PFC Kovic requested immediate transfer to WESPAC, Vietnam. When the form asked why, he wrote, "to serve my country." It's so much later now that it's hard to believe, but back then Ron and everybody in the battalion office had no doubts. PFC Kovic got orders in ten days and flew from Camp Pendleton to Okinawa to Da Nang Airfield and into his dreams.

At Pendleton, everything was serious. They were there to get trimmed into final fighting shape, and the marines slogged their hardest for three weeks. The last day was the time for the last lesson. It was the one the sergeant called "survival." It started with a rabbit. The rabbit was fluffy and white and shook its feet when the sergeant held it by the ears. "If you want to come back," the sergeant said, "you better learn this one real good." With that, he pulled his trench knife and gutted the bunny between kicks. The sergeant flopped the carcass in his hands and skinned it. Finally he took the guts and threw them out into the crowd. The pieces dropped in pitter-patters all over their helmets.

By Okinawa, the approaching reality of Vietnam was rising in short hairs all over Ron Kovic's arms. He was ready. It was his job to make the world safe for Sparky the barber and Scadato's delicatessen, and he wanted to do it better than anybody else. He was Massapequa's boy going to war, and he planned to be Audie Murphy and John Wayne all rolled into 150 pounds. In an Okinawa bar, the waiting hero got a glimpse into his future.

It was crusted on the boots of the marines sitting in the silent corners. It was yellow mud, and someone told Ron they were "in country." They'd been "down south," and that meant Nam with a capital *N*. Their uniforms were faded, and they all had a gaze, just a stare off past the walls. Ron didn't look for long. He wanted to do it for himself before he watched it on somebody else.

The next day, Private First Class Kovic got the chance he'd waited eighteen years for. From Da Nang, Kovic was sent in a C-190 to Chu Lai and into the administration office of the Third Battalion, Seventh Marines. Pretty soon he was out with the 3/7, hustling along with the captain's radio on his back. It was the old model PRC-10, and it carried like bricks. It was also a target. When they went out after the VC, the antenna stood out like a flag over the elephant grass. The VC sighted in on it and popped. As hard as the gooks tried, Ron never got hit. He didn't let the scattered whizzes and pings up off the dry ground get past his ears. Kovic looked for the action and moved as quick as he'd been taught. He got the feel for it on his first patrol.

The action happened down by a river. Some VC suspects had been sighted and chased into mud caves along the bank. They wouldn't come out so the marines were busy killing them where they sat. As Ron and the captain approached, he could hear the gas canisters sizzling and the sounds of M-16s. When they'd finished, the marines pulled the bodies into a fishing net. The net was tied to the back of an amtrac and dragged along in the mud to the village. The caravan passed Ron, and he saw the bodies were covered with slop and frozen in weird shapes.

The captain was standing a few steps away. He had two silver bars on his helmet, blue eyes and a face that never quite got the fear out of it.

"How'd you like it?" he asked.

"I liked it, sir," Ron answered. "I really liked it."

The captain shook his head and walked off for the landing zone.

★   ★   ★

Ron Kovic really did like it. Just like he knew he would back in Massapequa. He liked it so much he went right for its middle. After three months, PFC Kovic was a lance corporal, and he volunteered for what was called Recon. It was April, and Sgt. Jimmy Howard and a platoon from Delta Company had been surrounded on Hill 488 west of Chu Lai. Only eight grunts got back, so the reconnaissance outfit had to be what was called "rebuilt." The sergeant asked for volunteers, and Ron was the first to step forward. He'd heard about Recon.

Recon were studs. They were jungle thugs and said they ate Cong for lunch. Every mean thing Ron had ever heard, he'd heard about Recon. They were the light of the West in an ocean of darkness. Ron was ready for it.

Kovic fit right in at Bravo Company, second platoon. He was the radio operator and artillery field officer. Ron and seventeen others got up on Monday morning before light and painted themselves to look like tree stumps. The chaplain said a prayer in front of the choppers, and they were gone. Off to a set of lines on a map, hovering twenty feet over the long grass and jumping out one by one. As long as somebody back in the office didn't fuck up and drop them into a VC base camp, they were all right. Once down, the second platoon started moving. They kept it that way for five days. All day they stalked along under the canopy and across streams. The leeches dropped out of trees and began to hang on to their bodies, but they didn't stop. Their job was to look. If they saw large outfits, they broke radio silence and called in. That was Ron's job.

"Crepe Myrtle," he'd say, "this is Crepe Myrtle three. Over."

"Crepe Myrtle three. This is Crepe Myrtle," the radio answered. "Over."

"Fire mission. Coordinates 353/271, azimuth 270 degrees. Target: VC in open. Shell VT. Fuse quick. Over."

"Roger, Crepe Myrtle three," the radio said.

Then the shells walked in, blowing hunks of flesh and jungle left and right. Ron talked into the box and moved the explosions in and out and up and down and up until the lieutenant was satisfied. As soon as he was, the second platoon got their asses in gear. At this point the platoon was called "compromised." That means someone knew they were there. It was a fair assumption to make, and Recon was trained to make one response. They headed for a prearranged landing zone and told the radio. At the spot marked exit, they hacked the brush down and went out in the H-34s. The H-34 was a smaller chopper, and it took four to extract the whole platoon. Ron went on twenty-two of these patrols, five days out and dead-bone, sore-assed tired when you get back. His last one was his closest.

While the platoon was squatted, waiting in the loading zone, someone lobbed a Chicom grenade into the clearing and opened up. Whoever it was was in the tree line, and the marines returned fire blind. The air was full of lead, but nobody in the second platoon was hit. The lieutenant, the medic and Ron were always the last ones to leave. They leaned up against each other and drew 360 degrees with automatic fire. When they jumped in and the chopper lifted, Ron could hear the pops follow them up. The door gunner was chopping back with his M-60, and so was everybody else. Ron emptied his clip into the jungle and laid back. Nobody'd been hit. He was in Recon for eight months and not a hit in his outfit. He laughed, ripped the leech off his face and flung it past the gunner and out the door. "Woooowhee," Corporal Kovic said inside his helmet, "I'm a Recon motherfucker. Too fast for a bullet to catch, too good a marine to die."

When he got home, the Marine Corps gave Ron Kovic a commendation medal with a combat V and a promotion to E-4.

Ron had a good taste in his mouth right up to the time he left. He was tied in a knot with the second platoon, and he loved them the same way he loved his gun. It was tight, hairy, silent work they did together, and it made them close. Charging up the runway, to the plane back to the States, Ron sailed home to Massapequa to show the neighborhood his yellow boots.

★   ★   ★

The C-130 took him to a different world, miles away. It got old quick, and Ron missed Recon. His memories burned at him. Ron Kovic was stationed with a Hawk Missile Battalion, and his buddies were getting cut up in the jungle. That was no good. It pushed at him and pushed at him until it finally pushed him over.

A copy of *The New York Daily News* did the trick. The front page was covered with four longhairs burning a flag in Central Park. That pissed Ron off so bad, he sat on his footlocker and cried for the first time since he'd become a marine. When he'd finished, E-4 Kovic went down to the administration office and requested a transfer back to Vietnam. Transfer was denied four days later. Going back had come to be thought of as insane, and the sergeant stared when Kovic came in fourteen more times to repeat his request. By then he was considered crazy enough to return.

His new orders made Ron Kovic a full sergeant with three stripes on his arm. He was sent to Pendleton and staging battalion right away. Sgt. Kovic wanted to serve his country, and he meant it. It was the right thing to do. He knew it was, as sure as he'd been born. He trained a platoon and marched them all on the plane. They sang the Marine Corps hymn going up the gangway, and some cried. It was late in 1966, and Ron Kovic was twenty years old. He was going to the Third Division in the DMZ. From what he'd heard, the DMZ was a different kind of place from the one he remembered.

It sure enough looked that way on the plane he took to Dong Ha. No one talked. The only sounds were the marines loading their ammo magazines. When speaking broke out, the dirty ones said there was lots of "arty" up there. The shellings came like the mail, and it rained. When the arty wasn't falling, the Third Marines were up against the North Vietnamese Army in the wet slop.

Ron's base was at the mouth of the Cuaviet River, past Gio Linh. The Third Marines' job was sweeping an area called Charlie four. Khe Sanh was across the river and a place they called the Rockpile on past that. The country was all sand and stumpy pine trees, and the marines worked mostly off amtracs: steel boxes with a cave inside big enough to carry a squad. The camp was dug into bunkers, eight sandbags high. At night, Ron led a scout team outside the perimeter and laid ambushes 1000 meters from the wire. They sat in the rain and watched for the North Vietnamese Army (NVA). During the day, the scouts slept. At least they tried to. They had to ask arty's permission first. When it was arty's turn to talk, nobody slept.

As soon as the marines heard the crack with the whistle on the end of it, every son of a bitch with any sense ran for the bunkers. The rounds came in right on top, each one sounding like it had a ticket for the hairs on your ass. Noses bled and ears ached. A lot of the Third Marines got to keeping rosaries close by, to use in the shelters. The worst Ron ever saw was when they took 150 hits. As soon as the arty lifted, Ron grabbed a medic bag and ran out on the compound. He saw his own tent first, and it was just shrapnel holes held together with canvas threads. Past that there was a crowd where Sgt. Bodigga's supply tent had once been. Sgt. Bodigga never left the camp. He handled paper in his tent and had a rug on his floor. Whatever you wanted, Sgt. Bodigga could get if you just gave him a day. Ron pushed through the ring of marines and found a hole. No tent. Just a hole. In the bottom was something that looked like five or six bodies. They were all powder-burned and torn up. Ron reached in to find IDs and could only find Bodigga's wallet. After looking again, Sgt. Kovic realized that Bodigga was all there was in the hole...all those pieces were just Bodigga. Ron stacked Sgt. Bodigga on a stretcher and cried. Over his shoulder, in the motor pool, someone was screaming.

"McCarthy," they screamed. "They got McCarthy. Those motherfuckers. Those rotten motherfuckers. They got McCarthy."

McCarthy was from Boston, and he had blue eyes. When he was laid out with the rest of the dead, stripped naked in front of the command bunker with his loose parts piled next to him, McCarthy's eyes were open and looked straight up into the rain.

Ron saw him there and wanted to kill somebody. He wanted to kill somebody and use them to paste McCarthy and Bodigga back together. It didn't turn out that simple. As soon as Ron Kovic got to wanting that way, something happened to make him feel just the opposite. It was a night patrol.

A lieutenant took Ron's detail out to search for sappers across the river. There was a village on the far bank, and the colonel was worried someone would dive in and put a mine to the marine boats. A hundred meters from the village, the patrol saw the light of a small fire. It was inside a hooch, and it wasn't supposed to be there. The village had been ordered to keep lights out. The platoon spread out along a paddy dike and watched. Word was passed to hold fire, and the lieutenant set off an illumination flare. Just as the flare lit, someone to Ron's left fucked up and let go. That shot set the whole line on fire for thirty seconds at full automatic. When they were finished, Ron and Leroy were sent up to check the hooch.

Inside the broken bamboo, there was an old man with the top of his head shot away. Two kids were on either side of him. One's foot just dangled. The other had taken a round in the stomach that came out his ass. The hooch's floor was covered in blood. When the platoon crossed the paddy and saw it, the marines melted into lumps. Some dropped their weapons, and only Leroy talked.

"Jesus Christ," he whined. "What'd we do. We've killed an old man and some kids."

The lieutenant yelled to form up in a 360, but Leroy kept moaning and no one else moved. The villagers started to come out of their huts and scream at the marines. It took the lieutenant five minutes to round the patrol into shape. After they called a chopper for the kid who was still breathing, the platoon went inside the wire. Sgt. Kovic lay in his bunker all night and wanted to give it up. He wanted the referee to blow the whistle and call time out until he'd had a chance to think it over.

But wars don't work that way. Ron reported to the colonel in the morning and asked to be taken off patrols. The colonel said no. Instead, the platoon got a week in camp, and Sgt. Kovic was ordered to get his shit together and act like a marine.

★   ★   ★

The platoon didn't go back into action until January 20th. When they did, it was in the afternoon. January 20th started late but turned into a big day, about as big a day as there will ever be in the life of Sgt. Ron Kovic. It was a day that made all the ones after it very different from the ones that went before.

Word was that the NVA had the South Vietnamese Popular Forces pinned down by the village. Ron volunteered his men to take the point and lead the company's sweep. Another company was moving north from the river bank through the village graveyard. The platoon spread out and headed toward the tree line 100 meters off. Ron was on the right with just one man further over than himself. Everyone was out in the open when January 20th exploded. Ron couldn't forget it now if he wanted to.

"The people on the amtracs got hit first" is the way he remembers it. "I heard the pop...pop...pop as the mortars left their tubes and the crashing as they hit around the tracks. Then rounds started cracking around us. I couldn't tell if they were coming from the village or the tree line, so I fired both places. I was completely out in the open.

"All we could do was take ground and return fire. After a little bit, I heard a loud crack right next to me, and my whole leg went numb. A .30 caliber bullet had gone in the front of my foot and come out the heel. It took a piece out the size of a silver dollar. My foot was all smashed. I stayed standing as long as I could, but then it began to feel like it was on fire. I went to a prone position and kept using my rifle until it jammed from the sand.

"When I couldn't get a round into the chamber, I decided to stand and see where the rest of my platoon was. I slammed the rifle down and pushed myself up with it. Just as I got my arms straight, I heard a huge crack next to my ear. It was like getting hit with an express train. My whole body started vibrating. Another .30 caliber bullet had hit my right shoulder, passed through my lung and severed my spinal cord into two pieces. My whole body seemed to have left me. I felt like I was somewhere up in the air.

"I closed my eyes for just a second, then I started to breathe. My lung was collapsed so I just took little breaths. Slow little sucks. All I could think was that I didn't want to die. I couldn't think of nothin' else. I waited to die. I mean, I just waited for it all to black out, for all the things that are supposed to happen when you die. I couldn't believe what was going on. Where was my body? I must've been hit with a mortar. That was it, a mortar. It had ground up everything below my chest.

"Then I moved my hands behind me, and I felt legs. I felt legs, but they didn't feel back. They were my legs. There was something wrong, but I couldn't explain it. My body was there, but I couldn't feel it. Then I got real excited. It was still there. I wasn't going to bleed to death. My body was still there.

"The next thing I knew, Leroy was over me. He was bandaging my shoulder.

"'I can't feel my body,' I said.

"'It's all right, Sarge,' he said. 'You're gonna be all right. Pretty soon you'll be back in the States with all the broads.'

"When he got the bandage on, he split toward the tree line with rounds crackling all around him.

"After Leroy, I heard Palmer calling me from off to my left. 'Hey Sarge,' he said. 'We got to get the hell out of here.'

"'I can't move my legs,' I screamed.

"'Come on, Sarge,' Palmer kept yelling. 'Let's go. Let's get outta here.'

"'I can't feel my body,' I said. Then I heard a crack, and Palmer screamed.

"'Are you hit?' I yelled.

"Palmer yelled back. 'They shot my finger off. They shot my goddamned finger off.' After that I guess he left. I didn't hear him no more.

"I lay there for what seemed like hours. Once, somebody ran up in back of me. 'Hey,' he said. 'Hey, Sarge, you all right?' Then I heard another crack, and he seemed to fall on the back of me. I couldn't feel it, but I heard. Someone from my left yelled, 'He's dead, Sarge. They shot him through the heart.' He was a marine from the company who'd run all the way up. I yelled for everybody to stop coming. I don't know if they heard, but I yelled. I was being used as bait. Other than that, I felt nothing. I just wanted to live. I tried to calm myself. I felt cheated. Twenty fucking years old, and they were taking my life away from me.

"Then a black man came running up. He grabbed me and threw me over his shoulder. He started dragging me back. He was a big black man. Big black arms. Big black hands. All I can remember is staring up at the sky and the sky sort of spinning and jumping. I could just feel the top of my body. I felt the sun in my face and him picking me up and throwing me down. All the time he was yelling, 'You motherfuckers! Fuckers. Fuckers. Goddamned motherfuckers!' And me screaming the same thing. 'Motherfuckers! Motherfuckers!'

"Finally he threw me one last time in a hole, and a corpsman jumped in on my chest. He'd been running all over, and he was out of his head. I told him I felt I'd made it so far, and that was the roughest part. I told him I was gonna live."

By the next morning Sgt. Kovic had been given the last rites of the Catholic Church and gone on the operating table. He was in the intensive care ward at Marble Mountain in Da Nang. He'd been brought there by choppers, with tubes in his lungs and IVs all over his body.

Living meant doing everything right, so Sgt. Kovic listed his dos and don'ts on a Red Cross pad. He was going to be the perfect patient who recovers miraculously. The morphine helped. He got his syringe every 120 minutes. When he was waiting for his shot, Ron Kovic noticed that he couldn't feel his dick anymore. All day long, he explored his floppy body and checked to see if it had come back while he was asleep. It never did.

When the doctors asked Ron how he felt, he said he felt great. Good enough to leave intensive care anyway. In desperation, Sgt. Kovic finally stuck his thermometer in an ice bucket, and the reading was low enough to go to Japan.

Before the plane left Marble Mountain, a general came down to the ward, distributing Purple Hearts, bed by bed. The general's shoes were shined, and he had a private with him. The private carried a Polaroid camera and took pictures the men could send home to their families.

Ron Kovic lay three days in Yokosuka Naval Hospital with his catheter and his striker frame, and then he demanded a wheelchair. "I'm ready," he said. The doctors thought it was early, but Ron insisted. They brought the chair and lifted Ron into it. For half an hour he tried the chair. At the end of it, Sgt. Kovic puked all over himself and passed out. When he recovered, Ron decided to wait on the chair until he reached the States.

In the meantime, he'd concentrate. Ron kept a little chart of his progress each day. He swore to the doctors he was going to walk out. "If it's the last thing I do," is the way he said it. "Right out the fucking door." The doctors said that wasn't possible, but Ron wouldn't listen. He had to have something to want, and that was it.

When he wasn't wanting, Sgt. Kovic watched. There was pain all around him, but Ron knew it would pass. He figured out that most of the other lumps under the covers would heal. The pain would become a memory and then they'd leave, tall and strong again and whole. But he wouldn't. His wound couldn't. His shoulder would close up, and so would his foot, but that was all. The life in Sgt. Kovic's head would never touch his feet again.

One day, when he was lying back watching, the general brought a tour through the hospital. Bart Starr of the Green Bay Packers visited Ron's ward. He stood at the end of the bed.

"How's the war going?" the quarterback asked.

"Shitty," Ron said. "Pretty shitty."

★　　　　★　　　　★

After a while, the war had almost disappeared. The radio said everybody'd be home soon, and hospitals were just about the only thing Ron remembered. There was one in Anchorage, another in Virginia, one in New York State and then another that looked out on New Jersey. The last one was the Kingsbridge Veterans' Administration. It was summer by then, and Ron stayed at the Kingsbridge hospital eleven months the first time and then again for six more.

Sgt. Kovic now belonged to the Veterans' Administration. The marines discharged him with a Bronze Star and wished him well. The VA's job was to retrain certain kinds of ex-soldiers, and Sgt. Kovic was 100 percent retired. The first thing the VA tried to teach him was how to shit slowly, once every three days.

That's when they gave the enemas, every third day. Other than that you had to shit in your bed and lay on it. The enemas started at five in the morning. Tommy the Enema Man came by with his tube and dangled it under their noses. When everyone was awake, they each got a striker frame. Tommy and his helper rolled them all, twenty-four para- and quadraplegics, half the ward, into what was called the Blue Room. When it was full, the two white coats pumped all the stomachs up with soapy water. All twenty-four lay in there with their withered bodies and listened to their bowels hit the buckets like cow flop. When it was done, Tommy wiped each of their asses and rolled them into the shower.

Ron called it the car wash. The attendant ran a thin white strip of Phisohex down the middle of Ron's body and then hosed it off. When they were short-handed, the attendant sometimes had to leave in the middle of the scrub. The second time Ron got washed, he lay in the Kingsbridge shower for an hour waiting for the attendant to come back. All Ron did was try not to scream. He learned to lie on the tile and watch his body that wouldn't move and had started to shrivel.

Every third day Ron wanted to scream, and he never did. After a couple of months, the screams didn't even bother to cross his mind. Ron lay there and felt he'd been used up and thrown away, and no one was treating him like the marine he'd gone out there and been.

★   ★   ★

The more he looked around the ward, the more Ron felt it. C-3 was the sign over the door, and it was one big mirror. He saw his friends, and there he was. Propped up and flopped over, they weren't much to look at.

Ron noticed Mark more than anybody else. Mark was a nineteen-year-old head. He'd been a six-foot marine once. But then his truck hit a mine on the way to Khe Sanh, and Mark went out the window. He was paralyzed from the neck down. Mark got around by pushing his chin on an electric button that made the wheels on his chair spin. It was Mark who taught Ron how to fight the rats.

The rats were smallish, brown and came out at night. Just past 2:00 a.m., one crawled up on Mark's chest. He screamed. Then he screamed again. No one came. He screamed for three hours until an aide arrived and told Mark he must be drunk. From then on, Mark got Ron to lob his dinner rolls behind the radiator. That kept the rats eating all night and off their chests while Mark and Ron talked. Mark had been a high-school football player and asked Ron to look at the team picture and pick him out. Mark was proud and didn't take to being a loose sack of flesh very easily. He fought it as hard as he could.

He taught the rest of them to fight it too. Mark led the revolt in C-3. It started when the hospital staff canceled the paraplegics' party privileges. The VA said too many people were getting drunk. Mark was pissed as soon as he heard.

"I'm going to that fucking office," he said, and everybody agreed and got into a line behind him: all the paras and all the quads, rolling themselves however they were able and heading for the part of Kingsbridge that had carpets. There were some things they wanted to say. It was harder the closer they got to the front. The rugs were miring up around the wheels of Ron's chair like a Chrysler in the mud. A fat man in a blue suit came out into the hall and let them know where they sat.

"The president is doing everything he can to help you boys," he said. "All of us are doing everything we can."

"Do you think you could get the president to come in here and change my sheets?" one of the chairs asked.

The fat man didn't laugh. Ron asked him when was the last time he'd been on C-3. The fat man in the blue suit couldn't remember, but he was sure it was recently.

C-3 listened for a while and then went back up the hall to sleep. Mark couldn't. He lay up all night and listened to his plastic piss bag slop over onto the floor, and he hated it. He kept hating it until the day he would talk his friend in Chicago into sticking a needle through his vein. Mark would die with his eyes full of heroin and his body full of empty space. But that was much later, after Ron left the VA for the first time.

★   ★   ★

When Ron reached the doors, he left just the way he'd promised back in Japan. He walked. It wasn't like he'd pictured it, but it sure wasn't in a chair. He trained every day with braces until he could move on crutches and drag his strapped-up legs along. He scraped out the door to his mom and dad, and he felt proud. Every time he got up on his crutches, he felt that way. To Ron Kovic, he was tall and pretty, even if his spine did have a new bend to it. Ron walked like that all over the back yard in Massapequa. The doctors said he did it too much. He finally broke his femur when he was out on a walk and had to return to Kingsbridge.

This time there was an operation. When he got off the table, his right leg had a plate in it and was shorter than the other. The leg turned in, too, and wouldn't fit in his braces anymore. Ron screamed at the doctors.

"You ruined it," he said. "Now I can't walk anymore. I'll never get to stand up."

"It's all right," the doctors said. "You couldn't really walk anyway."

The second time Ron left Kingsbridge, he was pissed. He remembers it today, and he still gets angry. His jaw freezes up, and he talks louder than he means to. "It was like I'd swallowed a lie," he explains, "and then they rubbed my face in it. America made me. They made me, and I gave them everything I could give, and then

I wasn't good enough to treat like a man. I didn't want to be a good patient anymore. I was proud, and they wouldn't even let on I was still alive. I was something for a closet and a budget cut. I didn't feel lucky anymore. I was gonna live, and I knew how I was gonna live. I was living with a body that was already dead. That had to be worth something, but it wasn't. All it could get me was a seat out by the pigeons and the old men from World War II."

After a while, Ron couldn't sit on his anger any more. He moved to Los Angeles and called the office of Vietnam Veterans Against the War. While he dialed, he thought about Mark and a guy named Willie.

Willie was just a head too. To listen to Willie you had to put a cork in his throat and your ears next to his lips. As Ron was leaving Kingsbridge, Willie stopped him at his bed. Ron put the cork in and listened.

"Don't let them do it to anybody else," Willie said.

When the phone answered, Ron said he wanted to join and do anything he could to stop the war. Ron meant it. He manned tables and spoke at high schools. He told them how he'd been the Massapequa flash and the push-up body. He told them how he'd sung about the "halls of Montezuma" and the "shores of Tripoli" and how it was a lie. He told whoever would listen and half those who wouldn't.

Ron felt better than he'd felt in a long time. He liked the folks, like he was one of them. He didn't feel like a freak, and he wondered why it had taken so long for him to find out. His new life gave Ron a chance to meet his country again. One such meeting on Wilshire Boulevard drove the last of the bald eagle from Ron Kovic's mind. It happened in front of the headquarters for Richard Nixon's reelection.

The picket started at 11:00 a.m., and by noon there was quite a crowd and almost as many cops. And these weren't any run-of-the-mill-bust-a-drunk-on-a-street-corner cops. It was the L.A.P.D., and anybody west of Barstow knows the L.A.P.D. doesn't take no for an answer.

The ones Ron met were young, undercover and tried special hard. They moved in the crowd and took notes. Ron was up the block with a line of people who had wheeled over the cross street and blocked traffic. The blue line of police moved their way, and they scattered back to the sidewalk. As soon as the cops leaned to the cross street, the people on Wilshire did the same thing, and the police scurried back. It didn't take long for the L.A.P.D. to tire of the game. The captain gave an order to disperse, and the people decided to take it. The blue men had their clubs out and their goggles on: two very bad signs. The decision was made to go back to McArthur Park. Ron wheeled the word up to the cops.

"We're leaving," he said. "We're going to obey the order to disperse."

With that, the line of signs made its own slow way back down the boulevard. Ron stayed at the back, making sure everybody got out all right. It was then that he

met the L.A.P.D. up so close there was no way to mistake what he saw. The two long-haired ones came up from his back. The first one grabbed Ron's chair. The second said, "You're under arrest," and started banging the handcuffs on Ron's wrists.

"What are you doing?" Ron said. "We're leaving."

The back of the crowd saw what was happening and ran to help. That set off a whistle, and the blue line charged into a big circle with Ron inside. He was dumped out of his chair and onto the street. All Ron could think to do was shout.

"I'm a Vietnam veteran," he yelled. "I fought in the DMZ. I'm paralyzed. Don't you know what you're doing?"

The L.A.P.D. didn't shout back. The red-haired one pulled Ron's hands behind his back and locked them. Then the blue circle made a wedge and headed across the street with Ron in tow. A cop had each shoulder, and Ron's head bobbed up and down on the asphalt. The people who tried to help said they saw the police beat Ron's body with their sticks, but Ron didn't feel it. He felt the curb when his forehead hit it, and then all of a sudden he felt lifted up and into a squad car. They propped him up in the front seat. He immediately flopped over onto the dashboard.

"I have no stomach muscles," he panted. "With my hands in back of me, I can't sit up. I can hardly breathe, either." Ron had to talk in a grunt.

The cop shoved him up straight. "Sit up," he said.

Ron flopped back over. "I'm a veteran," he wheezed. "Don't you see what you're doing to me? I'm paralyzed."

"Sit up," the cop said and rammed Ron against the Ford's seat. Ron flopped back. "I said sit up you commie son of a bitch." The L.A.P.D. bounced Ron back and forth all the way to the station. At the booking desk, the cop asked the turnkey where to put the crippled one.

"Take him up on the roof and throw him off," the turnkey said.

They didn't. But it wasn't because they didn't want to. When Ron left five days later, the turnkey looked at him from behind his jowls.

"They shoulda let you die over there," he said. "You shoulda died and never come back."

★   ★   ★

Ron still had some people he wanted to see. All the vets did. That's why they went to Miami. They went in caravans and called it the Last Patrol. They were going to expose once and for all the lie of what they had fought for. They rolled into Miami and met lines of buses, tear gas and helmets. They came to see Richard Nixon, but only a few got the chance. Ron was one of that few.

It happened on the night the president came up from Key Biscayne to accept his nomination. Ron had tickets that got him into the lobby. A reporter pushed him through the first door, and his own wheely sprint brought him up to the back of the delegates. Then the security guard stepped up.

"You'll have to leave," he said.

"I've got a right to be here," Ron said. "I fought in Vietnam for it."

Nobody wanted to touch him with the TV cameras on, so the guards just tried to block him from sight. Ron shouted around them to the delegates. They had signs that said FOUR MORE YEARS, and they didn't really want to hear about it.

"You want to see your war?" Ron yelled. "Here it is. I'm your war in a package. I'm here. I'm real."

The nearby Republicans pretended not to notice. Ron felt stymied. He was blocked off. Fortunately, the word from Muller reached Ron through another vet. "Come on back," the vet said. "Muller's got passes for you, a place down front on the side."

Ron went back around and found who he was looking for. They were Bob Muller and Bill Wyman. Lieutenant Bob Muller had been leading a South Vietnamese unit when he took a bullet through his chest and spine. Bill Wyman's legs had been blown off at the knees by a mine. Ron Kovic, Bob Muller and Bill Wyman lined up wheel to wheel and waited for the president. He was on next. After Richard Nixon stepped into the footlights and the clapping died down, the three vets took deep breaths. With the first pause they shouted, "Stop the bombing. Stop the war."

That made the Republicans behind the chairs stare, but Richard Nixon didn't miss a step. The next time he paused, they did the same thing. Now the crowd around them was surly and embarrassed. The delegates began to chant, "Four more years!" to drown the three chairs out. They screamed and clapped, and one fat man with a red face spit on Ron's neck. Finally, the Secret Service came and made a ring around the vets. Moving in a circle, they carried the three chairs backward and formed a wall to screen out the cameras. Ron and Bob and Bill were taken to the rear entrance and put out. The security guard chained the door behind them, and they were left in the parking lot. When no one came to bust them, the three headed for the day's rally site.

Flamingo Park was empty when the three chairs wheeled into it. The cops had run everyone off. If that happened, the vets had planned to meet out at the municipal dump. Ron and Bob and Bill found everyone else waiting there. It was midnight, and the men of Chu Lai and Dong Ha and the Ai Shau Valley sat in the garbage and tried to figure out who was still in jail. The dump smelled of old fish and pepper gas, and all of them felt like they'd been there before.

★   ★   ★

If you want to find Ron Kovic, just go to the VVAW office in Los Angeles: take the Arlington off ramp from the Santa Monica Freeway and head for Pico Boulevard. The letters are painted on their storefront. I went in and found him. He looked up from writing a leaflet, and I asked him how he felt.

"In the last five years," he said, "I've felt tremendous pain and bitterness. I felt a closeness to no one but myself and my chair. I felt an anger I could never describe. I also felt a humility and compassion I could never explain. It was a tremendous sense of loss and a tremendous sense of gain. I felt I had lost a great portion of my body, but I'd gained a good deal of my soul. It was like I had to trade the one for the other."

Then I asked what he was going to do now that the war was over.

He laughed. "The war's not over," he said. "The war is between those who catch hell and those who give it out. Just 'cause it's not on TV don't mean they stopped giving it out. Ask somebody who's fought one. They'll tell you a war don't end just because somebody says so. A war isn't over until you don't have to live with it anymore."

For a lot of us that's going to be a long old time. Like Ron Kovic. Sometimes when he sits up at night, he can hear the war rumbling down in his legs. It makes a sound like the Long Island Railway flashing through Massapequa and heading west.

Funky Chic

by Tom Wolfe • January 1974

By October of 1969, Funky Chic was flying through London like an infected bat, which is to say silently, blindly, insanely and at night, fangs afoam...but with an infallible aim for the main vein...much like the Sideburns Fairy, who had been cruising about the city since 1966, visiting young groovies in their sleep and causing them to awake with hair running down their jawbones. Funky Chic, as I say.... So it happened that one night in a club called Arethusa, a favorite spot of the London *bon ton*, I witnessed the following. A man comes running into the gent's and squares off in front of a mirror, removes his tie and stuffs it into a pocket of his leather coat, jerks open the top four buttons of his shirt, shoves his fingers in under the hair on top of his head and starts thrashing and tousling it into a ferocious disarray, steps back and appraises, turns his head this way and that, pulls his shirt open a little wider to let the hair on his chest sprout out, and then, seeing that everything is just so, heads in toward the dining room for the main event. This dining room is a terrific place. It has just been done over in the white plaster arches and cylindrical lamps of the smart restaurant decor of that time known as Expense-Chit Trattoria. In the grand salon only, the waiters wear white shirts and black ties. The clientele sit there roaring and gurgling and flashing fireproof grins in a rout of leather jerkins, Hindu tunics, buckskin skirts, deer-slayer boots, dueling shirts, bandanas knotted at the Adam's apple, love beads dangling to the belly, turtlenecks reaching up to meet the mutton chops at midjowl, Indian blouses worn thin and raggy to reveal the jutting nipples and crimson aureolae underneath...The place looks like some grand luxe dining room on the Mediterranean unaccountably overrun by mob-scene scruffs from out of *Northwest Passage, The Informer, Gunga Din* and *Bitter Rice*. What I was gazing upon was in fact the full fashion splendor of London's *jeunesse dorée*, which by 1969, of course, included everyone under the age of sixty-seven with a taste for the high life.

Funky Chic came skipping and screaming into the United States the following year in the form of such marvelous figures as the Debutante in Blue Jeans. She was to be found on the fashion pages in every city of any size in the country. There she is in the photograph...wearing her blue jeans and her blue work shirt, open to the sternum, with her long pre-Raphaelite hair parted on top of the skull, uncoiffed but recently washed and blown dry with a Continental Pro Style dryer (the word-of-mouth that year said the Continental gave her more "body")...and she is telling her interviewer:

"We're not having any 'coming-out balls' this year or any 'deb parties' or any of that. We're fed up with doing all the same old things, which are so useless, and seeing the same old faces and dancing to so-called 'society bands' while a lot of old ladies in orange-juice-colored dresses stand around the edges talking to our parents.

We're tired of cotillions and hunt cups and weekends. You want to know what I did last weekend? I spent last weekend at the day-care center, looking after the most beautiful black children ... and learning from them!"

Or, as a well-known, full-grown socialite, Amanda Burden, said at that time: "The sophistication of the baby blacks has made me rethink my attitudes." Whereupon she described herself as "antifashion."

Antifashion! Terrific. Right away antifashion itself became the most raving fashion imaginable ... also known as Funky Chic. Everybody had sworn off fashion, but somehow nobody moved to Cincinnati to work among the poor. Instead, everyone stayed put and imported the poor to the fashion pages. That's the way it happened! For it was in that same year, 1970, that Funky Chic evolved into its most exquisite manifestation, namely Radical Chic, which I have had occasion to describe elsewhere ... socialites began to give parties for the Black Panthers (to name but one of many groups) at their homes, from Park Avenue to Croton-on-Hudson. Which is to say, they began to bring exotic revolutionaries into their living rooms and thereby achieved the ultimate in Funky Chic interior decoration: live black bodies.

It was at this point that fashion, on the one hand, and politics, on the other, began to interlock in a most puzzling way. The fashion of Radical Chic swept not only socialites but also intellectuals and cultivated persons of every sort in the years from 1968 to 1970. The situation began to contradict the conventional assumption of historians, which is that fashion is but the embroidery of history, if that. It is true that Radical Chic would have never become a fashion if certain political ideas and emotions had not already been in the air. But once Radical Chic became fashionable, it took on its own momentum. It had the power to create political change on its own, i.e., many influential people who had been generally apolitical began to express support for groups like the Panthers.

The conventional wisdom is that fashion is some sort of storefront that one chooses, honestly or deceptively, to place between the outside world and his "real self." But there is a counter-notion, namely, that every person's "real self," his psyche, his soul, is largely the product of fashion and other outside influences on his status. Such has been the suggestion of the stray figure here and there; the German sociologist Rene Konig, for example, or the Spanish biologist Jose M.R. Delgado. This is not a notion that is likely to get a very charitable reception just now, among scholars or readers generally. If the Bourbon Louises may be said to have lived in the Age of Absolutism, we now live in the Age of Egalitarianism (with the emphasis on the *ism,* if one need edit). Even people who lend themselves to the fashion pages, the people whose faces run through *Vogue, Bazaar, Harper's Bazaar* and *Town and Country* like a bolt of crisp white-glazed chintz, are not going to be caught out today talking about fashion in terms of being fashionable. They talk instead of ease, comfort, convenience, practicality, simplicity and, occasionally, fun and gaiety (for others to share). Right now I am looking at a page of photographs in *Bazaar* of a woman named Venetia Barker, a young English matron whose husband owns a stable of horses and a fleet of helicopters. She tells how two or three times a week she flies her own canary-yellow helicopter from their country home in Wiltshire to their townhouse in London in order to go antique hunting. Twice a week she flies it to Worcestershire to go horseback riding in the fox hunts. She speaks of the helicopter as a time-saving convenience, however, and of fox hunting in terms of mental hygiene: two days a week with horse and hound beats the psychiatrist any time in coping with the pressures of a busy modern life. "During the day," she says, "I wear what's most practical," items such as a Regency coachman's cape with three huge layers of flapping red overlaps about the shoulders plus leather pants by Foale and Tuffin of London. At night she changes "into something quite simple," which turns out to be outfits such as a black tunic gown by the good Madame Gres, slashed on the sides to reveal a floor-length scarlet slip and cross-laced black drawstrings, and surmounted at the bosom by a filigree diamond necklace with an emerald pendant the size of a Brazil nut. Convenience, health, practicality, simplicity…none of which means that the woman is being hypocritical or even cagey. She is merely observing a convention, a fashion taboo that is common to people at every level of income and status today.

The curious thing is that the same taboo makes fashion an even touchier subject for scholars. Louis Auchincloss once observed that academic writers seem to find the courage to write about society, in the sense of fashionable society, only from a great distance—either from across an ocean or across a gulf of a century or more in time, and preferably both. "Why can we find a hundred professors eager to explore the subtleties of the court of the Empress Theodora," he asks, "and not one to plumb the depths of a party given by Perle Mesta?" He also remarked, quite aptly, I would say, that nothing offers a more revealing insight into capitalism than the social life of Newport in the 1890s—"a crazy patchwork of borrowed values financed on a scale that would have made the Sun King stare"—and to this day the one serious study of it is by a Frenchman.

Auchincloss is a novelist, of course, and ever since the time of Richardson and Fielding, some 230 years ago, novelists have been drawn to fashion as an essential ingredient of realistic narration. This was out of sheer instinct and not theory. Early in the game they seemed to sense that fashion is a code, a symbolic vocabulary that offers a subrational but instant and very brilliant illumination of the characters of individuals and even entire periods, especially periods of great turmoil. And yet novelists who have dwelled on fashion in just this way have usually been regarded in their own time as lightweights— "trivial" has been the going word—scarcely even literary artists, in fact; even those who eventually have been judged to be literary giants of their eras. Dr. Johnson dismissed Fielding as minor, trivial, unserious to the the very end. He could not understand how any serious writer could wallow so contentedly in the manners and mores, the everyday habits, of so many rascals, high and low. Saint-Beuve continually compared Balzac to people like antique dealers, sellers of women's clothes and—this was one of his favorites—the sort of down-at-the-heel petty bourgeois doctors who make house calls and become neighborhood gossips. Balzac was not regarded as a major writer until after his death; he was not even invited to join the French Academy.

In our own time I don't have the slightest doubt but that Evelyn Waugh will eventually stand as England's only major novelist of the twentieth century (oh, all right, him and Lawrence). But during the last decade of his life his stock sank very low; so low, in fact, that he seemed finally to downgrade himself, judging by the opening chapter of *The Ordeal of Gilbert Pinfold.* In his writing he immersed so deeply in the fashion of his times that many critics regarded him as a snob first and an artist second. (I recall one English reviewer who was furious because Waugh had the hero of his final trilogy, Guy Crouchback, describe his father's funeral mainly in terms of how correctly everyone had dressed for the event despite the fact that it was wartime and the servants were out in the country.) John O'Hara's reputation has undergone a similar deflation over the past fifteen years. As for Louis Auchincloss—more than once he has set in motion characters who pursue the lure of Wall Street and Wealth and Family and Men's Club in the most relentless manner—only to see critics complain that the character is not believable: People don't conduct their lives in that way anymore. Auchincloss notes with some annoyance that they are saying "don't" when what they mean is "shouldn't."

Auchincloss identifies the moral objection that underlies the taboo as follows. At the very core of fashionable society exists a monstrous vulgarity: "The habit of judging human beings by standards having no necessary relation to their character." To be found dwelling upon this vulgarity, absorbed in it, is like being found watching a suck 'n' fuck movie. It is no use telling people you were merely there as a detached observer in the age of *Deep Throat*; in the case of fashion, too, the grubbiness rubs off all the same, upon scholars, no less than novelists, socialites and gossip columnists. Unlike a Balzac or a Gogol, the scholar seldom treats fashion as an essential ingredient of history. Instead, he treats it as comic relief, usually set apart from the narrative in an archly written chapter with a coy title such as "Bumpkins and Brummels: From Country Fair to Mayfair."

Today, in the age of Funky Chic Égalité, fashion is a much more devious, sly and convoluted business than anything that was ever dreamed of at Versailles. At Versailles, where Louis XIV was installed in suites full of silver furniture (later melted down to finance a war), one could scarcely be *too* obvious. Versailles was, above all, the City of the Rich. Hundreds of well-to-do or upward-hustling families had quarters there. The only proper way to move about the place was in sedan chairs borne by hackmen with straining trapeziuses. Anytime a notable of high social wattage gave a party, there would be a sedan-chair traffic jam of a half hour or more outside his entry way as the true and original *jeunesse dorée,* in actual golden threads and golden slippers, waited to make the proper drop-dead entrance.

One has only to compare such a scene with any involving the golden youth of our own day. I recommend to anyone interested in the subject, the long block, or concourse, known as Broadway in New Haven, Connecticut, where Elm Street, York Street, Whalley and Dixwell Avenues come together. This is near the heart of Yale University. Twenty years ago, at Elm and York, there was a concentration of men's custom-tailoring shops that seemed to outnumber all the tailors on Fifth Avenue and 57th Street put together. They were jammed in like pearls in a box. Yale was, after all, the place where the *jeunesse dorée* of America were being groomed, in every sense of the word, to inherit the world; the world, of course, being Wall Street and Madison Avenue. Five out of every seven Yale undergraduates could tell whether the button-down Oxford-cloth shirt you had on was from Fenn-Feinstein, J. Press or Brooks Brothers from a single glance at your shirt front—Fenn-Feinstein: plain breast pocket; J. Press: breast pocket with buttoned flap; Brooks Brothers: no breast pocket at all. Today J. Press is still on the case, but others of the heavenly host are shipping out. Today, a sane businessman would sooner open a souvlaki takeout counter at Elm and York than a tailor shop, for reasons any fool could see. On the other side of the grand concourse, lollygagging up against Brooks Health and Beauty Aids, Whitlock's and the Yale Co-op, are the new Sons of Eli. They are from the same families as before, averaging about $37,500 gross income per annum among the scholarship students. But there is nobody out there checking out breast pockets or jacket vents or any of the rest of it. The unvarying style at Yale today is best described as Late Army Surplus. Broadway Army & Navy enters Heaven! Sons in Levis, break through that line! That is the sign we hail! Visible at Elm and York today are more olive-green ponchos, clodhoppers and parachute boots, more leaky-dye blue turtlenecks, pea jackets, ski hats, long-distance trucker warms, sheepherder's coats, fisherman's slickers, down-home tenant-farmer bib overalls, coal-stoker strap undershirts, fringed cowpoke jerkins, strike-ball blue workshirts, lumberjack plaids, forest ranger mackinaws, Australian bushrider mackintoshes, Cong saddles, bike

leathers and more jeans, jeans, jeans, jeans, jeans. More prole gear of every description than you ever saw or read of in a hundred novels by Jack London, Jack Conroy, Maxim Gorky, Clara Weatherwax and any who came before or after.

Of course, this happens to be precisely what America's most favored young men are wearing at every other major college in the country, so that you scarcely detect the significance of it all until you look down to the opposite end of the concourse, to the north, where Dixwell Avenue comes in. Dixwell Avenue is the main drag of one of New Haven's black slums. There, on any likely corner, one can see congregations of young men the same age as the Yales but... from the bottom end of the great greased pole of life, as it were, from families whose gross incomes no one but the eligibility worker ever bothered to tote up. All the young aces and dudes are out there lollygagging around the front of the Monterey Club, wearing their two-tone patent Pyramids with the five-inch heels that swell out at the bottom to match the Pierre Chareau Art Deco plaid bell-bottom baggies they have on with the three-inch deep elephant cuffs tapering upward toward that "spray-can fit" in the seat, as it is known, and the peg-top waistband with self-covered buttons and the beagle-collar pattern-on-pattern Walt Frazier shirt, all of it surmounted by the mid-length leather piece with the welted waist-seam and the Prince Albert pockets and the black pimpmobile hat with the four-inch turn-down brim and the six-inch pop-up crown with the golden chain-belt hatband... and all of them, every ace, every dude, out there just *getting over* in the baddest possible way, come to play and dressed to slay... so that somehow the sons of the slums have become the Brummels and Gentlemen of Leisure, the true fashion plates of 1973, and the Sons of Eli dress like the working class of 1934...

...a style note which I mention not merely for the sake of irony. Just as Radical Chic was a social fashion that ended up having a political impact, so did Funky Chic. Radical Chic helped various Left causes. Funky Chic hurt them. So far as I know, no one has ever recorded the disruption that Funky Chic caused within the New Left. (Remember the New Left?) In 1968, 1969 and 1970 the term *counterculture* actually meant something. In those wild spitting hot-bacon days on the campus, counterculture referred to what seemed to be a fast rising unity of spirit among all the youth of the nation, black and white, a new consciousness (to use a favorite word from that time) that was mobilizing half the country, the half that was now under twenty-five years old (to use a favorite statistic from that time), under the banner of revolution or something not far from it. Yet at that very moment the youth of the country was becoming bitterly divided along lines of class and status. The more the New Left tried to merge them in a united front, the more chaotic and out of the question the would-be coalition became.

Funky Chic
Illustration by Tom Wolfe

Fashion was hardly one of the root causes of this division—that is another, longer story. But fashion was in many cases the cutting edge. Fashion brought out hopeless status conflict where there was no ideological conflict whatsoever. In 1969 I went to San Francisco to do a story on the young militants who were beginning to raise hell inside the supposedly shockproof compound of Chinatown. I had heard of a sensational public meeting held by a group called the Wah Ching, who were described as a supergang of young Chinese who had been born in Hong Kong, who emigrated to the United States with their parents in the mid-Sixties, who couldn't speak English, couldn't get an education, couldn't get jobs, who were ready to explode. They held a public meeting and threatened to burn down Chinatown, Watts style. So I came on into Chinatown, cold, looking for the Wah Ching. Right away, on the street corners, I see groups of really fierce-looking young men. They've got miles of long black hair, down to the shoulders, black berets, black T-shirts, black chinos, dirty Levis, combat boots. These must be the dread Wah Ching, I figured. So I worked up my nerve and started talking to some of them and right away I found out they were not the Wah Ching at all. They were a group known as the Red Guard, affiliated at that time with the Black Panthers. Not only that, they were not lower-class Hong Kong-born Chinese at all but American-born. They spoke English just like any other Americans; and most of them, by Chinatown standards at least, were middle-class. But they said they were allied with the Wah Ching and told of various heavy battles the Wah Ching were going to help them out in.

It took me about two weeks, but I finally arranged a meeting with one of the main leaders of the Wah Ching themselves. We were going to meet in a restaurant, and I arrived first and was sitting there going over all the political points I wanted to cover. Finally the man walks in—and I take one look and forget every political question on the list. He has on a pair of blue slacks, a matching blue turtleneck jersey with a blue shirt over it and a jacket with a leather body and great fluffy flannel sleeves, kind of like a suburban bowling jacket. This man does not add up. But mainly it is his hair. After all the ferocious long black hair I have been seeing in Chinatown— his is chopped off down to what is almost a parody of the old Chinatown rice-bowl haircut. So the first magnificent question I heard myself blurting out was: "What happened to your hair?"

There was no reason why he should, but he took the question seriously. He spoke a very broken English which I will not attempt to imitate, but the gist of what he said was this:

"We don't wear our hair like the hippies; we don't wear our hair like the Red Guards. We are not a part of the hippies, we are not a part of the Red Guard; we are not a part of anything. We are the Wah Ching. When we got to this country, those guys you were talking to out there, the ones who now call themselves the Red Guard, those same guys were calling us China Bugs and beating up on us and pushing us around. But now we're unified, and we're the Wah Ching and nobody pushes us around. So now they come to us and tell us they are the Red Guard and they've got the message and Chairman Mao and the Red Book and all that. They'll give us the message and the direction, and we can be the muscle and the power on the street and together we will fight the Establishment.

"Well, the hell with that. We don't need any ideological benefactors. Look at these guys. Look at the outfits they're wearing. They come around us having a good time playing poor and saying, 'Hey, brother.' Look at those berets—they think they're Fidel Castro coming out of the mountains. Look at the Can't-Bust-'Em overalls they got on, with the hairy gorilla emblem on the back and the combat boots and the olive green socks on you buy two for twenty-nine cents at the Army-Navy store. They're having a good time playing poor, but we are the ones who have to *be* poor. So the hell with that and the hell with them."

Here were two groups who were unified ideologically—who wanted to fight the old clan establishment of Chinatown as well as the white establishment of San Francisco—and yet they remained split along a sheerly dividing line, an instinctive status line, a line that might even be described by the accursed word itself, *fashion*. This example could be multiplied endlessly, through every instance in which the New Left tried to enlist the youth of the working class or of the slums. There never was a counterculture in the sense of any broad unity among the young—and this curious, uncomfortable matter of fashion played a part, over and over. I never talked to a group of black militants, or Latin militants, for that matter, who didn't eventually comment derisively about the poor-boy outfits their middle-class white student allies insisted on wearing or the way they tried to use black street argot, all the *man*s and *cat*s and *baby*s and *brother*s and *baddest*s. From the very first, fashion tipped them off to something that was not demonstrated on the level of logic until much later: namely, that most of the white New Lefters of the period from 1968 to 1970 were neither soldiers nor politicians but simply actors.

The tip-off was not the fact that the middle-class whites were dressing *down* in order to join their slum-bound brethren. The issue was not merely condescension. The tip-off was that when the whites dressed down, went Funky Chic, they did it *wrong!* They did it *lame!* They never bothered to look at what the brothers on the streets were actually wearing! They needed to have their coats pulled! The New Left had a strictly old-fashioned conception of life on the street; a romantic and nostalgic one somehow derived from literary images of proletarian life from before World War II or even World War I. A lot of those white college boys, for example, would go for those checkered lumberjack shirts that are so heavy and woolly that you can wear them like a jacket. It was as if all the little Lord Byrons had a hopeless nostalgia for the proletariat of about 1910, the Miners with Dirty Faces era, and never mind the realities, because the realities were that by 1968 the real hard-core street youth in the slums were not into lumberjack shirts, Can't-Bust-'Ems and Army surplus socks. They were into ruffled shirts and black-belted leather pieces and bell-cuff herringbones, all that stuff, macking around, getting over, looking sharp...heading toward the high-heeled pimpmobile *got to get over* look of Dixwell Avenue 1973. If you tried to put one of those lumpy mildew mothball lumberjack shirts on them—those aces—they'd *vomit.*

For years the sheer dividing line was a single item of clothing that is practically synonymous with Funky Chic: blue jeans. Well-to-do Europeans appreciated the chic of jeans—that primitive rawness! that delicious lubricious grip on the gourd and the moist skinny slither up into all the cracks and folds and fissures!—long before Americans. Even in the early Fifties, such special styles as London S.W.5 New Wave Habitat Bentwood Movie-Producer Chic and South-of-France Young Jade Chic and Jardins du Luxembourg Post-*Breathless* Chic all had at their core: blue jeans. Cowboy Chic, involving blue jeans and walking around as if you have an aluminum beer keg between your thighs, has been popular among young Parisian lollygaggers for at least fifteen years. Well-to-do whites in America began to discover the raw-vital reverse-spin funk thrill of jeans in the early Sixties. But until very recently any such appeal was utterly lost on black or any other colored street aces and scarlet creepers. Jeans were associated with funk in its miserable aspects, with Down-and-Out, bib overalls, Down-Home and I'm Gonna Send You Back to Georgia. Recently jeans have just begun to be incorporated in the Ace or Pimp look thanks to certain dramatic changes in jeans couture, such as the addition of metal-stud work, bias-cut two-tone swirl mosaic patterns and the rising value of used denim fabric, now highly prized for its "velvet hand" (and highly priced, just as a used Tabriz rug is worth more than a new one). In other words, the aces will now tolerate jeans precisely because they have lost much of their funk.

Well-to-do white youths still associate jeans in any form and at any price with funk, however, and Funky Chic still flies and bites the main vein and foams and reigns. The current talk of a Return to Elegance or the Gatsby Look among the young immediately becomes a laugh and a half (or, more precisely, the latest clothing industry shuck) to anyone who sets foot on a mainly white American campus, whether Yale or the University of California at San Diego. A minor matter perhaps; but today, as always, the authentic language of fashion is worth listening to. For fashion, to put it most simply, is the code of language of status. We are in an age when people will sooner confess their sexual secrets—much sooner, in many cases—than their status secrets, whether in the sense of longings and triumphs or humiliations and defeats. And yet we make broad status confessions everyday in our response to fashion. No one—no one, that is, except the occasional fugitive or spy, such as Colonel Abel, who was willing to pose for years as a low-rent photographer in a loft in Brooklyn—no one is able to resist that delicious itch to reveal his own picture of himself through fashion.

Goethe once noted that in the last year of his reign, Louis XVI took to sleeping on the floor beside his enormous royal bed, because he had begun to feel that the monarchy was an abomination. Down there on the floor he felt closer to the people. How very...funky....Well, I won't attempt any broad analogies. Nevertheless, it demonstrates one thing. Even when so miserable a fashion as Funky Chic crops up...stay alert! use your bean!

Faces: 1971–1974

Clockwise, from left to right:
The Mamas and the Papas
Nixon's farewell
Gay Pride parade
Jane Fonda
Joan Baez
A peace march
Carlos Santana
The art of sensual massage
Carl Sagan

Clockwise, from left to right:
Edgar Winter
The Doobie Brothers
James Taylor
Bob Marley
The Allman Brothers
Truman Capote
A Clockwork Orange

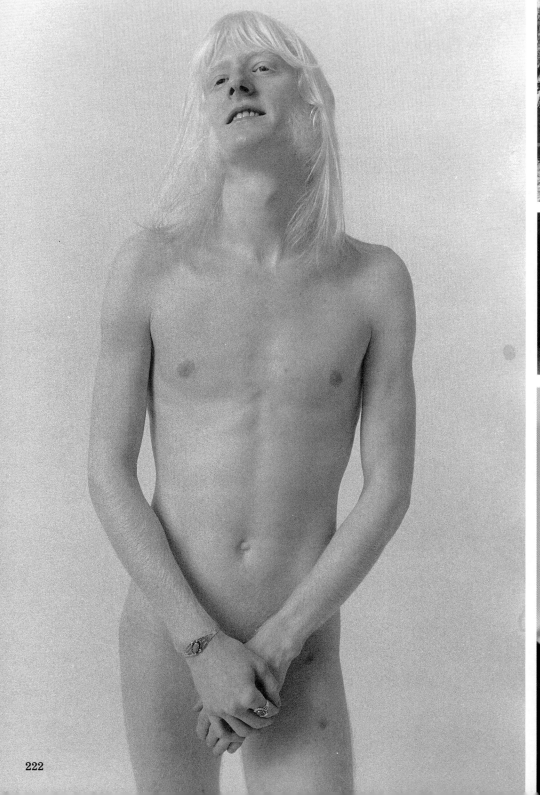

Clockwise, from left to right:
Hugh Hefner and Barbi Benton
G. Gordon Liddy
Ray Charles
Lily Tomlin
Elton John
Van Morrison
Ralph Bakshi's *Heavy Traffic*

Oh, baby this town rips the bones from your back
It's a deathtrap, it's a suicide rap
We gotta get out while we're young
'Cause tramps like us, baby, we were born to run
—BRUCE SPRINGSTEEN, *"Born To Run"*

1975–1979

They knew all the right people, they took all the right pills
They threw outrageous parties, they paid heavily bills
There were lines on the mirror, lines on her face
She pretended not to notice, she was caught up in the race
—DON HENLEY, GLENN FREY, JOE WALSH, *"Life in the Fast Lane"*

Voices

Marriage is an expression that to me suggests giving up, an expression of sacrifice and regret. I never wanted to get married, so I didn't make that sacrifice—it was a victory for me. To me, the worst curse that could happen to a person is to have a family.
—ORIANA FALLACI, *June 1976*

★   ★   ★

There is no more rock & roll. It's an imitation. We can forget about that. Rock & roll has turned itself inside out. Rock & roll ended with Little Anthony and the Imperials.
—BOB DYLAN, *January 1978*

★   ★   ★

Now we're in a period where the fundamental passion of the young is to snigger at the worn-out aspirations of the middle-aged. Snigger is the only word you can employ. We're in some sort of postfascisto, apathetic hippie beatdom. Everybody feels that somehow there is shit in the nectar. So you look for some ground on which to rally.
—NORMAN MAILER, *January 1975*

★   ★   ★

For most rockers, the only thing standing between them and total illiteracy is the need to get through their Mercedes-Benz owners' manuals.
—JIMMY THUDPUCKER, *February 1978*

★   ★   ★

I think it's irresponsible because the kids tend to think that because your music is hip, that your choice in political candidates is automatically good. I mean it curls my hair to think about some rock & roll group being able to give a candidate a quarter of a million dollars when they didn't even read the newspaper.
—LINDA RONDSTADT, *October 1978*

I don't want to grow up, but I'm sick of not growing up. I'll find a different way of not growing up. I have this great fear of this normal thing. You know, the ones that passed their exams, the ones that went to their jobs, the ones that didn't become rock & rollers, the ones that settled for it, settled for the deal! That's what I'm trying to avoid. But I'm sick of avoiding it with violence, you know? I've gotta do it some other way. I think I will.

—JOHN LENNON, *June 1975*

★   ★   ★

…What's coming is the following: so distorted an economic system that the apparent solutions produce all the wrong effects. Look at our surface transportation system; it's grinding to a halt in terms of congestion; it's ruining land planning; it's polluting the air enormously; it's depleting energy and other resources; and, in return, what are we getting for it? The lessons of Watergate are being forgotten with a rapidity only exceeded by Halley's comet.

—RALPH NADER, *November 1975*

★   ★   ★

The idea is that everything that was hoped for and attempted in the Sixties basically hasn't worked and couldn't work out. But who says it won't work? Who says there's something wrong with people dropping out? I think the world should be safe for marginal people. One of the nice things that happened was that a lot of people chose to be marginal and other people didn't seem to mind.

—SUSAN SONTAG, *October 1979*

★   ★   ★

It's a funny time for women. We demand a certain sensitivity. We've made our outward attacks at machoism, right, in favor of the new sensitive male. But we're just at the fledgling state of our liberty where we can't handle it. I think we ask men to be sensitive and equal, but deep down think it's unnatural. And we really want them to be stronger than us.

—JONI MITCHELL, *July 1979*

Malignant Giant

by Howard Kohn   March 1975

She was twenty-eight, a slight woman, dark hair pushing past slender shoulders, haunting beauty nurtured in a small-child look. She was alone that chilly autumn night, driving her tiny three-door Honda through long stretches of prairie. The Oklahoma fields lay flattened under the crude brush marks of the wind, the grass unable to snap back to attention. Every few miles a big-boned rabbit, mangled and broken, littered the roadside. A couple years back she had fired off a round of angry letters when sheep ranchers staged rabbit roundups, clubbing to death the furry army that had sprung up on the prairie. She was like that, poking her opinions where they weren't welcome.

In the early evening darkness of Wednesday, November 13th, 1974, Karen Silkwood was on an environmental mission of another sort. On the seat beside her lay a manila folder with apparent proof that records were being falsified at the plutonium plant where she worked. Waiting at a Holiday Inn thirty miles away were a union official and a *New York Times* reporter who had just flown from Washington, D.C., to Oklahoma City to meet with her.

They waited nearly an hour. Then they picked up the phone.

Karen Silkwood's body had already been found in a small rivulet along Highway 74 where rabbits often came to drink. Her car had swerved left across the highway, skittered about 270 feet along an embankment, smashed head-on into a culvert wing wall, lurched through the air and caromed off another culvert wall, coming to rest in the muddy stream.

Her death was ruled an accident; the police decided she was asleep at the wheel. But the union official was not satisfied. The manila folder was missing. And a private investigator discovered two fresh dents in the rear of her car: telltale marks of a hit-and-run.

★   ★   ★

Even in the dead of winter it can be a steamy eighty degrees in Nederland, Texas, a bottom-line speck on the map best known as the hometown of the late Tex "Hillbilly Heaven" Ritter. Nederland is tucked in the southeastern crook of the Longhorn State, a half-hour's drive from the Gulf of Mexico but within mosquito-flying distance of the bogs and bayous. It is a small town with a limited sense of local color. Its most exotic avenues are driveways paved with seashells from the gulf. A windmill-shaped museum pays tribute to turn-of-the-century Dutch ancestors.

But the most eye-watering landmarks of Nederland are the giant oil refineries obscuring the horizon, coughing out a gray, sinister fog. This corner of Texas produces ten percent of the nation's oil supply; it is Texaco-Mobil-Gulf country, where there are seldom discouraging words about an energy crisis. When the wind is right, which is often, a thick, fetid odor settles over Nederland, clinging to food and clothes, gagging unwary strangers.

Karen Silkwood never forgot the dirty air and sweet stench. When her teachers talked of a new technology that would eliminate the stink and mess of oil, she was captivated. The clean purr of nuclear power: that was the hope of the future. On her own time Karen enrolled in a six-week course on radiation. In her senior year she was accepted into her high school's advanced chemistry class, and her father, the town's premier house painter, dreamed of his daughter as a scientist. But when her mother, a gentle-faced housewife who moonlighted as a bank clerk, discovered Karen was the only girl in her chemistry class, there was a confrontation. "I thought she should be in something like home economics, and I told the chemistry teacher I wanted her out," she says. "But he finally made me change my mind. He said she was a better student than the boys."

Karen was an intense, serious girl who shunned the local teenage hot spots for library reading and volunteer work at a hospital. Her acquaintances remember only one irritating characteristic: she talked back to her teachers, correcting them with an uncanny firmness when they slipped up, say, on the atomic weight of tritium. "She was," says one old friend, "a very nice person who always wanted to be right about everything."

She graduated in 1964 with a college scholarship and best wishes from everyone. At nearby Lamar College, Karen pursued her science interests, deciding on a career as a laboratory analyst, perhaps in nuclear physics.

But before her sophomore year ended, she was whisked away from her studies by a good-looking guy with a promising future as a pipeline supervisor at Mobil Oil. It was seven years, three kids, one bankruptcy and a divorce later before she returned to her earlier ambitions. In August 1972 she had left her husband and children, reclaimed her maiden name and had taken a job away from the smoke-stacks of Texas as a laboratory technician for one of the nuclear elite, Kerr-McGee Corporation of Oklahoma City.

★   ★   ★

In downtown Oklahoma City, where Kerr-McGee's square-block head-quarters towers thirty stories above the modest skyline, the Kerr-McGee name is as imposing as its building. The late Robert Kerr, the company's cofounder, claimed to have been born in a log cabin and to have worked his way through college selling magazines. As company president, he prided himself on staying at cheap motels and eating baked beans in self-service cafeterias while fighting to keep unions at bay and workers at minimum wage. As Oklahoma governor in the Forties, he ran the state with the same frugality and didn't relax his tight fist until moving to the U.S. Senate in 1948. There, Kerr became the most powerful man in the senate, next to Lyndon Johnson. With Kerr's unflagging zeal, the energy industry won millions of dollars in tax subsidies. Nuclear research profited from fat bags of public dollars—to the exclusion of solar and geothermal research, in which Kerr-McGee had no interest.

Dean McGee, Kerr's successor as company board chairman, holds office and influence in such diverse interests as banks, power companies and the National Cowboy Hall of Fame. Recently McGee was named to a federal commission studying America's long-range energy needs. He is already looking ahead to the day when nuclear reactors will no longer use uranium. Future reactors will feed on a far more potent fuel: plutonium.

Uranium, like fossil fuels, is limited in supply; in forty or fifty years we are liable to run out. But plutonium is the love child of an ultimate alchemy: it can reproduce itself. Plutonium barely exists in nature; our present supply is entirely man-made. It was first discovered in the Forties among the waste products of fissioned uranium. Plutonium can take several forms, but it is usually a gray, soft metal, a slushy liquid nitrate or a fluffy yellow-green oxide powder fine enough to be inhaled. In any form it is "fiendishly toxic," according to one of its discoverers, Dr. Glenn Seaborg. As little as a millionth of a gram has induced cancer in lab animals, and some experts say that a softball-sized bag of plutonium, if properly dispersed, could visit cancer on every home on earth.

For years, plutonium was used exclusively for bombs. The nonmilitary inventory wasn't enough to fill a pair of size-ten shoes. But at the Atomic Energy Commission (AEC) in Washington, D.C., visionaries saw an incipient bonanza. So the AEC, encouraged by money and kind words from Capitol Hill, set out to make plutonium practical and profitable.

Kerr-McGee's plutonium plant, built next to one of its uranium plants (and within five miles of ninety-two gas and oil wells, two popular resort lakes and the churning Cimarron River), opened in 1970 shortly before 8583 fish turned belly-up in the river, following a big ammonia spill at the facility. Kerr-McGee had assured the AEC it could deal safely and circumspectly with the plutonium. But the AEC, a government agency in the curious role of both promoting and policing the nuclear industry, soon received numerous reports of irregularities and accidents at the Kerr-McGee plant.

In October 1970, two workers were contaminated when a radioactive storage container was left in the open for three days. Twenty-two more workers were exposed to plutonium in January 1971, when defective equipment allowed plutonium oxide to escape into the air. The protective "glove boxes" the workers used often had holes. Sometimes the Super Tiger and Poly Panther drums, specially designed to store the volatile liquid, unaccountably leaked.

One day a worker bent down to adjust a compressor unit; it exploded, ripping through his hand and tearing off the top of his face, spitting tissue over the ceiling. He died instantly. "When I got there," remembers a former lab technician, "they were washing the goo down the drain." Kerr-McGee, he feels, "didn't give a damn about the people who worked there—it didn't care whether its safety program was effective or not."

When Karen Silkwood arrived at the Kerr-McGee plant in late summer 1972, she was just divorced and eager to begin a career as a nuclear-laboratory technician. But after only three months of testing the plutonium fuel rods, Silkwood was outside the chain-link fence, marching with an on-strike placard.

The Oil, Chemical and Atomic Workers International Union (OCAW), representing international plutonium workers, was at loggerheads with Kerr-McGee. The company had managed to keep the unions out until 1966, three years after Senator Kerr's death. Now the OCAW was demanding a new contract with higher wages, safer conditions and better training. Kerr-McGee had replied with an offer worse than the old contract. Then, as soon as workers went on strike, the company rushed scabs onto the job, barely missing a beat in fuel-rod production. Among the inexperienced substitutes hired during the strike was the plant's safety officer.

On the picket lines, meanwhile, twenty-six-year-old Karen Silkwood was spending a lot of time with twenty-two-year-old Drew Stephens, a short-haired, brainy lab analyst with an easy smile. When he first came to work three years before, Stephens had expected to earn his forty-year gold watch from Kerr-McGee. But he had grown disenchanted after the rash of accidents and now lived for weekends, when he turned sports-car racer.

The strike lasted ten weeks. Those picketers whose jobs had not been lost to scabs returned to work in January 1973, reluctantly signing a new contract that stripped away many of their previous rights, including certain protections against arbitrary firings and reassignments. A few weeks later a plant employee was emptying a bag of plutonium wastes when a fire spontaneously erupted, shooting radioactive dust into the air. Seven workers sucked in the junk. But Kerr-McGee supervisors waited a day before calling in a physician. Four days later, the seven workers still had not been tested for contamination in their lungs.

Silkwood and Stephens shared in the outrage building in the plant. But they were now deeply in love, Stephens divorcing his wife of four years to live with Silkwood. They were enjoying the good times, tooling around in Stephens's tomato-red Austin-Healy Sprite, country rock blaring on the radio.

For Karen Silkwood, Oklahoma City was full of bright lights and good-time chances to catch up on what she missed as a teenager. She hung out at bars and rock concerts and learned how to get stoned. She was happy. Coming home one night, she told Stephens, "I feel like I'm in love with the whole world."

But after several months she moved out, jealous for her freedom, unwilling to risk another marriage. She wanted her own place and, after a money-poor marriage, indulged in a color TV, a $600 stereo, a Suzuki cycle and a Honda Civic hatchback. Silkwood and Stephens remained friends and part-time lovers, but her career was her first love. She retreated from the night scene to work overtime.

Then, in July 1974, Karen Silkwood became contaminated by a sudden swirl of airborne plutonium. She was not wearing a respirator to fit over her tiny, narrow face; it hadn't arrived.

Silkwood got involved in the union, OCAW Local 5-283. She looked to them as the only outlet for her growing frustration with management. When union elections came up the next month, Silkwood ran and won one of the three seats on the Local 5-283 steering committee. Fellow workers knew her as the spunky chick who talked back to her bosses. "Goddamnit, I am right and you are wrong," she once raged at a supervisor. "If you want to tell me what to do, you oughta learn how to do the job right."

Karen Silkwood and the other two steering committee members prepared a declaration of war against the company. New contract negotiations were due in a few months, and for the first time Local 5-283 was going to confront Kerr-McGee squarely on the issue of safety. The chronicle of accidents, safety abuses and other allegations was to be compiled into a formal list of grievances.

Silkwood helped interview workers in the dangerous production areas of the plant. The average age of the workers was twenty-five, and they came from nearby farms and small towns. Silkwood learned that several had no idea plutonium could cause cancer. They spun a grim tale of corporate callousness: new employees often were sent directly into production without safety training (one such worker had been badly contaminated and had quit the next day before receiving medical attention); production schedules sometimes forced workers to stay on the job even when the air wasn't safe to breathe—supervisors ordering them to wear respirators rather than hunting the source of contamination; and plutonium was sometimes stored in such casual containers as desk drawers.

With their grievances in hand, Silkwood and her fellow committee members, Gerald Brewer and Jack Tice, flew to Washington, D.C., for a meeting with the OCAW International. They arrived on September 26th and met Steve Wodka, an OCAW legislative assistant, a hard-nosed, stiff-talking man given to curt skepticism and impatient waves of the hand. Though only twenty-five, he was among the OCAW's best trouble-shooters. Wodka and his boss, Tony Mazzocchi, pumped Silkwood and the others for details, then the next day marched them over to the only place in town that could put the clamps on Kerr-McGee—the AEC. The AEC copied it all down and promised an investigation.

But Wodka was already considering another investigation. Silkwood had confided to him that for months she had suspected that the tests on the plutonium fuel rods destined for Richland, Washington, were being fudged. And, she said, she had recently heard about records being doctored. Kerr-McGee's plutonium plant might be defrauding the AEC, she had concluded, shipping inadequate or unsafe fuel rods to Richland.

"Both Tony Mazzocchi and I felt this was a very serious situation," Wodka says. "But we felt it was premature to bring it to the attention of the AEC. We had to have proof before we could make any accusations. So we asked Karen to go back to the plant, to find out who was falsifying the records, who was ordering it, and to document everything in specific detail."

Silkwood agreed to go undercover.

Back in Oklahoma, she revealed her new role to Stephens. She stood in his living room, crouching over the radiator vent to shake off the autumn chill, and jabbed a delicate brown finger into the air: "We're really gonna get those mother-fuckers this time."

"I told her to calm down, to forget about it," Stephens remembers.

Six days before Silkwood's Washington trip, Stephens had abruptly quit, riled by a sudden transfer. "When I first went to work there, I wanted to be the world's greatest laboratory technician. Now I never wanted to see the place again.

"But Karen felt differently. She wanted to reform the place. When she came back from Washington, she was really excited. This was her chance to do something. She figured things were really going to change."

On October 10th, two of the nation's leading plutonium experts, Dr. Donald Geesaman and Dr. Dean Abrahamson, arrived in Oklahoma City from the University of Minnesota, summoned by the OCAW International to conduct crash courses for Kerr-McGee's plutonium workers. The two professors were told that seventy-three workers had been internally contaminated by plutonium during the previous four years. (Dozens more workers had accidentally brushed plutonium or been sprinkled with it, but had washed it off their skin.) The seventy-three had been exposed to airborne plutonium; any inhaled into their lungs could not be washed out. The probability of cancer in such cases, Dr. Abrahamson warned, "is disturbingly high."

Karen Silkwood was one of those seventy-three, and she was shocked by Abrahamson's news. Silkwood grew moody and restless, working nights and unable to sleep during the days. She got a prescription for some sleeping pills. And she began to hunt for another job.

But first, she vowed to Stephens, she was going to get proof that Kerr-McGee was sustaining its plutonium plant through false and perjurious records. She had already collected some evidence, she said, and was certain she could get more. At one point, Silkwood reported to Wodka that she had obtained photographs proving the welding on some fuel rods was too weak. "They [company supervisors] are still passing bad welds no matter what the pictures look like," she said in a telephone conversation that Wodka taped. "I have a weld I would love for you to see, just how far they ground it down to relax the weld trying to get rid of the voids, the occlusions and the cracks." (Unsafe fuel rods, according to MIT physicist Dr. Henry Kendall, could lead to "an accident that would result in the release of huge amounts of radioactivity.")

Silkwood spent the weeks of October staying after hours, poring over files, recording every questionable procedure, building a dossier in a dogeared manila folder. She did not know then that other employees had noticed her spying and that the plant rumor mill was abuzz with suspicions about what she was up to.

On Tuesday, November 5th, 1974, Silkwood discovered she had been contaminated with plutonium again.

★   ★   ★

Rapidly, as if no time were left on the clock, Silkwood jammed the dime in its slot and dialed long distance. Washington. Steve Wodka. "Hello." An uncertain trickle started down her face. Her voice tottered. "Please come to Oklahoma," she said. "Something very weird is happening here."

Three times in the past three days Karen Silkwood had been contaminated with plutonium, and no one knew where it was coming from. A monitoring device had first discovered flecks of plutonium on her skin and clothing shortly after she reported for work November 5th. She had quickly stepped under a brisk shower. But the next day the monitor flashed on again. More plutonium on her skin. Another shower. On the third day the mystery repeated itself—and a nasal smear indicated she was also contaminated internally.

How much plutonium, she wanted to know, could a person ingest before it burned out her insides?

Wodka tried to reassure her and promised to fly in. Silkwood hung up and sought out her old lover. "She was damn near incoherent," says Stephens. "She was crying and shaking like a leaf; she kept saying she was going to die."

A team of Kerr-McGee inspectors, armed with alpha counters, full-face respirators, special galoshes, taped-up gloves and white coveralls, were meanwhile hunting the source of the plutonium. There had been no recent accident at the plant to account for her contamination. So, at Silkwood's request, they had trekked to her apartment. There the alpha counters commenced eerie gibberings. Plutonium, in small quantities, was everywhere. Outside on the lawn the inspectors filled a fifty-five-gallon drum with alarm clocks, cosmetics, record albums, drapes, pots, pans, shampoo, bed sheets. Alongside they stacked chairs, bed, stove, refrigerator, television, all items to be trucked to the Kerr-McGee plant for later burial in an AEC-approved site.

The plutonium trail turned hottest in the kitchen, inside the refrigerator. A package of bologna and a package of cheese were the two most contaminated items in the apartment. Apparently, the plutonium had been tracked around the apartment from the refrigerator. But no one could explain how two sandwich foods had become the source of the contamination.

The apartment was sealed off, and the AEC called in.

Silkwood, however, was more worried about the plutonium inside her than on the cheese and bologna. She kept popping the Quaaludes that had been prescribed a few weeks before. "The Quaaludes were just supposed to be taken for sleeping at nights," Stephens says. "But she was using them during the day, just to calm down. I'd never seen her so scared."

Wodka had jetted in from Washington and, after talking to Kerr-McGee and AEC officials, had helped arrange for Silkwood to fly to an AEC laboratory in New Mexico to be checked out for poisoning. On Sunday November 10th, five days after her first contamination, she boarded a Braniff airliner.

That same morning a front-page *New York Times* story reported that, according to the AEC's own internal documents, the AEC had "repeatedly sought to suppress studies by its own scientists that found nuclear reactors were more dangerous than officially acknowledged or that raised questions about reactor safety devices." One AEC study, kept confidential for seven years, predicted that a major nuclear accident could kill up to 45,000 persons and pollute an area the size of Pennsylvania. *Times* reporter David Burnham, who in 1970 interviewed Frank Serpico and broke open the New York police-corruption scandal, had sifted through hundreds of memos and letters and learned the AEC had a ten-year record of blue-penciling alarming data, soft-soaping test failures and glad-handing an industry that increasingly appeared not to know what it was doing.

The report gave scant comfort to Silkwood as she flew to Los Alamos, New Mexico, site of the world's first plutonium explosion during the A-bomb tests of World War II. With her were Stephens and Sherri "Dusty" Ellis, her roommate of the past few months, a blonde, rawboned, twenty-one-year-old rodeo champ. Ellis also worked at the plant but had refused to get involved in Silkwood's efforts to unmask the company. Now the three shared the same fears; all had been contaminated in the apartment.

For two days they underwent a "whole body count," a meticulous probing of skin, orifices, intestines and lungs, urinating at intervals into plastic bottles and defecating into Freezette box containers. After the first day, the three had cause for relief. Dr. George Voelz, the health-division leader, assured them they had suffered no immediate damage. Even Silkwood, by far the most infected, was told she was in no danger of dying from plutonium poisoning.

On Tuesday, November 12th, Silkwood called her mother to announce the good news about the tests, but added, "I'm still a little scared. I still don't know how I got contaminated. I feel like someone's using me for a guinea pig."

"I told her to come home," her mother recalls. "And she said she would. She said she was ready for a vacation . . . she just had to do a couple of things first."

After more body-prying tests at Los Alamos, the three travelers flew back to Oklahoma City, landing about 10:30 Tuesday night. Because the women's apartment had been gutted of furniture, they checked in at Stephens's bungalow. Silkwood wandered over to her favorite radiator vent, squatting and rubbing to warm up, then went to bed early. She had a busy day ahead. She had told Wodka she would give him the evidence she was collecting as soon as she returned from Los Alamos, and Wodka had set up a meeting with her and David Burnham, the *Times* reporter, who was winging in from the East Coast. The meeting was scheduled for Wednesday night at the Holiday Inn Northwest in Oklahoma City.

★   ★   ★

Wednesday morning Silkwood drove to work. Contract negotiations between Local 5-283 and Kerr-McGee had begun the week before and, as a committeewoman, she was supposed to take part in the bargaining. She spent the morning in negotiations, arguing the union demands for better safety training and higher injury benefits. In the afternoon she met for several hours with AEC inspectors, who were trying to unravel the mystery of her contamination.

At 5:15 p.m. she drove to Crescent, about five miles from the plant, and stopped at the Hub Cafe for a meeting, to discuss negotiations strategy with Local 5-283. Jack Tice, who headed the negotiating team, told the assembled union members that, as expected, Kerr-McGee was not budging off its hard line. Silkwood excused herself at about 6:00 p.m. to telephone Stephens, reminding him to pick up Wodka and Burnham at the airport and to expect her at the motor hotel about 8:00

p.m. She sounded normal, Stephens remembers, perhaps a bit excited about having an audience with *The New York Times*. At 7:15 p.m. Silkwood left the Hub Cafe and headed for Highway 74 and the Holiday Inn Northwest. A fellow union member would later swear in an affidavit that Silkwood, minutes before she left the restaurant, was carrying a manila folder an inch thick with papers. The folder, Silkwood told the union member, contained the proof that quality-control records were being falsified.

Thirty miles away, Wodka, Burnham and Stephens waited for that proof until 8:45. Then they picked up the phone; but for some reason the Holiday Inn lines were out of order, and another hour passed before the three could get through.

Meanwhile, at 8:05 p.m., a truck driver, rolling along the two-lane highway, spotted the white Honda, almost hidden in the muddy culvert. Silkwood had traveled about seven miles from the Hub Cafe, a ten-minute drive.

By the time Stephens, Wodka and Burnham learned the news from a local union member, the 1638-pound Civic hatchback had already been towed to Ted Sebring's garage in Crescent. And Silkwood had been pronounced dead on arrival at the Guthrie Hospital, the victim of multiple and compound fractures.

The three men raced to the culvert, only a mile from the plutonium plant, and prowled about, stepping gingerly through the mud, which in Oklahoma is the color of dry blood. All they could find were shards of aluminum trim, the orange roadside reflectors that had been trampled by the bouncing car and Silkwood's uncashed paycheck. Later they found the wreck locked up in Sebring's garage and peered at it through the window. They stopped at the home of union committeeman Jack Tice, one of the last to see Silkwood alive; Stephens called Silkwood's parents. Then they returned to the culvert, searching for an explanation in the tire tracks and the scraps of metal.

The explanation the State Highway Patrol offered was that Karen Silkwood, exhausted after driving 600 miles from Los Alamos to Oklahoma City, had fallen asleep and drifted off the road to an accidental death. Almost immediately the police had to alter their version when they were told Silkwood had gotten a full night's sleep only twelve hours before the crash.

The second official version was somewhat more convincing. Sometime during the afternoon of November 13th, Silkwood had gulped down at least one Quaalude from the vial in her coat pocket. Oklahoma City's chief forensic toxicologist, Richard W. Prouty, discovered .35 milligrams of methaqualone in her bloodstream, conceivably enough to lull her to sleep on the highway.

But that was not sufficient for Steve Wodka.

Silkwood had swallowed several Quaaludes in the past week without nodding out. Why would she fall into a trance on her way to a crucial meeting? And the proof of fraud she was supposedly carrying had disappeared. Her personal effects, listed by the medical examiner, included an ID badge, an electronic security key (for the plant), two marijuana cigarettes, a Kotex pad, two used Kleenexes, a Bradley Mickey Mouse pocket watch, a small notebook, her clothes, $7.00 in bills and $1.69 in change. But there was no manila folder heavy with Kerr-McGee documents.

Trooper Rick Fagan, however, had mentioned finding dozens of loose papers blowing about the accident scene when he first arrived. Fagan had plucked up the papers, he told his superiors, and shoved them into the Honda. According to the highway patrol's information officer, Lieutenant Kenneth Vanhoy, the papers were in the Honda when Ted Sebring hauled the car away. Presumably they were still there at 12:30 a.m.—five hours after the accident—when Sebring unlocked his garage for a group of Kerr-McGee and AEC representatives who said they wanted to check out Silkwood's car for plutonium contamination. But by the next afternoon when Stephens, Wodka and Burnham claimed Silkwood's car from Sebring, no papers were inside.

Wodka called Tony Mazzocchi at OCAW International. Mazzocchi agreed: an outside expert was needed to investigate the crash. Three days after Silkwood's death an auto-crash expert arrived in Oklahoma City from the Accident Reconstruction Lab in Dallas. A.O. Pipkin, an ex-cop, is a veteran of 2000 accidents and 300 court trials, a no-nonsense pro considered the best man around for piecing together an accident scenario. Pipkin examined the Honda and found two curious dents, one in the rear bumper, another in the rear fender. They were fresh; there was no road dirt in them. And they appeared to have been made by a car bumper.

At the scene, Pipkin noted that the Honda had crossed over the yellow lines and hit the culvert on the left side of the highway. If Silkwood had nodded into a stupor, he reasoned, she would have drifted to the right. In the red clay, Pipkin found something else the police apparently disregarded: tire tracks indicating the car had been out of control before it left the highway. Pipkin's disconcerting conclusion: Karen Silkwood's Honda had been hit from the rear by another vehicle.

★   ★   ★

On December 20th, five weeks after Karen Silkwood's death, Kerr-McGee temporarily closed its plutonium plant. These were trying days for the company. Supporters of Kerr-McGee found it necessary to print ads reminding Oklahomans that Dun & Bradstreet had recently named it among the five best-managed corporations in the country. But headlines kept popping up all over, thanks to *The New York Times* wire service, telling of a mysterious death, falsified records and ill-trained workers sent in to handle one of the world's most dangerous poisons.

Predictably, the plant shutdown ruptured the tentative alliance between the plutonium workers and local environmentalists. To Frank Murch, a middle-aged man with seven years invested in Kerr-McGee, the shutdown was a slap in the pocketbook: "You're damn right I'm bitter about this. I'm bitter at the environmentalists. It's a hell of a thing, putting this many people out of work." Some took to blaming the dead. One worker who earlier had talked about honoring Karen Silkwood with a special grave marker now spat at the mention of her name.

"Attitudes changed," says Gerald Brewer. "People started to blame Karen for getting thrown out of work right before the holidays." Brewer was one of the two union committee members who had accompanied Silkwood to Washington in September. In early January, after plutonium production resumed, Brewer was demoted and transferred to an isolated warehouse. Two weeks later he was fired. Brewer's apparent sin, besides his role in compiling the grievances, was his refusal to submit to a polygraph test that asked questions like, "Have you ever talked to the media?" Although of questionable legality, the polygraphs were required of most plutonium workers as a "security precaution" before they could return to their jobs. A Kerr-McGee official described company strategy in a conversation with Jack Taylor, ace reporter for *The Daily Oklahoman*: "We're going to tool back up slowly and hire people who are trustworthy and are not involved [in the union]." As for undesirables: "You don't have to tell them [anything]. You can just say, 'You didn't clear security.'"

Along with Brewer, five other workers who snubbed or failed the polygraphs were handed pink slips. Among the six was Dusty Ellis, the cowgirl who shared the contaminated apartment with Silkwood. After her roommate's death, Ellis initially cooperated with Kerr-McGee, refusing to talk to either the OCAW or the media. At one point she was seen, red-eyed and distraught, being escorted by two company detectives away from the Edmond Broadway Motor Inn where she had been staying, compliments of Kerr-McGee. Then Ellis, without explanation, aired a suggestion that Silkwood may have been pilfering plutonium from the plant. Shortly thereafter, Kerr-McGee reportedly offered Ellis $1000 as payment for any claims she might have against the company.

But Ellis turned down the offer. She began worrying that she had been more seriously contaminated than she had been told; her gums bothered her and she had trouble sleeping. In late December she hired a lawyer and threatened to sue the company for copies of all her health records. Three weeks later she was fired. Two weeks after that, in early February, Ellis told friends that twice someone had tried, and failed, to break into her new apartment.

During the month between the plant shutdown and the firings, the AEC had published the results of its investigation. (According to a *Daily Oklahoman* story, Kerr-McGee officials received a copy of the report well ahead of its official release, apparently in violation of AEC rules.) Company officials—who had been refusing comment since Karen Silkwood's death, except to say, "We will let the AEC speak for us"—pronounced themselves pleased with the findings.

On the question of falsified records, the AEC did locate one former worker who admitted using a felt-tip pen to touch up photo negatives that measured the welding on plutonium fuel rods. The worker, however, said he acted only to make his job easier and not under orders from Kerr-McGee. Without Silkwood's documents, the AEC reported, it could find no other hard proof. But the OCAW questioned whether the AEC was really looking. According to the OCAW, the AEC lied when it claimed to have interviewed a worker who disputed Silkwood's allegations of fraud. This worker, the OCAW said, had given the union a sworn affidavit that the AEC never interviewed him, and that he believes quality controls are not adequate.

On the question of plant safety, the AEC reported that twenty of the thirty-nine grievances it examined were true or partially true: plutonium had been stored in a desk drawer instead of a prescribed vault; in various incidents, employees had been forced to work in areas not tested for contamination or where leaks remained; in another, the company failed to report a serious leak that had forced it to close the plant in May 1974; generally, respirators had not been checked regularly for deficiencies; few workers had been properly trained.

Such disregard for safety, the AEC decided, merited no censure beyond adding these new citations to the trove already in the Kerr-McGee files. Kerr-McGee was free to resume its role in the AEC's fast-breeder program, a program that might have been seriously compromised had Kerr-McGee been forced to close up shop permanently.

Ilene Younghein and other environmentalists professed no surprise at the AEC's lack of action. The AEC had never summoned the courage to penalize Kerr-McGee in the past. The AEC had managed to levy only eight penalties during a twelve-month period, from 1973 to 1974, even though its inspectors had found 3333 violations. In 1972, during a hearing on nuclear safety, the AEC had given its scientists written instructions to "never disagree with established policy." And at a nuclear-waste dumping ground in Washington, the AEC has been in charge while half a million gallons of "hot" effluent, enough to fill four railroad cars, has been spilled onto the ground in numerous accidents since the 1940s, including one leak that dribbled 115,000 gallons out of a tank unnoticed for fifty-one days.

Over the years, the AEC had shrugged at multiple warnings that should have sounded sirens:

• A study by two AEC scientists in 1969 that predicted 32,000 more annual deaths from cancer if every American were exposed to the allowable radiation doses set by the AEC.

• An AEC-laboratory test in 1970 in which the key emergency safety system for conventional nuclear reactors failed to work in six out of six attempts.

• A 1974 AEC investigation that showed radiation levels in the lunchroom at a Tennessee nuclear plant were eight times too high.

• A *Science* magazine report revealing that a plant in Buffalo, New York, was recruiting beer-garden drones because conditions were too "hot" for regular employees.

• Accidents that spilled 1000 gallons of radioactive water into the Illinois River, leaked plutonium into Ohio's Erie Canal, sent radioactive dust out a chimney in a New York plant and increased the chances of cancer in hundreds of workers at dozens of plants.

• The 271 fires and 410 contamination cases at the AEC's only facility for mass production of plutonium parts used in atomic bombs, eight miles upwind from Denver, Colorado. In May 1969, this plant harbored the most expensive fire in industrial history; improperly stored cans of plutonium ignited and destroyed $50 million of delicate equipment. Over a year later, General E.B. Giller, director of the AEC's division of military applications, admitted the fire had been a "near catastrophe." Had it burned through the roof—and it nearly did—"hundreds of square miles could [have been] involved in the radiation exposure." *The Denver Post* has since reported that workers at the plant have a cancer rate seven times higher than the national average.

In some cases, the AEC has released data only after environmentalists filed lawsuits under the Freedom of Information Act. But the nuclear coverup seems to be coming unglued. And there is a new crisis of confidence in the nuclear industry. In January, *The New York Times* reported that because of recent criticism, the industry is nearly doubling its funds for lobbying politicians, reporters and labor officials.

There is even a question now whether nuclear power at its best can be efficient. During January 1974, the worst period of the energy crisis, twenty-two of the nation's thirty-one commercial nuclear reactors were closed down for all or part of the month. Even when they are operating, they provide less than ten percent of the country's energy needs. By contrast, science writer Isaac Asimov estimates that solar cells, say in the Mojave Desert, could supply the energy needs of the entire world.

More crucial is the issue of safety. Several nuclear plants have actually piled up more AEC violations than Kerr-McGee. And the Environmental Protection Agency has recently joined the growing queue of leading scientists and authorities who contend the AEC has greatly underestimated nuclear risks. It is not simply the past record that frightens them; it is the potential for future disaster. No fail-safe systems have been devised to meet the problems inherent in nuclear technology.

All her old clothes were under quarantine, suspected of plutonium contamination, so Karen Silkwood was buried in a new dress. No Kerr-McGee officials made the journey to Texas for the funeral, nor any AEC officials. Afterward Karen's parents returned to the green frame house where she grew up.

"Karen was fixing to come home." Her mother dabbed softly at her eyes. "She wanted to get away. She was so scared. I wish now I had made her come home when she called that day."

Her expression turned steely. "We never did appreciate Karen as much as we should have. I don't think anyone did. Even now they don't. Look what she did. She gave her life to save others."

Drew Stephens, who now works in a Volkswagen body shop, bought a holster, a box of cartridges and a .38 revolver shortly after the crash. He suspected he was being followed and that his phone was tapped. By spring, he says, he will be packing his van and heading cross-country. "There's nothing left for me here." His voice is muted. "Not unless they find who killed Karen."

At OCAW headquarters, Steve Wodka has found it difficult to return to other chores. The Silkwood case keeps nagging him. There are too many unanswered questions. For instance, how did Silkwood become contaminated a week before her death? For weeks afterward, Wodka kept the results of her Los Alamos tests scribbled on an OCAW blackboard, trying to puzzle out the mystery. The most logical explanation, he decided, was that Silkwood had been contaminated at the plant and unknowingly carried the plutonium home with her. But then the AEC reported that this would have been virtually impossible, given her duties at the plant during the time immediately preceding the contamination.

So now Wodka has come to believe she was poisoned. "Someone must have entered her apartment and placed the plutonium in her refrigerator," he says. "That's the only way it could have gotten on the cheese and bologna. We've heard from several sources, including the AEC, that Karen had been seen going through the files, looking for records. Someone apparently figured out what she was up to. One sure way of preventing her from gathering any more evidence would have been to poison her, maybe scare her into leaving."

Kerr-McGee officials have advanced a different conspiracy theory, passed along in off-the-record conversatoins with local reporters. Kerr-McGee suggests that Silkwood contaminated herself to embarrass the company. According to this theory, Silkwood smuggled a plutonium capsule out of the plant, either by swallowing it or slipping it up her vagina or anus—all suicidal maneuvers. But even assuming that Silkwood had become a frenzied zealot, this theory does not explain why she thought getting contaminated in her apartment would embarrass the company, or why the company would get red-faced over any contamination after seventy-three cases in four years.

Nonetheless, Oklahoma City media has popularized this theory. One state representative, a liberal, shakes his head. "I can't understand that dame, shoving plutonium up her ass like that." And some townspeople have added their own twist, announcing with a wink that "I hear she was a drug-crazy hippie who put this plutonium junk in her mary-jew-anna."

The OCAW International has pledged not to give up until the case is solved.

"Karen was a very unusual person," Wodka says. "She stood up to the company. She was outspoken. She was very brave, now that we look back on it; in many ways she was a lone voice. She was willing to go ahead when other people were afraid."

"She died for a cause," agrees Ilene Younghein. "She will be remembered as a martyr."

At the Nuclear Regulatory Division of the new AEC, she will be remembered, too. The commission has begun a file on her. It reads: SILKWOOD, KAREN… FORMER EMPLOYEE, KERR-MCGEE.

Stevie Wonder in New York

by O'Connell Driscoll   June 1975

There were four old ladies sitting in the lobby of the Fifth Avenue Hotel. They sat facing one another in a quartet of lackluster wing chairs, holding themselves as motionless as a photograph. One of the old ladies had a garishly painted scarf tied sportily around her neck. Her mouth was lost in an enormous circle of red lipstick, and her cheeks were made up to the color of a run-over peach. She fingered the tip of her scarf lightly, as if it were a corsage.

"This scarf..." she said suddenly. She stopped, out of breath, as if she had just run a great distance.

"Mary gave me this scarf," the lady with the red mouth declared. She tightened her grip on the scarf and flapped it at her three companions. "I think it's quite lovely, really."

Another of the ladies leaned forward and examined the scarf with interest. Her eyes swam around behind a pair of thick-lensed spectacles like tropical fish in an aquarium. She reached out a bony hand and nudged the lady sitting beside her, who gave the appearance of being dead.

"Mary," the lady with the fish eyes said, "Alice is speaking to you."

Mary awoke with a start, as if there had been a loud explosion. The lady with the aquarium spectacles pointed gently to Alice who was waving her scarf gaily in their direction.

"A lovely scarf," Alice repeated, "in my opinion."

Mary stared in terror at the lady with the lipstick mouth. Her hands tightened around the arms of her chair as if she were floating away. Her mouth began to tremble and open slowly, like a monster coming to life. A thin thread of saliva ran down her chin.

Stevie Wonder
Photograph by Annie Leibovitz

"Filth!" she cried out loudly. "Nothing but!"

Her words were drowned not immediately by the high-pitched sound of a radio turned to full volume. The music swept through the lobby like the heralding of trumpets, bringing with it an exuberant crowd of people executing an impressive Fellini-like costumed entrance.

Leading the pack was Stevie Wonder, wearing a pair of wire-framed aviator sunglasses and a black leather outfit intricately splattered with metal studding. He had a matching cap that he wore cocked smartly to one side, Dead End Kid-style. His head bobbed about freely on top of his tall, erect body, as if it were a broken spring.

Stevie's brother Calvin held his left elbow lightly, moving him through the lobby to the elevators. Pulling up alongside in a semijog was a heavyset black man wearing the bluest of all possible blue track suits with snazzy red and white piping running everywhere, a pair of white Adidas sneakers and a terrycloth tennis cap. He carried a combination radio-cassette player, which he held up to his ear and listened to intently every now and then, as if he were about to receive instructions from headquarters.

Following at close quarters was the rest of the entourage, several men with leather coats and embroidered briefcases and a sprinkling of ladies, some breathtakingly beautiful. Trailing the group was Ira Tucker, Stevie Wonder's general factotum. Tucker studied the lobby from behind a pair of lightly tinted heart-shaped glasses, apparently finding nothing of interest in what he saw.

The four old ladies turned their heads and watched Stevie Wonder's caravan trail away.

"Who was that?" the lady with the fish eyes asked.

"What?" Mary demanded in a shrill voice, nearly pulling herself out of her chair. "What is it?"

"I was asking," the lady with the fish eyes said in a loud, patient tone, "who was that tall Negro man who was standing here?"

Her voice carried through the entire lobby.

"Too much noise," Mary said to nobody at all. "Too much dirt, wherever you are."

"I'm not sure," said Alice with the lipstick mouth, "but I thought I recognized that young man. I've seen his picture." She tapped her forehead with one finger, a pantomime of thought. "I believe he's an athlete of some sort," she said at last. "A basketball player, unless I'm incorrect."

★   ★   ★

The hotel room was a low-level still life; everything within it was tainted by its dreary karma. The flowered drapes hung lifelessly by the windows like flags on a muggy day. The faded wallpaper and the worn out carpeting were testimonials to the unglamorous appointments of the Fifth Avenue Hotel.

The doorbell rang and two black men, one older than the other, came into the room. Ira Tucker gave them a wave of recognition. The older man had come to talk to Stevie about doing a documentary film. He wore a conservative suit offset by a Robin Hood-green turtleneck sweater. A blazing gold sunburst hung around his neck on a chain. The younger man was a writer for a black newspaper. He walked purposefully into the room, glancing all around him as if he expected to meet with something that would cause him displeasure.

Without rising, Tucker made the necessary introductions, and the two men settled down on the couch. Stevie disappeared into the bedroom and returned holding a large portable radio.

"Take a look at this, man," he said, handing the radio over to Tucker. "I just bought this thing today, but it doesn't work right. I think I should take it back."

Tucker turned the radio over in his hands and examined it with the closest attention. "What doesn't it do," he asked, "that it ought to do?"

"I can't get the police calls," Stevie told him. He stretched out his arm until he located the radio in Tucker's lap. "I can get everything," he said, "except the police calls."

He stroked the top of the radio with the tips of his fingers, as if he were petting a cat. "Cost me $500," he told everybody.

"Five hundred *dollars?*" Tucker shouted. "For a *radio?*"

"Well, see, it's not just...uh...an *ordinary* radio, you understand."

Stevie reached around in back of him, and his hand closed over the arm of a chair. He backed up slowly and sat down. "See, the thing is," he said, "with this radio you can get shit from all over the world. You can get Europe and every place. But no police calls."

"Man, Steve," Tucker said, "you are incredible. I mean you are really out there. What do you want the police calls for anyway?"

"It's not so much wanting them," Stevie said, "as not being able to get them. You know?"

"I can dig it," the young black newspaperman said suddenly. Nobody paid any attention to him.

"Otherwise," Stevie went on, "the radio works real good. This afternoon I was listening to the Dutch Top Forty. Shoo bop, dee doo bop, *bah*..."

"Dutch Top Forty," Tucker said. "Outasight. Were you on it?"

"Well, I don't know actually whether I was or not," Stevie said. "See, I was only tuned in for the top numbers...."

"Oh, *yeah*," Tucker said, "I dig it. You were only tuned in for the *top* numbers. And are you telling me, Steve, that you were not among the *top* numbers? Say that just ain't so, man."

"Yeah," Stevie said philosophically. "I guess their playlist is coming from a slightly different direction. Number One song was...uh...'Willie and the Hand Jive.'"

"'Willie and the Hand Jive?'" Tucker said. "Isn't that a goldie oldie?"

"No, this is a new thing. Eric Clapton."

"Rip-off reggae shit," the young newspaperman muttered with disgust.

"Eric Clapton loves your ass," Tucker told Stevie.

"Yeah?" he said, looking pleased.

"White folks have always ripped off black people's shit," the newspaperman said, his voice rising. "Just ask the Rolling Stones where they get their shit from. Chuck *Berry*, that's where!"

"Well, now," Stevie said, swinging his head toward the reporter, "that's not necessarily..." He fondled the radio in his lap and pulled his upper lip tightly against his gum like Humphrey Bogart. "That's not the best way of putting it," he said finally.

The reporter looked wounded. "How can you say that?" he asked weakly. "I mean just listen to what's being put out, man." He was beside himself with distress. "You should relate to this, man. After all, you're a black performer."

"You'll excuse me," Stevie said gently, "if I say that is not the case. I don't consider myself to be a black performer; I consider myself to be a performer who is...uh...black. That's a different thing."

"The difference between commitment and categorization," the filmmaker in the green turtleneck offered. "Perhaps."

"The what?" Stevie said.

"Well, you're black," the filmmaker said, edging to the front of his chair, "and you identify with that strongly. It's a dynamic part of your personality, which in turn," he flip-flopped his hands as if he were performing a magic trick, "you inject into your music. However, your music is not necessarily limited *by* or contained *within* the categorical boundaries of black music."

The man looked about him earnestly; his words hung in the air like freshly strung Christmas decorations. The room was a study in concentration for several moments.

"Exactly," Stevie said at length.

"Whatever it is," Tucker said, standing and stretching his arms, "it's cool. You got anything to drink up here, Steve?"

"I don't know, big brother Tucker," Stevie told him. "Why don't you just take yourself into the refrigerator box and see what's happening?"

Tucker edged his way into the kitchen and looked inside the refrigerator. "This is pathetic, Steve," he called back. "The best thing you got in here is a light bulb."

"There is, I believe, some apple juice," Stevie said, "someplace."

"I hope it's organic apple juice," Tucker said, taking a bottle out and holding it under his nose. "I can't dig it unless it's mother nature's own."

"Man, you gotta be kidding," Stevie said. "I got my own apple-juice-making machine in there. All electric and automatic...uses real apples and everything."

"I have to tell you, Steve," Tucker said, returning with a glass in his hand, "I'm impressed. A dude who has his own apple-juice machine is a dude who has arrived."

"Yeah, well, I'm not doing all this shit for nothing, you understand," Stevie said.

"Right on," Tucker said agreeably. "You're reaping the benefits of your station in life. It's the superstar hit."

"Superstar!" Stevie cried, clapping the arm of his chair. "You've been reading *Newsweek*, Tucker!"

"Now that," the reporter said, "that was a jive piece."

"*Newsweek* is out to lunch, man," Tucker said. "They think they discovered Steve last week or some such shit. Made him what he is today."

"Jive-ass piece," the reporter said again.

"Well," Stevie said, "see, the thing is...the thing is *this*." He settled back in his chair and folded his hands on his lap; he gave every appearance of having nothing further to say.

"What," Tucker asked after several moments, "is the thing?"

"They have it all fucked up," Stevie said simply. "I mean, *Newsweek* comes out with their story and everything, and there I am on the cover for America to see...which is cool...but it seems to me, as I understood the piece, that they missed the whole point."

"In what sense do you mean that?" the filmmaker asked.

"In the sense that they missed the point," Stevie answered. "They're going on about me, saying how I'm this and that and now I'm a superstar. Well, I say supershit! It was like...I mean it was as if they *decided* that black music was the thing that was going on *now*. It was as if they looked around and said, Hey! there's black music going on! And then...*then*...in attempting to understand this...uh... new-found thing, they had to go find some black cat who...ah...somebody who by what he *does*...uh...oh shit, Tucker," he said, snapping his fingers in midair, "what word am I looking for here?"

"*Symbolizes*," Tucker said. "They wanted somebody who symbolizes the phenomenon. Such as it is."

"Right!" Stevie said. "They're looking for a *symbol* of all this that they think is going on."

He threw his head back and grinned hugely.

"And that's me!" he shouted at the ceiling.

"Yes, maybe that's so," the filmmaker said evenly. "But on the other hand you must admit that your accomplishments have been impressive. We may be talking about specious labels here..." He looked around the room to see whether or not that was the case and received no response whatsoever. "Still," he went on, "I imagine that given contemporary standards you *are* a superstar, realizing of course the context in which that title is employed by the media and the need for the public to seek out and identify...or even to relate..."

The filmmaker's conversation slowed down, sputtered out and died, like a car running out of gas forty miles out of Las Vegas.

"Yeah, well forget that," Stevie said. "I mean no offense or anything. I'm not putting you down *personally*, I hope you understand. It's just that...well, look. People are always labeling you...as a performer...rather than listening to whatever it is you're doing and...uh...accepting you for what you are. I mean they're always trying to *comprehend* you, you see, and they think that by saying, hey, I got that cat's *label*—you understand?—that they have you all figured out. You can say...uh...well *this* dude here is obviously a rock singer...or this cat here is a country-western thing...you know? So now that I know what he *is*, I know *all about him!* Well, you don't know *shit!*

"It gets to be a ridiculous situation when I come out with a record and some people will say...my, my!...that doesn't *sound* like Stevie Wonder. Well, shit. How can I not sound like *me?* That's not my problem when that happens. That's the problem of somebody who has...ah...jumped to conclusions too quickly."

Stevie stood up and began to move across the room. "Some folks can't help but just trying to understand you a little too fucking fast," he said.

"Perhaps the public," the filmmaker suggested, "is conditioned to resist change."

Tucker drained the last of his apple juice and regarded the man good-humoredly. "You know you are really heavy, man," he told him. "I say that in all seriousness."

The filmmaker smiled uncertainly.

"It's not so much the public," Stevie said, hunting around in a stack of cassettes. "It's record companies…who naturally assume that they know everything there is to know…and they're telling you what you can and cannot do. What the public will *accept*. But, like, how do they know they won't accept something if nobody ever *does* it? Crazy things like that. Also, the people who write about performers and artists…"

Stevie turned his head and smiled at the young reporter. "Don't take this on a personal level," he told him.

The reporter hunched forward and rested his elbows on his knees; he looked as if he were carrying a great weight on his shoulders.

"People who write about performers can really get into some weird shit," Stevie said. "I don't know if either of you folks are familiar with my show but…uh …on this past tour I decided to do something a little bit…*different*. I thought instead of just going out and doing *all* Stevie Wonder's greatest hits and everything, I'd do some songs that I'd encountered along the way and that I admire very much. So I did 'Earth Angel,' the Penguin thing, and some Temptations stuff…'Ain't Too Proud To Beg'…and 'I Heard It Through the Grapevine,' 'What'd I Say' and just a lot of tunes that I really liked. You understand all this? Then I finished up with 'Finger-tips.' Right?"

Stevie began to clap his hands and dance around in the middle of the room. *"Everybody say yaayyyyyyy,"* he sang.

"Yay," Tucker said idly.

"And you wouldn't believe," Stevie said, still weaving about, "what some folks made out of that. People were saying…oh, goodness, that boy's all washed out. They said I was *lowering* myself because I was doing all this shit. Now, *I* was enjoying myself…and the audiences, they were enjoying *them*selves…and yet people seemed to take this as a sign that I was never going to do anything worthwhile again. Which is stupid, naturally."

Stevie danced over to the tableful of equipment and fed one of the cassettes into the tape deck. "Allriiiight!" he cried, as the music came out of the speakers. "It's Stevie…aghhhhhh!!…Wonder! Ba ba dee doo doo ba…"

He twirled around drunkenly, like a sailor coming back from shore leave.

"Will you look at this?" Tucker said. "Have you ever seen such grace?"

Stevie clapped his hands together happily and bounced around the room like a pinball. The filmmaker watched his performance with the detached curiosity of someone taking a bus tour through Europe.

"I tell you," Stevie said breathlessly, coming to a stop, "I love to perform. All this superstar shit can go out the window."

"But it's a platform, man," the reporter protested. "A place to stand…be heard..." He drove one fist into the palm of his other hand for emphasis.

"Well obviously you don't get the opportunity to perform," Stevie said, "if people don't know who you are. But when you start to believe the things you read about yourself...like when you begin thinking that you really *are* number one... that's when you begin to go nowhere. I mean if there really was such a thing as *number one*, well then whoever that lucky cat was would have no place left to go. You see? That's why I don't go for that whole thing. It's like...uh..."

"Limiting," Tucker said.

"Limiting," Stevie said. "Just like when you say I'm a black musician...you know...'Stevie Wonder does black music,' all of that. That's putting me in a particular box and saying...*stay...right...where...you...are!*"

Stevie whooped merrily and began to shimmy again.

"And you *know* I just have too much energy for doing that," he said.

"Don't you love the guy?" Tucker asked the two men on the couch. "He's a philosopher, man, in his spare time."

"I just dig audiences," Stevie said. "That to me is the most worthwhile thing about this whole business. Just people coming to have a good time and letting me sing for them. Tell the truth, Tucker, didn't we have a good time on this tour?"

"Pretty much," Tucker said. "But then again, there are some weird folks running around out there, Steve."

"Aw, c'mon," Stevie said. "They were terrific, every place we played. You know, I feel like those people...I think of them as my best friends in the whole world."

Stevie found Tucker's shoulder with his hand and gripped it tightly.

"You can't feel what all those crowds are like unless you're out in front playing for them. Because, man, when I look out at an audience," he said, tapping his sunglasses with his fingernail, "all I see are beautiful people."

★   ★   ★

The two people from Human Kindness Day sat in a booth in Feathers restaurant waiting for Stevie to come downstairs.

One was a muscular man with large sorrowful eyes and enormous hands; his hair was lined with ribbons of gray that ran like snail tracks to the back of his head. His partner was a frail, neurotically composed white woman whose eyes blinked constantly from unspoken anxieties. She drew aimless circles on the table with her forefinger and glanced around the restaurant with apprehension.

"He'll be down any minute," Ira Tucker said. He sat across the table from the two and watched the woman's blinking eyes.

"One thing you can depend on with Steve," he told them, "is that he'll always be late. That's his way of doing things. When we were in England last year, it took Steve three days to get on a plane and leave London. Each day we were supposed to split, and each day Steve just couldn't get it together enough to pack. But you just have to go with it. I sat in my hotel room the whole time watching one of the mellowest snowfalls I've ever seen."

The black man looked at Tucker with obvious sadness, as if there were far too many things in the world that could not be properly explained.

"At least," Tucker said, "I *think* it was snowing."

The woman with the blinking eyes pulled a Kleenex out of her purse and blew her nose; the story apparently offered her no consolation.

"When we were playing Detroit on this last tour," Tucker said, "Steve was forty minutes late in going on or something. Everybody's going crazy, you know, having heart attacks because Steve is just sitting in the dressing room trying to get his hair to look right. But I wasn't worried. I said, 'Listen, folks, there's no problem here, no reason to panic.' After all, Steve was in the place; eventually he'll go on and then everything's cool. Then a couple of weeks later, we're in Seattle. Rufus is onstage doing the opening act, and Steve is due to go on in thirty minutes, the only hang-up being that nobody's seen Steve since the day before. Suddenly, dig, as the tension mounts, the phone rings. Guess who? Steve! He was calling from L.A. to say he missed the *plane*. Missed the plane. And he's supposed to be onstage in thirty *minutes*."

Tucker took a pretzel from a basket on the table and munched on it with satisfaction.

"Man," he said, "that one just blew a lot of people away. And I said, okay... *now* we have a problem. *Now* anybody who wants to panic can go right ahead."

The woman from Human Kindness Day was visibly disturbed. She opened her mouth as if to speak, but no words came out.

"That," Tucker said, "is life with Steve."

The woman shivered and pulled her arms around herself. She looked away from Tucker in the direction of the adjoining booth; it was occupied by a young man with shoulder-length hair and a cowboy hat. She was amazed to find him waving at her.

"That man over there," she said. "He's waving at me. I've never seen him before."

Tucker looked at the young man, who then waved at him as well. Tucker saluted in return. "That's Robert Friedman," he informed the woman. "He digs people."

The woman's eyes were frozen on the young man like a deer caught in a car's headlights.

"Robert's a Village item," Tucker said. "He's into movies of a weird order; he's done stuff in Europe with Fellini and people like that...luncheon shit. He wants to be Steve's media coordinator."

Robert Friedman continued to smile benevolently. He had three Brandy Alexanders sitting in front of him. He would study them closely from time to time, smiling secretly to himself; then he would look up again and gaze out blissfully at the restaurant. When Stevie walked in, Robert called out to him.

"Robert?" Stevie said. He turned his head slowly, like a radar-tracking device. "Crazy Robert," Stevie said, edging closer to the booth. "What kind of trouble are you getting yourself into down here?"

"Well, I have three drinks here," Robert observed, "and I cannot decide which glass to drink from. Maybe..."

Robert looked up at Stevie, whose head was nodding with attention like an analyst's.

"...maybe I should just order a new one and have them take these away," Robert said.

"Yeah," Stevie said, after a moment's thought. "I *knew* it was you."

Tucker came over and took Stevie by the arm. He led Stevie over to the table and introduced him to the Human Kindness Day people.

"These folks, Steve, are terrific people. Don and Carol, this is Steve."

The black man who was Don took Stevie's outstretched hand and shook it firmly. Carol looked up and made a twittering sound, like a bird coming out of an egg.

"I'll leave you all to chat," Tucker said, easing Stevie into a seat. He pointed with his thumb in the direction of Robert Friedman. "I'm going over yonder to hang out with Buffalo Bob. Call if you need me."

"Ira," Robert said, squinting up under the brim of his hat, "I'm having a terribly difficult time relating, man."

"I can relate to you, pardner," Tucker said. "You're the midnight cowboy."

Robert nodded, "I think that chick at your table is about to flip," he whispered to Tucker. He stared at Carol and waved again. "She's got electric eyes, man."

Carol caught Robert's wave with the corner of her eye. She fluttered with her hand next to her face to shield him from view.

"Well," she said with a strained voice. "I'm so happy we finally have a chance to talk to you, Steve."

She paused for a response, but Stevie kept silent and pulled at an ornament hanging around his neck.

"I don't know how much you know about Human Kindness Day," she said. "We sent some literature—" Her partner cut her off with a sweep of his hand.

"Let me lay it on what we're basically about," he said. His large eyes strained outward from their sockets.

"Human Kindness Day is on the order of a celebration," he told Stevie. "A total concept thing. We gather as many voices as possible together and concentrate on the dynamic and beautiful power of human warmth: brothers and sisters rapping, tuning in on the goodness that surrounds them, conscious of problems but at the same time optimistic and looking forward, dig—seeking solutions. And we take all these positive things that are the result of people coming together and sharing themselves with others, and we reach out and say—yes!"

The black man closed his fist dramatically in midair, clutching at nothing. Stevie regarded him with the utmost gravity.

"We make one person the focus of the celebration each year," Carol said. "We dedicate Human Kindness Day to that person."

"And that person," Stevie said, "is...uh...me. Right?"

"We would be delighted if this year we could have Human Kindness Day honoring Stevie Wonder." She spoke as if she were reading off a theater marquee.

"The last two years," Don said, "we've had Dick Gregory and Nina Simone—"

"Everybody said Nina Simone wouldn't do it," Carol interrupted. "But I believe we touched her with our enthusiasm...."

Don silenced his partner again by restraining her arm.

"But this year," he went on, "we're trying for an even bigger event than we've had previously. That's why we want you to hook up to this, man. You have such a heavy impact factor. It would give us a national posture."

"Yes, well..." Stevie said. "See, that's the basic problem with what you're saying."

A spasm of alarm slithered across Carol's face.

"Problem?" she asked.

"That's right," Stevie said.

He ran his fingertips underneath his glasses and rubbed the corner of one eye.

"See," he said to them, "I've always tried to avoid doing the sort of thing you're speaking about—not that I don't think that what you're doing is a beautiful thing, you understand. But... if you're actually speaking about a day that is...ah... dedicated to brotherhood and love and kindness—which, as I say, is a very important thing. As a matter of fact, this sort of celebration is something of a personal dream for me—"

"I knew you would relate to this solidly," Don said.

"Well, to the concept, yes," Stevie said. "I relate to your *purpose*, you see. But as far as *honoring* me…uh…as far as making this a Stevie Wonder Day, so to speak…I think that's a mistake. Because that takes the focus—you understand what I mean by the focus?—it takes away from the real issue and the real concern, namely human kindness, and it puts it onto me…um…where it really oughtn't to be. Do you see my point here?"

"No, man," Don said quickly, "that's not the thing at all. This a function of the *community*, man. We've got schoolchildren in on this and everything. We run art contests, poster contests; kids write poems for this. It's far-reaching."

"It belongs to the people," Carol said.

"Exactly," Stevie said. "That's how it should be. However…" His head rolled suddenly from one side to the other, as if caught by a breeze. "…it has a way of getting away from the people and concentrating on *individuals*. Such as myself. What I am attempting to explain is how uncool that is. See, this is what is personally very upsetting about my…uh…*position* here. Because my inclination is to help other people whenever I can. I feel like that's a responsibility of mine, you know; I feel it necessary to give something back to people in return for all that they've given me. This is a compelling thing, you understand."

Carol's eyes were blinking spasmodically; her fortitude began to slip away, like water going down the drain. "We are also compelled," she told Stevie. A dreadful smile appeared on her face.

"Uh…yes," Stevie said. "Naturally you are. But as for myself, I know that from experience that when I become involved with something like what you're proposing to me now…suddenly…it's no longer a true thing. People forget about the violence going on in cities. People forget about the wars that are being fought. People forget about all the problems that they started out to deal with. Instead of the attention being where it should be—where it started out being—now you have Stevie Wonder in Concert. Now nobody wants to hear about what they can be doing to make the world a better place. They just want to hear me sing 'Superstition.' Which is not the way is should be."

"You don't have to perform," Don insisted. "That's not where we're at."

"But that's where I'm at," Stevie said. "That's what I *do*. That's what people *expect* me to do. And that's how I make my contribution, you see? That's my way of telling people what's on my mind…that's my way of telling them what *concerns* me. I want to make it clear to you that I take what I do very seriously; and since my accident, I suppose I take it even more seriously. Because from that point on I realized that I was just lucky to be *alive*…you know?…and it became very clear to me that it wasn't enough *just* to be a rock & roll singer or anything of that nature. I had to make *use* of whatever talent I have. So when I get on a stage and perform, I'm *saying* something to people, and I'm saying it in the way that's most effective for me."

Stevie paused and stroked the hair that curled under his lower lip with great concentration.

"When an audience comes to hear me perform," he said, "they know I'm not going to put them to sleep with my moral indignation, dig it? They know I'm going to do a show, which is why they came. So I give them their show; I entertain them, because I am an entertainer, regardless of what a lot of people think. I'm not a politician or a minister, but at the same time I can...ah...*enlighten* them a little."

Stevie placed his palms flat on the table and beat a light tattoo on its surface. "I speak through my music," he said, "because that's where my credentials are. And people know, when they hear me, that I'm not selling them anyone else's product. They know I'm speaking for myself."

Carol produced her Kleenex again and dabbed it under her nose. She allowed the tissue to dangle limply from her fingers and sniffed heavily.

"I think that chick is about to go bongos at any moment," Robert Friedman said, peering at her from his seat. "Is she stoned?"

"No, man," Tucker said to him. "She's just high-strung, that's all."

"I'm stoned," Robert explained. "But I maintain, Ira. That's important."

"Vital," Tucker said.

Robert Friedman nodded judiciously. "But sometimes," he told Tucker, "you absolutely cannot maintain. Sometimes it's impossible to relate."

Robert suddenly leaped to his feet. "How can anybody maintain in this hotel?" he demanded. "There's no way! The dam has broken, Ira. The shit is on the loose." Robert Friedman's cowboy hat fell off his head and crashed onto the table.

"Slow down, Hoss," Tucker said, handing the hat back. "The movie isn't over yet."

He felt a tug at his sleeve and looked up to see Stevie standing next to him. "Robert was about to get on his steed and ride off into the sunset," Tucker told him.

"Solid," Stevie said absently. "Listen, Tucker, I have to speak to you. I want to know where you get these people that you keep bringing to me."

"Those folks over there?" Tucker asked. "Why, they're from Human Kindness Day, man. Didn't they tell you what the hit was?"

"Yeah," Stevie said, "they want me to perform, Tucker. That's what they want."

"They don't want you to do any such shit," Tucker said.

"They *say* they don't," Stevie said. "They always *say* they don't. But then you show up and suddenly there's a piano and there's a microphone and how about doing just one small set? I mean that's how it always goes down, Tucker."

Stevie bent over and brought his head next to Tucker's ear; he lowered his voice to a whisper. "I mean, I tried to deal with the philosophy of the issue," he said, "but they just keep pushing the gig. It's upsetting me tremendously."

"Don't do anything you aren't getting paid for," Robert Friedman said. He had slumped back in his chair and had assembled himself into a configuration of serenity; his eyes were as flat and glassy as a skating rink.

"Okay," Tucker told Stevie. "I'll go back over there and straighten it out. But you know something?"

"Tell me," Stevie said.

"You're probably going to end up helping those nice people out. Do you want to know why?"

"Because I'm a good guy," Stevie said with a smile. "I'm a pussycat."

"No, man," Tucker said, standing up. "That's not it. You're going to do it because you're a committed person."

"Right," Stevie said. "I figured that was it."

Tucker put his arm around Stevie's shoulders and began to walk him back to his table. "Face it, man," Tucker said. "You gotta do what you gotta do. You're a professional, after all."

Stevie looked at Tucker and grinned furiously.

"A professional," he said. He stamped his feet in delight. "Ain't that just right!"

Tania's World

by Howard Kohn and David Weir   November 1975

Patty Hearst and Steven Weed were home in their Berkeley apartment watching *The Magician* on TV at nine o'clock on the foggy night of February 4th, 1974. The young couple lived together in something that used to be called sin and smoked an occasional joint. But in Berkeley they were considered straight.

Outside, a stolen 1964 Chevrolet Impala convertible pulled up in front and dimmed its lights. Donald DeFreeze, Willie Wolfe and Nancy Ling Perry emerged and moved silently to apartment number four. Perry rang the doorbell while De-Freeze and Wolfe waited in the shadows. Perry hunched over and held a hand to her face. "I just had a car accident out front. Could you…?"

Weed cracked open the door, and DeFreeze and Wolfe burst in, brandishing guns, knocking him to the floor and kicking him in the face with heavy boots. They grabbed Patty and carried her kicking and screaming to the waiting car. There they shoved her into the trunk with a brusque order: "Get in and keep quiet."

Patty was scared and half naked, but she stared hard-eyed at her kidnappers. "Don't give me any shit." Even in those first terrible moments, Patricia Campbell Hearst managed to summon up the daring and arrogance that had been her style through nineteen years of life as an heiress to the Hearst fortune.

Her parents had provided every indulgence, tolerated her dope smoking, her sneaking out to rock concerts at San Francisco's Fillmore auditorium and her faded blue jeans. When she couldn't accept the Catholic school discipline that required her to scrub toilets for breaking petty rules, her parents transferred her to a more flexible nonsectarian school.

It was there she met Weed, a math teacher and the school's most eligible bachelor. Two years later, when she was eighteen, she moved in with him. Her parents initially disapproved and Patty briefly worked at paying her own bills, holding a $2.25-per-hour job in a department store for four months. But when she gave that up to return to school, her father paid for her books, tuition and the out-of-wedlock apartment as well.

Patty was not used to discomfort. She was kept blindfolded in a stuffy, closet-size room with a bare light bulb and a portable cot. There were no windows, and it was hot. She lost track of time and didn't feel like eating. She was told her parents loved money more than her.

She was not raped or starved or otherwise brutalized. But Donald DeFreeze, the SLA leader known as Cinque, kept up constant intimidation. He berated her and her family for being part of a ruling class that was sucking blood from the common people.

"Your mommy and daddy are insects," he yelled. "They should be made to crawl on their hands and knees like insects if they want you back."

Patty tried to defend her parents. They had not hurt anyone. They were good people. Cinque was wrong. He had never met them. But Patty feared Cinque. He told her she'd be killed if her parents did not meet the SLA's demands, and she believed him.

So Patty grew impatient as the ransom negotiations bogged down. "I felt my parents were debating how much I was worth," she said later. "Like they figured I was worth $2 million but I wasn't worth $10 million. It was a terrible feeling that my parents could think of me in terms of dollars and cents. I felt sick all over."

★   ★   ★

Randolph Hearst was stunned. "You went ahead without even talking to me. I can't believe it!"

His wife, Catherine, stared defiantly. The Symbionese Liberation Army had threatened to kill their nineteen-year-old daughter if Mrs. Hearst accepted an appointment to the University of California Board of Regents. On the afternoon of March 13th, 1974, Governor Ronald Reagan phoned her with an offer.

"I can hold your appointment until this is all over," Reagan said. "I don't want to pressure you one way or the other. Do what you think is best for Patty."

Catherine told him, "I'll take it right now. I'm not going to give in to a bunch of hoodlums."

Randy (as he is called by his friends and employees), president of *The San Francisco Examiner,* the youngest son of William Randolph Hearst, heard about it on the radio. He confronted his wife late that night at their Hillsborough mansion: Patty's life was at stake. Catherine was adamant; she knew the stakes and she had done the right thing. Randolph Hearst swore at her and stalked out.

At the SLA's San Francisco hide-out twenty miles north, Patty also heard the radio broadcast. It was the final evidence that her parents had abandoned her. It became the pivotal moment in her change from Hearst to Tania.

Catherine had never forgiven Patricia for leaving Sunday mass, forsaking the Burlingame Country Club and moving in with Steven Weed, whom Catherine considered a charmless gold digger. To Catherine, it was Randy who indulged Patricia; he had been wrong to pay for her living with Weed then, and he was wrong now. It was his fault more than anyone's: if Patty had not been let loose in the radical life of Berkeley, none of this would have happened.

Patty was his favorite daughter. She was known as "Randy's spoiled brat." From the beginning he had been willing to reach an accord with the SLA. He set up the $2 million food giveaway over Catherine's objections. He liked the agent in charge of the FBI's San Francisco office, but had little faith that the FBI could find his daughter…or bring her back alive.

With his political clout and the family fortune, he felt better equipped to find Patty himself. His daughter was apparently in the hands of radicals; so he tried to hire the Left. In Berkeley's radical circles the word went out: for the right information Randolph Hearst was willing to pay a handsome finder's fee.

★   ★   ★

Steve Soliah took only a passing interest in the SLA. He spent his days painting houses and reserved his evenings for partying with friends and playing his guitar. But like many Berkeley people, Steve knew some of Patty's kidnappers secondhand. And his sister, Kathy, had waited tables with Angela Atwood.

Then on May 17th, 1974, Los Angeles police surrounded a grubby bungalow where the SLA was holed up. As the news spread through Berkeley, several friends and neighbors gathered with Steve in front of a black-and-white television set at the old house he shared with friends near the University of California campus. They could hear the barking of police gunfire long after there was no answer from the bungalow. Steve was twenty-six years old and had been living in the Berkeley area for three years. This was the first time he'd felt sympathy for people he regarded as violent revolutionaries.

"I feel sick," he said, flicking off the TV.

Kathy Soliah, a year older than Steve, felt a more personal outrage. Her good friend Angela Atwood was dead in the ashes, her body so burned that identification had to be based on her dental records. Kathy had met Angela a year before when both auditioned for roles in a local theatrical production of *Hedda Gabler.* Angela then had helped her get a waitress job at the Great Electric Underground restaurant in the basement of the San Francisco Bank of America world-headquarters building. They had quit their jobs together after the restaurant manager refused to alter uniforms they felt were demeaning.

In the days following the L.A. shoot-out, an anger welled up in the coffee-houses and communes of Berkeley. Many radicals had initially shunned comment about the SLA because of its violent tactics and because of suspicions that SLA leader Donald DeFreeze was a police agent. Now they spoke up at rallies that eulogized the six dead SLA soldiers as heroes in a progressive cause. Randolph Hearst saw the shifting mood and remarked acidly that, had the police not over-reacted, the SLA members "wouldn't have been martyrs but would have been seen as dingbats."

Kathy Soliah was among those most affected by the shoot-out. At a memorial rally for the SLA on June 2nd, Kathy pledged solidarity with the group. She began devoting her spare time to radical textbooks and long political discussions. During house parties, while Steve and others were enjoying the bonhomie, she would sit in a corner and talk politics with her boyfriend, twenty-six-year-old James Kilgore.

Kilgore, who wore a bristling handlebar mustache that belied a mild-mannered, intellectual nature, was Steve's good friend and house-painting partner. As Kathy and Kilgore both became more absorbed by the SLA, Steve was inexorably drawn in.

In the fall of 1974, Kathy helped plan a Bay Area Research Collective (BARC) conference called "Eat the Rich, Feed the Poor, SLA Knows the Score." Only a few people attended. Four months had passed since the L.A. shoot-out and indignation had dissipated. But the convention was a kind of homecoming rally for Patty Hearst.

Patty had spent the summer on a Pennsylvania farm with two other SLA fugitives, Bill and Emily Harris. They had been harbored by Jack Scott, the controversial sports author who had wanted to write a book about the SLA. But the three had split with Scott because of his aversion to violence and, in late September, they returned to California.

Patty and the Harrises had left California after the shoot-out because they couldn't find anyone willing to hide them. Standing up for the SLA at a demonstration was one step; risking a police siege by inviting the country's most wanted fugitives under your roof was an incalculable leap beyond that. The situation had not changed by the fall, except for the emerging boldness of the Soliahs, Kilgore and a few close associates who formed the SLA's "new team."

Two of their SLA comrades, Joseph Remiro and Russell Little, were awaiting trial for the SLA assassination of Oakland school superintendent Marcus Foster, and the fugitives decided to set up a base in Sacramento, the California state capital, only ninety minutes north of the San Francisco Bay Area.

With help from some members of the new team who knew the Sacramento turf, the Harrises moved into a dingy frame duplex about a mile from the Sacramento courthouse in November 1974. The front porch looked out onto the stark cement buttresses of Interstate 80. The expressway noise, which sometimes shook the windows, helped prevent eavesdropping by a fellow tenant who lived on the other side of a thin wall dividing the house. Steve Soliah loaned the Harrises his 1962 turquoise Corvair, which they parked in the back yard next to a pile of plywood, broken chairs and other junk. The Harrises left the grass and bushes untrimmed, and the house's peeling white paint blended into the unkempt neighborhood.

One of their correspondents was thirty-two-year-old Wendy Yoshimura, who had met the SLA fugitives through Jack Scott the previous summer. After sharing room and board at the Pennsylvania farmhouse, Wendy had returned to the Bay Area at the same time as Patty and the Harrises. She had been driven across country by twenty-two-year-old Margaret Turcich, a tall brown-haired waitress and close friend of Kathy Soliah. Instead of joining the SLA in Sacramento, Wendy decided to stay in San Francisco with Turcich.

Turcich and Kathy Soliah kept working as waitresses in the Bay Area; Kilgore and Steve Soliah continued to paint houses. And the Soliahs and Kilgore kept their addresses in Berkeley. Patty moved to Sacramento with the Harrises but, as another security precaution, took an apartment nearby. She regularly visited the Harris house, pedaling there on a ten-speed bicycle.

Patty still regarded the Harrises as family—they were her big brother and sister. For months they had protected and cared for her. But Patty began seeing a lot of Steve Soliah. The two became close friends and lovers. When Patty became depressed or tense, Steve could change her mood. Nothing seemed to upset him. Since her kidnapping, Patty had been living with intense, serious-minded people. Steve's capacity for humor was a welcome change. He was full of smiles and hugs. He had a full beard and golden hair to his shoulders. Friends called him a big teddy bear. He liked to get outdoors, go jogging or cycling. Patty had fun with him and felt somehow divorced from the reality of the SLA.

★   ★   ★

Randolph Hearst's well-bred ability to adapt to his guests and his self-deprecating sense of humor charmed nearly every radical who met him during his search for Patty. "I've never put in an honest day's work in my life," he liked to joke. "I don't really know what it's like out there." But during the long months of 1974 he called upon all the resources under his command: a newspaper, some considerable political influence and his Hearst inheritance.

In the first weeks after the kidnapping, Winnebagos and TV sound trucks clogged the street outside his Hillsborough mansion. The press had encamped for what they thought would be the duration. Someone at one of the television networks hit on the idea of nailing a portable phone on a convenient tree; the other two networks quickly installed phones on their own trees.

Hearst stayed calm through all this, shaking hands and chatting with anyone who might have word of Patty. He had three secretaries to answer all letters and phone calls, no matter how irrelevant they seemed. Several offers of help came from psychics, mystics, seers and ESP experts. Hearst expressed interest. Soon he was entertaining a host of rip-off artists. One swami set up an altar on the dining-room table, using one of Patty's shoes for inspiration. After a week of unanswered prayer the swami moved into the San Francisco Hilton where he ran up a $300 liquor bill on Randolph's tab. Another psychic asked to be thrown into the trunk of a car and driven away in a reconstruction of Patty's abduction.

Hearst didn't believe in the hocus-pocus. But he scrutinized the con men with the shrewd assumption that someone among them might be a real SLA informant dressed up like a Mama Crystal Ball to get past the FBI.

Hearst was willing to try almost anything to get Patty back. He debated one plan that involved hiring an ex-CIA agent to infiltrate the underground. The spy was to contact the SLA and offer an all-expenses-paid trip to Cuba, where they would be safe from the FBI. But Catherine vetoed the idea. She was afraid Patty might become a Communist. Catherine, however, wasn't around for most of the scheming. The constant tension unnerved her, and doctors ordered her to a sickbed.

Hearst's biggest clout was with *The San Francisco Examiner*, the leading survivor of the newspapers established by his father. Initially, he tried to placate the SLA by printing its long treatises. He also censored stories about Donald DeFreeze's history as a police informer and ordered one reporter not to investigate the SLA.

Later, another *Examiner* reporter used an old underworld contact, Mickey Cohen, to look for Patty. Mickey talked to a numbers racketeer in Cleveland who claimed to have seen her. But Mickey dropped out of the chase because, he said, he didn't want to see Patty end up in prison.

Most of Randolph's hope, however, was devoted to the world of political radicals. "Radicals may think I'm a reactionary asshole," he told one such activist, "but at least I'm a reactionary asshole who will talk to radicals."

Joanna Harcourt-Smith, the girlfriend of Timothy Leary, approached Hearst with a prospective trade: the imprisoned Leary for the kidnapped Patty. Joanna claimed that forty-eight-year-old Clifford Jefferson, a San Quentin inmate known as

Death Row Jeff, was considered a godparent of the SLA. He had introduced Cinque to some of the original SLA members and, according to his own court testimony, he had approved the SLA assassination of Marcus Foster.

Randolph quickly sidestepped Leary and Joanna and hired attorney Vincent Hallinan, the seventy-seven-year-old hero of the Thirties labor movement and the Fifties anti-McCarthy movement. Hallinan visited Death Row Jeff, and for a while the connection seemed promising. Jeff, hoping that Hearst's intervention might make life behind bars more bearable, agreed to help. But negotiations broke down with no visible result.

These failures frustrated Hearst. But they also changed him. For the first time he was dealing directly with people who lived on the edge of desperation. His own fears for his daughter seemed less anxious by comparison.

★   ★   ★

In October 1974, Bill Harris wrote a friend that he and the other SLA fugitives considered themselves at war with the system. But they were not "mad revolutionaries," he claimed. They were urban guerrillas trained to fight on, "sanely, calculatedly." At the same time, Harris added the title "General" to his adopted name Teko. Emily and Patty had accepted Bill as the group's leader after the death of Donald DeFreeze, a.k.a. Cinque. But Harris's new title signaled a renewed emphasis on militarism. He was now the official commander, in charge of his own army.

Harris had been born twenty-nine years before on an army base at Fort Sill, Oklahoma. From there he had become an Episcopal acolyte, a golfer, a thespian, a postgraduate in urban education and a U.S. marine in Vietnam. Vietnam was his introduction to violence. He came home bitter and no longer sure of his goals. With his wife, Emily, a schoolteacher he'd married while both were students at Indiana University, Harris moved to Oakland in 1972 and became active in the Vietnam Veterans Against the War (VVAW). There he met Joseph Remiro, a vet seemingly so deranged by Vietnam he used the antiwar movement to show off his combat training. Remiro once almost blew himself up while lighting gasoline he'd splashed around the fuselage of a display air-force jet in a city park.

But Harris was different. Friends remember him as quiet and rational, more interested in serious organizing than in violence. The Harrises began visiting Bay Area prisons, where both were profoundly affected by the black men in cages. In the spring of 1973 they met Cinque, a street tough from Los Angeles who had just escaped from Soledad prison. Cinque was being harbored by Remiro and other people they knew from their work in the VVAW and the prison-reform movement. To some old associates, Cinque was an unimpressive thug who had once robbed a prostitute of ten dollars, turned a buddy in to the police and frequently got drunk on plum wine. But to Remiro, the Harrises and a few close friends, Cinque was a charismatic prophet, whose talk of killing and kidnapping somehow made sense.

Meeting Cinque became a decisive juncture for the Harrises. Emily was completely entranced. "I am in love with a beautiful black man," Emily wrote in a letter to her mother. Suddenly Bill had to confront his own latent feelings of jealousy and racism. His response was dramatic.

Bill began affecting a black slang that mimicked Cinque's accent and ideas. He became Cinque's right-hand man in an army of four white men and five white women that included Emily and Remiro. Harris helped lead the nascent Symbionese Liberation Army team through boot-camp drills in the secluded hills above Berkeley and taught the women members how to load, shoot and break down army carbines that Cinque secured on the black market.

In the fall of 1973, Cinque began selecting targets for political assassination. His first choice was Charles O. Finley, the Oakland A's owner depicted on most sports pages as the petty tyrant of baseball. Cinque expected Finley's execution to produce a media splash for the SLA. But Cinque changed his mind when he heard that the Black Panthers were criticizing the conduct of Marcus Foster, the first black superintendent of Oakland's schools. "We're gonna waste that nigger," Cinque announced.

In January 1974, two months after Foster's execution with cyanide-tipped bullets, Remiro and roommate Russell Little were arrested while carrying one of the murder weapons. The two SLA soldiers were jailed and charged with the killing. That set into motion the kidnapping of Patty Hearst a month later. Patty was to be bartered for Remiro and Little's release. But before these negotiations ever began, Patty changed into Tania.

The SLA's illusion of growing military strength was soon shattered in a Los Angeles bungalow. Now, five months later, Harris was determined to replace Cinque and rebuild the SLA.

"The only high we get is from our actions," Harris said. On April 12th, 1975, a woman (later identified as Patty Hearst wearing a curly brown wig) drove a 1967 black-over-green Pontiac Firebird to a secluded garage in Sacramento. She told the manager she wanted to leave her mother's car there for about a week. She was nervous. She lit three or four cigarettes, stamping each out after a few puffs.

After she left, the garage manager remained suspicious of her behavior and was not surprised when the address she'd given did not check out. He called the Sacramento police. They arrived, discovered that the Firebird had been stolen earlier the same day in Oakland and decided they were onto something big—a gang of car thieves. Plainclothesmen were assigned to stake out the garage.

During the early morning of April 21st, however, the Firebird was driven away from the garage while the police weren't looking. Neighbors of Crocker National Bank in nearby Carmichael noticed the Firebird parked about six blocks from the bank that morning. Sometime after 8:00 a.m. it was moved next to the bank.

At 9:01 a.m., as the Carmichael bank opened for its early customers, four masked bandits shoved through the rear door and, without warning, shotgunned a forty-two-year-old woman waiting to deposit the weekend collections from the Carmichael Seventh Day Adventist Church. They ordered everyone else on the floor, kicking those who didn't move fast enough.

One bandit, a woman, looked at her wristwatch and began timing the operation: "Twenty seconds, thirty seconds . . ." The others scooped up $15,000 from the teller cages. When the count reached four minutes, all four fled outside and jumped into the Firebird. They abandoned the car a few blocks away and escaped in another car into the midmorning traffic.

The exact identities of the bank robbers, who wore wigs and covered their faces with ski masks and scarves, may never be known. But the FBI, in leaks to the media, has put forward the following allegations, based on fingerprints and other physical evidence:

Bill Harris, they say, was the gunman who murdered the woman customer. Emily Harris was the woman timing the action. Their accomplices were Steve Soliah and Patty Hearst. A fifth robber who served as the lookout was James Kilgore, Kathy Soliah's boyfriend.

According to police sources, this was the second SLA robbery in two months. On February 25th, two SLA members allegedly held up the Guild Savings and Loan Association in Sacramento for $3729. The next day a man identified as Bill Harris bought a 1966 Chevrolet station wagon with twenty-dollar bills apparently taken in the robbery. Soon after, Steve Soliah allegedly used crisp new twenties to buy a 1967 Ford Galaxie later recovered by police near Kilgore's apartment.

Harris had plans for a half dozen more bank holdups in Sacramento, according to police. The banks had been scouted, and detailed maps had been drawn. But the robberies were not carried out. Instead, as the Remiro-Little trial ended with guilty verdicts in early June, the SLA fugitives moved back to San Francisco.

Patty allegedly carried with her "bait money" from the April 21st robbery. As required by the Federal Deposit Insurance Corporation, the Carmichael bank had registered the serial numbers from a sheaf of bills and planted the "bait money" in a teller's cashbox where any bank robber would be sure to snatch it. Three months

later the FBI would find the money in a refrigerator cache at a San Francisco apartment where Patty lived.

★   ★   ★

When Jack Scott left the fugitives in September 1974, he believed he was finished with the SLA. He was living in Oregon with Portland basketball star Bill Walton and looking forward to writing about sports again. By now he counted himself a critic of Patty and the Harrises. He disagreed with their affinity for violence and disliked their preoccupation with themselves.

Yet part of his initial fascination remained. Being underground with the fugitives had been the most exciting time in his life. Then one morning in late fall he received a call from his parents in Las Vegas. His older brother Walter had just arrived with a request for money.

Walter was forty-one, nine years older than Jack. The two brothers had been political opposites since their days as high-school sports stars in Scranton, Pennsylvania. Walter had worked most of his adult life for a government that Jack felt was dangerously repressive. Walter had been a computer specialist and, he claimed, a hit man for various intelligence agencies. But now he needed money, he said, because he had been fired by the government after going on an unauthorized shooting spree that left three people dead in Egypt.

Working for the government was the major motivation left in Walter's life. His two marriages had fallen apart, and he was no longer close to any friends. His father, an unsuccessful businessman now managing a modern, middle-income apartment building in Las Vegas, did not know how to handle him. Walter's home-comings always seemed to cause trouble.

But Jack felt a loyalty to his brother. When Jack was a kid, Walter had coached him on how to run races and had helped him keep out of trouble. So Jack grabbed his checkbook and caught the next plane to Las Vegas. He had spent nearly $20,000 helping the SLA fugitives during his unsuccessful book venture. But he still had money left from the $40,000 given him in settlement earlier in the year for stepping down as athletic director at Oberlin College.

Jack loaned Walter $3000, and the two poured a few drinks. By the time their parents went to bed, both Jack and Walter were high. Walter talked boldly of his secret life as an assassin. Jack could not resist an urge to shock Walter with his own summer adventures at the Pennsylvania farmhouse. He had been fishing and sunbathing with Patty Hearst only a half-hour's drive from where the Scotts had grown up.

Patty Hearst
Photograph by AP/WIDE WORLD PHOTOS

271

"The cops were chasing all over the country for her and all the time she was there with me," Jack congratulated himself. "Would you believe it?"

Walter said he found it hard to believe. So Jack persisted, filling in dates and other details until he had furnished Walter with a story he could trade for countless favors from the FBI.

Even when he was living with the fugitives, Jack had tended to involve others in the experience. But confiding in Walter was Jack's worst mistake. In two months, Walter was again short of cash and relying heavily on the bottle. Twice while on binges he found himself tempted to sell Jack's secret. In early January he phoned the police in Washington, D.C. A few days later he called the FBI office in Philadelphia. He gave each the message that Jack Scott had harbored Patty Hearst, but he hung up before revealing his name.

The FBI, frustrated for months by the SLA case, routinely chased down the anonymous tips. Agents visited Walton's A-frame house in Portland to ask Jack and his wife Micki for a response. The Scotts feigned ignorance, and the matter was dropped.

Then on the Friday night of January 31st, Walter got drunk again and stopped by the police station in his home town of Scranton to see an old high-school buddy. "I've got the hottest fucking story in the world to tell you," he told Captain Clem Ross. "I know where Patty Hearst is."

Ross listened and, after Walter sobered up, marched him over to the FBI. This time Walter spilled the full account and then packed off to England and Ireland, flush with a fat informant's fee and the promise of a future high-paying government job.

With Walter's information, FBI agents soon discovered the SLA's farmhouse hide-out. Lab experts found fingerprints from Bill Harris and Wendy Yoshimura on broken glass, and a trained dog detected Patty's scent in a bed. The FBI had its first solid lead in the months since the L.A. shoot-out.

Federal grand jury subpoenas were issued for Jack and Micki. Jack learned of them February 26th when FBI agents showed up with the subpoenas at his parents' house while he happened to be visiting. The agents didn't spot Jack, however, and he took the opportunity to pick up Micki and disappear to think things through.

In the meantime, FBI agents chased down the rest of Walter's information and located Jay Weiner, a twenty-one-year-old sportswriter who had become friends with the Scotts while a student at Oberlin College. During the SLA stay at Pennsylvania, Scott had asked Weiner to serve as a backup for the fugitives in emergencies. Weiner had refused. But he had seen the fugitives, and he knew the story of Jack's involvement with the SLA.

Three FBI men found Weiner at 11:00 p.m. March 11th, as he was leaving a friend's apartment near the Oberlin campus. Weiner was backing out the driveway when the FBI car veered across his path. One agent jumped out, rushed over, pulled out his badge and flashed the gun in his shoulder holster.

"Are you scared?" he asked.

"Sure, I'm scared," Weiner replied. "What do you want with me?"

The agents brusquely escorted the short-haired young writer to a nearby campus-security office. There he sat sweating in a brightly lit room while the three agents took turns questioning him. Weiner felt alone and intimidated. The agents made him believe his whole future was in jeopardy. Three hours later he had confessed everything he knew about Jack.

But Weiner's disclosures, according to one FBI source, doused the agency's enthusiasm. He convinced them they were following a cold trail. The fugitives had left the farmhouse five months before, Weiner told the agents, and Jack had not seen them since.

Jack and Micki were still hiding out in tourist hotels under false names while they talked to attorneys about their legal status. On April 9th, six weeks after they had dropped from sight, they surfaced at a San Francisco press conference. But by then the FBI had lost interest in the Scotts. And the federal grand jury in Harrisburg, Pennsylvania, which had been studying charges against them, dropped its investigation after Weiner, angered by his FBI treatment, refused to repeat his testimony to the grand jurors.

But Randolph Hearst was very interested in Jack. A few hours after the Scott press conference, while Jack and Micki were watching themselves on the evening news, Hearst was on the phone to a friend of the Scotts.

"If it's at all possible I would like to meet with Mr. and Mrs. Scott right away." Hearst was tactfully urgent. "I understand they are good people who may be able to tell a father something about his daughter."

When Jack heard that Hearst wanted a private audience, he was excited. Patty had told him she did not feel her parents were equally "Pig Hearsts." Catherine was an irredeemable snob, Patty had explained, "but my father can be reasonable—he tries to understand why everyone isn't rich like him." Now Scott had a chance to see for himself.

But Jack was also leery, afraid the FBI might be using Hearst to trick him into a confession to be used against him in Harrisburg. In a second phone conversation the next morning, Randolph assured Jack's friend that the talk would be clandestine. "I give you my word the FBI will not know of it. This is something that concerns only me."

Scott still hesitated. He wanted to test Hearst's eagerness. He typed out a three-sentence statement that lauded Jack and Micki as "nonviolent, sincere people [who helped Patty] for humanitarian reasons." If Hearst would embrace the statement as his own, Scott bargained, he could have the meeting. The statement appeared the next day in a front-page story in the *Examiner.*

Jack was satisfied Hearst was in earnest. The next night Hearst met the two Scotts at the home of their San Francisco friend. Jack and Randolph quickly struck up a conversation about sports. The two were still talking and drinking vodka on the rocks two hours before dawn. Hearst was trying his best to put Jack at ease. Finally he asked about his daughter. "I'm really worried about Patty's health."

Jack answered cryptically. "If the person we're talking about was in fact your daughter, she was in good health when I saw her six months ago."

"What about being pregnant?"

"If that same person was Patty, she wasn't pregnant. That was a disguise."

"Isn't it true that Cinque was responsible for getting her pregnant?"

"No."

Randy asked only a few more questions. For the first time he was talking to someone who had been underground with Patty, and he didn't want to antagonize Jack. He was just happy to hear she was okay. At the end of the long evening Randy made a standing offer to Jack. "If there's anything I can do for you, let me know any time." Jack filed it away for a future day.

In early June he called Hearst for another conference. On July 11th, sixty-nine days before Patty would be captured, Scott dined with Randolph and Catherine Hearst at Senor Pico, a popular restaurant in Ghiradelli Square near Fisherman's Wharf in San Francisco.

Based on his talks with an SLA messenger, Jack had learned that Patty's loyalties were drifting away from the SLA. She was beginning to feel that the SLA's macho style did not fit in with her new sense of feminism. Patty had also expressed an awakening homesickness for her family; she had even talked of secretly visiting them. Jack kept most of this information to himself. But he hinted broadly to the Hearsts that he knew how to contact Patty and that she might be willing to return if the right arrangement could be reached.

Scott and Patty's parents drove the few blocks from Senor Pico to the Hearst's new apartment on Nob Hill, where they had moved after putting their Hillsborough mansion up for sale. Scott and Hearst continued their talk in the living room of the apartment while Catherine went into the bedroom.

As at their first meeting, Scott was careful not to say anything that could later become court testimony against him. But this time he was the aggressor, trying to sound out what Hearst's standing offer of last time actually meant. Jack felt that if Patty could surface with her new political beliefs intact, he could cut a deal and still retain his credibility as a radical. But he wasn't sure what he could get from Hearst—a lump sum for his expenses and legal fees or a long-term syndicated sports column in the Hearst newspapers or perhaps some other favor that could not be traced to a deal.

Hearst perceived Scott's motives for calling the meeting. Scott was the closest he had come to his daughter in more than a year of searching, and Hearst wanted to proceed scrupulously. He broached a hypothetical scenario for his daughter's return.

"What if Catherine resigned from the Board of Regents?" Randy asked. "Would that help convince Patty to come back?"

"It might," Jack answered.

Since their quarrel during the SLA ransom negotiations, Randolph had not said anything to Catherine about resigning her regent seat. But if it came down to a deal, he had decided, he was going to overrule any objection from her. He had never liked her ultraconservative contributions as a regent anyway. When some of her more vitriolic remarks at a 1972 regents meeting made headlines, *San Francisco Chronicle* columnist Herb Caen reported that Catherine was "catching a little hell on the home front." Catherine told another *Chronicle* reporter that Randolph "says the only time he wants to see my name in the paper again is in the obituary column."

Jack again stayed up drinking with Randy until the early-morning hours, a circumstance that so irritated Catherine she barged out of her bedroom at one point and confronted her husband: "What is he still doing here?" Jack left shortly after, unsure whether a deal would, or could, ever be worked out.

Then Randolph told Catherine of Jack's feeling that her resignation "couldn't hurt." "I will not," she snapped. "I don't trust that little weasel Scott for a minute. He's just like all those other glory seekers."

The FBI had maintained a watch on Hearst for any move that might indicate he was getting close in his pursuit of Patty. The day after the Senor Pico dinner, FBI agents dropped by the Hearst apartment to ask about the meeting. Randolph evaded the FBI's questions, anxious not to jeopardize his budding relationship with Scott. But the FBI anticipated Catherine's cooperation, and she provided an obliging account.

Yes, Scott was offering a deal: if Catherine resigned as a regent, he would appeal for Patty's surrender. Yes, he seemed to want money. Yes, he really seemed to know how to get in touch with Patty.

That same morning an FBI source tipped off a *Los Angeles Times* reporter to the talks between Scott and Hearst. The reporter phoned Catherine, and she volunteered her understanding of the proposed deal. The next morning, a Sunday, *The Los Angeles Times* featured a story about the discussion both Jack and Randolph had assumed would remain their secret.

Within hours other reporters started calling Jack for a response. He was enraged and demanded that Randolph deny the story. Hearst did so. But the Hearst-Scott negotiations had been effectively scuttled. The chances for Patty's return, Jack told Randolph, had been greatly diminished. The FBI did not think so. They had just stumbled across their most promising clue since the case began.

★   ★   ★

During the previous long months, according to the FBI's own account, it had checked nearly 50,000 tips, interviewed or spot-checked some 30,000 persons in the Bay Area alone and, at one time or another, employed 8500 agents—about seventy-five percent of the agency's field force. Fictional sightings of Patty Hearst, according to one source, had taken them as far afield as the Algerian embassy in Paris. They had put an Alexandria, Virginia, woman in a hospital for several weeks when they traumatized her by bursting unannounced into her apartment on a tip Patty was inside.

None of that produced the missing heiress. But now it was going to be different. Until Jack's July meeting with the Hearsts, the FBI had regarded his SLA connection to have been severed long ago. But if Jack now knew Patty's whereabouts—and Catherine had persuaded the FBI he did—then a fresh look at him was needed.

On July 29th the FBI sent twelve agents to Oregon to subpoena Jack and Micki before a new Harrisburg grand jury that had just reopened the Scott case. Micki called a Portland record store that evening to reserve two rock-concert tickets. When they arrived to pick them up a half-hour later, the agents were waiting with the subpoenas.

In San Francisco, the SLA fugitives were unaware of the future building for them. They were continuing their daily routine, jogging a mile, debating new actions and trying to mend the emerging split between Patty and the Harrises. The FBI itself did not know how close it was. But its agents had happened onto the right track. They decided that if Scott wouldn't lead them to Patty, his footprints might. They figured that the lead to Jack's current SLA connection could lie in his past SLA involvement. Two leads were left over from their earlier investigation of the Pennsylvania farmhouse: Wendy Yoshimura and a red Volkswagen.

The FBI's first hint of Wendy's ties to the SLA had been her fingerprints in the farmhouse. Although the FBI did not know how she happened to be at the farm, its California agents correctly assumed that Jack had met the SLA fugitives through Wendy or her friends. In their initial investigation, the FBI had turned up Wendy's boyfriend, Willie Brandt, a Berkeley radical sent to Soledad prison in 1972 for bombing a naval ROTC building. Wendy had gone underground after being accused of aiding in the bombing. Brandt could not be Scott's SLA connection because he was still behind bars. But agents guessed that a friend of Brandt's might be. So they rechecked the names on Brandt's list of prison visitors. One who stood out was Kathy Soliah, who had visited Brandt six times, had waited tables with slain SLA member Angela Atwood and had made no secret of her sympathies for the SLA.

The FBI knew of no prior connection between Jack and Kathy. But its New York agents were reinvestigating a red Volkswagen neighbors had noticed parked at the farmhouse the previous summer. Originally the FBI had traced the car to a New York friend of Scott's. Now the same agents rechecked the car's registration. The new name on it was Kathy Soliah.

On September 7th, Patty Hearst and Wendy Yoshimura rented a $180-a-month modern one-bedroom flat in a working-class section of San Francisco, about three miles from where the Harrises lived. General Teko was preoccupied with his latest strategy for the SLA: a bombing campaign in the Bay Area. He had gathered forty pounds of black powder, do-it-yourself bomb kits and helpful public library books like *The Science of High Explosives* and *Fuels, Explosives and Dyestuffs*. Recently they had ordered a box of bomb fuses from Western Reserve Enterprises, a mail-order firm in Independence, Ohio.

Both Harrises continued to excel at the disguises they wore during frequent excursions through the Bay Area, a territory they found easy to travel in after a year of living in unfamiliar places. They seldom bothered with elaborate disguises, preferring wigs, sunglasses, floppy hats and the casual clothes of the street. But when they used mascara, pencil shadow and brown lipstick to change the lines and complexions of their faces, they could have fooled any old associate who passed them by. For pseudonyms, Bill and Emily could choose from a selection of assorted credit cards, social-security cards, drivers' licenses, Blue Cross cards and other IDs they had received by filing phony applications and stealing purses.

Patty kept a similar assortment of disguises and fake IDs. But by late summer 1975, she had lost almost all fascination for the intrigue of the underground. Most of her time was spent away from the Harrises, who no longer seemed like the brother and sister she had once admired.

The new influence in Patty's life was Wendy Yoshimura, the small black-haired daughter of Japanese parents interned in the U.S. during World War II. Wendy had been born behind barbed wire, had grown up in Hiroshima after the atom bomb and had studied art in California before going underground. Patty had begun living with Wendy in June 1975 after returning to San Francisco.

The two often fell into long conversations about their fathers and former boyfriends. Wendy had become an articulate feminist during her three years underground and Patty began to appreciate Wendy's judgment. When Wendy initially criticized the SLA as sexist, Patty had defended Cinque and Teko. But over the summer her opinion changed. She was beginning to view the SLA as a gun-toting gang, heavy on machismo. In early September, Patty and Wendy set down their criticisms of Bill and the SLA in a seven-page letter. The two censured Bill for his machismo and suggested that the SLA's past violence had more to do with chauvinism than radical politics.

On the evening of September 14th, Patty and Wendy took the letter to the Harris apartment for a discussion. Bill read the letter and lashed out at Patty: "What does this mean? Are you trying to say you can be a better leader than I've been?" Before Patty could answer, Bill yelled at Wendy. "This fucking letter is all your doing. You don't even belong here. You're not part of our organization."

Emily sided with Bill. "This isn't a political criticism," she argued. "This is a personal insult to Bill. You're trying to hold him responsible for the things we all did."

The argument continued late into the night, keeping the next-door neighbors awake. Patty and Wendy returned home after deciding to seek the counsel of Kathy Soliah, who was herself both a feminist and an SLA supporter.

Kathy began commuting between the two SLA houses, acting as mediator in the dispute. The FBI agents who had been watching Kathy were puzzled by the additions to her itinerary. They jotted down the addresses—288 Precita and 625 Morse—and asked their superiors for extra surveillance teams.

Only one team was sent out. It chose the Precita house and set up a stakeout. On the afternoon of September 17th, a short, muscular man with a black beard emerged from the flat toting a load of clothes and headed toward a nearby laundromat. One agent crossed the street, walked casually past the man and nodded pleasantly while studying his face. The "make" fit General Teko. The agents phoned in and asked for orders.

Charles Bates, the FBI's San Francisco bureau chief, had suffered unceasing humiliations since the early days of the case when he sat sipping Randolph Hearst's finest liqueurs. Week after week, Bates had waited in his spacious office for the key telephone call, the case-breaking tip. Now suddenly the end was in sight. All that was needed was patience. He ordered his men to sit tight and keep a close watch.

The next morning, neighbors of the Harrises noticed four men in a green LTD pull up next door. Well-dressed men in other late-model cars also moved into the area. Bates was among them. Shortly after noon both Harrises left the house dressed in sweat clothes and tennis shoes for their daily jog around the neighborhood. Bates and his agents waited until 1:25 p.m., when the Harrises returned. Then they swarmed onto the street and handcuffed the couple.

Bates had hoped to spot Patty Hearst before making the arrests. But it seemed reasonable that she was hiding inside the Precita Avenue house. FBI agents rushed up the steps in grinning anticipation of the final SLA capture. No one was there.

Nevertheless, Bates drove back to his office flushed with victory and called a 3:00 p.m. press conference, in time to meet the deadline of the television reporters. A half-hour before the news conference, a mop-up crew of FBI agents and San Francisco cops checked out the Morse Street house that Kathy Soliah had visited. San Francisco police inspector Tim Casey and FBI agent Tom Padden knocked. Wendy Yoshimura came to the door and saw a gun pointed at her head. The cop raced in and caught Patty as she took a step toward the closet. He seemed as surprised as she was. "What are *you* doing here?" he stammered.

It was lucky timing for Bates. He was able to announce the end of the SLA hunt with an understated flourish before 100 assembled reporters.

★   ★   ★

Steve Soliah heard an initial radio report that the Harrises had been busted. He hurried to Patty's apartment and into the hands of police guarding the scene of the capture. He was arrested and later charged with harboring Patty.

That same afternoon, Patty, Wendy and the Harrises were arraigned at the Federal Building. The three women sat quietly, but Bill talked out loud at several points during the proceeding and turned often to survey the audience with a strange, uncomprehending smile. Neither Bill nor Emily talked to Tania. But as Wendy stood up from the defense table to be escorted away, she reached over and laid a comforting hand over Patty's.

Wendy was driven over the Bay Bridge to the Alameda County jail. Steve Soliah was locked in the San Francisco jail. Patty and the Harrises were taken down the peninsula to the San Mateo County jail. Kathy Soliah and boyfriend James Kilgore remained at large.

In the booking room, Patty was fingerprinted and asked the usual questions: name, age, date of birth, occupation. Emily Harris stood next to her as she answered.

"What do you do for a living?" the matron asked.

"Nothing."

"Are you a student?"

"No."

"Well, what are you?"

"Well, I don't do anything."

"Well, how do you make a living?"

"Well, I'm an urban guerrilla."

★   ★   ★

The petty bourgeois, "driven to frenzy" by the horrors of capitalism, is a social phenomenon which, like anarchism, is characteristic of all capitalist countries. The instability of such revolutionariness, its barrenness, its liability to become swiftly transformed into submission, apathy, fantasy and even a "frenzied" infatuation with one or another bourgeois "fad"—all this is a matter of common knowledge.
—LENIN

Mondo Brando

by Chris Hodenfield   May 1976

Marlon Brando's body was going through the motions, awaiting the return of his personality. It was miles away. He was reeling it in like a dancing sailfish.

His van was parked by the trees in a grassy field. Inside it was quiet. The air conditioner diced the air. Minutes had passed since our introduction, but he just sat on the edge of a bed, hands fumbling aimlessly with a hank of wires in a drawer. He picked up a screwdriver and turned it over carefully.

He was a hero whose vanity had surrendered. Beneath those wide oak-stump shoulders was a vast rippling cargo hold, 240 pounds on a five-foot-ten-inch frame. It was neat enough in here, a small brown space piled high with books on solar energy and Indian history. Cupboards were stacked with fresh T-shirts and clean towels, and the icebox was filled with Tab.

When at last he found what he was looking for—a cassette tape of Caribbean drum music—he eased across the bed and rested his head against the curtained window. The silvery-blond hair rolled over his ears. That face. He looks like an old medicine man. He appears as unmovable as the city planetarium. The concentration level is so high that when his distant manner suddenly evaporates and he questions you about your mother, ah, the arena gets hot.

He is, indeed, a presence. On the cowboy movie set of *The Missouri Breaks*, shot on the hot, dry plains of Montana, people seemed to be no more deferential to the actor than they'd be to any pharaoh about to exact tribute. Which is not the normal attitude for a hard-boiled movie crew. They'd see him walking in their direction, with that head balled up like a clenched fist, that forehead all knotted and complicated. People were embalmed with awe. Beethoven must have had the same air. The costar here, Jack Nicholson, had to laugh: "The man does scorch the earth, right? I mean for 200 miles in any direction. Not much leavin's."

Not for many moons has Jack Nicholson been second bill in a picture. I guess a guy will do some funny things for a million dollars. When Nicholson was a high-school kid in Neptune, New Jersey, his very last hero was Brando. Now they are next-door neighbors in Beverly Hills. Still, Nicholson will stare...at his neighbor.

"It's a big problem," Nicholson said, all glassy lizard grins. "I suddenly felt myself feeling an old symptom while working with Marlon, which is that he's so powerful, you fall so in love with what he's doing, that you want to do it yourself. I studied him then, and I find myself now, even when I'm working with him, wanting to emulate him." He grinned. "I think there's a well-known contest in the acting profession to see who can say the best stuff about Marlon."

Nicholson was one of the thousands of jaw-flexing young dogs who fell into the arms of the Method, nursing visions of *On the Waterfront* and *A Streetcar*

Named Desire. Elia Kazan, director of those two, turned out a couple more wonder boys, James Dean in *East of Eden* and Warren Beatty in *Splendor in the Grass.* They joined the ranks of Actors Studio toughs who were labeled Road-Company Brandos. Paul Newman. Vic Morrow. Harvey Keitel and Robert DeNiro are continuing the line.

Now Brando is fifty-two. His step is heavy with reputation. He has dried out in the air of scandal. A walking collection of headlines—a front-page banner on *The Los Angeles Herald Examiner:* NIGHTIE RAMPAGE JAILS BRANDO'S EX. *The Saturday Evening Post,* 1962, after *Mutiny on the Bounty* (an ill-prepared folly with a constantly shuffled script, three directors and an $18.5 million price tag): MARLON BRANDO: HOW HE WASTED $6 MILLION BY SULKING ON THE SET. *Time,* 1954, over a cover painting of Brando as Napoleon for *Desiree:* TOO BIG FOR HIS BLUE JEANS?

So we arrive at *Last Tango in Paris,* where the girl, Jeanne (Maria Schneider) looks at Brando's character and says, "I shall have to invent a name for you." Brando ("Paul") looks away: "Oh, God, I've been called by a million names all my life. I'm better off with a grunt or a groan for a name."

A one-human corporation who has had twenty-six years of the audience's karma invested in him. It's enough to make anyone suspicious of success. Brando is. The executive producer of *Missouri Breaks,* Elliot Kastner, employed everything but extortion to nail down his contract.

Rarely found in Beverly Hills, Brando is forever on the road, attending to his five children, taking them to Tetiaroa, his cluster of atolls near Tahiti, where a grunt or a groan is enough for a name. He builds windmills, methane-gas converters; he saves the turtles. He has funded a scientific study to raise cold-water Maine lobsters in Tahiti! He is as proud as a Republican farmer.

Reporters who ask for interviews find themselves presented with conditions. To talk about solar energy, or the American Indian, because Brando has received some undesirable dividends on his public image. Like the time he sat with some respected Indian leaders in a restaurant at a time when tensions were running high over the Wounded Knee trial and suddenly there appeared a woman with a plate of butter in her hand requesting a *Last Tango* performance. The actor crumpled. "Please, lady."

I wasn't in Brando's van five minutes, and I was playing catch-up ball. He does not take up a point and extrapolate to the far measures. He *starts* on a virgin asteroid and winds his way back to earth, free versing and free associating, leaving behind his poetic blur of images about the Russian troops hovering at the Mongolian border, and what starvation does to a baby's brain, and the time he drove through the African riverbeds during monsoon season....

He sat absolutely still, his shoulders parked on the pillow like a grand piano. The sad, brooding eyes drank in all the details. And as for the relationship between his body and the space around him, Bernardo Bertolucci's observation was very true. "We are usually dominated by space," the *Last Tango* director told Jonathan Cott, "but Brando strangely *dominates* space. Even if Brando is absolutely still, say, sitting on a chair...Brando has already taken for himself that privileged space. And Brando's attitude toward life is different from that of other people because of this fact."

Any mention of moviedom would be sidestepped very neatly. Finally I asked if he loathed the subject. "No," he said, shaking his head with no great commitment. The eyes darted, and the great train pulled into a distant station.

"Kazan is a performer's director," he said suddenly. "The best director I ever worked with. Because most actors...it's very lonely out there. Most actors don't get help from directors. Emotional help, if you're playing an emotional part. Kazan is the only one I know who really gives you help.

"Most of the time you just come like a journeyman plumber, and you gotta have your own bag of stuff, ready to go. But the people who perceive most delicately are Bertolucci and Gillo Pontecorvo [*Burn!*]. I never worked with, ah...the guy that did *Mean Streets*. Yeah, Scorsese, he's the best American director there is. He's a remarkable talent. He uses the actors very well, his intuitions allow him..."

He arrested his thought and glanced at my hands. I was twirling my sunglasses.

"What you're doing now, playing with your glasses and looking at me. Shaking your head in moments you don't plan on."

I stopped playing with my glasses, blinked and smiled.

"And blinking and smiling, moving your head. You see, all those are unplanned things. You don't know what you're going to do in sequence. And Bertolucci and Scorsese would allow you to do that. They put you in the psychological circumstances so that you would do all that stuff and that is...that's the essence of reality.

"Now the mere fact that I mentioned it set off a whole bunch of movements on your face. Because in some small measure you were frightened by it. Everybody has a very low threshhold of fear, and they carry it around and they don't know it. They don't know that they're being afraid if they do something like that. You talk to some people, and they'll hang on your eyes for maybe a twelve count, and they'll just *have* to get away. They can't stand eye contact. They'll look everywhere...and once in a while they'll give you a little flick just to make it look real.

"But they can't stand it. They're the only ones who know it, unless you're aware of the patterns of gestures.

"Shakespeare said something that was remarkable. You don't hear it very often. He said, 'There is no art that finds the mind's construction on the face.' Meaning that there is the art of poetry, music or dancing, architecture or painting, whatever. But to find people's minds by their face, especially their face, is an art, and it's not recognized as an art.

"We're just big computers is all. You inevitably store stuff up and for no reason at all. Right in the middle of a conversation, you'll start thinking of a short-handled hoe. It won't be related to anything, except something in your dreams has to do with a rubber telephone. 'Why was I thinking about a rubber telephone?'" He shrugged it off.

I told him that I had the impression that he was dredging up his own memories for *Last Tango*. Were they painful?

"No, because after a while it becomes a technical thing. I was putting things in my eyes to make tears in my eyes. I was making the right noises, the sounds of sobs. But, ah, I used to do that stuff straight. But it's too taxing."

He emphasizes such a point with a pincerlike grab at his chest. "For instance, now I don't even learn the lines. I don't learn them for a very specific reason, but..." He groped for a reason, and his eyes rested on me. "You see, you didn't know you were gonna look down just then."

I interrupted myself in mid-glance.

"You didn't plan on it, you just did it. And if you know your lines, very often, most of the time it sounds like, 'Mary-had-a-little-lamb-its-fleece-was-white-as-snow.' And people unconsciously *know* that you have planned that speech. And they know, for instance, that when you get up to leave and walk a certain, say, five steps to the doorway and then stop"—he pulled himself up and stopped at the bathroom door, suddenly a punk, slouching—"they *know* that you're gonna turn around and say, 'Why don't you ask Edith, then you'll find it in the shoebox.' And then walk out the door."

He disappeared into the bathroom. The theatrical voltage arrives at such a leisurely pace that it successfully dismantles your defenses.

He bounced back out of the bathroom. "But they already beat you to the fucking scene! So that doesn't keep them outta the popcorn. You always have to be ahead of the audience, or the audience is always ahead of you."

Still, I said, *Last Tango* seemed like more than technique.

He waved it off. "No, when you..." Suddenly, his face clenched and turned away.

Jesus, I thought, maybe I hit a sore spot. He was definitely disturbed. His lips taut, his eyes torn. A sob gurgled in his throat, and his shoulders shook. For an instant I was paralyzed. I stared at him.

Abruptly, his grief collapsed into a smile. "You just do that, you know. It just sounds like a bunch of tears. You make your face to go happy or to get mad. It's too costly to crank up. It's just too costly. If you can get by with a technical performance, nobody knows the dif. They can't tell."

I guess not, I said, wiping my palms on the bedspread. The key to his emotions seems to be in his upper lip. He has a very expressive upper lip. It lifts with a challenge, purses down when the irony of this earth gets serious. He cushions himself with irony.

I asked him if the *Last Tango* details were autobiographical.

"Oh, well, he [Bertolucci] had some cockamamie notion. What he wanted to do was sort of meld the image of the actor, the performer, with the part. So he got a few extraneous details. Played the drums, I don't know…Tahiti…so that the man is really telling the story of his life. I don't know what the hell it's supposed to mean. He said, 'Give me some reminiscences about your youth.' That made me think about milking a cow, my mother's getting drunk, one thing and another. He went, 'Wonderful, wonderful.'"

Brando grinned at the thought, leaned back and joined his hands behind his head. I said that several of my friends were upset because the elements were too outrageous. They couldn't take Brando in the role. It was too close.

"Not as far as I'm concerned. I would never, I'd never…there's a certain line you draw…I mean, in the days when I used to have to crank up emotionally, I would think of things that were very personal, but I would never exploit those in a film. For some goddamned check that came in at the end of the week. Or a director. He wanted to give that impression, so…"

He ruminated on a distant cloud. His jaw flexed.

"I don't think Bertolucci knew what the film was about. And I didn't know what it was about. He went around telling everybody it was about his prick!"

The laugh sounded like an asthma attack. "He looks at me one day and he says, you know…something like, 'You are the embodiment or reincarnation…you are the…symbol of my prick.' I mean, what the fuck does that mean?"

What did he see in the movie?

"I saw the picture about two years later. No, it was three years later, and I thought it was funny. I didn't know what it was about." He gazed emptily at the ceiling. "It was about a man desperately trying to find some meaning in life, full of odd symbols. He dies in a self-conscious way, in a fetal position. The woman shoots him at the end, and this whole thing was to have taken place over a three-day period. Impossible to have those transitions. It's a mythological tale; it doesn't happen in life."

I'd heard there were a lot of rugged stories around that movie, that it was an emotional pounding, that he'd never do anything like that again, that it took some recovery time.

"Naaah. As soon as they let go of your leg, then it's out to Tahiti or the desert."

The taped Caribbean drum music gave way to the crying jag of Carlos Santana. When you're around Brando for a while, you think not only of his comedic timing, but that he'd probably be a perceptive director. He's only directed once, a western called *One-Eyed Jacks* (after Stanley Kubrick was fired from preproduction).

Does he have any more taste for the job?

"I did it once," he said, shaking his head. "It was an ass breaker. You work yourself to death. You're the first one up in the morning... I mean, we shot that thing on the run, you know. You make up the dialogue the scene before, improvising, and your brain is going crazy."

I took it that he wrote the script.

"Yes. But it's better if you make it up, of course. Unless you're doing Eugene O'Neill. You can't wing that." He pulled up a dimply grin. "You can do it to Tennessee Williams, somebody that can write something. But you get in a picture with six guys like that, it's like an old whore in a lumber camp who's been fucked till she can't see straight."

The question is, how deep do you go with your improvisation?

"Well, it depends on what you're doing. If you're doing a hit-the-roof scene, you have to gas up, sorta. You don't have to kill yourself. When I first started, it was a movie called, ah... *The Men*. And I got there at something like 6:30, and by 9:30, when they were ready to shoot, I had shot my wad.

"If you do a scene any number of times, you just go dry. Unless you crank up very slowly to it. And then snap out of it at take thirteen. It all depends on the director; if he's fiddling around with this technical issue, there's no sense in cranking up. Because you know he's not going to print anything until the seventh take; he's just rehearsing himself.

"The trouble is, when you're playing one part, the director is playing another, and the writer is playing another part. Everybody's got a different idea. That's why it's better to get the signals straight up front. A lot of directors want to know *everything*. Some directors don't want to know anything. Some directors wait for you to bring everything to them.

"It's the no-talent assholes who get on your back, who think they're Young Einstein Misunderstood, or Orson Welles, or somebody like that. And you know

Marlon Brando
Photograph by Mary Ellen Mark/Archive Pictures

fucking well that when they say 'print,' that it's just thumbs-up-the-ass place. Those are the guys that are tough to work with.

"Chaplin you got to go with. [Charles Chaplin directed him in *A Countess from Hong Kong*.] Chaplin is a man whose talent is such that you have to gamble. First off, comedy is his back yard. He's a genius, a cinematic genius. A comedic talent without peer. You don't know that he's senile. Personally, he's a dreadful person. I didn't care much for him. Nasty and sadistic and mean…"

His voice trailed off. "*Oh, God.* He's like aaallll…. You got to stop them because that'll get on you. You got to stop them dead. But nevertheless you have to separate that personal life from that artistic life. One has *nothing* to do with the other. It's like writers, or anything else.

"You can't think that understanding people, or perceptive and sensitive people, are going to be perceptive and sensitive in other areas of human relationships. It just doesn't hold true. Talent has nothing to do with it, that's all. There are shits who are very understanding and extremely talented, and there are shits who are without a shred of talent. There's good guys on both sides."

There was a knock at the door. One of the press agents pulled himself inside with a fine, agreeable smile. A nice guy. He could read a will and get a lot of laughs. He said that I could come back the next day; they have a London correspondent outside who represents nine syndicated papers and he'd like five, ten minutes?

Brando pulled himself up and composed his face with businessman's calm. But his voice was pure bar-and-grill. "Well, I tell ya, I don't know the guy personally, and unless I have a clear contract of approval, I would not give him carte blanche to go home with a whole bunch of things. So tell him precisely that. Tell him if he presents to me a specific contract that I have approval of the full text and the nature of the interview, I don't care what he uses as long as it's real. But without a contract, I will not do an interview, and that's all I can do."

Smile nailed in place, the publicist attempted to spread a little butter on the situation. "Mostly he's doing a location story."

Brando winced. "I don't…in twenty years, I know what the angles are. They come in with a certain story angle, they're gonna write it no matter what you say, it'll be horseshit. So if he wants to do that, tell him I'd be perfectly delighted. Tell him that, tell him it's nothing personal."

The floating smile withdrew. Marlon returned. "This asshole, he's obviously a straight newsman…he might be a very nice guy, but in terms of policy, it just doesn't pay off. It's a waste of time anyway. We talked about that before. Sitting in a trailer and you come out from ROLLING STONE, we're rapping about 9 million things… there must be some purpose in your mind. I love to talk. But to talk for, or to be in print, seems so goddamned pompous. Making pronouncements of some kind. I guess that's one of the things that inhibited me from writing. It just seemed a pompous thing to do. When Van Gogh painted, for instance, he did it because it just said something to him that was irresistible. And he had to do that. That's a certain kind of artistry...."

The publicist reentered, with his certain kind of artistry. "No problems," he said, "we'll send everything to Alice."

That would be Marlon's secretary. "All right," Brando agreed, "have Alice call the lawyers and have them dictate the language and type it up and have him sign it."

The man's smile dropped. "You mean, do that now? He's going to leave today."

"Look, for anybody that I don't know, who doesn't pass muster, I'm gonna have to have a legal document."

"Well," the publicist said levelly, "this fellow is an established Hollywood correspondent."

"Then he's probably going to write a standard Hollywood correspondent piece."

The publicist backed out smiling. The last time I'd seen a smile like that, it was hanging on a steel hook in a butcher's window.

The door blew open again, and the event that transpired was a spiffy lesson on maneuvering this weary lion. It was his secretary, Alice Marchak, an elegant woman with exotic cheekbones. She was something of an older sister and bail bondsman to the actor, and was blunt with the news that he was not getting any day off. "They need you as soon as possible," she said. "Should I tell them you're ready?"

Brando, suddenly a kid, turned with a stage whisper. "That's a good lesson. When they tell you to go, *go!*" And he began to hoist himself up to get dressed, when the underassistant elbowed her way past Alice to confront the man. She had a flighty airline-stewardess charm and wore pink lipstick. She sighed helplessly. Brando leaned back.

"Do you want to hear my sad story?" she said to him, trying to laugh. "As you know, I am now a liar in your eyes. We got into a whole thing with this stunt that's going to take us far longer than we could take tonight. The only thing we could get today is scene 196, when you and Randy are first coming to the river. I'm *sorry*. What can I say?"

Genuinely mortified, she hurried out. He propped himself on an elbow to ponder the scene. Alice Marchak fussed with his overcoat.

"That's all such a painful collection of dog shit," he sighed, waving at the door. His voice was a low complaint. "There's no way she can just come in and say, 'Marlon, we need a shot of you coming in out of the woods, will you please get ready as quick as you can, please.' She's got to come in with the full Vaseline number first off. 'We're *terribly* sorry. I know you're going to hate me for this, and I know that I'm a liar and lower than a crock of shit.' And give you a fugging long explanation. She doesn't give a shit about me. She only gives a shit about what she thinks my position is. And she relates to that.

"Whereas, if I was driving the camera truck, it would be something like, 'Hey, listen asshole, get your buns over here because you got work to do, I got news for ya.' So you feel...utterly alienated from your society." He clawed the air with pinched fingers.

"One of the things I hate about working is that they won't let you be some overweight...middle-aged...fart who's walking down the street, who happens to be in the lumber business. They *insist* that you be somebody." His face aged with agony, then relaxed. He stood up to peel down for the costume change.

★   ★   ★

Ill winds raced in off the prairie that week, tearing off the windows and swallowing the city in a sheet of sand. Nerves got dragged on a razor strap. Dogs ran free. Idle persons turned to occult practices. Two FBI agents blew into town, and they had questions.

They were a pair. Casual knit suits and sensible black oxfords. They met Brando outside his mobile home, flipped their badges at him and stepped inside.

The movie crew was parked outside a postal warehouse. Inside, a nighttime campfire scene was set up in a bunch of phony shrubs. But no horse opera would operate while the leading man was held hostage by lawmen.

They had found the actor's fingerprints on all sorts of dangerous notions. Decades ago he had worked for the Jewish terrorist group, the Irgun Tzva'i Leumi. When Caryl Chessman was headed for the Green Room, Brando joined in a vigil outside San Quentin. He spoke at Bobby Hutton's funeral. And finally, he has joined hands with a gang of un-Americans, the Indians. In 1964, he was arrested with the Puyallup Indians while staging a fish-in for their river rights. Last year, when the Menominee Warrior Society took over a monks abbey in Gresham, Wisconsin, Brando dodged the law and joined them inside. Three sleepless nights later they walked out winners.

And it was no secret that he'd housed members of the American Indian movement, given them money and land. (The celebrated forty acres he gave to the Indians, which turned up with a $318,000 mortgage due, was settled recently. He saw to the note, and the Survival of American Indians Association took the land.)

Brando's plan to make a movie of the 1973 Wounded Knee uprising is certain not to paint a flattering, patriotic picture of our embattled FBI. And while the projected movie has been up and down hill, with the Indians sifting through directors and the investors waffling the money (Columbia Pictures dropped it from their schedule), the actor was still up for scrutiny. He would certainly know the whereabouts of Dennis Banks, who was, at that time, on the lam. (Banks was arrested January 24th, 1976.)

So the agents wanted to know if Brando would give shelter to any fugitive he might know. Brando, in turn, wanted to know if the agents would turn in another agent who illegally killed someone. They had a nice long talk.

By the warehouse door, an artist was painting a thick deck of cue cards for Brando. The top one read: TELL YOU WHY I THINK LIFE IS LIKE A MOUNTAIN RAILROAD. BECAUSE YOU DON'T KNOW WHAT SLEAZY SONOFABITCH HAS HIS HAND ON THE THROTTLE.

Brando broke into the sunlight, with a guiding arm for the agents. He took them inside to the campfire scene and secured a couple of director's chairs close to the action. Arthur Penn paced loosely among the shrubs. Brando was to sing, from a seated position, "Life Is Like a Mountain Railroad." The lyrics were taped to his mandolin. He had a faltering monotone so cracked you could strain spaghetti through it. He strangled the song fatally. The agents watched for a while and picked lint off their trousers.

That night Brando was anxious to scram. Get out of town, wash off the makeup, pull on the T-shirt, get this van moving. He knew there was a good place to camp out by the next day's location, an isolated ravine.

The blue shadows of scrub prairie pines grew in the long light of evening. We swung onto the interstate. Mike, a young, weary-looking driver hired to assist Brando on this picture, gunned ahead in the Jeep. Marlon didn't try to keep up, but steered the lumbering van in his own way. Slow and confident.

I asked about the FBI agents. They come around often?

"No, they're probably monitoring the phones, bugged the trailer, stuff like that. They're always around. They like to know what the hard line is, what the azimuth is that you're coming in on. But I never treat people as representatives of groups. I just treat them as people."

Wind sent shivers rolling through the van. He jerked the wheel.

"They don't have anything to go on, so what they do is they get tweezers, pick up a grain here and a grain there. They get 620 grains of information, and it starts to take shape. It doesn't always work out too good, you know. Their best chance is infiltration."

This sent him wandering off on a tangent about TV evangelists. "There's so many crazy people in influential areas, the craziness isn't even noticed. Craziness in the individual is much more noticeable than craziness in the society."

He gave a measuring look. "Do you remember telephone numbers?"

It's not my strong suit.

"My instinct—knowing the way they operate—the perfect setup is to get a guy from ROLLING STONE to work me over."

I had to laugh. But he shook his head and pressed on.

"That's the way they do it. They're really slick about it. You can't control guilt. It sneaks up on you, like a rabbit on a weasel. I would suspect myself if I was in the movement, if I was an Indian."

"There must be a limit to your participation," I said.

"It depends on how high the risk is. They figure, 'Well, he's gonna make a movie. *That* shows how liberal the country is. Everybody knows about the Indians anyway, what the fuck is he telling them for?' I went to Gresham where they're shooting real bullets twice a day. But they don't give credentials to naive people. They're smart people."

So what does this have to do with my memory for phone numbers?

He shrugged. "Some people have a memory for numbers, some have a memory for words, or for colors." He had a soiled look on his face. Then he saw the tape recorder balanced on my knees. "Oh, you got the machine! Yeah, it's picking up. Run it back a second."

I asked about the financing of his Wounded Knee movie.

"Oh, it's coming along. I thought about taking this to the movie companies, saying, 'Look, you people have done more damage to the livelihood of the American Indian's cause than any other group, outside the United States government, and you ought to kick in and do something about it, you know, keep your skirts clean.'

"The whole idea of the motion-picture industry is, don't offend anybody. Or you can't make money. So I'm scraping my ass to get financing for this film. People don't wanna spend $8 million for this. They're not gonna spend for something they think they're not gonna get back. And I don't know why not, because the truth is more dramatic than anything they could make up.

"They give you a nice runaround because they want to see you coming in next time with something that's palatable. They don't want to make an enemy out of you. As long as you're hot."

That sounds familiar. As long as you're hot.

"Yah," he said, leaning on the steering wheel. "I couldn't get arrested before."

Before *The Godfather*?

"Yeah, just about then. I mean, I could get arrested, but…it's a variable. When you been in about four stinkers in a row—" He drew back. "When you say stinkers, they could be artistically successful, but they don't turn into bucks—it starts to wobble.

"But films…it's funny. People buy a ticket. That ticket is their transport to a fantasy that you create for them. Fantasyland, that's all, and you make their fantasies live. Fantasies of love or hatred or whatever it is. People want their fantasies over and over. People who masturbate usually masturbate with, at the most, four or five fantasies. By and large.

"Most people like the same food, they like the same kind of music, and they like the same kind of sexual fantasy for a period of time, then maybe it changes. As it is in children. Who is it?" He drummed the dashboard. "Bruce Lee. That's the hero. Then you grow up and grow out of your Bruce Lee period, or your Picasso Blue Period, and go into another period.

"But with kids, because they outpower us, because they have no representation, because they are so dependent, all they think about is power. Dinosaurs or the Million Dollar Man, because they feel so helpless, because they have no way out of it, except fantasy. Because they are only that tall.

"And that's all films are." He had a concerned knit to his voice, like a preacher talking about his poverty. "Just an extension of childhood, where everybody wants to be freer, everybody wants to be powerful, everybody wants to be so *overwhelmingly* attractive that there's just no doing anything about it. Or everybody wants to have comradeship and to be understood.

"They become lullabies. They're 'tell-me-again-Daddy' stories. That's all television is: 'Tell me again, Daddy, about the good guy and the bad guy and the strong guy and Kung Fu and Flash Gordon.'" His voice grew soft. "People love to hear the stories, they love to hear the lullabies.

"Tastes change, but the function doesn't. I might as well be Jimmy Cagney in *White Heat*. The same story, the positive and the negative, the yin and the yang, the antihero.

"You know, so often, creative or positive things are accomplished for reasons that are totally irrelevant. They're done out of vanity, or out of anxiety or fear. There's a book written by Joseph Campbell. He was fascinated by symbols, not unlike Jung. He psychoanalytically treated the hero; the name of the book was *Hero with a Thousand Faces*." He gestured with an open hand, as if smoothing the ruffled air. "But *evil* has a thousand faces.

"We know so goddamned little about what makes us angry. Death is way down on the list of things that people are going to be afraid of, or care about. I was talking to an Indian kid, he was kicking Vietnamese out of airplanes. The intelligence officer asked questions that they wouldn't answer, so they kicked them out of airplanes. The kid got his head turned around, wound up shooting his commanding officer and hung him up on a cyclone fence through his wrist bones.

"Community spirit, patriotic spirit, it's just a big sell. The veterans who had their legs blown away, their jaws blown away in Vietnam..." The irritation rose. "They [Americans] just want to forget it. Go off like Major Hoople and think it didn't happen. They don't want to be reminded of it. Most people are expendable, and more than expendable; they're indifferent.

"There's no fooling. People are sheep. They'll just do any fucking thing. Anything. I mean, the sum total of everything I believe is the sum total of everything I've read, seen. I'm not told how to do it, it's just...something's influenced me. James Joyce or Schopenhauer or my Aunt Minnie.

"But everybody's looking for the man on the white horse, everybody's looking for the one who will tell the Truth. So you read Lao-Tzu, you read Konrad Lorenz, I don't know who else, Melville, Kenneth Patchen, somebody you think is not a bullshitter. Somebody who has the eyes of a saint and the perceptions of a ghost. They're gonna tell us the way, they're gonna show us. They never really do, and we run around being cheap imitations of all those influences." He shrugged in a resigned way. "But there isn't much of another way."

Spending a week around the guy, it was easy to stew about this massive acting talent going to waste. All those years he was making dog movies, and now he's got offers for every role going, from Aristotle Onassis to Papa Hemingway. When I asked about his present work ethic, he expelled a large, grudging sigh.

"I built a little house in Tahiti," he said at last. "Out of sticks and grass and palm trees, droppings. That gave me an enormous sense of satisfaction. Whenever I can physically achieve some simpler way of doing something.

"Work ethics are funny things. The Tahitians couldn't give three-ninths of two pieces of lizard shit about working.

"It's such a small planet now. I *used* to think that up in the hills of Afghanistan, where the Kurds were, it was light years away. You go to the interior forests where the Pygmies are now getting shafted. Same with the Masai, now split right down the middle between Uganda and Tanganyika. And Tanganyika says, 'Listen, you can't show your dick anymore.'"

The road gave way to rutted farm tracks. Mike, in the lead car, had disappeared. The tension seemed to be easing away from his shoulders. "I mean, where do you find hope?

"On the island, there's an ample opportunity to demonstrate that it can be done…to put these technologies together…with wind and methane and solar energy. I want to build it in my own house and then just make a little flick about that.

"I've got a little community developing down there, for an experimental hotel. I dropped a considerable amount of money in research and development. I invented a windmill, but to actually produce wind is quite a trick. My wife and kids are there."

We pulled up on a rise. Somewhere on these yellow fields was the campsite. Somewhere, Mike was out there taking corners. Marlon settled in his seat. "Is that the road he took? I got some glasses back there."

I got the binoculars. "Do you have 'journalist' on your passport?" he asked, scanning the plains. My passport doesn't say anything, I said. You mean the immigration cards?

"It must say something. I got so sick of writing 'actor' down on my passport that I wrote 'shepherd.' And it didn't make any difference. Except one dry English immigration officer." He set down the glasses and struck a Commander Schweppes pose. "'Haws your flawk, Mr. Brando?' I said, 'Doing very well.' 'I'm delighted to hear it.' Didn't smile at all."

He dropped back into gear and shoved off.

The Family, 1976: Portraits of American Leaders. A Portfolio by Richard Avedon

Gerald Ford

Hubert Humphrey

A. Philip Randolph

The Joint Chiefs of Staff:
General Fred C. Weyand,
Admiral James L. Holloway,
General George S. Brown,
General David C. Jones
and General Louis H. Wilson

Henry Kissinger

Nelson Rockefeller

Edward Kennedy

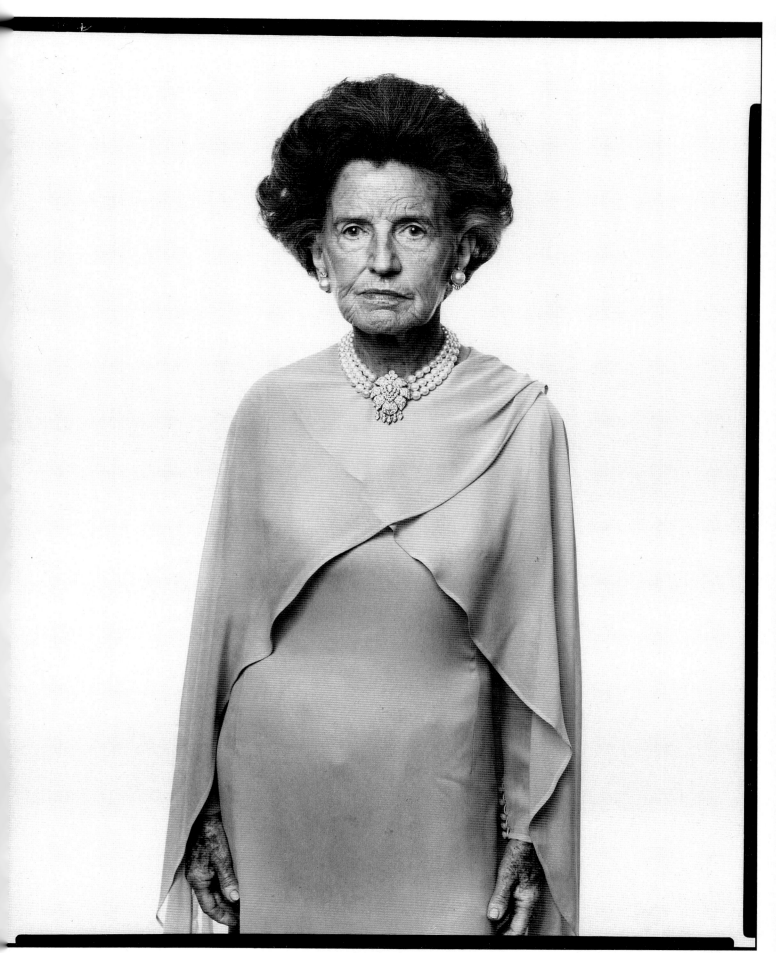

Rose Fitzgerald Kennedy

Rock Is Sick and Living in London

by Charles M. Young   October 1977

Instead of perfume there will be rottenness.
—ISAIAH *3:24*

Alittle before midnight, my taxi arrives at a club called the Vortex. The weather is atypically dry, and the neighborhood, like the rest of London, is a shopping district with its eye on the tourist trade. Half a block away, ten or twelve teenage boys dressed like horror-movie morticians jump up and down and hit each other. Their hair is short, either greased back or combed to stick straight out with a pomade of Vaseline and talcum powder. Periodically, one chases another out of the pack, grabs the other's arm and twists it until he screams with pain. Then they rush back laughing and leap about some more. Sitting oblivious against a building, a man dressed in a burlap bag nods gently as a large puddle of urine forms between his legs.

Shouting epithets at themselves in a thick proletarian accent, the boys finally bob down the street as another cab pulls up to the entrance. A man with curly, moderately long, red hair, a pale face and an apelike black sweater gets out. It is Malcolm McLaren, manager of the Sex Pistols, the world's most notorious punk band, whom I have flown from New York to meet and see perform. McLaren has been avoiding me for two days. I introduce myself and suggest we get together soon. He changes the subject by introducing me to Russ Meyer, the soft-core porn king of *Supervixens* and *Beyond the Valley of the Dolls* fame, who is directing the Sex Pistols' movie. "You're a journalist?" asks Meyer. "Do you know Roger Ebert? He won the Pulitzer Prize for film criticism, and he's writing the movie with me. You should talk to him. At *The Chicago Sun-Times*, he's Dr. Jekyll. With me, he's Mr. Hyde. He's really into tits."

McLaren seizes the opportunity to disappear into the Vortex and is lost to me for the rest of the evening. The dense crowd inside consists of a few curiosity seekers and 400 to 500 cadaverous teenagers dressed in black or gray. Often their hair is dyed shades of industrial pink, green and yellow. Several blacks, also drably dressed and with rainbow stripes dyed into their short Afros, speckle the audience. The music over the loudspeakers is about two-thirds shrieking New Wave singles and one-third reggae tunes, which the kids respond to with almost as much enthusiasm as the punk rock. The dancing is frantic as a band called the Slits sets up. The style is called pogo dancing—jumping up and down and flailing one's arms around. It is as far as one can get from the hustle, and it is the only way one can dance if one is wearing bondage pants tied together at the knees. Most are pogoing alone. Those with partners (usually of the same sex) grasp each other at the neck or shoulders and act like they are strangling each other. Every four or five minutes, someone gets an elbow in the nose and the ensuing punch-out lasts about thirty seconds amid a swirling mass of tripping bodies.

Unlike in American punk clubs, which occasionally become as crowded but where most people still try to avoid jostling each other, no one here hesitates to violate another person's physical space. Everyone is fair game for a push. The dance floor is phenomenally stuffed with sweating humans and getting more stuffed with each new song. Roadies onstage and a few fans hurl beer glasses at each other.

The Slits turn out to be an all-female teenage aggregation whose efforts almost any current American rock audience would reward with a shower of bottles. The guitarist stops in the middle of the fourth song to announce, "Fuckin' shit! Listen to this!" and plays an ungodly out-of-tune chord that no one else had even noticed in the cacophony. The singer, apparently the only one with pitch, has to tune the guitar for her. "Fuckin' shit!" explains the singer, plucking the strings. "We never said we were musicians." When the audience becomes restless, she calls them "wankers" (masturbators) and launches into a tune called, "You're My Number One Enemy."

The crowd loves it, dancing with even greater abandon—with the exception of one pogo stick who stops in midhop at the sight of my notebook and demands to know what paper I'm from. I say I'm American, not one of the wanking English press. "Well, maybe you're all right," he snorts in a barely understandable brogue. "At least you're not takin' fuckin' pictures. The newspapers all sensationalize it. We aren't fightin'. We're 'avin' fun."

The Slits draw an encore and invite their opening act, Prefix, a male group who shave their marble white bodies in emulation of Iggy Pop, to jam on "Louie Louie." The audience likes it so much that several of them storm the stage and nearly succeed in toppling the eight-foot stacks of P.A. speakers before the security men beat them into submission.

Heading for the exit, I recognize the Sex Pistols' drummer, Paul Cook, also weaving his way outside. Unaccompanied, he is wearing a sleeveless T-shirt, straight-legged blue jeans and dilapidated sneakers. The nose is wide, the skin pallid. Conditioned by six months of reports about the Sex Pistols' proclivity for violence, I half expect him to assault me. But his hand is limp as we shake, and his eyes do not meet mine when I introduce myself. He is, of all things, shy.

"It's just a laugh, not really that violent," he says when I ask him about their dancing. "You can take it which way you want: some laugh, some get paranoid. They want to prove they aren't posing."

"A lot of people have missed the satire," I say. "Some of the press are even trying to link you with the fascists."

"I can't be bothered with that shit," he replies. "It's just what they want to read into it. When we first started playing, before all the articles came out, people would come up and say they'd never seen anything so funny in their lives."

★   ★   ★

In the history of rock & roll, there is no stranger tale. In late 1971, Malcolm McLaren, then a twenty-four-year-old art student, and his wife Vivienne Westwood, who was either teaching or working for social security (she doesn't remember which), opened a boutique for Teddy boys called Let It Rock. They started with little money, but the shop proved an enormous success because of their shrewd buying of vintage rock records in discount bins and unused stocks of old clothes. The Teds' rigid conservatism proved boring, however, so McLaren and Westwood changed the name of their store to Too Fast to Live, Too Young to Die and catered to the rockers, another cultural fragment that favored chains, black leather and motorcycles.

McLaren was not, he says, at all interested in contemporary rock music, but was greatly impressed by the swagger of the New York Dolls when they visited Too Fast one afternoon in 1974. He followed them to a Paris performance and, from November 1974 to June 1975, tried to manage them when their old management and record company were mired in feuds. Burying their old image as trendy transvestites, McLaren dressed them in red leather, draped their amplifiers with hammer and sickle flags and asked the question in their advertising, "What are the politics of boredom?" This proved less than a hit with both public and critics. The Dolls hung it up forever in the middle of a gig in Florida, and McLaren flew back to England a sadder but wiser rock & roll manager.

Meanwhile, Westwood had changed the name of the boutique to Sex and was selling bondage clothes and T-shirts decorated with large rips and grotesque pornography (the government actually prosecuted them for their pictures). It became a hangout for budding punks who listened to the jukebox and stole the clothes. Among them were four proletarian kids—Steve Jones, Paul Cook, Glen Matlock and another guitar player—who wanted to start a band. McLaren suggested the name Sex Pistols. Jones began as the singer (Cook played drums, Matlock bass) but didn't know what to do with his hands, so they gave him a guitar, which he learned to play proficiently in two months. The other guitar player was given the boot, leaving an opening for a singer.

One of the regulars at Sex was a kid named John Lydon, who was distinguished on three counts: (1) his face had the pallor of death; (2) he went around spitting on poseurs he passed on the street; and (3) he was the first to understand the democratic implications of punk—rather than pay ten pounds for an ugly T-shirt with *holes* in it, he took a Pink Floyd T-shirt, scratched holes in the eyes and wrote I HATE over the logo. McLaren stood him in front of the jukebox, had him mouth Alice Cooper's "I'm Eighteen" and declared him their new lead singer. Jones noticed the mung on Lydon's never-brushed teeth and christened him Johnny Rotten.

From the beginning, the Sex Pistols had trouble finding venues for their chaotic performances. But Rotten, blessed with demented anger heretofore unseen outside a war zone, proved to be the spark that set off the forest fire of punk bands now raging through Britain. EMI, the largest and most prestigious English record company, signed them and released the Pistols' first single, "Anarchy in the U.K.," in November 1976. In a tune similar to the Who's "I Can See For Miles," Johnny Rotten declared himself an anti-Christ who wanted to destroy everything. The BBC was not amused and gave it no airplay. "Anarchy" was not even in the charts by December 1st when the Sex Pistols became household epithets in one night.

Appearing live on the British *Today* show at the supper hour, the Pistols responded to interviewer Bill Grundy's command, "Say something outrageous," by calling him a "dirty fucker" and a "fucking rotter." The newspapers put them on the front page for a week with screaming headlines like TV FURY OVER ROCK CULT FILTH and PUNK? CALL IT FILTHY LUCRE. Members of Parliament denounced them. "Anarchy" entered the charts at Number Forty-three, but record-company workers refused to handle it and EMI was fast buckling under the public pressure. The Pistols added to the outrage by refusing to apologize and by doing long interviews in which they denounced the star system and sacred luminaries like Mick Jagger and Rod Stewart for being old and rich. They went on tour, traveling around the country in a bus, arriving at gigs only to discover that they had been banned in the township. Out of twenty-one scheduled dates, the Sex Pistols played three.

On January 4th of this year, they flew to Amsterdam for a club date and got involved in an accident at Heathrow Airport. One witness claimed the Sex Pistols were doing something so disgusting that she could not repeat it for publication. Steve Jones claimed he had a simple case of indigestion, but the papers had a field day, and it became generally believed Jones had been vomiting on old ladies in the preflight lounge. EMI dropped them at a cost of 50,000 pounds and 5000 copies of "Anarchy" to break the contract.

WHAT A LONG STRANGE TRIP IT'S BEEN

Glen Matlock also left about this time, charging that the group was so manipulated by McLaren that they had become like the Monkees. The group charged Matlock with being into old farts like Paul McCartney. Sid Vicious, an old school chum of Rotten's, inventor of pogo dancing, reputed mean hand with a bicycle chain and totally inexperienced hand with a bass guitar, was the replacement.

On March 10th, A&M signed the Sex Pistols, advancing them 50,000 pounds, and dropped them a week later for another 25,000 pounds. In between, the Pistols were apparently involved in incidents of vandalism at the company's headquarters and in a pub fight with the head of programming for the BBC. It is also thought that A&M was the target of heavy pressure brought by disc jockeys, distributors and its own employees.

This summer they signed with Virgin for British distribution and released "God Save the Queen," a raunchy denunciation of the monarchy, just in time for the Queen's Silver Jubilee. The song quickly went to Number One on the *New Musical Express* charts. They followed up with a two-sided hit, "Pretty Vacant," an original about not caring for anything, and "No Fun," an Iggy Pop cover that Rotten starts as a sociology lecture and ends as a sort of hymn to the general worthlessness of the universe. They have just completed a much anticipated album, *Another Load of Bollocks from the Sex Pistols.*

In the meantime, the Sex Pistols are concentrating their efforts on a feature movie to take their message directly to their audience and bypass the journalists, record companies and disc jockeys. The boutique has been renamed Seditionaries to accommodate the new political mood, and its line of T-shirts now includes swastikas. Both Rotten and Cook were assaulted this summer by "patriots," who sent them to the hospital briefly.

★　　　★　　　★

"I felt like a sexless monster because at the time my head was shaved and I was wearing this vile tuxedo that was four sizes too big. I had no money to buy clothes, and people would run away when I walked down the street. It was a right laugh," says Sid Vicious in the lounge of the recording studio. Queen is recording at the same time, and Freddie Mercury's high-pitched howls waft through the not-quite-soundproofed door. "I didn't like fuckin' then, and I still don't. It's dull."

Vicious's voice has a tone of goofy absurdity, something like Ringo Starr's (though he'd hate the analogy), that elevates almost everything he says to high humor. Pencil thin, he is dressed in a black leather jacket with no shirt underneath and enormous black combat boots. His teeth appear not to have been brushed in several years. His hair is about two inches long and sticks straight out at odd angles. Several bright red scars highlight his solar plexus.

"One night nobody was payin' any attention to me, so I thought I'd commit suicide," he explains, belching loudly. "So I went in the bathroom, broke a glass and slashed my chest with it. It's a good way to get attention. I'm going to do it again, particularly since it doesn't work. They all said I didn't cut myself enough to be realistic and ignored me." Vicious laughs at the non sequitur, adding, "You better not make a fool of me in this article."

Vicious went to college, the English equivalent of American high school, with Johnny Rotten. "We were right thick cunts, we were," he says. "'E was the vilest geezer I ever met—all misshapen, no 'air, 'unchback, flat feet. Everybody 'ated 'im. Everybody 'ated me. We 'ated each other, too, but nobody else would talk to us, so we'd just get drunk and criticize each other. 'E used to tell people 'e 'ad to cut 'is piles off with a razor blade because they were 'anging out 'is pants, *and they'd believe 'im.* 'E used to tell them that niggers 'ad 'air on the roofs of their mouths. *They believed that too."*

Vicious dropped out of school after somehow finagling a scholarship ("I didn't know about the dole yet"), which he used to start some sort of illicit business that he declined to specify. He first touched immortality when attending the early Sex Pistols' concerts. "They were the only group I ever wanted to see," he says. "I didn't know how to dance, so I just jumped up and down and bashed people. Then everybody else started doin' it, but they didn't get it right, so I quit."

"Did you really get into all those fights attributed to you?"

"Don't believe everything you read in the press. If somebody starts with me, I try to mess them up, but I don't look for trouble."

"When did you first pick up the bass?"

"I never played seriously until I joined the group. Learned quite fast, I suppose. Before I started playing, I never really noticed the bass—couldn't tell it from a piano. I heard records as just a wall of sound. I'd have to think before I could pick anything out."

"It's true you hate the traditional rock stars who've made big names for themselves?"

"I absolutely despise those turds. The Stones should have quit in 1965. You never see any of those cunts walkin' down the street. If it gets so you can't see us that way, I don't want it."

"But the entire American music industry is poised to turn you into the next big thing. They'll suck out any integrity the band has."

"But how can they? I only know one way to live. That's like now."

"Will you have anything to sing about when you're rich?"

"I don't think we'll ever be millionaires. I don't really think about the future. I 'aven't got a clue."

★   ★   ★

Malcolm McLaren, who has a reputation for being two hours late for everything, is two hours late to meet me at his apartment. Vivienne Westwood ushers me into their bedroom, where I wait until she finishes cutting a half inch or so of her two-inch hair, presumably to make it stick out better. The room is modestly furnished in black and white, a constantly recurring color theme that—along with the incessant rain, bad telephones, warm beer, incompetent hotel service, yellow journalism, cretinous newspapers, lack of time with the band, money that weighs more than it's worth, cricket on television, geographically separate streets having the same name within London's city limits, riots between Marxist and neo-Nazi splinter parties, and a hangover—is convincing me to change my name to Chuckie Suicide and go Sid Vicious one better. The only color in the room is a poster of the equally depressing Red Ballet. The bookshelf includes Orwell, Dickens, de Sade and Wilhelm Reich's *The Mass Psychology of Fascism*. First in a pile of albums on the dresser is *The World of Billy Fury*.

Westwood appears a few years older than her husband and wears no makeup over her sheet-white skin. She wears a white blouse and black bondage pants tied together at the knee and thigh. Finishing her hair, she sits on the black bedspread and gives a history of her boutique. They are, she says, still awaiting a decision on the government suit against their pornographic T-shirts.

"We've always been about provoking," she says. "If you want to find out how much freedom you have, make some kind of explicit sexual statement and wait for it all to crash down around you."

She says Rotten was the first to rip his own shirt, but, contrary to some accounts, she gives Vicious credit for first using safety pins: "A mate who owed him money ripped up his apartment one night—shredded the rug, the walls, his clothes, everything. He had to use the pins to hold his trousers together."

When McLaren finally arrives after midnight, he is still wearing the mangy black sweater I saw several nights back. The long strings of matted wool keep reminding me of Johnny Rotten's piles hanging out of his pants. I asked why he presented the New York Dolls as Communists.

"It was just an idea that came out, like a can of new soup," he says. "Rock & roll is not just music. You're selling an attitude too. Take away the attitude and you're just like anyone else, you're like American rock groups. Of course, maybe there's just too wide a market there for a good attitude. The Sex Pistols came about because on the streets of Britain they're saying, 'What is this 1960s crap, paying five pounds to see some guy the size of a sixpence when I'm on the dole?' The kids need a sense of adventure, and rock & roll needs to find a way to give it to them—wham out the hardest and cruelest lyrics as propaganda, speak the truth as clearly as possible. Most bands won't do that sort of thing, but they must find a means to provoke."

"Aren't there easier ways to break a band?"

"I love to go the hardest route. It keeps you up. It keeps the truth happening. Too many of the new groups are getting sucked up by the record companies too early. The movement will get diluted.

"These record-company presidents, they're all whores. Two months ago, their doormen would have thrown us out. We sell a few records and they phone and want their pictures taken with us."

I ask why he places the press right down in the sewer along with record-company presidents.

"Because the music press are basically Sixties culture freaks. They imply we're not original, they try to maintain this facade of knowing every song, every riff, every lyric, as if they invented it. One recent headline had us as JOHN, PAUL, STEVE AND SID, like we were the Beatles! That's fucking disgusting! They were trying to make us *fun*. It shows the vampire nature of the Sixties generation, the most narcissistic generation that has ever been!"

The phone rings and McLaren answers. "What's that? Elvis Presley died?... Makes you feel sad, doesn't it? Like your grandfather died.... Yeah, it's just too bad it couldn't have been Mick Jagger."

★   ★   ★

When I call McLaren at home, he promises me a ride to Wolverhampton, a suburb of Birmingham, to see the first date of the Sex Pistols' "guerrilla tour" of Britain. Since they are banned everywhere, they will be playing under assumed names. Tonight it is to be the Spots, an acronym for "Sex Pistols on tour secretly." In the meantime, I make a phone call to Bernard Brooke-Partridge, Conservative member of the Greater London Council and chairman of the arts committee—the man primarily responsible for banning the Pistols in London.

"I will do everything within the law to stop them from appearing here ever again," he says. "I loathe and detest everything they stand for and look like. They are obnoxious, obscene and disgusting."

"Doesn't the question of who should decide what's disgusting in a free society enter here?"

"I am the person who decides," he says. "The electorate put me here. My power is not in question. If the Sex Pistols want to change the system, they are free to stand for election in my district."

"In the United States, the First Amendment to the Constitution says the government is not allowed to make such decisions."

"We have our own way of doing things here. The Sex Pistols are scum trying to make a fast buck, which they are entitled to do under the law. I am entitled to try and stop them. We'll see who wins.

"Now, I've seen many of the groups play. I've nothing against Mick Jagger and his ilk. Some of his gestures appeared lewd, and they were probably meant that way, but the audience was not tearing up the seats. I will say this for the Sex Pistols: there's one band that's a damn sight worse—the Bay City Rollers."

★   ★   ★

McLaren does not phone me back with instructions on how to get my ride, so I end up taking the train at the last minute. Wolverhampton turns out to be an industrial sumphole, resembling Cleveland if Cleveland had been built 200 years earlier. The Club Lafayette is in the middle of a tough, working-class neighborhood. Word has obviously gotten out, as a line five to eight persons wide extends around the block. Inside, it is already packed with people in their late teens and early twenties. Except for one kid who appears to have dyed his skin green (could it have been the dim light?) and a few others in punk paraphernalia, the crowd is dressed normally. They pogo to the recorded music, however, with even greater intensity than their counterparts at the Vortex. The fights are both more frequent and more violent. One battle seems to swirl around the entire floor, bodies tripping like a line of dominoes until it stops at the foot of the stairs in back, directly below Malcolm McLaren. A half smile on his lips, he is an island of serenity, magically untouched by the chaos.

"You've got to control yourselves a bit more," pleads the DJ over the loud-speaker, "or the Spots will not perform. Please be cool!" The crowd responds with what I'm told is a soccer chant.

At midnight, the Sex Pistols finally emerge from the dressing room. The crush around the foot-high stage is literally unbelievable and skirmishes with the security men immediately erupt. The ten-foot stacks of P.A. speakers are rocking back and forth and are dangerously close to toppling over. The band cranks up and Rotten growls the demonic laugh at the beginning of "Anarchy in the U.K.":

Rrrrrright nowwwww!
A-ha-ha-ha-ha-haaaa! I am an anti-Christ
I am an anarchist
I don't know what I want
But I know how to get it
I wanna destroy passers-by
Cause I wanna beeeeee
Anarchyyyyy.

Some kid has put his fist through one of the speakers, and a few more have escaped the security men to step on wires and knock over electronic equipment. The song is barely intelligible over the explosions and spitting noises from shorts, just the way anarchy ought to sound. The crowd pogos frantically. Paul Cook is completely hidden from view, but sounds fine, limiting himself to a basic repertoire of rock licks. Steve Jones's guitar work avoids frills but gets the job done with taste. His expression is deadly earnest—like a high-school basketball star stepping up for a crucial free throw—which he breaks only to spit on the audience every few minutes. Sid Vicious's bass playing is highly energetic and completely without subtlety. He's been up for two days prior to the gig and, hilariously, looks like he's trying to cop some z's between licks. Still clad in his swastika T-shirt, Rotten is perhaps the most captivating performer I've ever seen. He really doesn't do that much besides snarl and be hunchbacked; it's the eyes that kill you. They don't pierce, they bludgeon.

"You're bustin' up the P.A.," he says, more as a statement of fact than alarm, after the song is over. "Do you want us to continue?"

Several burly roadies join the security men to form a solid wall in front of the band. Rotten is completely hidden from view, so he climbs on top of a monitor and grabs the mike in one hand and the ceiling with the other for balance. Someone in the balcony pours beer on him.

The band manages to get through "I Wanna Be Me," "I'm a Lazy Sod" and "No Feeling" with the sound system relatively intact. "Pretty Vacant," their current hit single, draws an unholy reaction—the crowd shouting the chorus at the top of their lungs: "We're so pretty/ Oh so pretty/ Va-cant/ And we don't care!" For the first time I see Johnny Rotten crack a smile—only a brief one, but unmistakably a smile. Grasping a profusely bleeding nose, a kid collapses at my feet. Another pogos with his pants down. The "God Save the Queen" chorus—"No future/ no future/ no future for you"—sparks a similar explosion and closes the set. "No Fun" is the encore and, true to its title, blows out the entire P.A.

I grab a poster advertising the Spots and head for the dressing room. Uncool fan that I have become, I ask for autographs. Cook complies; Jones complies; Rotten complies; Vicious asks, "Why should I?"

"I don't know," I say. "I just wish you would. That was the most amazing show I've ever seen."

Vicious thinks a moment and signs it. "Usually I don't do this," he says. "For some reason, I'm glad you liked it."

I'm glad I liked it, too. Sid Vicious is about as close as rock & roll is going to come to Huckleberry Finn in this decade. I hope he can light out for the territories before he turns into just another ego. I can't dislike Malcolm McLaren for figuring out that reporters are vampires, lurking in the night, ready to suck out every last corpuscle of titillation, leaving the victim to spend eternity as a Media Zombie. If he were merely a manipulator, he wouldn't have chosen such genuine fuckups for the band. If he were merely a greedhead, he could have found an easier way to run the Sex Pistols for number-one group in the world. As it is, he chose not the politics of boredom, but the politics of division, Richard Nixon's way: amputate the wanking Sixties liberals from their working-class support. Kids destroyed schools to the tune of $600 million in the U.S. last year. That's a lot of anger that the Southern-California-cocaine-and-unrequited-love axis isn't capable of tapping.

And Johnny Rotten, it seems to me, told the entire United Kingdom he had to cut his piles off with a razor, and the damn fools believed him. America's get-well card is in the mail. It'll be a right laugh. But I keep thinking about that brief smile during "Pretty Vacant" at the Club Lafayette. Did that mean, "Look how great I am!" or "Look at them have a good time!"? Those have always been divergent roads in rock & roll. The Sex Pistols took the latter, the one less traveled, and that has made all the difference.

Mick Jagger:
The Rolling Stone Interview

by Jonathan Cott   June 1978

In their original Sixties incarnation, the Rolling Stones presented an eerie quality that combined the hustling menace of the spiv, the coolness of the dandy and the unpredictable amorality and frivolity of the Greek gods. And in such a guise, they exuberantly took on the role of the devil's advocate for what was then beginning to be thought of as the Love Generation—ridiculing the vices and hypocrisies of family and social life in songs like "19th Nervous Breakdown" and "Mother's Little Helper." But the Stones didn't stop there. As seemingly unassimilable voices of disengagement, they attacked the vice of the spirit of society itself in such songs as "Sympathy for the Devil" and "2000 Man."

As spoken and sung by their shining and narcissistic knight, Mick Jagger, the Rolling Stones presented themselves as beings of exalted indifference, innocent malice, careless cruelty—an ambiguous mixture of emotions revealing the disturbing yet fascinating quality of a child grown up too soon, like a six-year-old dragging on a cigarette. And it was this "child" who dangerously explored the ever-lurking but disapproved world of sex and drugs in such songs as "Under My Thumb," "Sister Morphine" and "Monkey Man."

Yet when the Stones were at their most exploitative, they seemed their most liberating, because we became aware of the reversal of that social and psychological pathology by which the oppressed identify with their oppressors: we sensed that the Stones, from their position of indifferent power, were singing in the voice of the hurt and abused, thereby magically transcending all humiliating barriers ("But it's all right now/ In fact it's a gas").

It is exactly this kind of playful yet powerful ambiguity that I have missed in the Stones' work during the past few years. But now we have 'Some Girls,' an album that draws on, in a remarkably unhackneyed way, the Stones' love for blues, the Motown sound, country music and Chuck Berry, and that combines and transforms these elements into the group's most energized, focused, outrageous and original record since the days of 'Between the Buttons,' 'Beggar's Banquet,' 'Let It Bleed' and 'Exile on Main Street.' And it is an album that thematically crystallizes the Stones' perennial obsession with "some girls"—both real and imaginary.

After years of standing in the shadows, the soul survivors are back on their own, with no direction home, sounding just like...the Rolling Stones.

You've been a Rolling Stone for about fifteen years. How does it feel?

What a funny question! It's a long time, maybe too long.

There are rumors that the Rolling Stones will break up very soon.

That's rubbish. They said it in 1969, too. They say it all the time.

Let's talk about "Miss You." I like the line "You've been the star in all my dreams."

Dreams are like movies, in a way. Or movies are like dreams.

You once sang, "I only get my rocks off while I'm dreaming."

I don't dream more than anybody else. But dreams are a great inspiration for the lowliest rock & roll writer to the greatest playwrights. Chaucer was a great one for dreams. He was a great one for explaining them and making fun of the astrological explanations. He used to take the piss out of most of them, but some of them he took seriously. Shakespeare, too, knew a lot about early English witchcraft and religion, and Chaucer had some sort of similar knowledge. Today we have psychiatrists to interpret dreams.

Have you ever been to one?

Never, not once. I've read a lot of Jung, and I would have gone to see him because he was interesting.

The title of your new album is the title of one of your most powerful and outrageous songs, "Some Girls", and I wanted to ask you about some of the girls in your songs. Here are a few lines taken at random from several of your older albums: "Who's that woman on your arm/ All dressed up to do you harm?" [from "Let It Loose"]; "Women think I'm tasty/ But they're always trying to waste me" [from "Tumbling Dice"]; "But there is one thing I will never understand/ Some of the sick things a girl does to a man" [from "Sittin' On a Fence"].

I didn't write all those lines, you know [*laughing*].

All right, we'll reduce the charge. But obviously, in your songs of the mid-Sixties, you were at pains to accuse girls of being deceptive, cheating, greedy, vain, affected and stupid. It was a list of sins. Whether you were singing about rejecting the girl ["Out of Time," "Please Go Home"] or about the girl rejecting you ["All Sold Out," "Congratulations"] or about both ["High and Dry," "Under My Thumb"], almost all the songs from that period...

Most of those songs are really silly. They're pretty immature. But as far as the heart of what you're saying, I'd say…any bright girl would understand that if I were gay I'd say the same things about guys. Or if I were a girl I might say the same things about guys or other girls. I don't think any of the traits you mentioned are peculiar to girls. It's just about people. Deception, vanity….. On the other hand, sometimes I do say nice things about girls [*laughing*].

Some of those other girls—"Ruby Tuesday," "Child of the Moon" or the girls in songs like "She's a Rainbow" and "Memory Motel"— are very elusive and mystical.

Well, the girl in "Memory Motel" is a real, independent American girl. But they are mostly imaginary, you're right. Actually, the girl in "Memory Motel" is a combination. So was the girl in "Faraway Eyes." Nearly all of the girls in my songs are combinations. "Some Girls" is all combinations. "Beast of Burden" is a combination. "Miss You" is an emotion—it's not really about a girl. To me, the feeling of longing is what the song is. I don't like to interpret my own fucking songs, but that's what it is.

On 'Some Girls,' it seems to me that you've taken all those "immature" feelings from the mid-Sixties and focused them into powerful songs like "Lies," "Respectable" and especially "Some Girls," which is a kind of exorcism of all those girls you used to sing about.

What you're saying is that there are two different types of girls in my songs: there's the beautiful dreamy type and the vicious bitch type. There are also one or two others, but, yeah, you're right—there are two kinds of girls…only I never thought about it before.

You don't have too many girls in your songs that share both qualities.

Ah, I see, I'm not integrating them properly. Maybe not. Maybe "Beast of Burden" is integrated slightly. I don't want the kind of woman who's going to drudge for me. The song says: I don't need a beast of burden, and I'm not going to be your beast of burden, either. Any woman can see that that's like my saying I don't want a woman to be on her knees for me. I mean, I get accused of being very antigirl, right? But people really don't listen, they get it all wrong. They hear "Beast of Burden" and say "Arrggggh!"

They sure heard "Under My Thumb" ["Under my thumb's a squirming dog who's just had her day"].

That's going back to my teenage years!

Well, it's both a perverse and brilliant song about power and sex.

At the time there was no feminist criticism because there was no such thing, and one just wrote what one felt. Not that I let it hinder me too much now.

How about your woman-in-bondage poster for your 'Black and Blue' album?

Yeah, we had a lot of trouble with that particular poster. As far as the songs go, one talks about one's own experience a lot of the time. There are a lot of women who are disgraceful, and if you just have the misfortune to have an affair with one of those...it's a personal thing.

And the "squirming dog" image?

Well, that was a joke. I've never felt in that position vis-à-vis a person—I'd never want to really hurt someone.

What about the groupies who are ready for anything? What about "Star Star"?

Exactly! That's real, and if girls can do that, I can certainly write about it, because it's what I see. I'm not saying all women are star fuckers, but I see an awful lot of them, and so I write a song called that. I mean, people show themselves up by their own behavior, and just to describe it doesn't mean you're antifeminist.

That bondage poster, though, was pretty blatant.

Well, there are a lot of girls into that—they dig it, they want to be chained up. And it's a thing that's true for both sexes.

But why use it to advertise a record?

I don't see why not. It's a valid piece of commercial art, just a picture.

Would you show yourself getting whipped and beaten?

Sure, if I thought it was more commercial than a beautiful girl!

People are obviously going to take a few of these songs on the new LP as being about your domestic situation.

Well, I actually mention "my wife" in "Respectable."

"Get out of my life/ Go take my wife/ Don't come back." And there's also: "You're a rag trade girl/ You're the queen of porn/ You're the easiest lay on the White House lawn."

Well, I just thought it was funny. "Respectable" really started off as a song in my head about how "respectable" a band we're supposed to have become. *We're* so respectable. As I went along with the singing, I just made things up and fit things in. "Now we're respected in society..." I really meant *us*. My wife's a very honest person, and the song's not about her.

But people will probably take this song, as well as the album, to be about you, in the same way they took 'Blood on the Tracks' to be about Bob Dylan or John Lennon's "I don't believe in Beatles" song to be about him.

But it's very rock & roll. It's not like "Sara." "Respectable" is very light-hearted when you hear it. That's why I don't like divorcing the lyrics from the music. 'Cause when you actually hear it sung, it's not what is, it's the way we do it.

Keith Richards once said something to the effect that rock & roll really is subversive because the rhythms alter your being and perceptions.

Music is one of the things that changes society. That old idea of not letting white children listen to black music is true, 'cause if you want white children to remain what they are, they mustn't.

Look at what happened to you.

Exactly! You get different attitudes to things...even the way you walk....

And the way you talk.

Right. Remember the Twenties, when jazz in Europe changed a lot of things? People got crazier, girls lifted up their dresses and cut their hair. People started to dance to that music, and it made profound changes in that society.... This sounds awfully serious!

To keep on the semiserious keel for a second, the song "Some Girls" seems to be about what happens when hundreds of idealized Twenties girls try to eat you up, destroy you—taking your money and clothes and giving you babies you don't want.

Well, it could be a bad dream in a way. I had a dream like that last night, incidentally, but there were dogs as well as girls in it.

I wonder what the girls and women, of all races, in the audience are going to think of lines like: "Black girls just want to get fucked all night/ I just don't have that much jam!" or "Chinese girls/ They're so gentle/ They're really such a tease."

I think they're all well covered—everyone's represented [*laughing*]. Most of the girls I've played the song to like "Some Girls." They think it's funny; black girlfriends of mine just laughed. And I think it's very complimentary about Chinese girls. I think they come off better than English girls. I really like girls an awful lot, and I don't think I'd say anything really nasty about any of them.

Are you running for president?

[*Laughing*] The song's supposed to be funny.

I couldn't help noticing that the way you sing lines like "Some girls they're so pure/ Some girls so corrupt" are perfect mimicries of Bob Dylan's phrasing and tone of voice during his 'Blonde on Blonde' period.

If that's how you think of it…yeah. Dylan's very easy to imitate. Sometimes I imitate Van Morrison too, for laughs. That song is a kind of a joke, too, but you haven't got it yet, so I'm not going to tell you.

"Some girls take my money/ Some girls take my clothes/ Some girls take the shirt off my back and leave me with a lethal dose." I wonder what those lines are about.

No reply [*laughing*]. "Some Girls" isn't really about me. I made most of it up just off the bat. I remember that when I wrote it, it was very funny. We were laughing and the phone was ringing, and I was just sitting in the kitchen and it was just coming out…and I thought I could go on forever!

The first time I heard it, I started making up my own lyrics: "Green girls get me anxious/ Blue girls get me sad/ Brown girls get me silly/ And red girls get me mad." It's like a kid's song.

[*Laughing*] That's why I said it wasn't serious. It's just anything that came into my head.

Do you remember the Beach Boys' "California Girls"?

Yeah, I love that song.

Well, it seems to me that instead of all the girls in your song being California girls, they've all turned into a different type of girl—and certainly from another state!

I know what you mean. I never thought of it like that. I never thought that a rock critic of your knowledge and background could ever come up with an observation like that [*laughing*].

You mean it's pretentious?

Not at all. It's a great analogy. But like all analogies, it's false [*laughing*].

"Some Girls" is full of New York City settings and energy.

Yeah, I was staying in New York part of last year, and when I got to Paris and was writing the words, I was thinking about New York. Hope they like it in south Jersey [*laughing*].

There's this gay garbage collector on Fifty-third Street in "When the Whip Comes Down," Central Park in "Miss You," the sex and dreams and parties and the schmattas on Seventh Avenue in "Shattered."

I'd written some of my verses before I got into the studio, but I don't like to keep singing the same thing over and over, so it changed. And I was noticing that there were a lot of references to New York, so I kept it like that. *Some Girls* isn't a concept album, God forbid, but it's nice that some of the songs have connections with each other—they make the album hold together a bit.

My favorite song on the album is "Beast of Burden," in which your voice and the filigreed interplay of the guitars bring back for me Otis Redding, Wilson Pickett, Smokey Robinson and even the early guitar solos of Peter Tosh.

I quite like it, but I didn't expect anyone to really go for it, certainly not as much as you. It's surprising. But I wonder what other people are going to think of the album. I mean, we've been knocked a lot recently—I don't really know what they expect us to do.

I've noticed that you can really hear the words on 'Some Girls,' whereas they're mostly buried on other albums.

During the mix, I kind of decide—if the words are good, we bring them up; if they're useless, then...

But on 'Exile on Main Street' the words were great, yet it was hard to hear them.

Yeah, a lot of people told me that. Maybe the rest of the band would prefer it if I weren't too loud, and I'm so good anyway [*laughing*]. But you know, people often interpret lyrics in ways you never meant. Sometimes I'm aware, when I write something, that a line can be taken in two ways, and I don't really want to say what everything is about. It's a lot more fun for people to interpret them in their own way.

I read somewhere that you bit off the front part of your tongue when you were a kid and that this was a kind of initiation rite.

[*Laughing*] Bullshit! I just bit a little bit off. That idea sounds as if it came from someplace like *Creem* magazine.

I heard that you were considering playing Antonin Artaud in a film. He once took peyote in Mexico and described the experience as the three happiest days in his life. This is what he said about that time: "Boredom disappeared, I ceased looking for a reason to live, and I no longer had to carry my body. I grasped that I was inventing my life, that this was my function and my raison d'être, and that I got bored when I had no more imagination." To me this quotation suggests you and your public persona quite a bit.

Strange, no? Uh-*huh*. I think it applies to most everybody, surely. But as Artaud said, he only had three happy days in his life. He was an unhappy person, and I'm not. I was just born happy, and he wasn't. But if I had the tiniest bit of the talent Artaud had, I'd be even happier than I am. I find him very interesting as a poet and in terms of his interest in theater and in cinema . . . and also interesting as an individual because he was so tortured. But I don't identify with him.

I don't continually question my reason to live—it's just a state of being. I'm just here. The real question is what you're doing with the living you're doing, what you want to do with that living.

What do you think you've been doing with the living you've been doing in the Seventies?

Wasting my time.

Yet during that time you also wrote "Time Waits for No One," which really is a powerful song that no one commented on that much.

I liked it a lot. But I don't see things in terms of years—the Sixties, the Seventies—it's just a journalistic convention.

Punk rock, too. I don't want to get into the accusations that the Rolling Stones gave in or up or whatever. It's sort of vaguely true, but it's not really true. To me, rock & roll just goes back to the basic things. It doesn't exist because other people *don't* come across. It exists because kids want to get up and play very simple. The punk-rock movement said things to get a lot of copy. It's just an excuse to say that Rod Stewart lives in Hollywood and spends millions of dollars. It was just a good line. It wasn't the real reason punk rock existed.

What song or songs have you heard in the past few years that really got to you?

Really got to me? Hardly any. I don't listen seriously to rock & roll today. I never really did listen to white English bands. I like Latin music, all kinds of Caribbean music—I prefer that to white rock bands. I recently saw Tuff Darts and the Jam, right? Tuff Darts are pretty good, but the music really didn't swing. It's like white people, you know what I mean? I liked disco music when it was very Latin, two or three years ago—it was all Latin steps.

Now it's Australian.

Right, Australian. I liked John Travolta.

How does his dancing rate with yours?

It's not really difficult to be a better dancer than I am. I think I'm a terrible dancer, and I'd love to have gone to school and learned it properly, but I don't have the time nor the discipline.

I once heard Nureyev on television say that you were a terrific dancer.

That's very kind of him because he's a great dancer. I can't dance a waltz or a quickstep. I just leap about, and sometimes it's very ungainly. It's hard dancing while you're singing.

You and Keith call yourselves the Glimmer Twins when you credit yourselves as producers. Someone once compared you two to Romulus and Remus.

[*Laughing*] We're very close, and we always have been. He was born my brother by accident by different parents. People don't know who does what. And it's very difficult for me to remember who wrote what particular verse or song. Rock reviewers say, "That's a typical Keith Richards song." But they don't know. They often get it wrong, and it makes me laugh.

How long have you known Keith?

Twenty-nine years.

How old are you?

Thirty-four. I met him when I was six. We lived on the same block for a while when we were kids. Keith and I went to the same school at one point, and we walked home together.

Sounds like "Hey little girl in the high school sweater."

[*Laughing*] Then I met him later on, and we really remembered each other.

When I listen to you on your records, I sometimes get the sense of a ten-to-fourteen-year-old singing, as if inside you were a young boy still. What age do you feel close to?

About eleven or twelve. Just prepuberty. I know it sounds immature [*laughing*], but one day I'll do it properly when I'm a big boy.

You once said that you didn't want to be singing "Satisfaction" when you were forty-two.

No, I certainly won't.

You often convey a feeling that combines the fearlessness and rambunctiousness that young kids have, and it seems to be a feeling that charms and bothers people.

It bothers them because they can't be like that themselves. I consider myself very lucky, and one of the reasons for that is that when I'm singing or acting or playing or anything, even at home, I feel just like a baby, like I'm ten or eleven or twelve. Whether that's my fantasy, whether it's right or wrong—I know that's something that other people can't do. I mean, I can act like a thirty-four-year-old, too—I've trained myself to act in this manner [*laughing*]—but when I'm playing, I can go back in time. I think that's true for many musicians and actors and dancers, and people envy that.

I was thinking of the lines in "As Tears Go By": "It is the evening of the day/ I sit and watch the children play/ Doing things I used to do/ They think are new." It must be amazing to you that there are all these kids who were three years old in 1964 and '65 and who are seeing you now for the first time.

Sure. When I was already in Los Angeles in my pink Cadillac, they were just three years old, and now I go out with them [*laughing*]. It feels all right.

Do you like older women?

No.

And not lying, cheating, vain, affected girls, either.

It's easy for me to write that kind of song because my talent seems to lie in that direction, and I can only occasionally come up with a really good love song. It's easier to come out with the other side of the coin. So I choose what I do best, that's all.

I remember your old song "Off the Hook": the girl's phone is always busy, you wonder what she's doing, and finally you just take your own phone off the hook.

People seem fascinated with whether your phone is on or off the hook—in your personal life, in other words. Why do you think that is?

It's amazing to me that people want to know about my soap opera. Not just mine, of course, but mine's been a very long-running soap opera for a rock & roll singer. I mean, people aren't interested in Roger Daltrey's soap opera. I'm not trying to put people down, I wish I didn't have a soap opera. Bob Dylan they're interested in now only because he's getting a divorce. Before they weren't—they didn't seem to care. He was just married and had a lot of children, and they didn't want to write about when he went out or whatever. No one was really *that* interested in any of the Beatles' soap operas, not to the extent that I go through it. Of course, John and Yoko did get attention in the late Sixties by making an exhibition of themselves, sitting in bed, et cetera. But I try to avoid publicity. I'm *running*.

I really don't like being a soap opera. It must be some sort of sexual interest. People who've got some kind of sexual attraction—and I hope I'm not being immodest by saying this—but when I was a kid I had it, I didn't have a problem getting girls. I did have a problem, though, until I started singing—I don't mind saying that. I got *nothing*. Maybe I was just shy.

It's that androgynous image that seems to attract both girls and boys.

Yeah, I don't think it did in earlier years, but maybe there was always room for the androgynous type. Anyway, all the guys have a feminine side. But most girls don't really fall in love with a completely gay guy, even though they like the feminine side showing. And vice versa with men. They like a woman who combines things, too. They don't want someone who's either butch or totally helpless.

But, as we said before, your songs don't always combine things. Maybe that's what gives the power to the songs.

Well, there is one song that's a straight gay song—"When the Whip Comes Down." But I have no idea why I wrote it. It's strange—the Rolling Stones have always attracted a lot of men [*laughing*]. That sounds funny, but they're not all gay. And, of course, I have a lot of gay friends, but I suppose everyone does in New York City, and what's that have to do with the price of eggs?...I sure hope the radio stations will play "When the Whip Comes Down." I don't know why I wrote it. Maybe I came out of the closet [*laughing*]. It's about an imaginary person who comes from L.A. to New York and becomes a garbage collector....But whatever, I don't like this gossip interest in me today at all. It upsets a lot of people, and it creates a lot of diversions in my life. I can ignore it in America—it's not so bad here—but in Australia and England there are so many competing gossip columns. I don't trust journalists, generally, because they don't write the truth.

'Some Girls' seems to be the first Rolling Stones album in years that presents a dramatic quality—as if each song were an element in a play.

I think *Some Girls* is the best album we've done since *Let It Bleed*. I hate to say that because usually I say I love all the albums, or I hate them all, or none of them means anything to me, don't bother me with it, et cetera. But I do think it's a good album, and I'm not going to be too modest about it. The reason perhaps why this album is so good is that we did forty-two songs [*laughing*], so we could cut the deadwood away. But there was a lot of good material.

Whatever you did, you certainly put it together right with this album.

Well, I just realized that we had to. People expect a lot more of us than they do everybody else.

Faces: 1975–1979

Clockwise, from left to right:
Van Halen
The Police
Norman Mailer
The Village People
Linda Ronstadt
Francis Ford Coppola and Martin Sheen
Ralph Nader
Three Mile Island

Clockwise, from left to right:
Bette Midler
The Eagles
Steven Spielberg and E.T.
Billy Joel
Tom Waits
Governor Jerry Brown
Richard Gere
David Bowie
John Travolta

Clockwise, from left to right:
Robin Williams
Jonestown
Jimmy Carter
Fleetwood Mac
Diane Keaton
Elvis's funeral
Robert DeNiro
Patti Smith

I can't believe the news today,
I can't close my eyes and make it go away.
How long, how long must we sing this song?
How long? Tonight we can be as one.
—U2, *"Sunday Bloody Sunday"*

1980–1987

I hear the ancient footsteps like the motion of the sea
Sometimes I turn, there's someone there, other times it's only me.
I am hanging in the balance of the reality of man
Like every sparrow falling, like every grain of sand.
—BOB DYLAN, *"Every Grain of Sand"*

Voices

In America, everybody is in show business…nobody isn't an actor. Everybody is aware of the camera, whether it exists or not, and it seems that everybody in this country aspires to be famous.
—STING, *September 1983*

★　　　　★　　　　★

People look at that guy Nicholson down there yelling and say, "What's he do?" Nothing—he sits around and complains. At least a guy in a nice pin-stripe suit down at the bank, he keeps the park clean, everything's cool. Who are these rabble-rousers? What do they do? Let's go back in there and let's buy shoes down at the conglomerate. Let's let the big guy in the pin-stripe suit run things, 'cause it'll be quiet then.
—JACK NICHOLSON, *August 1986*

★　　　　★　　　　★

It was kind of amusing. I knew that "Make my day" would have a certain amount of impact in the film, but I didn't realize it would become a sort of "Play it again, Sam."
—CLINT EASTWOOD, *July 1985*

★　　　　★　　　　★

Now is a great time for new religions to pop up. There are people who get religious about jogging, they get religious about sex, and you talk to some of these people who are avowed swingers—they'll bore your head off. God, it's just painful to listen to them. Health foods have become the basis of a religion. Let's see, ESP, of course, flying saucers, anything is fertile ground now. There's a new messiah born every day.
—TOM WOLFE, *August 1980*

★　　　　★　　　　★

In Britain, at the moment, we've got 2-Tone, we've still got punk, we've got mod bands, we've got all kinds of different families of music—each of which takes an enormous amount of adjustment. They're intense and very socially…jagged. They don't fit neatly into the existing society: they challenge it. And yet in America, kids seem to be quite happy. Rock, to them, is enough: establishment rock is enough.
—PETE TOWNSHEND, *June 1980*

Whatever power there is in the universe that creates and sustains meant for human beings to be almost hedonistic about it. I mean, get down and wallow in it. Enjoy life and be happy.
—DON JOHNSON, *November 1985*

★   ★   ★

I think what's happening now is people want to forget. There was Vietnam, there was Watergate, there was Iran. We were beaten, we were hustled, and then we were humiliated. And I think people got a need to feel good about the country they live in. But what's happening, I think, is that the need—which is a good thing—is gettin' manipulated and exploited. And you see the Reagan reelection ads on TV. You know: "It's morning in America." And you say, well, it's not morning in Pittsburgh. It's not morning above 125th Street in New York. It's midnight, and, like, there's a bad moon risin'.
—BRUCE SPRINGSTEEN, *December 1984*

★   ★   ★

It's very popular nowadays to think of yourself as a "liberal humanist." That's such a bullshit term. It means less than nothing. I think politics is an instrument of the devil. Just that clear. I think politics is what kills; it doesn't bring anything alive. Politics is corrupt; I mean, anybody knows that.
—BOB DYLAN, *June 1984*

★   ★   ★

I must say, since we're gettin' into drugs—and at the risk of sounding goody-goody again—that I do personally feel, from this perspective, today, that my favorite thing is to be clean and straight. I think you can enjoy your life better that way.
—PAUL McCARTNEY, *September 1986*

★   ★   ★

The only moment of satisfaction I've gotten from all this was when I saw the first Band-Aid boat. It was so big and so full of things. But when the history of Africa is written, it will have a lot to accuse the rest of the world of. Just as the Jews, without doubt, have a right to accuse the rest of the world for what they allowed to happen. I'm saying, I'd like to be one of the guys that saved people from the gas chambers or smuggled people out of the Nazis' control. I'd want to be like that.
—BOB GELDOF, *December 1985*

Lennon

by Scott Spencer   January 1981

It doesn't work. If I were writing a story about a man of his magnitude, and all I could come up with was a horrid little ending like that, I would have to say I didn't deserve to write it at all. How would it read? Once upon a time there was a man who heard music and poetry, and he told us what he heard, and people everywhere in all the kingdoms of the earth fell in love with what he made of himself, and he lived in a castle with his wife and child and had untold riches laid at his feet, and then one day a little man hid in the dark and with four jerks of the finger killed the man who made the music. What a pathetic conclusion. How utterly unworthy of the complexities, the possibilities. No one would publish such a thing. No one would represent it. You should throw it away. Quickly. Before someone reads it.

This is so difficult to write about. So dispiriting. I have a cigarette in my hand, and another one is smoking in the ashtray. There's loose change on my desk, a lucky stone from Massachusetts, a coffee cup, unopened mail, a bank deposit slip. Everything I want to say is receding from me. Everything these past twenty-four hours reminds me of death. It seems, whether we know it or not, we are in constant rehearsal for death: by forgetting, by sleeping, by looking away, by failing to hold the precious warm bodies we are meant to hold.

As a child, I would wait for my mother to come home. I'd peer out the window and see her walking down the street. And then I'd overturn a table, scatter magazines over the floor and fall in some dexterous approximation of a murdered corpse, waiting happily for her to discover me. Rehearsing, rehearsing. Half the games we played as children were about killing each other, choking each other, shooting each other, lunging out from hiding places to frighten each other: we were trying to learn the art of dying while we were still rightfully stupid enough to bear it.

Because he allowed us to know him, to love him, John Lennon gave us the chance to share his death, to resume the preparations for our own. Because we were so used to the way he thought, the habits, the turns, the surprises of his mind, we can enter him as we remember his last moments, to let it be us in the car, pulling up to the curb, opening the door, stepping out, breathing the night. Someone said he was happy that night, and we somehow know what his happiness felt like, and we can imagine ourselves resurgent, electric with energy.

Most of those who pass for heroes are not heroes at all. They are hidden from us, uncommunicative, of no final use. But because he was an artist, and a brave one, we knew him. We felt the rhythm of his thoughts. We knew what he meant, no matter what he said, no matter if we disagreed. He had the great moral transparency of genius, and so we could enter him at will. (This power he gave us surely must have terrified him.) And so we are there, feeling what he felt, having this sordid education in death forced upon us, rubbed in our faces. As far as I can tell from the daily papers, his last word was "Yeah." In the police car that took him to the emergency room, someone asked him if he was John Lennon, and he said "Yeah." There are compilations of the last words of the great and the famous, and some of them are real rousers. Yet John Lennon's simple syllable allows me to lean closer to the true and absolute reality of life running out, death hurtling forward, because with John Lennon, we somehow knew everything he meant, everything he implied: the sudden thrusts of meaning, the cast of his eye, the silences.

His death is everywhere. Like his life and his art, it is a unifying force. The astonishing—and for me, unduplicated—characteristic of his art was that it brought together people who may have had no other single thing in common. It was the only true mass phenomenon that's ever touched me. Through the Beatles—and I think, primarily through John—I was able to share with millions my thoughts and their thoughts, *our thoughts,* about growing old, falling in love, seizing happiness, transcendence. A genius can take an orange and a chunk of coal and create a unity. A genius like John Lennon can create a community of hearts and minds from 10 million separate appetites. Part of the grief we feel about his murder is our longing to once more belong to something larger than ourselves, to feel our heart beat in absolute synchrony with hearts everywhere. Passionate love can lift us out of our skin, can join us with another in a realm outside of time. Art can do the same, and when millions are lifted by an artist, he allows us to see one another in that moment as we never have before, never will again.

It was, of course, like the Sixties again, waking up, hearing of his death. There's no use injecting paranoia into something already so terrible, but it felt like the beginning of our new reactionary decade: history, as it fingers us in the chest, somehow able to reach back into the Sixties and renew the cycle of hideous assassinations. It's like a hurricane suddenly returning after it was supposedly spent at sea.

I am consoling myself now: He had a magnificent life. He fell deeply in love and knew enough about the heart and its lazy habits to never allow his essential connections to go stale. Like other great artists, he was a teacher. He taught us something about integrity. And risk. He taught us about speaking up against injustice. And he is an integral part of my most extravagant, far-flung dreams about the potential power of art. It is no inspiring feat to capture the attention of millions—*Dallas* can do that. But to capture the imagination of millions is an accomplishment on a wholly different scale. It is mythic. His life and our view of him were of course mucked up by all the byproducts of success, image making, celebrity and high finance. But his achievements always rose above the cheapness of publicity, the empty craziness of stardom. He proved that you can follow your vision, explore your talents, speak your mind—take any leap you dare. In a cautious age, John Lennon was uninterested in existing on any but his own terms. He sang and wrote what he believed, and he trusted us to listen. And he was right: we listened. Taking his lesson to heart, embracing his radiant example, ennobles the work *we* do. John's success, his awesome ability to communicate with millions—to say difficult things to people whom others felt were fit to hear only the emptiest words, to say emotionally vulnerable things to the most cynical and say them so well they could not be denied—remains a towering standard. He teaches us faith in oneself, confidence in and affection for the human community.

I am left with the one thing I wanted not to say, because it's so old and so fucking funereal: we are better people because of John Lennon. And now, when we need to be better still, and braver, with a deeper, more encompassing vision, losing him is terrifying. It just cuts so deeply. It's hard to believe our luck has gotten this bad.

John and Yoko: A Portfolio by Annie Leibovitz

December 3rd and December 8th, 1980

Bruce Springsteen and the Secret of the World

by Fred Schruers   February 1981

Bruce Springsteen, in the abstract, is just the kind of guy my little New Jersey home town schooled me to despise. Born seventy-seven days apart, raised maybe fifty miles apart, this beatified greaser and I grew up sharing little more than what came over AM radio. In Mountain Lakes, a community of 4000, we had a word for people like Bruce: Newarkylanders. The urban canker of Newark-Elizabeth was their state capital, but they lived and played along the boardwalked Jersey Shore. They wore those shoulder-strap undershirts some people called "guinea-T's"; we called them "Newarkys." They drove muscle cars and worked in garages and metal shops. They ate meatball subs made of cat parts for lunch, and after work they shouted at their moms, cruised the drive-ins, punched each other out and balled their girlfriends in back seats.

Our contempt for Newarkylanders cut almost as deep as our fear of them. We looked on them as prisoners, a subclass that would not get the college degrees and country squires we were marked for. But we realized that prisoners sometimes bust out of their cages with a special vengefulness. The fear was as real as a black Chevy rumbling down your tree-lined block, and inside are six guys with baseball bats and tire irons.

Bruce Springsteen has seen all this from the inside, he's seen the gates swing shut, he's watched people turning the locks on their own cages. You can hear it in his music, a music with shack-town roots; paradoxically, it saved him from that life. I could not have heard his songs, especially the earlier, wordier ones, and expected our meeting to boil down to the wracking Jersey nightmare of Joe College versus Joe Greaser.

While even among his ardent fans there are people who say Springsteen has gone to the well too many times for his favorite themes of cars, girls and the night, watching him perform the new songs, I came to believe he really was battering at new riddles: marriage, work and how people in America turn themselves into ghosts.

I would come to understand that this jubilant rock & roll cock of the walk never had cut it as Joe Greaser, that what had fathered his obsessiveness was doing time as a runty, bad-complected kid whom the nuns, girls and greasers had taken turns having no use for. There is finally something irrevocably lonely and restless about him. He's never claimed any different. Springsteen wants to inspire by example—the example of a trashed and resurrected American spirit. "You ask me if there's any one thing in particular," said E Street Band pianist Roy Bittan when we talked about Springsteen's commitment. "There's too many things in particular. He's older and wiser, but he never strays from his basic values. He cares more about the losers than the winners. He's so unlike everything you think a real successful rock star would be."

Springsteen comes down the ramp at the Minneapolis-St. Paul airport and looks down the empty corridor: "No autographs," he says in his characteristic parched cackle. "No autographs, *please.*"

This is exactly what he never says, of course, and when the tour party breaches the corridor's double door, he greets a pack of young, denim-jacketed guys familiarly. Some are holding copies of *The River,* released just this day and heading for Number One. As the entourage loads itself into a string of station wagons, a kid who has been hanging at the edge of the pack tells Bruce about a friend who's critically ill in a local hospital. Bruce tells the kid to get his friend's name to him through the record company. Doors are slamming and engines gunning. It's bitter cold. Just another stranger, I think.

Thirty-eight hours later, after performing "Out in the Street" onstage at the St. Paul Civic Center, Springsteen halts the show. "I met a bunch of guys at the airport yesterday coming in. One told me he had a friend who was sick. If that fella who told me his friend was sick will come to the side of the stage during the break, I got something for your friend backstage."

After the kid appeared, and was duly loaded up with autographed mementos, I pondered the gesture. Springsteen could have scribbled his good wishes on an album at the airport and been done with it. But he had left the benediction to be arranged in public. There's a lot of showman in Springsteen, and not a little preacher. Why had he let the anonymous kid slip so close to being forgotten, then given him his last rock & roll rites before the crowd?

"There's not much people can count on today," said Springsteen. "Everything has been so faithless, and people have been shown such disrespect. You want to show people that somehow, that somewhere, somebody can...I guess I just don't want to let them down. That's probably why we come out and play every night—there's that fear, 'cause then nothin' works, nothin' makes sense. As long as one thing does, if there can be just one thing that goes against what you see all around you, then you know that things can be different. Mainly it's important to have that passion for living, to somehow get it from someplace."

The inescapable cliché about faith is that it can always be doubted. That's the thing about Springsteen—if you pay any attention at all, his lyrics and his every stance will force you into a corner where you must decide whether you believe him or not. I had to believe he wasn't staging the benediction to pump up his image—in the tradition of Babe Ruth socking a homer for a dying child—but for the kid himself. Not to "rise and walk," but to offer something tangible—the momentary, empathetic suffering of this captive crowd of 15,000. And although most are in their wild age, perhaps some of them might even learn a little charity themselves.

Accuse Springsteen of being a star and he'll flick his hand like he's just been splashed with pigeon shit. He is eager to point out that he has the better deal in the meeting place between fan and star.

"I think the one feeling that's most unique to this job, the best part of the whole thing, is meeting someone like this guy I met the other night who had been on a bus ten hours. He's twenty-one years old, and he just grabs hold of me. We're in a room crowded with people. He's cryin' and he doesn't care. He says, 'It's my birthday,' and I ask, 'How old are you?' He says, 'I'm twenty-one, and this is the most important thing in my life.' And you know they're not kidding when they say it, because you look in their faces and they're so full of emotion.

"You meet somebody, and it's like an open well. In ten minutes I'll know more about him than his mother and father do, and maybe his best friend. All the things it usually takes for people to know each other just go away, because there's this feeling that it's so fleeting. They tell you the thing that's most important to them right away. It's a sobering thing, because you know that somewhere you did *something* that meant something to them. It's just a real raw, emotional thing; it's like the cleanest thing you ever felt. You have a communication, a feeling, and I don't know, you just gotta love the guy. If you don't, there's something the matter with you.

"And it ain't some starry-eyed thing, and it ain't some Hollywood thing, and it ain't some celebrity thing. This guy, he loves you, and what's more, he knows you in a certain way. That's the thing that makes me strong. I get strong when I meet somebody like that."

★   ★   ★

There is an obsessiveness to Springsteen—the underside of his manic off-stage energy—that can be a little scary. It seems to spring from flash fires that ignite in his very detailed memory. "There ain't a note I play onstage," he says late one night, "that can't be traced directly back to my mother and father."

We're riding in a rented Winnebago, rocking back and forth in icy crosswinds on a six-hour drive from Pittsburgh to Rochester, New York. We had started the drive at 3:00 a.m., an hour Springsteen takes to like a pup going for a walk. Still buzzed from a show that closed with Elvis's "Mystery Train," he merrily salts some fried chicken and picks up a remembrance. "It was a real classic little town I grew up in, very intent on maintaining the status quo. Everything was looked at as a threat; kids were looked at as a nuisance and a threat. And when you're a kid, your parents become fixtures, like a sofa in the living room, and you take for granted what they do." He lets out one of his oddly mournful laughs. "My father used to drive around in his car, and it would not go in reverse. Heh. I remember pushing it backward; that was just something you did, you didn't even think it was strange."

One of the things that makes Springsteen a whole different species of rock performer is his candor about the numbed, paralytic rage his father, Douglas Springsteen, a bus driver and sometime prison guard, converted to bitterness at a very early age. Bruce will stand on a darkened stage and remember out loud about coming into his house late at night, almost always seeing the kitchen light go on, to face his father. One day his aunt showed him a picture of his father, back from World War II, about to marry and start a family that would include Bruce and his two sisters. "He looked just like John Garfield, in this great suit, he looked like he was gonna eat the photographer's head off. And I couldn't ever remember him looking that proud, or that defiant, when I was growing up. I used to wonder what happened to all that pride, how it turned into so much bitterness. He'd been so disappointed, had so much stuff beaten out of him by then...."

Sitting in various arenas, ten years gone from my own home, I envy the teenage audience that is hearing Springsteen talk to them about that troublesome blood tie. For many, it is the first time anybody has nosed around in their feelings about their parents; paradoxically, Springsteen's anger seems to set beating, at least for a few moments, a kind of heartsickness that might turn out to be love for those parents. But it's not a Sunday-school rap: "...so much beaten out of him that he couldn't accept the idea that I had a dream and I had possibilities. The things I wanted, he thought were just foolish. People get so much shit shoveled on 'em every day. But it's just important to hold on to those things. Don't let anybody call you foolish."

He takes the Esquire he has absently, slowly been stroking, shrieks once and slams into "Badlands" and the cathartic, energized slide licks that sound like the hand of God reaching down to rip the tops off fleeing cars: "Poor man wanna be rich/Rich man wanna be king/And a king ain't satisfied/Till he rules everything...."

When he rocks back to goose out the taut guitar break in "Candy's Room," or jumps downstage with harmonica to race Clarence Clemons's sax to the end of "Promised Land," it's invigorating to notice that the guy can play, that despite all his steeplechasing and singing, he doesn't come off as a slacker on harp and guitar. Maybe that's because there's nothing ever casual about his attack.

★   ★   ★

At age nine, Springsteen saw Elvis on *The Ed Sullivan Show*. But in 1959, Bruce found guitar lessons to be "oppressive"—his hands were too small—and aspirations toward big-league baseball took over. "I wanted it pretty bad at the time. Every day from when I was eight till thirteen, I'd be outside pitching that ball." But the guitar fantasy wouldn't quit. "The best thing that ever happened to me was when I got thrown out of the first band I was in, and I went home and put on 'It's All Over Now' by the Rolling Stones and learned that guitar solo.

"I think when I first started, I wouldn't allow myself to think that someday... I just wanted to get in a halfway band, be able to play weekends somewhere and make a little extra dough, working at some job during the week or something. Which is what my parents used to say that I could do. That was allowed. I could do it on weekends, but it was impossible to see or think at the time."

Then it was bars and CYOs and clubs, in and out of various bands, playing, copping licks, going to the Village in New York City on Saturdays to catch matinees at the Cafe Wha.

"I don't ever remember being introduced to Bruce," says Miami Steve Van Zandt, who lived nearby and shared local guitar-hero honors. "I just remember I would go to New York, to the Village, and one day I saw him come walking down MacDougal. We looked at each other like, ah, 'You look familiar' and 'What are you doin' here?' It took a long time to become really close." Stints in bands called the Castiles, Steel Mill, Dr. Zoom and the Sonic Boom followed. And then there was Bruce Springsteen, leader of a band bearing his name.

He signed a management deal with a feisty entrepreneur named Mike Appel on the hood of a car in a dark parking lot. It was a signature that meant Springsteen and the band would not make any serious money until the 1978 tour for *Darkness on the Edge of Town,* his fourth album. "People always say, 'Gee, it must have been tough for you.' But I always remember bein' in a good mood, bein' happy even through the bad stuff and the disappointments, because I knew I was ahead of nine out of ten other people that I've seen around me. 'Cause I was doing something that I liked." Appel did get Bruce face to face with Columbia Records A&R head John Hammond. Bruce signed on with the label. After Jon Landau saw him perform at Harvard Square Theatre in 1974, Landau declared, in a review that was a landmark in both men's lives, that Bruce represented "rock & roll future." They became friends, and Springsteen asked Landau to come in the studio to help him and Appel produce *Born To Run.* Released in 1975, it quickly went gold.

★   ★   ★

Springsteen is happy in the front seat of anything, and he spends the ride from Rochester to Buffalo, New York, gazing at the sunny, snow-covered fields on either side of the highway. Arriving at the hotel, he tucks his cap under his sweat shirt's hood and invites me for a walk downtown in the "fresh [twenty-two degree] air." In high boots and a well-broken-in black cloth coat, he looks like a gravedigger off for the winter. He has pored over the local record store's entire cassette case (choosing collections by the Drifters and Gene Pitney) before the guys who work there recognize him. (The cassette I'd found in Bruce's portable player was Toots and the Maytals' *Funky Kingston.* Bruce confesses a love for reggae, a music he calls "too complex and too pure" for him to interpret.)

The guys behind the counter put on "Hungry Heart," which has plowed through the charts to Number One. It was a song Bruce originally didn't even want to have on the album until Jon Landau (now his manager) insisted. Bruce describes the song as an evocation of what the Beach Boys and Frankie Lymon used to do for him.

Still gimpy from a stumble he'd taken during a show in Washington, he walks on incognito until some jewelry-stand salesgirls corner him for autographs in a bookstore.

We cross the street to McDonald's. "Paradise," he calls it. "I never did get comfortable with places that got the menu in the window," he explains, making two Quarter-Pounders disappear. He looks contentedly around as the munching Buffalonians make no sign of recognizing him. "I love coming to these places where it's nothing but real."

Springsteen works hard at keeping his own life real. His mother is still doing the kind of secretarial work she began at age eighteen, and he predicted that his new money would not make any difference. "What's she gonna do—quit and run around the world and buy things? In a certain way, the money aspect of it is not very useful to them. I gave 'em some money one day and found out later on they didn't spend it. They thought that was gonna be the payoff, you know, there wasn't gonna be any more. They live around people like them [in San Diego]. The whole thing of driving your folks up to some big house and saying, 'This is yours,' they don't want that. Then it's not them anymore."

One theme that takes up a lot of room on *The River* is marriage and relationships—the ties that bind. "That's the hardest thing for me to talk about. I don't know, I'm in the dark as far as all that stuff goes. It took me five albums to even write about it. People want to get involved, not because of the social pressure, not because of the romantic movies that they grew up on. It's something more basic than that. It's very physical, and it presents itself. It's just the way men and women are.

"My mother and father, they've got a very deep love because they know and understand each other in a very realistic way. Whatever form relationships take is up to the people involved, I guess. But on the album the characters are wrestling with those questions—the guy in 'Stolen Car,' the guy in 'Wreck on the Highway,' 'Drive All

Night,' the guy in 'Sherry Darling,' even. It is a puzzle and a question. It's hard to separate it from all the impressions that are created in you as you grow older. That's why I wanted 'I Wanna Marry You' and 'The River' together, 'cause they're similar songs, similar feelings.

"Everybody seems to hunger for that relationship, and you never seem happy without it. I guess that's good enough reason right there. It just got to a point where all of a sudden these songs about things of that nature started coming out. I think you do tend to think about that particular thing around thirty. But even up till then, when I was writing all the earlier songs, 'Born To Run' and stuff, they never seemed right without the girl. It was just a part of wherever that person was going, that guy was going. It wasn't gonna be any good without her."

★　　　★　　　★

The night after John Lennon's murder, Springsteen was scheduled to play Philadelphia's Spectrum Arena. The band had been onstage at the Spectrum the previous night when the news came, but as organist Danny Federici put it, "They saved it from us till after the show." The next day, Miami Steve called the tour manager to see if the second night was going to be postponed. The answer was no. Steve was so upset he went to Springsteen shortly before the show, "saying that I felt really weird about going onstage, that I couldn't put it together. And he really just reminded me of why we do what we do, and how it was important to go out that night in particular. I wish I could remember exactly what he said, like, 'This is what John Lennon inspired us to do, and now it's our job to do the same thing for these other people, that today it was Lennon and tomorrow it might be me, and if it is....' That's how he does every show, like it was his last. That's the way to live. It's really lucky to be close to him at moments like that."

The band took the stage, most of them wearing black. Springsteen went to the mike. "If it wasn't for John Lennon," he said, "a lot of us would be in some place much different tonight. It's a hard world that makes you live with a lot of things that are unlivable. And it's hard to come out here and play tonight, but there's nothing else to do."

I've seen people digging firebreaks to save their homes, and I've seen some desperate fist fights, and, God knows, I've seen hundreds of rock & roll shows, but I have never seen a human being exert himself the way Springsteen did that night in Philly. His delivery of "Darkness on the Edge of Town" was raw with a mixture of anger, grief and determination. I'll remember "Promised Land" for the way the

Bruce Springsteen
Photograph by Annie Leibovitz

silhouettes in the top tier of the 18,500-seat arena were standing, striking the air with their fists. The crowd sang the refrain of "Thunder Road" so hard you could feel your sternum hum. "I've heard these songs a million fucking times," Miami would say the next day, "and it was like I never heard 'em before. I've watched him write, months and months of digging, but last night was a weird feeling, like you were in exactly the same place he was when he wrote them."

★   ★   ★

Springsteen works from the gut. There seem to be no planks of his ideology that are not nailed down by some hard-core, practical fact of life. There have long been hints that this lover of automobiles doesn't like the big oil companies; for the B side of "Hungry Heart" he chose "Held Up Without a Gun," which is partly about gas prices.

Yet many people were surprised when he made his passionate but furtive ideology explicit by joining the lineup for the No Nukes concerts at Madison Square Garden. While in Los Angeles in mid-1979, Bruce went to a Jackson Browne concert. Afterward, the MUSE people had a question for him. "They said they needed some help in New York City," he recalls, "and they asked, did we want to help out."

As he considers the politics of helping out, there seems to be a heavy, slow beat somewhere in his innards before every word he speaks. "There's too much greed, too much carelessness. I don't believe that was ever the idea of capitalism. It's just gotta be voices heard from all places, that's my main concern, and when you're up against big business and politics, you gotta have some muscle.

"People every day in different ways try to talk to people out there. Especially during the elections, they try to appeal to people's secret hearts, you know, with the American Dream. Really it's the human dream, and everybody knows by now that it ain't about two cars in the garage. It's about people living and working together without steppin' on each other.

"There's a cruel and cynical game that goes on," he continues, letting his hands fall open, as if they could catch hold of whatever is bugging him so deeply. "A game that people with responsibility play with these immense hopes and desires. It's disgusting the disrespect those people with responsibility can have. Like TV. You wonder what's going on in this [NBC chief] Freddy Silverman's head sometimes, like how can he do that? There's some good things on TV, but way too much of it is used to zonk people out.

"So that cynical game goes on; it's like the carrot-in-front-of-the-donkey game. The cynicism of the last ten years is what people adopted as a necessary defense against having tire tracks up and down their front and back everyday."

Springsteen pauses and looks across a table littered with chicken bones and empty soda bottles. Outside the hotel room, Lake Erie's gray expanse is whitening with the dawn.

"That was the spirit of rock & roll when it came in," he goes on, "talking to kids in their secret heart. To promise to somebody that things are gonna be all right—you don't ever have the room to do that. Then you're a politician. All you can do is say there's possibilities—some are gonna stand, some are gonna fall—and then try to say that the search and the struggle is a life-affirming action. Illusions make you weak. Dreams and possibilities make you strong. That's what I hope people get from our music. That's what I got from the Drifters, say, 'Under the Boardwalk.' As full as the singer's voice sounds, it always had that little sadness that made you love it, made you recognize it as being true.

"There's this movie, *Wise Blood* [from Flannery O'Connor's story, in which a young religious zealot from the deep South blinds himself]. One of my favorite parts was the end, where he's doin' all these terrible things to himself, and the woman comes in and says, 'There's no reason for it. People have quit doing it.' And he says, 'They ain't quit doing it as long as I'm doing it.'

"There's this thing that gets conjured up at night. In fact, to me it's different every night. I was always close to work. I found out very young what makes me happy. I stay very close to that. It just seemed like the secret of the world."

Modern Manners

by P.J. O'Rourke   November 1981

Cocaine and etiquette are inseparable; they go together like cocaine and, well, more cocaine. But why should courtesy be so important when "Sinus Highballs" are passed around? Why shouldn't we behave the way we behave with other drugs: burrow stupidly in the refrigerator as though we'd smoked marijuana or run naked through the streets killing policemen as though we'd taken PCP? There's no firm answer. Yet such behavior could not be less appropriate to the ingestion of "Alkaloid Chitchat Flakes."

Cocaine demands gentility from its partakers, perhaps because it's such a sociable drug. MDA is a sociable drug, but it makes people so sociable they'll screw a coffee-table leg. That's not good manners if the table has an expensive lacquered finish. Or it may be the price of "Talk Talcum" that inclines us to courtliness, though heroin, too, is costly, and repeated use of that turns people into Negroes (Reagan administration statistics clearly show). Most likely it's the special magic cocaine performs upon us all that ignites our civility and refinement. Cocaine makes us so intelligent, so quick, witty, charming, alert, well dressed, good-looking and sexually attractive that it would be unthinkable to be rude under its influence. True, there are exceptions. Cocaine doesn't always do that to you. But it always does it to me. And that's plenty of reason for people to behave.

THE FUNDAMENTAL REASON FOR SELF-SACRIFICE... AND HOW TO DEAL WITH IMPORTANT PEOPLE

The most important thing to understand about cocaine is, no matter how wonderful it makes us feel or how interesting it makes us act, it is bad for our bodies. This is the basis for all etiquette surrounding cocaine use. And this is why it's never bad manners to go off alone and fire some "Nose Nikes" and not share them. To risk your own health while protecting the well-being of others is the only honorable thing to do. For the same reason, when offered someone else's cocaine, you should Electro-Lux as much as possible—for their sake. If there isn't any left to take, they will be less inclined to destroy their mucous membranes, become psychotic, suffer heart palpitations and die from an overdose.

However, for reasons unknown to medical science, there are people cocaine does not harm. Important people who might be able to help someone's career are never injured by cocaine, no matter how much they're given. Neither are famous writers or actors or other personalities with whom many people would like to be friends. Also unaffected are extraordinarily good-looking, sexy people. In other words, the type of person reading this article seems to be immune from cocaine's deadly consequences.

The detrimental effect of "Cerebellum Blizzard" on others, though, cannot be overstated. There was a washed-up musician who hung around a well-known New York nightspot mooching drugs. He turned into a dangerous psychopath and tried to bore several people to death. My own younger brother took too much of my cocaine, and the result was a painful bloody nose. Another unfortunate case involved a vendor of the item itself. He had, no doubt, sampled too much of his own wares and began to threaten people with violence just because they owed him small sums of money… well, relatively small. A mysterious informant—who, honest, felt really bad about it—was compelled to turn him in to the police. (Jail is a famously discourteous place.)

THIRTEEN COMMON PROBLEMS OF ETIQUETTE EXPLAINED

1. How To Serve

Nothing is more awkward than taking out a vial of "Granulated Money" in a bar or restaurant and having everyone you know expect to get some. If you try to pass the "Powdered Trapeze Act" to some people and not to others, you may get hit over the head with a bottle. And that's bad manners. Instead, excuse yourself inconspicuously, saying something like, "Well, I sure have to go to the bathroom, and so do Robert and Susan and Alice, but Jim and Fred and Bob don't have to go."

Parties present the same problem. In the past, such secluded spots as coat closets and dark corners of the butler's pantry were used for spontaneous lovemaking. Nowadays, these nooks and crannies are crowded with people taking drugs. But there is still charm in an old-fashioned excuse. If you would like to give a "Peruvian Speed Bump" to Eileen, an attractive woman who's a power in the entertainment industry, but not to her unemployed boyfriend, Mark, you can always say, "Excuse me, Mark, I thought Eileen might like to blow me in the laundry room."

2. When To Serve

One of the delights of an "Adenoid Snack" is that it's appropriate at any time of night or day, often for several days and nights in a row, though perhaps everyone's favorite moment to take cocaine is right after a great deal of it has been taken already.

An increasingly popular time to make your snout play Selsun Blue with the "Dandruff of the Gods" is before an elaborate dinner. This brightens table talk, lets guests enjoy staring at the food and arranging little lumps of it in patterns on their plates, and gives the hostess many valuable leftovers. An oyster soufflé, for instance, can be reheated and fed to the pets.

Another favorite moment for an "Incan Pep Rally" is the second the dealer arrives with the gram. However, some people find it difficult to figure out when that will be. This is because cocaine dealers operate on Dope Dealer Savings Time, which is similar to Daylight Savings Time. Just as Daylight Savings Time is one hour later than Standard Time, Dope Dealer Savings Time is one hour later than you could possibly imagine anyone being.

3. What Implements Should Be Used?

There are any number of devices on the market for taking cocaine. Some are amusing or even useful in carefully measuring portions to make sure everyone gets too much. But most sophisticated drug users still prefer the rolled-up hundred-dollar bill. Better yet is a hundred-dollar bill folded over and placed inside a wallet. If you have a great many of these, people will find a way to get cocaine up your nose.

4. What Else Should Be Served?

Most people enjoy a couple thousand cigarettes with their "Face Drano." Others mix "Indoor Aspen Lift Lines" with multiple sedatives to achieve that marvelous feeling so similar to not having taken drugs at all. But everyone, whether he wants to or not, should drink plenty of whiskey or gin. If you smell strongly of alcohol, people may think you are drunk instead of stupid. Whatever you serve, overflowing ashtrays, wads of bloody Kleenex and empty Valium bottles can be arranged to make an attractive centerpiece.

5. Who Pays?

There's considerable debate about this. Some say the guest should pay for cocaine as a way of saying thank you to the host. Others say the host should pay for cocaine as part of the entertainment. Most people, however, say society should pay for cocaine by having to watch maniacally self-indulgent movies, fragmented TV sitcom plots and fractured and pathetic live performances by brain-boiled comedians and pop musicians wound up tighter than a Hong Kong wristwatch.

6. Topics of Conversation

…one of the things you're really getting into is cable TV which is going to be like the rock & roll of the Eighties because everybody's going to be hard-wired into 240 channels and there's this huge market for software already which is why you've gotten this programming-development deal together that like right now is a class at the New School but is almost sold to Home Box and is going to be an hour a day that's part news but like part entertainment too like this New Wave group that you've already done three minutes on with minicam on quarter-inch but you might turn that into a documentary plus maybe a docudrama for PBS because it's this sound that's sort of Western Swing but punk but ska which is all in this interview you got with the bass player that you're going to publish in this magazine you're starting which will be all the complete cable listings for all of New Jersey with public-access stuff that isn't listed anywhere plus like interviews too and….

Just because your mouth is moving much faster than your brain is no reason not to carry on an intelligent conversation.

7. Romance

If you have taken too much cocaine and are unable to become aroused, try talking into your partner's genitals. This gives a fair imitation of oral sex. However, if you have taken even more cocaine, try not to rape anyone you know.

8. An Important Question

If a man gives cocaine to a woman, is she then obligated to go to bed with him?

Yes.

9. Another Important Question

If a woman gives cocaine to a man, is he then obliged to go to bed with her?

Jeez, I didn't realize it was this late! I've gotta run—gotta get up and go to work in the morning. Plus I feel like I'm coming down with something. Mind if I do another line before I go?

10. How Is a Dealer Introduced?

It can be a problem knowing how to introduce your dealer. Is he a friend? Is he an employee? Or is he a dead pumpkin if he sells you another load of Dexamyl cut with Portland cement? In fact, there's no proper way to introduce your dealer socially, because no one *ever* deals cocaine. They just have a little extra. You see, a very special friend of theirs—who was in Peru on different business entirely—brought back, as a personal favor, some incredible rocks, which are also pure flake and happen to be crystals too (unless this gramette of alleged narcotics is so hopelessly filled with muck that it's indistinguishable from Nepalese temple hash, in which case it will be given an exotic name like Mudlark of the Andes and a spurious history having to do with Spanish conquistadors and Indian headhunters). So no one ever deals cocaine, but they'll give you this little extra they've got, for, you know, what they paid for it, which is unfortunately $150 a gram, but really, man, this is special stuff, like the Indians used to get by rubbing a coca bush between two Spanish conquistadors' heads.

11. Is It Polite To Refuse?

It's probably not bad manners to refuse cocaine. It might even be very gallant to turn down a spoonful of "Platinum Maxwell House," but it's hard to be sure, because, so far, it's never been done.

12. What To Wear

Many people believe it doesn't matter what they wear while taking a dose of "Brain Tabasco." Some people even take it in the nude (not counting a gold Rolex). But, as in every other social situation, clothes do matter. Richard Pryor is an example of inappropriate cocaine dress. If he had been wearing a nice, conservative Brooks

Brothers suit and an oxford-cloth shirt, he would have escaped most injuries. Unfortunately—as is so often the case in today's increasingly informal world—Mr. Pryor was wearing a polyester sport shirt decorated with Jamaican bongo drummers and dyed in colors visible only to bees. This went up like a torch. Wool, long-staple cotton and other natural fibers have superior flame-retardant qualities.

13. What Is the Polite Way To Refer to Cocaine?

Never call it "tootski."

John Belushi 1949–1982: Made in America

Compiled by Mitchell Glazer and Timothy White   April 1982

"Under the stars," she repeated. "I never noticed the stars before. I always thought of them as great big diamonds that belonged to someone. Now they frighten me. They make me feel that it was all a dream, all my youth."

"It was a dream," said John quietly. "Everybody's youth is a dream, a form of chemical madness."

"How pleasant then to be insane!"

"So I'm told," said John gloomily. "His was a great sin who first invented consciousness. Let us lose it for a few hours."

So wrapping himself in his blanket, he fell off to sleep.

—F. SCOTT FITZGERALD, "The Diamond As Big As the Ritz"

AGNES BELUSHI: I married Adam, John's father, in 1946, after he had returned from the war. He took a job at the Palm Grove Inn on the south side of Chicago, working his way up from busboy to manager of the business. From there, Adam got his own establishment, a place called Olympia Lunch. You'll remember that the Greek restaurant in the skits on *Saturday Night Live* was called the Olympia.

John was born in Chicago on January 24th, 1949, at 5:12 a.m. He weighed eight pounds, fourteen ounces. John was a full-blooded Albanian. His father was born in Qytetes, Albania, and moved to this country in 1934 at the age of sixteen; I was born in Akron, Ohio. John was baptized by Father Chaplain in the St. Nicholas Albanian Orthodox Church, and he was raised in the church.

John was an easygoing little boy, very quiet and well mannered, living in a world of his own. By the age of five, older people were relating to him like an adult, especially since he never really talked like a child. His voice was strong, deep and forceful. Unlike other boys his age, John was allowed and even asked to play with the older children.

ADAM BELUSHI: When John was a little boy, I used to tell him about life in Albania. We had no cars, of course, mostly cattle and donkeys and horses. I always loved to ride horses, and on Sundays, when John was young, we used to go horseback riding and bring a picnic lunch.

"Dad," he said one night, "someday I'm gonna be on television and make a cowboy movie, too."

I told him, "I came to this land from the old country because I heard that in America you can be anything you want to be. My own father came to Chicago to find work and the freedom to do what he wanted in life, and you can do the same."

JIM BELUSHI: John's first stage was the dinner table, and he had a tough audience.

Things could get a little tense at mealtime, and my father didn't like a lot of talk at the table. Whenever things heated up, we all looked to John for relief, and he usually provided it by turning his eyelids inside out. In one second, my mother would be laughing so hard you couldn't hear her anymore, my father's mouth would be stuck wide open while he pounded the table in hysterics, and the rest of us would be weeping with laughter.

Funny thing is, he was almost as quiet as my dad at the table, and the only time I remember him really speaking out when he lived at home was when our younger brother Billy was at the age when a little kid first begins to talk in a conversational way and usually gets ignored. Furious, John got up from the table one night and shouted, "Hey! Enough! Listen to Billy when he talks or he'll grow up with a stutter!" It was a highly unusual outburst, and everybody took it very seriously. From then on, Billy had listeners at the table.

AGNES BELUSHI: The family moved from Chicago to Wheaton when John was six and lived there throughout John's upbringing. John was an athlete. In grammar school, he joined the swimming team and was extremely good. In junior high, he was an undefeated wrestler. At Edison Junior High, he received the athlete of the year award, the American Legion award and the school's best actor award. At Wheaton Central High, John was the manager of the basketball team and captain of the football team, and he was the homecoming king. The other fellas on the football team called him "Killer" Belushi because of his determination, and he was a dedicated player who was always in bed by ten o'clock. He was also big on music, and we borrowed money when he was thirteen to buy him a blue drum set.

When he was moving to Chicago, he came to me one day and said that he and Judy Jacklin—whom John had been dating since he was seventeen and she was fifteen—were going to live together in an apartment there. "I love her, Mom," he said, "and I know I'll take good care of her." He knew how conservative our Albanian ways were, and he was afraid I wouldn't approve. I said, "John, will you do it anyway, no matter what I say?" "Yes, Mom," he said. "Our minds are made up."

ROB JACKLIN: John was about eighteen, attending the College of DuPage, and I was in grad school at the time of the 1968 Democratic National Convention in Chicago. Demonstrators were everywhere, and the city was under siege. I was watching the crowds on TV as they headed down Halsted Street, and at around Eighteenth Street they were met by National Guardsmen. They started firing tear gas, spraying it out as if it were coming from fire hoses. I saw a guy get toppled by the first blast of the gas, and I thought, "Whew, they nailed him, all right." About an hour later, the doorbell rang. It was John, and he was barely conscious. Turned out he was the poor soul I'd seen flattened on TV. That incident was very typical of John. If he was into something, he was right out there on the front lines fighting for it. By the way, it was also his first television appearance.

DEL CLOSE: During my days directing Second City, I was absolutely hung up on Belushi. He always worked at the top of his intelligence. He said to me once, "Del, you know why I'm so comfortable onstage? It's because that's the only place in the world where I know what I'm doing."

BRIAN DOYLE-MURRAY: John replaced me in Second City in 1971. Later, when I first came to New York, I slept on John and Judy's couch for three months. John and I were walking down Barrow Street in the Village one day, and a freak snowstorm hit. We were running in the street with our heads down when John yelled at me and threw me sideways, out of the path of a huge International Harvester truck that had come out of nowhere. The truck struck him, and he did a perfect tuck and roll over to the curb and got up. An ambulance came and took him to St. Vincent's hospital, but they found nothing wrong with him. John risked his life to save mine. He was that kind of man.

CHEVY CHASE: When I was on the road with John in *Lemmings*, we used to room together occasionally. I had a habit of putting my girlfriend's picture up on my bureau. John walked in one night, looked at the photo and said, "Oh, you've got one of her too, eh? I've got the version with the donkey in the picture."

LORNE MICHAELS: Once during one of the *Lampoon* stage shows, a heckler called John "fat," and he went backstage and cried. Sometimes he did everything he could to hide his sensitivity.

It was surprising that John got into showbiz at all. He said his high-school football coach once told him that if he acted in a play he might turn homosexual. Being almost raised by coaches, he had fears about doing drag skits. He had to be talked into some of his best bits, like Elizabeth Taylor eating the chicken. But sometimes it took more than simple coaxing to get John to act.

One week, on *Saturday Night Live*, we had built the whole show around John. He had been up with Keith Richards for three days when he arrived for the dress rehearsal. He was laid out on the couch in his dressing room, burnt out and moaning that he couldn't possibly go on. I was furious. The NBC doctor examined him and said, "His lungs are filled with fluid. If he goes on tonight, the odds are fifty-fifty that he'll die." Livid, I said, "I'll *accept* those odds." One of John's eyes popped open, the eyebrow raised, and he looked at me. Then he got up, changed into costume and did a great show.

JACK NICHOLSON: As I was getting ready to direct *Goin' South*, I realized I wanted a broadly comic character in the film, someone who would be very rambunctious, full of screaming and yelling and crazy bravado. Out of that notion evolved a character named Hector, a Mexican deputy—a rich caricature. Charles Shyer, one of the writers of the script, suggested that John would be good for the role. When John showed up on location in Durango in the hot summer of 1978, I told one of the assistants to take him over to the dentist and get him a gold tooth for the part.

"A gold tooth!" he said. "Why the hell do I need a gold tooth?"

"Trust me," I said. "Go to the dentist."

Naturally, he fell in love with that gold tooth and wore it everywhere. We developed a pretty close relationship while in Durango. John looked for dedication in people he liked, and he returned it in kind. Not many people would have come so far and been so enthusiastic about such a small role. On that first day, I asked him exactly why he had made the trip to Durango.

"Have you ever seen *Lawrence of Arabia*?" he asked.

"Yeah," I said, "I've seen it."

"Well," he said, grinning, "I came for you, Lawrence."

MITCHELL GLAZER: I met John when I did a magazine profile of him in December 1976. He was demanding. He wanted copy approval, picture approval, cover approval. He wanted my approval. Soon, the article was slipping away from me. I was falling prey to the Belushi Hijack Syndrome. It worked like this: John called from the *Saturday Night Live* office for the fifth night in a row, at, say, three or four in the morning. By then, my sleep patterns were shot, deadline approached, and I still hadn't interviewed the man. "Hey, What're ya doin'?" John said. "Listen, get up here right now. Bring your tape recorder and a bunch of tapes. I'm ready to do the interview." Just as I set the receiver down, the phone rang again. "Listen, why don'tcha stop off at a deli and pick up a sandwich—no, two sandwiches. Whatever you want, and hurry."

So it was predawn (*his* time) at Thirty Rockefeller Plaza (*his* turf). The anonymous room—a jumble of clothes, crumpled legal paper and assorted macho hardware—was in shadows. John leaned back in his chair, one eyebrow leaping dangerously. "Well, I thought about it for a while," he sighed, "and I don't need to do the interview after all."

The scary thing was that I was starting to like the guy a lot. He was completely irresistible. There would be a knock at your door; you'd cautiously open it just a crack, and suddenly all the elemental forces of nature would blow into your apartment, use your phone and suck you out into the night. One evening after the article was done, the phone rang in my living room at the instant my live-in girlfriend was throwing me out.

"Hey, what're ya doin'?" John said.

"Well, uh, well, actually, John…oh, Gayle and I are, y'know, breaking up."

"Good. I'll be right over to get ya. You can stay in the back room. Hey, bring your Stones records. Mine are all fucked up. See ya in five minutes."

That was five years ago. My Stones records are still in his basement.

SANDY ALEXANDER: I met John at the Lone Star Cafe in 1977. I didn't know who he was, but he knew I was the leader of the New York chapter of the Hells Angels, and he wanted to meet me. He invited me to come over to the NBC studios and see the show, and we became good friends.

JOHN LANDIS: *National Lampoon's Animal House* was a low-ball project in Hollywood when I was asked to develop it. I read the script and loved it, but the studio said no movie unless I got this guy named Belushi to play Bluto Blutarski. I flew to New York and arranged a meeting with John at the Drake Hotel. He came up to my room, ordered ten shrimp cocktails, twenty beers and ten Perriers. John threw out ideas. I said no to all of them, thinking that I was losing my star and my movie.

"No?" he said.

"No," I said.

"Good," he said. "I was just teasing you. I'll do the film." He got up and left, and then, of course, all the food and drink arrived.

MORT COOPERMAN: A lot of people tried to use John, and there was a lot of criticism concerned with what John should be, as opposed to appreciation of what he was. The story of the birth of the Blues Brothers band is a case in point. I saw the whole thing go down in my club. John spent a lot of time at the Lone Star Cafe because it was near his house and because so many of the acts coincided with his musical tastes. He came by one afternoon early in 1977 and said he wanted to do a Blues Brothers thing with Danny on *Saturday Night Live,* and he wanted to keep it going but wasn't sure how. I put him together with Doc Pomus, who got him in touch with Roomful of Blues, a consummate blues band that had been struggling along for some time. They worked things out, made preparations and did a show at the club. The audience response to John and Danny was enormous. Technically it was obvious that neither John nor Danny was in a league with Roomful of Blues, but the crowd loved their good humor and spirit. After the show, Belushi went up to one of the band members, who was a little drunk and asked, almost like a litle boy, "How did I do?" The fella replied, in so many words, "You *sucked.* You were total shit, and you should never have gone onstage." Belushi caved in. "But they *liked* me." he said. The band pissed on him because of an ego crunch; the crowd was more interested in the fun John and Danny had whipped up than in the band's technical expertise, and they resented it. What made matters worse was the band's interview with *The Soho Weekly News,* in which they ridiculed John and Danny for not being blues archivists.

Those were the kinds of things that reduced John's natural joy, broke his heart and isolated him, after he'd started out as open and giving as a schoolkid. John was one of the biggest blues fans I'd ever met. He'd been after me for some time to book John Lee Hooker into the club, and when I did, John came by and asked me to introduce him. Hooker was standing there dressed in black, a woman on each arm and wearing dark shades.

I said, "John Lee Hooker, this is John Belushi."

"Hi," he said blankly, shaking John's hand.

"You know, John Belushi. I'm on TV."

Another blank stare from Hooker. Then he peered closer through his shades and smiled. "Oh, yeah," said Hooker. "You one of them Muppets, ain't ya?"

John loved it. A year or so later, Hooker was signed for the Blues Brothers movie.

RAY CHARLES: I not only worked with John on the Blues Brothers film, I also worked with him on *Saturday Night Live.* He was the kind of guy who would volunteer to sit with me and help me prepare my lines, since I obviously could not rely on cue cards. John was a loyal fan of rhythm & blues, and I know for a fact that the Blues Brothers got a hell of a lot of people back into R&B. They especially helped people like Aretha Franklin and me reach the young kids who might not have even known we existed. During recent European and Asian tours, I met any number of young people who got hip to the music through the Blues Brothers film and records. Man, we owe him.

JAMES BROWN: When John and Danny invited me to be a part of the Blues Brothers film, they helped me get myself going again. I was going through a bad period at the time, having trouble getting my records released. They opened the door again for me, and for so many other performers, by getting us rediscovered and appreciated again. John flew in to watch me cut my stuff for the soundtrack album. He knew I was having problems with my career, and he said, "How can I help?" He was *there* for me, understand?

JIM BELUSHI: John worked extremely hard for years in order to make it, and he almost isolated himself completely from the family. In 1978, after the first Blues Brothers concert, I went backstage to congratulate John, and I said to him, "John, I've handled the family for years, explained why you're never calling or writing. I've done my part, and now it's your turn."

"You're right," he said. "Okay, I'll take it from here." After that night, he called everybody in the family, fixed them up financially, bought Mom and Dad a ranch so high in the California mountains that Dad said he felt like he was back living in the hills of Albania. John was suddenly back in touch, and he stayed that way, but the change was so dramatic and forceful it scared everybody half out of their wits.

ROSIE SHUSTER: The weekend before the Blues Brothers movie began production,

John and Judy and Danny and I went to a resort in Wisconsin. The trip was supposed to be for relaxation, with the four of us sharing a tiny cabin. But a horde of fans descended on the place, and we ended up jumping out the back window into thorn bushes and beating a hasty retreat to a drive-in movie, which John watched with his head down.

It was difficult for John to relax as his success escalated. The responsibilities of his dynamic, samurai side became difficult to maintain. There were signs of desperation there, because a part of John always wanted that little cabin in the woods with his friends. It just got tougher to get back as time went on.

DR. HUNTER S. THOMPSON: Even though he was a bit of a monster, he was our monster, as well as a damned good person you could count on for help in the dark times. There was a ten-day period one recent summer when I sought refuge with him. We fooled around in his speedboat, dug clams and steamed them, and he lifted me out of the pit with his considerable powers as a host. The most drugs we did was a little pot, and he seemed as peaceful as I'd ever seen him. The last time he visited me, he caught my neighbor a bit off guard by "borrowing" his truck for a spell. But, hell, he brought it back in pretty good condition. As far as I'm concerned, John is welcome at my house any time, dead or alive. For me, John's epitaph is: THIS MAN WAS THE REAL THING. HE NEVER NEEDED PROPS.

LARRAINE NEWMAN: John was typecast as an uncouth, boorish slob with no discipline, so you were constantly impressed to discover he was just the opposite. The sweet, loving, boyish John in *Continental Divide* was described by some critics as unconvincing, but it was a very real side of him. Granted, it was not the *only* side. He could be so damned dogmatic when he wanted you to share something with him. When we were both working on Steve Martin's last TV special, we had another one of our fights about his musical tastes. He was playing Fear in his dressing room at an inhumane decibel level, and I went in and said, "Damn you, John, you don't know anything! You're just a faddist and an obnoxious pain in the ass!"

"Well," he said, "whose music do you like?"

"Johnnie Taylor," I snapped.

He rummaged through his records, found a Johnnie Taylor album and gave it to me. I was kinda startled, but that was John. He'd get you nuts and then turn around and do something sweet.

TOM SCOTT: "I know you," John said when he hired me for the Blues Brothers band. "You played wimped-out music with George Harrison and Joni Mitchell."

The burdens of being John's buddy could be fairly exotic. John was in Los Angeles in 1981, when Judy's birthday rolled around. He called up my wife, Lynn, and me one night to invite us to a party at their rented house in Beverly Hills. He asked if

we'd be kind enough to pick up a cake big enough to serve forty-five people. No problem. He hung up and then called back.

"I want it to be a surprise. Could you call most of the people for me?" No problem. He hung up. Called back. "Could you guys come a *little bit* early to greet the guests? I won't be there and the house will be locked, but you can crawl in the back window and unlock the front door." Er, no problem. Goodbye.

Hello again. "And could you entertain the people with some of the make-out music you play on that horn of yours?" No prob—yeah, sure. See you tomorrow night. Bye.

The phone rang again.

"Tom?"

"Yeah, John."

"I never said it would be easy being my friend."

RICHARD BELZER: About a month before his death, John came by my apartment in Hollywood. I wasn't home, so he rang my neighbor's bell. They opened the door and freaked out. He went inside, and they had wine, ate and talked, and then he took a nap on their couch. When I got home, my neighbors were out walking the dog. They said, "John's asleep inside. Wake him gently." I went in, got him up, and we hung out. It was incredible. There was always room at the inn for John Belushi.

BERNIE BRILLSTEIN: John was in constant motion, not simply because he was hyper, but because he was actively searching for something, and that something was family attachments. Feeling a closeness to his friends and their friends was a consuming passion in his life, and he could never get enough involvement in that process, whether it meant taking my children on a daylong tour of London or calling an old friend from the past to tell him he wasn't forgotten. One of the biggest pleasures of his life was orchestrating big meals and social gatherings among friends. Two weeks before he died, he and Tino Insana hosted a pizza party—Tino cooked—out in L.A. for friends, and John kept saying it reminded him of Sunday dinner with his own family. John was the Man Who Came to Dinner; he always wanted Sunday supper with his loved ones, and he could never line up enough of them. He was much more of a traditionalist and a romantic than he'd ever care to admit.

The ironies in John's death are so painful, and some are downright eerie. As a favor to Tino, who is in the cast of *Police Squad*, he agreed shortly before his death to do a cameo on the show in the celebrity-death segment they have at the opening of each episode. To do a takeoff on a prediction Michael O'Donoghue once made that John would be found floating dead in a swimming pool one day, the people at ABC shot a scene of John being found just that way. Of course, they yanked the segment after his death, but it said a lot about John's sense of humor about himself. With John,

John Belushi
Photograph by Annie Leibovitz

the last laugh was usually his, but it always came from an unexpected place.

CARRIE FISHER: Most of all, I liked those little unexpected get-togethers with John. He once sat with me for three hours in a Beverly Hills beauty salon while I had my hair done, and he was like the world's largest puppy, charming the whole place. Another time, he wanted to take me to Disneyland, and I said, "Forget it, John. Going there with you would be like going there with another Matterhorn!" John was his own Disneyland—with better rides.

DAN AYKROYD: The thing that killed John was not a habitual element in his list of pleasures. Three packs of cigarettes a day, a bottle of Courvoisier, la cocaína, maybe, but jones was not his jones. People, the man who grasped me, danced with me, met my eye and planned the future was not a junkie. As a prop, the hypo made us laugh. It was not a tool in his life.

The Sixties and the Woodstock legacy applied a subcultural legitimacy to the consumption of drugs for both mind expansion and mind impairment. John and, in fact, all of us from *Saturday Night Live* were participants in that new social phalanx. It was the touch of the hippie, the beatnik, the hipster that helped us to impart a weird, novel approach to our work.

John and I often discussed the roots of hip comedy in the bohemian and American beat scene. He did a character called Shelly Bayliss: a guy in a black suit, white shirt and black tie…with shades on…a stone hipster in a suit…a suit to fool the cops…shades to hide his eyes. Wear a suit, look straight, and everything will be all right. Add a hat, and you have the uniform of the Blues Brothers. These were roles, *not* the way we wanted to live our lives. John knew the full implications of the hipster's addiction, and it's not the way he wanted to go out. The John I knew could only have been assisted into oblivion during the course of an experiment. He hated needles and could never have inserted a hypo into himself. He wasn't that good a mechanic.

The full rewards of knowing and being with John will never be totally understood by even those who loved his work, don't care how he died and are just sorry he's gone. To these people, I say his sweetness and generosity were as big as his appetite for life.

There is a picture of John that was taken during a recording session with Ray Charles in Chicago. John is smiling and has put his hand up to his mouth because he'd slipped up on a note. It captures his essence. This is the John I'll remember—a powerhouse with a big, warm, sensitive, vulnerable guy inside.

DON NOVELLO: Five Reasons Why John Belushi Went Straight to Heaven:

• About two months ago, John and I were working on *Noble Rot* in his office at Paramount Studios. There was a record on the turntable, and it was turned up *loud.*

The producer and director of the film walked into the office. One of them asked John to turn down the music. I think only people in our generation know what the phrase "turn down the music" represents. I saw the look that shot across his face. I knew the hair was rising on his neck. He walked over, lifted the needle from the record, started the song from the beginning and turned up the volume twice as loud as it was before. In my opinion, if God is the kind of fellow I think he is, this one act alone should grant John automatic admission into Heaven.

• He sent money regularly to relatives in Albania he never saw.

• He put together his old high-school band, and they played in January at an open-mike night at the Central in L.A. He loved having his high-school buddies onstage with him in Hollywood, doing the same songs they played together fifteen years before in Illinois. Who could ask for a better thing to be said about someone in his position than that he didn't forget his old friends?

• He did great cartwheels.

• He was the best at everything he did. He walked into every room he entered like he was on horseback. He had to be, and he always was, number one. But he didn't mind being the *second* most famous Albanian—second in line behind Mother Teresa. He wasn't threatened by her popularity. He knew as hard as she might try or as blessed as she could get that she could never sing "Louie, Louie" as well as he.

It was a joy to have known him and an honor to be his friend, and we all know that God now has his hands full.

Michael Jackson:
Life in the Magical Kingdom

by Gerri Hirshey   February 1983

It's noon, and somewhere in the San Fernando Valley, the front shades of a row of condos are lowered against a hazy glare. Through the metal gate, the courtyard is silent, except for the distant splat of a fountain against its plastic basin. Then comes the chilling whine of a real-life Valley girl. "Grandmuth*er*, I am not gonna walk a whole *block*. It's *humid*. My hair will be *brillo*."

"Not what you expected, huh?" From behind a mask of bony fingers, Michael Jackson giggles. Having settled his visitor on the middle floor of his own three-level condo, Michael explains that the residence is temporary, while his Encino, California, home is razed and rebuilt. He concedes that this is an unlikely spot for a young prince of pop.

It is also surprising to see that Michael has decided to face this interview alone. He says he has not done anything like this for over two years. The small body of existing literature paints him as excruciatingly shy. He ducks, he hides, he talks to his shoe tops. Or he just doesn't show up. He is known to conduct his private life with almost obsessive caution, "Just like a hemophiliac who can't afford to be scratched in any way." The analogy is his.

"Do you *like* doing this?" Michael asks. There is a note of incredulity in his voice, as if he were asking the question of a coroner. He is slumped in a dining-room chair, looking down into the lower level of the living room. It is filled with statuary. There are some graceful, Greco-Roman type bronzes, as well as a few pieces from the suburban birdbath school. The figures are frozen around the sofa like some ghostly tea party.

Michael himself is having little success sitting still. He is so nervous that he is eating—plowing through—a bag of potato chips. This is truly odd behavior. None of his brothers can recall seeing anything snacky pass his lips since he became a strict vegetarian and health-food disciple six years ago. In fact, Katherine Jackson, his mother, worries that Michael seems to exist on little more than air. As far as she can tell, her son just has no interest in food. He says that if he didn't have to eat to stay alive, he wouldn't.

Michael Jackson
Photograph by Bonnie Schiffman

"I really do hate this," he says. "I am much more relaxed onstage than I am right now. But hey, let's go." He smiles. Later, he will explain that "let's go" is what his bodyguard always says when they are about to wade into some public fray. It's also a phrase Michael has been listening for since he was old enough to tie his own shoes.

★   ★   ★

Let's go, boys. With that, Joe Jackson would round up his sons Jackie, Tito, Jermaine, Marlon and Michael. "Let's go" has rumbled from the brothers' preshow huddle for more than three-quarters of Michael's life, first as the Jackson Five on Motown and now as the Jacksons on Epic. Michael was just eleven in 1970 when their first hit, "I Want You Back" nudged out B.J. Thomas's "Raindrops Keep Fallin' on My Head" for Number One.

Michael says he knew at age five, when he sang "Climb Every Mountain" in school and laid out the house, that something special was going on. Now, at twenty-four, Michael Jackson has one foot planted firmly on either side of the Eighties. His childhood hits are golden oldies, and his boyhood idols have become his peers. Michael was just ten when he moved into Diana Ross's Hollywood home. Now he produces her. He was five when the Beatles crossed over; now he and McCartney wrangle over the same girl on Michael's single "The Girl Is Mine." His showbiz friends span generations as well. He hangs out with the likes of such older kid stars as Tatum O'Neal and Kristy McNichol and ex-kid star Stevie Wonder. He gossips long distance with Adam Ant and Liza Minnelli, and he has heart-to-hearts with octogenarian Fred Astaire. When he visited the set of *On Golden Pond,* Henry Fonda baited fishhooks for him. Jane Fonda is helping him learn acting. Pen pal Katharine Hepburn broke a lifelong habit of avoiding rock by attending a 1981 Jacksons concert at Madison Square Garden.

Even E.T. would be attracted to such a gentle spirit, according to Steven Spielberg, who says he told Michael, "If E.T. didn't come to Elliott, he would have come to your house."

★   ★   ★

Cartoons are flashing silently across the giant screen that glows in the darkened den. Michael mentions that he loves cartoons. In fact, he loves all things "magic." This definition is wide enough to include everything from Bambi to James Brown.

"He's so magic," Michael says of Brown, admitting that he patterned his own quicksilver choreography on the Godfather's classic bag of stage moves. "I'd be in the wings when I was like six or seven. I'd sit there and watch him."

Michael's kindergarten was the basement of the Apollo Theater in Harlem. He was too shy to actually approach the performers the Jackson Five opened for—everyone from Jackie Wilson to Gladys Knight, the Temptations and Etta James. But he says he had to know everything they did—how James Brown could do a slide, a spin and a split and still make it back before the mike hit the floor. How the mike itself disappeared through the Apollo stage floor. Recently, for a refresher course, Michael went to see James Brown perform at an L.A. club. "He's the *most* electrifying. He can take an audience anywhere he wants to. The audience just went bananas. He went wild—and at his age. He gets so *out* of himself."

Getting out of oneself is a recurrent theme in Michael's life, whether the subject is dancing, singing or acting. As a Jehovah's Witness, Michael believes in an impending holocaust, which will be followed by the second coming of Christ. Religion is a large part of his life, requiring intense Bible study and thrice-weekly meetings at a nearby Kingdom Hall. He has never touched drugs and rarely goes near alcohol. Still, despite the prophesied Armageddon, the spirit is not so dour as to rule out frequent hops on the fantasy shuttle.

"I'm a collector of cartoons," he says. "All the Disney stuff, Bugs Bunny, the old MGM ones. I've only met one person who has a bigger collection than I do, and I was surprised—Paul McCartney. He's a cartoon fanatic. Whenever I go to his house, we watch cartoons. It's real escapism. It's like everything's all right. It's like the world is happening now in a faraway city. Everything's fine.

"The first time I saw *E.T.*, I melted through the whole thing," he says. "The second time, I cried like crazy."

A tug of war between the controlled professional and the vulnerable, private Michael surfaces in the lyrics he has written for himself. Two of the Jackson-written cuts on *Thriller* take on a wary, defensive stance. "They eat off you, you're a vegetable," he shouts in "Wanna Be Startin' Somethin'." "Beat It," a tense, tough dance cut, flirts with paranoia: "You have to show them that you're really not scared/You're playin' with your life/This ain't no truth or dare/They kick you/Then they beat you/Then they tell you it's fair."

Yes, he says, he feels used, declining specifics, saying only that in his profession, "They demand that, and they want you to do this. They think that they own you, they think they *made* you. If you don't have faith, you go crazy. Like not doing interviews. If I talk, I say what's on my mind, and it can seem strange to other people's ears. I'm the kind of person who will tell it all, even though it's a secret. And I *know* that things should be kept private."

For his own protection, Michael has rigged himself a set of emotional floodgates, created situations where it's okay to let it all out. "Some circumstances require me to be real quiet," he says. "But I dance *every* Sunday." On that day, he also fasts.

This, his mother confirms, is a weekly ritual that leaves her son laid out, sweating, laughing and crying. It is also a ritual very similar to Michael's performances. Indeed, the weight of the Jacksons' stage show rests heavily on his narrow, sequined shoulders. There is nothing tentative about his solo turns. He can tuck his long, thin frame into a figure skater's spin without benefit of ice skates. Aided by the burn and flash of silvery body suits, he seems to change molecular structure at will, all robot angles one second and rippling curves the next. The bony chest heaves. He pants, bumps and squeals. He has been known to leap offstage and climb up into the rigging.

At home, in his room, he dances until he falls down. Michael says the Sunday dance sessions are also an effective way to quiet his stage addiction when he is not touring. Sometimes in these off periods, another performer will call him up from the audience. And in the long, long trip from his seat to the stage, the two Michaels duke it out.

"I sit there and say, '*Please* don't call me up, I am *too* shy'," Jackson says. "But once I get up there, I take control of myself. Being onstage is magic. There's nothing like it. You feel the energy of everybody who's out there. You feel it all over your body. When the lights hit you, it's all over, I *swear* it is."

He is smiling now, sitting upright, trying to explain weightlessness to the earthbound. "When it's time to go off, I don't want to. I could stay up there forever."

Alas, he is still at the dining-room table in his condo. But despite the visible strain, he's holding steady. And he brightens at a question about his animals. He says he talks to his menagerie every day. "I have two fawns. Mr. Tibbs looks like a ram; he's got the horns. I've got a beautiful llama. His name is Louie." He's also into exotic birds like macaws, cockatoos and a giant rhea.

"Stay right there," he says, "and I'll show you something." He takes the stairs to his bedroom two at a time. Though I know we are the only people in the apartment, I hear him talking.

"Aw, were you asleep? I'm sorry...."

Seconds later, an eight-foot boa constrictor is deposited on the dining-room table. He is moving in my direction at an alarming rate.

"This is Muscles. And I have trained him to eat interviewers."

Muscles, having made it to the tape recorder and flicked his tongue disdainfully, continues on toward the nearest source of warm blood. Michael thoughtfully picks up the reptile as its snub nose butts my wrist. Really, he insists, Muscles is quite sweet. If anything, the stranger's presence has probably made Muscles a trifle nervous himself. He's coiled around his owner's torso; his tensile strength has made Michael's forearm a vivid bas-relief of straining blood vessels. To demonstrate the snake's sense of balance, Michael sets him down on a three-inch-wide banister, where he will remain, motionless, for the next hour or so.

"Snakes are very misunderstood," he says. Snakes, I suggest, may be the oldest victims of bad press. Michael whacks the table and laughs.

"Bad press. Ain't it *so*, Muscles?"

The snake lifts its head momentarily, then settles back on the banister. All three of us are a bit more relaxed.

"Know what I also love?" Michael volunteers. "Manikins."

Yes, he means the kind you see wearing mink bikinis in Beverly Hills store windows. When his new house is finished, he says he'll have a room with no furniture, just a desk and a bunch of store dummies.

"I guess I want to bring them to life. I like to imagine talking to them. You know what I think it is? Yeah, I think I'll say it. I think I'm accompanying myself with friends I never had. I probably have two friends. And I just got them. Being an entertainer, you just can't tell who is your friend. And they see you so differently. A star instead of a next-door neighbor."

He pauses, staring down at the living-room statues.

"That's what it is. I surround myself with people I want to be my friends. And I can do that with manikins. I'll talk to them."

All of this is not to say that Michael is friendless. On the contrary, people are clamoring to be his friend. That's just the trouble: with such staggering numbers knocking at the gate, it becomes necessary to sort and categorize. Michael never had a school chum. Or a playmate. Or a steady girlfriend. The two mystery friends he mentioned are his first civilians. As for the rest…

"I know people in show business."

Foremost is Diana Ross, with whom he shares his "deepest, darkest secrets" and problems. But even when they are alone together, their world is circumscribed. And there's Quincy Jones, "who I think is wonderful. But to get out of the realm of show business, to become like everybody else…"

To forget. To get out of the performing self.

"Me and Liza, say. Now I would consider her a great friend, but a show-business friend. And we're sitting there talking about this movie, and she'll tell me all about Judy Garland. And then she'll go, 'Show me that stuff you did at rehearsal.' " He feigns a dance move. "And I'll go, 'Show me yours.' We're totally into each other's *performance*."

This, Michael does not find odd, or unacceptable. It's when celebrity makes every gesture a performance that he runs for cover. Some stars simply make up their minds to get on with things, no matter what. Diana Ross marched bravely into a Manhattan shoe store with her three daughters and had them fitted for running shoes, despite the crowd of 200 that convened on the sidewalk. Michael, who's been a boy in a bubble since the age of reason, would find that intolerable. He will go to only one L.A. restaurant, a health-food place where the owners know him. As for shopping, Michael avoids it by having a secretary or aide pick out clothes for him. "You don't get peace in a shop. If they don't know your name, they know your voice. And you can't hide."

He won't say love stinks. But sometimes it smarts.

"Being mobbed *hurts*. You feel like you're spaghetti among thousands of hands. They're just ripping you and pulling your hair. And you feel that any moment you're gonna just break."

Thus, Michael must travel with the veiled secrecy of a pasha's prized daughter. Any tourism is attempted from behind shades, tinted limo glass and a bodyguard's somber serge. Even in a hotel room, he hears females squeal and scurry like so many mice in the walls.

"Girls in the lobby, coming up the stairway. You hear guards getting them out of elevators. But you stay in your room and write a song. And when you get tired of that, you talk to yourself. Then let it all out onstage. *That's* what it's like."

No argument—it ain't natural. But about those store dummies? Won't it be just as eerie to wake up in the middle of the night to all those polystyrene grins?

"Oh, I'll give them names. Like the statues you see down there." He motions to the living-room crowd. "They've got names. I feel as if I know them. I'll go down there and talk to them."

A restless rhythm is jiggling his foot. Michael is apologetic, explaining that he can sit still only for so long. On an impulse, he decides to drive us to the house under construction. Though his parents forced him to learn two years ago, Michael rarely drives. When he does, he refuses to travel freeways, taking hour-long detours to avoid them.

First, Muscles must be put away. "He's real sweet," Michael says as he unwinds the serpent from the banister. "I'd like you to wrap him around you before you go."

This is not meant as a prank, and Michael will not force the issue. But fear of interviewers can be just as deep-rooted as fear of snakes, and in consenting to talk, Michael was told the same thing he's telling me now: *Trust me. It won't hurt you.*

We compromise. Muscles cakewalks across an ankle. "You truly believe," says Michael, "with the power of reason, that this animal won't harm you now, right?

But there's this fear, built in by the world, by what people say, that makes you shy away like that."

Having politely made their point, Michael and Muscles disappear upstairs.

★   ★   ★

HI, MICHAEL.

A few such girlish messages are scratched into the paint of a somber security sign on the steel driveway gate at his house. There is a fence, dogs and guards, but girls still will loiter outside, in cars and in bushes.

As Michael conducts the tour of the two-story Tudor-style house, it's clear that the room he will sleep in is almost monkish compared to those he has had designed for his pleasures. "I'm putting all this stuff in," he says, "so I will never have to leave and go out *there*." The "stuff" includes a screening room with two professional projectors and a giant speaker. And then an exercise room, a room for video games and another with a giant-screen video system. In addition, there is a huge chamber off the back-yard patio, which has been designated the Pirate Room. It will be not so much decorated as populated. More dummies. But this set will talk back. Michael has been consulting with a Disney technician, the very man who designed the Audio-Animatronics figures for the Disneyland ride Pirates of the Caribbean. If all goes well, he will install several scowling, scabbard-waving buccaneers, wenches and sea dogs right here.

Pirates is one of Michael's favorite rides in the Magic Kingdom. And Disneyland is one of the few public spots even he cannot stay away from. "I tried to go just last night, but it was closed," he says with some disbelief. If you live in the fun house, you usually don't have to worry about such things. Michael has sung it himself: "Life ain't so bad at all/If you live it off the wall."

★   ★   ★

When we arrive back at the condo, Michael finds that a test pressing of "The Girl Is Mine" has been delivered. This is business. He must check it before release, he explains, as he heads for a listen on the stereo in the den. Before the record is finished, he is punching at phone buttons. In between calls to accountants and managers, he says that he makes all his own decisions, right down to the last sequin on his stage suits—the only clothes he cares about. He says he can be a merciless interviewer when it comes to choosing management, musicians and concert promoters. He assesses their performances with the rigor of an investigative reporter, questioning his brothers, fellow artists and even reporters for observations. Though he truly believes his talent comes from God, he is acutely aware of its value on the open market. He is never pushy or overbearing, but he does appreciate respect. Do not ask him, for instance, how long he has been with a particular show-business firm. "Ask me," he corrects, "how long they've been with *me*."

Those who have worked with him do not doubt his capabilities. In the studio, Michael's nose for things is so by-your-leave funky that Quincy Jones started calling him Smelly. Indeed, *Off the Wall*'s most memorable cuts are the Jackson-penned dance tunes. "Don't Stop 'Til You Get Enough," the album's biggest-selling single, bops along with the appealing give-and-go between restraint and abandon. The arrangement—high, gusting strings and vocals over a thudding, in-the-pocket rhythm—is Michael's signature. Smelly, the funky sprite.

It works. Such a creature as Michael is the perfect pop hybrid for the Eighties. The fanzine set is not scared off by raunchy lyrics and chest hair. But the R-rated uptown dance crowd can bump and slide right along the greasy tracks. *Thriller* is eclectic enough to include some African chants and some ripping macho-rock guitar work by Eddie Van Halen. It is now being called pop-soul by those into marketing categories. Michael says he doesn't care what anybody wants to call it. Just how it all came about is still a mystery to him, as is the creative process itself.

"I wake up from dreams and go, 'Wow, put *this* down on paper,'" he says. "The whole thing is strange. I feel that somewhere, someplace, it's been done and I'm just a courier bringing it into the world. I really believe that. I love what I do. I'm happy at what I do. It's escapism."

Again, that word. But Michael is right. There is no better definition for good, well-meaning American pop. Few understand this better than Diana Ross. Her closeness to Michael began when she met the Jacksons.

"No, I didn't discover them," she says, countering the myth. Motown head Berry Gordy had already found them; she simply introduced them on her 1971 television special. "There was an identification between Michael and I," she says. "I was older, he kind of idolized me, and he wanted to sing like me."

She has been pleased to watch Michael become his own person. Still, she wishes he would step out even more. "He spends a lot of time, too much time, by himself. I try to get him out. I rented a boat and took my children and Michael on a cruise. Michael has a lot of people around him, but he's very afraid. I don't know why. I think it came from the early days."

Michael's show-business friends, many of them women not thought of as especially motherly, do go to great lengths to push and prod him into the world and to keep him comfortable. When he's in Manhattan, Ross urges him to go to the theater and the clubs, and counteroffers with quiet weekends at her Connecticut home. In notes and phone calls, Katharine Hepburn has been encouraging about his acting.

Michael has recorded much of this counsel in notebooks and on tape. Visiting Jane Fonda—whom he's known since they met at a Hollywood party a few years ago—on the New Hampshire set of *On Golden Pond* proved to be an intensive crash course.

"In some ways," Fonda says, "Michael reminds me of the walking wounded. He's an extremely fragile person. I think that just getting on with life, making contact with people, is hard enough, much less to be worried about whither goest the world.

"I remember driving with him one day, and I said, 'God, Michael, I wish I could find a movie I could produce for you.' And suddenly I knew. I said, 'I know what you've got to do. It's *Peter Pan*.' Tears welled up in his eyes, and he said, 'Why did you say that?' with this *ferocity*. I said, 'I realize *you're* Peter Pan.' And he started to cry and said, 'You know, all over the walls of my room are pictures of Peter Pan. I've read everything that [author J.M.] Barrie wrote. I totally identify with Peter Pan, the lost boy of Never-Never Land.'"

★   ★   ★

All children, except one, grow up.

This is the first line of Michael's favorite book, and if you ask Katherine Jackson if she finds this similar to what happened in her own brood of nine, she will laugh and say, oh yes, her fifth son is the one.

Five children—Maureen, Tito, Jackie, Jermaine and Marlon—are married and have families. LaToya is a very independent young woman. At thirteen, Janet was starring as a self-possessed ghetto twerp on the sitcom *Good Times*. Youngest brother Randy, at twenty, is already living on his own. Michael is sure he'd just die if he tried that.

"LaToya once told me she thinks that I overprotected them all," Mrs. Jackson says. "But under the circumstances, I truly don't think so."

Marriage had brought her from east Indiana, just outside Chicago, to the chilly industrial town of Gary. A growing family had forced Joe Jackson to disband the Falcons, an R&B group he had formed with his two brothers. The guitar went into the closet, and Jackson went to the steel mills as a crane operator. The family budget didn't have a lot of slack for toys, but there was an old saxophone, a tambourine, some bongos and a homey patchwork of songs from Katherine's childhood. What she could remember, she taught her children. "It was just plain stuff," she says, "like 'Cotton Fields' and 'You Are My Sunshine'."

Baby Michael, who liked to flail on the bongos, surprised his mother one day when she heard him imitating Jermaine's lead vocals in his clear toddler's falsetto. "I think we have another lead singer," she told her husband. The brothers agreed.

"He was so energetic that at five years old, he was like a leader," says Jackie, at thirty-one the oldest brother. "We saw that. So we said, 'Hey Michael, you be the lead guy.' The audience ate it up."

By the age of seven, Michael was a dance monster, working out the choreography for the whole group. Local gigs were giving way to opening slots at larger halls in distant cities. When Motown called, Joe took the boys to Detroit, and Katherine stayed in Gary with the rest of the children. She says she never really worried about her children until she went to a show and heard the screams from the audience. "Every time I'd go to a concert I'd worry, because sometimes the girls would get onstage and I'd have to watch them tearing at Michael. He was so small, and they were so big."

There have been some serious incidents, too, one so chilling and bizarre it landed a young woman in a mental institution. So Katherine Jackson has made it her business to talk to some of these wild, persistent girls. What is so very crazy, she says, is that they do it in the name of love. "There are so many," she says. "You have no idea what's really on their minds. That's why it's going to be so hard for my son to get a wife."

Michael is aware of, if not resigned to, the impossibility of that task. He might like to have children in the future, but says he would probably adopt them. He has borne, with patience and good humor, the standard rumors of sex-change operations and paternity accusations from women he has never seen. But clearly they have affected him. "Billie Jean," on *Thriller,* is a vehement denial of paternity ("the kid is not my son"). In reality there has been no special one. Michael says that he is not in a hurry to jump into any romantic liaison.

"It's like what I told you about finding friends," he says. "With *that,* it's even harder. With so many girls around, how am I ever gonna *know*?"

★   ★   ★

"Just here to see a friend."

Michael is politely trying to sidestep an inquiring young woman decked out with the latest video equipment. She blocks the corridor leading to the warren of dressing rooms beneath the Los Angeles Forum.

"Can I tell my viewers that Michael Jackson is a Queen fan?"

"I'm a Freddie Mercury fan," he says, slipping past her into a long room crowded with Queen band members, wives, roadies and friends. Freddie invited Michael. Though they are hardly alike—Freddie celebrated a recent birthday by hanging naked from a chandelier—the two have been friendly since Michael listened to the material Queen had recorded for *The Game* and insisted that the single had to be "Another One Bites the Dust."

"Now, he listens to me. Right, Freddie?"

"Righto, little brother."

Freddie waves his cigarette at the platters of fruit, fowl and candy. "You and your friends make yourselves comfortable." Moments later, Michael is questioning a dancer he knows about the recent crises of a fallen superstar. Michael wants to know what the problem is. The dancer mimes his answer, laying a finger alongside his nose. Michael nods and translates: "Drugs. Cocaine."

Michael admits that he seeks out such gossip and listens again and again as the famous blurt out their need for escape. "Escapism," he says. "I totally understand."

But addictions are another thing. "I always want to know what makes good performers fall to pieces," he says. "I always try to find out. Because I just can't believe it's the same things that get them time and time again." So far, his own addictions—the stage, dancing, cartoons—have been free of toxins.

Something's working on Michael now, but it is nothing chemical. He's buzzing like a bumblebee trapped in a jelly jar. It's the room we're in, he explains. So many times, he's stretched and bounced and whipped up on his vocal chords right here, got crazy in here, pumping up, shivering like some flighty racehorse as he wriggled into his sequined suit.

"I can't stand this," he fairly yells. "I cannot sit still."

Now Michael is boxing with the bodyguard, asking every minute for the time until the man mercifully claps a big hand on the shoulder of his charge and says it: "Let's go."

Mercury and company have already begun moving down the narrow hall, and before anyone can catch him, Michael is drawn into their wake, riding on the low roar of the crowd outside, leaping up to catch a glimpse of Freddie, who is raising a fist and about to take the stairs to the stage.

"Oooh, Freddie is pumped," says Michael. "I envy him now. You don't *know* how much."

The last of the band makes the stairs, and the black stage curtain closes. Michael turns and lets himself be led into the darkness of the arena.

Palm Beach
Illustration by Ed Sorel

A Dog Took My Place

by Hunter S. Thompson   July 1983

*Notes from the Behavioral Sink and Other Queer Tales from Palm Beach
…Wild Lies and Relentless Perjury…A Fishhead Judge Meets a Naked
Cinderella…Dark, Dark Days on the Gold Coast, Long Nights for Animals*

There is a lot of wreckage in the fast lane these days. Not even the rich feel safe from it, and people are looking for reasons. The smart say they can't understand it, and the dumb snort cocaine in rich discos and stomp to a feverish beat. Which is heard all over the country, or at least felt. The stomping of the rich is not a noise to be ignored in troubled times. It usually means they are feeling anxious or confused about something, and when the rich feel anxious and confused, they act like wild animals.

That is the situation in Palm Beach these days, and the natives are not happy with it. The rich have certain rules, and these are two of the big ones: maintain the privacy and the pipeline at all costs, although not necessarily in that order. It depends on the situation, they say, and everything has its price, even women.

★   ★   ★

There are no jails or hospitals in Palm Beach. It is the ultimate residential community, a lush sand bar lined with palm trees and mansions on the Gold Coast of Florida—millionaires and old people, an elaborately protected colony for the seriously rich, a very small island and a very small world.

There are hideous scandals occasionally—savage lawsuits over money, bizarre orgies at the Bath and Tennis Club or some genuine outrage like a half-mad eighty-eight-year-old heiress trying to marry her teenage Cuban butler—but scandals pass like winter storms in Palm Beach, and it has been a long time since anybody got locked up for degeneracy in this town. The community is very tight, connected to the real world by only four bridges, and is as deeply mistrustful of strangers as any lost tribe in the Amazon.

The rich like their privacy, and they have a powerful sense of turf. God has given them the wisdom, they feel, to handle their own problems in their own way. In Palm Beach there is nothing so warped and horrible that it can't be fixed, or at least tolerated, just as long as it stays in the family.

The family lives on the island, but not everybody on the island is family. The difference is very important, a main fact of life for the people who live here, and few of them misunderstand it. At least not for long. The penalty for forgetting your place can be swift and terrible. I have friends in Palm Beach who are normally very gracious, but when word got out that I was in town asking questions about the Pulitzer divorce trial, I was shunned like a leper.

The Miami Herald called it the nastiest divorce trial in Palm Beach history, a scandal so foul and far-reaching that half the town fled to France or Majorca for fear of being dragged into it. People who normally stay home in the fall to have all their bedrooms redecorated or to put a new roof on the boathouse found reasons to visit Brazil. The hammer of Palm Beach justice was coming down on young Roxanne Pulitzer, a girl from the wrong side of the tracks who had married the town's most eligible bachelor a few years back and was now in the throes of divorce. Divorce is routine in Palm Beach, but this one had a very different and dangerous look to it. The whole lifestyle of the town was suddenly on trial, and prominent people were being accused of things that were not fashionable.

A headline in *The Denver Post* said PULITZER TRIAL SEETHING WITH TALES OF SEX, DRUGS, OCCULT. *The New York Post* upped the ante with TYCOON'S WIFE NAMED IN PULITZER DIVORCE SHOCKER and I SLEPT WITH A TRUMPET. The Boston *Herald American* made a whole generation of journalists uneasy with a front-page banner saying PULITZER WAS A DIRTY OLD MAN.

Some of the first families of Palm Beach society will bear permanent scars from the Pulitzer-versus-Pulitzer proceedings. The Filthy Rich in America were depicted as genuinely *filthy,* a tribe of wild sots and sodomites run amok on their own private island and crazed all day and all night on cocaine. The very name Palm Beach, long synonymous with old wealth and aristocratic style, was coming to be associated with berserk sleaziness, a place where price tags mean nothing and the rich are always in heat, where pampered animals are openly worshiped in church and naked millionaires gnaw brassieres off the chests of their own daughters in public.

★   ★   ★

I arrived in Palm Beach on a rainy night in November, for no particular reason. I was on my way south, to Miami, and then on to Nassau for a wedding. But it would not be happening for two weeks, so I had some time to kill, and Miami, I felt, was not the place to do it. Two weeks on the loose in Miami can change a man's life forever. It is the Hong Kong of the Western world. Not even the guilty feel safe in Miami these days.

Money is cheap on the Gold Coast, and there is a lot of it floating around. A thirteen-year-old boy recently found a million dollars' worth of big, finely cut diamonds in a brown bag on the railroad tracks near Hollywood. His aunt made him turn in the loot, but nobody claimed it, and his neighbors called him a fool. Which was true. There is no place for Horatio Algers down here on the Gold Coast; hard work and clean living will get you a bag of potato chips and a weekend job scraping scum off the hull of your neighbor's new cigarette boat.

There is a whole new ethic taking shape in South Florida these days, and despite the rich Latin overlay, it is not so far from the taproot of the old American Dream. It is free enterprise in the raw, a wide-open Spanish-speaking kind of Darwinism, like the Sicilians brought to New York a hundred years ago and like the Japanese brought to Hawaii after World War II, and not really much different from what the Israelis are bringing to Lebanon today. The language is different, the music is faster, the food is not meat and potatoes, but the message is still the same: Rich is strong, poor is weak, and the government works for whoever pays its salaries.

★   ★   ★

The Palm Beach County Courthouse is not much different from others all over the country. It is just another clearinghouse on the street of broken dreams, a grim maze of long corridors full of people who would rather not be there. Young girls wearing neck braces sit patiently on wooden benches, waiting to testify against young men wearing handcuffs and jail denims. Old women weep hysterically in crowded elevators. Wild Negroes with gold teeth are dragged out of courtrooms by huge bailiffs. Elderly jurors are herded around like criminals, not knowing what to expect.

Only lawyers can smile in this atmosphere. They rush from one trial to another with bulging briefcases, followed by dull-eyed clerks carrying cardboard boxes filled with every kind of evidence, from rusty syringes to human fingers and sworn depositions from the criminally insane with serious grudges to settle.

The Pulitzer divorce trial was held in a small hearing room at the end of a hall on the third floor. There was no room for spectators, and the only way to get one of the nine press seats was to be there in person at seven o'clock in the morning—or even earlier, on some days—and put your name on the list. Under Florida law, however, Judge Carl Harper was compelled to allow one stationary TV camera in the courtroom so that the trial could be watched on closed circuit in a room across the hall, where anybody could watch the proceedings in relative comfort, with cigarettes and doughnuts from the courthouse coffee shop.

These were the bleacher seats at the Pulitzer trial, a strange and sometimes rowdy mixture of everything from CBS producers to lanky six-foot women with no bras and foreign accents who claimed to be from *Der Spiegel* and *Paris Match*. It was a lusty crowd, following the action intently, sometimes cheering, sometimes booing. It was like a crowd of strangers who came together each day in some musty public room to watch a TV soap opera like *General Hospital*. On one afternoon, when Roxanne Pulitzer lost her temper at some particularly degenerate drift in the testimony, the bleachers erupted with shouting: "Go get 'em, Roxy! Kick ass! That's it, Rox baby! Don't let 'em talk that way about you!"

Some people made notes, and others played constantly with tape-recording equipment. A man from the *National Enquirer* came in one day but left quickly and never returned. "We don't need it," he said later. "It's too serious."

★   ★   ★

On the surface, the story was not complex. Basically, it was just another tale of Cinderella gone wrong, a wiggy little saga of crime, hubris and punishment: Herbert "Pete" Pulitzer Jr., fifty-two-year-old millionaire grandson of the famous newspaper publisher and heir to the family name as well as the fortune, had finally come to his senses and cast out the evil gold digger who'd caused him so much grief. She was an incorrigible coke slut, he said, and a totally unfit mother. She stayed up all night at discos and slept openly with her dope pusher, among others. There was a house painter, a real-estate agent, a race-car driver and a French baker—and on top of all that, she was a lesbian, or at least some kind of pansexual troilist. In six and a half years of marriage, she had humped almost everything she could get her hands on.

Finally, his attorneys explained, Mr. Pulitzer had no choice but to rid himself of this woman. She was more like Marilyn Chambers than Cinderella. When she wasn't squawking wantonly in front of the children with Grand Prix driver Jacky Ickx or Brian Richards, an alleged Palm Beach coke dealer, she was in bed with her beautiful friend Jacquie Kimberly, 32, wife of seventy-six-year-old socialite James Kimberly, heir to the Kleenex fortune. There was no end to it, they said. Not even when Pulitzer held a loaded .45-caliber automatic pistol to her head—and then to his own—in a desperate last-ditch attempt to make her seek help for her drug habits, which she finally agreed to do.

And *did,* for that matter. But five days in Highland Park General Hospital were not enough. The cure didn't take, Pete's attorneys charged, and she soon went back on the whiff and also back to the pusher, who described himself in the courtroom as a "self-employed handyman" and gave his age as twenty-nine.

Roxanne Pulitzer is not a beautiful woman. There is nothing especially striking about her body or facial bone structure, and at age thirty-one she looks more like a jaded senior stewardess from Pan Am than an international sex symbol. Ten years on the Palm Beach Express have taken their toll, and she would have to do more than just sweat off ten pounds to compete for naked space in the men's magazines. Her legs are too thin, her hips are too wide, and her skin is a bit too loose for modeling work. But she has a definite physical presence. There is no mistaking the aura of good-humored out-front sexuality. This is clearly a woman who likes to sleep late in the morning.

Roxanne blew into town more than ten years ago, driving a Lincoln Continental with a sixty-foot house trailer in tow, a ripe little cheerleader just a year or so out of high school in Cassadaga, New York, a small town of 900 near Buffalo. After graduation from Cassadaga High, she got a job in nearby Jamestown as a personal secretary to the general counsel for the American Voting Machine Corporation (AVM)—a serious young man named Lloyd Dixon III, who eventually committed suicide. His father, who was later sent to prison, was president of AVM at the time and took such a shine to the new secretary that he hastened to marry her off to his other son, a callow youth named Peter, just back from the air-force reserve.

The newlyweds hauled their trailer down to West Palm Beach, where young Peter had often spent winter vacations with the family, and set up housekeeping in a local trailer park. They both enrolled in local colleges and lived more or less like their neighbors. But the marriage turned sour, and the couple soon separated. The trailer was sold to gypsies, and Roxanne got half, which she used to finance the rest of her education at West Palm Beach Junior College. After she graduated, she went immediately to work for a local insurance agency, selling policies.

That is where she met Randy Hopkins, who at the time was also selling policies to supplement his income as an heir to the Listerine mouthwash fortune. Everybody in Palm Beach is an heir to something, and there is no point in checking them out unless you want to get married. Hopkins was the real thing for Roxanne, and soon they were living together.

These were the weird years in Palm Beach, with a sort of late-blooming rock & roll crowd, champagne hippies who drove Porsches and smoked marijuana and bought Rolling Stones records and even snorted cocaine from time to time. Some ate LSD and ran naked on the beach until they were caught and dragged home by the police, who were almost always polite. Their parties got out of hand occasionally, and the servants wept openly at some of the things they witnessed, but it was mainly a crowd of harmless rich kids with too many drugs.

It was in the heat of the mid-Seventies that Roxanne Dixon moved in with Randy Hopkins and took herself a seat on the Palm Beach Express.

One of Hopkins's good friends at the time was Pete Pulitzer, a forty-five-year-old recently divorced millionaire playboy who bore a certain resemblance to Alexander Haig on an ether binge. Pulitzer was also the owner of Doherty's, a fashionable downtown pub and late-night headquarters for the rock & roll set. Doherty's was a fast and randy place in the years when Pete owned it. John and Yoko would drop in for lunch, the bartenders were from Harvard, and Pete's patrons were anything but discreet about their predilection for dirty cocaine and a good orgy now and then.

It was the place to be seen, and Pulitzer was the man to be seen with. He had his pick of the ladies, and he particularly enjoyed the young ones. When his friend Randy Hopkins introduced him to Roxanne one night, he liked her immediately.

★   ★   ★

All the evidence in the case was trundled around the courthouse in a grocery cart that some bailiff had apparently borrowed from a local supermarket. It contained everything from family tax returns to the tin trumpet Roxanne allegedly slept with while trying to communicate with the dead. The cart was parked next to a Xerox machine in the county clerk's office on all days when the court was not in session, and under the curious provisions of Florida's much-admired public-records statute, it was open to public inspection at all times. The contents of the cart were shuffled and reshuffled by so many people that not even the judge could have made any sense of it by the time the trial was over, but journalists found it a source of endless amusement. You could go in there with a satchel of cold beers on a rainy afternoon and whoop it up for hours by just treating the cart like a grab bag and copying anything you wanted.

I spent a lot of time poring over copies of the Pulitzers' personal tax returns and financial ledgers submitted as evidence by the Pulitzer family accountants, and I have made a certain amount of wild sense of it all, but not enough. I understood, for instance, that these people were seriously rich. Family expenditures for 1981 totaled $972,980 for a family of four: one man, one woman, two four-year-old children and a

to wonder why it is full of naked people every morning. The gardener will not be comfortable with the sight of rope ladders hanging from the master-bedroom windows when he mows the lawn at noon, and any chauffeur with the brains to work a stick shift on a Rolls will also understand what's happening when you send him across the bridge to a goat farm in Loxahatchee for a pair of mature billys and a pound of animal stimulant.

Nakedness is a way of life in Palm Beach, and the difference between a picnic and an orgy is not always easy to grasp. If a woman worth $40 million wants to swim naked in the pool with her billy goat at four in the morning, it's nobody's business but hers. There are laws in Florida against sexual congress with beasts, but not everybody feels it is wrong.

"My roommate fucks dogs at parties," said a sleek blonde in her late twenties who sells cashmere and gold gimcracks in a stylish boutique on Worth Avenue. "So what? Who gets hurt by it?"

I shrugged and went back to fondling the goods on the shirt rack. The concept of victimless crime is well understood in Palm Beach, and the logic is hard to argue. No harm, no crime. If a pretty girl from Atlanta can sleep late in the morning, have lunch at the Everglades Club and make $50,000 tax-free a year fucking dogs in rich people's bedrooms on weekends, why should she fear the police? What's the difference between bestiality and common sodomy? Is it better to fuck swine at the Holiday Inn or donkeys in a penthouse on Tarpon Island? And what's wrong with incest, anyway? It takes 200 years of careful inbreeding to produce a line of beautiful daughters, and only a madman would turn them out to strangers. Feed them cocaine and teach them to love their stepsisters—or even their fathers and brothers, if that's what it takes to keep ugliness out of the family.

Look at the servants. They have warts and fat ankles. Their children are too dumb to learn and too mean to live, and there is no sense of family continuity. There is a lot more to breeding than teaching children good table manners, and a lot more to being rich than just spending money and wearing alligator shirts. The real difference between the Rich and the Others is not just that "they have more money," as Hemingway noted, but that money is not a governing factor in their lives, as it is with people who work for a living. The truly rich are born free, like dolphins; they will never feel hungry, and their credit will never be questioned. Their daughters will be debutantes and their sons will go to prep schools, and if their cousins are junkies and lesbians, so what? The breeding of humans is still an imperfect art, even with all the advantages.

Where are the Aryan thoroughbreds that Hitler bred so carefully in the early days of the Third Reich? Where are the best and the brightest children of Bel Air and Palm Beach?

These are awkward questions in some circles, and the answers can be disturbing. Why do the finest flowers of the American Dream so often turn up in asylums, divorce courts and other gray hallways of the living doomed? What is it about being born free and rich beyond worry that makes people crazy?

Nobody on the Palm Beach Express seemed very interested in that question. Instead, the community rallied around poor Pete Pulitzer when the deal started going down, even through eighteen days of weird courtroom testimony that mortified his friends and shocked half the civilized world. The most intimate aspects of his wild six-year marriage to an ambitious young cheerleader from Buffalo were splayed out in big headlines on the front pages of newspapers in New York, Paris and London. Total strangers from places like Pittsburgh and Houston called his wife at home on the telephone, raving obscene proposals. Vicious lawyers subpoenaed his most private belongings and leaked whatever they pleased to giggling reporters. His privacy was violated so totally that it ceased to exist. At the age of fifty-two, with no real warning at all, Herbert Pulitzer became a very public figure. Every morning he would wake up and go downtown with his lawyers and hear himself accused of everything from smuggling drugs to degrading the morals of minors and even committing incest with his daughter.

The only charge Judge Harper took seriously, though, was Roxanne's "adultery," which was defined so many times by so many people that it came to be taken for granted. No adultery was ever proved, as I recall, but in the context of all the other wild charges, it didn't seem to matter.

★   ★   ★

He told me that if I didn't sign those documents, he would take my children. He said he had the power, the money and the name. He said he would bury me.
—ROXANNE PULITZER *in court, November 15th, 1982*

The husband was never pressed to confirm that quote. The judge performed the burial for his own reasons, which he explained in a brutal nineteen-page final opinion that destroyed Roxanne's case like a hurricane. In the end she got even less than her lawyer, Joe Farish, whose fee was reduced by two-thirds. He got $102,500 for his efforts, and the wife came away with $2000 a month for two years, no house, no children, a warning to get a job quick, and the right to keep her own personal jewelry and her own car. The whole package came to not much more than Pulitzer had spent on the day-to-day maintenance of his boats in 1981, which his accountants listed as $79,000.

The $441,000 the couple spent that year on "miscellaneous and unknown" was four times what the wife was awarded as a final settlement after six and a half years of marriage and two children. It was nothing at all. A little more than $100,000 on paper and in fact less than $50,000. There are dentists all over Los Angeles who pay more alimony than that. But we are not talking about dentists here. We are talking about a dashing millionaire sportsman from Palm Beach, a wealthy jade of sorts who married an ex-cheerleader from the outskirts of Buffalo and took her to live sex shows and gave her jars of cocaine for Christmas.

In a nut, Herbert "Pete" Pulitzer rented the Best Piece of Ass in Palm Beach for six and a half years at a net cost of about $1000 a month in alimony, and when it was over, he got the house and the children, along with everything else. That is not a bad deal, on the face of it. The *worst* piece of ass in San Francisco goes for at least a hundred dollars a night at the Siamese Massage Parlor, and that can add up to a lot more than $1000 a month. Dumb brutes. Women so mean and ugly that you don't want to be seen with them, even by a late-night room-service waiter. There is a bull market for whoremongers all over the country these days, and the price of women is still not going up.

Judge Harper had run the whole show with an evil glint in his eye, enduring a shit train of perjury from both sides and day after day of relentless haggling and posturing by teams of Palm Beach lawyers and a circus parade of rich fools, dumb hustlers and dope fiends who were all getting famous just for being in his courtroom —where smoking was not allowed, except for the judge, who smoked constantly.

That should have been the tip-off, but we missed it. The judge had made up his mind early on, and the rest was all show business, a blizzard of strange publicity that amused half the English-speaking world for a few months and in the end meant nothing at all.

★   ★   ★

Toward the end of the trial, it rained almost constantly. Logistics got difficult, and my suite overlooking the beach at the Ocean Hotel was lashed by wild squalls every night. It was like sleeping in a boathouse at the end of some pier in Nova Scotia. Big waves on the beach, strange winds banging the doors around like hurricane shutters, plastic garbage cans blowing across the parking lot at thirty miles an hour, darkness in chaos, sharks in the water, no room service tonight.

It was a fine place to sleep—wild storms on the edge of the sea, warm blankets, good whiskey, color TV, roast beef hash and poached eggs in the morning … Fat City, a hard place to wake up at six o'clock in the morning and drive across the long, wet bridge to the courthouse in West Palm.

One morning when I got there too late to make the list for a courtroom seat and too early to think straight, I found myself drifting aimlessly into a dimly lit bar on the fringes of the courthouse district, the kind of place where lawyers and bailiffs eat lunch and the bartender has a machine pistol and the waitresses are all on probation, and where nobody reads anything in the newspapers except local gossip and legal notices.

The bartender was trying to find limes for a Bloody Mary when I asked him what he thought about the Pulitzer divorce case. He stiffened, then leaned quickly across the bar to seize my bicep, and he said to me: "You know what I think? You know what it makes me feel like?"

"Well…" I said, "not really. I only came in here to have a drink and read the newspaper until my trial breaks for lunch and—"

"Never mind your goddamned trial," he shouted, still squeezing my arm and staring intently into my eyes.

I jerked out of his grasp, unsettled by the frenzy.

"It's not the goddamned Pulitzers," he shouted. "It's nothing personal. But I know how those people behave, and you know how it makes me feel? Like a goddamned animal!" he screamed. "Like a beast. I look at this scum, and I look at the way they live, and I see those shit-eating grins on their faces, *and I feel like a dog took my place.*"

"What?" I said.

"It's a term of art," he replied, shooting his cuffs as he turned to deal with the cash register.

"Congratulations," I said. "You are now a Doctor of Torts."

He stiffened again and backed off.

"Torts?" he said. "What do you mean, *torts?*"

I leaned over the bar and smacked him hard on the side of his head.

"*That's* a tort," I said. Then I tossed him a handful of bills and asked for a cold beer to go. The man was slumped back on his rack of cheap bottles, breathing heavily. "You whore-face bastard," he said. "I'll kill you."

I laughed. "Shit eyes! People like you are a dime a dozen!" I reached over and grabbed him by the flesh on his cheek. "Where is your dog, swine sucker? I want to *see* the dog that did this to you. I want to *kill* that dog." I snapped him away from me, and he fell back on the duckboards.

"Get out!" he screamed. *"You're* the one who should be on trial in this town! These Pulitzers are nothing compared to monsters like you."

I slapped him again, then I gathered my change and my mail and my newspapers and my notebooks and my drugs and my whiskey and my various leather satchels full of weapons and evidence and photographs. I packed it all up and walked slowly out to my red Chrysler convertible, which was still holding two feet of water from the previous night's rain.

"You skunk!" he was yelling. "I'll see you in court."

"You must be a lawyer," I said. "What's your name? I work for the IRS."

"Get out!" he screamed.

"I'll be back," I said, lifting a small can of Mace out of my pocket and squirting it at him. "You'd better find a dog to take your place before you see me again, because once I croak these scumbags I'm working on now, I'm going to come back here and rip the nuts right off your ugly goddamned body."

The man was still screaming about dogs and lawyers as I got in my car and drove off. People in the street stopped to stare, but when he begged them for help, they laughed at him.

He was a Doctor of Torts, but in the end it didn't matter. A dog had taken his place anyway.

★   ★   ★

Long after the Pulitzer divorce case was finally over—after the verdict was in and there were no more headlines, and the honor of Palm Beach had been salvaged by running Roxanne out of town; after all the lawyers had been paid off and the disloyal servants had been punished and reporters who covered the trial were finally coming down from that long-running high that the story had been for so long that some of them suffered withdrawal symptoms when it ended. . . . Long after this, I was still brooding darkly on the case, still trying to make a higher kind of sense from it.

I have a fatal compulsion to find a higher kind of sense in things that make no sense at all. We were talking about hubris, delusions of wisdom and prowess that can only lead to trouble. Or maybe we are talking about cocaine. That thought occurred to me more than once in the course of the Pulitzer divorce trial. Cocaine is the closest thing to instant hubris on the market these days, and there is plenty of it around. Any fool with an extra hundred-dollar bill in his pocket can whip a gram of cocaine into his head and make sense of just about anything.

Ah, yes. Wonderful. Thank you very much. I see it all very clearly now. These bastards have been lying to me all along. I should never have trusted them in the first place. Stand aside. Let the big dog eat. Take my word for it, folks. I know how these things work.

In the end it was basically a cocaine trial, which it had to be from the start. There was no real money at stake: Peter Pulitzer ended up paying more money to lawyers, accountants, "expert witnesses" and other trial-related bozos than Roxanne would have happily settled for if the case had never gone to court in the first place.

★   ★   ★

I am living the Palm Beach life now, trying to get the feel of it: royal palms and raw silks, cruising the beach at dawn in a red Chrysler convertible with George Shearing on the radio and a head full of bogus cocaine and two beautiful lesbians in the front seat beside me, telling jokes to each other in French.

We are on our way to an orgy, in a mansion not far from the sea, and the girls are drinking champagne from a magnum we brought from Dunhills, the chic and famous restaurant. There is a wet parking ticket flapping under the windshield wiper in front of me, and it bores me. I am giddy from drink, and the lesbians are waving their champagne glasses at oncoming police cars, laughing gaily and smoking strong marijuana in a black pipe as we cruise along Ocean Boulevard at sunrise, living our lives like dolphins.

The girls are naked now, long hair in the wind and perfumed nipples bouncing in the dull blue light of the dashboard, white legs on red leather seats. One of them is tipping a glass of champagne to my mouth as we slow down for a curve near the ocean and very slowly and stylishly lose the rear end at seventy miles an hour and start sliding sideways with a terrible screeching of rubber past Roxanne Pulitzer's house, barely missing the rear end of a black Porsche that protrudes from her driveway.

The girls shriek crazily and spill champagne on themselves, and the radio is playing "The Ballad of Claus von Bulow," a song I wrote last year with Jimmy Buffet and James Brown that makes me nine cents richer every time it gets played on the radio, in Palm Beach or anywhere else. That is a lot of money when my people start adding it up. I am making ninety-nine cents a day out of Palm Beach alone, and ten times that much from Miami. The take from New York and Los Angeles is so massive that my accountant won't even discuss the numbers with me, and my agent is embarrassed by my wealth.

But not me, Jack. Not at all. I like being rich and crazy in Palm Beach on a pink Sunday morning in a new red Chrysler convertible on my way to an orgy with a magnum of French champagne and two gold-plated lesbian bimbos exposing themselves to traffic while my own song croaks from the radio and palm trees flap in the early morning wind and the local police call me Doc and ask after my general health when we speak to each other at stoplights on the boulevard.

The police are no problem in Palm Beach. We own them, and they know it. They work for us, like any other servant, and most of them seem to like it. When we run out of gas in this town, we call the police and they bring it, because it is boring to run out of gas. The rich have special problems, and running out of gas on Ocean Boulevard on the way to an orgy at six o'clock on Sunday morning is one of them. Nobody needs that. Not with naked women and huge bags of cocaine in the car. The rich love music, and we don't want it interrupted.

A state trooper was recently arrested in Miami for trying to fuck a drunk woman on the highway in exchange for dropping all charges. But that would not happen in Palm Beach. Drunk women roam free in this town, and they cause a lot of trouble. But one thing they don't have to worry about, thank God, is the menace of getting pulled over and fondled by armed white trash wearing uniforms. We don't pay these people much, but we pay them every week, and if they occasionally forget who really pays their salaries, we have ways of reminding them. The whole west coast of Florida is full of people who got fired from responsible jobs in Palm Beach, if only because they failed to understand the nature of the Social Contract.

Which brings us back to the story, for good or ill. Not everybody who failed to to understand the nature of the Social Contract has been terminally banished to the West Coast. Some of them still live here, and every once in a while they cause problems that make headlines all over the world. The strange and terrible case of young Roxanne Pulitzer is one of these, and that is the reason I came to Palm Beach, because I feel a bond with these people that runs deeper and stronger than mere money and orgies and drugs and witchcraft and lesbians and whiskey and red Chrysler convertibles.

Bestiality is the key to it, I think. I have always loved animals. They are different from us, and their brains are not complex, but their hearts are pure, and there is usually no fat on their bodies, and they will never call the police on you or take you in front of a judge or run off and hide with your money.

Animals don't hire lawyers.

Sting:
The Rolling Stone Interview

by Kristine McKenna   September 1983

"I'm quite interested in finding me again," Police singer and bassist Sting confessed to the press last summer. "I used to be the same sort of person onstage that I was in private life, but now it's sort of a monster. He looks wonderful with the lights and the crowds, but in the kitchen it's a bit much. I'm just trying to find out who is the real me—is it this monster or someone more normal? Right now, he's a bit worn at the edges."

The past year has been a stormy one for Sting. In July 1982, his wife of seven years, actress Frances Tomelty, was testifying on his behalf in the court case he'd filed against Virgin Music to regain the publishing rights to his early material. Then, just weeks later, Sting's marriage appeared to be finished (though he has since said he still loves Tomelty and that she "transformed my life and was a catalyst in my becoming something completely different"). The grapevine began buzzing with stories suggesting that Sting was beginning to succumb to the perils of rock stardom: Sting, flitting about the globe with a new girlfriend, actress-model Trudy Styler. Sting, attending such questionable events as a party thrown on the French Riviera by Saudi arms dealer Adnan Khashoggi. Sting, having the obligatory rock-star-scuffles-with-photographer episode at a London airport. Such erratic behavior may be par for the course for successful rock stars, but it is alarmingly out of character for Sting, a man known for his unshakable cool.

Now thirty-one, Sting (Gordon Matthew Sumner) was raised in Newcas-

tle, England, the eldest of four children. "I was brought up on a street of terraced houses, and at the bottom of the street was a shipyard where they built tankers," he has recalled. His father was a milkman, his mother a hairdresser. He was educated by Jesuits, whom he credits with being "responsible for my venomous nature." At twenty-four, Sting married Frances Tomelty while still teaching school in northeast England. A self-taught musician, he was playing bass in a jazz combo at night when he was "discovered" by drummer Stewart Copeland. After adding guitarist Andy Summers to the lineup, the Police released the first of their five albums in 1978.

Sting describes himself as a melancholy person prone to radical mood swings, and though that may be true, he presents a formidably tougher face to the world. He is a voracious reader. He says he "cannot operate without a guitar or a piano around," and he's currently composing a symphony on synthesizer. He's had parts in four movies—'Radio On,' 'Quadrophenia,' 'Artemis '81,' 'Brimstone & Treacle'—and has just finished a role in 'Dune,' a science-fiction film directed by David Lynch, who also did 'Eraserhead' and 'The Elephant Man.' The very picture of youthful vitality and health, Sting doesn't smoke, eats balanced meals, drinks in moderation and works out every day.

All of this activity doesn't leave him much time to hang out with the chaps at the corner pub, and he is a somewhat solitary man. One gets the impression that Sting finds the action in his own head more engrossing than most of the people he meets, and he is singularly self-contained.

It's unusual to meet someone who genuinely likes himself, but Sting seems not just at home in, but pleased with, the skin he's in, even while admitting that he's capable of a certain ruthlessness. He has incredible drive—to excel? to win? for approval?—that I imagine could turn ugly should circumstances back him into a corner, and he has little time or patience for losers. Yet he seems to have the Big Picture clearly in focus. He is aware of the absurdity of rock stardom, the arbitrary whims of fate and the role luck has played in his life.

You **recently said, "Being famous is becoming increasingly nightmarish." Can you elaborate on the fears associated with fame?**

I saw *The King of Comedy* the other night, and it really struck home. I walked out of the theater, and there was a crowd of people waiting to come in. They all started to shout, "Hey, it's Sting!" I'd just seen Jerry Lewis brutalized by a fan, and I felt vulnerable.

I walk on the street a lot more than many performers I know because I feel it's my right. I don't have bodyguards and limos, because you have to maintain some kind of grown-up autonomy or you end up a baby.... Still, *The King of Comedy* frightened me, and the end of the movie, where Pupkin [Rupert Pupkin is the character played by Robert DeNiro] becomes famous, really pissed me off. I wanted Jerry Lewis to just wipe the floor with him. I wanted Pupkin to fail as a comedian because he'd taken such a liberty with a man's life. But I realized that I saw the film from an isolated point of view. The rest of the audience seemed to find the idea funny of tying up a famous person and torturing him.

Do you think most people feel hostile toward celebrities?

I think it's very ambiguous. And in America, everybody is in show business, and fame is almost within everybody's grasp. All the taxi drivers are showbiz taxi drivers, and nobody isn't an actor.

Those generalizations might be true of New York and Los Angeles, but there are vast stretches of America that have nothing to do with those two cities.

That isn't true. Every walk of life in America has its counterpart in television. There are situation comedies and dramas about every walk of life, and everyone has a kind of stage rhetoric that he or she uses. Everyone is aware of the camera, whether it exists or not, and it seems that everybody in this country aspires to be famous. It's a human trait to want to be watched and be the king of the walk, but I find it to be less the case in Europe than in America. But, then, America is the most technologically advanced country in the world, and the people here are inundated with images.

You once described America as being attractive as a concept. What's your concept of this country?

Unlike most Americans, I think I've probably been to most of America. When the Police started, we were touring America and staying in motels, dives, bordellos and everything else, so I have a fairly good knowledge of the place as a traveler. I think America is still very young and naive, and therefore I think it's quite dangerous politically. There are forces at work here that could take over, and Reagan is a step in that direction. I'm not saying Reagan's a demon—he's a victim. He's a sad case because he believes in what he's saying, but he's no more responsible than you or I. He just points to a general weakness in society.

How has success changed you?

I've been successful for about five years, but I've also aged five years, so I probably would've been more mature regardless of the degree of success I've achieved. I sometimes wonder if I wouldn't be more mature had I not had success. When you're a rock star, you're allowed to be a petulant child and many other things you're supposed to grow out of.

At the same time, isn't there a large responsibility that comes with the kind of success you've had?

People talk about the pressure and the responsibility, but it's no worse than your average car worker. He's under pressure to pay the mortgage and make sure his wife has a coat. No, I don't subscribe to the school of "Oh, the pressure."

What's the most widely held misconception about success?

That it brings you happiness. It doesn't, and I don't think anything does. But I don't think happiness is necessarily the reason we're here. I think we're here to learn and evolve, and the pursuit of knowledge is what alleviates the pain of being human. And everybody *is* in pain, but if you're learning something, your mind is diverted elsewhere.

When I interviewed you in 1979, you said, "Success always necessitates a degree of ruthlessness. Given the choice of friendship or success, I'd probably choose success." Do you still feel that way?

[*Laughing*] I have massive success and no friends. Actually, I do have very few friends. Partly, I go for quality as opposed to quantity. I would say I have three very close friends. The public tends to imagine that rock stars have millions of friends. I don't.

Are you friends with the other members of the Police?

It's not an easy relationship, by any means. We're three highly autonomous individuals, and a band is an artificial alliance most of the time. There are obviously tensions, but I think there's a great love between us and a genuine respect. I can't think of two musicians I'd rather play with. But none of us is easy to work with. It's not all buddy-buddy, and it never was.

So you're not a team player?

I don't think history is made up of mass movements or teams. History is made up of individuals. At least that's how I read history. It's not mass ideologies.

Then how does the group arrive at decisions?

Violence... I'll argue till the cows come home about something I believe in, and so will Andy and Stewart. *Synchronicity* went through all kinds of horrendous cogs and gears to come out, emotionally and technically, the way it did.

Did it come out the way you wanted?

My feeling before we made the album was that we had to change our sound, because there were a lot of clone groups who sounded a bit like us. That's flattering in a way, but I thought we should try to sound a little different, so we pared away the things people have come to expect in our music. Reggae, for instance, is more buried in the undercurrent of the music than it might have been in the past. I think this is a more refined record than we've previously made.

The title of the album refers to coincidence and things being connected without there being a logical link. For instance, in the title cut there's a domestic situation where there's a man who's on the edge of paranoia, and as his paranoia increases, a monster takes shape in a Scottish lake, the monster being a symbol for the man's anxiety. That's a synchronistic situation. They're not connected logically, but symbolically and emotionally they are. There's a song called "King of Pain," which is a series of analogous statements about the soul: "There's a little black spot on the sun today/That's my soul up there . . . /There's a dead salmon in a waterfall . . . / There's a butterfly trapped in a spider's web." They're all images of entrapment and pain. The single, "Every Breath You Take," is a very sad song, and it makes *me* sad, but it's a wonderful sadness. It was written at a time of awful personal anguish, and it was a great catharsis to write that song.

What do your songs say about you?

My personal life is in my songs, in an archetypal form, of course. At the same time, I regard myself as quite a complicated person, and there are very complex things going on in my head. Many of the songs seem quite contradictory, and I seem to be two people: on the one hand, a morose, doom-laden character, and on the other, a happy-go-lucky maniac. I am as ambiguous as Martin, the character I played in *Brimstone & Treacle,* and I didn't have to delve too deeply into myself to excavate him. He's definitely an exaggerated version of me. The songs are also very folded in because there's no point in stating the obvious. You implicate the audience and draw them in by forcing them to discover things. So, to a certain extent, the songs are abstract, but if I look at them closely I can see that I'm writing about my private life.

And what have you learned about yourself?

Every day I see myself behaving in a way that, on reflection, is a reenactment of my childhood. I'm becoming increasingly aware that I *am* my mother and father.

You don't seem to recall your childhood with much fondness.

No, and I'm glad of that because it gave me a fighting spirit. I didn't have an unusually bad childhood, it's just that I have a certain mentality that made childhood very painful. I remember just aching—there was just an ache all the time. Heart-ache. It wasn't my parents' fault, it's just the way my brain was working.

Were you raised in a liberal environment?

That's a very relative term, but yeah, I suppose I was, and I didn't want to be at the time. I think kids desire reactionary parents. You know, your parents should be strict and make you do certain things. If they don't, you wonder, "Am I being brought up right?"

Did you have a religious upbringing?

I was raised Catholic. And in the rock world, which is hedonistic and, on the surface, very existential, it sets you apart to have had an upbringing that was rooted in magic and religion. I'm not a devout Catholic, and I don't go to mass, but I'm not sure I've broken away from it. All that was inculcated into my brain as a small child—that there is a heaven and hell, mortal sins and venial sins—is inside my psyche and will never come out. I'm not raising my kids Catholic, but I sometimes wonder whether I should. I think human psychology is such that we invent gods and demons anyway, and the Catholic ones are tried and tested archetypes. The ones we invent for ourselves are much more dangerous, in a way. The power of projection is so rife in the world.

Why do you think people need to create gods and demons?

Everyone does it, and even the most devout agnostic has deep within his unconscious a need for a god and a devil. I don't know why, but it is deep within our history as a race. I think you have to come to terms with the gods and demons who populate your unconscious and your dreams.

That dreams actually mean something is a recent realization for me. I think they do present some kind of coherent picture. I didn't used to dream, but I dream a lot now, and I keep a record of my dreams. My dreams tend to redress the balance of my life. For instance, if I've been particularly mean to someone, I find that I'll subsequently dream about that person in a very exalted state. My dream is telling me to reassess that person. Or if I fall in love with someone, she'll appear in my dream as a witch. So in a sense, dreams are an equation between your conscious and unconscious lives.

You once commented that "the rock star myth pleases me at the moment, but I don't believe in it, and I'm sure I'll tire of it eventually." Have you tired of it?

I never lived the rock-star myth and never had any desire to. It doesn't take much imagination to get wild every night, and there are many performers who do live that myth publicly. I saw a few of them on the news the other night at a press conference for the Us Festival. There was [Clash aide] Kosmo Vinyl bellowing [*Sting feigns an excellent Cockney accent*] "Eh, yeah, you ca' be sure the Clash e' gon' be sayin' somfink!" What, I wondered, are they going to be saying? Ranting the thoughts of Karl Marx while they rake in the dollars strikes me as slightly ambiguous. I've no respect whatever for the Clash, and I once did.

Well, whom do you respect?

I can't think of anyone offhand... I've said all along that the blueprint for rock stardom has been thoroughly written about and the pitfalls are obvious.

Have you stumbled over those pitfalls?

We're talking about drugs, right? Drugs are a symbol for all the bad things associated with stardom. Drugs are always there when you're down. Drugs are very much a symbol, and you have to control them. I don't take drugs anymore.

Why not?

Because one day I realized that I was saying they weren't a problem for me, and I stepped back and thought, "That's a very sad psychology. I'm kidding myself." So about a year ago, I decided to stop them altogether. I wasn't a heroin addict or anything like that. It's just that the drugs are around and you take them, and then you start taking them on your own as well, and that's dangerous. Then·you start lying to people and lying to yourself. They're so insidious and available, and when you're feeling vulnerable, they're there. But you just mustn't. I don't believe people who say, "I can handle it. I've been taking drugs since I was twelve." It's wrong, and as puritan as it might sound, they're not even that much fun.

What kind of image do you think people have of you?

What surprises me is that people see me as arrogant. To a certain extent, I am, but any artist worth his salt has arrogance. It's a prerequisite of being stage-worthy. You have to have a certain air of "Watch me, because I'm really good." But I'm quite humble in many ways [*laughing*], self- effacing and modest.

You recently told an interviewer that you like being photographed and you like the image side of what you do. Isn't that a questionable thing, manufacturing and selling larger-than-life images to the public?

Yes, it is, but it seems to be a prerequisite of making music. You either become Greta Garbo and put a sack over your head, or you play the game to a certain extent.

Have you always liked the way you look?

No. Some mornings I wake up and I hate myself. But I feel confident that I can manufacture a face or look given a couple hours of preparation. It's all mental.

Would you describe yourself as a vain person?

I'd admit to it, but I wouldn't describe myself as vain.

Is vanity a vice?

In the business I'm in—he said defensively—it's a necessity. You have to have a certain amount of vanity to get onstage. If I don't think I look good, I don't perform very well. If I'm fit, toned up, don't look tired and I've done some preparation, I perform better. People pay money to *see* you, so if I had to perform tonight, I'd be going through a certain regime—work out, take a bath, don't eat any rubbish, get a good night's sleep. Stage performance is more athletic than musical. Well, that's not true, but a large percentage of what you do is leap up and down in time to the music.

You once commented that pop music is a useful form, and it has its function. What do you see as being its function?

At its best, it's subversive. Ostensibly, it confirms the system, makes money and generates an industry, but underneath it's very anarchic. That's not to say that it'll turn over society, although it has helped to do that in certain cases. The Beatles and the hippie thing were very influential in the Vietnam War, for better or worse. I'm not saying that it's a good thing America lost—everybody lost. But it was a war where for the first time people questioned the adage "My country, right or wrong." And I think that was probably a good thing.

As on the last album, 'Ghost in the Machine,' many of the songs on 'Synchronicity' seem to have political undertones.

I'm against politics with a capital *P*, but I think we have to come to terms with the reality of nuclear power. It's no good to say let's get rid of it, because we'll always have that knowledge. I really dislike this Luddite mentality of "Let's get back to nature and get rid of nuclear power," because we never will. We have to make those things safe...and the only way to do that is to clean out the gangsters and criminals who are running our world. And they are criminals. They're greedy, frightened, and they are endangering us....We will be blown up, you know. The age of the domestic H-bomb is years away. Humans make the mistake of believing that it's their right to survive. Species die out on this planet all the time without anybody noticing. The planet will still be here, and we must lose this attitude of divine right, that something will save us, which we've developed over the centuries. The Martians aren't going to come down and save us. God isn't going to save us. We are in great danger, and it's easy to get diverted from that awareness by everyday life. And every time we spend a million dollars on defense, that danger increases. Those weapons are intended for use. And what on this earth is military superiority about? Superior to what? As a species, we're too bound up in what we consume, ignoring what consumes us. It's a madness that we have to sort out.

You seem to have a fairly pessimistic view of the human condition.

No, I have a realistic view. I would like the future to be better, and I think we have to live as if there will be a reasonable future for our children. But I can't close my eyes to the fact that we must do something soon. Maybe it will take a disaster to bring us to our senses. I just hope that we learn from it and that it's not on my head.

Even though your previous films haven't been box-office smashes, do you think you've reached a point where your name guarantees a degree of commercial success for your film?

I'd rather it didn't. I didn't want to arrive in Hollywood with an air of "Here I am, Hollywood! You've all been waiting for me to appear!" I've sort of come in from the underside and played in films that were left field. I was surprised *Brimstone & Treacle* was even screened in America, much less distributed. I want to continue to approach it that way. So, in a sense, I don't want to use my name, 'cause it's an albatross around my neck. It may be attractive to one segment of the cinema-going public, but to another, it's not. Who wants to see *String*? In a movie? String! Never heard of it! What is it? Would your mother go see String in a movie? I'm proud of being a rock musician, but I don't want to be branded. When I'm in a film, I want to act.

Is it easy to make the transition from rock to film?

They're obviously related, and though music may have given me a confidence that somewhat prepared me for being in front of a camera, making transitions is the hardest thing for a performer to do. And you know, you don't have to have the intelligence of a brain surgeon to play rock & roll. The opposite is the general rule, in fact.

Doesn't rock require a particular kind of savvy?

No. Some of the best rock performers don't have any sense at all. And I think the performers who have managed to make the transition from one form to another are unusually clever. David Bowie and Bobby Darin both did it quite skillfully. Bobby Darin was a great singer and a great actor. And *The Man Who Fell to Earth* was a clever thing for Bowie to do.

Does your move into film mean you're no longer challenged by the Police?

It's still hard work. It's not easy to be in a group. It's like marriage without sex. The only lubricant we have is music, so the music has to be good.

Isn't money a lubricant?

More money isn't. If any of us felt we couldn't go on together, money wouldn't be a factor. I've got enough money, which is not to say I don't enjoy making it, because it's fun to make money. But the reason we stay together is because we still work as a band. As I've said all along, it might break up tomorrow. As soon as it becomes a drag, then that's it— I'll walk out.

What's the most important thing you've learned since the Police have become so popular?

To be more cagey. Candidly, the other article you wrote in ROLLING STONE quoted some things I said about my childhood that hurt my family deeply. ["I come from a family of losers... and I've rejected my family as something I don't want to be like."] I learned a big lesson there and had to work very hard to repair the damage done by the article. It wasn't your fault; it was purely my own arrogance and lack of thought. I've become more aware of the possible consequences of what I say to the press. My family was completely unprepared for the media onslaught they were subjected to. I'm protected from it, but the innocent bystanders—my kids, my wife—were crunched by it. There's no way I can protect those around me from my career, and I have to live my own life. But there is a balance you can strike between being selfish in the right way and protecting those around you.

How much does the public have a right to know? There are those who would argue that performers are rewarded very lavishly for what they do and part of what the public pays for is the right to vicariously share in the lives of famous people.

To a certain extent, I agree. But that can go too far. I've seen that become genuinely destructive, not to me, particularly, but to those around me, and it's no fun.

Last May, you told 'Trouser Press,' "If I could get away with it, I wouldn't do any more interviews." Why do you still do them?

This particular interview is useful. But I don't want to get up on a soapbox …it's not my desire to confess, and there aren't any burning social issues that I feel I have an exclusive handle on. The important things I have to say are in the songs in a veiled, symbolic form. And what I have to say like this—you make of it what you will. I don't have a half-life. I am fairly straight down the middle. I'm no angel, by any means, but I consider myself to be relatively normal, and I have normal needs.

So you don't feel compelled to comment on or defend yourself against things that are written about you?

They're not writing about me. They invent a life, and it just doesn't get to me. It might get to people who aren't as sophisticated in their defenses as I am, but they're not writing about me. They don't know me, and they never will.

Tough shit.

Bob Dylan:
The Rolling Stone Interview

by Kurt Loder   June 1984

So here he is once more—but <u>who</u> is he? A forty-three-year-old divorced father of five (one is his ex-wife Sara's daughter, whom he adopted), Dylan divides his time among California, where he owns a sprawling, eccentric heap of a house; Minnesota, where he maintains a farm; and the Caribbean, where he island-hops on a quarter-million-dollar boat. While in New York—a city to which he soon hopes to relocate again—he caught a gig by his former keyboardist Al Kooper, dropped in on a recording session for ex-J. Geils Band singer Peter Wolf and hung out with old pals Keith Richards and Ronnie Wood of the Rolling Stones. Despite his spiritual preoccupations, he insists that he's no prude ("I think I had a beer recently") and that his religious odyssey has been misrepresented in the press. Although he contends he doesn't own any of his song-publishing rights prior to 1974's 'Blood on the Tracks' ("That's Keith's favorite"), he is probably quite well-off —"Some years are better than others" is all he'll say on the subject—and is known to be extraordinarily generous to good friends in need. He apparently does not envision any future retirement from music. When I asked if he thought he'd painted his masterpiece yet, he said, "I hope I never do." His love life—he's been linked in the past with singer Clydie King, among others— remains a closed book.

As we spoke, a drunken youth approached our table for an autograph, which Dylan provided. A few minutes later, a toothless old woman wearing hot pants appeared at our side, accompanied by a black wino. "You're Bob Dylan!" she croaked. "And you're Barbra Streisand, right?" said Dylan, not unpleasantly. "I only wondered," said the crone, "because there's a guy out front selling your autograph." "Yeah?" said Dylan. "Well, how much is he askin'?"

People have put various labels on you over the years: born-again Christian, ultra-Orthodox Jew. Are any of those accurate?

Not really. People call you this or that. But I can't respond, because then it seems like I'm defensive, and, you know, what does it matter, really?

But weren't three of your albums—'Slow Train Coming,' 'Saved' and 'Shot of Love'—inspired by some sort of born-again religious experience?

I would never call it that. I've never said I'm born again. That's just a media term. I don't think I've ever been an agnostic. I've always thought there's a superior power, that this is not the real world and that there's a world to come. That no soul has died, every soul is alive, either in holiness or in flames. And there's probably a lot of middle ground.

What is your spiritual stance, then?

Well, I don't think that *this is it,* you know—this life ain't nothin'. There's no way you're gonna convince me this is all there is. I never, ever believed that. I believe in the Book of Revelation. The leaders of this world are eventually going to play God, if they're not *already* playing God, and eventually a man will come that everybody will think *is* God. He'll do things, and they'll say, "Well, only God can do those things. It must be him."

You're a literal believer of the Bible?

Yeah. Sure, yeah. I am.

Are the Old and New Testaments equally valid?

To me.

Do you belong to any church or synagogue?

Not really.

Do you actually believe the end is at hand?

I don't think it's *at hand.* I think we'll have *at least* 200 years. And the new kingdom that comes in—I mean, people can't even imagine what it's gonna be like. There's a lot of people walkin' around who think the new kingdom's comin' next year and that they're gonna be right there among the top guard. And they're wrong. I think when it comes in, there *are* people who'll be prepared for it, but if the new kingdom happened tomorrow and you were sitting there and I was sitting here, you wouldn't even *remember* me.

Can you converse and find agreement with Orthodox Jews?

Yeah, yeah.

And with Christians?

Oh, yeah. Yeah, with anybody.

Sounds like a new synthesis.

Well, no. If I thought the world needed a new religion, I would *start* one. But there are a lot of other religions, too. There's those Eastern religions, you know. They're happening, too.

When you meet up with Orthodox people, can you sit down with them and say, "Well, you should really check out Christianity"?

Well, yeah, if somebody asks me, I'll tell 'em. But you know, I'm not gonna just offer my opinion. I'm more about playing music, you know?

Your views apparently seemed clear to many record buyers. Were you frustrated by the commercial resistance— both on record and on the road—to your fundamentalist-influenced music?

Well, after the '78 gospel tour, I wanted to keep touring in '79. But I knew that we'd gone everywhere in '78, so how you gonna play in '79? Go back to the same places? So, at that point, I figured, "Well, I don't care if I draw crowds no more." And a lotta places we played on the last tour, we filled maybe half the hall.

And you don't think that was because of the material you were doing?

I don't think so. I don't think it had to do with *anything.* I think when your time is your time, it don't matter what you're doin'. It's either your time, or it's *not* your time. And I didn't feel the last few years was really my time. But that's no reason for me to make any kinda judgment call on what it is I'm gonna be. The people who reacted to the gospel stuff would've reacted that way if I had done, you know, "Song to Woody."

You think so?

Yeah, I know it. I can usually anticipate that stuff—what's going on, what's the mood. There's a lotta young performers around. And they look good and they move good, and they're sayin' stuff that is, uh, *excitable,* you know? Face it, a lotta that stuff is just made and geared for twelve-year-old kids. It's like baby food.

Do you follow the political scene or have any sort of fix on what the politicians are

talking about this election year?

I think politics is an instrument of the devil. Just that clear. I think politics is what kills; it doesn't bring anything alive. Politics is corrupt; I mean, anybody knows that.

So you don't care who's president? It doesn't make any difference?

I don't think so. I mean, how long is Reagan gonna be president? I've seen like four or five of 'em myself, you know? And I've seen two of 'em die in office. How can you deal with Reagan and get so serious about that, when the man isn't even gonna *be* there when you get your thing together?

So you don't think there's any difference between, say, a Kennedy and a Nixon? It doesn't matter at all?

I don't know. It's very popular nowadays to think of yourself as a "liberal humanist." That's such a bullshit term. It means *less* than nothing. Who was a better president? Well, you got *me*. I don't know what people's errors are; nobody's perfect, for sure. But I thought Kennedy—both Kennedys—I just liked them. And I liked Martin…Martin Luther King. I thought those were people who were blessed and touched, you know? The fact that they all went out with bullets don't change nothin'. Because the good they do gets planted. And those seeds live on longer than that.

Do you still hope for peace?

There is not going to *be* any peace.

You don't think it's worth working for?

No. It's just gonna be a false peace. You can reload your rifle, and that moment you're reloading it, that's peace.

Isn't it worth fighting for that?

Nah, none of that matters. I heard somebody on the radio talkin' about what's happenin' in Haiti, you know? "We must be concerned about what's happenin' in Haiti. We're *global* people now." And they're gettin' everybody in that frame of mind—like, we're not just the United States anymore, we're *global*. We're thinkin' in terms of the whole world because communications come right into your house. Well, that's what the Book of Revelation is all *about*. And you can just about *know* that anybody who comes out for peace is *not* for peace.

But what if someone is genuinely for peace?

Well, you can't be for peace and be *global*. It's just like the song "Man of Peace." But none of this matters, if you believe in another world. If you believe in *this* world, you're stuck; you really don't have a chance. You'll go *mad*, 'cause you won't see the end of it. You may wanna stick around, but you won't be able to. On another level, though, you *will* be able to see this world. You'll look back and say, "Ah, that's what it was all about all the time. Wow, why didn't I *get* that?"

That's a very fatalistic view, isn't it?

I think it's *realistic*. If it *is* fatalistic, it's only fatalistic on this level, and this level dies anyway, so what's the difference? So you're fatalistic, so what?

In "Union Sundown," you say the Chevrolet you drive is "put together down in Argentina by a guy makin' thirty cents a day." Are you saying he'd be better off without that thirty cents a day?

What's thirty cents a day? He don't need the thirty cents a day. I mean, people survived for 6000 years without having to work for slave wages for a person who comes down and…well, actually, it's just colonization. But see, I saw that stuff firsthand, because where I come from, they *really* got that deal good, with the ore.

In Minnesota, in the Iron Range, where you grew up?

Yeah. *Everybody* was workin' there at one time. In fact, ninety percent of the iron for the Second World War came out of those mines, up where I'm from. And eventually, they said, 'Listen, this is costing too much money to get this out. We must be able to get it someplace else.' Now the same thing is happening, I guess, with other products.

What was it like growing up in Hibbing, Minnesota, in the Fifties?

You're pretty much ruled by nature up there. You have to sort of fall into line with that, regardless of how you're feeling that day or what you might want to do with your life or what you think about. And it still is like that, I think.

Were you aware of any anti-Semitism there when you were a kid?

No. Nothing really mattered to me except learning another song or a new chord, or finding a new place to play, you know? Years later, when I'd recorded a few albums, *then* I started seeing it in places: "Bob Dylan's a Jew," stuff like that. I said, "Jesus, I never knew that." But they kept harping on it; it seemed like it was *important* for people to *say* that—like they'd say "the one-legged street singer," or something. So after a period of time, I thought, "Well, gee, maybe I'll look into that."

Was Hibbing an oppressive place? Did it just make you want to get out?

Not really. I didn't really know about anything else except, uh, Hank Williams. I remember hearin' Hank Williams one or two years before he died. And that sort of introduced me to the guitar. And once I had the guitar, it was never a problem. Nothing else was ever a problem.

Did you get to see any of the original rock & roll guys, like Little Richard, Buddy Holly?

Yeah, sure. I saw Buddy Holly two or three nights before he died. I saw him at the Armory. He played there with Link Wray. I don't remember the Big Bopper. Maybe he'd gone off by the time I came in. But I saw Richie Valens. And Buddy Holly, yeah. He was great. He was incredible. I mean, I'll never forget the image of seeing Buddy Holly up on the bandstand. And he died—it must have been a week after that. It was unbelievable.

How did you take to the guitar?

First, I bought a Nick Manoloff book. I don't think I could get past the first one. And I had a Silvertone guitar from Sears. In those days, they cost thirty or forty dollars, and you only had to pay five dollars down to get it. So I had my first electric guitar.

I had a couple of bands in high school, maybe three or four of 'em. Lead singers would always come in and take my bands, because they would have connections, like maybe their fathers would know somebody, so they could get a job in the neighboring town at the pavilion for a Sunday picnic or something. And I'd lose my band. I'd see it all the time.

That must have made you a little bitter.

Yeah, it did, actually. And then I had another band with my cousin from Duluth. I played, you know, rock & roll, rhythm & blues. And then that died out, pretty much, in my last year of high school.

And after that, I remember I heard a record—I think maybe it was the Kingston Trio or Odetta or someone like that—and I sorta got into folk music. Rock & roll was pretty much finished. And I traded my stuff for a Martin that they don't sell anymore, an 0018, maybe, and it was brown. The first acoustic guitar I had. A *great* guitar. And then, either in Minneapolis or St. Paul, I heard Woody Guthrie. And when I heard Woody Guthrie, that was it, it was all over.

What struck you about him?

Well, I heard them old records, where he sings with Cisco Houston and Sonny

[Terry] and Brownie [McGhee] and stuff like that, and then his own songs. And he really struck me as an independent character. But no one ever talked about him. So I went through all his records I could find and picked all that up by any means I could. And when I arrived in New York, I was mostly singin' his songs and folk songs. At that time, I was runnin' into people who were playing the same kind of thing, but I was kinda combining elements of Southern mountain music with bluegrass stuff, English-ballad stuff. I could hear a song once and know it. So when I came to New York, I could do a lot of different stuff. But I never thought I'd see rock & roll again when I arrived here.

Did you miss it?

Not really, because I *liked* the folk scene. It was a whole community, a whole world that was all hooked up to different towns in the United States. You could go from here to California and always have a place to stay, and play somewhere, and meet people. Nowadays, you go to see a folk singer—what's the folk singer doin'? He's singin' all his own songs. *That* ain't no folk singer. Folk singers sing those old folk songs, ballads.

I was tellin' somebody that thing about when you go to see a folk singer now, you hear somebody singin' his own songs. And the person says, "Yeah, well, *you* started that." And in a sense, it's true. But I never would have written a song if I didn't play all them old folk songs first. I never would have *thought* to write a song, you know? There's no *dedication* to folk music now, no *appreciation* of the art form.

Do you notice that you've influenced a lot of singers over the years?

It's phrasing. I think I've phrased everything in a way that's never been phrased before. I'm not tryin' to *brag* or anything—or maybe I am [*laughs*]. But yeah, I hear stuff on the radio, doesn't matter what kinda stuff it is, and I *know* that if you go back far enough, you'll find somebody listened to Bob Dylan somewhere, because of the phrasing. Even the content of the tunes. Up until I started doin' that stuff, nobody was talkin' about that sort of thing. For music to succeed on any level…well, you're always gonna have your pop-radio stuff, but the only people who are gonna succeed, really, are the people who are sayin' somethin'. I mean, you can only carry "Tutti Frutti" so far.

Were you aware of punk rock when it happened—the Sex Pistols, the Clash?

Yeah. I didn't listen to it all the time, but it seemed like a logical step, and it still does. I think it's been hurt in a lotta ways by the fashion industry.

You've seen the Clash, I understand?

Yeah. I met them way back in 1977, 1978. In England. I think they're great.

How about Prince—have you ever run into him in Minneapolis?

No, I never have.

Have you met Michael Jackson yet?

No, I don't think so. I met Martha and the Vandellas.

Do your kids tell you about new groups: "You gotta check out Boy George"?

Well, they used to, a few years ago. I kind of like everything.

Are your kids musical?

Yeah, they all play.

Would you encourage them to go into the music business?

I would never push 'em or encourage 'em to. I mean, I never went into it as a *business*. I went into it as a matter of *survival*. So I wouldn't tell anybody to go into it as a business. It's a pretty cutthroat business, from what I've seen.

What do you tell your kids about things like sex and drugs?

Well, they don't really ask me too much about that stuff. I think they probably learn enough just by hangin' around me, you know?

You had a drug period at one time, didn't you?

I never got hooked on any drug—not like you'd say, uh, "Eric Clapton: his drug period."

Ever take LSD?

I don't wanna say anything to encourage anybody, but, uh, who knows? Who knows what people stick in your drinks or what kinda cigarettes you're smokin'?

When people like Jimi Hendrix and Janis Joplin started dropping away, did you look upon that as a waste?

Jimi, I thought, was a big waste. I saw Jimi…oh, man, that was sad when I saw him. He was in the back seat of a limousine on Bleecker Street, just…I couldn't even tell then whether he was dead or alive.

Do your old songs still mean the same to you as when you wrote them?

Yeah. It's like it was just written yesterday. When I'm singin' the stuff, sometimes I say, "Wow! Where'd these lyrics *come* from?" It's *amazing*.

Do you still look back on some of it as protest material? Or did you ever see it as protest material?

I think all my stuff is protest material in some kinda way. I always felt like my position and my place came after that first wave, or maybe second wave, of rock & roll. And I felt like I would never have done the things I did if I just had to listen to popular radio.

It always seemed to me that you were sort of infallible in your career up until 'Self Portrait' in 1970. What's the story behind that album?

At the time, I was in Woodstock, and I was getting a great degree of notoriety for doing *nothing*. Then I had that motorcycle accident, which put me outta commission. Then, when I woke up and caught my senses, I realized that I was workin' for all these *leeches*. And I didn't wanna do that. Plus, I had a family, and I just wanted to see my *kids*.

I'd also seen that I was representing all these things that I didn't know anything *about*. Like I was supposed to be on acid. It was all storm-the-embassy kind of stuff—Abbie Hoffman in the streets—and they sorta figured me as the kingpin of all that. I said, "Wait a minute, I'm just a *musician*. So my songs are about this and that. *So what?*" But people need a leader. People need a leader more than a leader needs people, really. I mean, anybody can step up and be a leader, if he's got the people there that want one. I didn't want that, though.

But then came the big news about Woodstock, about musicians goin' up there, and it was like a wave of insanity breakin' loose around the house *day* and *night*. You'd come in the house and find people there, people comin' through the *woods*, at all hours of the day and night, knockin' on your door. It was really dark and depressing. And there was no way to *respond* to all this, you know? It was as if they were suckin' your very *blood* out. I said, "Now wait, these people can't be my fans. They just *can't* be." And they kept comin'. We *had* to get out of there.

This was just about the time of that Woodstock festival, which was the sum total of all this bullshit. And it seemed to have something to do with *me*, this Woodstock Nation, and everything it represented. So we couldn't *breathe*. I couldn't get any space for myself and my family, and there was no help, nowhere. I got very resentful about the whole thing, and we got outta there.

We moved to New York. Lookin' back, it really was a stupid thing to do. But there was a house available on MacDougal Street, and I always remembered that as a nice place. So I just bought this house, sight unseen. But it wasn't the same when we got back. The Woodstock Nation had overtaken MacDougal Street also. There'd be crowds outside my house. And I said, "Well, fuck it. I wish these people would just *forget* about me. I wanna do something they *can't* possibly like, they *can't* relate to. They'll see it, and they'll listen, and they'll say, "'Well, let's get on to the next person. He ain't sayin' it no more. He ain't givin' us what we want,'" you know? They'll go on to somebody else. But the whole idea backfired. Because the album went out there, and the people said, *"This* ain't what we want," and they got *more* resentful. And then I did this portrait for the cover. I mean, there was no *title* for that album. I knew somebody who had some paints and a square canvas, and I did the cover up in about five minutes. And I said, "Well, I'm gonna call this album *Self Portrait."*

Which was duly interpreted by the press as: This is what he is....

Yeah, *exactly.* And to me it was a *joke.*

But why did you make it a double-album joke?

Well, it wouldn't have held up as a single album—then it *really* would've been bad, you know. I mean, if you're gonna put a lot of crap on it, you might as well load it up!

In the Sixties, there was feeling that this society really was changing. Looking back, do you feel it changed that much?

I think it did. A lot of times people forget. These modern days that we know now, where you can get on an airplane and fly anywhere you want nonstop, direct, and be there—that's recent. That's since what, 1940? Not even that—after the war, it was. And telephones? *Forget it.* I mean, when I was growin' up, I remember we had a phone in the house, but I also remember there was a party line of maybe six other people. And no matter when you got on the phone, you know, there might be somebody else on it. And I never grew up with television. When television first came in, it came on at like four in the afternoon, and it was off the air by seven at night. So you had more time to...I guess to think. It can never go back to the way it was, but it was all changing in the Fifties and Sixties.

My kids, they know television, they know telephones. They don't think about that stuff, you know? Even airplanes: I never rode on an airplane until 1964 ·or somethin'. Up till that time, if you wanted to go across the country, you took a train or a Greyhound bus, or you hitchhiked. I don't know. I don't think of myself as that *old,* or having seen that much, but....

What do you make of music videos? Do you think they're all that important?

Uh, to sell records, yeah. But videos have always been around. David Bowie's been makin' 'em since he started. There was one thing I saw on video, and I thought it was great. Then I heard the record on the radio, and it was *nothin'*, you know? But video does give you something to hook on to.

Are your best friends mostly musicians?

My best friends? Jeez, let me try to think of one [*laughs*].

There must be a few.

Best friends? Jesus, I mean, that's…

You've got to have a best friend.

Whew! Boy, that's a question that'll really make you think. Best friend? Jesus, I think I'd go into a deep, dark depression if I were to think about who's my best friend.

There have to be one or two, don't there?

Well, there *has* to be…there *must* be…there's *gotta* be. But hey, you know, a best friend is someone who's gonna die for you. I mean, that's your best friend, really. Yeah, I'd be miserable trying to think of who my best friend is.

Since you've spent a lot of time in the Caribbean, you must be familiar with Rastafarianism.

Not really. I know a lot of rastas. I know they're Bible-believing people, and it's very easy for me to relate to any Bible-believing person.

Well, what if someone is born in a place where there are no Bibles—the Tibetan mountains, say. Could they still be saved?

I don't know. I really don't. Allen Ginsberg is a Tibetan—a Buddhist, or something like that. I'm just not familiar enough with that to say anything about it.

Speaking of Allen Ginsberg, doesn't the Bible say that homosexuality is an abomination?

Yeah, it does. It says that.

And yet Ginsberg's a good guy, right?

Yeah, well, but that's no reason for *me* to condemn somebody, because they drink or they're corrupt in Orthodox ways or they wear their shirt inside out. I mean, that's *their* scene. It certainly doesn't matter to *me*. I've got no ax to grind with any of that.

Were you up in Minnesota when they tried to pass that antiporn law in Minneapolis? The contention was that pornography is a violation of women's civil rights. What do you think?

Well, pornography is pretty deeply embedded. I mean, it's into everything, isn't it? It's too far gone. I mean, if you start makin' laws against porno magazines and that kinda stuff, well, then where do you draw the line? You gotta stop the prime-time television shows also.

Any thoughts on abortion?

Abortion? I personally don't think abortion is that important. I think it's just an issue to evade whatever issues *are* makin' people think about abortion.

Well, I mean, when abortion's used as a form of birth control.

Well, I think birth control is another hoax that women shouldn't have bought, but they did buy. I mean, if a man don't wanna knock up a woman, that's *his* problem, you know what I mean? It's interesting: they arrest prostitutes, but they never arrest the guys *with* the prostitutes. It's all very one-sided. And the same with birth control. Why do they make women take all them pills and fuck themselves up like that? People have used contraceptives for years and years and years. So all of a sudden some scientist invents a *pill*, and it's a billion-dollar industry. So we're talkin' about money. How to *make money* off a sexual idea. "Yeah, you can go out and fuck anybody you want to now, just take this pill." But who *knows* what those pills do to a person? I think they're gonna be passé. But they've caused a lot of damage, a lot of damage.

So it's the man's responsibility? Vasectomy's the way?

I think so. A man don't wanna get a woman pregnant, then *he's* gotta take care of it. Otherwise, that's just ultimate *abuse*, you know?

But the problem is not abortion. The problem is the whole concept behind abortion. Abortion is the end result of going out and screwing somebody to begin with. Casual sex.

But is it taking a life? Is it a woman's decision?

Well, if the woman wants to take that upon herself, I figure that's her business. I mean, who's gonna take care of that baby when it arrives—these people that are callin' for no abortion?

In regard to these feminist sympathies....

I think women rule the world, and that no man has ever done anything that a woman hasn't allowed him to do or encouraged him to do.

In that regard, there's a song on 'Infidels' called "Sweetheart Like You," in which you say, "A woman like you should be at home.../Takin' care of somebody nice."

Actually, that line didn't come out *exactly* the way I wanted it to. But, uh...I could easily have changed that line to make it not so overly, uh, *tender*, you know? But I think the concept still woulda been the same. You see a fine-lookin' woman walkin' down the street, you start goin', "Well, what are you doin' on the street? You're so fine, what do you need all this for?"

A lot of women might say they're on the street because they're on their way to jobs.

Well, I wasn't talkin' to that type of woman. I'm not talkin' to Margaret Thatcher or anything.

Are you in love at the moment?

I'm *always* in love.

Would you ever marry again? Do you believe in the institution?

Yeah, I do. I don't believe in *divorce*. But I'm a strong believer in marriage.

One last question. I think a lot of people take you for a pretty gloomy character these days, judging by your photos. Why reinforce that image by calling this latest album 'Infidels'?

Well, there were other titles for it. I wanted to call it *Surviving in a Ruthless World*. But someone pointed out to me that the last bunch of albums I'd made all started with the letter *S*. So I said, "Well, I don't want to get bogged down in the letter *S*." And then *Infidels* came into my head one day. I don't know what it *means,* or anything.

Don't you think when people see that title, with that sort of dour picture on the front, they'll wonder, "Does he mean us?"

I don't know. I could've called the album *Animals,* and people would've said the same thing. I mean, what would be a term that people would like to hear about themselves?

How about "Sweethearts"?

Sweethearts. You *could* call an album that. *Sweethearts.*

With a big smiling picture?

Yeah.

The Bonfire of the Vanities

by Tom Wolfe   September 1984

The Great White Defendant.... Bellows of Rage from the Brutes...
A Rigoletto from the Sewer...Captain Ahab's Complaint

The next morning, as it turned out, was the morning Larry Kramer decided that things had to change. He was not driven to this decision by anything as terrifying as the unspeakable business with the Perdidos, although that was always somewhere in the back of his mind. No, this time it was just an ordinary workaday piece of nastiness outside the courthouse, just another harmless bellow of rage from the brutes.

As usual, he had walked up 161st Street, up the hill, in his Nike sneakers, past all the deep-fry short-order joints, trying to hold his breath as the exhaust vents pumped their zephyrs of rancid fried ground-haunch-meat grease in his face, carrying his slippery white plastic bag from the A&P with his black oxfords and his rain hat and his filthy raincoat and the rest of his subway camouflage gear, and he was getting ready to cross Walton Avenue. The Bronx County Building—the Island—was right there, right across the street, right in front of him.

The sun above and the shadows below brought out the mighty muscles in the figures in the sculpture on the corner, twenty or thirty feet above the sidewalk. They remained mighty and majestic, because they were too high up for the graffiti roaches to reach them. Ulysses, Jason, Agamemnon, Hercules, Zeus, Thor, Loki, Truth, Justice, Labor, Industry, God, Freedom, Immortality—whoever they were—if they ever came down from there, they wouldn't survive long enough to walk over to 159th Street and get a blue Sharksicle or a cellophane bag of Pepitos.

Just down Walton Avenue, Kramer could see three blue-and-orange Corrections Department vans in a line, waiting to enter the Bronx County Building's service bay. The vans brought prisoners in from the Bronx House of Detention, Rikers Island and the Bronx Criminal Court, a block away, for appearances at Bronx County Supreme Court, the court that handled serious felonies. You couldn't see inside the vans, because their windows were covered with a wire mesh. Kramer didn't have to look inside. There would be the usual job lots of blacks and Latins, plus an occasional young Italian from the Arthur Avenue neighborhood and a few Irish bozos from families that didn't get out of the Bronx when the getting was good or some other white stray who had the miserable freaking luck to pick the Bronx to get in trouble in.

"The chow," Kramer said to himself. Anybody looking at him would have actually seen his lips move as he said it.

In about forty-five seconds, he would learn that somebody was, in fact, looking at him. But at that moment, it was nothing more than the usual: the blue-and-orange vans, and him saying to himself, "the chow."

Kramer had reached that low point in the life of an assistant district attorney in New York when he is assailed by Doubts. Every year, 40,000 people, 40,000 incompetents, cretins, schizophrenics, alcoholics, drug users, perverts, gang runts, layabouts, slobs, sluts, psychopaths, good souls driven to some terrible terminal anger and people who could only be described as stone evil were arrested in the Bronx. Four thousand of them were indicted and arraigned, and they entered the maw of the criminal justice system—right here—through the gateway into the Island, where the vans were lined up. That was 300 new cases, 300 more pumping hearts and morose glares, every day that the courts and the Bronx County District Attorney's office were open. And to what end? The same stupid, dismal, pathetic, horrifying crimes were committed day in and day out, all the same. What was accomplished by assistant D.A.s, by any of them, through this relentless stirring of the muck? The Bronx crumbled and decayed a little more, and a little more blood dried in the cracks. The Doubts! One thing was accomplished for sure: the system was fed. And these vans brought in the chow. Fifty judges, thirty-five law clerks, two hundred and forty-five assistant district attorneys, one D.A. and Christ knew how many criminal lawyers, legal-aid lawyers, court reporters, court clerks, court officers, probation officers, social workers, bail bondsmen, special investigators, case clerks, court psychiatrists—what a vast swarm had to be fed! And every morning the chow came in, the chow and the Doubts.

Kramer is about to cross the street when a big white Pontiac Bonneville comes barreling by, a real boat, with prodigious overhangs, front and back, the kind of twenty-foot frigate they stopped making about 1980. It comes screeching and nosediving to a stop on the far corner. The Bonneville's door opens with a sad torque pop, and a judge named Myron Kovitsky climbs out. He's about sixty, short, thin, bald, wiry, with a sharp nose, hollow eyes and a grim set to his mouth. Through the back window of the Bonneville, Kramer can see a silhouette sliding over into the driver's seat vacated by the judge; that would be his wife.

The sound of this enormous old car door opening and the sight of this little figure getting out moves Kramer in a way he doesn't understand at first. These gigantic Bonnevilles had been considered luxury cars a decade ago. Today, they, like the big Cadillacs and Lincolns, are the cars of the greasers with the open shirts and gold chains twinkling in their chest hair, the cars you always see heading out of Manhattan, across the Willis Avenue Bridge or the Fifty-ninth Street Bridge, back to the Bronx or Queens. Judge Kovitsky comes to work in a greaser yacht practically ten years old. Supreme Court judges make $65,100 a year. After taxes, they have less than $40,000. For a sixty-year-old man in the upper echelons of the legal profession in New York, it's…not right. And this man whose car goes *thwop* every time he opens the door is at the top of the hierarchy here on the Island, and he, Kramer, occupies some vague middling position. If he plays his cards right and ingratiates himself with the Bronx Democratic organization, this—*thwop*—is the eminence to which he might aspire three decades from now.

These thoughts are going through Kramer's head as he walks across the street, when it begins:

"Yo! Kramer!"

It's a huge voice, and it's a black voice. Kramer can't tell where it's coming from.

"You redheaded cocksucker!"

Whuh? It stops him in his tracks. A sensation, a sound—like rushing steam—fills his skull.

"Hey, Kramer, you little redheaded piece a shit!"

It's another voice, also black.

"Yo! Fuckhead!"

They're coming from the back of the van, the blue-and-orange van. It's no more than twenty feet from him.

"Yo! Kramer! You Hymie asshole!"

Hymie! How do they know he's Jewish? Why would they—it rocks him.

"Yo! Kramer! You faggot Goldberg! Kiss my ass!"

"Aaaayyyy, maaaaan, you steeck uppy yass! You steeck uppy yass!"

A Latino, that one! The very barbarism of it twists the knife in a little further.

"Yo! Shit face!"

"Aaayyyyy! You keesa sol! You keesa sol!"

"Yo! Kramer! Eatcho muvva!"

"Aaaayyyy! Maaaan! Fokky you! Fokky you!"

It's a chorus! A rain of garbage! A *Rigoletto* from the sewer, from the rancid gullet of the Bronx!

Kramer is still out in the middle of the street. What should he do? He stares at the van. He can't make out a thing. Which ones? Which of them…from out of that endless procession of baleful blacks and Latins.…But no! Don't look! He looks away. Who's watching? Does he just take this unbelievable abuse and keep walking to the Walton Avenue entrance of the building while they pour more of it all over him, or does he confront them? Confront them? *How?* Then he sees Kovitsky. The judge is on the sidewalk about thirty feet from the entrance.

"Hey! You baldheaded worm!"

"Aaayyy! You steecka balda ed uppas ol! Steecka balda ed uppas ol!"

Bald? Why bald? Kramer isn't bald. What—they've spotted the judge. Now they have two targets.

"Yo! Kramer! What you got inna bag, man?"

"Hey, you baldheaded old fart!"

"You shiny old shitfa brains!"

They're in it together, him and Kovitsky. Kramer keeps walking across the street. He feels like he's underwater. He cuts a glance at Kovitsky. But Kovitsky's no longer looking at him. He's walking straight toward the van. His head is lowered. He's glaring. You can see the whites of his eyes. His pupils are like two death rays burning just beneath his upper eyelids. Kramer has seen him like this in court.

The bozos inside the van try to drive him back:

"What you looking at, you shriveled little pecker?"

"Yaaaagghhh! Come on! Come on in, wormdick!"

Kovitsky walks right up to the van and tries to stare through the mesh. He puts his hands on his hips.

"Yeah! That's right! Come on, man!"

"Visiting hours, bro'! We'll give you a fucking visit!"

Now Kovitsky walks to the front of the van. He turns those blazing eyes on the driver.

"Do...you...*hear*...that?" says the little jurist, pointing toward the rear of the van.

"Whuh?" says the driver. "Whattya?" He doesn't know what to say. (Christ! Forget it, will you? Go inside the building! Go put on a robe!)

"Are you fucking deaf?" says Kovitsky. "Your prisoners...*your*...prisoners....You're an officer of the Department of Corrections..."

He starts jabbing his finger toward the poor bewildered bastard.

"*Your...prisoners....*You let *your prisoners* pull...this *shit*...on the citizens of this community and the officers of *this court?*"

The driver is a swarthy white man—Italian, Greek, it's hard to say—short, pudgy, around fifty, a civil-service lifer...and all at once his eyes and his mouth open up, without a sound coming out, and he lifts his shoulders, and he turns his palms up and the corners of his mouth down.

It's the primordial shrug of the New York streets, the look that says, "Egghh, whattya? Whattya want from me?" And in this specific instance: "Whattya want me to do? Crawl back in that cage with that fucking buncha animals and shut their faces?" It's the New York cry for mercy, unanswerable and undeniable.

Kovitsky stares at him and shakes his head. Then he turns and goes back to the rear of the van.

"Here come Goldberg!"

"Chew my willie, yo' Honor."

Kovitsky stares at the window, still trying to make out his invisible abusers through the heavy mesh. Then he takes in a deep breath, and a tremendous snuffling sound is heard in his nose, and there's a deep rumbling in his chest and his throat—it seems incredible that so volcanic a sound can come out of such a small, thin body—and he...*spits*. But *spits* is scarcely the word for it. He hocks a lunga. He propels a prodigious gob of spit toward the window of the van. It hits the wire mesh and hangs there, a huge runny yellow oyster, part of which begins to sag like some hideous virulent strand of gum or taffy with a glob on the bottom of it. And there it remains, gleaming in the sun for those inside, whoever they may be, to contemplate at their leisure.

It stuns them. The whole chorus stops. For one strange feverish moment, there's nothing in the world, in the heavens, in the universe, in all of astronomy, but the cage and this one gleaming, oozing, pendulous sunlit gob of spit. Then, keeping his right hand close to his chest so that no one on the sidewalk can see it, the judge shoots them a finger and turns on his heels and walks toward the entrance to the Island.

He's halfway to the door before they get their breath back.

"Yeggghh, fuck you too, man!"

"Yeah...you wanna...shiiiit...you try that..."

But their hearts aren't in it anymore. The grisly esprit of the prison-van uprising fizzles in the face of this furious blazing little steel rod of a man.

Kramer hurries after the judge and catches up with him as he's going in the Walton Street entrance. He has to catch up with him. He has to show him that he was with him all along. It was the two of them out there, taking that insidious abuse.

Kramer touches his shoulder. "Hey, Judge! I don't know how you did it, but..." He starts to say, "...you shut up those bastards," but he stops short, for fear of sounding as if he thinks he's on intimate terms with Kovitsky, who not only outranks him but is twice his age.

"Nice class of defendant we get here," says Kramer. "Did you hear what they said to me?"

Kovitsky stops and looks Kramer up and down, but distractedly. Mainly he looks right through him. It's as if his thoughts are a long way away.

"Fucking useless...," says the judge, quietly but still seething. Kramer realizes he's talking about the driver of the van. Then the judge lets his breath out and looks down.

"Well, the poor son of a bitch. He's terrified. And what's he gonna do...." He seems to be talking more to himself than to Kramer.

Kovitsky is still talking. He's still talking about this fucking whatever and that fucking whatever. The profanity doesn't even register. The courthouse is like the army. From the judges down to the guards, there's one all-purpose adjective or participle or whatever it should be called, and after a while it's as natural as breathing.

The two of them were barely fifteen feet inside the Walton Avenue entrance. It had never been intended as anything other than an employees' entrance, and even now there was no reason why the sad citizens whose lives drew them into the Bronx County Building had to come in this way. Why didn't they use the front entrance—that great staircase on 161st Street—a staircase practically a block wide, leading up to a majestic Moderne entrance of brass and marble? They could enter these halls with God's sun upon their faces and the Jazz Age exuberance of the Style Moderne in their shanks! And as they opened those great brass doors, they could gaze upon mahogany walls and marble floors and German Expressionist foliations of brass and malachite. But no, this was the Bronx in the 1980s, and they all came squeezing into the Walton Avenue entrance, which brought them in at basement level. The light of the City Bankrupt, namely, the fluorescent tube, gave the scene a tubercular-blue glow.

"…this Goldberg business," says Kovitsky, and then he gives Kramer a look that demands a response.

Kramer doesn't know what the hell he's been saying.

"Goldberg?"

"Yeah! 'Here comes Goldberg,'" says Kovitsky. "'Wormdick!' What difference does it make? 'Wormdick.'" He laughs without the slightest gaiety. "But 'Goldberg.' That's poison, that's hate. They're anti-Semitic. Anti-Semitic! And for what? Without the Yiddeshe, they'd still be looking up shotgun barrels and laying asphalt in South Carolina."

Kovitsky's talking about the Yiddeshe and liberalism or something or other, and Kramer is looking into his face and nodding to beat the band and not hearing a word, and out the corner of his eye, he can see an extraordinary figure walking out of the door to the Landlord and Tenants Court, a giant, in fact, a young white man, probably six feet five, well over 250 pounds, grossly fat but powerfully built, bursting like a length of bratwurst out of the glistening liverish layer of flesh that covers his huge frame, wearing a stiff-brimmed black hat and a long black coat and a wild black beard and a pair of corkscrew curls that hang down from his temples, on either side of his head, just beneath the brim of the hat.

He was a Hasidic Jew—but what a giant of the breed! Kramer knew who he was. He was known as the Seven Day War. He worked for landlords in the Bronx, collecting rents. He went door to door. Collecting rents, door to door, in the Bronx, was as dangerous a job as existed in the United States in the 1980s. Soldiers of fortune, suicide-squad terrorists, underwater demolition experts, those Indians who build bridges, those Texans who put out fires in offshore oil wells, those commandos who invade prisons on foreign soil to spring their comrades, those decoy policemen who sit on park benches at night waiting for muggers to attack—they were all nellies, lulus, sweetie pies, cotton balls next to people who went door to door collecting the rent in the Bronx. But...the Seven Day War loved it! On he clomped, this liver-white giant in his outlandish—literally outlandish—costume, pounding up and down stairs, pounding on doors, his *peyes* bobbing up and down, the pale sausage of his face glistening with sweat. And the dark faces of the Bronx, eternally behind in the rent, quaked, as if it were Samson himself, an invincible hulking vestige of the days when the Jews ruled these hills and stairwells and sunken-living-room apartments.

Suddenly an alarm sounded. A frantic ring filled the hall. It pounded your ears in waves. Judge Kovitsky had to raise his voice to be heard, but he didn't even look around. Not even Kramer batted an eye. The alarm meant a prisoner had escaped or some skinny little thug's brother had pulled out a revolver in a courtroom, or some gargantuan tenant from 174th Street had grabbed a 130-pound Jewish hearing officer in a hammerlock. Or maybe it was only a fire. The first few times you heard the alarm in the Island, your eyes darted around and you braced yourself for the clatter of a herd of guards wearing leather shoes and waving .45s, running along the marble corridors trying to catch some nutball in striped sneakers who, jacked up by fear, does the hundred in eight-four. But after a while, you ignored it. It was the normal state of red alert, panic and disarray in the Bronx County Building. All around Kramer and the judge, people were swiveling their heads in every direction. Oh, their sad, dark faces....They were entering the Island for the first time, on Christ knows what sad mission.

All at once Kovitsky is motioning toward the floor and saying "...is this, Kramer?"

"This?" says Kramer, desperately trying to figure out what the judge is talking about.

"These fucking shoes," says Kovitsky.

"Ah! Shoes," says Kramer. "Ah! They're running shoes."

"Is that something Weiss thought up?"

"Noooo," says Kramer, chuckling as if moved by the judge's wit.

"Christ, every kid who sticks up a Red Apple's in court wearing these goddamned things, and now you guys?"

"Nooo-ho-ho."

"You think you're gonna come in my Part looking like that?"

"Nooooo-ho-ho-ho! Wouldn't think of it!"

"Christ, I got enough trouble with the lesbian activists, without you guys."

"No, look, Judge, I've got my—"

"You ever run into Myra Grabrotchky?"

"Yeah, I know who you mean."

"She comes into my courtroom wearing some kinda goddamned camouflage suit. She looks like a hijacker. I tell her, 'You wanna practice law in this courtroom, you'll dress like a lady.' You know what she says to me? She says, 'I'm a lesbian.' *I'm a lesbian!* So I told her, 'Miz Grabrotchky, it so happens...that the *Court*...has athlete's foot...but you will observe...that the *Court...nevertheless!...*wears *shoes*'."

The alarm keeps ringing. And the new people, the new sad dark faces who have never been inside this glum citadel before, look all about with their eyes wide and their mouths open slightly, and they see a baldheaded old white man in a gray suit and a white shirt and a necktie and a young redheaded white man in a gray suit and a white shirt and a necktie just standing there talking, yakking, shooting the breeze, and so if these two white people, so obviously a part of the Power, are just standing there, without so much as lifting an eyebrow, how bad could it be?

★   ★   ★

To get to the office of the Bronx District Attorney, you went to floor 6M, *M* for mezzanine. When you got out of the elevator and looked down the hall, you could see a wide entryway, framed in mahogany and marble in the best Moderne style of the 1930s. A counter and a gate kept people from walking unannounced into the complex of offices beyond. Behind the counter, at a desk, sat a uniformed guard armed with a .45. He served as the receptionist. He was also supposed to serve as a deterrent to the random berserk vengeance of the Bronx.

Over this princely portal were some large elegant Roman-style brass letters, which had been fabricated at considerable expense to the taxpayers of New York and cemented to the marble facing with epoxy glue. The brass letters gleamed: RICHARD A. WEISS, DISTRICT ATTORNEY, BRONX COUNTY.

Every time Kramer got off the elevator and saw this grand gauche proscenium, he laughed to himself. The A stood for Abraham. Weiss was known to his friends and his political cronies and the newspaper reporters and channels 2, 4, 5, 7, 9 and 11 and his constituents—most especially the Jews up around Riverdale and

Pelham Parkway and Co-op City, who were the core of his support—as Abe Weiss. He hated the nickname Abe, which had originated in his boyhood. It sounded too…too …Jewish. A few years back he had let it be known that henceforth he preferred to be called Dick, and he had practically been laughed out of the Bronx County Democratic organization; and to Abe Weiss, to be laughed out of the Bronx County Democratic organization or separated from it in any fashion whatsoever would be like being thrown off the back of a Christmas cruise ship in the middle of the Atlantic. So he was Richard A. Weiss only in *The New York Times* and over this doorway.

The guard buzzed Kramer through the gate with an unenthusiastic nod, and the young assistant D.A. made his way back to the Homicide Bureau, carrying his slippery white shopping bag. Kramer shared an office and its one window with two other assistant D.A.s in their thirties. There was just enough room for three metal desks, a secondhand table bearing a Mr. Coffee machine, an old coat stand with six savage hooks sticking out from it, four filing cabinets, three swivel desk chairs and the legs of the three young men, which took up a lot of room because these three young men were always sitting down in the swivel chairs with their legs crossed in the bull triangle position. In the bull triangle position, you put the ankle of one leg on top of the knee of the other leg. The idea is that a prize Angus such as yourself couldn't get his legs crossed any further if he tried.

When Kramer walked in, his two confreres, Frank Andriutti and Jimmy Caughey, were already there, sprawled back in their swivel chairs, their legs cocked in the bull triangle, their jackets off and hung with perfect give-a-shit carelessness on the coat rack, their shirt collars loosened and their necktie knots pulled down an inch or so. Andriutti was rubbing the back of his left arm with his right hand, as if it itched. In fact, he was feeling his triceps, which he pumped up at least three times a week by doing French curls with dumbbells at the New York Athletic Club. He also liked the fact that when he reached around behind one of his mighty arms with the other hand, it made the latissimi dorsi muscles of his back fan out so wide they practically split his shirt, and his pectorals hardened into a couple of mountains of pure muscle. So he rubbed his itching triceps about 120 times a day, on the average.

Still rubbing them, Andriutti looked at Kramer as he walked in and said: "Jesus Christ, here comes the bag lady. What the hell is this fucking A&P bag, Larry? You been coming in here with this fucking bag every day this week." Then he turned to Jimmy Caughey and said, "Looks like a fucking bag lady."

Caughey was also a jock, but more the sinewy triathlon type, with a narrow face and a long chin. He just smiled at Larry, as much as to say, "Well, what do you say to that?"

Kramer said, "Your arm itch, Frank?" Then he looked at Caughey and said,

"Frank's got this fucking allergy. It's called Triceps disease." Then he turned back to Andriutti. "Itches like a son of a bitch, don't it?"

Andriutti let his hand drop off his triceps. "And whatta these *jogging* shoes?" he said to Kramer. "Looks like those girls walking to work at Merrill Lynch. All dressed up, and they got these fucking rubber gunboats on their feet."

"What the hell *is* in the bag, Larry?" asked Caughey.

"My high heels," said Kramer.

He took off his jacket and jammed it down, give-a-shit, on a coat-rack hook in the accepted fashion and pulled down his necktie and unbuttoned his shirt and sat down in his swivel chair and opened up the shopping bag and fished out his black oxford shoes and started taking off the Nikes.

"Well, don't let Captain Ahab see this," said Caughey. And then to Andriutti: "He'll have Jeanette issue a fucking directive."

"No, he'll call a fucking press conference," said Andriutti.

"That's always a safe fucking bet."

And so another fucking day in the fucking Homicide Bureau of the Bronx Fucking District Attorney's office was off to a fucking start.

Caughey had started calling Abe Weiss "Captain Ahab," and now they all did. Weiss was notorious in his obsessive quest for publicity, even among a breed—the New York District Attorney—that was publicity mad by nature. Weiss's legendary predecessors in the office of Bronx District Attorney, Burt Roberts and Mario Merola, had certainly not been bashful when it came to the press. But they had also been known as strong and effective district attorneys. Weiss never went near a courtroom. He spent entire days doing nothing but playing the machinery of publicity in New York City.

Jimmy Caughey said, "I was just in seeing the Captain. You shoulda—"

"You were? What for?" asked Kramer, with just a shade too much curiosity—and incipient envy—in his voice.

"Me and Bernie," said Caughey. "He wanted to know about the Moore case."

"Any good?"

"Piece a shit," said Caughey. "This fucking guy Moore, he has a big house in Riverdale and his wife's mother lives there with 'em, and she's been giving him a hard time for about thirty-seven fucking years, right? So this guy, he loses his job. He's a bond trader, and he's making $400,000 or $500,000 a year, and now he's outta work for eight or nine months, nobody'll hire him, right? So one day he's puttering around out in the garden, and the mother-in-law comes out and says, 'Well, the water seeks its own level.' That's a verbatim quote. 'You oughta get a job as a gardener.' So this guy, he's out of his fucking mind, he's so mad. He goes in and tells his wife, 'I've had it with your mother. I'm gonna get my shotgun and scare her.' So he goes up to his bedroom, where he keeps this twelve-gauge shotgun, and he comes downstairs and heads for the mother-in-law, and he's gonna scare the shit outta her, and he says, 'Okay, Gladys,' and he trips on the rug, and the gun goes off and kills her, and—*ba-bing*— Murder Two."

"Why was Weiss interested?"

"Well, the guy's white, he's wealthy, he lives in a big house in Riverdale."

Kramer and Andriutti contemplated this piece a shit without needing any amplification. Every assistant D.A. in the Bronx, from the youngest Italian just out of St. John's Law School to the oldest Irish bureau chief, shared Captain Ahab's mania for the Great White Defendant. Kramer had been raised as a liberal. In Jewish families in New York, liberalism came with the Similac and the diaper service and the Mott's apple juice and the Instamatic and Daddy's grins in the evening. And even the Italians, like Frank Andriutti, and the Irish, like Jimmy Caughey, who were not exactly burdened with liberalism by their parents, couldn't help but be affected by the mental atmosphere of the law schools, where, for one thing, there were so many Jewish faculty members. By the time you finished law school in the New York area, it was, well…fucking *impolite!*…on the ordinary social level…to go around making jokes about the *yoms*. It was worse than morally wrong, it was…*in bad taste.* So it made the boys uneasy, this eternal prosecution of the blacks and Latins.

Not that they weren't guilty, mind you! One thing you learned after two weeks on this job was that ninety, ninety-five percent of the defendants who got as far as the indictment stage were guilty. The caseload was so overwhelming that most of the time you didn't even try to bring the marginal cases forward. They hauled in guilt by the ton, those blue-and-orange vans. But the bellowing bozos behind the wire mesh barely deserved the term *criminal*, if by criminal you have in mind the romantic notion of someone who has a goal and seeks to achieve it through some desperate way outside the law. No, they were simple-minded incompetents, most of them, and they did unbelievably stupid, vile things.

Kramer looked at Andriutti and Caughey, sitting there with their legs cocked in the bull triangle. He felt superior to them, and yet he desperately wanted to be accepted by them. He was a graduate of Columbia Law School, which was a rare thing in the ranks of assistant district attorneys in the Bronx, and they were both graduates of St. John's, which was standard…dead-on standard. But they were all three sitting here in this Good Enough for Government Work office at $32,000 to $42,000 a year, instead of down at Cravath Swaine & Moore or some such place at $132,000 to $142,000, for the same reason: they had been born a million miles from Wall Street, meaning the outer boroughs, Brooklyn, Queens and the Bronx. To their families, their going to college and becoming lawyers had been the greatest thing since Franklin D. Roosevelt. And so they sat around in the Homicide Bureau talking about this fucking thing and that fucking thing and using *don'ts* for *doesn'ts*, as if they didn't know any better. They knew, all right; it was just that in this world, the paths of glory took turns stranger than any the WASP comma checkers at Cravath Swaine & Moore had ever dreamed of. The three of them had made it to Homicide, the elite corps of this little-known army of 245 assistant district attorneys in the Bronx. If you were in Homicide, that meant you knew, or were supposed to know, how to deal with the most evil of all crimes—and the most fascinating to the press. And there you got down to an unspeakable truth. So what if a couple of Latin drug dealers get in an argument and pull knives, and one of them says, "Let's put the weapons down and fight man to man." And they do, whereupon Mr. Manly Honor pulls out a second knife and stabs the other fellow in the chest. So what if two black guys are in a group of guys drinking and taking cocaine and playing a game called the dozens, in which the idea is to see how rudely you can insult the other fellow, and one of them pulls out a revolver and shoots the other one through the heart and then collapses on the table, sobbing and saying, "My man! My man Stan! I shot my man Stan!" The press couldn't even *see* these cases, and to deal with such crimes was to be part of the garbage-collection service, necessary and honorable, but anonymous.

Kramer stopped smiling. Abe Weiss wasn't all that funny. He was merely more obvious and candid about things than they were, and he had an election coming up in a county that was eighty percent black and Latin. Consciously or not, they were all doing the same thing he was. They were sitting there waiting for a beast which in the Bronx seemed as rare and exquisite as the unicorn. They were all waiting for the Great White Defendant.

Yeah, Frank and Jimmy could laugh at Abe Weiss all they wanted. Nevertheless, Abe Weiss had made sure an entire city knew his name. And on whose lips was the name Larry Kramer? Some poor sad invisible bozos bellowing inside a blue-and-orange van. It was at that moment, leaning back in a swivel chair with his right ankle resting on his left knee, that Kramer decided the time had come to light up the sky.

Jack Nicholson: The Rolling Stone Interview

by Fred Schruers   August 1986

Jack Nicholson's Hollywood Hills home perches above an empty ravine—a rare prospect amid these overbuilt hills of dirt and scrub. On the hot afternoon when I arrive, a chain-link fence is being installed (not, I'm later told, at Nicholson's instigation) on the winding driveway he shares with Marlon Brando. Despite the fence and an electronic inspection of visitors, Nicholson's complex—two houses, a row of carports topped by a basketball hoop, and a deck equipped with a pool and a commanding view—doesn't have the aspect of a fortress. Inside, the walls are crammed with oils by the likes of Soutine, Matisse and Picasso, but the mountain breeze and the informality of the furnishings lend the house the air of a tropic bungalow.

I am informed that Nicholson is in the Jacuzzi, recuperating from an exercise session, and I take a stroll around the deck as John Coltrane's recording of "My Favorite Things" wafts from discreet outdoor speakers. When I turn toward the house, the man himself is in the shadowy interior. He shakes hands and apologizes assiduously for the delay. Dressed in baggy white slacks and a short-sleeved sport shirt, he looks unostentatiously stylish—even when he seats himself and his pants legs hoist off his Adidas to reveal fluorescent-orange socks.

He'll talk here for the next three hours, using few gestures but often hunching forward in his seat to bear down on a point. The force of his passion when he's talking about things that make him angry can be a mite scary: he begins to clip his words off, curl his lips back over his teeth and close sentences with "pal."

Jack Nicholson doesn't have a lot of competition as the modern movie star for America's everyman, a man who does his work spectacularly well largely without indulging in the pomposities and fits of temperament associated with other great movie actors. Often seen as a hard-partying, no-bullshit street guy from Jersey, he nonetheless maintains the seignorial distance we expect of pop royalty. When the paparazzi catch him, he shrugs it off and lets the flashbulbs glint off his shades, telling us what he wants to with the set of his notoriously expressive mouth.

He is heir to the alienated brooding of Brando and James Dean, but having incorporated their inarticulate (if brilliant) posturing in his craft, he has gone on to stand up onscreen in service of the great line, *from "You know, this used to be a hell of a good country," in 'Easy Rider,' to "Heeeeere's Johnny!"—a marrow-chilling and hilarious ad-lib—in 'The Shining'. In between there's been plenty of time for other unforgettable outbursts, like his rebuke to the waitress with the problematic chicken salad in 'Five Easy Pieces' ("Yeah, I want you to hold it between your knees"), or his abrupt attack on a nasty bartender in 'The Last Detail' ("I am* the motherfucking shore patrol, motherfucker!")*

His Oscars for Best Actor in 'One Flew Over the Cuckoo's Nest' and Best Supporting Actor in 'Terms of Endearment' as well as his six other nominations are Hollywood's official tributes to a maverick who has never pandered to it.

Do you feel that packaging is one of the reasons people are saying that movies are losing their magic?

There are millions of ways, but it's all—see, our country is becoming corrupted little by little by conglomeration and conglomerative thinking. Coca-Cola—look at Columbia [Pictures]. Coca-Cola owns them. Coca-Cola also owns part of Tri-Star. Coca-Cola runs its business based on market share. Period. That's the way they run it. And baby, you or I ain't going to change it. Because it's back in Atlanta. It has nothing to do with any one movie. And that's where the business is being corrupted.

All these guys you read about in the newspapers who are the heads of the studios—I predicted this four or five years ago, when they were trying to cut my prices—all these deal makers are making themselves the stars now. They're on the covers of magazines. Their salaries are now quotable. Why? Because it isn't about movies anymore.

Hasn't the movie industry been flirting with that kind of conglomeration since it began?

When Harry Cohn and Louis B. Mayer and Darryl Zanuck and these people ran the business, I wasn't working, so I don't know if I would have been better off or not. But at least they were making movies....Every guy who was the head of a studio was also a gambler. They weren't making market shares with back-off sales and cross-financing and cross-collateralization. There's nobody that gambles now. Everybody's going for the big whamola all the time. Before this, the debate was whether you should go ahead and make a movie—whether or not you thought it was going to be profit making—because the movie made a valid statement. Well, that debate's not even on anymore. Anybody who tells you it is on is lying or doesn't understand the situation. Because there's nobody left to take that kind of chance.

Do you see a link between these new multiplex cinemas with their tiny screens and the banality of the studio film product?

You know, I like the big silver, I really do. The world is going to miss the movie-going experience. I know I still prefer going to a theater that's got a decent screen in it. If you can't see that it's more fun to sit and watch a movie at the Paramount theater in New York than to sit in a bowling alley with this little postage stamp—well, then I can't explain my point. The point is, your life, the moviegoer's life, has been degraded by this thing.

Maybe that's why so many people would rather stay home and watch movies on television.

You know, television is not a support group for the movies; it's a competitive industry that's been devouring the movies like a cancer since I came out here in the Fifties. And I happen to be anachronistically in love with the movies, so I deeply resent the whole video thing. Everybody says it's great for the labor pool. I didn't get in this to be in a union labor pool; I got in this thing to be an artistic, expressive person. The movies have sold their future so cheap for so long it's almost amateurish to comment on it.

You seem to be saying that the decline of the movies is an index to our descent into some kind of Orwellian nightmare.

It's so clear it's a joke. All you've got to do is drive across America. Go to Kansas City and see old Kansas City down *here*, and then there's this six-lane highway that goes around it, and you've got plastic light boxes that say Radio Shack and Chicken Bicken and Roller Skate World. That's what America looks like today. I don't like what the light box has done to America at night—turned everybody into a fucking pinball-machine moth. If they had just outlawed these light boxes, the world would simply look bigger. But we can't even get them to stop acid rain—how can you get them to think about what's beautiful? Because what's beautiful is all that counts, pal. That's *all* that counts.

But the corporations that built those franchise strips will tell you they're creating jobs.

Okay. All right. Life used to be work until five o'clock and then you were meant to have some fun, some nourishment, some leisure. Americans don't understand leisure. They don't have a clue. They understand work; they understand play; they understand love; they do not understand leisure. Literacy is dropping. These are not redeemable things. These are our lives. I don't know what the minimum wage is today, but what you give up by putting up that light box, with bugs all over this world and graffiti up your keister...if you gave a kid the insight he would need to be a purer person at fifty, do you want to give that up for $200 a week?

Is labor God? Is a job God? People vote like it is. Ronald Reagan is a vote to return to the company store. People look at that guy Nicholson down there yelling and say, "What's he do?" Nothing—he sits around and complains. At least a guy in a nice pin-stripe suit down at the bank, he keeps the park clean, everything's cool. Who are these rabble-rousers? What do they do? Let's go back in there and let's buy shoes down at the conglomerate. Let's get our movie down at the conglomerate. Let's let the big guy in the pin-stripe suit run things, 'cause it'll be quiet then.

Well, pal, that hasn't ever worked in the past. And it ain't gonna work in the future. Dream on, dream on. I can't do nothin' about it. I understand numbers. I'm going to reach fifty years old next year. I just turned forty-nine. There ain't time for me to turn this around.

I did my part. I screamed my ass off for ten, fifteen years. I paid those dues, too. I'm not giving up. But I'm not going out there and try to rake people up....The professional man says, "Hey, man, you can't take conglomeration out. The Japs got monopolies." The guy in the third grade knows if he gets a B minus on a spelling test, what his job is going to be at Mitsubishi twenty years later. That's it, it don't change. That's what a monopoly is.

But, pal, if we're not a nation of idealists who fight against these things, I guess it's because we don't understand what it's costing us anymore. Anyway, I wasn't going to talk this wild. But you get the picture.

Don't you see your job as simply making quality movies about people's real emotional lives?

I still make the movies I want to make. I'm just talking about—where's the soil for them? Where's the informed intelligence? I'm doing fine. You know, you don't want to see this as so huge that you begin to dysfunction. But I have to whip up a foam in my spirit, or I'll just stop seeing where it's at, too.

Social graces don't come—they're not innate. You learn them, develop them. Once you're past the high-school prom, what you do on your own is what gives your life quality. *You* have to learn how to dance. *You* have to learn how to read a book. *You* have to learn how to appreciate music, to enrich your mind in order to have a conversation.

I heard someone call himself a conservative anarchist; I wonder where you feel yourself to be on the political spectrum.

I guess you'd call me a liberal, certainly through my earlier years of involvement. I was flat-out anti-capital punishment. However, I agree with Reagan about terrorists. These people are not criminals against the United States. They're criminals against the world. And this is a degradation of all mankind. In World War II, you tortured the man; in Vietnam you tortured the man's children in front of him. This is an indication of an overall decline in civilization.

Despite all this, friends point out your "positiveness."

There are many areas for optimism as well. I'm a simple person in my job. I don't want to do what I accuse other people of doing, not taking the time to smell the roses. Something very wonderful has happened to me. I don't want the fact that I see this endless din and gloom in the world to make me incapable of expressing something that's quite frankly wonderful. I'm a very fortunate—statistically impossible to describe how fortunate—person to be where I am and do what I do.

And you feel your work can help make a difference.

My first acting teacher said all art is one thing—a stimulating point of departure. That's it. And if you can do that in a piece, you've fulfilled your cultural, your sociological obligation as a workman. What you're supposed to do is keep people vitally interested in the world they live in. The thing I originally wrote so pretentiously as a young person, *Ride in the Whirlwind*, was about the Sisyphean mountain. You push that boulder up, it rolls down. You push it up again. Man's dignity is in the trip down the mountain, returning to his labors. This is where artists are supposed to be of use, to make people not necessarily happy but enrich their vitality.

And, not incidentally, your own.

I start thinking, "Hey, Jack, nobody ever *needs* you." You've got to remember that. You're alone, that's it. Friendships are a boon, love is a boon. Contacts with other human beings and events—these are all boons. You've got to do your part as well as you can.

My life is enriched by my friends—[screenwriter-producer] Don Devlin, my partner Harry Gittes. We've been communicating for thirty years. They're all still in my life, none of them has quit to become a hangman. They're doing these things I talk about. You don't talk to these people and get pap. They're in there. They don't give a fuck—I mean, my closest friends probably have less of a consensus about adoring my movies than any other group. They fight with me about it. Now I don't think that means they don't like me anymore, don't want to see me do anything. Quite the contrary. I hope I take what's positive, or at least stimulating, and grow from it.

It's almost like film sets represent a portable Utopia to you. Did you have that same sense of community growing up along the New Jersey Shore?

I grew up through age five there in Neptune. I lived on Sixth Avenue in Neptune, and Fifth Avenue was Neptune City, so it's that close. But Mrs. Nicholson understood the difference, and when I got to a certain point of school age, she moved to Neptune City, this slightly...*affluent* is the wrong word, but just a little better situation for a kid.

To reiterate your situation so we've got things straight: You never met your natural father. Your real mother, June, was the woman you believed to be your sister. The woman you call Mrs. Nicholson—Ethel May, whom you called Mud—was in fact your grandmother, and her husband, presented as your father, was this hard-drinking guy who was never around. The third woman in the triumvirate that raised you was June's sister, Lorraine. Plenty of company, but no real father.

Well, I had Shorty. He was married to Lorraine. That, believe me, is as good a father as anybody's ever going to get or need. I can be as hard on my family or friends as anybody—I'm fairly objective—but there's nobody much that's impressed me as much as Shorty. Simple guy, but many is the poem I've written in my mind to the higher feelings he promoted in me—which he would have no ability whatsoever to articulate.

Now, Shorty's not what a civics class would pick out as a role model. He was a featherbedded railroad brakeman, you know, who went to gin mills and drank and sat around all day with his shirt off and bullshitted. Everybody did love Shorty. He was the first all-state football player from the region, and he stayed right there in Neptune. He wasn't a hidden man. It's not sentiment—this guy was advanced. Shorty just had a grasp—innate, not a conscious ability—about life. I hope I've got it.

Your natural father was someone you never met and didn't even know about till around 1975.

Both grandmother and mother were deceased before this particular group of facts came to my attention. I was very impressed by their ability to keep the secret, if nothing else. It's done great things for me. I mean, I don't have to question the abortion issue in my mind. It's an open-and-shut case where I'm concerned. As an illegitimate child born in 1937, during the Depression, to a broken lower-middle-class family, you are a candidate for—you're an automatic abortion with most people today.

So it's very easy for me. I don't have to get into the debate of when does the thing come alive. And I'm very pleased to be out of it, 'cause it's not an easy issue.

They sound like a formidable group of women.

These were strong women—made their own way in a period of time when it just wasn't done that much. They did it without connections. In fact, Ethel May Nicholson was disinherited for marrying an Irish Catholic, because her family was Pennsylvania Dutch rock-hard Protestants, and that just wasn't done. I guess she got married very young, too. And never saw much of that very wealthy Pennsylvania family again in her life.

My basic model for women is an independent woman. There was no grandeur in that for me, because it was that way from the beginning. You know, here was Mud, and she carried everybody on her back like a tiny little elephant, and it didn't seem to faze her. She marched right through it. They all had a lot of style and a lot of fun. The neighborhood idolized all of them.

Mud was the patron saint of the neighborhood, and anybody who had a problem, they'd come running over to her beauty shop—"Ethel, da-da-da," and she'd figure it out. I'm very fortunate to have had that very unusual environment to grow up in. Very free, very trusting. A lot of responsibility—not heaped on you, but just by definition of the situation.

Once you moved to Neptune City, what was the scene like there?

I started high school in 1950. Cool was invented in this period. Rock & roll did not start with Elvis Presley. In fact, to that age group, Elvis Presley was a secondary figure to Ray Charles. And, you know, Johnnie Ray. That's when all that stuff really got rolling. It wasn't as explosively widespread, but that was the seminal period of it. And peer group was everything. There was not a lot of visible rebellion, aside from the DA haircut and stuff.

How did you dress?

I used to like to go to school in a pair of navy-blue cuffed pegged pants, a black or navy-blue turtleneck sweater, maybe a gray coat over it and a black porkpie hat that I'd gotten from the freeway in a motor accident that involved a priest. So it had a lot of juju on it. I wore it flat out like a rimmer. That was one way.

Now, when we had the dances and everything, you just got the greatest suit you could get a hold of. Always pegged, pleats, blue suedes, thinnest tie, shoulders, one button in front. But we did everything. My friends, we'd go to New York on weekends, get drunk, see ball games, bang around…school was out, we just went to the beach all summer. And had fun, got drunk every night. It was the age of the put-on. Cool was everything. Collars were up, eyelids were drooped. You never let on what bothered you.

And at the beach you'd try to pick up girls who came in from Camden or something?

Teaneck. And when you got to be a lifeguard—which I did later—why, you were the prince of summer. You know, it didn't do me much good, but a lot of guys made a lot of hay with it.

Did you wear oxide on the nose, sunglasses, the whole bit?

You bet. Where I worked in Bradley Beach, a boat stayed just outside the breakers and kept people in. You'd stand up in the boat, Mr. Cool, and look at everything. I used to "boat" people, standing up with a black wool coat, no matter how hot it was, big white nose, big white lips and a prisoner's hat. They'd just gotten mirrored sunglasses in. Must have been the funniest sight of all time. I was sixteen years old, but I thought I was like death itself [*laughs*], guarding these people.

Then you got the girls…

It was a great chance to impress the girls. But like most people of that generation, I didn't think I was adept at anything. It takes a while to find out all them people were lying to you [about their exploits]. If you're a certain kind of guy, you don't lie about it. I could never make up any stories like that. It definitely was a different period, from the point of view of how adolescents go through the rites of spring.

You went straight from there to California at the age of sixteen.

I came here because it finally had occurred to me that I didn't want to work my way through college. I already thought I was lazy, and I had been working since I was eleven. I scored very high on the college-board examinations, so there was a certain interest in me academically, but I had a poor deportment record, and I never really hit the books or anything. And since my only relative in the whole world was June, who was out here, I came out to look around. I don't think I left Inglewood the first six months that I came to L.A. I went to the race track, went to the pool hall.

June was living there with…

With her children, alone. So I'm wondering what I'm gonna do, and then I got a job in the cartoon department at MGM, and I saw every movie star known to man in that period. I had crushes on Grace Kelly, on Rita Moreno.…

What's striking about your early days is how the first friends you made are still in your life.

[Cartoonists] Bill Hanna and Joe Barbera, through the studio's talent department, got me started at the Players' Ring Theater as an apprentice, and from there I went into classes with Jeff Corey, where I met Robert Towne [screenwriter], Carol Eastman, John Shaner, who wrote *Goin' South*—many of the people who are still in my life today.

Not long after leaving MGM you got the lead in 'Crybaby Killer,' a picture produced by Roger Corman, king of the B movies.

And, I thought, "This is it—I'm meant to be an actor." Then I didn't work for nine months, a year. I didn't make another penny. I'm living on unemployment, this and that, and I went into Marty Landau's acting class, which is where I met Harry Dean Stanton. I'd seen Harry around just as a kind of Porsche-driving, troubled night person. We started hanging out together. I met my ex-wife, Sandra Knight Nicholson, in that class, and Millie Perkins. Again, people still in my life today. Don Devlin and Harry Gittes came into my life around in here, in a house we ran over at Fountain and Gardner, which was the wildest house in Hollywood for a while.

Your family was transplanted to California by now?

By now Mud had come to California; she had contracted a fatal disease. She was sort of nursed by June, and then in the middle of it, irony had it, June got cancer and died before Mud did. I went away on *Ensign Pulver*, and June died while I was flying to Mexico. And the day I got back from that job, six or seven weeks later, was the day my daughter was born.

When did you end up in Laurel Canyon, rooming with Stanton?

When Sandra and I elected to get divorced. I was doing two jobs at the time, and a lot of it was the pressure from that. I hadn't worked for a while, and I remember I was out on the lawn with [actor] John Hackett and we were doing a brake job on my Karmann Ghia, and that day I got two jobs. To write a movie [*The Trip*] and to act in one [*Rebel Rousers*]. The scene in *The Shining* comes out of this time, where I say, "Whenever I'm here and you hear me *typing*..."

The scene where he tells his wife to leave him alone when he's working?

Yeah. Later on, with Stanley Kubrick, we wrote that scene together...sort of the climactic scene of my marriage, because I was under such pressure to get this script out, and I was acting in *Rebel Rousers*, an improvisational movie with Harry

Dean and Bruce Dern. I think it's the only movie of mine I've never seen. Really the whole period was incredibly long hours of work, meeting a writing deadline and getting up and doing an acting job. Most of my divorce is written into *The Trip*.

How old was your daughter when you divorced?

Jennifer was about five.

She's now about twenty-two?

Yeah. She went to high school in Hawaii, and I didn't see much of her. I see a lot of her now. She's starting to work now as an apprentice art director in movies. I'm very impressed by her.

What have you told her about men?

Not too much, because she's been around me a lot, and I don't hide too much from her. So she oughta have a pretty good picture.

The overwork that precipitated your divorce kicked off a very productive period for you.

It was an overlapping thing. I guess from there I was in. There were very few gaps. I'd been part of this very fertile underground film movement that really only existed in this period. I guess we kind of came up above ground and spread out.

I got in *Easy Rider* because I had done all these other nonunion or underground movies. I had produced the westerns [*Ride in the Whirlwind* and *The Shooting*, both in 1965] in the middle of my marriage. Bert Schneider and Bob Rafelson [the coproducers of *Easy Rider*] thought I was a good actor but had me out with them all the time on locations, primarily to help with production.

I knew the movie was going to be huge because I had done a motorcycle movie that did $8 million, $12 million, which was an enormous gross in those days. Dennis Hopper had had one, Peter Fonda had had one. Regular Hollywood hadn't tumbled to this yet. It was a progression in this genre, like *Stagecoach* was to the western—kicked it up one more notch.

That's putting it quite humbly; people at the time thought it defined the war between straight and counterculture.

Yes, my character was a bridging character.

In any event, 'Easy Rider' won Hopper the best new director award at Cannes and made you a hot property. You took full advantage of it.

I was ready. I was seasoned. I knew immediately—well, "I've worked so hard to become a known actor that now that it's happened I've got to follow that line."

What's the one essential thing you would tell a novice actor today?

Well, I wouldn't give him any rules, because it would be like knowing a little law. I try to tell them where the freedom lies, rather than the restraint. This is where unpredictability comes from, this is where the fortunate accident comes from.

Perhaps something like the famous chicken-salad speech in 'Five Easy Pieces'?

First-person autobiography. In those days, I used to do that sort of thing.

Coffee-shop waitresses seemed to bust a lot of chops back then.

Hey, I don't want to hear it *today*.

We've talked a lot about that sterilized, buggy, overlit environment out there, and your hope that the work you do runs counter to that. Is there any other way to be a corrective to that?

Well, there is more that I do. The main thing that I, that you, can do, is *be* it. *Be* it. That's the main thing you can do.

Faces: 1980–1987

Clockwise, from left to right:
Prince
Laurie Anderson
Arnold Schwarzenegger
Sandinistas
Bishop Desmond Tutu
Eurythmics
Richard Pryor

Clockwise, from left to right:
Bill Murray
Sean Penn
Jesse Jackson
Culture Club
Cocaine
Chrissie Hynde
John Cougar Mellencamp
Duran Duran
Cyndi Lauper

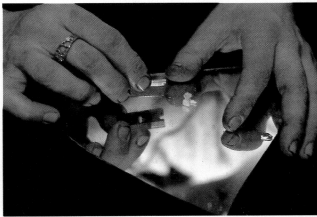

Clockwise, from left to right:
Sade
Tina Turner and Mick Jagger
Run–D.M.C. and Aerosmith
Whitney Houston
Huey Lewis
Max Headroom
Ronald Reagan
David Byrne

460

RICHARD AVEDON
Richard Avedon is one of America's foremost
photographers. Renowned for his work in *Harper's
Bazaar* and *Vogue*, he has also been a contributor to
ROLLING STONE since the publication of "The Family"
in the magazine in 1976. His books include
Observations (text by Truman Capote), *Nothing
Personal* (text by James Baldwin), *Portraits, Avedon:
Photographs 1947-1977* and *In the American West*.
He lives in New York City.

JONATHAN COTT
Jonathan Cott was ROLLING STONE's first London
correspondent; he is currently a contributing editor.
He is also the author and/or editor of fifteen books,
including *Forever Young*, a collection of his
conversations for ROLLING STONE. His most recent
books are *The Search for Omm Sety* and a second
collection of conversations called *Visions and Voices*.
He lives in New York City.

TIMOTHY CROUSE
A former associate editor at ROLLING STONE,
contributing editor Timothy Crouse is the author of
The Boys on the Bus, which grew out of his reports
for ROLLING STONE on the media coverage of the 1972
presidential campaign. He has also written for *The
New Yorker, The Atlantic* and *Esquire*. He lives in
New York City, where he is currently at work on a book
and a musical comedy.

DAVID DALTON
A former London correspondent and contributing
editor at ROLLING STONE, David Dalton is the author
of such books as *James Dean: The Mutant King, The
Rolling Stones: The First Twenty Years* and *Piece of
My Heart: The Life, Times and Legend of Janis
Joplin*. He is currently working on a mythical history
of the early kings of Athens, Greece, called *High
Daddy and Sons*. He lives in New York City with his
wife and son.

O'CONNELL DRISCOLL
Besides his work for ROLLING STONE, O'Connell
Driscoll has contributed articles to such publications
as *Playboy* and *The Los Angeles Times*. He lives in
Los Angeles with his wife and two children.

JOE ESZTERHAS
A former associate editor at ROLLING STONE, Joe
Eszterhas is a screenwriter, whose film credits
include *Jagged Edge, Flashdance* and *FIST*. He lives
in San Rafael, California.

DAVID FELTON
A former associate editor and contributing editor at
ROLLING STONE, David Felton has been an
investigative reporter for *The Los Angeles Times* and
a contributor to *The Washington Post, The
Washington Star* and *Esquire*. He has also written
scripts for such television shows as *Square Pegs* and
Faerie Tale Theatre. He is currently writing
screenplays in New York City.

MITCHELL GLAZER
A former executive editor of *Crawdaddy* magazine,
Mitchell Glazer is currently writing screenplays. He
lives in New York's Greenwich Village with his wife.

DAVID HARRIS
A former contributing editor at ROLLING STONE,
David Harris is the author of *I Shoulda Been Home
Yesterday*, a memoir of his experiences in prison as a
conscientious objector, 1969-1971; he had been a
founder of the Resistance, a draft-resistance group at
Stanford University, where he was a student-body
president in the Sixties. Harris is also the author of
The Last Scam, Dreams Die Hard and *The League*.
He is currently working on a biography of William S.
Paley, which will be published by Bantam Books. He
lives in Mill Valley, California, with his wife and two
children.

GERRI HIRSHEY
ROLLING STONE contributing editor Gerri Hirshey
won the ASCAP Deems Taylor Award in 1984 for her
interview with Michael Jackson. She is also the author
of *Nowhere To Run: The Story of Soul Music* and the
style columnist for *The Washington Post Magazine*.
She lives in New York City.

CHRIS HODENFIELD
Chris Hodenfield has worked in every ROLLING STONE
office—Los Angeles, San Francisco, London,
Washington, D.C., and New York—and has served at
various times as a West Coast editor, film columnist
and contributing editor for the magazine. He is
currently living in L.A. and working on books and
screenplays.

JERRY HOPKINS
ROLLING STONE's first Los Angeles correspondent,
Jerry Hopkins has also been a Europe and Africa
correspondent and a contributing editor for the
magazine. He is the author of seventeen books,
including *No One Here Gets Out Alive*, a biography of
Jim Morrison, which he wrote with Danny Sugerman.
He lives in Honolulu with his wife and three children.

HOWARD KOHN
A former senior editor and Washington bureau editor
for ROLLING STONE, Howard Kohn is the author of
Who Killed Karen Silkwood?, which was based on his
investigative reporting for the magazine. His latest
book, *The Last Farmer* (Summit Books), is based on
another of his ROLLING STONE articles, "My Father's
Farm." He lives in suburban Washington, D.C., with
his wife and two daughters.

ANNIE LEIBOVITZ
ROLLING STONE's chief photographer from 1973 to
1983, Annie Leibovitz started as a part-time
employee at the magazine while still studying at the
San Francisco Art Institute in 1969. Some of her best
work appears in the book *Annie Leibovitz:
Photographs*. She currently contributes to such
publications as *Vanity Fair, Vogue* and *Time*. She lives
in New York City.

KURT LODER
Kurt Loder, a senior editor at ROLLING STONE, is the coauthor with Tina Turner of *I, Tina*. He lives in New York with his wife and son.

MICHAEL LYDON
One of the original editors at ROLLING STONE, Michael Lydon is the author of the books *Rock Folk, Boogie Lightning* and *How To Succeed in Show Business by Really Trying*. He is also a singer, guitarist, composer and comedian. He lives in New York City.

GREIL MARCUS
A former records editor and book columnist at ROLLING STONE, Greil Marcus is currently a contributing editor at the magazine and a music columnist for *The Village Voice* and *Artforum*. He is also the author of *Mystery Train: Images of America in Rock 'n' Roll Music*. He lives in Berkeley, California.

KRISTINE McKENNA
Kristine McKenna has written regularly on the arts for *The Los Angeles Times* for the past ten years. She is a former music editor at *Wet* magazine, and she has contributed to *Musician, Interview* and *The New York Rocker*. She lives in Los Angeles.

P.J. O'ROURKE
P.J. O'Rourke is ROLLING STONE's foreign affairs editor and a former editor of *National Lampoon*. Some of his best articles have been collected in the book *Republican Party Reptile: The Confessions, Adventures, Essays, and (other) Outrages of P.J. O'Rourke*. He lives in New Hampshire.

CHARLES PERRY
The first full-time paid employee at ROLLING STONE (April 1968), Charles Perry subsequently served as a copy chief, poetry editor and contributing editor at the magazine. He is also the author of *The Haight-Ashbury: A History* and a restaurant columnist for *The Los Angeles Times*. He lives in Los Angeles.

FRED SCHRUERS
Fred Schruers, a former associate editor at ROLLING STONE, is currently a contributing editor at the magazine. He also writes for *GQ, The Village Voice* and *The Washington Post*. He lives in the New York area.

SCOTT SPENCER
Novelist Scott Spencer is the author of *Endless Love, Waking the Dead* and the forthcoming *Secret Anniversaries*. He lives in upstate New York with his wife and two children.

RALPH STEADMAN
English illustrator Ralph Steadman began his series of collaborations with Hunter S. Thompson for ROLLING STONE with "Fear and Loathing in Las Vegas." His work has also appeared in the books *Sigmund Freud, America, I, Leonardo* and his autobiography, *Between the Eyes*. He's currently working on *America II* and a book about God. He lives in Kent, England.

HARRY SWIFT
Harry Swift is the pseudonym of a prominent yet sometimes modest man of letters, who lives in New York City.

HUNTER S. THOMPSON
Hunter S. Thompson has been ROLLING STONE's national affairs editor since 1970. His reports for the magazine have spawned such books as *Fear and Loathing in Las Vegas, Fear and Loathing on the Campaign Trail* and *The Great Shark Hunt*. He is also the author of *Hell's Angels*. He lives in Aspen, Colorado.

DAVID WEIR
A former associate editor at ROLLING STONE, David Weir is the author of the books *Circle of Poison* (with Mark Schapiro) and *Raising Hell* (with Dan Noyes). His latest, *The Bhopal Syndrome*, is published by Sierra Club Books. Weir is also a cofounder and executive director of the Center for Investigative Reporting in San Francisco, where he lives with his wife and three children.

TIMOTHY WHITE
A former managing editor of *Crawdaddy* and a former senior editor at ROLLING STONE, Timothy White is the author of several books, including *Catch a Fire: The Life of Bob Marley* and *Rock Stars*. He is currently writing a social history of Southern California. He lives in New York City.

TOM WOLFE
The chief architect of New Journalism in the Sixties, Tom Wolfe is the author of such contemporary classics as *The Electric Kool-Aid Acid Test* and *Radical Chic & Mau-Mauing the Flak Catchers*. In 1973 he began a series of articles on the NASA astronauts for ROLLING STONE, which eventually became the book, and later the movie, *The Right Stuff*. From the summer of 1984 to the summer of 1985, he wrote his first novel, *The Bonfire of the Vanities*, chapter by chapter in consecutive issues of ROLLING STONE; the book is published by Farrar, Straus and Giroux. Wolfe lives in New York City with his wife and two children.

CHARLES M. YOUNG
A former associate editor at ROLLING STONE, Charles M. Young is currently a music columnist for *Playboy*, a contributor to *Musician* and a news writer for MTV. His first book, *Blowin' Chunks: The Incompleat History of Punk Rock and Other Stuff*, will be published by Doubleday/Dolphin. He lives in New York City.

Praise for these other novels of delightful contemporary romance by *USA Today* bestselling author
Kieran Kramer

YOU'RE SO FINE

"Kieran Kramer writes a sexy, sassy Southern romance with heart."
—Jill Shalvis, *New York Times* bestselling author

"Kramer dishes up another delightful contemporary romance that is deftly seasoned with sassy Southern wit, snappy dialogue, and plenty of smoldering sexual chemistry. Readers who fell in love with Susan Elizabeth Phillips' *Dream a Little Dream* (1998) or *Ain't She Sweet?* (2004) will definitely want to add Kramer's latest sexy, sparkling, spot-on love story to their reading lists."   —*Booklist*

"Filled with smart, believable characters and fresh, witty storytelling. A sexy, poignant romance wrapped in Southern charm and lightly accented with Hollywood glamour."
—*Kirkus Reviews*

"A superbly written, powerful, and touching book."
—*Fresh Fiction*

SWEET TALK ME

"The perfect combination of good-natured sass, sultry sexual tension, and hint of Southern crazy. I loved this book."
—Tracy Brogan, author of *Crazy Little Thing*

"A sweetly sexy love story that is everything a romance should be . . . a knockout!"   —*Booklist* (starred review)

"The banter between these characters was fun to read and I loved the tension that flowed between them . . . a great read to lose yourself in for a few hours."

—*Night Owl Reviews* (Top Pick)

"Readers who enjoy works by Nora Roberts and Luanne Rice will want to give Kramer a try. This reviewer predicts that the beaches this summer will be covered with copies of *Sweet Talk Me*."

—*Library Journal* (starred review)

Christmas
AT TWO
LOVE LANE

KIERAN KRAMER

St. Martin's Paperbacks

This is a work of fiction. All of the characters, organizations, and events portrayed in this novel are either products of the author's imagination or are used fictitiously.

CHRISTMAS AT TWO LOVE LANE

Copyright © 2017 by Kieran Kramer.

All rights reserved.

For information address St. Martin's Press, 175 Fifth Avenue, New York, NY 10010.

ISBN: 978-1-250-11104-3

Our books may be purchased in bulk for promotional, educational, or business use. Please contact your local bookseller or the Macmillan Corporate and Premium Sales Department at 1-800-221-7945, ext. 5442, or by e-mail at MacmillanSpecialMarkets@macmillan.com.

Printed in the United States of America

St. Martin's Paperbacks edition / October 2017

St. Martin's Paperbacks are published by St. Martin's Press, 175 Fifth Avenue, New York, NY 10010.

10 9 8 7 6 5 4 3 2 1

This story is for every woman who needs reminding she's already beautiful—right here, right now.

"You can be gorgeous at thirty, charming at forty, and irresistible for the rest of your life."
—Coco Chanel

ACKNOWLEDGMENTS

To my editor, Eileen Rothschild: You're a rock star! You've made this book better in every way, and your unflagging support has meant the world to me. I'd also like to thank Jennifer Enderlin, who has always had my back. Jen, your dedication to bringing the world wonderful books inspires me to write true and hard, to fight for my dreams. To Annelise Robey, my sunshine of an agent, I owe a huge debt of gratitude for believing in this journey I'm walking. I never feel alone, thanks to you.

I'd also like to thank The Sustainability Institute of Charleston, SC, for providing me with an idea for my story and for making it their goal to transform our local community for this generation and the next. To learn more about their work to reduce our environmental footprint and conserve energy, please visit http://sustainabilityinstitutesc .org. Thanks, especially, to the lovely Katherine Westmoreland Richards for her dedication to this effort.

May women continue to strive to be heard in the world of letters. Thanks to all the female writers who have come before me and made my path possible.

CHAPTER ONE

Macy Frost was a sixth-generation Southern belle, a hard-working business owner, and an avid college basketball fan—and she wasn't fond of pears. But she liked what pears *meant* on that sunny, cold afternoon in December, when the sound of Mariah Carey singing her famous Christmas anthem drifted in from Roastbusters, the tiny coffeehouse at the top of Love Lane.

Pears meant success!

When you were a founding partner at the most prosperous matchmaking agency in Charleston, South Carolina, a town made for romance, lots of satisfied clients sent holiday gifts. And since Thanksgiving, Macy had received *four* Harry & David fruit samplers, *three* boxes of Godiva chocolates, and a wall calendar featuring twelve state-of-the-art refrigerators from Joe, the Lowcountry's most prosperous household appliance dealer.

Joe's business calendar wasn't very exciting, but she loved it anyway—because he was married now with two kids, thanks to Macy's matchmaking skills, and Cupid.

She had an inside track, actually, when it came to the game of love. Thomas Winston Frost, the first of her ancestors to settle in Charleston in 1703, declared in a letter to his children that he was a direct descendant of Cupid himself. Thomas was a successful judge, well-loved, and skilled in matchmaking. He found a spouse for every one of his seven siblings and eight children.

So Macy liked to believe that she was Cupid's direct descendant too, and took a special delight in wearing Thomas's beautiful gold signet ring stamped with the family crest he'd brought over from England. The crest was emblazoned with a heart and arrow and the family motto in Latin: *"Dives in caritate,"* which meant "Rich in love."

The Frost family tree was filled with people who had a spark for matchmaking. Macy's father, her grandmother, and her great-grandmother were considered gifted in the love-and-marriage department. From the time she was a little girl, Macy had wanted to be Cupid's assistant herself.

So what that she hadn't found her soulmate yet? She'd barely noticed! She was having too much fun to worry about it.

That day—the pear day—she sat on the front edge of her massive desk, propped herself on her palm, slung one booted leg over the other, and bit into a juicy Anjou. A few pearls of juice trickled down her chin, and she let out a fake moan, fake because pear skin was always a little too bitter for her. But she didn't care. She wanted to show Oscar, her orange tabby cat sprawled like a playboy across the desk blotter behind her, what luscious, in-your-face triumph looked like.

"Must be a really good pear," a dry masculine voice announced from the door.

She stopped chewing. Whoever it was had said "pear" like someone from the Northeast—New York or Boston— and she was charmed. The voice woke her up the way an invigorating shower did, or an extra firm handshake. It occurred to her that she might not be having as much fun as she thought. She might be bored. Bored senseless! Showing off to a cat! Being happy about refrigerator calendars!

She turned toward the door.

A man channeling a young George Clooney—down to the amused expression in his eye—stood there in a black overcoat and a gray pinstriped suit, one broad shoulder on the doorjamb and his hands in his coat pockets. His bold stare beneath those jet eyebrows wasn't exactly proper, according to Charleston standards. But Macy liked it, although she was loath to admit it. She tried not to imagine him lounging next to her and feeding her grapes on a long barge sailing down the Nile and then ravishing her beneath a blazing hot sun. But she gave up and let the thought bloom while she took in the rest of him.

Beneath his open coat and jacket, his tapered waist and flat stomach appealed to her. So did his black hair, cut above his collar but slightly unruly at his temples. And there was the merest glimmer of a five o'clock shadow on his jaw, which looked chiseled out of desert sandstone. Damn him for being so handsome and virile when she was making a fool of herself with Oscar who, let's be frank, was one of her very best friends.

"So you're Macy Frost." Sexy. Bossy. Two words she'd write at the top of his file.

"Who are you?" She wouldn't give him the satisfaction of confirming his assumption, not until he introduced himself.

"Deacon Banks." He crossed the threshold.

Without asking!

She put down the pear, slid her bottom off the front of her desk, and quickly maneuvered herself behind it, picking up a pen along the way to look official, busy, and unbothered, never once totally giving him her back.

Her first-impressions meter registered off the charts

already. The man had spoken only six words, and already she wondered if there was a woman in Charleston who could take him on. She thought of Evelyn, the hard-edged, glamorous librarian at the main library on Calhoun Street, who was smarter than everyone and opinionated. Evelyn could hold her own with Deacon Banks.

But could they be a love match?

No, Macy could see that already. Evelyn would hate his gorgeousness. Evelyn would want a noble, hawk-nosed man with a slight stoop signifying his deep brooding nature.

Beneath his impressive garb, Mr. Banks—Macy guessed—was all action, a guy's guy who played pick-up basketball after work and got hot wings delivered on a regular basis. At the most, he might have a passing knowledge of excellent wine to impress women and season tickets to the symphony. But he'd go just to network and would leave at intermission, or pass his tickets around to clients.

Yet somehow he'd figured out a way to get around the very precise Miss Thing at her antique King Louis XV *bureau du roi* and matching strawberry-silk-covered chair in the parlor off the front hall.

Macy stood straight and told herself that she was one hundred percent back in charge. Maybe Mr. Banks was here to sell her something. . . .

Instantly, she felt calmer. And disappointed.

"Nice place." His six-foot-oneish, solid frame cast a shadow across the Persian rug as he sauntered all the way up to her desk and scratched Oscar's ears.

Oscar was a terrible security cat. He burst into loud purrs and shut his eyes.

I'm sorry, but—Macy almost said but didn't because Ella Mancini and Greer Jones, her business partners, had made a three-way pact with her not to apologize so much.

"Whatever you're selling, I'm not interested. Miss Thing should have told you—"

"I'm not selling." Deacon Banks stayed flat-footed where he was, carelessly rubbing Oscar's forehead, his fingers smooth and steady, not twitching the way hers were.

"Oh," she answered.

"Is there really someone here named Miss Thing?"

"Yes." Macy wouldn't say more. Couldn't say more. She was tongue-tied.

"This guy," her unscheduled visitor said of Oscar, who was still preening, "looks almost exactly like the cat I had growing up. King Bean. The best mouser ever."

Mous-ah evah.

His accent was adorable, and he liked Oscar. And he'd named his cat something as curious and likeable as King Bean. But she wouldn't ask him more. She had a job to do.

She nudged Oscar off the desk. "So what is it you want, Mr. Banks?" She wouldn't ask him to sit. And she wouldn't sit, either.

He sat anyway, in front of her desk, in another beautiful vintage French chair, this one upholstered in an eye-popping, high-end, turquoise-saffron-and-white-patchwork fabric. He leaned forward, his hands curved and dangling between his knees, like he was on a basketball bench waiting to get called into the game.

Which appealed to her, of course. Anything about basketball did.

"I hear you're a social butterfly with a local pedigree," he said. "Just the person I need to talk to."

Wow. His friendly tone probably got him a lot of attention and phone numbers from women in New York or Boston or New Haven or wherever he was from. But it didn't affect Macy. At least not the way he probably hoped.

"I *do* have a lot of friends," she answered him. "People

I care deeply about. And yes, my family has been in Charleston a long time. But I'm earning my own way in this world. Social butterflies and pedigrees? *U-G-H,* ugh to terms like that."

He arched one brow. "You really had to spell that out?"

"It felt good to, yes." A shudder would have done as well, but she was a Southerner, which meant she loved being a little over the top when the situation called for it. "Now why are you here, exactly?"

"I'm in town until the end of December"—his eyes told her he was conflicted about this fact—"and I'd like to line up a string of striking, sophisticated dates. Good conversationalists. Women with style. It would also help if they have serious social cache here in Charleston."

"I'm sorry." She couldn't wait to tell him why. "We're not a dating service. We're in the serious business of finding people the love of their lives. Nothing less."

Take *that,* Mr. Banks!

"I'm not interested in love." He spoke with utter assurance. "This arrangement is strictly temporary, a way to burn time while I'm here. I'd like to hire you to screen potential candidates. I've got an hour to spare today to write up the contract. *This* hour."

She should have told him guys who talk like that fall the hardest. But she was busy being irritated at his indifference to her actual skill set and her business's core mission, of which she was very proud.

"Please take a look at that wall." She flung a well-manicured hand (nails painted in Deborah Lippmann's "It's Raining Men") toward a mosaic of frames holding photos of couples who'd married as a result of working with her. " 'Strictly temporary' and 'burning time' don't match what we do at Two Love Lane."

He gave the wall a cursory glance. "But you're a businesswoman. You make deals."

"Yes, I *am* a businesswoman. In fact, we have a special metric system here at Two Love Lane that's garnered national attention."

"Oh, yeah?"

She loved talking about what she and her partners did. "We developed unique algorithms that rate compatibility and soulmate status to such an accurate degree, we've been featured on the *Today* show. So now we have clients from all over the United States. Soon we're going international. We had to, after a European prince and a few Hollywood people showed interest."

"*No.*"

"Yes." She had to admit, she was extremely excited about their royal and celebrity connections. Even the Chamber of Commerce was proud of Two Love Lane and had given them a special award at their last luncheon. If Mr. Banks was being sarcastic with that *no,* she'd show him to the door.

"Can I get in on this?" he asked. "Buy some stock? Become a partner?"

Oh, good. He sounded impressed. "I'm afraid not," she said. "I already have two partners."

Get in line, is what she really wanted to say. Now that they were doing well, they fielded calls from interested backers all the time.

"Sure," he said, "but do these partners share your obvious passion for the brand?"

Macy had to chuckle. "Ella has more passion in her pinkie finger than you'll find in a whole room full of suits. When she's not here, she's at the Dock Street Theatre. She loves to act and has a special fondness for musicals. You'd think she'd be all about Ella, since she gets a lot of lead roles. But she's not. She reads people like no one else."

"Whoa. I'd like to meet this Ella. And your other partner?"

"Greer is a total brainiac dressed like a Bond girl. Every charlatan's worst nightmare."

"You're not presuming *I'm* a charlatan, right?"

"I never presume."

Mr. Banks grinned. "I'm enjoying our chat, Miss Frost. May I ask another question?"

"Of course." She was enjoying the Q&A session too, although she didn't want to admit it.

"Why are you three in the matchmaking biz?" His furrowed brow made him look terribly serious all of a sudden.

"That's easy," she said with genuine feeling. "We believe in love, and we can't imagine doing anything else."

"Yes, but"—he leaned forward—"I can see in your eyes there's something more."

She was shocked. There *was* something more. How had he seen that? "You're astute, Mr. Banks."

"Why, thank you."

She decided to be cryptically honest, if that was possible. "One of us broke someone's heart really badly. Matchmaking relieves the guilt. Another one of us had her heart broken, and it derailed her professionally. Connecting other people for a living makes her feel empowered again. And the third one of us has never truly been in love because she holds back. She immerses herself in the love business to live vicariously."

"You won't say who's who?"

"I'd rather not." Inside, she still felt off-kilter. He was looking at her as if he could see right through her. Could he tell which one of the three she was?

"Cancel your lunch date," he said. "I'll take you out."

That well-defined mouth, tipped up on one side, hinted at fun. Fun was not a good idea. Exhaustion was Macy's constant companion lately, but she had to stay focused on riding this wave of success Two Love Lane was experiencing. And she certainly wasn't going to whine about it or cave, in any way, to anybody.

"No thanks." She went to the door and opened it, her hand holding the glass knob so hard that her Cupid signet ring dug into her finger. "I'm afraid I'm out of time to chat. Thanks for coming by. And good luck."

He gave a sexy shrug. "I'll pay double your fee today after I lay out more details about our potential arrangement at lunch. Work with me, Miss Frost. I don't usually have to beg, so I can't promise my offer will be open for long."

She was hungry, and she loved the idea of adding a big, fat sum to Two Love Lane's PayPal account. But, "The answer is still *no*," she said.

There was the merest beat of silence.

"Got it." He grinned. "If you change your mind, I'll be at Fast and French."

Her favorite local lunch spot, on Broad Street. A little hole-in-the-wall straight out of Paris, with a bar where people dined elbow-to-elbow and a few high tables squeezed in the back. Most tourists didn't know about it.

"I won't change my mind." No way, no how, even though she adored the croq monsieur and the daily soup, which was never overly salted—the hallmark of an excellent chef, in her mind. She always told her friends it was the hallmark of an excellent chef, and they were tired of hearing her repeat herself.

It was one of her weird quirks, but everyone had a few, didn't they?

"Come and sit with me anyway," said Deacon Banks. "I'd love to hear more about your fair city."

She loved how he said "fair city." She loved anyone who loved Charleston. Nevertheless, she said, "I'm busy. But thank you."

He stopped right next to her and shot her a mysterious,

testosterone-infused smile, like something James Bond would bestow upon a woman he wanted to seduce. But since everyone knew James wanted to seduce everyone, Macy wasn't biting.

She frowned up at him.

"Good-bye, Miss Frost." He sounded as if he was in a good mood. Unfazed by her frown. Excited to go to Fast and French by himself to partake of their excellent soup, which he wouldn't appreciate the way she did, because she could tell he was a hot-wings man, through and through.

After he left, Oscar walked a figure eight through her legs. "Sorry," she said, "he's not my type."

But something compelled her to throw on her favorite white A-line winter coat, zip through Miss Thing's parlor—which she noticed was empty—and fly down the front brick steps and through the iron gate. She told herself she was running in her boots down a cobblestone alley—risking two twisted ankles—only because she had to have a bowl of that deliciously seasoned Fast and French soup. And if she happened to tell Deacon Banks it wasn't overly salted, then so be it. He'd simply have to listen.

CHAPTER TWO

Deacon heard the measured, gritty tap of heels-on-sidewalk behind him and hoped it was who he thought it was. Last he'd seen her, Macy Frost had turned him down for lunch. Footsteps could belong to anyone, right? Why did he think these particular footsteps had extra oomph? Character? Pizazz? Why did he think they sounded exactly the way Macy Frost's footsteps would sound? He didn't know her well enough to guess.

But he was right.

It was slightly ridiculous that he was not only satisfied but *happy* that she fell into step next to him. She looked like she'd just come off a runway in Paris in over-the-knee boots, her sunshiney blonde hair caught up in a high ponytail. He couldn't help thinking that there was no way she could have Ubered two blocks over that fast. *She'd had to have run to catch up to him.*

The idea appealed to the caveman in him. It was hot. *She* was hot. Time to get a grip. Be the savvy businessman he was and not a guy in heat.

"I thought I'd join you, after all." She sounded cool and relaxed, but he knew better. Her cheeks were a little flushed from her haste to meet up with him.

"Nice." He'd learned long ago that when you want to find out about someone, let them do the talking. Besides, he could listen to her all day. Her Southern accent was light, elegant even. But she also had game. From the athletic way she carried herself, he could tell she'd have been the girl to go climb trees with the boys in the neighborhood. Or beat them in a sprint across the school playground.

She had a long, sexy stride. They walked in silence for a few beats, and then she said, "My client was sick. She had to cancel."

"Oh."

"And none of my friends could go to lunch at such short notice."

He was amused. "That's the most unflattering *yes* to an invitation to lunch I've ever received. But I'll take it."

She dropped her head for a second—abashed, he supposed—then looked back up again, keeping her gaze straight ahead. "I know I said I wasn't interested in finding out more about you. But I've changed my mind."

"Just like that."

"Yes." *Click-clack-click-clack* went those boots.

"No explanation?" This walk down Broad Street was the best thing he'd done in weeks. The sun was out, he was with a beautiful woman, and all was well with the world. After lunch he'd worry about business.

She shrugged. "I want you to hire me."

"You do?"

She nodded. "But on my terms. I want a shot at finding you your soulmate. I know time is short. You're here a month?"

"Leaving New Year's Day. So less than, actually."

Her chin came up. "I think I can do it, even if you don't. Everybody has a soulmate."

"Do *you*?"

"Somewhere."

"Ah." They kept walking. "On what basis do you believe all this stuff?"

"I just know."

"Woman's intuition?"

"Perhaps." She chuckled. "But there's more. I'm good at what I do. I see connections other people don't."

"You're very interesting, Miss Frost." Understatement of the year for him. "But my answer to your proposition is no. *N-O*, no."

She gave him the side-eye. He could do the spelling thing too.

"I don't see the benefits of having a soulmate," he said. "I mean, there's Tinder. Not that I've used it. Finding companionship isn't a problem for me if I get lonely."

"I get that. But there's more to love than sex."

"I wouldn't know."

"You've never been in love?"

He shrugged. "Not more than puppy love." He was a busy man.

"You must have gotten hurt to be so certain real love isn't for you. What happened?"

"That's awfully personal." Let her feel nosy. Maybe she'd move on to a different topic.

"My interest is entirely professional," she said. "Everything I can learn about the human condition makes me a better matchmaker."

"For other people. Not for me. Although the offer is still open for you to line me up some dates."

"Just tell me why you don't believe in love."

"Let's talk about football. Been to a Panthers game?"

A fire hydrant and a parked red Beemer later, she said, "Mr. Banks, come *on*," and cast a glance at him from beneath those thick lashes, her mouth turned up just a little.

Southern girls and their charm! He hated to admit it,

but he was a sucker for it. At least her brand of it. "All right, then," he said. "I'll tell you why I don't believe in love. But only if you call me Deacon."

She laughed. "You can call me Macy. But it'll cost you. You need to tell me—"

"Why I don't believe in love," he finished for her. "Okay, here goes. Four of my good friends are already on their second wives or divorced from their first wives. None of them are over thirty-five."

"Interesting."

She didn't act shocked or anything. Deacon supposed matchmakers must hear all kinds of stories. "One of those guys called me the other day and said he's ready to divorce wife number two and move on to number three."

She shook her head. "Maybe it only means you run with a crowd that doesn't understand that love and commitment feed on each other. Hang around different people."

He wasn't used to people talking back to him, but he liked it. "These are good guys."

"I don't doubt it." A wintery gust of air swept down the street, and she dug her hands deep into her coat pockets. "But when social media makes you think there's always someone better around the corner, it's no wonder romance is dying."

"From a business perspective, it makes no sense to me that you'd want to stay in a dying trade."

"A calling is something you have to do, even if you don't get paid for it. That's what matchmaking is for me. I make what money I can. I enjoy what I do."

She sounded so serene, so confident, saying that. There was a part of him—a very stupid, illogical part—that envied her. But he'd never say it out loud. Because then he'd have to admit to himself that the privileged life he led— one he worked seven days a week to maintain—wasn't perfect the way it was.

Half a block later, they were at Fast and French. Inside, a huddle of suits and a few hipster types had their backs smashed up against the storefront window.

"Don't worry," she said at the door, "we'll only wait about five minutes, ten at the most. People get in and out. They need to get back to class or work."

So did he. Besides running his empire via phone, he had to deal with the problem of his aunt, her strange mission, and whether or not he could save her from herself. But it was hard to focus on the day's goals when they waited elbow-to-elbow near the cash register in a gaggle of customers.

Deacon didn't like the besotted thoughts running through his head when he was near Macy. She smelled like flowers. He found it much more intoxicating than the fragrance of bread wafting his way and the rich scent of French press coffee in the carafes scattered across the counter. That flower smell made him want to pull out her chair for her and charm her with his wit and intelligence—before sleeping with her and even *after.* . . .

You're not going to sleep with her. Idiot.

He hated his conscience. It always showed up when he least wanted it to, but he nearly always succeeded at shutting it up.

Five minutes later, they were seated at a high-top table with two older women, and placing their order.

"And two wine punches each, please," Macy told the waiter with equanimity, then turned to Deacon. "We'll drink the first one so fast that we'll need a second one right away. You'll see."

Slamming wine punches, whatever those were. Maybe that was hard-core in Charleston. In Manhattan, it would be a double martini at his plate. "I'm willing to give it a try," he said to be nice.

The waiter came quickly with their four punches, one

of which they each downed immediately, much to the consternation of the elderly woman beside Macy.

"I like it." Deacon wasn't lying. "It's refreshing, the way Hawaiian Punch was when I was a kid. But not too sweet. Just right."

"I know," Macy said, out of breath as she stuck a paper straw into her second punch.

"So how'd you get into matchmaking?"

"It's a long story." She winked at him.

Wow. He thought women winked to get you to shut up only in old Cary Grant movies. And he'd never seen sucking on a straw as a speech-avoidance strategy, but she worked it, and it was hot.

"Got it," he said. "No prying."

"Someday I'll tell you." She smiled like *Mona Lisa*.

She was beautiful, with a champagne sparkle in her light brown eyes, which he'd immediately been captivated by at her office, especially by the golden rim around her pupils.

When their food came a few minutes later, he enjoyed seeing her expression brighten at the oblong oval platters with bowls—soup-and-sandwich combos—placed in front of them.

She leaned closer. "Try your soup."

"I will." He also had a gooey croq monsieur alongside it. He took a bite of that first. "Mmmm. Amazing."

"It is, isn't it?" She bit her gorgeous lower lip.

"The best croq monsieur I've ever had outside of France."

"Told you this place was good." She ladled a spoon of soup into her mouth, and a blissful expression came over her face.

God. She had no idea how alluring she was. None. He started thinking even wickeder thoughts than the ones already in his head.

"This soup," she said, "it's really . . ."

"Let me try mine." They'd both gotten the daily special, curried lentil.

She stopped talking, and her eyes widened as he sampled it—she seemed a little intense, actually. He couldn't put his finger on what was going on.

"The hallmark of . . ." she began as if she were delivering a very important fact, but another diner brushed by her chair.

"Sorry, Macy," the guy said, sliding behind her.

Macy had to yank her coat toward her so it wouldn't fall on the floor or dislodge her purse, which was hanging over the chair. "No problem, Frank," she replied cheerfully.

Deacon held out his hand. "Deacon Banks."

Frank shook it. "Frank Hathaway. Take care of this girl. Thanks to her, I met the love of my life."

"Is that so?" Deacon saw Macy go pink.

"Macy's the best." Frank grinned and moved past them.

"You've got fans," Deacon told her.

"Frank's a sweetheart. He used to be such a wild man, too."

"Oh?"

"He had a seriously roving eye when he was single."

What man didn't?

"I almost despaired of him," Macy went on. "And now his wife Bitsy's about to have their second set of twins. *Love*"—she stabbed a finger on the table, like a CEO making a point—"turned him around."

Huh. There was no romance, no frills in her tone. She was all business.

It was true that Frank hadn't acted as if he'd had a ball and chain around his ankle. But weren't pregnant women grouchy? And how did one handle *two* sets of twins? What happened to poker nights? And sleeping in late? And sex whenever you wanted it and with whomever you wanted?

"I've never had soup this good," Deacon said to avoid thinking about the plight of married men, which surely involved changing dirty diapers and buying tampons.

Macy stopped adjusting her purse and coat and swung her gaze back to him, her face glowing. "Really? You like the soup?"

"Usually it's too salty, no matter where I go—"

"Whether it's New York or Chicago," she said. "I've never been to L.A., or Paris, but I'll bet you—"

"I've been to both." He ate another spoonful. "Even in Paris, they oversalt the soup. Okay, maybe a Michelin-starred restaurant on the Left Bank didn't. But everywhere else . . ."

She sat silently looking at him.

"Are you okay?"

"I'm fine." She wore an endearing grin that made Deacon ridiculously happy.

"I'm not a foodie," he warned her. "I don't take pictures of what I eat and put them on Instagram." Heaven help him if he ever did.

"Neither do I." She kind of squirmed in her seat. "But you have to admit, perfectly seasoned soup on a cold day is one of life's great pleasures."

"True. So is good wine." He did like wine, so he wasn't lying. But when it came to life's greatest pleasures, nothing was better than sex. Especially outside in a field in the daylight. Or down a dirt road in the cab of a pickup truck.

Neither of which he'd done. It was cold up North. And people didn't drive pickups. He had the sudden creative longing to do those things in Charleston with Macy, but there were no fields and an awful lot of Beemers and Lexuses. Plus, she might not be into him like that, and he'd better stop thinking about sex and Macy and pickup trucks before he drove himself crazy.

She took a hearty bite of her open-faced sandwich, smeared with chopped green olives, and chewed with the impatient intensity of someone who really loved to eat but also loved to talk. After another provocative sip of her second glass of wine punch through that straw, she said, "What exactly do you do?"

"I buy tech companies. Boutique acquisitions are my favorite."

"How did you get into that?"

He winked. "It's a long story." He loved giving her a taste of her own medicine.

"Oh." She was a good sport, playing along. "So you're here on business?"

"No, actually. I'm with my aunt Fran," he said, "to help her settle in. I'll stay in touch with the New York office every day, but I'm officially on vacation."

"You're here for your *aunt*?"

"Yes."

"She moved *here*?"

"She did. You seem surprised."

"Not surprised. But I thought you were here for *you*. It never occurred to me—"

"That I have family? And that I'd do stuff on their behalf?"

"Um, yeah. I guess."

"I do have a heart."

"As you should," she replied thinly, not willing to be apologetic but knowing she should be, which he found amusing. "Tell me more about her."

"Sure." He leaned closer as the noise in the room rose to a crescendo. "She grew up on Staten Island, but she's lived the past thirty-five years on the Upper East Side of Manhattan. She's a recently retired talk show host with a penchant for saying, 'Really? *Really?*' to all her guests. I guess you'd say she's famous for that. She occasionally acts in films and commercials and runs her social circle like a dictator. But she needs new pastures. She saw—"

"Wait. Are you saying your aunt is *Fran Banks*?"

"I am."

"Oh. My. *God*. She's interviewed all the biggest personalities in politics and show biz! About personal things. She can be very hard on people."

"That's her shtick. She's quite a talent, don't you think? She has five Emmys to prove it."

Macy clapped her hand to her forehead. "I don't believe this. She's interviewed the president! And so many of the cast from *Game of Thrones*! She even hosted *Saturday Night Live!* Not once but twice."

"Three times, actually," he said.

"She wasn't a family-oriented entertainer—"

"For a daytime talk show host, she kept the bleep censor alive and well, didn't she?"

She laughed. "How did she get away with kissing every man on her show? She'd lay one right on them! No one seemed to mind. I don't understand it."

"Me either," he said. "She gets away with a lot."

"She's doing adult-diaper commercials right now."

"That she is."

"They're pretty good, actually. Considering the topic. She never shies away from the awkward stuff."

"She's a brave lady."

"I had no idea she had a family. She talked about her dogs but never about her family."

"For such a nosy person, she's pretty private," Deacon said. "But let's get back to why she's here. She saw a reality show about Charleston. It has lots of drama and good-looking people in big houses."

"You mean *Bless Your Heart*?"

"That's it. And now she wants to be a Southern belle

six months of the year, from October to March. So she bought a condo."

Macy moved closer. "You're kidding."

"No." He liked being almost nose-to-nose with her. "Aunt Fran claims she also bought this place because some olden-days Bankses are from here. I kinda think she's making it up."

Macy thought for a second. "I don't know of any Bankses in our local history books or even present time, believe it or not, and it's obviously a common name. You can't ask your father?"

"No. He died when I was two."

"I'm sorry."

"Yeah. So did my mother."

"Oh no. I'm *really* sorry."

"It's okay," he said. "I don't remember them. It was a car accident. Aunt Fran's my father's sister. She brought me up. She's the only family I have."

"Wow. She did that with the big career she had?"

"Yes. And you probably know she's had her share of divorces, too."

"Oh yes," Macy said. "None of them famous, interestingly enough."

"She has a thing for doctors. She's a closet hypochondriac and fell in love with hers all the time."

"Really?" Macy chuckled. "So you had step-uncles? Did any of these doctors become father figures?"

"Nah. They never stuck around long enough. The craziest part is that Aunt Fran says she still believes in love."

"How many doctor husbands did she have?"

"Four."

Macy smiled. "I like that she still believes."

He shook his head. "I don't get the fairy tale obsession. And honestly? I think it's a sham. People who love love are as self-interested as the rest of us."

"Hmmpph. You're so cynical."

"With good reason. This is the important detail I didn't tell you in your office because, quite frankly, it's embarrassing." He got up close to her ear, which was like a small seashell, perfect and delicate, and lowered his voice. "Aunt Fran wants me to marry a Charleston girl. Not for love, although that's what she claims. She thinks if I marry into a local family, she'll become society's darling down here."

Macy drew back, staring at him with those big brown eyes. "Excuse me?"

He laughed. "The plain and simple fact is that Aunt Fran needs the spotlight, even in retirement. She wants to be Scarlett O'Hara's mother-in-law. Those dates you'll set up for me—which you and I will make sure go absolutely nowhere—are my Christmas gift to her."

That was it. Plain and simple.

CHAPTER THREE

So there you had it. His aunt wanted Deacon Banks to marry into Charleston society. Macy thought it was a crazy plan, honestly, considering how tight that group was and how difficult it was to get in—except for the fact that it just might work.

Sure, Deacon was "from off," as they said around town, but he was also rich, good-looking, charming, and funny. Maybe—just maybe—she could find him his own Scarlett O'Hara.

"Wow, so that's why you came to my office." She remembered how determined he'd been to get his way, and now she saw his persistence in a new, more forgiving light. "You're doing this for your aunt."

"When she's happy, I'm happier too," he admitted. "So I told her I'd go see you at Two Love Lane. She was ecstatic. But she can't ever know my heart's not in it."

"Oh." Macy didn't like that. She stirred her straw slowly in her glass and tried to think what to do.

"What?"

"Well, if you're faking it, she'll be disappointed in the end. So what good is this supposed Christmas present?"

"It buys me time."

Kara and Kiki Montagu squeezed past and stared at
Deacon. He ignored them, and Macy pretended not to see
them. They always asked her to their designer trunk shows,
where they'd try to sell her a five-hundred-dollar blouse
or a thousand-dollar dress. All her money went to her
house and business, so T.J. Maxx was her jam—that and
Goodwill for the ball gowns she needed each year during
the debutante season.

"My aunt," Deacon continued seamlessly, "has a fragile ego, like a lot of celebrities. She thinks she doesn't have
much to offer outside the TV business, and everyone will
find out she's a phony. If she stays busy this month, she'll
figure out she doesn't need me to marry a Charleston girl to
become a success here."

"I've got great news," Macy said. "She's a slam dunk
for fitting in here. She's interesting. Entertaining. Smart.
Not to mention well-connected professionally. Those qualities will serve her well in Charleston."

"I'm happy to hear that."

His grin jolted Macy down to her nude Victoria's Secret
seamless low-cut briefs. She came to a decision. "I'm a
businesswoman too—as you've pointed out."

"Yes?"

"So I'm renewing that proposition I made to you on our
walk here. I'll find you these dates you're looking for. Per
your wishes, I'll tell them you're only interested in having
fun while you're visiting your aunt for a few weeks, a fact
I'll make very clear because I don't want anyone's heart
broken. But I'm going to do my very best—for your aunt's
sake and my own—to find you The One."

"The One?" He put finger quotes around the phrase.

"Your Scarlett O'Hara." She sucked on her straw again,
draining her glass a little noisily. "There's a caveat, of
course. I'm accepting your offer to pay me double what I

charge my regular clients." Did he really mean it? Now was the time to find out.

He didn't blink an eye. "Great. But here's *my* caveat. I'm not going to help you. No wheedling data out of me to feed into your algorithms."

"It'll be fun to wing it again," she said. "Before the algorithm and Two Love Lane, I still made matches. Lots of them."

"What was your secret in the good ol' days?"

Other people might make fun of her for accepting her ancestor's belief that he was related to Cupid, so she rarely shared her theory about her matchmaking heritage. "Let's just say it's a gift that runs in the family."

"I see." The twinkle in his eye made her a little breathless. "I'm going to shell out a lot of money to be your burst of nostalgia. *You* should be paying *me*, don't you think?"

She laughed. "Spoken like a true negotiator."

He shrugged, grinned. "I'm an enigma wrapped inside a puzzle. So said my last three girlfriends—but in much more colorful language. I doubt you'll get a handle on me."

It felt a little bit like they were flirting. And she was loving every second of it, even though she wasn't supposed to flirt with clients. "I can see that you'll be a challenge." She strove to sound as professional as she ever had. "Does that make you feel better?"

He got a cool, assessing glint in his eye. She was already coming to recognize that look as his New York CEO face. "Honestly? People do their best work for me when I'm not easy on them. And that's how I get to know them, too. Their weaknesses. Their strengths. Whether or not we can ever work together again."

"That makes sense."

He leaned in so close, they could kiss if she bent forward just a few inches. "I have a few phone calls to make," he said. "But I'd love to continue our conversation some-place more quiet. What do you think?"

Something arced between them. He wasn't—he couldn't be.

Was he actually coming on to her?

Yes, of course, he was. Her instincts were always on target, and she'd been flirting too. "I've got to get back to work," she said, her tone light. There. That interrupted the moment, whatever it had been.

"You're a noble soul, Macy."

She stood. He did too. "I'm going to charge you triple now," she told him. "For pushing your limits."

"You wouldn't dare." He helped her on with her coat.

Something seemed inevitable. A kiss. She could feel it hovering between them and was shocked at herself for longing to kiss a man she barely knew, especially *this* man. He was her client. And he was so different from the men she was used to dating. He had that New York accent, for one. And his fashion sense was classically masculine, elegant in a big-city way. He'd never wear a bow tie or a seersucker suit, the two most popular looks for guys in Charleston. Over his dead body, she was sure.

He followed behind her as they wended their way through chairs to the register. It took them five minutes to go twenty feet because she felt compelled, being a social person, to stop at every table and say hello, plus introduce him as "Deacon Banks, a visitor from Manhattan." She didn't say "*friend* from Manhattan," or "*businessman* from Manhattan."

On purpose.

Everyone was nice enough. But she could see their wheels spinning. Who was this guy, really? Why was he with her? Was he looking for love?

Let them wonder.

A few of the women seemed to assume he was fair game

on the singles market since he was with a professional matchmaker. Then again, Southern women in general made feminine-and-flirty an everyday art form.

"I'm getting my aunt settled into her new condo," he told them.

The small but fascinating fragment of news about his aunt was enough to get the other diners asking a string of questions, but Macy was adept at cutting everyone off before they got details.

"We've got to run," she said, and her friends fell right into line.

"You go on, you busy young lady," the older people said affectionately, or "Talk to you at So-and-So's party Thursday night," the younger ones replied, letting her off the hook because she was well-liked in this town—by everyone, that was, except for a woman about her age with strawberry-blonde hair, a slender nose, and a high forehead who had reminded Macy of Queen Elizabeth I reincarnated for as long as she could remember.

"Hello, Celia." For the first time that day, Macy felt sort of bummed, which was natural, she supposed, since Celia Waterford wasn't at all fond of her. Not one little bit.

"Macy." Celia inclined her head. Her pursed lips might as well have formed the words *Get the hell out of here.* But then, shockingly, she turned and said, "Hello, Deacon."

"Celia," he said. "Nice to see you again."

They'd met? How? Celia was the one person Macy knew she'd never, ever be friends with. Everyone else had a fighting chance.

When they got to the register, Macy whispered, "I'm not going to ask how you know her."

"Fine," he replied.

Surely he could tell she really wanted to know. But he wouldn't fess up. Instead, he insisted on paying for lunch.

"You didn't have to, but thank you," she said.

"My pleasure."

"Pleasure." That word coming from Deacon Banks took on a slightly improper—but delicious—meaning, at least to Macy. "You'll have a good time in Charleston," she told him. "I promise. Shall we shake on it?"

"Sure." He grinned, his eyes two pools of deep blue beneath his dark brows.

She found she didn't want to release his palm, pressed flat and warm against hers. But she retreated first, proud of herself for doing so. He opened the door for her, and she stepped over the threshold in her boots, which held her currently wobbly knees steady. "Where's your aunt's condo?" she asked him on the sidewalk. The lampposts on Broad Street had been festively adorned with wreaths for at least a week, but for some reason, the Christmas spirit had passed her by, until that very moment. It hit her willy-nilly, which was always the best time for it to strike.

"At One South Battery," he said.

She felt heat spread to her toes and her ears, her chest and her forehead. The Battery was the tip of the peninsula, facing Charleston harbor, where all the big, historic homes were. The first shots of the Civil War had been fired there.

She lived on the Battery too.

"The house has three stories, but it's sideways," he said. "Each floor has been made into a separate condo, and there's an elevator onto these amazing porches—"

"Piazzas," she interjected. "They allow for sea breezes. And most houses here are sideways. They take up less street space that way. In the old days, it saved on taxes."

She could say all that in her sleep. She was talking for talking's sake so she didn't have to think about what was actually happening—a shakeup in her predictable, comfortable life that was bothersome and possibly cataclysmic, if her intuition was right, as it usually was.

"The taxes, I'm sure, are going to be sky-high," he replied, but it might as well have been *blah blah blah*. All she could think about was the fact that she wanted to step closer to him and run away at the same time, which was of course, impossible. "This place wasn't cheap. It's very nice. Aunt Fran got the middle floor."

"Your aunt Fran is going to be my next-door neighbor." There. It was out. Like a rock dumped into a still pond. She was glad, too. Now she couldn't think of kissing Deacon Banks against the front window of Fast and French.

"What a small world." He wasn't nearly as rocked by the news of her home's proximity to his aunt's new place as she was. "But this is a small town, right?"

"Yes, but *still*." Didn't he see how potentially inflammatory this was? Didn't he care? Did she not inspire in him the same volatile, very wrong feelings *she* was feeling—about him? "I live right *there*. My bedroom window looks onto your aunt's piazza."

Where he would be periodically standing for the next month, if not to bask in the winter sun then to look over the balcony at the palmetto trees and the magnificent harbor, at the people walking dogs along the Battery wall. She'd see him through the sheer panels on her bedroom window as she put on or took off her clothes, getting ready either for work or for bed.

"Is that so," he said easily, and fell in beside her as she walked east on Broad.

"Wait a minute." She stopped, so he did too. "You *knew* already."

He tugged on his ear. "Well, yeah. Aunt Fran's realtor told us a little bit about all the neighbors."

"I'll bet it was Sherry. She sells most of the real estate south of Broad Street. That's how you knew to come looking for me at Two Love Lane."

"Yes."

And then it hit her. "You asked Sherry out, didn't you?"

"No. But Aunt Fran did, on my behalf. In the middle of the closing, she told Sherry that she and I would hit it off in the romance department."

"Sherry just lost her husband to cancer. Not even three months ago."

"So we discovered when she had to leave the room for a few minutes to compose herself. The whole thing was painfully embarrassing for me and far worse for Sherry. See what you and I are up against? Aunt Fran's like Godzilla. She must be stopped."

Macy liked how they were already a team. "Sherry knows Two Love Lane doesn't deal in short-term flings. I hope she told you so."

"Of course." He paused on the sidewalk near a house Macy had always loved. It had a glossy hot-pink front door. "She said you're in the serious business of finding people love. Aunt Fran was verklempt at the possibilities, but I hoped that since we're going to be neighbors, maybe you'd help me out on my terms instead."

"Is that why I was going to regret not working with you?" Macy asked. "Because we'd be neighbors?"

"Sure," he said. "Wouldn't you be embarrassed going out to get the paper in the morning and seeing me there, all alone, rejected, and dateless, on Aunt Fran's piazza?"

"I would not."

"Besides, I'm paying you a lot of money to help me out. Maybe you could use it to work on your house. It has that slight lean to the right, toward my aunt's place. By next year, she might be able to crawl over her balcony rail through one of your windows." He chuckled.

"My home," Macy said quietly, "which my dear grandmother left to me, has gone through the Revolutionary War, the Civil War, and two hundred years of occasional hurricanes. And let's not forget the massive earthquake in

1886. I love the tilt, and the engineers say the foundation is perfectly fine. It's not going anywhere."

"Sorry. No offense meant. I figured you were putting your spare cash into the business, is all."

"You're ninety-percent right," she said, "but around here, we do our best not to talk about money. Some of the oldest, most distinguished families are poor as church mice. Now let's change the subject. Tell me how you know Celia Waterford." Knowledge was power.

"Only if you tell me more about your family."

"Fine." She'd just have to wait another minute to find out about his connection to Celia. "My parents are academics. They teach at the College of Charleston." She couldn't help hesitating. She barely knew this man, and she was a private person in some respects.

"You look so serious all of a sudden," he said.

His face was so open and interested, she'd be honest with him. "I didn't have the perfect childhood, but no one does, right?" She shrugged and smiled. "Mom and Dad meant well, and my sister Anne and I turned out just fine, thanks to them. We're both hard-working, happy people."

"You get together a lot?"

"Yes. I see them almost every week, at least for a cup of tea and sometimes lunch or supper."

"Nice," he said. "I think it must be the hardest job in the world, to be a parent. That's why I'm in awe of my aunt. She's definitely not perfect. Things were rocky at times, when her marriages didn't work out. But she's incredible all the same, and I credit her with a lot of my success." He grinned. "Tell me more about your family. It makes this place seem more real to me."

She liked that about him. "My parents are still in the house I grew up in," she said. "It's north of Calhoun, a fifteen-minute walk from here, in the garden district. A neighborhood called Wraggborough. Anne is married to Kyle Wright, a doctor at the Medical University of South Carolina, which is here in Charleston. I set the two of them up."

"Nice."

"Lucy and Sam are their two children. They're three and five. Anne stays home with them, but she's working on her master's degree part-time and volunteers at the kids' school a lot. I see the kids every chance I get. They live a few blocks away from me."

But it was time to get back to Celia, who'd been hovering in Fast and French like a spider dangling on a gossamer thread. "How do you and Celia know each other?"

"She's my aunt's social consultant."

"Is that what Celia says she is now?" It was utter ridiculousness. Except it wasn't. Celia had what it took: polish, flair, connections, and a last name that carried weight in Charleston.

"She has a business card," Deacon said, "and a book out."

"About being the hostess with the mostest." Macy refrained from rolling her eyes. "It's in all the tourist shops."

"She made a guest appearance on *Bless Your Heart*. She taught one of the female stars how to throw a dinner party. Aunt Fran looked her up after she saw that and fell in love with the way she folds napkins."

"Of course. That female star, by the way, is actually from Tennessee. She moved here last year. Except for one or two locals in the cast and the gorgeous scenery, there's nothing particularly authentic about that show."

"Well, Aunt Fran's paying Celia a small fortune to get her invited to the best dinner parties and social events in town."

"I hope Celia didn't overdo it. Maybe I'd better go back in there and talk to her."

"Please let it go. I've got it under control—"

"You mean, Celia has your aunt under *her* control—"

"You and I had such a nice time at lunch. Didn't we?"

Macy stopped and thought. He was right. They *had*. "I suppose."

"You're helping me out," he said. "And there was the wine punch. And that soup. I'm glad you made me order it."

"You did like the soup?" She was pleased, but she couldn't help feeling suspicious of him.

"I loved it. I can't wait to go back for more."

How he'd figured out that talk of the soup would soothe her both baffled and upset her because he didn't *know* her. But maybe he wasn't at all aware it would make her feel good. Maybe he just really liked the soup. He should. The whole world should like the soup.

It was time to go. "I'll see you tomorrow before noon at Two Love Lane," she said. "You'll sign the contract and pay me fifty percent of your fee. I have meetings in the afternoon."

She didn't say "please" on purpose. Before he could object to any of her demands, she walked away, her ponytail swinging back and forth in time with her hips.

"I'm busy tomorrow!" he called after her.

She smiled to herself. She knew he'd hate to be bossed around and would want the last word.

"What a shame," she called back lightly without turning around. "I'm booked the rest of the week." She wiggled a few fingers in a semblance of a wave, her special signet ring saying "Rich in love" in Latin twinkling in the sun. "If you change your mind, I'll see you at ten sharp tomorrow."

He didn't answer—playing his own cat-and-mouse game, no doubt—but she wouldn't look back. He wanted her to. She could feel his eyes still on her. She was sure women always looked back at him. In fact, they probably walked away backward so they could stare adoringly at him and blow him kisses full of sexual promise.

Not her. She turned the corner, chin up, and was out of his sight.

Deacon Banks might be the boss among his social and professional set in New York City. But Charleston was different. *She* was the one with clout here. He'd have to figure out a way to deal with that fact before tomorrow morning.

CHAPTER FOUR

But when Macy got back to Two Love Lane, no one was there. Forty-five minutes passed—forty-five tortured minutes, since she couldn't stop thinking about how crazy she'd been to take on a client who didn't want to find love. Not only that, when she was around him, she had a difficult time thinking about business. Instead, she thought about wanting to kiss him. That didn't bode well.

But Greer, Ella, and Miss Thing had yet to show up.

"Where could they be, Oscar?" she asked after she'd finished filing a whole stack of bills and correspondence for Miss Thing. "We never take two-hour lunches! And they're not answering my texts."

Oscar didn't care. He was perched atop a table in front of a window, watching a squirrel taunt him from a branch.

"This has never happened before," Macy said. Oscar's tail swept the table's marble surface, and his ears flattened, whether because of her or the squirrel she had no idea. "We don't act this way here, Oscar. We know our mission."

But she'd strayed from hers today by agreeing to work with Deacon Banks, hadn't she?

She plopped herself into Miss Thing's spindly ivory

chair with the strawberry-pink goose-down seat cushion and the padded back and stared at the computer screen in front of her. A beautiful photo of Two Love Lane's exterior, a shot taken far enough back to encompass the gate, the front garden, and the brick pavement leading to the front porch, was the screensaver. It never failed to move her, that sight. Two Love Lane was one of the most charming houses in Charleston. It was home to hearts that needed connection. And it seemed to call people. It had even called Oscar. He'd shown up on Macy's first day of work three years before.

To make herself feel better, she clicked on the mouse, activated the computer screen, and typed in the company's website. When she hit ENTER, the webpage blossomed before her eyes, a gorgeous site that went straight to a colorful, polished video introduction, narrated by a melodious, gently bred Southern voice—Miss Thing's, in fact.

Welcome to Charleston, where sea breezes always blow, where palmettos, stately oaks draped in moss, and an abundance of headily scented gardens grace every street—a place to hold your dreams close and believe in love with your whole heart.

On a beautiful spring day, turn the corner from bustling East Bay Street, lined with those famous pastel-colored mansions, the ones comprising Rainbow Row, and enter a sun-dappled, cobblestoned alley with one—just one— house tucked at its end. It's been there over two hundred years, and it already knows you better than you know yourself. Its old glazed windows on each of its three stories beckon your wounded heart, which is suddenly, crazily hopeful as you walk through black-lacquered wrought-iron gates forged with love by a Revolutionary War-era craftsman.

Tread the intricately patterned brick path winding between blazing pink azaleas and blue hydrangeas, which crowd the mossy fountain topped with a chipped plaster cherub spouting water from its mouth. Ascend broad granite steps, their edges worn smooth and round from over two centuries of booted and slippered feet, onto a painted wood-planked piazza, where lazily spinning fans hang some fifteen feet above your head. Ring the tinny old bell and wait before the tall mahogany door for one of the three owners of Two Love Lane, or their charming assistant, to invite you inside.

When you cross the threshold, sit down in one of the elegant, private sitting rooms with Ella, Greer, or Macy and sip on a crystal glass of sweet iced tea sprigged with mint. Open up, slowly but surely, under the kind, rapt attention of your hostess. Sense, too, what the house is saying—that hearts have always hungered for connection here, long before you were born, and will do so long after you're gone.

You're not alone, in other words. Two Love Lane is the perfect place to start your journey toward your romantic destiny.

Macy sighed with pleasure. "*This*," she said. Watching that video never failed to remind her of the treasure they all had in Two Love Lane. It was special, and so were her partners and Miss Thing.

As if on cue, familiar voices sounded from outside and sharp heels ascended the steps. They were back, her best friends, who were also her professional colleagues. They'd all met at the College of Charleston. Greer, Ella, and Macy had shared a room as undergrads in one of the dormitories, a gorgeous yellow Victorian with a big wraparound porch. Greer had been a math major. Ella had studied theater. Macy had been the business major of the group. And Miss Thing had been their house mother.

Miss Thing, who was fun, clever, and had her own unique style, never put herself first, so one day the three girls devised a creative plot to set her up with her big crush . . . the president of the school, a handsome, confident man named Harold. There were some missteps—the girls had a learning curve, as did Miss Thing—but after a couple of months, the couple wound up marrying and being very happy. Miss Thing went from cooking supper for a bunch of hungry students to attending fancy sit-down dinners with Harold and hosting her own cocktail parties at the president's mansion.

Harold was powerful and respected, but Miss Thing wouldn't give up her original name, and he supported her completely. They were both so proud that hundreds of students she'd fed and coddled still stayed in contact with her. She was a campus legend. She'd always be "Miss Thing" to so many.

After the three girls graduated, they went their separate ways. But every time they got in touch, they shared matchmaking stories. It seemed once they'd had that success with Miss Thing, they were on a roll. Greer excelled at figuring out probable romantic outcomes for her circle of friends. Ella, too, had a real flair for bringing out the most attractive qualities in her friends' personalities. Macy, a born networker, was good at sensing potential connections.

But one day three years ago, Miss Thing called to say her wonderful husband had died unexpectedly. The three girls, devastated by the news, reunited in Charleston to console their dear friend. It was then that Miss Thing reminded them that they shared a special gift. She urged them to consider helping other people find true love, the way they had helped her and Harold.

Macy, Greer, and Ella had several heart-to-heart talks about their own romantic lives: what had gone right, what had gone wrong, and what they wanted to see happen for themselves in the future. It was then that they realized they wanted to help others with similar dreams.

Staring them in the face was their true calling: being matchmakers.

So that week, the girls devised their business plan. Greer and Ella moved back to Charleston, Macy found them the house, which they'd use as their office, and Two Love Lane, the matchmaking business, was born.

Miss Thing, who never revealed her age, had always aspired to dress like Elizabeth II. In winter, if it was cold enough, she wore matronly matching coats and hats she bought off eBay from her online pal Tommy, a cross-dressing clothes hound in England obsessed with Her Majesty. Today the coat and hat were emerald green, and the coat had a giant pearl brooch on the lapel. The hat sported a small peacock feather.

"Oh, my land, I got a facial," Miss Thing announced with a dismissive wave of her hand, her standard, preemptive "this is gossip" gesture. "I was at that new place on Society Street. I heard Faye Burton is secretly flying to New York each month to meet a lover half her age." She brushed by Macy and put her hat and pocketbook on her desk, right next to a pink feather duster. "My, my face feels tingly!" she added brightly as she took off her emerald coat. Beneath it she wore a matching sheath.

Macy couldn't believe she wasn't apologizing for being gone so long.

Ella, her glossy black hair cut in a blunt bob that fell right above her shoulders, came in next. She was five feet two, beautifully proportioned, voluptuous and sexy, in love with the Kardashian sisters' style. Today she had on black from head to toe: form-fitting pants, a plunging top that stopped an inch past where the matrons of Charleston wished it would, a cropped jacket, and suede ankle boots. The only thing that wasn't black was her scarlet-red boho handbag and the big ruby on her right index finger.

She was followed by Greer, who favored a Wall Street

look, with edge. Beneath her trench coat, her tailored gray trousers and matching vest showed off her tall, slender frame. The sexy white blouse and dangling red-and-gold-striped bow tie hanging around her collar added some fun to the look. As usual, she wore her signature black horn-rimmed glasses and carried one of her collection of leather briefcases instead of a handbag. Today's was the vintage Chanel black caviar one with the signature gold clasp. Her light brown hair was scraped back into a chignon.

Ella stopped short, presumably at the expression on Macy's face. Greer bumped into Ella's back.

"You didn't have fun, Macy?" Ella's smile faded.

"We were so hoping you would," Greer chimed in, her brow puckered.

Miss Thing was already at the bookshelf, swiping it briskly with the pink feather duster. "I had a feeling when I woke up this morning and saw a cardinal land on my windowsill that something big was going to happen today." She paused. "And it did. Mr. Banks came to our office, and my morning improved drastically! I so hoped you were going to have fun, sugar. Didn't you?" She looked expectantly at Macy.

Macy didn't want to admit it, but she *had* had fun. "Why would you ask me if I had fun with a client? What's going on, ladies?"

"But did you?" Greer persisted.

"I did," Macy said. "I mean . . . I had a fairly good time. As professional meetings go."

"That's all?" Ella's mouth hung open. "He was *gorgeous*."

"Having a good time was not the point." Heat spread up Macy's neck. "This was *business*."

"You're right," said Greer. "But I couldn't help myself. From the moment he walked in, I didn't think of him as a client."

"Neither did I," said Ella.

"Me either," echoed Miss Thing. "I thought of him as someone special."

"All our clients are special," Macy reminded them.

"I know," said Miss Thing. "But he was different."

"He was." Ella nodded. "I don't understand it myself. It was more than his good looks."

Greer tapped her index finger against her pursed lips. "I can't put my finger on it either."

Neither could Macy. She felt entirely the same way! But should she admit that? Someone had to pull in the reins and get the team back to professional mode. "Every single person who walks over our threshold should be considered a potential business client," she said. "So let's put aside your reactions to him, and please help me understand better who he is. Do any of you know him?"

"Not a bit." Miss Thing shrugged her shoulders. "He came in today and asked to see you, and—"

"You let him through without telling me." Macy wasn't one to get riled easily. But why on earth would Deacon have gone to such lengths to get her alone, and how had he managed it so well?

"Oh honey pie, I'm sorry." Miss Thing lowered her duster. "He was charming. Didn't you think so? And watch out. You don't want to lose your grandmother's pearl ear bob. Oscar will bat it right under a couch, and we'll never see it again."

Macy had been fiddling with her earring because she was jumpy, for good reason. She strode to the window and looked out at the cobblestones glowing in the afternoon sun, then turned back to face her friends. "I'm trying to understand how you could have abandoned your post, Miss Thing, without telling me. It's not like you. And then you two"—she looked at Ella and Greer—"you disappeared for a long while too."

"We told Miss Thing it was okay for us all to go," said Ella.

"He was a difficult man to turn down," Greer said.

"He was impossible to resist," Miss Thing insisted.

"I get it." Macy swallowed her chagrin. "He was handsome and . . . and sexy."

"Oh, but it was more than his sex appeal." Ella giggled.

"Abundant though that was," Greer tacked on because they couldn't let that go now, could they?

"He gave us each gift certificates." Miss Thing smiled dreamily. "That's how I got my facial."

"And I got one to the Peninsula Grill," Ella crowed, "good only for today. Enough money on it for lunch for six. I couldn't resist calling five of the backstage crew from the theater. How often do starving artists get to eat at such a nice place?"

"I got sucked in too," Greer said. "He gave me a certificate to the Apple Store. I could buy up to three laptops to donate to the elementary school, but the deadline was today at one p.m. I couldn't pass up that opportunity."

"Mr. Banks *bribed* each of you to leave us alone together?" Macy stared at them. "What if he was a serial killer? I was a sitting duck!"

"We trusted him." Miss Thing flicked her feather duster on top of a lamp shade.

"Why?" Macy threw up her hands. "He's a total stranger!"

"He Googled himself for us," said Ella. "We saw a picture of him with his aunt—Fran Banks! No wonder he has such star quality. She's beautiful. And charismatic."

"If a bit bossy for my taste," Greer added.

"She can be downright nosy," Miss Thing said, "which we all are, but she doesn't try to hide it. Someone needs to teach her manners." Being impolite was anathema to Miss Thing.

"Are we so starstruck by celebrities that the people who know them get a free pass to barge into my office?" Macy asked.

"He didn't barge, did he?" Miss Thing blinked several times, her palm curved above her heart. "He told me he'd be gracious."

As Ella drew a wand of scarlet Chanel lip gloss over her lips, she somehow managed to say, "His eyes were genuinely warm and friendly. He's no sociopath." She tossed the lip gloss back into her purse. "And when he said he was desperate to make his aunt happy, I felt sorry for him. I like a man who loves his family."

"Pfft," Macy replied.

Greer chuckled. "I have to admit, I'd had a tedious morning. Nothing was going right. I was so happy to deliver those laptops to the school."

"And I love the Peninsula Grill's she-crab soup," Ella enthused. "Our new lighting technician is a fan of Huguenot Torte. And we all enjoyed the good-looking waiters. They surf, most of them. They've got awesome tans."

Macy covered her face for a moment, then dropped her hands. "He did all this just to get you out of here?"

Miss Thing nodded. "Not only was he sex on a stick and lots of fun, Mr. Banks was determined."

"*Miss Thing.*" Macy had to suppress a smile and stay stern. "It's his determination factor that bothers me. *We're* in charge here. Not a stranger."

"Mr. Banks told us he needed your undivided attention," Ella said. "I get the feeling he's used to bossing people around."

"That's an understatement," Macy said. "He obviously inherited some of his aunt's chutzpah. He was like a dog with a bone. But I managed to get rid of him."

"You did?" Greer's face fell. "Before you heard him out?"

"No." Macy thought back to how stubborn she'd been about not eating with him at Fast and French. "I listened, but I said no to helping him."

"Shoot." Ella wore a wistful expression. "I was hoping we'd see him around the office."

"Me too." Miss Thing's shiny brooch trembled as she gave a little shiver. "He was all man."

Macy was irked, to be honest. Deacon Banks had won over her colleagues, big-time.

"So that's that?" Greer asked, her tone heavy with disappointment.

"No, actually." Macy braced herself for something loud and raucous. "I changed my mind and went after him."

"You did?" Greer's face lit up.

"That's my girl!" Miss Thing clapped her hands madly.

"Woohoo!" Ella put her hands in the air and pumped her arms, like she was dancing to Beyoncé. "I would have chased him, too!"

Macy couldn't help grinning. Her colleagues occasionally went a little nuts. But so did she. She had that very morning, as a matter of fact. "After he left here, I chased him down the street, and we had lunch at Fast and French."

"You literally *chased* him?" Greer asked.

Macy nodded. "And these boots don't do great over cobblestone. I chased him for three blocks."

Greer laughed. It was one of Macy's favorite things about her. She had a big honk of a laugh. *Hah! Hah-hah-hah!* Nothing prissy about it. Sometimes it made Macy jump, but it was always worth it.

Everyone started laughing then. You just couldn't help it when Greer did. After they all caught their breath, Greer said, "I liked the guy, personally."

"So he's likeable," Macy said. "But I'm not sure I should have agreed to work with him."

Greer still had high spots of color on her cheeks from

laughing so hard. "Why wouldn't you work with Mr. Banks? He's eye candy. Rich. Powerful. He could bring us some good connections in New York. So could his aunt! What if she's really happy with what you accomplish with him? She could tell all her Hollywood friends about us—"

Macy shook her head. "I can't ask for referrals in this case."

"Why not?" A small squiggle appeared on Miss Thing's freshly massaged brow.

"Because he's not a willing client." Macy spoke bluntly—the ladies were getting carried away. "He's doing this under duress."

Ella's mouth dropped open. "But he told us it would make his aunt happy to see him settle down."

"It wouldn't make *him* happy," Macy replied. "He flat out said he's not interested in commitment."

"Oh dear," said Miss Thing. "I had such high hopes since he cleared the decks here just to speak to you uninterrupted. I assumed he was desperate for you to find him a love match."

"No, not at all." Macy wasn't happy to admit that fact. "I think he learned from his aunt how to catch people off guard. He probably guessed he wasn't a typical client. He assumed I just might throw him out, which I did, at first." Guilt assuaged her. "I don't know why I went after him, honestly."

"What's done is done," said Greer.

Miss Thing nodded. "Your instincts are always on target."

"You're very kind." Macy cast a grateful smile around the room. Because really, how lucky was she to have such nice, supportive friends? And when they smiled back at her, she felt fresh resolve. She could do this.

"So here's the situation," she said. "I've got to set Mr. Banks up on lots of dates because that's his Christmas gift to his aunt. Casual dates that go nowhere. That's not what we do. But I agreed on one condition."

"Which is?" Ella asked.

"I get to try to find him his One and Only anyway."

"We're Two Love Lane," Greer said. "That's what we do."

"He agreed to my terms, but he also said he's not going to cooperate in the soulmate search." Macy lifted and dropped her shoulders.

"That won't stop you," said Miss Thing.

"Yes, recruiting potential dates should be fairly straight-forward," Greer said.

"But finding someone who will turn out to be the love of his life in less than a month?" Ella sounded skeptical.

Macy bent down and scratched Oscar's ears, her favorite thing to do when she needed time to calm down. "I know it seems impossible. But I want to try."

"I can see why you'd enjoy the challenge," said Ella. "I'm proud of you."

"So am I," Miss Thing chimed in.

"Me too," Greer said, "but who's his perfect match?"

Nerves struck Macy hard. She gave up on Oscar's ears and started fiddling with her earring again. "I have no idea." And she truly didn't.

"Let's sit on the couch," Miss Thing said.

It was their thinking spot sometimes. And sometimes it was simply their place to be a united team.

They squeezed in. The only way they could fit was to link arms. Everyone sighed a cozy sigh, their legs all crossed in the same direction.

"The house is listening," said Ella.

They were quiet for a second. Some winter birds chirped and tweeted in the camellia bushes behind the house, and a hanging shutter on the front porch creaked. Macy felt the peace of the house wrap them up and hug them.

"Maybe it sounds corny, but I think the house is rooting for us," whispered Miss Thing.

Greer wasn't into mojo, karma, magic, and feelings. She liked numbers and was very practical. But she was also a good sport. She started their secret three-squeeze handshake, which meant *I love you*, and passed it down to Ella, who passed it to Macy. Macy passed it to Miss Thing, who then patted Oscar, who'd leaped up onto the sofa arm.

He meowed and jumped down, only to strut across the Persian carpet with his tail in the air. Oscar wasn't into corny. Not one bit.

CHAPTER FIVE

Deacon sat on the sofa in Aunt Fran's new condo, the middle floor of a two-hundred-year-old mansion cut into three layers like a luscious cake. He was restless in the secret way that all men are when they're waiting on couches for women to tell them what to do.

After all, when he was staying with Aunt Fran, he was no longer the intuitive, ruthless tech entrepreneur who'd made a name for himself buying start-up companies and transforming them into success stories. He was merely Deacon, the garbage taker-outer; Deacon, the wine-cork remover; Deacon, the lover of all things cooked by George, who was Aunt Fran's houseman; and Deacon, the repository for his aunt's hopes and dreams for him. Those included a devoted wife, a home with tea towels in the kitchen, a job that allowed him to take a vacation whenever Aunt Fran stayed at her house on Nantucket, and a strong peppering of dogs and babies in the mix.

At the moment George was buying up Charleston's champagne stock before the holiday stampede, and Aunt Fran was talking to Celia Waterford in the kitchen about who was who in Charleston. Aunt Fran still couldn't believe that the people featured on *Bless Your Heart* weren't the crème de la crème of local society.

"Most of the people on that show aren't even from here," Celia insisted. "However, there's one local on it, Trent Gillingham, who's a notorious jerk. But he's from a good family, so people endure him."

"Oh no. He's my favorite!" Aunt Fran talked much faster than the people in Charleston did, with an impatient but good-humored edge. That was normal in New York City—where life was always colorful and busy, busy, busy—but it was very noticeable here. "I was hoping he was misunderstood. He's really that bad?"

"Yes." Celia rolled her eyes. "He's high on himself. Always has been. Never worked a day in his life and drinks too much."

"Deacon, do you hear that?" Aunt Fran practically shrieked.

"I heard!" Of course, he'd told her a million times already that the show was a total set-up. He went back to focusing on testing out a video game one of his smaller companies had recently produced, but all he could think about was the fact that Macy Frost was next door. He knew she was home from work. When he'd sat on the porch smoking a cigar with George, he'd seen her walking down the street with a bright-orange tote bag on her shoulder zipped shut except for a little hole where the face of that cat he'd met at the office peeked out at the world.

"Deacon, could you come get this wine?" Aunt Fran called.

"Sure." He stood, braced himself to enter the kitchen—because the very-much-married Celia was clearly interested in him, and he already knew he wasn't interested in *her*—and put on a polite, neutral expression.

"What's wrong with you?" Aunt Fran ribbed him. She

really meant, of course, that he'd been impolite not to join in the conversation earlier.

"Nothing," he replied, feigning innocence. "I didn't want to interrupt any social strategy sessions." That was his way of reminding the two of them that they were on Celia's office time, and that Aunt Fran had better pay attention since she was shelling out big bucks for Celia's social advice.

Celia leaned on the butcher block countertop. She wore clothes that reminded him of the British royal family when they were roughing it at one of their lesser castles in the country: silk scarf; cashmere sweater; pants made of something warm but expensive; and fine leather boots with good, discreet hardware and elegant stitching. "So you had lunch with Macy Frost?"

"I did." Deacon wasn't fond of answering "yes" or "no." It was a quirk of his. He had no idea how this habit had ever started. Most of the time, he wasn't even aware of it. He only became cognizant of it when he was annoyed at having to answer unwelcome questions, as he was now.

While a roast popped and sizzled in the oven, he poured the three of them a glass of red wine. He handed one to each of the ladies, raised his own glass, and said, "Cheers."

"Cheers," Aunt Fran said with such fervor, he knew she was very happy. She was the Evel Knievel of the Upper East Side. Moving to Charleston six months of the year was her version of a rocket-motorcycle jump across a canyon.

He was glad he had come. She deserved this.

Celia merely inclined her head and clinked.

Each of them took a healthy sip.

"Mmmm," Celia said. "So tell me more, Deacon." Her tone was sophisticated-playful. Not quite flirtatious but bordering on. "Are you *friends* with Macy?"

"She's Aunt Fran's new neighbor," he said, "so, yeah."

"She has such an eccentric family." Celia gave a little chuckle.

"I thought Southerners prided themselves on their eccentric families," said Aunt Fran.

"To some extent." Celia sighed. "We do draw a line, however. Wyatt and Melanie Frost were always quite careless with those girls, letting them run around barefoot and in bathing suits in the summer along the Battery wall, like wild things for all the tourists to see."

Deacon thought of Macy and how awesome she seemed. He suspected being a wild child had been the making of her.

"You sure do have a lot of interest in Macy's life," Aunt Fran said lightly.

Celia lifted a delicate shoulder. "Welcome to Charleston. Everybody's interested in each other here. And Macy and I—let's just say we have a long history."

"Hopefully, a nice one." Aunt Fran poured Celia another glass of wine. "Especially since Deacon hired her to help him dip his toe in the local dating pool. It could be Deacon meets a nice girl through Two Love Lane."

"Could be," Celia said doubtfully, sending him an enigmatic smile. But he got the message, all right. He was flattered, but he wasn't interested. He didn't sleep with married women. And even if she were single, Celia didn't intrigue him that way.

"Actually, I'm doing this for Aunt Fran," he said. "It's my Christmas present to her."

"It was all I wanted." Aunt Fran gazed at him fondly. "But you're going to take it seriously, right? You're over thirty now. Time to fall in love and settle down."

"I'll think about it," he said. Then he added, "The world's greatest aunt calls *all* the shots at Christmas" and wrapped an arm around her shoulder. He never cringed at expressing devotion to the woman who'd taken him on when she'd been only twenty-eight and he'd been in the midst of the terrible twos.

Aunt Fran wriggled away. "He loves to make me cry and embarrass myself."

Celia laughed the tinkling bell laugh that some of the more glossy women of Deacon's acquaintance in New York learned at Swiss boarding schools.

"How long has your family been here?" Aunt Fran asked their guest—her employee, although surely Celia would no doubt balk at being reminded of her hired status.

"Since seventeen hundred," she replied smoothly. "Robert Waterford, from Essex, England, was the first Waterford in the United States."

Somehow from that little speech, Deacon knew she'd always been the teacher's pet. He also doubted she'd ever gone camping or slept on the beach and woken up with sand and the taste of stale vodka in her mouth. She'd always known what to say and when. Was Celia a robot with no heart, or did she only have really proper manners? He hoped, for his aunt's sake, it was the latter.

"What about Macy's family?" Aunt Fran asked.

"They've been here almost as long as mine has," Celia replied.

That flimsy word "almost." It carried some weight in the diss department.

It was time to change the subject. "You've got to go see Yo-Yo Ma this Friday," Deacon told his aunt.

Aunt Fran laughed. "Why, that was out of the blue!"

"Not really. Macy told me to tell you."

"She's right, you should go, Fran," said Celia. "It's too late to get tickets, but Walter and I have a box. I'd love if you'd sit with me. Walter will be out of town at a medical conference." She smiled at Deacon. "The both of you, of course. Everyone will see you, and you'll probably get some party invitations out of it."

"I'm *there*," said Aunt Fran, draining her glass. She then set it with force on the counter to illustrate her extreme enthusiasm. "How about you, Deacon? Or will you be on a hot date?"

"I don't know," he said, which was true.

"The seats will be available," Celia reiterated. "If you have a date, bring her along."

Aunt Fran patted Celia's arm. "You're worth every bit of money I'm paying you."

Celia didn't thank her. "Remember," she said, "don't ask anyone else about their net worth. And if you want invitations, please steer clear of asking those funny personal questions you're known for. I don't care how curious you are, Fran."

"Good Lord," said Aunt Fran with excitement. "How am I going to hold myself back? Everyone in Manhattan—and let's face it, around the country—loves when I'm slightly outrageous."

"There are a lot of rules in Charleston," Celia said. "Are you sure you want to toe the line?"

Deacon took a swig of wine. Funny. Macy had said Aunt Fran would sail through any social tests in Charleston with flying colors. Toeing the line was not his aunt's natural way.

Aunt Fran's eyes shone with anticipation. "It'll be a nice change of pace for me. My celebrity doesn't give me a pass here."

It was true she could go anywhere in New York and get easy entrée.

"How about following one rule?" Deacon said. "Be yourself."

Celia frowned. "That's all well and good, but—"

"Don't worry." Aunt Fran patted Deacon's arm. "I'll be fine. Celia, how do people dress here? Can I wear my caftans?"

"Caftans are acceptable for Southern matriarchs." Celia sounded like she was reading from a book.

"Thank God." Aunt Fran brushed pretend sweat off her brow. "I'm a matriarch. Aren't I, Deacon? Of our little family?"

"Of course, you are," he said. "And you wear what *you* like."

Aunt Fran laughed. "I have to admit, I wouldn't mind impressing that hunk Trent Gillingham from *Bless Your Heart*. I don't care that he's half my age and sleeping with all his female costars. Will we see him around?"

"Sure," said Celia. "Most everywhere I go. Consider yourself my plus-one to any party Walter can't attend. I also plan on calling some friends and getting them to add you to their invitation lists—there are plenty of dinner and cocktail parties over the holidays, sometimes several a night."

"I can't wait." If Aunt Fran had had a tail, it would have been wagging.

"It will happen, I promise." Celia's queen-bee confidence was palpable. "You'll feel like a Charlestonian before you know it."

If you toe the line, Fran, was the understood end to that sentence. Deacon didn't like it. But if it made his aunt happy to play Celia's game, who was he to interfere?

There was a buzz on the intercom.

"I'll get it!" Aunt Fran grabbed a bowl of nuts and walked briskly out of the kitchen. "Come on, you two! Sit in the living room. It's probably the delivery boy from the Bull Street Market. He's coming over today or tomorrow to discuss regular meat-and-milk deliveries—fresh off the farm—with George."

"She's a hoot," Celia murmured over her shoulder.

"She's interesting, all right." Deacon wasn't sure about the word "hoot." Was that good? Or bad? Why hadn't

Celia smiled when she used it? Would Aunt Fran's brand of intelligence and personality—honed over years of chatting up taxi drivers and celebrities, hosting swanky cocktail parties at her Manhattan apartment, chairing various charitable boards, attending every Knicks home game, and fighting off the competition in the entertainment world—be appreciated here?

But it was too late to worry, and too soon to tell. What was done was done, and he was here to help her make the best of it.

"It's Macy Frost," the voice said from the intercom. "From next door. I brought you a homemade coconut cake to welcome you to the neighborhood."

Macy was coming up. Deacon felt a surge of happiness that had nothing to do with cake. It was about the girl bringing the cake.

Aunt Fran pressed the intercom button. "Holy crap, Macy. A cake?"

"Tone it down," Celia whispered.

Aunt Fran's face fell. She pressed the intercom button again. "I mean, uh, George will be ecstatic," she said meekly. "I'll send Deacon down."

Deacon already had his hand on the doorknob. "Yourself," he told his aunt. "That's what you'll be when we come back."

"Fine, but I'll also avoid asking uncomfortable questions." Aunt Fran pointed to a wingback chair. "Sit, Celia."

Celia sat.

"No stirring the pot," Aunt Fran promised her. "No using bad words. Although avoiding 'asshat' might be hard. It's so much fun to say. And there are so many asshats in the world." She plopped down on the sofa. "Witches with a capital *B*, too. Don't take this wrong, but you're a little bit of one, Celia, aren't you?"

Oh, God. Would Celia last? Deacon kind of hoped she

wouldn't. He took off down the stairs. His only exposure to Southern ways was *The Andy Griffith Show*. He'd never had coconut cake, but he was sure he'd keep it all to himself if he baked one.

But this was Macy. Maybe this wasn't an Aunt Bea–type gesture. Maybe she'd made this cake to get to know him better—so she could get deets on him, to use to find his soulmate.

Not a chance in hell!

But look how quickly she was on the move. He was impressed.

On the ground floor, there was a locked inner double door. On the other side, Macy waited in a tiny tiled foyer with three ancient brass mailboxes. Another set of double doors loomed behind her, at least fourteen feet high. Behind those was the blue of the harbor and a splash of pale winter green from a palmetto tree on the Battery wall.

In her hands was a magnificent cake.

Deacon unbolted the inner door, and she stepped inside the main hallway.

"Wow," he said. The toasted coconut on top of the cake curled like wood shavings. "That's beautiful."

She was beautiful, glowing with pride but even more with excitement. She liked to make people happy. That was obvious.

"I brought you the contract to sign, if you want to," she said. "It's in my purse. You can read it and sign it and stick it through my mail slot tomorrow morning. It'll save you a trip back to my office."

She made a quarter turn.

He pulled a rolled sheaf of papers from her purse. "Will do."

So it was official.

"I love that tiny foyer." Her voice echoed off the staircase and walls. "You don't need a key to get into it. If there was a thunderstorm, I could stand in there to get out of the rain. Or if I were a kid and just wanted to find out what it was like to be in one of these big houses, I could go in there and pretend. I've always liked tiny places." She paused. "I miss phone booths, even though they were already on the way out when I was born. I got to stand in one once at Disney World. A British one painted red. I liked it as much as some of the rides."

He was unduly charmed by every little thing she said. "That tiny foyer is where the UPS guy leaves George and Aunt Fran packages," he said. "I found five this morning. The mail carrier opens it every day to get to the mail boxes too."

"My house doesn't have that."

"You have the phony front door leading onto your porch."

"Onto the *piazza*," she said with a smile.

"Okay, piazza." He'd agree to anything she wanted to call it.

"I have to keep my fake door locked, though," she said. He was gratified that she'd decided to ignore his slow learning curve and keep teaching him about her way of life. "Otherwise, tourists walk right in. The real front door is halfway down the length of the piazza."

"How does the UPS man leave packages? Or the postman?"

"They can't. They leave me a note. And then I have to figure out how to pick the packages up. Or I take my chances the next day and leave the outer door unlocked. That way they can open it and leave the package on the piazza. Neither way is particularly comfortable."

"What a funny town. In a good way. There are secret places all over."

"Yes, like Love Lane."

"I never would have found it. I would have stopped at

Roastbusters, but Sherry the Realtor told me about the tiny jog around the corner past the hydrangeas, and there it was." They started toward the stairs. "You were nice to bake a cake."

"Thank you."

"Maybe it's about more than being nice." He had no idea why he wanted to taunt her, except that he felt the same way he did when he chased his crush around the playground as a kid, supposedly to pull her ponytail. He wanted to be near her, talk to her, listen to her. To see how her emotions moved across her face. "Could it be a strategy of yours—to get over here and get intel on me from Aunt Fran as fast as you can?"

"Oh, I did it for both reasons," she said, blithely. "To learn more about you, yes. But I also want to welcome your aunt. I enjoy baking. I have a trick. Mix four layers at a time in my KitchenAid—enough for two cakes—bake them, wrap them, and keep them in the freezer. I only had to make the icing when I got home from work."

"Clever." He couldn't get enough of her. "Can I hold it for you?"

"Oh, no thank you. I've got it."

They walked up the wide staircase side by side, and neither of them said a word. It was a bit awkward. But he felt awkward. He was lusting after a wholesome Christmas elf. Luckily, it only took ten seconds to reach Aunt Fran's door.

"Aunt Fran looks forward to meeting you," he finally said, and made the decision then and there to make mad love to his next-door neighbor, the sooner the better. She'd forget all about finding him a soulmate, and she'd have just enough energy afterward to arrange the dates he needed to satisfy Aunt Fran.

"No," Macy said.

"No, what?"

"I know what you're thinking."

"You do?"

"You want to have a fling with me to pass the time while you're here. And maybe I'd forget all about my plan for you, to find you a soulmate. That's an old and tired strategy, wouldn't you say? Men have been avoiding commitment forever that way. Through sex."

"I suppose you're right. And it's really fun."

"Well, look into my eyes."

"I'm looking." They were that fantastic color, the brown and gold of deep autumn.

"It's never gonna happen."

"Really?"

"Really." She lifted her chin. "The door, please."

"Yes, *ma'am*." He swung it wide open, proud that he'd said "ma'am." He'd heard it about a thousand times already in one day. "Watch out for the Corgis," he added.

But it was too late. They rushed at Macy and began sniffing her pink Chuck Taylors.

"Come in, come in!" Aunt Fran said a little belatedly, standing up from the couch. Deacon noted that she looked quite pretty in a shockingly peach caftan she must have quickly changed into while they were downstairs.

Celia stood, reluctantly, it seemed.

When Macy saw her, she seemed to freeze for a second, the same way she had at Fast and French. She set the cake on a table, petted the dogs swarming around her, and said, "Hello, Miss Banks."

Fran had always kept her maiden name.

His aunt strode over—ever on stage, her head held high, her shoulders thrown back—to share an air kiss with Macy. The dogs scattered, content that their mistress had taken over the welcoming duties. "Call me Fran."

"Only if you call me Macy."

"Of course." Aunt Fran got busy examining the cake from all sides, oohing and aahhing over it.

Macy wore a pretty little sweater over her shoulders. Beneath it was a faded purple band T-shirt. "Hello, Celia."

"Hello, Macy." Celia was polite, and no more.

"This cake is enchanting," Aunt Fran told Macy. "You made it?"

She was doing well so far. "Enchanting" was an elegant word.

"I did make it." Macy sounded a little out of breath, as if she'd just finished making her creation—which she had—and now had to return home to brush all the leftover coconut flakes off the counter and wash the frosting bowl.

Aunt Fran made her "shocked" face. The daytime talk show audience loved it. Her brows shot up. Her chin flattened. Her mouth hung open, and her eyes registered intense astonishment. "Really? *Really?* And you're not *married*?"

In some ways, Aunt Fran was too predictable for words. Old-fashioned, too.

"No, I'm not," Macy said.

Her little "no" must have saddened his aunt because she put a palm over her heart. "Are you kidding me? When you make such good-looking cakes and are so beautiful yourself?" She didn't wait for an answer—as usual. "What's wrong with the single people of Charleston?" She made another famous face—her "I-know-your-deepest-secrets" expression, the same one that had made Beyoncé, LeBron James, and Scarlett Johansson laugh and then reveal a juicy detail about their lives. "Maybe you have a married lover you don't want to tell us about."

Aunt Fran waited. Her expression this time was indescribable. But if Deacon had to try, he'd say she looked as if she had to use a public bathroom and there were too many people in line.

If they didn't like that look in Charleston, then too bad.

Although he did feel a little sorry for Macy. But she was tough. She could take it.

Celia was frozen in her seat, a fake smile pasted on her lips.

Macy stole a quick glance at Deacon—what could he say?—then she smiled kindly at his aunt. "I actually *don't* have a married lover. Sorry."

See? She was a trooper.

"That's a travesty," his aunt replied sternly. "You're prettier than any of the girls on *Bless Your Heart*. And they're always bragging about their conquests."

"*Fran*," Celia tried to interject.

"Not that I have a problem with those girls and their sex lives." Aunt Fran spoke right over her paid consultant. "But I would think the men of Charleston would fall over themselves to win Miss Macy Frost, maker of cakes."

Deacon wondered if Macy wished she could go home and watch TV or make more cakes. Most people probably would want to disappear at this point.

But she rallied. "That's very kind of you," she said. "I *think*."

Good for her!

"You're getting too personal too fast, Fran," said Celia.

"Oh, I meant it as a compliment." Aunt Fran waved a hand. "You've got that all-American girl thing going on, Macy, with hidden depths. Like Jennifer Lawrence or Emma Stone. Not Reese Witherspoon. She comes across as prissy. You're not prissy. Celia's prissy. I couldn't handle two prissy women at once."

"Get used to it," Celia said blandly. "You're in the heart of prissy country."

"Shit," said Fran. "Then I'm screwed."

Deacon laughed. Macy giggled.

"She needs to stop," Celia said.

"Oh, right." Aunt Fran's expression was an odd mix of fear and bravado, which was what Deacon loved about her.

"Well, um," Macy said, "you asked about the eligible guys here, Fran, and the truth is I haven't met any I'm seriously interested in. Maybe I'll change my mind at some point."

"I like a discerning woman," Aunt Fran insisted. "I know a fellow"—She gave Deacon a theatrical nudge in the side, and he grimaced. He wasn't a *fellow*! He was a man! A hot-blooded one, too!—"who'll meet your criteria for the perfect guy."

"Don't listen to my aunt, but do stay for dinner, Macy," said Deacon. It went against his best interests, but sooner or later, she was going to grill Aunt Fran about him. He might as well be there.

"Yes, you must stay," echoed Aunt Fran. "I'll get George to set another place. If he ever gets back. He's enjoying all the Southern people."

As if he were on an alien planet.

Macy chuckled. "I can stay for dinner, thank you very much. But don't get your hopes up, Fran. Deacon's hired me through Two Love Lane. I don't date my clients."

"Why not?" His aunt picked up one of her Corgis, the wriggly one named Whitney, kissed his nose, and put him back down.

"We want them to feel we have their best interests at heart," Macy said, "not our own."

"She's the consummate professional." Celia swung a leg over her knee in lazy fashion. "I suppose."

"Thanks for the ringing endorsement, Celia." Macy's tone was only slightly dry.

"My pleasure." Celia kept that leg swinging.

Deacon felt serious tension developing.

Macy looked at Fran. "I'm sorry. I feel like we're on

Bless Your Heart right now, with Southern-fried conflict. But ours isn't contrived."

"I thought I sensed something going on." Aunt Fran gathered her Corgis close. They panted in unison, their ears pricked up.

Deacon felt for Macy.

Celia stood. "Perhaps I should go."

"Oh, no," said Aunt Fran. "It could be that real Charleston drama is even better than the television version." She patted the seat next to her. "Sit, Macy. Tell us what's going on. You have a right to defend yourself against Celia's lukewarm support. You sit back down, too, Celia, and let her do it, since you brought it up. Deacon, pour us all a glass of wine."

"My pleasure." All he could think of at the moment, however, was getting Macy away from Celia and his meddling aunt and onto the porch—the *piazza*—where they would look out at Fort Sumter together. He'd watch her profile. And admire her figure. All while she was talking to him in that absurdly husky-yet-sexy voice.

Of course, the Corgis would be there, scratching themselves and yawning and wagging their tails. They ruined the daydream, in a way, which made it easier for Deacon to focus on pouring everyone wine.

Macy sat gingerly next to Aunt Fran, almost on the head of a sleepy Corgi named Bubbles. "I feel like I'm on your talk show."

Aunt Fran laughed. "My talk show was fun. You have nothing to fear. And maybe everything to gain." Gareth, the fattest Corgi, put his snout in Aunt Fran's lap, and she petted him fondly, like the Wicked Witch might pet her favorite flying monkey.

One really shouldn't mess with Aunt Fran. She was a strange mix of adorable senior citizen and, well, evil incarnate.

Deacon handed Macy a nearly brimming glass of a good Australian shiraz. "Don't let my aunt bully you. Or let Bubbles put you in a corner."

Macy giggled.

He had to figure out a way to make her do it again. His fingers touched hers when she accepted the glass. And he liked it. Very much.

"Now I know where you get your intrepid nature," Macy said.

No one had ever told him he had an intrepid nature. Tech magazines had called him "adventurous," but there was something so much more noble and glamorous about being called "intrepid."

"You might as well tell them," said Celia from her corner of the boxing ring that was Aunt Fran's living room.

"Or you will, I assume," Macy replied.

Celia shrugged. "They'll find out somehow."

"Spill the beans, my dear," Aunt Fran commanded Macy.

"Oh, all right." Macy sighed. "Once, long before I had a matchmaking service, I set two people up. I had a friend—"

"An acquaintance," Celia interrupted her, "who was born here but went to boarding school far away."

"Obviously, *you*, Celia," said Aunt Fran, in her best listening mode. She was the most impressive as an interviewer when she listened.

"Yes," Macy went on, "it was Celia. She was at the end of her rope about men. So I promised I'd help her find the right guy, and I thought I had. But I found out these two were wrong for each other a week before the wedding. I told her"—she paused and looked guiltily at Celia—"that she should reconsider the whole plan."

"It was none of Macy's business," said Celia. "But she had to butt in."

"What happened?" asked Aunt Fran.

Celia took a swig of wine. "The day after I talked to Macy, the groom"—Deacon could tell Celia wanted to call him a very bad name, and he wished she would—"decided to call off the wedding."

"Was it the wrong decision?" Aunt Fran rivaled Katie Couric and Barbara Walters when she felt like appearing deeply, professionally involved in ferreting out good gossip.

"At the time, I thought so," said Celia, "and for several years afterward."

Macy looked miserable. "I'm really sorry."

"What happened to the son of a bitch groom?" Aunt Fran asked.

"Fran—" Celia attempted to rebuke her.

"We're in private," Fran said. "And you hate him, right?"

"Yes, but you don't say so. It's not *done*."

"You poor Southern society people." Aunt Fran shifted in her seat. "To be so constrained."

"We're happy that way," Celia said. "Anyway, my fiancé decided he was in love with another woman."

"Who?" asked Fran. "Macy? It must be. Your resentment is obvious."

"No," said Macy. "It was someone else. He told me because he was too cowardly to tell Celia. He wanted me to do it for him, and I had no choice. He was going to leave town without telling her."

"Well, that takes the cake!" said Aunt Fran.

Poor Celia. She sat unmoving and silent as a fencepost.

"Lemme tell ya, sweetheart," Aunt Fran went on to say, "you lost nothing—*nothing*—when he left the picture." Her voice became gentle. "And you shouldn't kill the messenger. I'm sure Macy didn't relish sharing such horrible news with you."

Celia sighed. "I know. It's not *your* fault." She looked stonily at Macy.

Macy's pink cheeks were pale now. "I knew he was preoccupied. I knew he wasn't treating you the way a loving groom should treat his future wife. But that was all. When I found out he was in love with that other woman—well, I was shocked. And devastated, on your behalf."

"Where is he now?" Deacon felt for Celia. He needed to ask at least one question to show he was paying attention.

"Married to that woman," Celia enunciated properly but with disdain. "They have three children."

"Surely the devil's spawn," said Aunt Fran helpfully.

"They're living in Atlanta." Celia sat up a little higher.

"Which Sherman burnt," his aunt said agreeably.

Celia shook her head. "It's best not to refer to the War Between the States."

"That's what you call it here?"

Celia nodded.

"Okay." Fran smiled. "You sure you don't still resent Macy?"

"It would be a waste of my energy." Celia put her wine glass on the coffee table.

"I hope you're not suggesting Macy's not worth your time." Aunt Fran, ever the troublemaker, eyed Macy with a sympathetic eye.

Celia addressed the abstract portrait of a naked woman behind Aunt Fran's head. "It's galled me to see her set up shop as a matchmaker. If she's so good at it, why couldn't she tell that the man she'd meant for me was in love with another woman?"

"I'm right here, Celia." Macy raised her hand. "I have no excuses. I simply didn't sense what was going on, and it's probably because I didn't hang around you two very much. I told you I'm sorry."

"And you're married now," said Aunt Fran to Celia. "Aren't you happy?"

"Of course." Celia glowered, appearing the opposite of a woman deeply in love with her husband.

Aunt Fran put a proprietary hand on Macy's arm. Dogs squirmed between them. "Part of being any sort of professional is recognizing when you're in over your head."

"Duly noted." Macy met Deacon's gaze. Why was she smiling at him with her eyes? Like they were in on one gigantic joke together? Every other young, single female of his acquaintance pegged him as either a scoundrel or the answer to all their prayers. Of course, he was both. He had the feeling Macy understood that.

It was terrifying.

Which was why he said to his aunt, "I'm not staying for supper, after all. Tell George to take my place at the table."

And he ran away to Upper King Street, where all the happening bars were, and endured the flirtations of college girls by buying them all drinks and sending them on their way so he could play pool and smoke cigars in the alley until two in the morning with a bunch of fraternity boys who dubbed him "Old Man."

CHAPTER SIX

Macy's life felt completely different now that Deacon and Fran Banks were in town. The air was softer. The sun was shinier. Everything Southern that she'd grown up with took on a fresh appeal, thanks to Fran's marveling. Like grits. Macy had a sudden, new affection for them. They were corn—corn ground down to tiny white specks that together tasted amazing with a pat of butter and a sprinkle of salt!

She had no idea she'd been in a rut *at all* until the Bankses came along.

In the bubble bath last night, after she'd given Fran the coconut cake, she decided she'd been like a sad, rusted bicycle that had been chained to a tree so many years that the chain was embedded in the tree bark. And someone had come along with a big chainsaw—a really loud one—and cut through the chain, or maybe even the tree.

That description might be a little extreme, but it was how Macy felt. She was moving again. Forward.

The next morning, she walked out her front door after breakfast with Oscar on her arm in his tote bag. Deacon's contract had been pushed through her mailbox onto the wooden planks of her piazza. There was some kind of tan stain on it. She sniffed. Bourbon. He must have read it at a bar and signed it in a drunken stupor.

Even so, she was happy. The way he'd skipped out on them last night at dinner, she'd had her doubts he'd go through with their business arrangement. So had his aunt.

"I don't know why he's so skittish about settling down," Aunt Fran had said over a gorgeous roast beef. "But he made it very clear to all of us tonight that he plays by his own rules. I'm sorry, Celia and Macy, that he abandoned us."

"He doesn't need to settle down," George had said, wiping his mouth with a linen napkin. "The world is Deacon's oyster. More wine, ladies?"

George had been a highlight of the evening, even if Celia was still her cold self. Macy didn't care, though. Oh . . . that was a lie. She did care. She still felt horribly guilty about Celia's breakup. But what could she do? Celia had moved on. The offending gentleman had moved on. So had Macy.

But at least the night wasn't a total bust. She'd met Fran, who was challenging and fun, and George. Already she felt as if she'd made two new good friends, and they were right next door.

So was Deacon. For Macy's own sake, she needed to get to work on finding him dates—and maybe his soulmate—as fast as possible. He was a terrible temptation. George and Fran told her stories last night of all the women who'd thrown themselves at Deacon because of his charm and had their hearts broken.

Macy had long since passed her bad-boy phase. She was proud of that fact. Yet last night, getting ready for bed, tipsy from the delicious shiraz, she wondered where he'd gone. She'd even peeked out the window when she turned off the light at eleven thirty to see if she could see through one of the windows on Fran's piazza into her living room, which was still well lit.

And then she realized that she was spying, and that it was an awful thing for a good neighbor to do.

So now she shut her sidewalk front door behind her and started her walk to work, saying in her head, *I'm a professional, I'm a professional*, in time with her steps. Oscar, meanwhile, stuck his head out of his carrier bag and sniffed the salty sea air flowing over the Battery wall.

"Psssst!"

She looked back and up. There was George, leaning over Fran's piazza railing, his head almost blocked by the green, waving fronds of a tall palmetto tree.

"Good morning!" Macy called to him.

He was thin, wiry, of indeterminate age—somewhere between thirty and forty-five, she guessed—and fond of colorful clothing. Today he wore a golden-yellow kerchief wrapped around his head, and the same large gold ring in his left ear that he'd worn last night. He'd donned another pair of flowing silk pants, Wedgwood blue (they'd been scarlet the evening before). His shirt was an ivory silk with voluminous sleeves.

Last night she'd discovered that he lived in a fifth-floor walkup in the Hell's Kitchen area of Manhattan and commuted by subway to Aunt Fran's penthouse on Central Park every morning, preparing her breakfast at nine and leaving at seven each evening after cooking her supper.

"Deacon's hung over," he said. The gusty sea breeze almost stole away his words.

"I guessed that." She held up the contract. "It smells like bourbon."

George chuckled. "Maybe you can find some Southern belles who'll set him back on his heels. Fran says *she* needs a challenge—well, Deacon does even more. Take it from me."

"Thanks for the heads-up," Macy called up to him and

readjusted her tote bag. Oscar hated when she dawdled and was squirming.

Fifteen minutes later at her office, she started working on creating a master list of thoroughly vetted dates for Deacon. It shouldn't be hard, but it *was*.

"First, the ideal candidate has to meet his requirements," she told Ella and Greer.

"Which are?" Greer was poised at the whiteboard in Two Love Lane's conference room with her favorite purple marker.

"She should be striking, sophisticated, and an excellent conversationalist," Macy said. "And she shouldn't be seeking real romance. Which means she'll be satisfied with a fun date with an emotionally unavailable out-of-towner."

"Our clients are all about emotional availability," said Ella, "so we need to go outside our office files to find these women."

Macy agreed. "Let's look at our own personal contacts."

"To our phones," Miss Thing announced like a military commander in charge of a campaign.

So they sat for fifteen minutes scrolling through their phones and scribbling down potential prospects. In the end, they had eight names. Greer wrote them on the whiteboard.

It was time to dive in and make some calls.

In the end, four women out of the eight called were okay with a fun date that led nowhere.

"I love all four of these ladies," Macy said. "We know them personally. We can vouch for each of them having their own special qualities."

"They'll have fun," Greer predicted. "And who knows? Maybe sparks will fly."

"That's what I'm hoping." Macy high-fived everyone then picked Oscar up and kissed the top of his head, which he pretended to hate. "We're on our way," she told her furry friend.

And she was glad. She was having too many naughty thoughts about Deacon as it was. Let some other woman think them instead.

Later that night, when Macy got home, Fran's piazza was empty, but pale blue light streamed from the living room windows. Someone was watching television. Company would be nice, and Macy was tempted to go over, but she really needed a good night's sleep.

"Macy?"

Her heart stopped for a flash of a second. It was Deacon. He must have just come outside. She looked up and felt warm all over at the sight of him. Caught in the soft glow of a gas lamp burning by the front door of Fran's house, he was such a pleasure to look at, especially with that lazy smile. "Hi," she eked out.

"You okay?"

"I'm fine," she said, although her throat felt a little tight. She wasn't sure why. Fatigue, probably. And the stress of worrying—just a tad—about how she was going to find him a soulmate when she couldn't stop daydreaming about him herself.

"Come on over," he said. "We're just about to have some more of that coconut cake. It's really good."

"I'm so glad. But I"—she couldn't think—"I need to go to bed."

There was a pause. "Okay."

"Hey"—she strove to sound excited—"we compiled a master list of fabulous women you can take out."

"Uh-huh." He sounded wary.

"Remember you're doing this for Fran."

"I know."

"You'll have a good time. I'm sure of it." And she was.

"Right."

"Tell you what," she said. "Come for breakfast tomorrow. I can fill you in."

"What time?" He perked up a little.

"Eight?"

"See you then." He smiled.

She liked the dimple that appeared in his left cheek. "Good night." Her keys jangled in the lock as she practically forced the fake piazza door open.

While she unlocked her front door, she wondered what had happened to professional Macy. She was still frazzled when she fed Oscar and had a bowl of leftover turkey soup she'd made the day before. So she took a soothing bath, and while she was in it, got lost in a fabulous novel by Dorothea Benton Frank, whose stories about Charleston always made her laugh, and sometimes cry, but in a good way.

Even so, when she pulled the plug and watched the bubbles go down the drain, something was still a little off.

"Let's go." She unceremoniously scooped Oscar up from one of his favorite watching places—the top of the toilet lid, which she'd covered in a hideous shag carpet material for the cat's comfort. "You're sleeping with me tonight."

He didn't object. He was too smart for that. He waited until she'd arranged a fuzzy lap quilt decorated with a snowy scene for him on the other side of the double bed and slid beneath the sheets herself before he bolted.

"Don't you know it's almost Christmas?" she called to him. "You're supposed to be extra nice! Especially with everything that's going on!"

Oscar was there when it all started—the day Deacon Banks had shown up in her office. She adjusted her pillow several times and tried to sleep, but it was a long time coming. Just the thought of Deacon sent warm, longing feelings through her. She imagined them making love in her bed. It was the best fantasy ever. It didn't matter that she had an agenda for him, that he was her client. She was crushing in a big way for the first time in ages.

But she knew she couldn't just have a fling and walk away. She had a life that she cherished and wanted to protect.

CHAPTER SEVEN

Deacon woke up starving. His first coherent thought was *Breakfast at Macy's*, but he wasn't thinking about toast and eggs, or bagels and coffee. Even as his stomach growled, his imagination lingered on the curve of Macy's cheek, the spark in her eye, the way she laughed.

He couldn't wait for breakfast because he liked her. Macy was a cake baker, a matchmaker, and a society girl who didn't seem to notice she was cut from a different, spectacular cloth. She was a wild thing. He saw it in her eyes—a barefoot girl who marched to her own drummer. And he wanted to get to know her better.

Way better.

He rubbed his jawline and decided against shaving so he could slip out before George started puttering around the kitchen. He and George were Aunt Fran's two favorite men. They were like brothers, antagonizing each other one minute, best pals the next. This morning, Deacon didn't want to deal with the man's sly brand of humor.

But just as he was about to close the front door behind him, George showed up in the living room.

"Morning," he called to Deacon in a singsong voice, as if he'd caught him out.

Which he had.

Deacon sighed and opened the door again. "Not a good way to start the day, seeing you."

"The feeling's mutual. You make me feel ugly, you brute, with my bedhead and your *GQ* hair." George was in a multicolored robe Aunt Fran had brought him back from a safari trip. "Where ya headed? Not out for a run, obviously."

Deacon was in jeans, an old L.L.Bean sweater, and a button-down with a frayed collar. "Over to Macy Frost's for breakfast. And a rundown of the women she's lined up for me."

George gave a short laugh. "I like Macy, but this dating scheme is just a tad ridiculous."

"Agreed."

"Why are you doing it then?"

Deacon hated starting off the day feeling testy, but he was moving in that direction. "It was Aunt Fran's greatest desire. She told me in front of you. So why are you rubbing it in?"

"Because it's the pot calling the kettle black. It will be a cold day in hell when Fran ever settles down, after all the bad luck she's had. So why is she wishing that on you? It's a little weird. And hypocritical. I kinda thought you'd remind her of that."

"You want me to tell her those husbands who didn't appreciate her were a waste of her time? You really think that would go over well?"

George scratched his chin. "No."

"I owe her, George," Deacon said. "It's kind of heroic, actually, that she has the energy to hope for me in the romance department, in spite of giving up for herself."

George nodded slowly. "I guess I see your point. We have to get her having hope for herself again."

"Not a bad idea. Do you think she moved here to investigate a new crop of men?"

George shook his head. "She's bored, is all. But you wouldn't know about that, would you? You're the guy everybody wants to hang out with."

"I could say the same about you."

"Good thing we run with different crowds, brother."

"I'd hate to fight you for top-dog status," Deacon said, his mood improving. "I have no idea who'd win."

George lofted a brow. "If the competition's about who can pick out the prettiest shelf paper or bake the best roasted chicken, I would."

"By a landslide." Deacon winked and shut the door.

When he knocked on Macy's real front door less than a minute later—the sidewalk one was ajar, presumably just for him—Macy yelled, "Come into the kitchen!"

He hoped she had something besides yogurt and granola. He was spoiled at his aunt's house, thanks to George. No cold breakfast for him.

At least there was hot coffee. He followed the smell of it past the foyer with a stately, simple staircase into a formal dining room that looked like it was straight out of the olden days except for the modern silver vase filled with poinsettias on the sideboard. He pushed open a swinging wooden door into a vast kitchen with a large brick fireplace at the other end. Strung across its mantel was a line of paper reindeer.

"So I fancy myself a Waffle House cook in another life." Macy wore a Santa hat and a half-apron with snowmen stitched all over it. She was busy making waffles, toast, fried eggs, bacon, and hash browns.

Sunshine and breakfast with an honest-to-goodness elf. George couldn't top this. "Merry Christmas to you, too," he said. "I should have worn *my* Santa hat."

"It's on the table," she said.

Sure enough, it was. He put it on. She laughed.

"What's the Waffle House?" he asked.

"A Southerner's favorite place to eat breakfast at two in the morning." She smiled. "You have to be a little bit drunk when you go."

"Ah. Sounds fun."

"We'll have to try it sometime." She had a twinkle in her eye.

"I'd love to."

With the flick of a wrist, she shut the lid on the waffle iron. "How do you like your eggs?"

He loved her expert confidence. "Over easy is fine. Wow. This is some breakfast."

"Thanks. Grab yourself a cup of coffee." She had a whole coffee bar set up.

"I think I want to come over every day for breakfast now."

"I'll do this another time for George and Fran, too," she declared. "But today we need to tackle some business."

"Sure. In our Santa hats?"

"We have a lot to be jolly about, right? Fran will be thrilled you're getting started on delivering her Christmas present." Her eyes were bright. Wide open. Honest.

He was a little disappointed she was so excited about the idea. "Fine," he said. "But first I have to say, this place is awesome."

"Thanks. It needs some work. But it's all mine. And I mean to make my grandmother proud by keeping it up for future generations of my family."

"Yeah, sorry what I said about the tilt. Good for you for taking care of a special house like this."

"It's seen a lot. So has Two Love Lane." She was busy with the eggs, and then the next second she was pouring orange juice and flipping hash browns.

"You own that property, too?"

"I do. With my two business partners and best friends, Greer and Ella."

"Real estate is a great investment. In fact, sometimes I wonder why I went toward the tech sector. I love houses. I always loved *Monopoly*."

She grinned. "I liked *Clue*."

"Great game. You got a billiard room here? Or a conservatory?"

"No, thank God." She stirred a few pots. "And no neighbors named Colonel Mustard or Professor Plum."

"That's good." He liked how light things were.

She opened a cupboard and brought out two mismatched plates. Apparently, she was done cooking. Everything was hot, steaming, or fried to a golden crisp, and smelled fantastic.

Of course, nothing smelled as good as her flower scent, the one he'd liked the other day. He was tempted to lean in. And he did—

Just as she turned around to face him.

He pulled back.

"Wow," she said, looking adorable in her Santa hat. "You're right there."

"You smell good," he said. Like an idiot.

But it made her blush. "I do?"

"Yes. Like flowers."

"Thank you." She gave a light sigh. "All I can smell is bacon."

"Really?" He lifted his chin. "You sure you can't smell my new soap on a rope? Aunt Fran got it for me in the British Virgin Islands."

She made a skeptical face. "Really, Banks?"

"Why not, Frost?" He crossed his arms. "Soap on a rope is key to leading a manly life."

She shot him a small grin and leaned in. "Mmm," she said. "It's very nice."

"Why, thank you." This was the point where he'd usually try to kiss the girl. He always knew what the next step would be.

But not with Macy.

"Is there anything here you don't like?" she asked expectantly, hovering over the food.

"Uh, no. I like it all." He meant her, of course. But he still wasn't sure exactly why. He'd met many gorgeous, charming, smart women over the years, several of whom were amazing cooks. What was it about this one that threw him off kilter?

"I'm glad you're not a picky eater," she said, her manner brisk. "Have a seat. I put a file from Two Love Lane next to your place setting. You can start looking through it while I dish up."

So he did. He sat, and it felt like home with the little blue vase and the single lush pink blossom in it. His ancient floral linen placemat had to be from the 1950s or early '60s. Macy had paired a faded red linen napkin with it. He also had a fork lying primly on the left, with a seashell pattern on its end, and a matching butter knife, blade turned in, on the right.

Damn, that cutlery was heavy.

"That's my grandmother's sterling silver," she said.

"You use it every day?"

"Sure do."

So she was old-fashioned but eclectic, too. He couldn't call her formal. She was too warm for that. George would love her style.

"What kind of flower is this?" He eyed the blossom in the vase and thought how well it went with Macy's personality. It was sunshiney and open but elegant, too.

"A camellia from my back garden." She poured two glasses of orange juice from a glass pitcher.

"You didn't squeeze that juice, did you?"

"Of course," she said, and held up an old hand juicer. "Good for my grip."

"You play tennis?"

"Yes. But badly. As for camellias, they bloom in winter. Aren't they gorgeous?"

"Yes." He wanted to play tennis with her—that morning. Too bad she had to work. He opened the file on the women, and words, words, words leapt out at him. He didn't feel like reading. He wanted to talk. But he tried to read the file because this was business, and she clearly wanted to keep it so.

He perused the names and photos at the top of each page: Tiffany (cuddling a kitten; absurdly pretty). Louisa (outdoorsy in hiking boots). Rena (dark-eyed; holding an artist's paint brush in front of a canvas). Barney (wearing glasses and a ponytail; definitely pretty).

But anyone could be pretty. Go to any makeup artist and be transformed. It took someone special, someone different, however, to be striking. It meant something intriguing in a woman's personality was revealed on her face. He much preferred to keep company with a woman who could claim his attention that way.

Although gorgeous didn't hurt. Gorgeous kicked off that instantaneous man reaction in him which had everything to do with sex and nothing to do with long-lasting rapport.

Macy was gorgeous. But she was also striking. That was a deadly combination when Deacon wanted to keep thinking bachelor thoughts.

"Barney's an interesting name," he said.

"*Barney* is short for Barnwell, a surname in her family," Macy explained. "Barney's great. You'll love her. She's a firefighter."

"For real?"

"Yes. She's got some great stories to tell."

A few seconds later, she brought over his plate with everything on it. Somehow he was supposed to eat all that.

"Do you prefer real maple syrup or the fake kind?" she asked.

"Either." He liked how she fussed over him.

"I like Log Cabin," she said, "and I will never change. But I have both."

While she retrieved them, she asked if he wanted blueberries and/or whipped cream on his waffle, or just butter, along with his preferred syrup.

"Just butter, please."

"That's how I like my waffle." She beamed. It was too early in the morning to tolerate people beaming at him, but somehow he liked when she did. And he was glad he'd pleased her.

What was wrong with him? Everyone understood why he'd want his aunt's approval, considering that she gave up so much just to raise him. But *this* girl . . . he barely knew her.

She sat down opposite him and slathered her waffle with butter. Then she poured Log Cabin syrup all over it and sighed. "I love breakfast," she said. "Please dig in."

So he did. Their eyes met across the table. He read sheer enjoyment in hers. And he was happy too. Food was good.

But so was sex. And a man eating a delicious breakfast opposite a beautiful woman who'd cooked it for him and fussed over him would also be thinking about sex with her.

He tried not to. They talked about the nice weather for December. He'd never had such a temperate holiday season. She told him about the Christmas boat parade that night. She ate a piece of bacon with obvious gusto. And then another.

"I'm sorry you have a bacon allergy," he said with a straight face.

"Yeah. It's terrible." She chuckled.

They had a companionable ten seconds together watching Oscar roll on the floor, hoping for some tummy scratches. Deacon took the file folder and scratched him behind the ears with it.

Macy rubbed Oscar's belly with the tip of her shoe then looked up at Deacon. "Hey, your aunt should have a little boat parade party."

"She is," he said. "Celia arranged it."

"Oh, great! I'll gladly watch it from your balcony." She paused. "Not that I'm inviting myself."

"Don't be silly," he said. "We're neighbors. Aunt Fran was going to ask you today, so I will, instead."

She was quiet. Some sort of awkwardness descended where it really should not be, not after their happy little breakfast. She took a few sips of coffee without speaking. He made another cursory glance through the papers in the file, but none of those women interested him at all. He was sure they were perfectly nice and would make for enjoyable dates for any man. But his heart wasn't in it.

What was he doing in Charleston? That question popped into his head, even though he already knew the answer: He was here to give his aunt a month of his time. He'd carved out this time, just for her. Everyone he worked with had prepared themselves. So had he.

Yet he didn't know what to *do* with so much unscheduled time. He wasn't comfortable with it. He had too much time to think. . . .

But he didn't even know about what.

"You seem really tense right now," Macy said. "Is something upsetting you? Is it this dating thing?"

He shook his head and focused on his over-easy egg.

She took another bite of hers. "No date has to last longer than two hours. Honestly, if one of these women isn't your type at all, the date could be concluded in an hour and a half. That's considered long enough to be respectful and polite."

"Fine." But it wasn't fine. He wanted to go on a date with *her*. He didn't want her to be his so-called tour guide at Waffle House. He wanted more.

When Deacon knew something, he confronted it head-on. But for some reason, with Macy he felt he had to tread carefully. Maybe it was because she was Southern, and he felt like an outsider here. He didn't want to step on toes and totally ruin his chances with her.

He wanted that chance.

She kept eating. So did he.

Suddenly, she put her fork down. "I've heard from Fran and George that you've had a lot success with women."

He lofted a brow. "And I'm sure that's just how they explained it."

She smiled. "They said you love 'em and leave 'em. Actually, that they leave you because you're not into commitment."

"That's more accurate."

"But is dating itself hard for you? Plenty of CEOs know what to do in the boardroom but have a difficult time partnering on a date—the give-and-take that's required. So they never bother to learn. I mean, powerful men often have women waiting in line, so dating isn't something they need to put a lot of thought into."

He put his fork down, too. "Do you really think I might have that issue? Not knowing how to be a good date?"

She popped a blueberry in her mouth with her fingers. "I'm not sure. You were awfully demanding in my office. But that was business. So was Fast and French. I have no idea how you'd be on a real date. It's something to watch out for, is all."

"Duly noted." She was in pro matchmaker mode. He wanted her back as Macy the wannabe Waffle House cook.

"It's also okay," she said, "not to be familiar with or *like* this artificial way of dating. Blind dates are hard."

"I've been on blind dates. That's how I met my last girl-friend."

"Oh, okay," she said. That weird awkwardness was back. She pressed her napkin to her lips, then stood, her coffee mug in her hand. "Can I get you a refill? Coffee? Juice?"

"No, thanks." He stood too, and followed her to the counter, but held back a ways. "Thanks for a great breakfast."

"You're welcome." She smiled at him over her shoulder. "Don't forget your file, okay?"

"Right." He strode quickly back to the table and picked it up.

When he turned back around, she'd lifted her mug to her lips, and all he saw was her eyes, which were deep, and warm, and bright beneath her Santa hat. He knew then that he'd keep that image of her forever, might even dream it at some point.

She put the mug gently on the counter and said, "I think these four women are all great."

"I'm sure they are."

"Feel free to set up follow-up dates on your own. And you might even meet someone else at one of the parties you'll no doubt be invited to. This goes without saying, but ask out anyone who seems interesting to you."

"Right." Except he couldn't ask *her* out. Not yet. And she was the one he wanted to take to dinner, pull out a chair and buy a glass of champagne for. He wanted to woo her, the old-fashioned way.

She went to work rinsing their dishes and putting them in the dishwasher. "I've got one more thing before I have to head out. You know how I get to work on finding you a soulmate?"

"You like to remind me of that." He put the leftover orange juice and the butter in the fridge before grabbing a paper towel, dampening it, and wiping down the Log Cabin bottle.

She shut the dishwasher. "There's something bothering me about this so-called arrangement."

"And that is?"

She turned to face him, her hands behind her back on the counter. "I can't work my end well when you're not being honest with me."

"I'm being truthful," he insisted.

She pushed off the counter. "I'm not so sure."

He pushed in both chairs at the table.

She put on a jacket that hung from a wooden coat tree in the corner. "You said you'd never been in love as an adult—I'm talking the serious, non-puppy type of love between possible soulmates."

"I understand."

"But is it true? Or it is fun to let people assume it's true? Maybe you get something out of having a playboy image."

He removed his Santa hat. "Thanks for breakfast."

"You're welcome." She took hers off, too. Then she picked Oscar up, who was rubbing against her leg, and put him in his tote, slung it over her shoulder, and grabbed her purse. "I don't expect you to be forthcoming about your present. But I do expect at least a foundation of truth about your romantic past when we work together. It's only fair."

"You're right." He knew he was trying her patience.

They walked outside together into blue skies and mild temperatures for December. It was a gorgeous day. Too gorgeous with that big yellow sun in his face to lie any longer.

"What the hell," he said, stopping on the pavement beneath his aunt's house. "Shakespeare said, 'Love is merely a madness.' I wouldn't know. I've never been in love. Real love, the soul-searing kind. And so if people want to call me a bad boy for that, it's better than being known as that loser guy with no heart and no luck."

CHAPTER EIGHT

Standing there in the sunshine on that glorious day, Macy couldn't help it—her mind was blown. Deacon was like *her*. She was so excited, she just said what came to her: "Do you like hot wings?"

"Hate 'em."

"Basketball?"

"Love it."

"I do, too. I have season tickets for the men's basketball team at the College of Charleston. I don't play myself, but I know the rules better than the refs. And sometimes, I lose control and yell at them."

"You 'lose control.' " He laughed. "You're funny. How about you think the refs suck? And you're the boss and they'd better listen up, or you'll knock 'em over?"

"Yeah." She felt so happy that someone understood.

"I'd love to see you at a game."

"How do you know Shakespeare?"

"Same way most people do. School. And Aunt Fran. We read the comedies and the tragedies together. She got me into musicals, too, believe it or not. It's hard not to love 'em when you live near Broadway."

Macy laid her hand on his arm. "I've never been in love either."

"Really? *You're* the matchmaker who's never been in love?"

"Yes." She could see the shock in his eyes and shrugged. "I've had a million crushes, all right? But not the real thing. I recognize what love is, though. Otherwise, I could never do what I do."

"Wow." He peered intently at her. "You're definitely not the type I'd think had never been in love."

"There is no type for that," she said. "It is what it is. It doesn't mean people like you and me aren't suited for love. It just means we haven't found it yet."

"Or maybe we don't want it and don't miss it. I fall in that camp. I'm happy the way things are. "

"That's not another line to pacify the critics?"

"Nope. It's the truth." He gestured to Oscar's tote. "May I? I'd love to walk off breakfast with you two."

"Sure. Thanks."

Oscar retreated into his little nylon canvas cave when Deacon took over carrying him. But Macy liked it. No one else had ever carried Oscar before. And she'd never had someone tag along with her as she walked to work. She liked the change-up.

"I've been in a serious relationship twice," Deacon said. "They wanted to make it permanent. Have babies. Move in next to family. And that was when I realized I didn't love them. I just liked them a lot."

Macy sighed. "I know the feeling."

"Besides, I'm crazy about my work."

"I get you there too."

"Most women I meet are looking for either a money grab or a power alliance or both." He spoke in a careless, cool manner, blissfully unaware that Macy was seeing deep beneath his alpha-male exterior to a sensitive soul. "Being related to Aunt Fran makes me even more of a so-called catch. She's got a lot of cash and influence in her own right."

"I can see how having a famous person in your family might have its perks, but also its serious drawbacks," Macy agreed. "On a smaller scale, I'm in somewhat of the same dating boat in Charleston. I come from a well-connected family. I'm never sure if a guy likes me just for me." It was a heady confession to make. It was scary too. She wished she could grab his hand.

And then he grabbed *hers*. He squeezed hard and pulled her across Broad Street. "We're a lot alike, aren't we?"

"I guess we are," she said, her heart pounding in her ears. She knew in that second, her crush was not just dialed up to a ten. She was all the way to eleven with this guy.

When they reached the curb, he dropped her hand, and she had about half a second to regain her composure. She reminded herself that he was only being a gentleman, taking her hand the way a friend would when you're talking and you don't want to lose track of the conversation, and bang—next thing you know, you're yanking that friend across a busy street.

Oscar's face had come back out. His whiskers twitched at the smell of Deacon and salt air. They were coming up on Roastbusters.

Deacon was quiet. But he was thinking. Macy could tell. There was a serious cast to his expression, an alertness with which even Oscar, who thought he was a lion on the prowl, couldn't compete. They passed a narrow street lined with tightly squeezed old houses that ended at a pier on the harbor. In the distance, the Ravenel Bridge, with its two white triangular towers, gleamed against the blue sky.

"Here's the really big thing you need to know," Macy

said. "You have to believe you're naturally lovable. My grandmother told me that many a time, and I still struggle with it myself. It's easier said than done when you're not sure of people's motivations. But you have to trust your instincts. You'll recognize the opportunists."

"Believe me, I do." Deacon gave her the side-eye. "You're good at giving advice. I also like how you admit you don't always take it yourself."

She smiled. "Just don't let anyone make you a cynic. Cynics are terrible at falling in love." She wondered if that was why *she* hadn't fallen in love. She asked her sister every once in a while if she thought so too. Anne would always say, "Don't be silly. Of course, you're not a cynic!"

But what if she was? Sometimes Macy worried about that at night, when things didn't seem as bright and optimistic as they did during the daylight hours.

"I'm already a cynic," Deacon said. "Which means the odds are against me."

"But not impossible," Macy said. "And you're *not* too far gone. A full-fledged cynic doesn't carry a cat in a tote bag."

That was why she wasn't a cynic either, she assured herself. She loved life. She loved walking to work and smelling the fresh air. She loved her cat, and she wasn't afraid to do crazy things like carry him around with her.

Deacon kept his gaze straight ahead. "So I guess there's hope for you too, huh?"

That drew her up short. Had he guessed that she had her moments when she wasn't entirely sure that dreams came true, even when you believed in them with all your heart? They were at the corner of East Bay and Love Lane. The cobblestone alley glittered with dew and sun.

She didn't want to go. "Thanks for walking with me."

"My pleasure," he said.

There was that word "pleasure" again, sounding like

candy from his lips. And he was so good-looking, she could hardly breathe. His grin—broad and bright—was framed by dark stubble and that dimple in his right cheek. His blue-eyed gaze was honest and confident yet somehow vulnerable too. The mix was super sexy. She shot him an awkward smile. "I'll take Oscar now. He enjoyed seeing things from a little bit higher up, I'm sure."

They made the switch and walked down Love Lane to the gate in front of the house. Deacon squatted to look at the ornate ironwork.

"It's beautiful, isn't it?" Macy never got tired of looking at that gate.

"Stunning." He ran his fingers over the two interlocking hearts formed so gracefully in the middle of the design. "I wonder if there's a story about these hearts."

"I've always wondered the same thing."

"This is a work of art," he said.

"It is." The wonder in his voice moved her. "Some master craftsman made it by hand back in the day."

"Around the Civil War?"

"No. The Revolution."

"I'm in awe. Honestly." He squinted up at her. The morning sun dappled his hair with golden highlights.

She smiled. "I always like when newcomers appreciate what we have here. Everything has a story. It hasn't always been pretty, I know. There's a long history of pain and suffering in Charleston." Just thinking about the different stories of the people who'd walked Love Lane's stretch of cobblestone over the centuries made Macy emotional. "But there has always been love here too, and bravery and hope, in spite of the tragedies we've endured. We have Mother Emanuel leading by example today."

"I feel that." His expression was sober, thoughtful. "I wish—"

"What?"

"I wish I could leave a mark. The way this master craftsman did with this gate over two hundred fifty years ago."

"You'll do great things," she said out of the blue. She couldn't help herself. She believed in him somehow. She saw sincerity and a generosity of spirit in his eyes.

He laughed. "What do you mean?"

"Don't be so worried." She opened the gate. "Let life happen." She needed to get away because talking to him made her want to play hooky at work. "See you later."

But he grabbed her wrist before she could take another step. "You're fun to be around, Miss Matchmaker Lady."

Uh-oh. Macy felt that buzz of awareness between them, the same one she'd felt in her office, at Fast and French, in his aunt's foyer, over her own breakfast table, and when he'd held her hand crossing Broad Street. Was she destined to feel it every time they met?

"Thanks. You are too," she said, and slid her wrist from beneath his palm.

"See you on the piazza tonight." He turned away, whistling, and started walking back up to Roastbusters.

She couldn't take her eyes off him. "That was nice," she murmured to Oscar, "and probably not a good idea. Let's go."

Her office was a place to hide. A place to think. To recover. And to plan exactly how she was going to keep her head on straight because Deacon Banks was messing with it very badly. And he wasn't even trying that hard.

However, when she got inside, past Miss Thing, who was on the phone but winked at her, a big bouquet of gorgeous purple and pink hothouse tulips awaited Macy on her desk. She put Oscar's tote bag down. He ran out and leapt onto her blotter.

"Don't you dare," she told him, when he immediately bit into a pink petal.

She pushed him off, and her heart pounded when she read the card: I KNOW BREAKFAST IS GOING TO BE DELICIOUS. AS WAS THE COCONUT CAKE. THANKS FOR BEING A GREAT NEIGHBOR. ~DEACON BANKS

"Fudge," she said out loud. Who cared that he wasn't from here? A gentleman was a gentleman. And a handsome devil was a handsome devil. . . .

She dared not forget that he was both.

CHAPTER NINE

Deacon had run eight miles that afternoon—mapping out a route across the huge Ravenel Bridge and back, then around the Battery, up and down beautiful side streets, and around Colonial Lake before returning home. Then he turned right back around to buy a ten-foot North Carolina Fraser fir at a church parking lot on Wentworth Street. It was supposed to be a quick-and-easy errand, but he wound up having words with Trent Gillingham, the local jerk on Aunt Fran's favorite show. Trent had wanted the same tree.

"I'm Trent Gillingham," he'd said, "from *Bless Your Heart*, and I saw this tree first."

He put his hand on the tree trunk Deacon had already claimed as his own. Deacon was only waiting for the tree lot guy to bring back his change. "I'm Deacon Banks," he said, "from Manhattan, and no, you didn't see this tree first. It's mine. Go find your own."

Trent glowered at him and gave the tree trunk a little push with his palm. Luckily, Deacon had anticipated such a tantrum and had already tightened his hold on the tree. It didn't move.

Trent stalked off.

"Merry Christmas, buddy!" Deacon called after him.

What an idiot.

Back at Aunt Fran's, he told the story, and instead of being upset at Trent's rudeness, Aunt Fran wanted to know where her favorite television hunk had touched the trunk, and then she wondered if Deacon should have given it to him.

"No," Deacon said. "He was a brat. And I'd already paid for it anyway. Why are you so obsessed with this guy again?"

"He's handsome, and he has such a great accent," she said.

"There are plenty of guys in Charleston with the same accent," said George, who was helping Deacon put the tree in its stand.

"And ones closer to your age," Deacon chipped in.

Aunt Fran sulked for a minute, but only until Deacon gave her some spiked egg nog. Then they all got busy putting on the lights and decorating the tree, after which Deacon and George strung the balconies with lights—all in preparation for the parade of boats that night.

And Christmas, of course. But the cocktail party spurred them on.

Now Deacon was freshly showered, the last of the pungent tree sap scrubbed off his fingers, and on the piazza again in a sweater and jacket. A light wind blew off the harbor a mere hundred feet away. It was pleasantly cold—not nearly Christmas cold, but he liked it anyway. The seventy-five-year-old bag boy at Harris Teeter had told him that morning that it was more mild a Christmas than usual, but any day they'd get polar temperatures.

"You just never know with Charleston," the old man had said with a cackle, then stopped and looked at the plastic container he was putting in the bag. "You're getting a lot of olives and cheese and crackers, aren't you? Throwing a party? Are some pretty girls attending? I see you're not married."

"Yes. It's a small cocktail party. During the boat parade." People around here liked to talk. And take their time bagging groceries. And ask you personal questions.

"Of course." The bag "boy" chortled. "You gotta good place to watch it?"

"Sure do. Right over the Battery wall. On a . . . piazza."

"Fancy that," the guy said with robust cheer. "The Battery. In one of those big mansions?"

"Yes. My aunt has a condo in one."

"Good for your aunt. Is she a sweetheart?"

"Oh yeah. Sweet as can be."

"Then you tell her 'Merry Christmas' from Peter, especially if she's single." He winked and put a box of crackers in the bag.

"She *is* single, as a matter of fact." Deacon grinned. "I'll tell her."

Walking back to the Battery with a bag in each arm, he decided he didn't mind the menial errand or chatting with strangers. They were good distractions, but more than that, he was having fun living in the low-key zone.

As usual, he had a lot on his mind. Sales figures. Profits. Staffing problems. Scaling the businesses he'd bought across the country. If he really wanted to, he could be on his phone and his computer all day, or flying out to the West Coast or Chicago for meetings.

But he knew the best—the very best—business people in the world took time off—a sabbatical of sorts. A chunk of time to reflect, to renew, to discover new aspects of themselves and their talents maybe they didn't even know they had until they stopped for a little while and let themselves catch up.

So he forced himself to let it all go.

It felt weird and exhilarating. He was on *vacation*. He was with his aunt. If he was thinking about work, he couldn't carry on a decent conversation with her or anyone at her party. Now he watched his aunt's guests drink, eat, and chat while waiting for the boat parade to start. His own drink was gone, and he wondered where Macy was. He felt immature waiting for her like a high school boy, but so be it. She liked the tulips. She'd texted him to thank him. He'd texted back that he was glad she liked them, but he couldn't text her again without a good reason. The only good reason he could think of was to talk about women she'd set him up with—and he didn't want to do that.

He'd just have to be patient.

George was at the bar, pouring ice into a bucket. Deacon headed his way. Celia threw him yet another searing glance, but he ignored her. What was she thinking? Did she assume he was interested in an affair? Where had that come from? Especially when her husband, who seemed like a perfectly nice guy, was standing right next to her.

Aunt Fran appeared at his elbow. "I'll take a martini," she told George.

"You're in Charleston," George said. "New rules. Men go to the bar for you and bring you your drink." He made the martini and passed it to Deacon. "Give this to your aunt."

Deacon handed it to her.

Aunt Fran pushed it away. "No way. I get my own martinis. You drink that one, George, and make me another."

"I'll be glad to." George threw it back and got to work shaking up another. "You sure are stubborn."

"There's only so much I can change." Aunt Fran poked Deacon in the side. "You look a little preoccupied."

"Some small part of me still believes I'd better behave," he said, "or I'll get coal in my stocking."

"Impossible," his aunt said, and picked up her new martini. "I brought you up right. Can you guess what I'm giving you for Christmas?"

George shoved a fresh drink Deacon's way. "Maybe a book or two on politics, history, or some celebrity biography," Deacon said. Most of them came from the green room on her set, former interviews she'd done. But she'd have them autographed to him, which was nice.

Her eyes flew wide. "Absolutely not," she lied. "What else?"

"My annual suit."

"Well, of course. This time we'll get it at Charleston's premier men's store. It's called Berlin's, and the locals tell me people fly down from New York just to shop there."

She'd been giving Deacon a new suit every Christmas since he was three years old. They'd always gone to Bloomingdale's on Third Avenue when he was a kid. Later, he graduated to a custom tailor on Broadway.

"And of course, we'll have our usual beef tenderloin dinner," she said, "although Celia says we have to have oyster pie also. She's giving George the recipe. Afterward, we'll do the usual."

Which was watching *Mame*. They did every year. Aunt Fran had raised her sibling's child, just as Auntie Mame had, so the show was near and dear to their hearts.

"I could use a little Christmas right this very minute," Deacon said, paying homage to their favorite tune in the show, as he kissed his aunt's cheek.

She smiled. "I wish Macy were here."

That was exactly what he was thinking . . . Macy would be a little Christmas for him.

But he was in Charleston to protect Aunt Fran and to advance her interests. So he did his best to be the nephew she could be proud of at the party. He especially enjoyed meeting retired marine colonel Ed Block, appropriately named because he came across as an immoveable force.

Colonel Block had a tendency to jut out his chin and clench his jaw, like Marlon Brando in *The Godfather*. "I smoke a cigar and drink bourbon in my library every day at seventeen-thirty hours sharp," he informed Deacon in a thick Southern drawl. "If it's nice out, we retire to the brick patio. I live around the corner. Feel free to stop by."

A petite redhead with a short, sophisticated haircut came up to the railing.

"These lights are pretty spectacular," she said.

"They are," Deacon agreed. From big sailboats, shrimp trawlers, motor yachts to modest johnboats and a few Sunfish, the boats were all covered with lights. It was a very merry display, and a twinge of honest-to-God Christmas spirit snuck up on Deacon. He shot his new companion a friendly smile. "Hi. I'm Deacon, Fran Banks' nephew."

"Hey, back." The new arrival stuck out her hand and smiled. "I'm Penelope Gordon. I work at the Historical Foundation. Macy Frost told me to meet her here, but I see she hasn't arrived yet."

"She'll show up at some point, I'm sure." If she didn't, Deacon's budding Christmas spirit would take a hit. "Thanks a lot for stopping by."

Penelope was attractive. And personable.

"My pleasure. I talked to your aunt about your family history here in Charleston." The diminutive redhead gave a pretty shrug and smiled. "She actually didn't have anything to tell me beyond the surname Banks. Supposedly, one of your family members came here at some point."

"It's more like an old family rumor," Deacon confessed.

Penelope nodded sympathetically. "Every family has them. And sometimes they turn out to be true. I'll see what I can find out."

"You're kind to do that."

Ten minutes later, he and Penelope were still chatting. Boats streamed slowly by. Drinks were refilled. The talking on the piazza got louder. Out on the street, the crowd shifted, grew, and one group starting singing Christmas carols.

"So how are you and Macy friends?" Penelope asked.

"She's setting me up on dates through Two Love Lane," he said. "I'm doing it for my aunt. It's a Christmas present."

Penelope laughed. "I get the impression you're not ready to settle down yet, Deacon Banks."

"You read me well. But the truth is"—he hesitated—"aw, never mind."

"No, tell me." Penelope had such a friendly face.

"Well, all right," he said. "If I'm going on any dates while I'm here, I'd rather go out with Macy than her clients."

Penelope's expression softened. "Why?"

"I really like her," he confessed.

"My oh my." Penelope cocked her head. "That's so sweet. Thanks for confiding in me."

He shrugged. "I'm not trying to be sweet. And I don't think it's particularly gallant of me to be talking to one lovely woman about another one."

"No, no." She waved a hand. "I like your honesty. And I feel like we're already friends, don't you? A little Christmas cheer in a cup and a nice boat parade go a long way to breaking down barriers, wouldn't you say?"

"I'm honored you think so," he said. "And I agree, friend." He grinned and raised his glass to her.

"To friends." She smiled and raised hers back. "Look, I want to help you here. Macy is very professional, so I don't think she'd ever go out with you when you're her client."

"You're right."

"But you can't back out of your deal, correct? I mean, your aunt is counting on you for this gift?"

"Yes. Not only that, Macy has this burning desire to find me my soulmate. So both ladies would be devastated. One personally, the other professionally."

Penelope laughed. "What a quandary. But I've got an easy solution. Do you have the phone numbers of the women Macy's setting you up with?"

"I do."

"May I see them?"

"Sure."

Penelope perused the names on his phone. "I know three of the four. And that's no big deal. She'll be on board after I talk to her."

"What do you mean?"

Penelope grinned up at him. "I'm going to tell them we need to conspire with each other to get you and Macy together. Whatever it takes. We all love her. And she's always putting other people first. It's time for her to have some fun."

"You'd do that?"

"Of course. And I don't mind helping you out either. You're my first friend from New York City."

"I'm blown away. Thanks."

Penelope chuckled. "I'm looking forward to this, Deacon. Big-time."

"You rock. Really." They clinked glasses again.

"Hey, she's here," Penelope said, "and she's heading our way."

Deacon turned. Sure enough, Macy was on the other side of the piazza.

"Work with me when she comes over, okay?" Penelope asked him.

"Will do."

"Hey, you two." Macy squeezed in between them at the railing.

"Hey, yourself." Penelope bumped her hip with her own.

"Now we've got ourselves a real party," Deacon said. "Can I get you a drink, Macy?"

"Not just yet, thanks," she said. "Let me look at the boats."

So they did. The twinkling lights on the water, the people lining the Battery wall, it all added up to a spectacular, heartwarming sight.

"I had to help my sister wrap presents for thirty-five teachers," Macy said. "But I'm not gonna lie. I enjoyed every minute of it. I'm a good-cheer junkie."

"Me too," said Penelope. "Life's too short to live it any other way. What about you, Deacon?"

"Sure." He raised his glass of bourbon. "Cheers."

"Not that kind," Macy teased him.

"I like the other kind too," he insisted. "The feel-good, Christmas kind that's supposed to last all year. Like Charles Dickens said."

"I love a well-read man," Penelope stage-whispered to Macy.

Macy laughed. "He is, honestly. Ask him about any Shakespeare play."

"I'd love to," said Penelope, "but I have to run. Hey, I'm bummed because I have reservations at FIG tomorrow night that I have to give up. My friend is too busy to go, and I am too, honestly. You know how hard those are to get, Macy. I had to book six weeks out."

"Yes," said Macy. "FIG's so good, it's almost impossible to get in unless you plan way ahead."

"That's too bad," Deacon said.

"How about you two take them?" Penelope looked between them both.

Deacon wished he could laugh out loud. She was a fast mover.

"I don't know." Macy sounded skeptical.

"If it's that good . . ." Deacon put down his bourbon. "I wouldn't mind." He tried to sound nonchalant.

"I don't know." Macy's forehead puckered.

"Oh, come on," said Penelope. "It's always amazing. You'll be at work all day, Macy. Won't it be great to walk to FIG afterward for a glass of wine and a fantastic meal? The reservations are early. Six o'clock. They're the only ones I could get."

Six o'clock was definitely not the dating hour.

Macy's shoulders relaxed. "Okay."

"Fine by me." Deacon was playing it cool.

Penelope grinned. "Thanks, y'all. I would have felt so bad cancelling. It's FIG!" She bade her farewells, and that was it.

Deacon had a date with Macy.

"We need to talk," Macy said.

"I know what you're going to say."

"You do?"

"You're going to tell me FIG isn't a date. And of course, it's not. I'm your client."

Macy relaxed. "Exactly."

"It's only a six o'clock reservation." He struck a casual pose against the balcony railing. "Nothing romantic about that."

"True. In fact, we'll call it a practice date. I'll check out your style."

"You saw it at Fast and French."

"But that was business. And daytime. This is dinner at a white-tablecloth restaurant. A different vibe."

"I don't really need help dating," he said.

"I know that. But maybe we do things a little differently in Charleston. I could give you tips. And it never occurred to me to add Penelope to your dating list because she recently came off a bad breakup. But I think I should."

"You're the expert," he said.

"She's so smart and pretty. And nice."

"Yep." She was selling Penelope hard.

"I think she might like you."

"You think?" He had to fight to sound truly interested.

"Sure."

"Too bad she's not my type," he said.

Macy's grin faded. "She's not?"

"Nope." He kept his eyes on the long line of festive boats.

"Do you have a type?" Macy asked.

"Sure." He drained his glass. "Likes to bake cakes. Asks too many questions. But she's sexy and sweet, so she can get away with it. We'll go from there." He was going faster than he'd planned. His Christmas drinks had loosened his lips.

"I have no idea which of the women on your list like to bake." So she was going to pretend she didn't know he was talking about her. "But all of them are sexy. And to heck with sweet. They're reasonable, friendly, and mature."

"Those are great qualities. But let me clarify sweet. I actually mean she's got to be flexible about kissing." He knew it was high school talk. But he had a crush. A big one. "I'll want to kiss her in front of her parents. Or at a football game. Or when she's coming out of the shower."

"Hmm."

His body was begging him to get close to Macy Frost. His mind couldn't stop thinking about her. And his heart was clamoring for her attention. He wanted to put his arm around her badly, to pull her close, to kiss her temple, murmur sweet nothings in her ear.

But he knew that he'd not want to stop there. He'd want to kiss her mouth. Run his hands down her sides, relish the curve of her hip. Lose himself in her body.

"You ready for that drink yet?" he asked her.

"Sure. But I really just want a Coke."

But George was out of Coke.

"No worries," said Macy. "I have some at my house. Let me go get it."

"Thanks, doll," said George.

"I'll go with you," Deacon said.

"Great." She gave a lighthearted shrug.

They chatted easily down the stairs about nothing special. But when he opened Fran's front door for her, and she passed beneath his arm, he wanted to reach out, pull her close, and kiss her.

Not yet, though. He wanted to be mature about it—and cool, and respectful—but waiting was driving him crazy.

Outside on the sidewalk, she wrapped her arms around herself. "It's getting colder."

"I love it." He liked walking with her to her house. And there was no place he'd rather be when he followed her onto her piazza, through her foyer and dining room, and into her kitchen.

She grabbed two liters of Coke from the pantry. "Here we go."

"Let me," he said, and took them from her but put them down on the countertop.

It was time.

"Uh-oh," she said. "A kiss is coming, isn't it?"

"I want it to." He tugged on her hands. "Do you?"

She hesitated, then nodded. "Oh, why not?" she said, and put her hands on his chest. "It's a party."

"It's always a party being around you. Did you know that?"

She blushed. "I was talking about your aunt's party."

"I'm talking about you," he said. "Not that damned piazza and George behind the bar and all those people Aunt Fran is trying to charm."

Macy gave a slight shake of her head.

"You're beautiful," he murmured, just before lowering his mouth to hers.

The kiss was searing hot. And it went on. And on. Macy's hourglass figure fit perfectly within his arms. Her mouth was perfection. He wanted her badly. She was a hot kisser, giving as good as she got, so maybe she wanted him too.

"Wow," she said, finally pulling back.

He would like nothing better than to pick her up and lay her down somewhere, strip off her clothes, and make love to her.

"We can't," she said. She always knew what was on his mind.

"I want," he said.

She groaned. "No. I was stupid to kiss you."

"You're not stupid."

"You're so cute. And . . . and sexy."

"So are you."

She backed up a step. "We just can't."

"Tell you what." He tugged on her hands and pulled her close again. He couldn't tell if she was acting shy or wary—or both. "You're fired. You can keep all the money, but this arrangement isn't working."

Her eyes widened, but she quickly recovered her professional cool. "What about your aunt? Your promise to her?"

"Here's a compromise that will satisfy her: You and I go out. I don't want to see those other women." He squeezed her hand. "You feel it, don't you? *I want you in my bed*."

To hell with playing games, using Penelope and the

other women to help him win Macy over. He could do it himself. And in a lot less time.

He believed in honesty.

She stared at their interlocking fingers, hesitated, then pulled her hand away and looked up at him. Her eyes held a glint of shock. But he saw regret there too, which made the flame of his crush hotter than ever.

"Deacon"—she had the grace to hesitate again—"you're tempting. I gave in to a kiss, and it was worth it. Believe me. But I don't want to get involved with a guy who doesn't even live here and who has said he's emotionally unavailable."

She was smart. Of course she was. Smarter than he was. "Maybe this isn't practical," he said. "But we could have a lot of fun. And I'm not heartless, you know. I like you. I like you a lot."

"I like you too, but I'm not into Christmas flings," Macy said simply. "Neither am I necessarily interested in getting into a relationship. I'm a busy woman. I'm happy. Fulfilled. It would have to take a heck of a situation for me to change course—I mean, love with a capital L and all that it involves. You get that as an entrepreneur yourself. Don't you?"

"Of course. But I don't have to like it."

"Look." She smiled softly. "Our business arrangement will work if you give it a chance." She picked up the two liters of Coke. "Please? For your aunt's sake?"

"Okay," he said, and took the Cokes from her again. This time he held onto them. "The arrangement stands." He had no desire to continue with their agreement. But he would. To keep her and his aunt happy. But if he was going to have to jump through a million hoops to do so, he refused to feel guilty about trying to make the experience a lot more enjoyable for himself. He'd go along with Penelope's plan. What Macy didn't know wouldn't hurt her.

And maybe, just maybe, it would work.

* * *

So Deacon was completely into her, Macy realized. That was the problem—and the delight of her heart. She was an evil, wicked, terrible matchmaker. But she couldn't think about how amazing that kiss was or dwell on her own shortcomings for long.

She had a phone conference to get through with a client on business in Jamaica. He really wanted to talk to her about one of the women she'd set him up with. He was starting to fall for this woman, he told Macy, but he had reservations. He didn't like her dog. It was too small. Yet this potential soulmate of his was obsessed with it. What could he do? He only liked big dogs. . . .

All in a day's work for Macy.

After convincing him to give the woman and her small dog at least another week's try when he returned home, Macy popped her head into Greer's office. "Heading out to Roastbusters and then to pick up a new skirt I bought at Nancy's on King Street. I had to get it altered. Wanna come?"

Greer pushed up her glasses. "I wish. I'm too busy. Thanks, though."

Macy wasn't ready to tell anyone she'd kissed Deacon, but she was dying to talk to Greer and Ella about her fake date with him—What should she wear? Was it okay to spray on a tiny bit of perfume when this was only a practice run?—but she didn't want them to know she was actually excited. She was a professional, right? She was all about that.

Macy found Ella's office door shut with a Do Not Disturb sign on the knob. Loud noises she couldn't decipher emanated from within, something like a hammer pounding. Or two blocks being hit together. And then a mysterious whining noise, followed by a thump—and another thump.

She sighed. Ella was apparently off-limits at the moment.

She went to Miss Thing. She wouldn't dare talk to her about the date. Their office manager saw through Macy every time she tried to hide something—and darned fast. Oscar sat on a chair next to Miss Thing, his tail flicking relentlessly. He was obsessed with her pink feather duster, which he knew was hidden in her lower desk drawer.

Miss Thing was resplendent in a nubby yellow Chanel wool jacket and skirt finished with white stitching on the sleeves and breast pockets. At the moment, she was updating the December calendar on Two Love Lane's website. Each day, she added a holiday dating tip.

"What's going on in Ella's office?" Macy asked.

Miss Thing lowered her crystal-studded reading glasses. "Some secret Christmas activity."

"I'll say."

"Have you heard anything more from that young man, Deacon Banks?" The sharp gleam in Miss Thing's eye didn't bode well.

"Sure, I've seen him." Macy braced herself. "He's my neighbor."

"He *is*?"

"Yes." She did her best to sound dismissive and picked up some paperwork from Miss Thing's desk. "What's this? The bill from the landscaping company?"

"They fixed the hose out back so it doesn't leak anymore."

"Good. I see the equipment charge. But where's the labor cost?"

Miss Thing ripped the paper out of her hands. "Mr. Banks is your *neighbor*?"

Macy sighed. "Yes. His aunt bought a condo in the house next to mine. I can see directly onto their piazza from my bedroom window."

"Oh my heavens." Miss Thing started waving the landscaping bill in front of her face as if she were about to burst into flames. "So what's happened? Have you been over there? Have they come over to see you?"

"Yes, I've been there, several times now. And Deacon—"

"You call him Deacon?"

"That's his name."

"Yes, but—my goodness. That was awfully fast."

"Not really. I tend to call all my clients by their first names within the first couple of meetings—unless they prefer a more formal interaction."

"Still." Miss Thing blinked. Her mouth, lined in a deep fuchsia matte lipstick, tilted up in a tremulous smile.

"Miss Thing. You must remember something."

"Yes?"

"We are a business here. Deacon Banks is my client. Please don't forget that. Our reputation rides on our commitment to our mission, that we are professional matchmakers who put the needs of our clients first. Whether I'm attracted to Deacon Banks or not doesn't matter."

"You *are*?"

"Of course!" Macy put her hands on her hips and tapped her foot on the floor. She was feeling quite . . . flustered. Yes, that was the word. "Let's stop talking about it. Okay?"

"Whatever you say." Miss Thing's tone was smug as she abandoned the landscaping bill and started polishing her white princess phone with a lace handkerchief. Oscar stood, his pupils widening, and watched that handkerchief wiggle all over the phone.

Macy put on a brittle business smile. "See you in a little while. I have errands to run." Of course, she loved Miss Thing, but gossip didn't pay the bills. She escaped to the vast entry hall, where she inhaled a deep breath, put on her coat, slung her purse over her shoulder, and prepared to exit the house.

"Oh, Macy dear?" Miss Thing called to her.

"Yes?"

"Do you have somewhere to be tonight? Where you'll see Deacon?"

"Yes. How did you know?"

"I can just tell. Have you kissed him yet?"

"*No!*" she lied, slamming the door behind her.

Thank God for Roastbusters. Two Love Lane was equipped with a coffee machine, but there was nothing like the slow drip they made at the coffee house, and nobody beat Roastbusters at making peppermint cocoa.

Macy had been getting it a couple times a week since Thanksgiving.

"Extra hot, please," she told Andy, the owner and main barista. "Extra whipped cream too, if you don't mind."

"Right." Andy winked.

"And no lid, please," she added.

"*Right*, Macy." He laughed.

"Sorry. Oh, and—"

He put both his palms on the counter. "Don't you think I know your holiday order by now?"

"I suppose you do."

He leaned closer. "You don't want a lid so you can really pile on the whipped cream. You like it extra hot because you take it back to work and get so busy, you forget about it, and it cools down, and your microwave is broken and you refuse to fix it because your mother doesn't believe in microwaves. *You* do, but you feel guilty about liking them."

"I've told you that?"

"Several times."

She blushed.

He went on. "You like half a pump of peppermint instead of a whole pump, and you like me to put a cherry on top, even though cherries and peppermint don't go together that well. You tell me that too. You say, 'Andy, they don't go together well. But I don't care. I like them.'"

"Oh." She could feel her blush deepen. "I guess I do say that."

Andy laughed. "We don't *do* drinks with cherries on top, Macy."

"You don't?"

"Nope. I keep a jar just for you."

"You do?"

"Yes. And you know why?"

"Why?"

"Because I like you, that's why. The first time you came in and asked for a cherry on top, I felt terrible telling you we didn't have any. I pretended we normally stock them. And that night I went to Harris Teeter and bought a jar."

"For me?"

"Yes, for you. Because I like you."

"*Andy.* Oh my gosh. I like you too." She was so touched.

"You keep coming in here and being you, Macy. It makes my day." He slid her peppermint cocoa across the counter. The whipped cream on it was so high, the cherry jiggled.

"Thank you, Andy. I-I—"

"Go on, now. You don't have to tell me I'm your favorite man. I already know I am. You can go do your errands. I can tell you're in a rush. Or something exciting is going on."

What was exciting? She couldn't remember. And then she thought about seeing Deacon that night at FIG. It was embarrassing, but she was excited about *that*. She tried to tell herself she was excited because she loved the food there. But the truth was, she wanted Deacon to see her in her beautiful new skirt from Nancy's on King Street.

"Andy, can I admit something to you? And will you promise not to tell?"

"When have I ever told your secrets?"

"You're right." She leaned closer. "Sometimes I'm the worst matchmaker ever."

"No, you're not," he said stubbornly. "You're a wonderful matchmaker. Go on, now."

She sighed with gratitude and started walking away then turned around. Something had occurred to her. "Are you married? Or in love?"

He laughed again. "I'm in love with *life*. And that's good enough for me. Are you trying to set me up, Miss Matchmaker? This is a first. You've held back until now."

"Well, yes, but only if you want me to. I just think you'd make someone a wonderful partner."

Andy's face grew serious. "I had a wonderful partner," he said. "But that was many moons ago. It was a big enough love to last me a lifetime. Now I'm passing it on to all my customers." He pointed to her cup with his right hand, his palm up. "That love is in your peppermint cocoa."

Her heart swelled. "I can tell." She gave him a quick smile, and he turned away, got back to work.

She was lucky, so very lucky.

CHAPTER TEN

Deacon's ears were cold. They never got cold unless it was really winter.

"Now it's really winter," he told George. They were drinking bourbon on Aunt Fran's piazza. Not too much—Deacon was meeting Macy at FIG. "If it stays like this, we can have Christmas here and not feel funny."

"Yeah," said George. "I don't know if I could do a summertime Christmas, although Peter, my new best friend at Harris Teeter—"

"The seventy-five-year-old bag boy?"

"One and the same." George inhaled on a cigar downwind from Deacon, who didn't want the smell on his coat—for Macy's sake. "Anyway, Peter says last year he wore swim trunks outside on Christmas Day. It was seventy-two degrees."

"Whoa."

"And we still have a ways to go. Peter said we could easily have a hot Christmas."

"No way," said Deacon. "We brought the New York weather with us. It's going to be cold."

"No snow, though, and that's fine by me." George

stretched his legs out and sighed the sigh of a contented man.

"I'll miss the snow." Deacon watched an elderly couple,
bundled up and holding hands, strolling along the Battery
wall. "But I'll be fine as long as it's good and cold to the
point I go inside and want to sit by the fire."

"And drink bourbon," added George helpfully.

"Yep, I think this might be our last piazza bourbon. It's
time for fireside bourbon."

"You'd think." George stubbed out his cigar. "But we'll
probably drink too much fireside bourbon, enough that we
can't feel the cold. And head out to the piazza again."

"You can't beat the view." Deacon admired the white
caps scudding across the harbor. The fronds on the palmettos waved their leafy fingers. Dogs trotted, people gazed
over the water. But he was nervous. He was going to go
on a date with Macy. A trial date, where she was going to
critique his readiness to go on dates with the women she'd
chosen for him.

After a few more minutes of sipping and people-
watching, the two men stood.

"Have a good time tonight," George said.

"I will."

"I know." George chuckled.

Deacon wasn't feeling on his game when he set out for
FIG. The truth was, he'd never had to work for any sort of
approval from women. Tonight would be his first time.
And the irony was, tonight was the first night he wasn't
feeling exactly confident.

His cell phone rang about a block from the restaurant
door. It was Penelope.

"Hi," he said, surprised.

"Hi," she said back. "I got your number from Macy. I
told her I needed to talk to you about your Banks ances-

tor. But of course I'm calling about the women on your list.
I've spoken to all of them. They can't wait to get you together with Macy. So be prepared. They all have their
own ideas."

"Will she figure it out?"

"Hopefully not. But even if she does, so what? She'll
find out her friends care about her."

"True, but I promised her I'd behave and follow through
on our agreement. She might not appreciate that things
changed without her permission."

"Deacon, stop worrying. You're doing the right thing.
By the way, I Googled you. Everything looks good. I don't
want Macy to get hurt."

"Definitely not. But fair warning: I like Macy but I also
like being single. My life is complicated. If that doesn't sit
well with you and the other ladies, you might want to call
off this operation."

"Operation Macy?" Penelope laughed. "No way. We
want her to have fun. Everything else is up to you two."

"Thanks." He hung up and opened the door to FIG.

"Deacon!" There was Macy, looking gorgeous. She had
a cranberry-colored martini in her hand.

No way in hell was this a practice date, he decided. It
was going to be real. He kissed her cheek. That was what
he'd do on any first date. But it felt awesome to touch his
lips against her soft skin. It gave him a craving to make
out with her right then and there.

"How are you?" he said close to her ear, and couldn't
believe how glad he was to see her.

"Good," she murmured, and looked up at him from beneath thick lashes, almost as if she was feeling shy. "I got
a pomegranate martini. Want a sip?"

"Guys don't drink pomegranate martinis."

"Don't be that way." She grinned. "Just give it a taste."

"Okay."

She held it up to his lips. He took a sip. "It's actually not bad."

"It's delicious," she said, and took another sip herself. Her lips were wet and shiny. She was sexy, and if he kissed her right now, he'd taste that martini.

So he did. He kissed her, tasting her mouth with his tongue, and the jolt of desire that shot through him nearly knocked him off his feet.

She pulled back, her eyes wide and luminous. "First-date kisses don't happen that fast," she whispered.

"I couldn't resist," he said low. "I'd love to ravish you right here and now, but I'm a gentleman."

"Deacon—"

"But seduction can wait," he told her. "I want to hear what you have to say. I want to see what you get to eat too, and what kind of wine you like. I want to hear you laugh."

She inhaled a deep breath. "You're very . . ."

"What?"

"Sexy," she said, and took a large gulp of her martini. "Oh, this is a terrible first date. We're not supposed to act so . . . hot and heavy."

"I think that makes for a great first date."

"People should take it slowly."

"Why?" he asked.

"So true friendships can evolve."

"Macy, I don't want to be your friend. I want to be your lover."

Her neck turned a pretty pink. "Lovers *should* be friends."

"Fine, but who said the friendship has to come first? Sometimes the best way to get to know someone is in the sack. It's more exciting that way." He took in the peep of décolletage he could see and grinned.

"Deacon, you *are* a playboy, and this conversation is inappropriate. I hope no one can hear it." She looked around, her forehead marred with a single squiggle. But the place was busy. The ambient noise was as effective as cotton stuffed in a person's ears.

"We're fine." He chuckled and took her elbow. "No grading me until the end of the night, okay?"

"Okay." She gripped her martini glass tighter.

"Follow me," a friendly host said, and led them to a quiet corner table, where he put down two simple menus. "Enjoy your meal, folks."

Deacon pulled out Macy's chair. He told her she looked beautiful. He asked the host to bring her another martini. But he did those things because he really wanted to, not to get a good grade on his dating report card.

When the host left, Macy smiled at Deacon, a sparkle in her eye. "I always love this place. And it's been a long day. It feels good to be here."

"I'm glad we're here too."

There was the slightest pause.

"Tell me about your day—" they both said at the same time.

Macy laughed and unfolded her napkin, placing it in her lap. "You first."

"Okay," he said. "Aunt Fran had me running all kinds of errands for her. The funniest one was buying pimento cheese. Celia told her about it. It's my new favorite food. It's so orange. And good. Especially on Wonder Bread."

Macy laughed. "You don't have pimento cheese in New York?"

"No. We're missing out. What's going on with you? Something beyond pimento cheese concerns."

"You sure you want to know?"

"Yes. Lay it on me."

A college-age server with a high ponytail came by and took their order, but as soon as she retreated, Macy said, "There's this client who runs all over me. And I have no idea how to turn that situation around. The truth is, I'm intimidated by her, even though I have no good reason to be. I'm the one who knows what I'm doing. But she's very powerful and used to getting her way."

Deacon let that sink in while he munched on a cracker smeared with pâté. "Okay." He wiped his mouth with an overlarge linen napkin. "Let's create a list of *good* reasons to be intimidated by someone. Are there any?" He grabbed a receipt out of his shirt pocket. "Got a pen?"

"Sure." She pulled one out of her purse. "Better education," she said right away.

He turned the receipt over and wrote that down. "Wealthier," he added, and scribbled that down too.

"Better-looking," she said.

"Better social skills." He was trying to keep up.

"Which ties in with more confidence." She put her chin on her hand and watched him write.

"Anything else?"

"Better athlete?

"Okay." He wrote that down and pushed it across to her. "Look at this list."

She perused it.

"Do you feel like you're back in high school again?"

She chuckled.

"We don't have to be those people anymore," he said.

The server brought them their entrées, which smelled delicious.

"You're right." She inhaled the delicate aromas of steaming rice and curry on her plate and smiled.

"Before we chow down," he said over his own plate of homemade pasta with prosciutto, "let's pretend we're rebutting that list to some really fantastic teenagers with low self-esteem. What would you tell them about better education?"

"Easy." She let out a breath. "Just because someone has

a more recognizable degree or a higher level of formal education, doesn't mean they will go further in the world than you."

"Agreed," he said. "And common sense, which is much too rare, has nothing to do with education anyway. It's found in every segment of the population."

She leaned toward him, her eyes sparkling. "About wealth. We know money can't buy you love."

"That's right." He picked up his fork. "You can't take it with you, either. Money, that is. Maybe you can take love . . . or make love."

She leaned on her fist. "You've got a one-track mind."

"Not fair." He shot her a lazy smile. "This is an enjoyable conversation."

"That it is," she murmured. "So what will we tell these teens worried about beauty? That it's in the eye of the beholder?" She picked up her fork too.

"Yep, and good looks have nothing to do with changing the world."

"As for social skills and confidence, we'd tell them you can develop those." She took a bite of her entrée and closed her eyes. "This is delicious."

She was so sexy. "And it takes all kinds to make the world go 'round anyway," he added. "What if we were all extroverts? How exhausting would that be?" He sampled his entrée too, and put his fork down to savor it. "This is excellent."

"Isn't it?" She leaned in. "You know what? I like shy people. I'd tell those teens who are shy not to worry about it."

"I agree. I like shy people too."

She smiled. "As for sports, anyone can become an athlete. How about the paralyzed man who walked across the Ravenel Bridge last year in the 10K fun run? He wore an exoskeleton. He crossed the finish line too."

"Wow. Good story." Deacon eyed her. "So Frost. Tell me more about this woman who intimidates you."

Macy put down her fork and eyed him back. "There's nothing to tell, Banks," she said quietly. "Thanks for helping me remember that it's all in my head."

They fist-bumped across the table then raised their wine glasses.

"God, you're going to get a big head over this, but you're doing awesome on this date," Macy said. "You'll be a hit with all the ladies here."

The thought didn't give him pleasure. "I want to be a hit with *you*," he said.

She sighed. "You *are*."

"I am?" He grabbed her hand and kissed the back of it.

She shook her head. "But it doesn't matter." Her voice was low. "For all the reasons we've already discussed."

"I'll take it," he said. "I'll take anything I can get from you."

She smiled again. "You're incorrigible. And—and the opposite of boring."

He laughed. "So are you."

She waved a hand.

"You're most definitely the most exciting woman I've ever been around," he said.

She shook her head.

"I'm not flattering you." He wished she believed him. "These things are true."

"I'll think about them," she said noncommittally, and was clearly relieved when the server showed up.

After much discussion of the various options, they came to a conclusion: two coffees—one with extra cream for Macy—and they'd split the sticky sorghum cake with walnuts and amaretto ice cream.

"So," Macy said, once they were alone again.

Deacon exhaled a deep breath. "I want to thank you for something."

"For what?"

"You brought us a cake when my aunt arrived. You've been nice to George and to the Corgis. And now I know where to get the best soup in the world—at Fast and French. You've made me feel at home here in Charleston. And my family too."

She laughed. "But that's just what people do . . . we're kind to one other. We look out for our neighbors."

He shook his head. "I haven't gone out of my way to look out for anyone, really. Sure, I give my employees good bonuses and I try to make their workplace enjoyable. We partner with charities too. But I rely on my assistants to send flowers, to buy cards. I even get them to call my aunt for me."

"Surely you visit Fran."

"I do. But not as often as I could. Or should."

Macy shot him a sympathetic look. "Don't be so hard on yourself.

The server brought over the sorghum cake and smiled. "Enjoy. It's on the house."

"My goodness." Macy's eyes widened in delight. "That's so sweet of the kitchen. I'm not sure why . . . I don't have a birthday. Deacon, do you?"

"No." But he soon would. And dammit, he'd be thirty-three. Anyone that age had no excuses left. You either accepted the mantle of full-time grownup or looked like an idiot rejecting it.

"Actually, it's not the kitchen," the server said. "Two customers sent it over. They just left. Lisa and John?"

Macy smiled. "Aw, the Tatums. That was so nice. Thanks."

"No problem." The server went on her way.

"Lisa and John are old clients who wound up marrying," Macy explained. "They just had their first baby."

"You're good at what you do. Really good. And I admire that."

"Thanks." She wore a self-conscious smile that warmed his heart. It was obvious people didn't tell her often enough she was amazing.

Well, he was going to change that.

They both dove into the sticky sorghum cake. And after the bill had been paid—Deacon insisted on handling it—they walked home together slowly. It was cold.

He took her hand. "Let me," he said before she could pull hers away. "It's perfectly acceptable first-date behavior."

She stole a quick glance at him. "Okay."

He relished every moment of that walk.

At her door, she took her hand back and tucked it into her coat pocket. "I had a great time," she said.

"So did I." He didn't want her to go in.

The waves shushed and slapped against the Battery wall behind them.

"So we'll dissect this date tomorrow?" he asked.

She shrugged. "That was the plan."

But he could tell she felt some reluctance about going back to thinking of this evening as a test. He grinned. "I won't keep you in suspense. You were a fantastic date. I don't have a single complaint or critique."

She gave a little hop. "Really?"

"Really."

"Except for one thing," he added.

The wind blew down the street, soft and cool.

"What is it?" she asked him.

"That martini kiss was too quick."

Her eyes widened. "Banks," she said in a jokey voice. "You were doing so well. We even held hands. I mean—"

"The kiss is the most important part of a date. We all know it."

She took a step back. "I think so too. There has to be chemistry. But I don't need to evaluate you that way. All I need—"

"Shush," he said, and tugged on her free hand.

She came down a step. Now she was looking up at him.

"Let me kiss the pretty girl I just had a great time with."

"Okay," she whispered.

Time slowed down. Way down. He leaned in, channeled his more innocent high school self, and kissed her lips— just her lips—lingering only long enough to let her know he wanted way more. She was like candy, her mouth soft and sweet, and it killed him to pull back. But he did.

"Good night," he told her, his hands in his pockets.

"Good night," she returned softly.

He tossed her a wink and turned away.

"Deacon?"

He was dying to look back, but he wouldn't. Instead, he gave her a thumbs-up. "It was a ten!" He could feel her staring at his back.

"But we didn't even . . ." she called after him.

He turned around. "Get very far?"

She wrapped her arms around her middle. "Um, yeah."

"I really want to. But I'm saving that for when we're not kissing under first-date testing conditions."

"Oh," she said. "Right. Not that we'll—"

"Yes, we will," he said. "Someday." There was a beat of silence, a yawning gap between them filled with possibilities. "Sleep well, Macy."

A smile tugged at her lips. "You too." She opened her piazza door, and he watched it shut behind her.

This woman, he thought. *This one*.

He was crazy about her.

CHAPTER ELEVEN

After her practice date with Deacon, Macy's intuition kept telling her: *You and Deacon are a match. You and Deacon are a match!*

She'd always trusted her gut before. Why not? She was sure Cupid was one of her ancestors. Matchmaking ran in her blood. She had proof she was good at it. And dinner at FIG had been . . . magical. She had no other word. They'd conversed so easily about things big and little. Everything seemed right. And the whole time, she'd wanted to kiss him badly. How could she not? After their searing kiss of the night before?

It was a shock how natural and fun it felt, that pomegranate martini kiss. And then there was the innocent, perfect kiss at her door. She remembered feeling that everything was out of her hands. It was as if she were simply watching as this powerful thing—whatever it was—bloomed between her and Deacon while the inky night sky sparkled with stars above their heads.

She tossed and turned in bed that night. Why couldn't she sleep?

Was Deacon her soulmate?

She turned on her bedside lamp. It was two a.m. Staring

at the signet ring on her hand, she decided she'd check with the algorithms in the morning. She didn't have all of Deacon's data. But she'd been around him long enough to make some good guesses. She'd get Ella and Greer involved. They'd all played with the algorithms before to test out friends, family, and even celebrity couples.

Finally, she slept. But at nine o'clock the next morning, she was huddled with Ella and Greer around the desktop computer in Greer's office. The screen darkened, then brightened. Colors, numbers, and a block of text popped up.

"No, no, no," said Macy, her heart pounding.

"You were right," Greer said, and squeezed Macy's arm. "You're a match."

Macy closed her eyes. "I'm not ready for a match—for so many reasons."

"Look," said Ella.

Reluctantly, Macy opened her eyes. Ella pointed at the screen. "Not only are you a match, you two got the gold star."

A gold star meant that there was a high likelihood that the couple in question would make a commitment to each other within the year.

"No," said Macy. "He's my client, first of all. I'm not supposed to date my clients! And he's from New York. He's going back soon. Did I mention we have very little in common? Can you imagine a guy who attends every Yankee home game at a Southern debutante ball? And here's the real kicker—he doesn't even believe in love! He wants a fling. A Christmas fling."

She sat in Greer's chair.

Greer blew out a breath. "All I know is that you need to stop acting like love is for other people and not for you too."

"Yeah," said Ella. "And so what if you start with a fling? It could be fun."

"I like him, I admit it," Macy confessed, a hitch in her voice. "A fling—I could probably use one."

"Couldn't we all!" Greer exclaimed.

Macy put her hand over her eyes. "I don't know what to do."

"It's okay to be afraid," Ella said.

"We're here, always," said Greer, "to back you up."

"Thanks," Macy whispered. "Maybe I'll ignore whatever it is between us. Swipe left, like on Tinder."

"You could," said Ella. "You could be like two ships passing in the night. But I don't want you to run away. Not if this is something *real*."

"You need to work with him," Greer reminded Macy. "But he'll be gone in a few weeks."

"Right." Macy's heart felt heavy.

"How can you set him up with other women now?" Ella asked.

"What's done is done," she said. "I'm a professional. I can't very well call these women and say, 'Sorry. He's mine.'"

"I don't see why not. They're our personal friends," said Greer. "Maybe you're in love. The real deal. And if the feeling is mutual, you don't need to worry about those other women being in the picture."

"That's right," said Ella. "Let's call them."

Macy shook her head. "Let's not. It can't be love. Not this fast. I feel sure of that. We've barely even kissed. All told, under ten minutes of kissing time is not long enough to figure out such heady stuff."

"Okay, so maybe we're jumping the gun," Ella admitted.

"Just never say never," Greer added.

"Okay." Macy felt a little better.

A beat of silence passed, and then there was a sharp knock at Greer's office door. "Yoohoo! Y'all need to get back to work." Miss Thing was always jealous when she was left out of conversations.

"Is something happening out there?" called Ella.

"No. But Oscar needs petting. And I'd like to show you my new shoes."

The trio in Greer's office exchanged amused glances.

"We'll be out in a minute," Macy called. "And I'll tell you everything. I promise."

"Thank God," said Miss Thing through the door. "You three are my girls! I must know all!"

Their little huddle broke up. Macy was back to being on her own. But at least she knew she was loved. And if she ever had a problem, she could come to her friends at Two Love Lane.

CHAPTER TWELVE

Christmas was so close. Every radio station DJ and TV news anchor in Charleston was warning the public to "Get your last-minute presents now!" the day Deacon walked inside the fire station on Wentworth Street.

The redhead who stuck her hand out for him to shake had a natural glow, and she had quite the grip. Barney Fulton was a firefighter. "So, Deacon, I'm just *thrilled* to meet you!" she said.

"Great to meet you too." He'd never met a female firefighter, and it was exciting to meet her at the station.

She laughed. "Man, if I'd known you were this good-looking, I wouldn't have agreed to help you go out with Macy."

"Who paid you to say that?" Deacon grinned.

"And that New York accent to boot. Say 'Saturday.'"

"Saturday."

She giggled. Why, he wasn't sure. "Now say 'water.'"

"Water."

She laughed. "I love it! You sound like someone from *The Godfather*."

"And I'm not even Italian." He winked.

"Macy's meeting us here, and then she thinks we're heading to lunch, right?" Barney had a very slow, deliberate way of speaking, like she was eating spoonfuls of molasses. It was cute.

"That's the plan," he said. "We're heading to Tzasiki's."

"Good." Barney was all business now. "So when she shows up, the boys will invent some kind of emergency for me, and she can just take my place."

"You're a real sport," he said.

"I know!" She clapped her hands.

"Macy's pretty unpredictable," he said. "I haven't known her long, but I sense she keeps everyone on their toes."

"Yes!" Barney rolled her eyes and laughed. "It took me forever to convince her to meet us here. That's not her protocol. But I told her I was shy and needed her to break the ice between us."

Barney? Shy? "I'm shocked it worked," Deacon said.

"It barely did." Barney chuckled. "I had to tell her some fake story about a childhood birthday party that had scarred me for life and made me shy on the inside."

"Wow," Deacon said. "I appreciate all the effort you're going to."

"Not a problem. Just remember, we've got to be prepared if she tries to beg off. Knowing her, she'll say she's got to eat lunch at the office."

"I wouldn't be surprised."

"No matter *what*," Barney said, wagging her finger, "we're not going to let her escape."

"Duly noted." Deacon caught a glimpse of some of the male firefighters in a back room. One had a clipboard, and several others surrounded him. "They know what's going on?"

"Yep, and don't be surprised when I act real interested in you in my fake-shy way."

"Um, okay."

Barney grinned. "We don't want her to suspect this is a set-up. And we need her to get a little jealous besides."

"Gotcha."

She leaned to the right, her eyes on the street. "Oops! She's coming. Let's act real excited about each other now." She immediately moved closer, pretending to show him a piece of equipment on one of the trucks.

"Hey, y'all!" It was Macy. She was wearing another pair of sexy boots. Deacon thought she looked gorgeous, professional, and very kissable.

Barney turned around. "Oh," she said quietly. "Hello, Macy." She put her chin down. Pushed some invisible dirt around with her boot.

"Is everything okay, Barney?" Macy's eyes registered concern.

Barney looked up. "Oh, um, yeah! Actually, I'm fine. I'm enjoying meeting Deacon here."

Deacon had to try hard not to laugh. Barney had better just give up the shy act. He wasn't sure her acting skills were up to par. "Hi, Macy."

"Hi." She smiled at them both. "So I'm glad you've gotten to chat before I arrived."

Deacon nodded. "Barney's great. She's got a fascinating job."

Barney looked up at him with a little fake hero worship that was really inappropriate considering *she* was the firefighter. "I'm so glad we're going to lunch. Deacon's got a lot of interesting stories about his job in New York."

Not really. Not compared to the stories he was sure Barney had to tell.

"Great!" Macy *did* look happy. "In that case, I'm heading back to work. You two have fun."

She turned to go.

"Wait!" Barney called after her. "Since you're here, I wanted you to see our new truck."

"Oh, of course!" Macy turned right back around without a moment's hesitation. No one could turn down a tour of a new fire truck.

Deacon caught her gaze and she instantly blushed. That was a great sign. Maybe she was remembering the kiss on her doorstep. Or the super-sexy martini kiss. Or maybe she was thinking back to when they hungrily kissed in her kitchen with open mouths and hands all over each other.

"Hop in, Macy." Barney opened the passenger side door of the massive truck and then moved around to the driver's side.

Deacon took Macy's hand—he loved holding her hand—and helped her up the steps.

She settled herself into the seat. "This is totally awesome," she told Barney, who was now behind the wheel.

Deacon watched from the floor. Macy looked down at him but then quickly away. He knew he'd have to walk a fine line with her. Was he doing it right? Or was he blowing it?

He had no idea. He could only hope he'd get to take her to lunch today to try to win her over some more.

"We're proud of this truck," Barney said, and gave a firm tap of the horn. Macy jumped. Deacon flinched. As if on cue, three male firefighters came out.

Oh. So the honk was Barney's secret code.

"Barney, we have an emergency," one of the guys said as if he were a very bad actor in a very bad movie.

"Oh?" Barney called down to him.

Hopefully, Macy wasn't catching on.

Another firefighter jerked his thumb to the open station door. "Gotta go to the restaurant around the corner. They had a small stove fire. It's out, but they want someone to check on it for insurance purposes. We're cleaning out the portable water tanks, so you'll have to go."

At least that guy sounded pretty authentic, Deacon thought.

"You'll need the truck, right?" Macy fumbled with the seat belt to get it out of her way and slid down to the floor.

Deacon caught her around the waist when she landed. For a second, when she looked up at him, he thought he could see in her eyes that she wanted to kiss him again— as badly as he wanted to kiss her.

"I'll walk," Barney called down to her. "But this means I can't go to lunch. Sorry, Deacon." She opened the driver's side door, jumped out, and came around to stand with them.

"I understand," he said, and tried to look disappointed but mature—because no one should stand in the way of a firefighter doing her duty.

"Darn." Macy winced. "We'll have to reschedule your date."

"I'll check my calendar." Barney grabbed a coat from a hook on the wall and put it on. She grabbed her helmet next. "Technically, I don't need these, but people love it when I show up this way." She grinned as she put her helmet on.

"You do what you have to do," said Macy.

And then—shocker—Barney came up to Deacon and kissed him on the mouth, lingering for a few seconds. "I will *definitely* reschedule," she said in a flirty voice, and then strode out the station door.

"She told me she felt shy," Macy said, shock in her tone. "*That* wasn't shy."

"I think it's because we got along like . . . like two houses on fire," said Deacon with a chuckle. The truth was, there hadn't been a single spark.

"Fine." Macy lifted her chin. "I'm heading back." Her tone was brisk, no-nonsense. "We'll talk soon."

"Sure you don't want to join me for lunch?"

For a split-second, she hesitated. "No, I really can't," she said. "I've got shopping to do for my Toys for Tots party."

"I didn't know about this party." He definitely wanted to know more. "Tell me about it."

Her expression lightened. "We do it every year at Two Love Lane. My specialty is finding gifts for the older kids who come. Most people forget about them. They buy stuff for the little ones."

She was a sweetheart. If she were a real elf, she'd win awards. The more he was around her, the more he realized how much catching up he had to do in the good-cheer department.

Barney reappeared at the station door. "Oh," she said, "I meant to ask you to take my place at lunch, Macy. I feel terrible backing out on Deacon like that."

"He understands," Macy insisted.

"Of course I do," Deacon said. "Macy's buying Christmas presents for teenagers coming to her Toys for Tots party. No way am I going to hold her up from that."

"She'll need to eat before she does all that spending. Right, Macy?" Barney wasn't giving up.

"No, not really." Macy looked at her watch. "I-I need to get going."

"Come on now," Barney insisted. "It's your civic duty to help me not feel guilty about abandoning Deacon. Do it for the fire department. And *then* go shopping. I'm counting on you, Macy." She winked and left.

Macy cut her eyes at Deacon then looked toward the open firehouse door. Barney was definitely not coming back. "Um, I guess I should go with you. For Barney's sake."

Deacon waved a hand. "I'm fine. You go play Santa for a good cause."

Macy seemed to think about it some more. "Christmas shopping takes me forever. I'm always starved by the end of it."

Was she wavering?

"I'll bet," said Deacon. "Well, I'm heading home to eat with George and Aunt Fran. See you later." He waved to the guys in the back. "See ya, fellas!" They waved back and wished him a good day. He started walking. And hoping. . . .

"Wait," Macy said quickly.

Shazam! At the door Deacon had to pretend he wasn't super excited when he turned back around. "Yes?"

"I can't let Barney down," she said. "And I-I'd love to have lunch with you."

"You would?"

"Sure." She lifted and dropped her shoulders. "Sorry I'm being . . . weird."

"Not weird, exactly." He grinned. "I'm wondering if maybe you regretted kissing me is all."

"No." She turned redder than Santa's suit. "You know. No big deal. We're friends. It's fine."

"Okay, then." He stifled a grin. She was struggling. But he was glad—it meant she wasn't indifferent to him. "Shall we head to Tsaziki's?"

"Okay." She finally smiled, and it made his day. Apparently her heart was a little lighter. She waved good-bye to the firefighters, and then they both started out.

"You must be disappointed Barney can't come," she said. "She's quite a woman."

"She sure is," he said. "Gorgeous. Funny. And sweet."

"Right," said Macy, sounding slightly unsettled. Even disappointed.

His heart swelled with happiness. She liked him. Maybe she was a little jealous. *Three cheers for Barney!* "Too bad I have no interest in her at all," he added.

Macy stopped walking. "Really?"

He stopped too. "Really. She's nice. Accomplished. Perfect for someone else. Hope she'll be okay when I wind up being too busy to take her out again."

"Wow," said Macy.

They started walking again. He glanced her way. She had a funny look on her face. She seemed a little rattled. Vulnerable. Something about her eyes, and the way her lips were slightly parted.

He noticed she didn't try to convince him to go out with Barney again, so he was making progress. Not only that, thanks to Barney, he was on date number two with Macy. And she had no idea.

Never eat a gyro in front of a guy you want to impress, Macy realized too late, just a half hour after Barney left her stranded at the fire station with Deacon. First of all, you had the onions to deal with. She forgot to tell the waiter to leave them off, so she pulled them off herself and hoped Deacon didn't think she was doing it in anticipation of a kiss later.

No, she was totally not going there. No kisses, no way.

Which immediately made her want to kiss him.

But back to the problem of gyros on dates—not that this was a date, of course—there was that sauce, as well as the abundant lettuce and tomato. It wasn't easy looking elegant eating a gyro, so Macy gave up. She wolfed it down, eating it with a few little moans of pleasure. She allowed herself that luxury because Deacon said, "I hope you don't mind, but the only way to eat a gyro is to really go for it." And then he took a big chomp out of his, promptly losing a chunk of tomato in his lap.

She was full, and happy. They laughed a lot, and at one point, when she dropped her napkin and went to pick it up, he bent down too, and they knocked heads—not hard enough to see stars but enough that they both said, "Ow."

"You've got a hard head," he said, wincing and grinning.

"So do you." She chuckled.

And they sat and looked at each other for a few seconds, their hands to their skulls.

"Sorry for being such a klutz." He was smiling now, a sweet smile.

"I'm sorry too," she barely eked out. Because the truth was, he was adorable, and the right thing to do, it seemed to her, was to lean across the table and kiss him in apology. It took everything in her not to do so.

He paid the bill when she wasn't looking—it was her turn, she protested—and when that had been settled, she grabbed her purse. "I guess I should go now. The shops are calling."

She wanted to ask him to go with her. But then he might get the wrong idea. And she might too. He was an awful temptation, this bad boy who was heading back to New York after Christmas.

He stood with her. "Do you need any help? I'm trying to earn my Good Cheer badge in a serious way."

Yes! a voice within her cheered. But she couldn't show him how excited she was. "Sure," she said. "I'd love the help. But I'm warning you—once I start shopping, I don't slow down."

"I'm good with that," he said. "I'll hold all the bags."

She couldn't remember the last time she'd been shopping with a guy, and for him to be so accommodating was really flattering. It made her want to lean into him, put her hands on his chest, and give him a slow, hot kiss.

Help me, Santa! she thought in her head. Like an idiot. But she was a fool around Deacon Banks. She never should have eaten gyros with him. She should have let him go home and have lunch with George and Fran.

"Guess what," she said. "I don't think I'll have any bags."

They'd crossed George Street and were walking down Meeting Street.

"Why not?" Deacon asked.

"We're going to the Bicycle Shoppe." She turned to him. "The big kids love getting bikes. Or electronics. This year I want to do bikes."

His eyes lit up, which made her even more excited. "Great idea! I'd love to contribute some."

"The more the merrier," she said.

His hand brushed against hers, and she had this overwhelming urge to grab it and lace her fingers through his, the way they'd done walking home from FIG. But that had been a practice date. He'd been playing a part. She reminded herself she was contracted to find him casual dates with other women, no strings attached. He wasn't interested in a real relationship.

Somehow, that sort of cynicism didn't fit the man she'd come to know. But she had to take him at his word. She never wanted to be one of those people who imagined qualities she cherished in other people. That was naïve.

Thirty seconds later, they were at the bike shop door. He opened it for her, and when she walked past him into the shop, she smelled his cologne. It was light. Manly. She imagined him buying it at a discreet men's shop somewhere in Manhattan. And then she imagined him taking it home and putting it on in front of the bathroom mirror, naked except for a towel wrapped around his waist.

"Something up?" he said, like a kid.

She'd been caught looking at him. Having naughty thoughts about him. "Nothing," she replied lightly as she picked up a bike's price tag. The owner was behind the counter, helping a customer with a bike lock. Two other customers milled around the store. The bikes were lined up in gleaming rows, all colors of the rainbow.

"You were thinking something," he said over her shoulder. He was too close for comfort.

She giggled. And couldn't believe she had. She wasn't a giggler. But around him, she'd become one. "I can't say," she said. "Santa would give me coal in my stocking."

"Hmmm," he said back. "You've intrigued me."

She gathered herself and looked him in the eye. "I need to buy twenty bikes. Would you look for the kind boys ride? And I'll look for the girls' bikes? I try to keep the colors fairly neutral, except for one or two pink or purple ones. Most need to be beach bikes. But we can get a few that shift gears. We can't go too expensive because then the bike is more likely to get stolen. Just pick out your average, quality bike, something teens would be proud to ride."

"Will do," he said.

The owner was free then and came over. Macy and Deacon exchanged holiday greetings with her, a lovely woman in her seventies who'd owned the shop for forty years. Her name was Laura, and she wore blue reading glasses on a pearl chain.

"So glad you're back," Laura said to Macy. "Just rip off the tags of the ones you want. I'll reduce the price fifteen percent and deliver them the morning of the party. And please throw in two extra bikes, my gift."

"Thanks so much." Every year Macy marveled at the generosity of people at Christmastime. But the most heartening thing of all was how happy their expressions and voices were when they talked about helping her with Toys for Tots. Each year she witnessed over and over that it was giving that brought people joy, much more than receiving ever did, just like her parents had taught her. "We'll need bike locks too, and gift certificates for helmets. I always let the kids pick those out."

"Excellent." Laura beamed.

Macy looked at Deacon. "I always want to cry when I see the bikes lined up at the party."

"I can see why," he said. "This is . . . this feels really good. Please let me pay for them. You're going to the effort of having the actual party. I'd love to donate all the bikes this year."

"Oh, I can't do that. I'm touched by your offer. Truly. But that's a lot of money."

"Not in the big scheme of things. It's a drop in the bucket. I wish I could buy a bike for a thousand kids. Please let me do this."

"Okay." She could tell he really needed to. "Thank you, Deacon."

He grinned from ear to ear. "Thank *you* for letting me."

She gave into impulse. She hugged him. He hugged her back. And she felt it—the Christmas spirit, lifting them both. She could hug him all day. . . .

But after only a few seconds, she pulled back. "That was it," she said. "That's all the shopping I have to do today."

"You did great." His gaze was warm, steady.

She felt very close to him then. He felt like a real friend. But she didn't know how to tell him. She hoped the hug had conveyed something of her feelings to him.

At the counter, Laura finished the transaction and said, "Hey, you two. Would you like to take two of my rental bikes to Waterfront Park? It's a nice day."

Deacon looked at Macy. "I'm game."

"I have some work to do," she said, "but sure. You're very kind, Laura."

She was crazy to hang out with Deacon even longer. But she couldn't help herself.

So they rode bicycles, and it was sheer, simple fun. She'd forgotten how easy it was to have fun. She'd been working too hard. When they got to the fountain, they got off and walked the bikes around the edge, where large drops of water splashed against the concrete sidewalk, and headed down the pier. They passed the big swinging benches and finally came to the railing overlooking Charleston Harbor and Fort Sumter.

The water was a navy blue, flecked with white caps. The wind was light. And the sun felt really good.

"I'm always so happy coming out here," Macy said.

"It's great." Deacon seemed to be soaking it all up. "I can see why my aunt wants to live here six months of the year."

"You do? You really like it?"

He looked down at her. "I really do." He turned his gaze to the Ravenel Bridge, its two diamond-shaped spans gleaming in the sun. "It's not New York, of course. But who wants a New York vibe down here? It would be out of place. I love my home town, but it feels good to go somewhere so mellow. And beautiful."

"And still with lots happening," Macy said. "This town has tons of energy."

The wind lifted the hair off his forehead. "I feel it," he said.

They shared another smile, and Macy decided to broach another topic. "So, since we're not rescheduling with Barney, should we talk about Louisa?"

"No need," he said. "I've already called her. We're good to go."

"Oh, okay."

"I've talked to all the women on your list," he said. "So you and I don't need to mention them again. I promise. I got it covered. You did your job."

"But—"

"You gave me their names and numbers," Deacon said. "And we've got dates arranged."

"You do? Already? With all of them?" Her face heated. Somehow, she felt stupid for not being more actively involved.

"Isn't that what I was supposed to do?" He took out his phone and showed her his calendar.

She gave a little laugh. "I thought you'd need me to facilitate—"

"Nah," he said. "You can relax now. I've got it covered."

"That's terrific." She smiled a bit wanly. "You have a lot going on. And these are only first dates. It could be you decide to go out with someone again."

"Could be."

She was horrified that she felt jealous. And regretful that she'd ever decided to be his matchmaker.

"What with these dates and Aunt Fran's party schedule, I'm going to be busy," he said. "I don't know when I'll get time to hang out with you much. But George is always looking for someone to chat with, so please feel free to come over any time. Unless you're going to be as busy as I am. We might run into each other at parties. Right?"

"Yes, we probably will." And she didn't want to. The last thing she cared to see was him with his arm around a date, or if he were escorting Fran, flirting with available women at parties with lots of spiked egg nog and bourbon flowing. But she hated admitting that to herself. It terrified her that she wasn't thinking like a matchmaker—at all. "Shall we go back?" she asked him.

"Sure."

They began walking the bikes back down the pier, past the benches, and approached the fountain. He seemed a little more distant. She wasn't sure why, but she couldn't very well *ask* him, could she?

Of course, she could. She turned to him. "Anything on your mind?" The fountain was loud. Actually, it was *really* loud.

He grinned. Maybe he hadn't heard her.

"Anything on your mind?" she asked again, yelling the words this time.

He squinted at the sun, then back at her. "Yes," he yelled. "*You*."

She couldn't have heard him right. "What did you say?" she shouted.

"You!" He said it the way a football captain calls plays to his teammates. He looked serious. But in the zone. And then he pointed at her.

She pointed at her own chest. "Me?"

He nodded. Amusement gleamed in his eye. He was a devil. An outright devil. He was trying to discombobulate her. Maybe. Or maybe she was freaking out all on her own. She didn't know what to think.

"Oh," she finally said, then nodded. "All right then." She started pushing her bike again.

But she'd only moved a few feet when his big, warm palm covered her hand.

"I've been wanting to do this all afternoon." He ran a thumb over the back of her hand. Then he pulled it off the handlebar and held it, raised it slowly to his lips, and kissed it. "I have no desire to go out with any of those women. I'm only doing it because I don't want to let you down. I know how seriously you're taking your mission."

"You do?"

He nodded. "Yes. And I admire your dedication. Especially when you're dealing with a scalawag like me. You used to have pirates here, right?"

She nodded. "Yes, we did. And somehow the word 'scalawag' is perfect for you."

He kissed her hand again, then looked back up at her, and she felt lifted out of her skin by the desire she saw in his eyes.

"You and me," he said. "That's what I want to see happen."

She didn't pull her hand back. All she could think was that her house was only two blocks away, and there was nothing she'd like more than to ride their bikes there, invite him inside, and stand in the hall and kiss. And then she'd lead him upstairs and they'd strip down and make mad, passionate love.

But that was a ridiculous thought. Deacon was only being flirtatious. And yes, kissing the back of her hand had a certain Old World charm about it too. She might even say it felt chivalrous to her. It was a sexy kind of chivalry, one that women went crazy for.

"I didn't know Yankee men could rival any Southern gentleman when it comes to charm," she said.

"That's because you haven't gotten to New York as much as you should."

"You're right. I've never been."

"Whoa."

"I know, I can't believe it myself," she said.

"Why don't you come up sometime? I'll show you around."

Did he have to look so boyish and adorable when he said that? She cleared her throat. "Uh, that would be nice."

She started walking her bike down the steps to the street. It would be more than nice to visit him in New York. It would be sexy and hot and romantic! And then she'd go home, and he'd stay in Manhattan, and he'd go back to his bachelor lifestyle.

She mounted her bike again. "Ready?" Even in December, there were lots of pedestrians and cars, so she'd take as many back streets as she could to get back to the Bicycle Shoppe.

"As I'll ever be," he said, back on his own bike. His

jacket disguised the muscles in his upper arms, but his pecs showed to excellent advantage as he leaned on the handlebars.

"Let's go." She could mean that in more ways than one if she wanted to. She sensed all she'd have to do was crook a finger and he'd show up in her bed every night until he left town.

But it had to remain a fantasy. Clearly. One of those holiday daydreams to get her through all the parties with the couples snuggled in front of fires and singing Christmas carols together—or retreating to an unused bedroom or even a bathroom and making hot holiday love with no one the wiser.

Being single wasn't bad. It also wasn't easy, especially around Christmas. She shouldn't let that lead her into a Yuletide fling she'd regret later.

But her hand still tingled from that kiss. . . .

CHAPTER THIRTEEN

Tiffany was Deacon's next date.

"You're going to love her," Macy told him. She was over at Fran's house, supposedly helping George make shrimp and grits for supper—the quintessential Charleston dish—but George couldn't be trusted in the kitchen. He'd had too much of a really good wine he'd found at Harris Teeter, and so Deacon had put him on the sofa to watch *Jeopardy* with Fran.

"I'll help," he told Macy. She looked sexy in her little Christmas apron she'd brought from home.

"Good," she said, her face flushed from the heat off the stove. "Can you chop up that bacon? And then I need you to stir these grits."

"Sure." He rolled up his sleeves. He couldn't help thinking they made a good team. "Can I get you some more wine?"

She lifted her glass to her lips. "Mmmm," she said. "This is really good. But I'm fine for now." She put it on the counter and smiled at him.

Little did she know how much that smile lit him up inside. "All right," he said, and grabbed a knife to chop up the bacon. Easy peasy. When that was done, he went to the stove to replace Macy as the grits stirrer.

Being that close to her was tough. He wanted to put his hands around her waist from behind and kiss her neck, where those little tendrils hung down so enticingly.

"Got it?" she asked him, and moved aside to let him get at the wooden spoon sitting inside the pot of bubbling goo. That's what it looked like to him. But he'd never tell her.

"Got it," he replied, and took her place.

"Shrimp takes only a few minutes to cook," she said, and started peeling it raw. He noticed the heads were already off. Her nimble fingers handled the shells and tails with ease. "I always buy fresh off the dock at Shem Creek. I freeze plenty for out of season."

"Thanks for sharing it with us."

"My pleasure. I have many more pounds where these came from. I have to have shrimp and grits at least a couple times a month. Somehow it grounds me. You have anything like that?"

"Yep. There's a pizza place in my neighborhood, Frantoni's, that makes incredible upside-down pizza."

"What's that?"

"They put the cheese on the crust first, and then the sauce on top. I don't know why it tastes so good that way, but I wake up craving it. If I don't have it at least every other weekend, my life falls apart."

They both laughed and locked gazes. Damn if he didn't want to stop stirring those grits and go over and kiss her.

"Keep stirring." She knew exactly what he was thinking. She bent her head and got back to peeling shrimp. "Anyway," she said like they were old friends, "Tiffany's a writer. She grew up in Nantucket, so you two will have some geography in common, I'm sure."

"I love Nantucket. What kind of writing does she do? In her file, it just said she was self-employed in the arts."

"Essays, mainly. Enjoyable nonfiction pieces she writes for magazines, mainly about gardening. Flora and fauna. She moved down not too long ago to be near her sister. The sister owns a candle shop on Society Street."

"That's interesting, I guess. A whole store full of candles."

"That's where you're meeting Tiffany."

"Really?" Deacon was surprised. "When we texted, we decided to go to a bar for drinks." He'd been planning on calling Tiffany that night to strategize how to get Macy there.

"I encouraged her to do something more exciting," Macy, ever the matchmaker, said. "So y'all are going to make candles at her sister's shop instead. One section of the store is devoted to classes."

"Oh."

Macy laughed. "You don't sound too excited."

Deacon loved hearing her laugh. "Can you come with us? This seems like a chick thing."

"That's not fair. Guys like candles too."

"You're right. I'm into candlelit dinners. And candles in the bedroom." He waited for her to object, but she didn't. "A naked woman by candlelight is a beautiful sight."

"Oh yeah?"

He heard a bit of sass and sizzle in her tone. "Yeah," he said, his voice roughening at the thought of seeing her naked. "I'm not a crafts person, though."

She laughed again. "This is some conversation. 'Not a crafts person.'"

"And your problem with that is . . . ?"

"You make doing crafty things sound so awkward. And dull."

"I will never make a wreath with a hot glue gun. Ever. And I sure as hell thought I'd never make a candle."

"Aw, you can handle it. It's a good icebreaker."

"I'll do it," he said. "For you."

She looked over at him again. "Not for me. For your aunt. And yourself. You might like Tiffany."

"I told you—"

"You don't know in advance that you won't connect with her."

"Yes, I do."

She peeled her last shrimp and washed her hands under the faucet. "You can't know that."

"Sure, I can. I'm already thinking of someone else. And that someone is you."

She dried her hands on a tea towel. "But we've never even—"

"Never what? Made a candle together? Come with me, and we will."

"No." She folded her arms over her beautiful breasts. "I was going to say we've never even . . . you know. You can't like me enough to say you've sworn off all the other women in Charleston."

"Did Maria and Captain von Trapp even get to first base before they knew they had the hots for each other?"

She laughed aloud. "So you really do know musicals. Can you sing?"

He kept stirring. "I'm the best tenor on the planet, at least in my own head. I sing in the shower every morning and wonder how Broadway has done without me all these years. I'd make a helluva leading man. I see myself as Yul Brynner with lots of hair."

"Oh my God." She was giggling again.

He loved that. "You want to check on these grits? Make sure I'm stirring them right?"

She came over, carefully, it seemed, as if she were afraid he'd be the Big Bad Wolf and eat her up. She peeked into the pot. "You can stop. They're done." She looked up at him with a distinctly amused, if frustrated, light in her eye. "You're a real troublemaker, you know."

"Thank you." He put the spoon down. And this time he did place his hands at her waist. "I'm glad you came over to cook shrimp and grits for us."

She looked at his mouth. "Me too. Will you ever sing for me?"

"Only when we're in the shower. I could arrange that. Tomorrow morning? Your house?"

She turned a deep red. "*No.*"

They both listened to *Jeopardy* for a few seconds. Alex Trebek was insulting a contestant. Aunt Fran said, "Alex, you never came on my show, and now I know why. You're a pill. A real pill."

George was snoring.

Jeopardy went to commercial, its theme song making Macy and Deacon both grin for some reason.

"What a weird and wonderful holiday this has been so far," she said softly.

"And to think before I came here, I didn't even know you existed," he said. "If I'd seen you on *Bless Your Heart*, I would have taken the next plane down here to meet you, long before Christmastime. Maybe even Halloween."

She smiled. "I like that we met now. You dressed up for Halloween—"

"I was a vampire this year," he interrupted her.

She chuckled. "You as a vampire, and pumpkins, and my favorite candy together . . . that might be too much awesomeness for me to handle." Her eyes were luminous.

"This ex-vampire wants to kiss you," he said.

And he did. This time it was slow, and it was sexy from the very beginning. Nothing innocent or young about it. They were two adults, and Deacon wanted Macy. He hoped he was making that clear. She, he was happy to sense, wanted him too, judging by the way she wrapped her hands around his neck and moaned a little against his mouth. He hardened against her, and she didn't move away.

She clung even closer, tilted her chin so he could get better access to her neck.

If only George and Aunt Fran weren't there—and Alex Trebek. The *Jeopardy* theme, the most unromantic song in the world, came back, and so they finally came up for air.

"Uh-oh," she said low. "We shouldn't have done that."

"I disagree. We totally needed to do that." He ran his hand down her back and back up to her waist. "You sure you won't come with me and Tiffany?"

"No." She pushed gently against his chest, and he released her. "I'm not babysitting you and Tiffany." She sighed. "I need to cook the shrimp."

"Okay," he said, and felt his body—heated and ready for sex—slowly surrender its primal need, at least for the moment. Macy was obviously unsettled. Maybe even upset. He got that. They were crossing lines that she'd had no intention to cross. She'd told him so, and—poof—those lines were gone. "Is there anything else I can do to help in here?" he asked her, putting every ounce of understanding that he could into those words.

She sent him a bright smile, but he could tell it was contrived—pure Southern politeness. He'd learned in the short time he'd been in Charleston that you didn't show your backside. You kept up a front. You retained your dignity—and your graciousness—at all costs.

"Please call Fran and George to the table in five minutes," she said. "If you want to check the wine in the meantime, that would be good. I brought over a nice pinot grigio to go with the shrimp."

"Okay, then." He put on his own brisk air, more to accommodate her need for distance than to express any discontent on his part—and how much his body felt wrecked by lust and longing. He walked out into the living room. "Shrimp and grits in five," he said.

George and Fran were quite the pair.

"Who are Salt-N-Pepa!" George was awake again and yelling at the television set.

"Salt and Pepper, Alex!" Fran cried at the same time.

"You lost," said George. "You forgot to put it as a question. And they're Salt-N-Pepa. No *R* on the end, you nerd."

"I hate you." Fran hit George with a couch pillow.

"Guys," Deacon told them. "Forget about *Jeopardy*. Go wash up. Macy's been working hard in the kitchen."

It was like rounding up two puppies. But eventually, everyone got to the table. Macy was there, beaming as she handed around plated shrimp and grits.

"Mmm-hmm," said George. "This smells divine."

Everyone dug in.

"And tastes like a million bucks," said Fran.

Thankfully, their *Jeopardy* fervor was forgotten.

"This is really good," Deacon said. And it was. Even the grits, which were smooth and creamy, not gooey at all. The shrimp were plump and swimming in some kind of delicious gravy. He could see why Macy had to have this a couple times a month.

"I'm glad you like it," she said. "It's nothing fancy. I use bacon, not tasso, and whatever tomatoes I have on hand to help round it out." She put down her fork. "I hate to leave the party, but I have to go."

"Where?" Deacon suddenly completely lost his appetite.

"I just got a call in the kitchen," she said. "An unexpected one. I'd never abandon one event for the other, I promise, unless it's a really big deal and I can trust the people I'm with not to take it wrong. Which I do you. But I have a date I don't want to miss."

"You *do*?" Deacon said like a disappointed high school boy.

Fran and George exchanged delighted looks.

"Of course she does," said George.

Fran waved a hand. "Honey, go paint the town red."

Macy laughed. "It's not that kind of date. My sister's sick, and she needs me to come over and bake eight dozen cookies for school tomorrow. Then I have to decorate them." She stood, seemingly reluctant to go. Her gaze was a little strained. "See y'all soon. I knew you'd understand."

"Have a great time." Deacon hated to see her go, but he was beyond thrilled she didn't have a real date. "I mean, have as much fun as you can baking cookies."

"Oh, it's fun, all right," said George, "especially if there will be single guys there for you to feed raw cookie dough to. Any chance of that, my dear?"

"No," said Macy.

Good, thought Deacon.

"The single men here are idiots," said Fran. "Complete fools. Macy should have had ten marriage proposals by now."

"Exactly," said George.

Deacon agreed, but that was a touchy subject. "I'll walk you downstairs," he said, feeling wooden all of a sudden.

"Oh, no." Macy's smile was equally forced. "I'm fine."

That was a "no" if there ever was one, and Deacon had the thought that maybe this cookie caper was entirely made up. But he hoped not. Because that would mean she didn't want to hang out with him and his kooky family.

Yes, George was family. And so were all those roly-poly Corgis.

"Okay, then," he said. "I guess I'll let you know later how my candle-making date goes tomorrow."

"Right," she said, and walked meekly to the door, like she'd forgotten something.

"Spit it out," said Aunt Fran. "Is there something else you'd like to say, Macy?"

"No." She sounded firm.

"Are you sure?" Fran asked.

Macy nodded. But she looked completely miserable. "Bye," she squeaked.

When she shut the door behind her, Fran pointed her fork at Deacon. "You're a fool," she said.

"What do you mean by that?" He felt his blood rise.

But Fran wouldn't say. George stayed silent too, although he wore such a smug expression, Deacon was annoyed. "Stop that," he told him.

George quit chewing and glared at him. "Don't blame me."

"For what?" Deacon was really pissed now.

"For your idiocy," George replied, then looked at Fran. "This meal is delicious."

"It is," she said serenely.

It was superb. But Deacon sure as hell wasn't going to eat it around these two *Jeopardy*-loving fools. He picked up his plate. "I'm eating in the kitchen."

"Suit yourself," Fran replied airily.

"Be that way," said George. "Do nothing and sit back like a king on your throne."

And then they both laughed. Laughed! As if Deacon was a joke—as if his love life was too.

Maybe you are, a voice in his head taunted him. *And maybe it is*.

"I've never had a joke of a love life!" he called out to them. "And if I'm a king, you're the court jester, George, and you're the mean old nurse, Aunt Fran, the one who doesn't do anything when she sees trouble happening except smirk and talk to the king like he's the baby she used to take care of. Well, he's not."

They didn't say a word. All he heard was the clinking of knives and forks against china and the pounding of his miserable heart.

He wanted Macy to feed him raw cookie dough.

Maybe it wasn't too late!

Maybe that whole time she'd wanted him to come with her, but she hadn't been sure how to ask, particularly as they were eating her specialty dish. He *was* an idiot, not to see her dilemma.

He strode out into the dining room. "I'm going. Don't wait up for me."

"We won't," said Aunt Fran, her eyes alight.

"Later, gator." George raised his wine glass to him.

Deacon wouldn't tell them what he was up to, but he knew they knew. Because when he shut the door behind them, Fran said, "We love you!" in a semitrembling voice and George said, "Good night, Deacon!" in the sweet, simple tone that meant they'd been on his side the whole time.

CHAPTER FOURTEEN

Deacon got his cookie dough. Macy plopped some right into his mouth the night of the cookie baking at her sister's house. But she also fed her sister's dog some cookie dough, so Deacon didn't feel particularly special. Her sister's husband was in the kitchen too during the whole floury, buttery shebang, so nothing romantic happened. But at least Deacon had made the effort to be there. He could tell Macy appreciated it by the way her face lit up when he caught up with her on her walk down East Bay Street toward her sister's house on Tradd.

"It's you," she'd said.

"Uh-huh," he said back.

They pretended he was just being helpful. But he knew—and he was sure she knew—that he was making an extra effort to chase her. It was the classic old-fashioned chase men took up when they wanted to be with a special woman. He was proud to join that fraternity.

And being at her sister Anne's house was easy. The kids, Lucy and Sam, were fun. So was Kyle, the brother-in-law. It was a low-key endeavor with lots of holiday music keeping them going through the scary parts, like rolling out the dough to the right thickness, which Deacon had never had to do before since he'd never made cookie dough.

"It's not hard," Macy assured him.

"That's what she said," he replied. Kyle laughed, but Macy had never seen *The Office*, so she didn't get it.

Deacon had been all ready to walk her back home when they finished up at eleven thirty, but she decided to spend the night and wake up with the kids in the morning to feed them breakfast. Anne would be in no shape to, and Kyle had to head to the hospital at five.

So Deacon walked home alone. But he didn't feel alone. He felt like maybe some Christmas elves were busy making a surprise for him since he'd been so helpful that evening. He hoped the surprise would be Macy, wrapped in nothing but a big red bow. But he knew that elves didn't think like grown-ass men with sex on the brain. So he suspected he might get a book. Or socks.

He got home and saw a text from Tiffany: *Looking forward to messing with Macy tomorrow. I have a plan to get her there. You need to be surprised too, or she'll catch on. Trust me?*

Sure, he said, willing to go along on the adventure. *Looking forward to it.*

"Tell me," said George. They were in the kitchen drinking late-night Irish coffees in glass mugs—as if they needed caffeine and alcohol at midnight, or fancy glass mugs for that matter—George was totally into presentation. "You look like you have a delicious secret you need to spill."

So Deacon told him how Macy's clients were going to cooperate with him to get Macy and him together.

"Together?" George asked. "As in in the sack? Or as in connecting with your true love and getting married?"

"You got whipped cream on your lip."

George ignored him. "Are you turning into Jimmy Stewart before my very eyes? Or are you still Bruce Willis?"

"Neither," Deacon said. "I'm more like Ryan Gosling." He reached out and swiped the fleck of whipped cream off George's lip.

George swatted at him. "You are no Ryan Gosling. I'd say you're Channing Tatum. You're noble enough. But you still ooze bad boy."

"I'll take it."

"Why didn't you tell me this devious plan a lot sooner?" George cocked his head like a seagull on the Battery wall.

"I wasn't sure if it was the right thing to do. And you'd have let me know."

"Damn straight. But I happen to think it's a great idea. So much more exciting than going on deadly dull blind dates. And Macy likes you. I can tell. I don't know why she's so gun-shy, though. Could it be you already threw out Christmas-fling signals? If so, you were talking to the wrong girl."

"Yes, I threw out Christmas-fling signals." Deacon was abashed. He so rarely was.

"*Dumb*," said George. "But understandable. She makes a helluva cake. That alone is a tremendous aphrodisiac."

"Well, I'm ramping up my game," said Deacon, "and trying seriously to get her attention. But I'm a little uneasy about tomorrow. I have no idea what Tiffany is going to do at this candle shop."

George laughed. "You and candles. It doesn't compute."

"I know."

"It's time for you to get out of boss mode and let other people help you out. So embrace this clearly romantic undertaking."

"Actually, I'm finding it refreshing—humbling, even—to allow strangers to come to my aid." It felt like putting on a new coat that you were sure wouldn't fit or look good, but not only did it fit, you looked awesome in it.

"That's what the Christmas season is all about." George

was twitchy but waxing sentimental. No wonder. It was his third Irish coffee.

About two in the morning, when Deacon finally got to sleep, he dozed off thinking that so far in Charleston, he'd sucked at coming to anyone else's aid, except Aunt Fran—and maybe those kids he'd bought bikes for. But that was too easy. He needed to think about what else he could do and for whom, something hard that challenged him. *No way do I want those elves to stop working on my present*, he thought, and then he was out like a light with a smile on his face.

The next day at work, Macy was busy, so busy that she had to cut short her lunch with her parents at a deli on King Street. They'd all converged there from their offices. She hugged them good-bye right after her BLT but before the gooey, giant brownie her dad ordered for them all to split.

"We understand," her mother said with a smile. "We have afternoon classes to teach anyway. So don't worry. Do what you have to do."

"I've got your mother to keep me company," her father said, beaming.

"Is this a date now?" Macy's mother teased him.

"You bet," her father said back, and kissed her.

Macy loved how happy they were together. "Be good, you two!" She blew kisses at them.

"We love you!" they called after her.

She hurried on her way, buoyed by the meet-up. One of her couples was on the verge of getting engaged, and the guy wanted her help figuring out how to make it a moment in time his beloved would never forget. Macy had been on the phone all morning trying to arrange for him to pop the question inside a chic private art gallery after it was closed for the day. It took forever, but finally, after lunch, she got permission from the owner. She also arranged for a local restaurant to serve a romantic meal in the gallery, beneath the future bride's favorite painting, which the future groom had already arranged to purchase for her.

"Yay," she murmured, right as she hung up with the restaurant's chef. But the next second her phone vibrated. Please, she thought, *don't let that be anyone messing up all the plans I just made.*

But it wasn't. It was Tiffany. Her heart sank anew. Why was Tiffany calling? She was supposed to be at the candle shop with Deacon. Macy wanted that date to work out. She was too into Deacon herself. He was dangerous, and she was in no place to date a dangerous man. She had Two Love Lane to worry about. And . . . and . . .

And she was afraid of falling in love. She'd screw it up. She just knew it. And then she'd be among the brokenhearted, and that wouldn't do. Pain hurt. She was a wimp. She was much better at arranging other people's happily ever afters. To hell with her own. She'd make do with chocolate. And great shoes.

"Tiffany," she said smoothly. "How goes it at the candle shop?"

"Macy, Deacon is an absolute doll," Tiffany said in a low tone. "And we just started making our candles. But—" She hesitated.

"But what?" Macy felt her temples throb with anxiety.

Tiffany gave a little cry. "My sister is driving me crazy. She keeps looking over my shoulder. It's like being watched by your parents at a middle school dance."

"Wow. Sorry I suggested it. Can you go somewhere else? Do candles another day."

"It's too late. Deacon likes making them. He's into it, Macy."

"He *is*?"

"Yes! Either that, or he's into my sister. And I think my sister has the hots for *him*. I'd better just leave."

"Please don't. Deacon would never treat a date poorly. Flirting with your sister would be awful of him. I'm sure he's not. He's just being kind."

"How can you be sure?"

Macy really couldn't. But she knew him. Somehow, she did. "I just know," she said, feeling a little sheepish. "Can you take your sister aside and ask her to go back to the workroom or something?"

"She doesn't have a workroom. Everything is stored up front. She'll be hovering no matter what."

"Ask her to leave the store. You know how to make candles. You don't need her."

"She needs to close out the register and shut down her equipment. I've never done any of that."

"Tell her to leave for half an hour. A coffee break."

"There are other people in the class. They'd think it was weird if she left. And we have coffee here."

"I see." Macy didn't know what to do.

"I'm leaving," said Tiffany.

"Please don't do that!"

"I don't want to stay. My sister doesn't have a boyfriend either. She's always wanted what I wanted. And she's ruining this date."

"Do you . . . do you want Deacon?"

"Who wouldn't? He's totally hot. And his enthusiasm for candle making is adorable. He's terrible at it. But at least he acts like it's fun."

"I didn't think he was into crafts, but I was hoping he'd give this a shot. I'm so glad. Stay, Tiffany. Ignore your sister."

"Impossible. Someone needs to finish my candle. I'm going home."

Click.

"Darn it!" Macy immediately dialed Deacon.

"Hi," he said. "I'm making a grapefruit-scented candle, and it rocks."

Macy couldn't help but chuckle. "Um, that's good."

"We should come back here together sometime. You should make one."

"I will." Macy's heart warmed that he wanted her to go there with him. "Hey, is Tiffany gone?"

There was a pause. "She's talking to her sister in a corner. They're waving their hands around."

"Tiffany thinks her sister likes you."

Deacon gave a short laugh. "I think she does too."

"Oh no."

"I tried to fob her off. But she's pretty persistent. Invading my space and all that."

"Tiffany's leaving."

Deacon sighed. "I can't say that I blame her. Wait. Here she comes."

Macy waited. She heard voices, several "good-byes."

Deacon came back on the line. "She asked me to finish her candle for her. She won't let her sister do it."

"I'm sorry it didn't work out. She's not mad at you, is she?" Macy asked.

"No. She gave me a hug. She fibbed and said she had a terrible headache. I told her I'm sorry she's leaving."

"Well, now you know why she left."

"I want to go too," he murmured low. "I mean, I'm here with these other people in the class. But the sister . . . she's, um, heading my way. She has a glint in her eye. Too bad because I was having fun. Candle making is cool. You can accidentally explode things. And of course there's fire. All these wicks are getting a pretty good flame. I stuck my finger in one for *four* seconds."

"Why are men fascinated by explosions? And fire? And daring themselves to do dumb things?"

"Because it's fun?" Deacon guessed.

"Don't leave your candle," Macy said. "I'll come down and finish Tiffany's for her and fend off her sister so you can finish yours."

"Whew. Thank you."

"I'm glad to help. And sorry it didn't work out with Tiffany. You can always reschedule."

"Nah," he said. "No way do I want to come between two sisters. And she's made it clear she's done."

"All right." Macy tried to sound like the disappointed matchmaker. But deep inside . . . she was glad.

And wouldn't you know it? She loved making candles too.

But Deacon was better at it.

"Sorry," he said, on their walk back home.

"No, that's okay." Macy's candle—Tiffany's, really— was lopsided. She brought it home anyway. She'd give it to Tiffany next time she saw her.

"How'd you do that?" Deacon asked. "I mean, it was sitting on a flat table, like mine."

"I have no idea how it happened. Something went . . . crooked."

"It's hard to mess up candles," Deacon said.

"You're impossible," she said back.

"But I'm a good candlemaker. I'm going to ask Tiffany's sister if I can do bubblegum flavor next time."

They arrived at her door.

"Candles don't come in bubblegum flavor," she told him.

"Mine will," he replied.

"It can't happen," she said.

He got extra close to her. "Sure it can."

She sighed. "You need to back away."

"You really want me to?"

"Everyone across the street is looking at us. A whole bunch of tourists."

"So? They've never seen people kiss before?"

"We're not—"

And then they were kissing, each of them holding their own candles in a bag. And in that kiss was such longing and wishing and frustration and hot, carnal desire that when a police siren was suddenly heard, Macy was sure someone was coming to arrest them for a public display of affection of the highly erotic kind.

She gladly would have gone to jail for that kiss.

CHAPTER FIFTEEN

"I think this is our last piazza bourbon," Deacon told George. "It's time for fireside bourbon."

George laughed. "You've said that already. But we keep coming out here."

Deacon sighed. "I like Yo-Yo Ma, but I hate to leave." No man wanted to dress up in a tux, sit in a box at the symphony, and make small talk when there was a college football game on television, a stocked bar, pimento cheese on crackers, and fireside bourbon.

The only bright spot for him was that Macy was coming over to attend the concert with Fran, and he'd get to escort them both as far as the lobby of the Gaillard, where they would meet up with Celia, their hostess, and he'd linger behind and wait for Louisa, his blind date.

His blind date who wasn't a blind date, that is. It was a complicated operation, but Louisa had it all figured out, how she'd ditch him and leave Macy with no choice but to step in.

Speaking of which—the totally in-the-dark object of his desire came walking down her front porch steps at that very moment in a gown the color of a well-circulated penny.

"Get a look at that," said George.

"Whoa." Deacon couldn't take his eyes off the plummeting neckline until he noted that Macy also wore an unbuttoned dramatic black coat with a big, furry collar that made him think of Cruella de Vil—in a good way, an erotic way that he was appalled and turned on by. So he tried to focus on the little shiny things holding her blonde curls together, baubles that picked up the last few rays of sunshine.

She was a Southern goddess who looked like she might have a whip hidden in the folds of that coat, and now she stopped on the sidewalk below their piazza and looked up at them. "Hey! How are y'all?"

"Fantastic!" said George with more verve than usual.

"Very well, thanks," said Deacon. "I'm looking forward to our evening."

Macy beamed. "I'm excited, too! I can't wait for you to meet Louisa. You'll love her, Deacon."

She couldn't hear George's diabolical chuckle. "If she only knew," he murmured.

"Shut up," Deacon hissed, then said to Macy, "I'm sure I'll enjoy Louisa's company"—he felt generous, and slightly liquored up—"if she's a friend of yours." And he meant it. Any friend of Macy's was a friend of his.

"She's wonderful," Macy assured him while he tried not to ogle her cleavage, which he could drop a peppermint down if he merely stuck out his arm and released one from his fingers. There was a bowlful of the red-and-white striped sweets on the piazza, and he was sorely tempted.

"Fran said you'd have me a drink prepared." Macy squinted up at George, having no idea how close she'd come to getting a free piece of candy in addition to a free drink. "Is that right?"

"A mere drink, milady?" George called down to her as if he were in a Shakespeare production. He loved attention, especially from beautiful women and men—and passing tourists, several of whom stopped across the street on the

Battery wall to watch the goings-on at the glamorous mansion with three piazzas.

He put his hands on the balcony railing and tossed his head, which made the sweeping curl on his forehead drop over his eye, lending him a Hollywood look. "*Au contraire!* I made a special, one-of-a-kind cocktail to commemorate this beauteous evening."

"Awesome!" Macy's surfer-girl exclamation broke the dramatic spell. But George didn't care because she was clapping, and she hadn't removed her gaze from his.

The people across the street clapped too. One even whistled.

George turned to Deacon, "God, I love this town," he said.

Deacon still wanted to drop the peppermint down Macy's gown and then run downstairs to the sidewalk and fish it out himself. With his mouth. What else was he supposed to think about when her luscious breasts were on such classy display?

"This cocktail," George continued to explain to Macy in his Shakespearean tone—because he really didn't know when enough was enough—"is to celebrate Fran's debut in Charleston society, Deacon's date tonight with a Southern belle, and most important of all, our neighbor Macy's kindness in putting up with the motley, needy, dare I say 'panting' crew next door. And I'm not talking about the Corgis."

The tourists, thankfully, moved on, their attention diverted by two yellow labs trotting toward them, their tails at full wag; a horse-and-carriage ensemble carrying even more tourists; and the blood-red of the setting winter sun.

"You belong here, George." Macy laughed up at him, then winked at Deacon.

Damn. That wink went straight to the high school crush center in Deacon's brain and then down his body, testing the elastic stretch of his very expensive boxer briefs. Indeed, if Aunt Fran were to come out onto the piazza, he'd feel compelled to turn the other way.

"What's this illustrious beverage called?" she asked George.

George hesitated but a second. "The Yo Yo Ma-garita," he declared.

Deacon groaned. "Really?"

"I made that up right this minute," George said, "and I think it's pretty clever." He turned back to Macy with a delighted smile. "The secret ingredient is a splash of limoncello! Get it? *Cello*?"

Deacon shook his head. George glared at him, but brightened again when Macy said, "Of course I get it! You clever man!"

George chortled. "You'll be hearing Yo-Yo Ma's cello inside your head if you drink too many. Which might be a good thing, depending upon what he's playing. God forbid, it's a dirge. Or a march."

Macy laughed. "I'll be right up."

"I'll meet you downstairs." Deacon was resigned to appearing dull at the moment. No red-blooded male could compete with George at his most charming. No one.

"I'll be waiting in the little foyer," she announced to Deacon with not an ounce of flirtation in her tone, sadly.

"We'd better have tequila," he warned George. "And limoncello."

"Of course we do." George waved a dismissive hand at him. "Now stop taking out your sexual frustration on me, and go open the door for the person who's *really* making you crazy. 'Kay?" He turned on his heel and hurried inside to whip up his new alcoholic creation.

And Deacon went to get Macy. He didn't even mind any more that he was missing a good football game. He was recording it anyway. Earlier that afternoon, he'd decorated the cubbyhole of the foyer with real mistletoe from a nearby sea island farm. He'd picked it up at Harris Teeter, his new favorite social hangout.

"Don't tell me any scores," he said to George on his way out the front door, which was now covered on both sides with sparkly Christmas wrapping.

"Shut up and rescue that magnificent creature downstairs. She belongs up here, surrounded by Corgis on the burgundy velvet couch. And you'd better prepare yourself. Your aunt is on pins and needles. She thinks no one will like her tonight. I'm relying on you to see to it that she feels like a star."

"George, she *is* a star."

"I know, but she forgets."

Ten seconds later, Macy announced, "I see it," when Deacon unlocked the hall doors.

She should. The sprig of mistletoe was attached to a ribbon slowly spinning from the ceiling inside the tiny entryway.

Behind him, jazz music played from the first-floor condo belonging to a mysterious young man he'd glimpsed only twice. A few feet behind Macy, on the other side of the outer doors, two tourists discussed the oyster po-boys they'd had for dinner as they walked by.

Deacon crossed the threshold into the matchbox-sized chamber, his back squeezed against the brass mailboxes, and shut the doors to the hallway behind him.

They were now in an area about as big as an airplane bathroom.

Yes, it was a bold move. And he had no idea how Macy would react. Her ebony coat and gown took up almost the whole space—that, and his heady wonder at her utter gloriousness.

"Sorry, Frost." His dazzled appreciation grew as he

inhaled her flower scent and touched one of the dangly pearl earrings she wore. "You know the rules."

"Good try, Banks." She smiled up at the mistletoe, and a wispy black piece of fur from her coat caressed her cheek. "Those rules don't apply when one of the kissers is employed by the other."

He couldn't help himself. He allowed his gaze to sweep over her plunging décolletage and back to her face. "Perhaps it's too early for mistletoe anyway. I think the tradition goes back to pagan mating rituals that took place at the winter equinox, which isn't for a few days." Her pupils widened.

Ah. He'd gotten to her. An intoxicating, invisible heat rose between them.

"Shall we go upstairs?" He held out his arm.

"Good idea." She took it without the slightest hesitation. He'd hoped that maybe he'd knocked her off her game and she'd need to lean—heavily—on him. Apparently not.

Their moment was over.

As they ascended the stairs, she said, "I can't wait to see what Fran is wearing," the way women do when they want to stick to innocuous topics rather than listen to you pointedly suggest making out beneath the mistletoe.

Deacon played along. "It's a gown she says she borrowed from Rita Wilson and never gave back."

"*The* Rita Wilson? Who appeared in *Sleepless in Seattle*? And married Tom Hanks?"

"The very same."

"She was also in an episode of *The Brady Bunch*," Macy informed him. "She played a rival to Marcia during cheerleading tryouts."

He stopped on the stairs. "We really ought to talk out here more often."

She smiled but said nothing. She knew just when to pull

those *Mona Lisa* moments. He could never predict them. They drove him mad.

Once in the condo, they were swept up by all things Fran, like two trees sucked into a giant tornado. Deacon had no interest in George's special cocktail. He never veered from bourbon, Scotch, and beer. But Macy and Aunt Fran threw back two Yo-Yo Ma–garitas apiece.

Afterward, Deacon called Uber—Aunt Fran despised limos—and helped the ladies inside a small compact car. The driver peppered Aunt Fran—the first celebrity he'd ever picked up in his car—with questions about Harrison Ford and Denzel Washington, his two favorite actors. He didn't care that Deacon had to sit in the front seat on top of a pile of newspapers.

Deacon didn't care either, honestly. He was glad his aunt was already having so much fun. Macy too. Together, they were slightly scary, especially post-tequila.

Deacon hated to admit it, but he felt cozy in the Uber car. He didn't like words like "cozy." He associated it with furry bunnies and babies' bedrooms. But that was how he felt. He didn't want to get out. Maybe they could ride around for a while and talk about non-work-related things with his two favorite women.

Wow. That was a big thing to admit. But it was true. Macy and Aunt Fran were his favorites. His number ones. He'd do anything for either of them. He wasn't sure he liked knowing there were now two women in his life who commanded that sort of devotion from him. But before he could think about it more, they were at the Gaillard Center.

Cars whizzed by in both directions. "Thanks for the ride," he told the driver.

"You're welcome." The guy jumped out to help Aunt Fran, who'd sat directly behind him. They chatted and laughed and took their time.

It was inelegant to rush in Charleston.

Deacon took Macy's hand. It was warm. Her slender fingers curled around his when he helped pull her up and out. When she stood her full height, he felt possessive all of a sudden and didn't want any other man to get close enough to inhale her flower smell or cast secret glances at the tops of her breasts, so gracefully displayed in her dress and framed by that amazing coat.

She almost left her purse behind, a glittery little thing, but he saw it on the floor and handed it to her.

"Thanks," she said, and clutched it to her stomach.

"I hope you'll enjoy yourself tonight." He meant it too. She had no idea she'd be sitting next to him, no idea that Louisa wasn't going to show, that in effect, he and Macy would be on a date. He didn't feel guilty either, because a woman who looked as glorious as she did in that gown should have a man who admired her escorting her into what was sure to be a wonderful performance.

The air was chilly. He was glad of his topcoat. And now he had Aunt Fran on one arm and Macy on the other. The impressive, well-lit Gaillard Center stood before them. Somewhere inside was Yo-Yo Ma—and Celia, demanding attention, because they would be sitting in her box.

Meanwhile, he was sure his arrangement with Louisa would go off without a hitch.

But for the thirty seconds it took to walk inside, he simply enjoyed the pressure of the ladies' fingers on his coat, and Macy's hip occasionally brushing his. He also reveled in their small talk.

"I love theater boxes," said Aunt Fran, wobbling a little in her heels. "Important things always happen there. Apart from Abraham Lincoln's assassination, I mean."

Aunt Fran, he thought with affection. She was so odd sometimes.

"Such as?" asked Macy.

"Romantic liaisons," Aunt Fran said. "Scandalous assignations. Covert affairs."

"Oh." Macy leaned a little more into him, the better to speak to his aunt. "I should learn more about that theory, being a matchmaker."

"You should." Aunt Fran's tone was chipper. "And occasionally, people's futures are crushed—or made—in theater boxes." She was on a roll.

"How do you know all this?" asked Deacon.

"Edith Wharton." Aunt Fran laughed softly. "But really, everyone knows. You probably just haven't thought about it. Small spaces—wherever you have a lot of compressed life forces—are powerful places. Theater boxes, tree houses, gondolas, ship cabins, train berths."

"Phone booths," added Marcy.

"Yes," said Aunt Fran. "Don't discount them. Superman used them to great effect."

Deacon exchanged a quick look with Macy. Did postage stamp–sized foyers with dented brass mailboxes and frosted door panes count? How about compact Uber cars, where big truths snuck up on a guy with no warning?

She sent him a small, tense frown, which he easily read. She'd made that phone booth comment, so surely she was thinking about the foyer at Aunt Fran's house too and the kiss that never happened beneath the mistletoe.

He had only two more strides before he'd be required to open the door to the Gaillard Center and release both his aunt and Macy to their adoring fans—and Celia.

He stopped abruptly. "I just wanted to say that I'm a very lucky man to escort you two gorgeous creatures inside." He looked first at Aunt Fran, who beamed up at him, and then at Macy, whose smile was tense.

"No, we're the lucky ones." Aunt Fran patted his arm.

"You're very kind," said Macy primly.

Where was the confident matchmaker? The masterful cake maker and waffle baker? The hot tamale taking up too much space in the foyer in her black coat and sexy copper-colored dress?

He didn't know. But he missed her already.

"You think we'll be okay?" Aunt Fran asked him. "These are very intimidating people here in Charleston—kind, generous, but they don't suffer fools."

"You've dined with a U.S. President," he reminded her, "arm wrestled Sylvester Stallone, and sung harmony with Paul Simon. You'll do great."

"Of course you will," echoed Macy, sounding spirited.

He relinquished both their arms to open the door. Aunt Fran walked through and was instantly engulfed by Celia and her posse. Macy swiftly followed, and Deacon was right behind her.

She turned all of a sudden. "If you go out with Louisa afterward—" Her expression was stark.

"Everything will be fine," he assured her.

She hesitated a moment, then blurted out "Just don't kiss her" and took off into a blur of colorful gowns and black tuxes before he could ask her if that was the matchmaker in her talking, or the siren under the mistletoe who'd turned down his kiss and might possibly regret it.

CHAPTER SIXTEEN

Where did Macy go after she made that ridiculous remark to Deacon?

To a small room, of course, where big things happen. Fran would need to add it to her list: a stall in the ladies' bathroom. What woman hasn't cried there? Or hidden there? Or snuck makeup on there? Or seen her boyfriend's name on the wall there—with some other girl's—and realized that life, as she knew it, was over?

Yes, Macy went straight to the ladies' room at the Gaillard Center, before anyone could catch her to say hello, and threw herself into the farthest stall and locked the door with shaking hands. Somehow, she managed to pull out her cell phone and dial Greer.

"Hey." Greer sounded happy. She'd stayed at home that night to write Christmas cards. "Aren't you at the Gaillard?"

"Yes. And I—" Macy didn't know where to start.

"What's wrong?" Greer's voice filled with concern.

Macy closed her eyes. A toilet flushed nearby, and she didn't even care. Usually, she got in and out of public bathrooms pronto because she was a priss about such things. But that night . . . well, let the toilets flush—all of them at the same time, even. She couldn't have cared less at that point.

"I can't talk long," she said. "I'm in the ladies' room—"

"Tell me," Greer insisted.

"Okay." She drew a breath. "I think I'm officially in a bad place with this matchmaking assignment. The one with Deacon."

"I'm not surprised," Greer said. "How so?"

"I told him not to kiss Louisa. I never tell people that. I hope he thought I meant that first dates should be very low-key, platonic, get-to-know-you sessions. But that's not what I meant at all."

"What *did* you mean?"

"That I'd be jealous if he kissed her."

Greer laughed. "You two are a match. A gold-star match. Of course you'd be jealous."

"We were walking together. He was holding my arm on one side, and his aunt's on the other. And I felt it emanating from him, as bright and clear as the moon tonight. He was with the two women who *completed* him. His surrogate mother . . . and, um, me." Her voice cracked a little.

"Don't cry," whispered Greer. She sounded like she wanted to cry herself.

Macy was glad her friend understood how significant the moment was. "But he's so good at being a bachelor. Not that there's anything wrong with that when you're up front about it, which he is. He doesn't like commitment. But I . . . I don't want to get hurt." She stared at the hook on the stall door.

"You know what I've told you about that," said Greer. "You have to get over it."

"I wish I could."

"So where do you go from here? I think we should call Ella."

"I don't know." Macy sighed. Confusion wasn't a good

feeling, especially when you were out in public in a gown that you hoped a special man would notice—and he was on a date with someone else you'd set him up with.

Ten seconds later, Ella was on the line, and Greer filled her in.

"If you're that afraid to take a chance with him," Ella said, "you can keep trying to match him to someone else while he's here. It won't be easy, but you have to decide what to do. Only you know your heart."

"You're right." Macy leaned her back against the stall door. She felt herself getting embarrassed all over again.

"Just go up to that theater box and don't think about it for a while," Ella suggested. "The answer will come to you eventually."

"You got this," Greer chimed in, "especially if you stay relaxed. Try to enjoy yourself."

"Thanks, you two." Macy said good-bye and, after a quick glance in the bathroom mirror, checked her coat in the lobby. And then she got a text from Louisa: *Can't make it. So sorry!*

"Aw, shoot," she said out loud to no one. No matter what, she decided, she'd enjoy herself. She'd stay relaxed if it killed her!

A minute later, an usher escorted her to Celia's side of the box. There were three rows of stadium-style seats, two seats per row. Fran sat in the front row, an empty seat beside her, presumably Macy's.

Celia sat next to Deacon in the second row. "Our party of six is down to four," she said. "My cousin doesn't feel well." Celia was extra glamorous with an up-do and long, thick, false eyelashes. Her silver gown, with a square neckline and capped sleeves, was spectacular too, in a British monarch sort of way.

"And Louisa had something come up," Deacon added.

Macy was flummoxed. "She just texted me. I wonder what it was?"

"I have no idea." Deacon didn't appear fazed in the least. "I'm sure she's okay."

"And you'll have plenty of company," Celia told him as she patted his arm.

"All right then." Macy took her seat, feeling self-conscious. She was the matchmaker, the coordinator of these dates for Deacon, and so far none had panned out. He was paying her good money, and she felt she hadn't earned it.

But what else could she do now apart from enjoying the performance? She took Greer and Ella's advice and focused on the grand space before her—the dramatic ceiling overhead, the other boxes, the crowd below, and the solitary figure on stage with a glossy brown cello—and squeezed Fran's hand, just once.

Fran squeezed back.

So what that Celia and Deacon were sitting so close together behind them? Celia was married. Off-limits. Taken. And Yo-Yo Ma's music was magnificent. That was what Macy would think about.

At the intermission, Fran took her aside in the hallway. "Can we talk about Celia? Her body language right now is shouting that Deacon is all hers."

It was true. Celia and Deacon were looking up at a plaque on the history of the Gaillard space. She had her arm hooked through his.

"And she'll carry that body language back to the box," Fran said, "where it's dark and all sorts of things can go on, mere inches behind our backs. Aren't you going to fight for him?"

Macy gave a little huff. "Of course not. He's supposed to be on a date with someone else. And Celia is *married*."

"So? You're awfully naïve."

"Deacon would never—"

"I know. But Celia will try. And you're okay with that?"

"No. It's—it's inappropriate for anyone married to cheat."

Fran laughed. "You make it sound like you don't care that she's specifically angling for Deacon."

"It's not my business."

"You should make it your business," Fran said. "Louisa's not here. The squeaky wheel gets the grease. And Celia is the squeaky wheel tonight."

Macy took a cleansing breath. "Don't take this the wrong way, Fran, because I find your nephew quite charming and attractive, and someday he'll make another woman very happy if he ever decides to settle down—but Deacon is not my type."

"Come on, Macy." Fran put a hand on her hip and looked her over. "You're better than having a *type*. That's what people say who are afraid of commitment and won't admit it. You're as bad as Deacon is. Maybe worse. Because at least he admits he's running from it."

"*Fran*."

"Yes?"

"Please don't use your television tactics on me."

"Oh, you can take it."

"And even if he were my type—"

"Macy, you're doing it again. Showing your own disdain for commitment with these easy-out words that mean *nothing*—"

"Even if I felt Deacon and I were, um, compatible . . . how many times do I have to tell you? He's my *client*."

"So? I was a true professional, and I kissed every single one of the male guests on my show. And you know I didn't settle for a peck on the cheek. I'll never regret it."

"I remember. The whole country does, and good for you. But whoever wants to be with me will have to make a real effort to get my attention. I'm not going to run after him."

"Good for you," Fran said. "But what about the shy men? You're going to make them jump through that hoop? A lot of them are unfairly overlooked because so many girls have to have the dog-and-pony show, which doesn't last, my dear, let me tell you. Roses, flights to San Francisco for dinner, all that *Pretty Woman* crap. Go for the humble. A guy who's a bit nerdy. Someone who sees the real you and can't afford helicopter rides."

"Are you saying your nephew is humble, slightly nerdy, and not rich?"

"No. He's none of those things. You're so lucky." Fran slapped Macy's arm, which she promptly rubbed to take the sting away. "I was actually talking about every other man in the world, if you're foolish enough not to go after Deacon." She rolled her eyes.

Macy would be patient. "You're full of a lot of advice, Fran. Maybe you should take it and find your own man."

"I'm not looking."

"Well, neither am I. And as for Celia, I've learned not to engage with her anymore. It's what she wants. Deacon can take care of himself." She tucked her phone in her satin-lined clutch. "Louisa's not answering my texts. She left no explanation about why she didn't show, which is so unlike her. Something's not right here, and I want to get to the bottom of it."

"Fine," Fran said, "but I'm making Deacon go with you. I have to get him away from Celia. This is a good excuse. Maybe you could get to know each other better."

"We don't need to," Macy said. "Just be patient. Let him find someone on *his* terms, with my oversight, if he wants it."

* * *

Considering the company he was keeping at the moment—
Celia, who had attached herself to his arm—Deacon almost decided he'd made a huge mistake turning over his
life for one month to his aunt as a Christmas gift. But then
he remembered Macy, who was standing near a potted palm
talking to Aunt Fran during intermission.

He led Celia toward his two favorite ladies.

"I'm going to find Louisa," Macy said when they arrived. "Something's fishy about her not being here."

Deacon felt a pang of anxiety. Very slight. Hardly noticeable. But it was there. He wasn't one to dissemble. And
here he was doing just that. If Macy found out how he and
his dates had been colluding to disrupt her matchmaking
plans for him, she wouldn't be happy.

But he wouldn't be happy if he went along with those
plans!

He was stuck between a rock and a hard place.

"You gotta go for it," George had told him that night
before he'd left the house. "All's fair in love and war."

"I never said I loved her," Deacon had replied. "You
can't love someone you've only just met."

"It's obvious the musicals you grew up on were wasted
on you," George said. "You're never allowed to sing Freddy's song from *My Fair Lady* ever again." He literally
pushed Deacon toward the door. "Someday you'll come to
your senses."

Now he had to wonder if George was right. He was only
stirring things up. No plan, no commitment. And he was
missing something about life and love, clearly. All he knew
was that singing in the shower was as far as he wanted to go.

"You're being a bit paranoid, Macy," Celia said, still
clinging to Deacon's arm.

"I know Louisa." Macy's tone was firm. "She didn't explain why she stood Deacon up. Which means something is off."

"She probably got cold feet about going on a blind date and didn't want to say so," Deacon said. "That's understandable."

"Whatever," said Macy. "I'm going. Thank you, Celia, for the invitation to your box. I hope you won't mind I'm leaving early."

"That's fine," Celia said.

Of course it was fine with her, but it wasn't fine with Deacon. Macy was supposed to stay. He was supposed to make this night into a date with her.

His diabolical plan was backfiring.

Now he was stuck with Celia.

Macy turned on her heel. Her copper gown swayed behind her, back and forth, in time with her hips, like a cobra in a straw basket dancing to the sound of the snake charmer's pipe.

"I'm going with you," Deacon insisted.

Macy stopped and looked back at them. "Not necessary. Really."

"I will too, then," Celia said.

"I'd appreciate it if you stayed here with my aunt," Deacon said as cordially as possible, but he really wasn't asking. No way was she coming along.

"All right," said Celia, sounding sulky. "But you're going to miss the rest of the performance."

"I'm glad you're going." Aunt Fran smiled at him.

"Louisa was supposed to be my date, after all." He felt foolish pretending to be concerned, when he knew very well Louisa was off having a good time at an oyster bar over the Ravenel Bridge. But he was desperate too, a new state of mind for him.

"I'd actually prefer going alone." Macy's chin was high.

"But thanks for the offer. Just in case Louisa isn't feeling well, we don't want to overwhelm her. I'll keep you posted via text."

And she took off down the stairs, her skirt hitched up in her hand, without even waiting for a reply.

Deacon caught up with her on the curb. She was already in her big Cruella de Vil coat. Good thing too. It was cold enough to see his breath—a first for him in Charleston.

"I told you . . ." she started reprimanding him, but she was so busy punching in numbers, presumably calling Uber, that she trailed off.

"Louisa is my date," he explained once again. "I'm going."

"She's *my* responsibility." Macy narrowed her eyes and kept punching.

"She can take care of herself." He took her arm.

"Wait!" She stumbled along beside him.

"There's a line of cabs on the street."

She finally looked up from her phone and walked with a little more interest. "You can let go now."

"Maybe I don't want to."

She sent him a sideways glance that he knew was meant to intimidate him. "You're my client. And I've set you up with some amazing women."

"Amazing, huh? So amazing I'll fall in love with one of them? Like on *The Bachelor*?"

"If you ever get to have a real date with one of them, I think there's a solid chance of that. Maybe not in love, but close enough that you'll want to continue seeing whoever it is and fly back down here from New York on your private jet."

"I don't have one of those."

"Really?"

"I fly commercial. Always." He opened the door to the cab and helped her in, then got in himself. She was already giving the driver the address. They sat thigh-to-thigh as the cabbie took off toward Louisa's. "Disappointed?"

"No. What does flying in a private jet have to do with someone's value as a human being?"

"A lot, if you're into monetary worth."

"You're right. Some people are."

"And I've met an awful lot of those people," he said.

"That's no excuse to hide from love."

"Is that a line in a song?"

"No."

"It should be. About those dates you've arranged . . ."

"I'm sorry we're batting oh-for-three right now," she said. "I'm embarrassed, truthfully."

"Don't be. Maybe I don't want amazing. Maybe I prefer ordinary."

She didn't say anything.

Neither did he.

"Are you saying *I'm* ordinary?" she finally asked.

"Why would you assume I'm talking about you? I mean I like you, but I was talking more about a type. Not a specific person."

"Never mind. And 'type' is a lazy term. That's for people who can't commit. They use 'type' as a rationalization so they can get away with rejecting everyone."

"Really? When did you come to that conclusion?"

"Your aunt told me so." Macy smiled.

"So she was talking to you about me."

"Maybe she was talking to me about *me*."

He liked how she flirted. "All I'm saying is that I prefer to be with someone who doesn't need to prove herself."

"That's not the same as 'ordinary.'"

"I meant it in a good way. 'Ordinary' as in real and relatable. Isn't it exhausting to have to be amazing all the time?"

"Are you saying *I'm* amazing?"

He saw the mischief in her eyes. "The question was rhetorical," he said with a grin. "But are you fishing for a compliment? Because I'm not sure if I'm supposed to answer yes or no, considering I said amazing is exhausting. Somehow I don't think you want to be called exhausting."

"Then don't answer. Celia likes you, you know."

"I know." Macy's flower smell got to him, as it usually did. He wanted to grab her hand, raise it to his lips, and kiss it.

"What will she do if she outright propositions you, Deacon, and you reject her? Will she seek revenge?"

"No," he said. "I think she'd cry, and not about me. About something else. It's like she has a splinter in her foot she can't get out. I have no idea what it is, apart from some dissatisfaction with her marriage. Do you?"

"No." Macy bit her lip at that and looked out the window. "She was like this long before she got married." She reached into her sparkly bag for the fare, but he beat her to it and handed the driver some cash.

"Shall we?" He took her hand, and she scooted across the seat to his door.

He helped her out and put his hands on her waist when she sought her balance on her heels. He kept holding her because it felt right, as if his hands belonged just there . . . and he wanted to keep looking at her.

Already he was forgetting life before Macy. Or not exactly forgetting, but wondering how he'd ever had fun. He'd been Macy-less and hadn't even realized it.

She looked right back, little flecks of champagne sparkle in her light brown eyes. "Louisa," she said. "I really, *really* think you're going to like her."

Punch to the gut. Did she always have to play matchmaker?

"Let's go see if she's in," he said.

"She'll be furious that we came. What if she really did

get cold feet and she's watching TV? She'll be embarrassed."

"Let's hope that's not what happens." He prayed that Louisa was still out and unreachable by phone or text.

They managed to get down the cobblestone lane arm-in-arm because really, those stones were murder, especially on a woman in heels. There was one light on at Louisa's house, on the first floor. They knocked on her glossy red door.

She wasn't there. No surprise. At least not for him.

"Shoot," said Macy, and looked behind her at Colonial Lake, shimmering in the moonlight. "I don't know what to think."

"Let me call her," Deacon said.

"Fine. Maybe she'll answer for you."

And she did. The conversation was short and sweet. Deacon said Macy wanted to talk to her. Louisa explained to Macy that yes, she'd gotten cold feet at the last minute, and that state of mind, combined with an opportunity to catch up with an old friend in town for the weekend, made her ditch her date with Deacon. She apologized profusely.

"It's okay," Macy said into the phone. "Sorry I came to your house looking for you. I wanted to make sure everything was okay."

Deacon sensed her relief. And her professional disappointment.

When she ended the conversation, she handed him his phone and shrugged. "Oh, well. She asked if we could check her flat iron while we're here. She's afraid she left it on. The key's under the back mat."

"Sure." This was not a part of the plan, coming to Louisa's house, going inside. Macy was supposed to sit next to him at the concert. That was all.

But he'd wing it.

"You were right," Macy said. "She decided she didn't want to go on a blind date. It's that simple." She headed down a stone path on the side of the house. "I'm glad I checked. When I walked into the box and saw you and Celia together, an alarm bell went off in my head. I thought Celia might have bullied Louisa into not coming tonight."

"No. Absolutely not." This set-up, Deacon noted, might be getting out of hand. "Celia's difficult, but she's not diabolical."

Macy shot him a wry look. "She'd love to wreck my matchmaking plans. And she seemed awfully happy to be hanging on your arm."

"She might be jealous of you and infatuated with me— or she might just be bored with her life. I think it's the latter. Hey, what's a flat iron?"

"It straightens curls or waves."

"Why would anyone want to do that?"

"For a change of pace, I suppose," said Macy.

"Do *you* have a flat iron?"

"Of course!"

"You mean, your hair's not really straight?"

"No, it's straight. But even if you have straight hair, you use a flat iron sometimes. Because flat irons can make it straighter." She sent him a *duh* look.

Women and their mysterious grooming habits. At least for a few seconds he wasn't thinking about the nape of her neck, which was mighty tempting to nuzzle. She was a mere six inches in front of him, lifting the gate latch.

Once through, she traipsed around back like Goldilocks through the woods—he followed in his manly stride, which was actually sexual frustration masquerading as chivalry—and they entered the house through a patio door.

"I like it," he said. It was decorated in a traditional style, lots of hunting prints and old furniture, but with a smattering of modern art. A Christmas tree with some wrapped gifts beneath it stood in a corner.

"Me too. I'll just run up to her bathroom and check things out and be right back down."

"Great." He stood there with his arms folded and tried to ignore the powerful temptation to go after her.

"Deacon?" Macy called down.

"Yes?"

"Could you come up? You're not going to believe this!"

"Sure." He bounded up the stairs—ignoring how happy he was to be beckoned—and saw an open door, some light pouring from the room, and the edge of Macy's ebony coat and copper skirt.

"She *did* leave on her flat iron," she said when he arrived, pointing to the bathroom counter. "This is the first time I've known someone who thought they left something hot on and actually did."

"She's lucky."

"She is, but that's not what I wanted to show you." She inclined her head. "Come here. Into her bedroom."

"Really?"

"She won't mind."

They walked in. Three bright, shiny, new tricycles sat on one side of the room with big foil bows tied to them: one silver, one red, and one green. Giant tags hung from the handlebars with names written in magic marker: Jake, Tommy, Marcus.

"She's got triplet nephews," Macy said. "They're coming for Christmas. They live in Savannah."

"Wow. That's really nice."

Macy blinked and hugged herself. "Yes. It is."

"You want kids?"

She laughed. "Sure. Someday. But even if it never happens, I have Lucy and Sam, my niece and nephew. How about you?"

"It's not something I've ever seriously contemplated."

"Why, do you think?"

He shook his head. "I don't know."

She nudged his shoulder with hers. "You have to know. Is it because you were an only child?"

He crouched by a tricycle, his coat puddling around him, and ran his hand over the seat. "Maybe."

She sat down on the floor next to him.

He looked over at her. "I just always thought I'd stay busy. I think I've always been afraid to slow down."

"You mean, with Fran, you never relaxed? Had family time?" She hugged her knees close. "Was her career always paramount?"

He sat all the way down too, and shook his head. "She was wonderful at sitting with me and reading."

"Shakespeare."

"Exactly. Or E. B. White. Or Louis Sachar. We'd watch TV shows too, and DVD movies, or play board games. But I always got the feeling that we were running from something."

"Oh," Macy said.

A beat of silence went by.

"I think we were always running from the sadness of my parents not being there," he said. "Every birthday, every holiday, every milestone at school—I felt their absence. I didn't want to. But I think Aunt Fran felt it, and so I did too. She's not one to hold back when she feels something."

"I can imagine."

"Poor woman, she tried. I never saw her actually lose it. Never even heard her cry in her bedroom. But I sensed it in her. There was a hole in the fabric of our family she never wanted to look at. She never wanted me to either."

"I can see why. Did you ever go visit your parents' graves?"

"A couple of times. Once when I'd gotten out of the hospital with a pretty severe case of tonsillitis. I was about eight, and for some reason, it took me a while to recover. At the cemetery, Aunt Fran held my hand so tightly it hurt, and I pulled away, went running down a path. But she caught me and brought me back. We left flowers. The next time, I'd turned twelve, and she gave me a lecture about becoming a man while we were there. Both times, I remember we got out as fast as we could. And right before college, I went by myself without telling her. But nothing happened. I mean, I didn't know how I was supposed to feel." He paused. "I haven't been back since."

Macy put her hand over his. "I'm sorry."

He turned to her. "You should probably move your hand."

"I don't want to," she said stoutly, the way a good friend would.

"You'll regret it," he warned her.

She didn't blink. "You will."

He laughed. "You're brave."

"So are you."

And then he leaned over and kissed her.

CHAPTER SEVENTEEN

Macy knew it was the wrong thing to do, kissing Deacon.

Wrong, wrong, wrong.

But she did it anyway because sometimes wrong was actually right. She didn't know how to explain this truth, but when it came, there was no denying it. It was real. It was complete. It was massive, like a thunderstorm that moved over the prairie, and when it came, it occupied your body and soul and you thought you'd be afraid of it, but you weren't. You knew all along you were meant to be in it, and then you realized you actually *created* it.

You ruled the storm.

And she had to be honest. She didn't just give in to Deacon. She signaled him with her body language, with her eyes, with every cell in her body screaming for him to touch her, to kiss her, to do more . . . way more.

She invited him in, past her big coat with the wispy feather collar, and the tightly zipped gown, and her beautiful French bra and panties set from Bits of Lace on King Street.

And once they got started, there was no stopping them. . . .

Here was the tacky part, although she wouldn't apologize: she rummaged through Louisa's bathroom counter drawers for condoms. She didn't want to ask Deacon if he had one. Because then that might mean he was intending to use it with Louisa.

"I have one already," he said when she brought in the shiny foil packet.

She was crushed. "You do?"

He laughed. "Not for Louisa," he said. "Every decent single guy carries them."

She laughed too. Of course he was right.

They stayed in Louisa's bedroom, on top of their coats on the floor. They were bad houseguests—they weren't even houseguests!—and they didn't care. They made love in different, crazy positions that just happened, like they were channeling the Kama Sutra.

More than once.

All in half an hour.

She had already decided Deacon was the best lover she'd ever had when she caught sight of a tricycle and the clock on Louisa's bedside table.

"We need to go," she said on her back, still panting and so pleasured she didn't want to move.

Deacon was busy running his hand up and down her side, from her bare shoulder down to her hip. She felt curvy and attractive. "You're right," he said.

And then he pushed her palms back on the coats, positioned himself over her, and kissed her, just kissed her, until she felt like that adored queen on the barge on the Nile that she'd wanted to feel like ever since she first saw him.

Finally, he pulled back. "This was a long time coming."

"I barely remember getting undressed." She sat up, her breasts exposed, no sense of modesty. "We've only known each other—" She snapped her fingers to signify how short the time had been.

"And every second that's gone by has been torture.

Because this was meant to happen. You know it as well as
I do. We've been dancing around it."

"Even at Fast and French you felt tortured?"

"Don't remind me. Yes."

"How about when I was sitting on my desk eating a
pear?"

"God, yes. You drove me crazy."

She laughed. "That's very kind of you."

"Kind? I'm not kind," he scoffed, but it didn't come out
harshly. Somehow, it was sexy. Friendly. Even intimate. He
stood up and held out his hand.

She took it and was taken straight back to that feeling
of him grabbing her naked rear end with his greedy man
fingers while he kissed her senseless.

"Okay, you're not kind," she said. "Neither am I, actually." She allowed him to pull her up.

And then he tricked her. He sank to his knees on the
coats, leaned over and kissed the round of her right butt
cheek.

Wow. Standing above him, she knew where he was
headed, but she didn't feel an ounce of awkwardness. He
was right. This was really meant to happen.

What he did was very, very good. She was tempted to
scream, "Yo-Yo *Ma*," but that would have been too funny
and distracting at just the wrong time.

How could she reconcile all this intimacy—that clearly
went beyond the physical—with the fact that Deacon didn't
believe in love? Her colleagues at Two Love Lane were all
about her getting together with him, but wouldn't they also
be a little disappointed in her for putting her personal life
ahead of the business's priorities?

But she was that missing piece in Deacon's jigsaw
puzzle. The cherry on top of his sundae. The reason for him
to stop running.

She knew it, but she didn't know if he would ever know it himself. She was sure he thought she was hotter than hell and a fabulous (temporary) sex partner. But he might never figure out that she was home for him.

So she had to do her best to forget that he was home for her.

Hot little tears sprang to her eyes, but she held them at bay.

He'd finally gotten to his feet. Her limbs, understandably, felt weak and floppy, plus she had trouble remembering how to put her clothes on.

"Raise your arms," he said. He'd managed to yank on his tuxedo trousers and now put her gown over her head and pulled it down for her. When he zipped her up, he kissed the back of her neck. "That's my special spot," he said.

"All yours," she murmured, still lost in a sexual haze.

"We overstayed our welcome." He helped her on with her coat.

"Welcome, shmelcome," she said, which wasn't clever at all but she didn't care because it said everything about living in the moment, where nothing stuck and you were free.

She adjusted Deacon's bowtie, then fished her handbag from a woven straw basket filled with clean laundry Louisa had yet to fold. She had a vague recollection of throwing her purse there to get it out of the way. It had come open, and her round compact hairbrush had fallen out, the Dollar Store kind that flips open with plastic brush bristles that pop out. She stuffed the disc back in her clutch and hoped her cool up-do wasn't totally destroyed.

For some reason they were both somber at the curb at the end of the cobblestone street when they waited on the Uber car. But then Deacon turned her toward him. "I'm sorry," he said, and pushed her hair back from her face. "I didn't mean to seduce you. When I joined you upstairs, I was—"

"I know." She looked up at him. His palm felt good on the side of her face. And he was so gentle. "It's okay."

And what she meant was that it was worth it. She was horrified at herself for believing that, but she would not regret what they had done.

He'd set a new standard for her.

Maybe he got that—because his mouth tipped up, and then he kissed her. Very gently. He held her like she was a piece of her grandmother's fine bone china. His lips were toasty warm, keeping the cold night at bay. She was ready to go home with him and crawl into his bed and not get out for several days.

She knew very well that she was in something way over her head.

"Is that our Uber car?" She forced herself to retreat from being the lover back to fellow pedestrian.

Deacon threw his arm around her shoulder and squeezed. "Wouldn't you know it?" He looked down the street like a little kid waiting on a Christmas parade. "We got the same guy who'd picked us up from my aunt's house."

"You liked him," she said.

"I did."

The car pulled up. "Yo," the driver said.

Yo-Yo Ma, Macy thought. It was the theme of the night.

He looked slightly bewildered. "You didn't go to the concert?"

"We did," Macy said briskly, "and we're on our way back." She looked at Deacon in a whole new way now. She'd always thought he was sexy, but she'd lifted the hood and seen the engine. How was she supposed to not remember his mad skills every time she saw his mouth or his eyes or his hair, which she'd played with while he'd buried himself in her?

"We had pressing business," he said.

"Yes. Totally pressing," she added.

They were being silly. But it was fun.

When they got out at the Gaillard, Deacon reached into the car before he shut the rear passenger door and handed the driver a hundred-dollar bill. "Merry Christmas, a little early."

A brisk wind lifted Macy's coat and swirled beneath her gown and up her legs, making her shiver, especially when she remembered the hot hands that had caressed her naked thighs so recently.

The guy paused, then shoved the bill in his pocket. "Thanks, man," he said. "I'll give this to my mom. She finally paid off the mortgage on her decrepit little house— the one I grew up in—but she pays heating bills like she has a twenty-room mansion."

"Why?" Macy couldn't help asking.

"She's got no insulation, I guess. And she can't afford to get it fixed up. Almost all her pension goes to medications."

Deacon took out his wallet. "Here." He gave the driver another couple of hundred-dollar bills.

Macy had to admit she was slightly dizzy at the sight of all that cash. She was business-rich and cash-poor herself.

The driver shook his head. "No, man. But thanks."

"I want to help your mom," Deacon insisted.

"You tourists need to take care of yourselves," the guy said. "Not be too generous. There are some very bad people, even in a nice place like this, just waiting to take advantage of you."

"I know that," Deacon said. "But sometimes you take a chance. And I'm not worried. I know where this is going."

The driver scratched his ear. "I don't know."

Deacon shoved the bills forward another couple inches. "Come on. It's not charity. This is friend to friend."

The guy finally took the money. "I can't thank you enough," he said soberly.

Macy smiled. "We're all just paying it forward, you know?"

"I'll pay it forward too." The driver allowed himself a small grin. "I promise."

Deacon crouched lower to make better eye contact. "You're already doing it. Helping your mom is important."

That touched Macy's heart. Deacon had lost his mother at such a young age. And he had done really well taking care of the one he'd been blessed with in her place.

"This is a good night," the guy said. "Mom will love hearing this story. She'll make me tell it to her at least three times."

Deacon looked at Macy, and she looked at him, and all felt right in Macy's world. It was an awesome feeling.

"Merry Christmas, you two." Their friendly driver waved.

They waved back.

How different the walk was this time when they made their way to the Gaillard Center's main entrance!

Deacon had a contented half-smile on his face.

"That was nice of you," Macy said.

He shrugged. "I did it to impress a certain good-cheer enthusiast I know."

A car whizzed by, the sounds of "Rudolph the Red-Nosed Reindeer" floating out the window in that out-of-tune way that happens when sound waves meet speed.

"I don't think so," she said. "You would have done it without me there. Admit it."

"I will, but only if you tell me what you were thinking after he said his mom would want to hear the story three times."

She stopped walking. "You really want to know?"

"I do."

"I was thinking that there is no better feeling in the world than giving. Seriously. Making someone else happy is addictive, and I wish I could feel like that *all* the time. Not just at Christmas."

They started walking again.

"I was thinking the same thing," he said.

"At the same time." She wished she could hold his hand. She wanted to.

"Hate to ruin the Hallmark moment"—he shot her a wicked grin—"but I also feel that way about great sex. Like the kind we had today. Maybe I'll get coal in my stocking for saying so."

"Um, no. You could never get coal for what you did at Louisa's house."

"Oh yeah?"

They stared at each other for a few drawn-out seconds. Inside, she shivered, remembering how locked into each other they'd been.

"I propose we get naked together every day," he murmured low. "Morning and night. You live right next door. I can slip in and out of your house, easy. And our Christmas will be merry and bright."

"*Deacon.*"

"I know what you're going to say." He held open the door for her to the lobby. A rush of warm air swept past her into the night. "You think I'm only about having a fling. You regret our little interlude at Louisa's. And you think we need to put back up those walls."

"Because we're neighbors." She made a beeline for the coat-check room. "And you're my client—my challenging client who doesn't believe in love."

He checked his coat too.

They didn't speak to each other again until they were all alone walking up the stairs. "I can't regret what we did today," he said. "And I wasn't thinking only about myself. I was thinking about you."

"Which I find very . . . sweet." He'd been a thoughtful lover. She couldn't deny that.

"So we'll forget we made mad, passionate love several times on the floor of a stranger's house?"

Tingles shot up her spine. "Yes," she said awkwardly. "As we both know, healthy adults can have sexual lives that don't necessarily lead to intimacy. It's a drive, like hunger, and thirst—"

"Macy." Deacon laughed softly. "I'm the last person you have to explain that to. I get it."

"Of course." She couldn't help feeling stupid.

"Don't feel guilty about having sex with me and leaving it at that. I'm a big boy."

"I know." She felt how red her cheeks must look.

He opened the door to the box. She went in first, and he followed. Aunt Fran and Celia sat together in the front row. Macy and Deacon took their seats behind them. She didn't look at Deacon, nor he at her, as far as she knew. They were well-behaved. Clapped appropriately. Made sure their knees didn't touch.

I am a professional, she told herself over and over, even as the juncture between her thighs was pleasantly sore from the vigorous sexcapade she'd participated in not an hour before with her client, the hottest man in the world.

Her *client*.

Who was an amazing lover.

Her client.

Who wanted to sleep with her every day he was here during the holidays.

I am a professional, she reminded herself once more when the lights came up at the end of the performance.

And then Celia turned around, and Macy made a decision.

CHAPTER EIGHTEEN

Deacon wished the lights hadn't come up. He was still thinking about what a fierce, enchanting lover Macy had been at Louisa's house. And here she was, sitting next to him—lush and beautiful—and Celia and his aunt were staring at him, and he was trapped. Trapped by good intentions. Trapped by his own folly in that he should never, ever have put pleasing his aunt above being authentic with her. He owed her that. But he hadn't bothered to really show up in his personal life in a long time. He'd been too busy with work. He'd become a mere cliché of the dutiful nephew, and look where the guilt had got him.

Celia cooed, "Deacon, you owe me a drink. You missed almost the entire second half." She didn't even look at Macy. "Shall we go to the Grand Bohemian?"

"That's a fabulous idea, Ceels," Macy said, sounding perky. Sickeningly perky.

And "*Ceels*"? What was that about? Deacon played it cool, but it wasn't hard to guess that Macy was trying to make Celia crazy.

"I'm up for a mojito," Aunt Fran volunteered. "Any word from Louisa?"

But his aunt wasn't even listening. Her eyes were on someone behind Deacon's head.

It was Colonel Block entering the box. "I saw you from across the way during intermission," he called down the stairs. "But you had too many admirers. I've come to say hello."

"Aren't you the courteous gent?" Aunt Fran yelled up to him.

He seemed to notice her for the first time. "Oh, hello, Fran. You have your share of admirers too, of course. I'd say for sheer numbers they wouldn't even fit into this auditorium. But I was speaking to my friend, Mrs. Turnwell. Have you two met?"

Deacon turned and saw a lovely woman about his aunt's age on the other side of the box's aisle.

Mrs. Turnwell smiled at his aunt. "No, we haven't. How do you do?"

"Very well, thank you," Aunt Fran said. Deacon could feel her chagrin and embarrassment. "Lovely to meet you."

"Likewise." Mrs. Turnwell looked up at the colonel with bright eyes. "You going to the hunter trials in Aiken next weekend? My granddaughter's riding."

"With bells on." He chuckled.

"Good. I'll see you then," Mrs. Turnwell said gaily, then turned back to her party.

The colonel's chuckle trailed off, and he glared at nothing in particular.

"Would you like to have a drink with us, Colonel?" Deacon called up to him.

"Only if you're not too busy," Aunt Fran added. She wasn't being sarcastic, as Deacon expected she'd be after playing second fiddle to the lovely Mrs. Turnwell.

"I suppose I could do that," the colonel replied.

"You stay there," Aunt Fran said, excitement in her voice. "I'll come up to you."

Uh-oh. Deacon saw the signs. She was getting a crush. Why, though? The colonel wasn't exactly exciting. Nor was he a doctor, her usual infatuation.

"Louisa was eaten by an alligator," Deacon said matter-of-factly to his aunt as she passed him and Macy on the steps.

"Oh, good," Aunt Fran said, her eyes still on the colonel.

Damn. She had a *serious* crush!

Macy leaned toward Deacon a mere half-inch. He could see right down her dress. Of course, he looked. No sane man wouldn't. "When we get to the Grand Bohemian," she said, "I'll want to order a Manhattan with two cherries." She picked up her fancy little purse, took out her lipstick and compact, and ran the lipstick over her mouth.

Operation Shameless Flirt was fascinating to watch.

"Celia," she went on, dropping her lipstick back in her purse, "I hope you'll tell us about your husband's latest missionary work. He's such a hero, going to Haiti all the time. Isn't that where he is tonight?"

"No," Celia said flatly. They began their walk up the box steps. "He's at a medical conference."

"We should FaceTime him," Macy said. "From the Grand Bohemian." They were out in the hall. "Let him see for himself that his wife is out on the town enjoying herself."

"I don't think so," said Celia, who was beginning to sound perturbed.

Deacon noted that his aunt was still talking to the colonel, but the old military man had brought over more friends, which was nice to see.

Macy laid a hand on Celia's arm. "By the way, thank you so much for the box seats."

"You're welcome." Celia's smooth brow never changed, but there was a hint of wariness in her tone.

"Shall we go, ladies?" Deacon suggested, as well he should. These two were miserable around each other.

"I've decided to head on home." Celia shot them a brittle smile. "Have fun." She took off down the stairs.

"What was that about?" Deacon asked Macy.

She shrugged. "I realized when she was blatantly ignoring me after the lights went up that I was letting her do it. I always have. I've let her treat me poorly."

"So you caught her attention by flirting with me, huh? Good thing I don't mind being objectified."

Macy stopped, her mouth falling open. "You weren't my pawn."

"Sure I was." He arched a playful brow. "Celia's too."

She bit her lip. "I *did* treat you like a pawn."

"It's especially galling after you told me we needed to stay in the friend zone." He was secretly amused, of course.

"I should be appalled at myself." Macy put her hand over her heart. "But I'm not," she added, "because it worked. Celia left."

"You're bad," Deacon murmured an inch from her ear. If they faced each other, they'd have to kiss. That was how close they were. And he liked it.

"Stop," she said. "Everyone will guess what happened at Louisa's."

"I hope they do." He steered her toward his aunt and the colonel, who were alone at the moment. The others in the group had drifted off.

"All set for Toys for Tots?" the colonel asked Macy.

Her expression brightened. "I am, Colonel, but I haven't heard yet how many marines you're sending me. I only want to know so I can be sure I have the proper number of scarves for them."

"Scarves?" asked Aunt Fran.

"Miss Thing enjoys knitting scarves every year with the Marine Corp seal on them," Macy explained. "To give to the marines who come help us."

"I normally send two," Colonel Block said, "but everyone fights over your party and those scarves, so I'm sending three this year."

"Excellent." Macy beamed.

"Deacon and I would love to crash the party," Aunt Fran said.

"Oh, please come," Macy said. "Everyone's invited. We do it every year. The only requirement is to bring a new, unwrapped toy. We're collecting for infants all the way up to fifteen-year-olds."

Aunt Fran smiled. "We'll be there."

Of course, they would. Deacon couldn't wait to see all those bikes lined up. And he wanted to be there for Macy. Sure, she'd have marines helping her, but maybe he could do something to help out too.

"It's next Saturday, noon to two," Macy said. "We'll have a cocoa and coffee bar set up from Roastbusters and lots of Christmas cookies that I spend a whole two days making with my business partners in the kitchen at Two Love Lane. We've got some carolers coming, and we might even have Santa Claus." She tossed a conspiratorial grin at the colonel.

"You're an imposing man," Aunt Fran said, "who can be jolly if you want to be—not that I've seen that yet."

The colonel lowered his brow. "I'm always jolly, madam."

"Should we put two and two together then?" Aunt Fran asked. "I'm guessing you have a red suit in your closet."

"I'll never tell," the colonel replied stiffly.

"Oh, lighten up, Frances." Aunt Fran laughed.

"My name isn't Frances," the colonel said with great dignity.

"It's an expression," Aunt Fran explained.

The colonel sniffed and stared off into the distance. "Pardon me for not recognizing it."

Aunt Fran shrugged. "No wonder, since you're sitting on such a high horse."

Macy's eyes widened, and she looked to Deacon. *Let's get outta here*, her expression said.

"Let's go, everyone." Deacon led the way down the stairs, Macy's arm wrapped through his.

It felt right, so right, he had to think about something else. But what? It was impossible when she was this close. Not even the friction between Aunt Fran and the colonel could really bother him.

"What *is* your first name?" Aunt Fran asked the colonel as they crossed the vast hall.

"Frederick," the colonel replied.

"I'll call you Freddie." Aunt Fran was a mischief-maker.

"I prefer Frederick," the colonel shot back.

Aunt Fran tried unsuccessfully to block a yawn. "I can't wait to get into a warm taxi. Or Uber car. You like Uber, Colonel?"

"No. Nor do I like taxis. I like to travel under my own power."

"So how do you get to New York? Flap your arms?" Aunt Fran obviously thought her own joke was very funny. She laughed.

Deacon and Macy exchanged a look. *Whatever*, hers said, her eyes twinkling. He agreed. It was the colonel and Aunt Fran's problem, not Deacon and Macy's. He had her arm. She stayed close. He was happy.

The colonel glared at Aunt Fran. "I don't go to New York."

That was like cold water poured on Aunt Fran's head. "That's crazy," she said.

"I'm hardly crazy," said the colonel.

"I think you are." She huffed. "Anyone who misses out on New York is nuts. But I'll forgive you, Colonel. Curmudgeonly behavior aside, you've got your good points."

"Please elucidate," he replied drily.

"I'm not telling. You'll have to charm them out of me. And since that's not going to happen, they stay in the vault." Aunt Fran lifted her chin.

The colonel glared at her.

This was how older people flirted? And fought? Deacon squeezed his fingers gently around Macy's arm. She stifled a giggle. "So," he said briskly, "we're off to the Grand Bohemian."

"One of my favorite places." Macy wanted to sound upbeat too.

"That sounds good," said Aunt Fran coolly. "I'm a bohemian, unlike the colonel here." She strode like a queen toward the exit door.

"Hey!" Colonel Block called after her. "I've been a bohemian plenty of times."

"What would you know about letting loose?" she flung over her shoulder at him.

She was holding her own. Deacon wasn't surprised, but he wondered if the colonel was.

"I suggest we take a brisk winter's walk there," the colonel said outside. "It's only on Wentworth Street. It's good for your soul, to be out in the cold."

"This isn't cold, Colonel," Aunt Fran said. "This is balmy compared to Manhattan at this time of year."

"Which is why you left," he replied smugly.

"Absolutely not. It had nothing to do with snow and everything to do with seeking new adventures."

He harrumphed. "As if we're some sort of exotic creatures below the Mason-Dixon line."

"Well, to me you are," Aunt Fran said, "especially here in Charleston. What's a Huguenot torte? And do I really need to eat grits every day at breakfast?"

"Yes to both," the colonel said. "And MoonPies and Goo Goo Clusters. They weren't invented here in Charleston, but they're true Southern delights."

"As is Cheerwine," Macy chimed in, "which comes from North Carolina. Where Pepsi was created too."

Deacon was glad the cold, fresh air had blown away at least some of the older folks' animosity by the time they'd reached the Grand Bohemian Hotel. They went up the elevator to the rooftop bar, where several fires flickered heartily at chic, Scandinavian-inspired hearths, and took seats at one of the long, rectangular pits.

When the beverages came, including the colonel's rum and Coke, Macy remembered something. "Coca-Cola is from Atlanta."

"Ah, yes." The colonel took a big sip of his drink.

"But you don't have good New York pizza." Aunt Fran had managed to sit almost in the colonel's lap. And interestingly enough, he hadn't scooted over.

"And our bagels," said Deacon, "are the best in the world."

"I've heard they're delicious," Macy agreed.

"But are they as good as a Southern biscuit?" The colonel eyed the flames thoughtfully. "I wouldn't know. I've never had a bagel, much less one from New York."

"We know." Aunt Fran pretended to yawn. "You've never been there."

The colonel's brows lowered again.

"Maybe we should invent a dish that combines the best of New York and Charleston," Macy said quickly.

She was brilliant. And Deacon liked brilliant.

Aunt Fran's mouth fell open. "I love it! We'll make it into a contest."

"A contest it is." The colonel looked a little less unhappy.

"I'm not a real cook." Deacon was a take-out king. "But I'm an excellent taster."

"We'll have teams." The colonel pointed his drink in Deacon's direction. "You're on Macy's. And Fran"—he hesitated—"you're on mine."

"Keeping your enemies close, Colonel?" She patted his knee, and he didn't flinch. "Never mind. This way the best of both worlds will be sure to be represented on each team."

Deacon and Macy shared another amused look. Did the colonel and his aunt like each other? Or hate each other?

"The winner will be announced on New Year's Day, after my annual cannon firing," the colonel declared.

Aunt Fran laughed. "You've got to be kidding me. You're firing a cannon?"

"A small ceremonial one." The colonel drew himself up. "It's the highlight of the year in Charleston."

"It's the colonel's thing," Macy whispered to Deacon. "And he thinks it's everyone else's too. He takes it personally when someone's not in town for it."

But Deacon wasn't thinking about the colonel's cannon ceremony. He wished he could lean over and kiss Macy. Run his hand over her thigh. Hold her fingers and squeeze them, hinting at sexy promises for later that night.

"Who will judge?" Aunt Fran's very good point reluctantly brought him back to the topic at hand. "No contest is worth its salt without fair, impartial judges."

"George," Macy said instantly, "because he's from New York. And how about Mrs. Beauchamp?"

Deacon remembered she was the elderly librarian who'd been to his aunt's boat parade party.

"A fine pair," said the colonel. "But we need a tiebreaker judge."

"Penelope Gordon," Macy suggested.

"Perfect," said Aunt Fran.

"Penelope's a delight," the colonel agreed. "A true gem of a lady. She'd make an excellent wife." He looked pointedly at Deacon.

"Let's not get ahead of ourselves," he said. "I'm only here for a few weeks. Besides, she's Macy's friend too."

Here he was sitting with Macy—whom he'd just slept with—and the old folks were trying to marry him off to one of her good pals.

"Penelope's modest. And quiet," said the colonel.

Aunt Fran lifted a shoulder and let it drop. "That's not always a good thing."

"Oh, yes it is." The colonel's "Ho Ho Ho" wasn't exactly friendly.

Aunt Fran sat up higher. "I suppose you're right, Colonel. Choosing a quiet, modest mate makes a lot of sense, especially if you're scared to have someone stand up to you." She shrugged. "Luckily, Deacon's not intimidated by anyone."

The colonel drew in his chin. "What are you implying, Miss Banks? You think I'm scared of *you*?"

"You wouldn't be that unusual," she said. "Even the commander of our armed forces—the President—confessed he's scared of me. I think he was kidding. Because at the dinner I shared with him and his family at the White House, he and I cracked jokes all night." She turned a gimlet gaze on him, raised her glass, and took a sip.

The colonel drained his rum and Coca-Cola. "Well, then. That's a fine memory you have." He sounded sincere.

"Yes, it is." Aunt Fran was on fire.

"I'm impressed," said the colonel.

"You are?" Aunt Fran squeaked.

He chuckled. "Of course!"

Aunt Fran's mouth dropped open, but she quickly shut it when Deacon winked at her. She chuckled. "You keep me on my toes, Colonel."

"Likewise," he said with a grin.

Aunt Fran had won that round, and she was very happy, which made Deacon happy for her.

"Back to Penelope," Macy said helpfully. "She'll be fair. So she's our final judge."

"I'll have a New Year's Eve luncheon." Aunt Fran's tone brooked no arguments. "They'll taste the dishes there."

"We have a plan," the colonel said.

Maybe, just maybe, he and Aunt Fran could be friends. At least Deacon hoped so. He liked the colonel, despite the dicey last half hour.

Macy's eyes lit up. "Hey, it's Rena!"

Two women about Macy's age both stopped walking toward the exit.

"Hey, yourself," one of them said with a big grin. "We were in the corner. Didn't see y'all."

So this was Rena. She was pretty. Over the next few minutes, Deacon saw she had a bubbly personality.

"Still on for tomorrow?" she asked him.

"Looking forward to it," he said.

"You'll love the RKW. It's my favorite art gallery," Macy said, and grinned at both of them. She was in full-on matchmaker mode, which Deacon must endure, despite everything that had gone on between them. It was his fault too. He was the one who'd said love was for naïve people. Not that he was in love. But he liked Macy. A lot.

A *lot* lot.

"I haven't seen the latest exhibit, so I'm extra excited," said Rena.

After a flurry of farewells, she and her friend took off.

"Such lovely Southern belles you'll be meeting this month, Deacon," said Aunt Fran.

The colonel cleared his throat. "The loveliest Southern belle is right here—Miss Macy Frost."

"Of course." Aunt Fran smiled at her. "But she's not available, sadly for us. She's helping Deacon find dates through Two Love Lane."

"What does a man of Deacon's good looks and status need with a matchmaker?" asked the colonel. "That makes no sense to me."

Deacon felt none too happy. "It's a gift," he said, "to Aunt Fran. From me. She'd like to see me settled down."

The colonel narrowed his eyes at Deacon's aunt. "You're making a big mistake interfering like this. Love can't be forced."

"I know." Aunt Fran shook her glass and looked at the ice as she did so. Maybe she regretted putting her nephew in a corner, asking for a gift like this. "I'm not pressuring Deacon. But I'm hoping Macy can help him see that "commitment" is not a dirty word. That's all."

"Hmmph," said the colonel. "Nothing wrong with being single either."

"Amen to that, Colonel." Deacon winked at him.

"Don't you dare get involved in *my* romantic life, Macy," the colonel warned her.

"I wouldn't dream of it, Colonel." Macy's smile was affectionate. "Not unless you come to see me at Two Love Lane."

A twinkle appeared in the older man's eye. "Don't need to. The odds are in my favor."

The colonel was a player, Deacon saw, and couldn't help tipping up the corner of his mouth in amusement.

"So there are that many older widows and divorcees in

Charleston?" Aunt Fran asked her sofa mate a little acer-
bically.

"Yes," the colonel said, "and you left out the ones
who've never married. I don't like to call 'em old maids
because they're not dowdy in the least. They're usually rich
and have chosen to stay unattached because they're having
too much fun traveling and working and doing their thing.
They're loving life. Like *you*, Macy. But a couple decades
older."

"Well," Aunt Fran said drily. "It's nice to know you
won't contemplate dating someone Macy's age."

"Of course not." The colonel's brows formed a storm
cloud over his nose. "What do you take me for? A silly old
man? I want a woman of experience."

"I like how you think." Aunt Fran sounded outright
saucy.

The colonel's ears turned pink. "I'm speaking of *life* experience, madam."

"There are all kinds of life experience, Colonel."

"As I well know," he replied.

"Do you?" Aunt Fran said silkily and sent the colonel
a frank stare.

Macy suppressed a laugh. Deacon was in awe of his
aunt's ballsy approach to flirting. Or dissing. He couldn't
tell which one it was. Surely that antagonistic chat between
the two older people wasn't good for their blood pressure,
but maybe it was good for their souls.

They had a good walk home. Everyone was mellow.
Deacon was sure the clear night sky bursting with stars
had something to do with it, as well as their conversation
about Yo-Yo Ma and what a talent he was. The colonel was
the first to say good night, and he seemed reluctant. Deacon and Macy dropped Aunt Fran off next. She couldn't
stop talking about the colonel and how difficult he was,
but her color was high and her eyes were blazing. Finally,

Deacon escorted Macy to her own front door, the fake one that led onto her piazza.

She looked up at him. "This was some night."

"That it was."

She wrapped her arms around her feathery coat. The wind off the Battery blew her hair.

"Could you believe my aunt and the colonel?" he asked her.

"No." Macy laughed out loud, her gaze on the harbor, glinting with moonlight and starlight. "They're funny together, aren't they?"

"Yes." He couldn't think of what else to say. She was so damned gorgeous.

Their eyes met.

"Don't even think about it," she said firmly.

"I'm thinking about it." He put his hands deep in his coat pockets. "It would be so easy. And no one would know. I won't be able to sleep. I'll tell you that much."

"One word." She smiled. "*Rena.*"

An instant bad mood descended. Deacon hated not getting his way, not being in charge, and being ensnared by his own plans that were now working against him.

Macy's phone rang and she glanced at it. "It's awfully late for my sister to be calling me. I'd better take this." She opened her massive front door. "I had fun tonight. Really. But we need to move forward." She spoke softly, but the words were damned final.

"Understood."

She looked at him hard for a second. "I'm glad you understand," she said, then gently shut the door. Her heels clicked over the piazza floor. "Anne? Is everything all right?"

There was the rattle of her keys in the actual front door. She laughed. "Oh, good. I just wondered. It's kind of late. Tell me more."

The front door opened, and she went inside, talking all the way, and then shut the door behind her.

Deacon had never had anyone tell him to get lost after he'd just made love to her. He'd always been in charge of his relationships—hell, even of his one-night stands.

It was very clear that Macy was doing just fine without him.

He actually chuckled aloud walking back to his aunt's door, thinking about it. It felt better than he imagined it would be to be taken down a notch.

In fact, the notion that he couldn't control everything was actually pretty invigorating. If he really took it to heart, he could relax. Let life happen more. Stop trying to construct it all around him, like a city—a fortress—to protect himself.

He stopped on the sidewalk, hands in his tuxedo pants pockets, thumbs out, to look out at Fort Sumter, which seemed to float within a silver haze in Charleston Harbor. The battles this town had seen. The pain. The suffering. And not only during wartime. Yet it was stronger and more beautiful than ever. Rebuilt. Renewed. A real community, open and alive.

Not a ghost town.

"Huh," he said aloud. Because something came together for him at that moment. A flash of an idea. Something for himself, to keep him occupied while he was here, since he couldn't have Macy.

But the thing that excited him the most was that it was something for everyone else too.

Everyone else, his steps seemed to say as he walked. *Everyone else*. He felt free, slicing through the cold winter air with a brain, body, and heart designed to strive, to battle uphill, to fight until the end—

Because that was when one's finest hours were to be had, not when you were resting on old laurels, or doing something you were merely good at. You had to *love* what you did.

But it was even simpler than that.

"You have to love," he said, looking up at the stars.

And everything else would fall into place.

CHAPTER NINETEEN

Macy couldn't help wondering: How did you *do* Christmas while you were working hard to be at the top of your profession and while you were fighting intense attraction to the wrong man? Especially after you'd slept with him and he wanted to keep it going?

How could you drink that peppermint cocoa with extra whipped cream with a pure heart when you weren't telling your colleagues and best friends the whole truth? How could you honestly stand with Miss Thing and dance the South's favorite dance—the Shag—to "Jingle Bell Rock," letting her lead, while you wondered if you were possibly sabotaging your own business because you couldn't pull yourself together?

And how did you think about what Christmas really meant—peace and love—when you were making selfish choices?

In the big scheme of things, Macy's problems were tiny, she knew. But they involved other people. She could *hurt* other people.

So those problems did matter.

To be honest, she didn't think she'd really hurt Deacon. The guy propositioning her at her front door wasn't exactly looking for a deep relationship. He had no idea—at least as far as she could tell—that she was his perfect match. His heart was nowhere on the line. So even though rejecting his sexual advances felt like deprivation and hardship, she knew she hadn't scarred him.

She was glad when Anne called her and gave her an excuse to leave him on the sidewalk. Anne only wanted to tell her a funny story about the kids, but it was good to hear from her.

Macy told her what had happened between her and Deacon. Who better to confess your deep secrets—and your misgivings—to than a loving sister?

Bottom line, Anne didn't judge her. She understood. She was even a little jealous and determined that she and Kyle get back to that level of physical passion. But she worried about Macy too. Anne wanted to know if she was emotionally involved, as in falling in love with the guy, which Macy assured her she was not. It wasn't true, but if she said it often enough, she hoped it could be.

The next day was cookie-baking time at Two Love Lane. Macy had been mixing the dough up for three days straight at home after work. So all she and her colleagues had to do was roll the dough out, cut it into Christmas shapes, bake the pieces, cool them, and decorate them.

They would then put them in the freezer and take them out later for the party. They always wanted this part out of the way so during the last few days before the event, they could focus on the rest of the logistics, call people to make sure they were coming, and do a last-minute advertising blitz.

But today, Macy was worried. How would her friends take her news about sleeping with Deacon? She was obligated professionally to tell them she'd compromised the business by doing so. But she also wanted their personal advice.

She had other things to cover first. She stepped into Greer's office.

Greer put down a pair of scissors.

"What are you doing?" Macy was curious.

"Cutting out magazine pictures, is all."

"Of what?"

Greer shrugged. "Random stuff. Sometimes I create collages."

"I had no idea." Macy liked that she still didn't know everything about Greer.

"I do have an artistic side," her friend said, coloring a bit.

"I'm sure you do." Macy smiled. "I'd love to see your work sometime."

"Okay." But Greer still seemed a little defensive. Or worried.

Maybe Macy was worrying her. She wouldn't be surprised. She was about to slink out of her friend and business partner's office feeling horribly guilty when Greer came around her desk and sat on its edge. "Is there anything on your mind?" She looked at Macy thoughtfully.

"There are things I need to address with y'all," Macy said, her stomach in knots. "You, Ella, and Miss Thing."

"Right now?"

"If that's okay."

"Let's do it."

Miss Thing was packaging peanut butter cups and a copy of *Vogue* to send to her clotheshorse friend in England when Macy asked her to go with them to Ella's office.

"Sure." Miss Thing wore a double-breasted light-blue jacket with gold frogs and a matching blue skirt. Macy recognized it as a knock-off of one of the queen's outfits.

Once more, Ella's door was closed, a DO NOT DISTURB sign dangling from the knob.

"It's always closed these days," Miss Thing whispered.

Macy leaned close to the wood panel. "I don't hear it

now, but last time there was a squeaking noise. And some thumps. And a sound like sticks being hit together. Do y'all have any idea what she's up to?"

"No," said Greer. "I asked her outright. And she told me with a straight face that she has no idea what I'm talking about."

"Me too," said Miss Thing. "It's making me a little crazy. She says she has the 'Do Not Disturb' sign up for a little privacy, is all."

"Let me knock and see what happens." So Macy knocked. "Ella? Ella, are you in there?"

"I'm here." Their friend's voice had an edge to it. "What's up? I have my sign on the door. It must be an emergency, right?"

"Well, no." Macy did her best to sound blasé, but Ella was stressing her out. "Can we come in? We're all here."

"Not now." Ella's tone was firm.

"Will you come out then?" Greer sounded more demanding than Macy had. "We're about to work on the Christmas cookies. And we really do need to get those done."

"Right." Ella's voice sounded small. "Sorry, I forgot. Give me five minutes."

"We'll meet you in the kitchen, dear," said Miss Thing.

"Okay." And then there were knockings. And thumps. And that damned squeaking noise, like nails on a chalkboard.

In the kitchen, Macy asked the others, "What the heck is going on in there?" She had no idea.

Miss Thing shook her head. "I can't check when she's not here. She keeps the door locked. And she's meeting all her clients in the Green Room."

The Green Room was their upstairs drawing room.

"It's got to be something for Christmas," Greer suggested.

Miss Thing's brow puckered. "Do you remember last summer when y'all went on that two-week vacation together without her?"

Greer and Macy looked at each other. They would never forget that trip.

"We can't really call it a vacation," Macy said.

"No," Greer echoed weakly.

They'd gone to France to learn exotic flirting and love-making tips from a Parisian expert to share with their shyer clients. And then to Italy for Greer to pick up the latest matchmaking theories of compatibility from a premier Roman agency known for its uncannily high matchmaking rate. They'd had to invest a good bit of money to gain this access, and the only reason they got it was because Ella was second cousins with the CEO.

And, um, things happened. But they got out alive and smarter about matchmaking, so that was all that mattered.

"Whatever you want to call it," Miss Thing said, "the whole time you were gone, Ella did the same thing. Locked herself in her office, and made all those strange noises. In the *summer*. So I don't think this has anything to do with Christmas."

Greer made a face at Macy, and Macy made one back at her. It was their "What's going on with our best friend?" face.

"I hope she tells us soon," Macy said. "I'm going crazy wondering. She said she didn't want to go on that trip last year, even though it was her own cousin we were going to see."

"I know," said Miss Thing. "And while you were gone, she seemed as happy as a clam. So I don't think she resented your trip, but it does make me wonder why this secretive stuff started during that time."

Greer's right eyebrow arched high. "It's like she needed us to be gone."

"I know." Macy almost shuddered.

They exchanged another look: the "Should we be scared of our best friend?" face.

And then they both laughed it off.

"We're being stupid." Greer grabbed four aprons off several hooks on the wall.

Macy pulled out four rolling pins from the kitchen drawer. "Poor Ella. It would hurt her feelings to know we're thinking something odd's happening in there."

"But it *is* odd." Greer opened a cupboard full of cookie sprinkles, sugar, flour, and icing bags. "She won't tell us."

"Let's wait until Christmas," said Macy as she tore a big sheet of wax paper off a roll. Miss Thing took it from her and laid it flat on the table. And then they did it again. "I'm sure it will all be revealed on December twenty-fifth."

Ella seemed perfectly fine when she met them in the kitchen. They rolled out some cookies, at least six pans' worth, and put two at a time in the oven to bake. With their buttery scent wafting from the AGA stove, Macy sat down at the kitchen table.

"Miss Thing, you're hearing this for the first time. I spoke to Ella and Greer last night while I was at the Yo-Yo Ma concert."

"I'm all ears." Miss Thing loved a good gossip.

"I have a huge crush on Deacon Banks."

"And you slept with him," said Miss Thing, "and now you're having second thoughts."

Macy felt the blood drain from her face. "How did you know?"

"Honey, it's written all over you."

Greer and Ella stared slack-jawed first at Miss Thing, then at Macy.

"You two had sex?" Ella asked Macy.

"Were you drinking?" Greer sounded like Macy's mother.

"No." Macy was blushing so hard, she felt almost dizzy. "We left the concert to find Louisa, and at her house—"

"You wild things," Miss Thing said with relish. If she'd had her way, she'd put Barry White on the speaker system.

"But how could you tell?" Macy felt desperately exposed.

Miss Thing giggled. "Don't think I was being psychic or anything."

"Of course, you weren't. What clues did you uncover?" Greer loved Benedict Cumberbatch, who played the logical Sherlock Holmes on the BBC.

"You have a hickey on your neck," Miss Thing said proudly. "It's the size of a golf ball. About three inches beneath your ear, so you must not have seen it in the mirror, sweetie."

"No!" Macy slapped the side of her neck.

"Wrong side, sugar." Miss Thing chuckled as Macy tried to cover the other side. "No one gets a hickey like that during a demure getting-to-know-you make-out session."

"Oh my gosh." Macy was stupefied. "I don't remember getting a hickey at *all* . . . but things were so hot, I couldn't even remember my name."

"Lawsey me." Miss Thing fanned herself.

"Move your hand, Macy." Greer craned her neck to see Macy's neck better. "People really get hickeys? I thought they were a myth. They just seem so useless."

"I agree." Ella stood up and took a gander too. Macy let them. She figured it was her punishment. "Once I had a boyfriend in high school who wanted to give me one, and I said no. I was like, *why*?"

"That's because the art of the hickey is known only by expert lovers." Miss Thing occasionally liked to show off her bedroom know-how. "Most people get 'em wrong, and those sorts of hickeys look tacky. Yours, Macy, looks *good*."

"Give me a break," she protested.

"No." Miss Thing nodded firmly. "It does. I'm envious."

Macy started laughing with Ella and Greer.

Miss Thing joined in. "Oh, sex is funny!"

Which made them laugh even more.

"Wait," Macy said, wiping her eyes, "now that I think about it, I do sort of remember feeling like a vampire was seducing me, and I loved it, in a dark, erotic way, and—"

"That's enough," said Miss Thing. "I'm already a little faint just thinking of Deacon Banks in a suit and being proper in my office, speaking to me about the weather. I can hardly sit up straight thinking about him naked and practicing his lovemaking skills."

Macy felt herself getting redder by the second. "I wonder if anyone else noticed? After the concert? Colonel Block, Celia, Deacon's aunt Fran . . ."

"The colonel can't see well," Ella reminded her. "He once thought the mayor's wife was an old military buddy. He saw her across the library floor and called her Sergeant Wilson. And when she wouldn't come over, he got upset. I had to tell him."

Everyone laughed again.

Greer shook some cookie sprinkles in her palm and licked them up. "Who knows about Fran Banks?"

"She would have said something to me," Macy said. "She's not the type to shy away. I think she had eyes only for the colonel last night."

Ella checked the cookies in the oven. "That leaves Celia."

Macy put her face in her hands. "She didn't see much of me after the lights went up at the auditorium. She went home. And I barely saw Rena and her friend at the Grand Bohemian." She sat up extra straight. "Wouldn't Deacon have noticed too? And asked me to hide it somehow?"

"He was probably noticing your boobs." Ella was such a tease. "They looked extra fantastic in that dress."

"True," said Greer. "And if he noticed your hickey, he was probably super proud of it and didn't want you to cover it up."

"Even in front of his aunt?" Macy couldn't help her voice getting shrill.

"Men," said Miss Thing, and looked at each one of them as if she'd just revealed the answer to all the world's mysteries.

Yes, *men*.

"So let's get back to the serious question," said Greer. "Has sleeping together changed things between you two?"

"All I know is he walked me home last night and tried to come in," Macy said. "He said he hoped we'd continue our sexual connection until he went back to New York. *Twice a day*."

"Geez, Macy!" Ella stood back up and peeked at the cookies in the oven. "Do you have to torture us like this?"

They were all single.

Greer's gaze was serious. "Does anyone else know you had this little tryst, apart from your sister?"

"No." Macy was nervous. "I hope you don't think I've compromised Two Love Lane's mission. I mean, I did—"

Greer patted her hand. "You're too hard on yourself is what you are, Macy Jane Frost."

"I agree," said Miss Thing. "You should rule your work and not the other way around."

"That's right." Ella wore a little crown of flour because she'd tried to get the bag out of the cupboard and it had fallen out, right on top of her, and a poof of the white stuff had settled in her hair. "We created Two Love Lane together. We can never let ourselves forget that this company's foundation is made of real people—the four of us and our clients. And we all have our own hopes and dreams. We're not perfect, not any of us."

"Two Love Lane is *not* composed of contracts and

money," Greer declared in that authoritative way she had that always reassured Macy when she needed a boost of confidence. "Those are strictly by-products."

"Okay." Macy felt a little hitch in her throat. "Thanks, guys."

They worked and worked making cookies for three more hours, stopping only long enough to take a break to pet Oscar, who wouldn't leave them alone, and to eat a quick lunch of Miss Thing's homemade chicken salad wraps and strawberries.

By the time they finished for the day, they had two hundred beautifully decorated cookies.

"We rock, if I do say so myself." Miss Thing's lips were dyed green from eating too much icing.

"At this rate, we'll be done by noon tomorrow." Ella beamed. "That leaves a whole half day to Christmas shop."

"You mean, you haven't shopped yet?" Macy exchanged a lightning fast look with Miss Thing and Greer.

"No." Ella laughed. "You know I don't shop until fairly late."

So she definitely wasn't wrapping Christmas gifts in her office.

"Later today," Macy said, "I'm hoping to get a report on Deacon's museum date with Rena. They're at a special exhibit at the RKW."

"Which is so gorgeous since that remodel." Miss Thing was a volunteer there.

Greer cocked her head. "You can handle getting the low-down on that date?"

"Of course," said Macy. "Especially since we haven't gotten past the hot sex phase of this relationship and probably never will. He's said outright he's not ready for love. And I'm not either."

"Give him a break if he doesn't fall for Rena," Ella said. "I think he's stuck on you."

Macy nibbled on the edge of a cookie she'd messed up. "He won't be the first client I've failed at connecting with someone. Although I have to admit, it's frustrating."

Her life would be so much easier if Deacon Banks fell in love!

CHAPTER TWENTY

Not a minute later in the cookie-covered kitchen at Two Love Lane, Macy got a text. "Oh, no," she said. "Rena's ears must be burning."

"Don't let it be more trouble," said Miss Thing. "Aren't they at the RKW as we speak?"

"They're supposed to meet right about now." Macy squinted at the text.

"Have any of his dates worked out yet?" Ella asked.

"No, we've had very bad luck so far," said Macy, and drew in her chin. "I don't understand this. I think she meant to send it to someone else."

Greer peered over her shoulder. " 'Good luck!' " she read out loud. " 'I hope it works out.' "

Macy shook her head. "I guess she means she hopes her date with Deacon works out. I should write her back."

"Wait." Ella's eyebrows shot up. "Let's see if she texts anything else to you first."

Macy didn't even get a chance to reply to Ella before another text came through from Rena. " 'Peter said he doesn't mind at all,' " Macy read out loud, " 'especially since you're making such a big donation.' "

"That's weird," said Greer. "I wonder if she means Peter

Donovan, who runs the museum's foundation. And who did Rena really mean to send this text to?"

"I have no idea," said Macy. "I'm really confused now." She texted: *I'm not sure what you mean, Rena.*

Rena wrote back: *Peter's calling Macy in about fifteen minutes. He'll coax her to come down and accept the free membership. Meanwhile, I'll twist my ankle and scoot.*

Twist her ankle?

Scoot?

Macy's heart beat so hard, she could hardly speak. "Something really fishy is going on. I think Rena meant to send this text to Deacon. Could you read this to everyone?" She handed the phone to Greer with a trembling hand and sat down.

"Sure." Greer read the message out loud.

There was silence.

"Wow," said Ella. "Sounds like Rena's planning on pretending to twist her ankle so she can leave the RKW."

"I think Deacon is bribing people again to get his way," said Macy. "I should have known. My gut told me at the very beginning he was trouble when he bribed y'all to leave the office."

"What's going on, exactly?" asked Miss Thing. "Is he trying to make it so you show up on this date instead of Rena?"

"It appears that way." Macy's cell phone rang. "It's the RKW."

"Take it," said Greer.

It was Peter Donovan. He told her that her name had been submitted in a lottery at their last fundraising dinner, and they'd picked the winner that morning. She'd won a free lifetime membership to the RKW. "But I need you to come right now to pick it up," Peter said. "Your friends Deacon and Rena are here. They watched our director pick a name out of a hat and volunteered to pick up the prize for you, but we can't do that. Sorry."

"Peter," Macy said, "I'm sorry. But I have to decline the prize."

"Really?" He sounded like his collar was too tight.

"Yes," said Macy, "because I know full well Deacon Banks arranged this, and I'm not playing his game. Please tell him so. And tell Rena I'm so sorry she twisted her ankle."

"She did?" Peter sounded concerned. "She looked just fine a minute ago."

"You might want to ask her about that ankle," Macy said. "Good-bye, Peter." And she hung up.

"Oh my," said Miss Thing.

Macy looked around at her friends' concerned faces. "Deacon was obviously working not only with Rena but with Barney, Tiffany, and Louisa. Somehow he managed to get me instead of them on each of those dates."

"Because he's crazy about you," Miss Thing said.

"Obviously," added Ella.

"And your friends love you so much, they cooperated," said Greer. "I know it looks really bad, but don't be too mad, Macy."

"Of course, I'm angry," Macy said quietly. "I feel manipulated." She took a deep breath. "The worst of it is, he's paying me a hefty sum to set him up with these women."

"And then intentionally sabotaging the dates." Miss Thing shook her head. "I can see why you're upset. But it's flattering too, sweetie."

Macy shook her head. "I don't feel flattered. I feel duped."

"He's sure to come by and try to explain," said Greer.

"With a huge bouquet of flowers, I'll bet," said Ella.

"His intentions were good," said Miss Thing. "Are you

going to forgive him, Macy? I hope you do. No one is perfect all the time."

Macy couldn't speak for a moment. There was a big lump in her throat. "How can I forgive him?" she finally said. "He's broken my trust."

"But he did it because he likes you," said Ella. "I'm not saying that's right, but it's understandable."

"He was desperate," Greer added. "You're not easy, Macy. You do realize that, don't you? You're intimidating. And you're stubborn. You were holding him at arm's length. He was being creative. I actually admire that in him."

"I get it," said Macy. "But none of that excuses him going behind my back." Her eyes filled with tears. "Excuse me, ladies. I want to go home."

They all hugged her tight and begged to go with her.

"No. I just want to be alone. But thanks." She felt empty, as if all the time she'd spent with Deacon was a joke. The whole time, he'd been pulling strings behind the scenes—so what was actually real between them? What *could* be real?

Nothing.

Deacon did come by to find Macy. He left Rena and Peter at the museum and went straight to Two Love Lane. The women said she'd gone home and wasn't in a good state. He figured as much, and inside he felt helpless and angry—at himself. He stopped by Harris Teeter, picked up a huge bouquet of pastel roses in varying degrees of pink, yellow, and cream, and rang and rang the doorbell at Macy's fake door. He texted too.

But she wouldn't answer.

He was screwed. He knew it. Inside, he felt hollow, as if a big piece of his heart was missing. But he wouldn't give up. He couldn't.

"I have to explain why I did it," he told George in private back at Aunt Fran's house. "It's because I really care about her. I like her more than any woman I've ever met. She's special. And I wanted to spend time with her."

"I get it," George said, "and I egged you on, didn't I? I was so damned glad to see you interested in someone! But obviously Macy feels you forced the situation. She probably thinks you've been bossy and manipulative. Hindsight's twenty-twenty."

"Hell, I don't know what to say to make it right," Deacon said. "Maybe I've messed things up so badly she'll never talk to me again."

The awfulness of that possibility kept him up all night. The next morning, he waited by her front doorstep and caught her going to work, Oscar in the tote bag on her arm.

"I don't want to speak to you," she said, and looked straight ahead.

He put his hands in his coat pockets and kept pace with her. "I'm sorry, Macy. I didn't mean to hurt you. Everyone just wanted it to work out between us, is all."

"Everyone?" She still wouldn't look at him.

"Yes. The ladies and I. My dates."

"They were all in on it," she said without emotion, which was scarier than her acting angry.

"Yes," he replied. "Penelope too. She's the one who gave me the idea."

For the first time, she hesitated. "Penelope?"

"The night of the boat parade. I confided in her that I didn't want to go out with anyone in Charleston but you. And she came up with the idea, which I gladly latched onto. So please don't blame her. It's my fault."

Macy sighed. "I can't believe this."

"It was meant to be innocent," he said.

"Lying to me is not innocent."

"I'm really sorry. It made sense to me at the time. I knew it was a gamble. But I can see now I shouldn't have taken it."

They crossed Broad Street together. How different it was this time from the last time, when he'd held her hand! They might as well have been a million miles apart.

"So that night at Louisa's," she said quietly, "you knew before we got there that Louisa was fine. And yet we still went."

"I didn't know what else to do. You were on a mission."

She winced. "And then we made love." She gave a short laugh. "I guess you felt your plan was working pretty well."

He ran a hand through his hair. "You make it sound so tawdry. It wasn't like that. I liked you! I wanted to be with you. We never planned that part out. Ever."

"You wanted to be with me at any cost?" she asked him. "Even if it meant losing my trust?"

"I see now that I was arrogant," he said. "But I want to remind you of one thing. It doesn't excuse my behavior, but I think it matters in the big scheme of things."

"What?"

"I told you several times in no uncertain terms I wanted to back out of our arrangement. But you would have none of it. You kept insisting you wanted to find me a soulmate. You also tried to lay a guilt trip on me about my aunt and her expectations. You wanted to be my matchmaker—at all costs! Why? What motivated you? The money? Your pride? And how do you think I felt about that after I'd been so honest with you about my feelings for you?"

She hesitated. "I-I'm sorry."

"I felt I had no choice but to try anything I could to get your attention," he said. "I'm not saying what I did behind your back was right. But my heart was in the right place. Was yours, Macy, when you kept advising me to go out with those women? I wonder if you were more worried about checking another client off your list than actually seeing me for who I am—a guy who really likes you. A guy who made it very clear he didn't want to be your client, almost from the get-go."

"My heart"—her voice rose, and Oscar retreated into his nylon cave—"was always in the right place. I cared about you. I did. I didn't want to be selfish—"

"How is it selfish to allow yourself to like me back? To let me come to your house after what we did at Louisa's and make love to you again? How is it selfish to let yourself be happy?"

"I allow myself to be happy," she insisted, but her voice cracked.

"You do? You could have fooled me. You're always doing everyone else's bidding."

Her jaw looked square and hard. "You should really go now. I'm returning your check."

"I don't want it. You earned that money. You put your professional life above your personal one. I can appreciate the sacrifice that took. I do it myself all the time, but I'm not going to anymore."

"I don't want your money," she said. "Our contract is invalid."

"Fine," he said. "Donate it to Toys for Tots."

They came up to Roastbusters.

"I can't simply get over this, Deacon," she said quietly. "You knocked me off my game not only personally but professionally."

"I'm really sorry. I never wanted that to happen."

She blinked back tears. "You were my client. I should have listened to your wishes instead of plowing ahead. I'm sorry too."

The stared at each other.

"You should go," she whispered.

"All right." He turned on his heel and left her.

Oscar meowed, long and loud. Hearing that broke Deacon's heart somehow. But he wouldn't turn around. Macy had made it clear where she stood.

"Deacon!" she called after him.

For a split-second hope flamed in his heart. He stopped and turned around.

"Feel free to come to the Toys for Tots party," she said, blinking fast. "I really appreciate your buying all those bikes."

"Aunt Fran can handle it," he said.

"And"—she swallowed hard—"we never made a final decision on the food samples for the colonel's contest. Which of the three did you like the best?"

Deacon had done the shopping, and Macy had assembled ingredients. He told her his own preference in as few words as possible. "But choose your favorite."

"That was my favorite too." Her face was somber. "So I guess we're set."

"I won't be around for it."

"You won't?"

"No. If we win or lose, it's all on you." He shrugged and crossed the street.

He might as well have crossed the Rubicon. There was no turning back.

CHAPTER TWENTY-ONE

Macy got a call the very next day from Penelope.

"It's my fault," Penelope said. "Please forgive Deacon."

Macy gripped the phone. "I don't want to talk about it, Penelope. Thank you for caring about me. I know you meant well."

"So did he," Penelope said.

"He misled me," Macy explained patiently. "Did he ask you to call me?"

"Absolutely not. He can fight his own battles. I just happened to see him at Harris Teeter and asked him how things were going, and he told me."

"He'd better not get the other girls to call me."

"He's not like that," said Penelope. "He's a stand-up guy, Macy. I'm sorry how things worked out between you two."

"Thank you for thinking of me," Macy said.

"Or course." Penelope hesitated. "I feel terrible about this."

"Please don't." Macy suppressed a sigh.

"He's the real deal, Macy. Don't give up on him, okay?"

"There's nothing to give up on," she said quietly. "There's nothing between us at all." It had all been fake, a game Deacon had set up. "So feel free to continue hanging out with him, Penelope. You two have become friends, and I don't want to stand in the way of that."

After five more minutes of attempting to sway Macy to call Deacon or go see him, Penelope quit trying.

But a few days later, Macy saw Deacon and Penelope together on King Street. She was carrying a bunch of shopping bags. Deacon had some too. They were talking. Penelope was smiling. At least they weren't holding hands.

Even so, it felt like someone had stabbed Macy through the heart.

Fran and George knocked on her door one night, asking her to come over. They both admitted that Deacon had told them the situation.

"He's not perfect," said Fran. "And he's leaving so soon. Please don't let this stand between you."

"He's crazy about you," said George. "And I encouraged him in his shenanigans. I told him all is fair in love and war."

"You shouldn't have," Macy chided George.

"I know that now. Come over and have a drink. Let's all make up."

"It's more complicated than that," Macy said. After hugging them both, she begged off. "You can come over here, though. Any time."

But when they left, she knew she wouldn't be calling them to do that. It hurt too much to see them without Deacon. And she didn't like to think of him leaving. Despite everything, she'd miss him. Every adventure she'd ever had had always been an event, or a place.

Not a person.

But Deacon himself felt like the adventure, all on his own.

That was why she'd miss him.

Charleston's charms would dim—just a fraction, she assured herself—when he went back to New York.

CHAPTER TWENTY-TWO

A few days after Macy said she was done with him, Deacon saw Penelope again at Harris Teeter. She shyly asked him if it would be okay to go a Christmas party together—as friends, she assured him—and he said, of course it was. At the very least, he owed it to her for being so supportive. Plus, she was still doing research for him into his family tree.

After the party, which was tame verging on dull, he walked Penelope home, kissed her on the cheek, and didn't make any definite plans. When he headed back to the Battery, he was caught by the light at the corner of East Bay and Broad and had to wait. To distract himself from the fact that he'd lingered on that corner with Macy a few times, he pulled out his cell phone and checked his messages. He'd received nothing from New York, for the first time since he'd arrived in Charleston. His colleagues were finally getting the message: Leave him alone.

He called George.

"You're already done with your date?" George asked.

Deacon could hear barking in the background. "Yes. And it was fine. So don't get on my case. I'll be home in a minute. Wanna go out and play some pool?"

"No. I need to work on the Colonel Block problem and babysit the Corgis. Bubbles has a stomachache. She ate too many cream puffs. I put them out on the piazza to stay cool because the fridge is too full, and she got out there and gobbled them up."

"Oh God no. Where's Fran?"

"Playing bridge at Mrs. Beauchamp's. Although I think it's strip poker. Mrs. Beauchamp may be ninety, but you ought to hear her talk about living in Paris when she was an exotic dancer back in her twenties."

"Wait—she's a librarian."

"And your point is? Are you making assumptions about librarians that are totally unfair and wrong?"

"No—"

"She became a librarian later. And she's the best damned one in Charleston."

"Have you been drinking?"

"You would too, if you'd been here for dinner. Colonel Block still hasn't figured out Fran has a crush on him. I don't think she has either. She thinks she hates him, and vice versa. He waxed poetic about my pork roast, but he didn't say a word about Fran's new hairdo or false eyelashes."

"He's old, George. Give him a break."

"Those lashes were a bitch to put on. Fran's used to her makeup man at the studio in New York. She said I had fat fingers. That woman knows how to hurt a guy's feelings. She hurt the colonel's too. She told him he needed his bushy eyebrows worked on. She's right, of course, but that was low."

"I'm about a block away. Maybe I'll keep walking."

"No, come home."

Home. Deacon found that the grand living quarters his aunt had purchased had become a home of sorts. "Maybe this is the way old people do relationships."

"Not on your life," said George. "My grandparents were lovey-dovey until the end. Are you almost here? Whitney, Francine, and Gareth need you. They're feeling neglected. Bubbles is getting all the attention. And that's because she smells really bad."

Oh God.

"What should I do about the colonel?" George couldn't stop talking. "Pull him aside and tell him outright that a diminutive Yankee television personality has the hots for him?"

"Aunt Fran would hate our interfering. And so would he. No, we have to make it so he's intrigued somehow."

"Tonight she told him everything she knew about nineteenth-century artillery."

"What does she know about that?"

"Next to nothing. She thought she was trying to upstage him, but you and I both know she actually wanted to impress him. Listening to her recite from *The Encyclopedia of Cannons* was as boring as watching Kardashian women discuss shopping. Or salads. They're always eating salads."

"George, get back on track. Did the colonel like what Aunt Fran had to say?"

"He couldn't hear a damned word. He left his hearing aid at home."

Deacon couldn't help laughing. He was walking past a garden that even at night in the winter was stunning. Maybe it was the statues illuminated from below, or the perfectly manicured topiaries, or the shadowed brick wall. It exuded mystery and elegance, and he had a sudden yearning for Macy, the most elegant woman of his acquaintance—when she wanted to be. She was a mystery all the time, he decided, feeling slightly bitter about it.

But who was he kidding? Deep inside, he loved that about her. Life was never dull around Macy. He missed her terribly.

"Old people are adorable, aren't they?" George chuckled. "The worst part is we can't strategize with your aunt about this crush as long as she won't admit she has one."

"Maybe she'll talk to Celia."

"No. Fran is persona non grata with Celia at the moment."

"Why?"

"Today they were at some Christmas luncheon on the Isle of Palms held by an elite book club, members only, but the president made an exception for Fran since Celia begged. So they were discussing the latest thriller by some well-known guy, and Fran said over her shrimp salad that she thought this author was a jackass. She'd had him on her TV show once, and he was rude to her crew, and she couldn't wait to get him off the set."

"Okay, so?"

"So his wife is a member of the book club. She was sitting right across from Fran."

"No way. He lives in Charleston?"

"Yes. A lot of writers do, actually. And CEOs of big corporations in New York. They fly down on the weekends."

"Poor Aunt Fran. Such bad luck."

"Deacon, she *knew* he lives in Charleston!"

He groaned. "Are you sure?"

"Yes."

"She couldn't have known his wife was there, though. Let's give her that."

"Sure," George said. "But you don't diss locals when you're a guest or a newcomer—or both, as she was."

"Okay, but we both know what she was thinking. She was trying to find a way to connect. That story was her 'in.' "

"I get it. But they saw it as her showing off. And being rude. And she'd have gotten the same reaction in New

York. It's not just a Southern thing. People object to loud-mouths. And harsh as that term is, that's what Fran is."

"She's made millions off that mouth." Deacon wished he knew what to do. "But she's not perfect. And if she says the guy was an asshole, I believe her. She's reliable that way."

She'd called Deacon one the other night, as a matter of fact, for messing things up with Macy.

"Well, the wife was none too happy," George said, "and Celia was caught in the middle. She told Fran she was taking a few days off from socializing with her and that Fran had better think long and hard about how many party invitations she wants to receive here."

"Great."

George sighed. "Don't worry too much. She'll rally."

"She always does." Deacon turned the corner and saw George standing on the condo balcony, lit up with soft white Christmas lights. A dog snout poked through the railing. That was no doubt stinky Bubbles, and she'd better stay there for a while.

George waved. "I guess we can get off the phone now. I'll have a bourbon waiting. Cigars too."

"Maybe skip the cigars."

"You're going to invite Macy over, right?"

"No. Get over it."

"She can sit downwind."

"She hates me." And Deacon clicked off before George could agree.

CHAPTER TWENTY-THREE

Can you come over? It's a love emergency. And not about Deacon.

The text from George showed up exactly when Macy was about to step out of her clothes into her pajamas. It got her in the deeply personal, naked soul space where she admitted to herself—and no one else—that she was so crazy about Deacon, the rest of her life was going to suck without him in it. She needed to make her bedroom a no-cell-phone zone, she decided, a place of total peace where she could go and not think about her dark, miserable future.

"Oh, who am I kidding?" she told Oscar. "I'll be thinking about him anyway."

Oscar turned around and showed her his bottom, his tail high in the air.

I'm pretty tired, she texted George. *Sorry.*

I know you think D's into Penelope. But he's not. He's only seeing her to please you, George texted.

Oscar was sitting at her window, looking out at the moon and harbor.

But Penelope is awesome, she texted back to George. *Maybe it's meant to be.*

Oscar's tail whipped slowly back and forth, but he wouldn't look at her. He could tell she was a liar. *She* wanted Deacon—

For herself!

But only when she was a silly fool, half-dressed and standing in a moonbeam. At all other times, she was logical. And professional.

That's bullshit talk, George texted back.

It was. She had to stop lying to herself.

We need your help with Fran and Colonel Block, George added in a new text. *Especially now that Fran offended a bunch of Celia's friends. Everyone loves the colonel. Go figure. The man is impossible!*

Macy couldn't help laughing. *Is this really a love emergency?*

YES!!!! George wrote back.

Hmmm, all caps. Lots of exclamation points.

Ok, I'll help, she texted him.

Just put up with Deacon, ok? He insists on being involved, George texted.

Ok, she wrote. Oscar leapt down from his porch and left the room, disgusted by her wishy-washiness, she was sure.

We're on the piazza now, George texted. *Open your window.*

Wow, she could hear them laughing. They must have just come out. She wished she felt like laughing. Deacon had a lot of nerve to be so carefree.

She raised her window. A cloud of steam formed in front of her mouth. "Hello," she said in a serious tone.

The guys' laughter stopped.

"Hi." Deacon was bundled up in his Patagonia jacket.

"Lean out a little further." George beckoned her with his cigar-holding hand, an arc of red flashing through the night. He wore a Burberry scarf over a cape. All he needed was a Sherlock Holmes hat. He got close to the rail himself and told her the situation between Fran and Colonel Block in detail.

She was acutely aware that Deacon stood there saying nothing, but she pretended not to notice him.

"So what should we do?" George asked her.

"Boot camp for lovers," she said. "But you have to go for it one hundred percent. You can't be soft on either one of them."

"What the hell?" George put out his cigar on a plate.

Deacon dug his hands deeper into his jacket pockets.

"We employ it only on rare occasions at Two Love Lane," Macy said, "but I'm thinking the colonel and Fran are the perfect candidates for it. It's an uncomfortable way to wake two people up who might be made for each other but don't want to acknowledge their feelings or aren't sure how to make a move."

Deacon and George looked at each other.

"I'm in." Deacon was being just as somber and boring as she was. Both of them were probably annoying George no end.

"I am *so* in," said George, chuckling.

Twenty minutes later, they were at the colonel's around the corner. Somehow on the way over, Macy and Deacon had declared a truce. They weren't exactly talking to each other, but since she was giving directions to both him and George, there was a semblance of normalcy between them.

"We need to leave it on his piazza," Macy whispered to her crew of two. "But someone will have to get inside the grounds." The spiked wrought iron fence was ten feet tall and flanked by two brick pillars.

Deacon peeked into the bag she'd brought. "This is terrible. If someone ever gave it to me, I'd seriously run in the opposite direction."

"Which is precisely the point." She couldn't help a devious chuckle.

"He'll never forget who sent it to him." George chortled like a naughty schoolboy.

"Bingo," she said. "But on the off chance that he likes it—because a rare few people do—we still have step two." She handed George the thing that would set the whole boot camp experience in motion.

"Wish me luck." George lifted the bag up and down. "It weighs a ton. If I drop it on my toe, it'll break my whole foot."

"Seriously," she said happily, "it would. Deacon, please give him a lift."

"You're both crazy." Deacon paused. "And I like it."

She refused to say thank you. "You'll do great," she assured George instead, and kissed his cheek. "Is the note still attached?"

"Yep." George put his foot in Deacon's hand and was boosted to the top of the brick pillar with his booty slung over his shoulder in a bag. He slid down on the other side until his feet made contact with the porch railing.

"Careful," Deacon warned him from the gate, then sidled closer to Macy and said, "Why didn't we wait until morning and just knock on his door?"

She ignored the thrill that went through her at his proximity. "Because I like George. I wanted him to have some adventure in Charleston so he could go back home to Manhattan and tell the story."

Deacon shook his head. "You're a strangely thoughtful person. What about a story for me?"

She shot him a droll look.

"Right. I've had my story. And I probably shouldn't talk about it."

That story was much too hot—and painful—to handle. She conveniently moved on. "We do have another reason we're dropping this off tonight. The note I left attached to it tells the colonel to go to your house for breakfast."

"It could have said lunch."

"No, it has to be breakfast," she said. "An *early* breakfast. And I know the colonel gets up early. I've run by his house at five and seen his lights on. He gets the paper, so he must come outside to pick it up. So he should get the note in time."

"Why breakfast, though?"

"In boot camp, you get up early. You're *raw* at that time of day. No time to put on your usual layers of identity. You're just you."

"I'd like to see you at that time of day. How about I pop over and wake you up one morning?"

"Have you been drinking?"

"A little."

"We're not on joking terms anymore, remember? But let me just say, in your dreams you'll pop over."

"My Christmas dreams." He was wicked.

"You're going out with Penelope."

"We're friends," he said.

"That's good. She's very nice."

"Yes, she is."

Macy felt a pang of anxiety at that.

"But back to Operation Boot Camp," he said. "Tell me more. Because I'm assuming I'm going to have to get up early too, to make sure it happens."

"You will," Macy said. "And you'll see first-hand how much Fran likes the colonel, based on how much she's willing to throw off the covers and get out of bed when she hears that doorbell and finds out he's downstairs."

"She can always take a nap later."

But Macy wasn't fooled. If she wasn't done with him, she would think it cute how worried Deacon was about his perfectly independent and resourceful relative. "She'll be fine," she assured him.

"She'll hate not having a chance to put on makeup." He wouldn't give up.

That was sweet. But she wouldn't get sucked in by his apparently soft heart. "Do recruits put on mascara and blush at boot camp before they work out at sunrise?"

He lofted a brow and looked vaguely like Chris Pine playing Captain Kirk. She nearly swooned but managed to hold it together. "I always appreciate a good rhetorical question," he said. "But new military recruits also aren't in their late fifties and former TV personalities."

"Not having time to fuss will work to Fran's advantage," Macy assured him. "She'll look more approachable when she's not all dolled up."

"If the colonel sees her in her bathrobe, she'll have a fit."

"Make sure he does."

"You're tough."

She laughed softly. "Not tough. Just goal-oriented. We want these two to snap out of their stubborn fog, right?"

He gripped the wrought iron fence with his left hand and peered through at George. "I bought her that bathrobe fifteen years ago, and she refuses to let me get her a new one."

They watched George tiptoe back toward them as if he were trying to complete a spy mission without being shot. He navigated the porch rail, pulled himself up on the pillar, like a giant brown moth in that cape of his, and slid back down on their side of the fence.

"Mission accomplished," he told them triumphantly, his cheeks bright red from the cold, and maybe the exertion too.

"Great job!" Macy fist-bumped him because a high-five might have been too loud.

"I have to say you're evil." George wore a Cheshire cat

grin. "You even got a label on that thing that says 'Fruit-cakes by Fran.'"

Macy lifted and dropped her shoulder like a boss. "She'll get over it. Eventually."

"Who ever knew fruitcake could become a weapon of sorts?" Deacon took her elbow and they crossed a street. Every time he touched her, a *zing!* went through her body, charging her sexual batteries to the max.

If she were a true professional, she'd locate the off switch. But she had no idea where it was. Every fiber of her being responded to his touch.

"That letter was pretty outrageous." George couldn't keep the delight out of his voice.

She pounced on the chance to stop thinking about Deacon. "Dear Colonel," she quoted from the note, which was still in her head, "I have something on my mind I'd like to discuss with you. Nothing worrisome. But it would mean the world to me to see you at breakfast tomorrow at oh-six-thirty sharp. Meanwhile, I hope you enjoy the fruitcake I made especially for you. Warm regards, Fran Banks."

"What *does* Fran want to tell him?" George asked her.

Macy had to be honest. "I don't know, but the colonel will be very flattered. I can just see him racing over there to find out. She'll come up with something on her mind. Hopefully, something good."

Deacon shot her a skeptical look. "She's more likely to say, 'What the hell is going on?' Aunt Fran doesn't beat around the bush. If she's thrown off-kilter, she corrects things fast."

"She'll be mad as a hornet and call foul *if*"—Macy raised an index finger—"if she doesn't have that crush on him. She won't give two hoots about how awkward the situation would make the colonel feel. Because she got used, pranked, or whatever you want to call it."

"But if she's crazy about him," George said excitedly, "once she realizes she's been set up somehow, she'll play along. She won't want to hurt his feelings. Or embarrass herself."

"Or lose her chance to win points with him," Macy clarified. "We'll see how motivated she is to turn the fruitcake and early breakfast situation to her advantage."

"But if it goes poorly," Deacon said, "be prepared. The proverbial you-know-what will hit the fan."

"But if it goes well," Macy reminded him, "she'll be so fluttery and happy, it won't even occur to her to call you two out."

"You mean call out the three of us," Deacon said. "All for one, and one for all, right?"

She wanted to, but she wouldn't smile at him. "Okay, so I'm the so-called mastermind. Later on, I'll take credit for that, if they start dating. Meanwhile, we're taking a little risk."

"I like how you say 'little,'" George said. "This is Fran Banks, who makes celebrities and world leaders cry and never takes the blame."

"Thank you." Deacon reached out and squeezed the fingers of her right hand—only for a second—and she reveled in the sensation, in the hot-pink, flowers-and-balloons, impulsive part of her brain, where her logical self didn't come out and play.

And then she quietly put a few inches between them.

"So when do I have breakfast on the table?" George was practically skipping with glee.

"Six thirty sharp," Macy told him, "and please make sure the table looks amazing."

"No problem. I'll put out the best silver and china. I've got gorgeous hothouse yellow roses ready to be put in a vase tomorrow morning."

"Serve something plain and tasteless, preferably," she advised Fran's right-hand man.

George laughed. "You're killing me."

"This is boot camp." Macy put on her best stern military persona. "Shock and awe is involved. I suspect the curmudgeonly colonel will rise to the occasion. For him, adversity builds character. Let's see how Fran does."

"Yes, Sergeant." George saluted her. "I'll make watery cream of wheat. With lumps in it."

"Excellent." She tried hard not to notice how perfect Deacon's profile was. "And the coffee should be ghastly. Cold, or too strong, or something to make them wince."

"You've got to make a secret pot for the kitchen staff," Deacon warned George.

"You're in charge of cold toast," Macy told Deacon. It was fun to order him around. "In case the colonel asks for some. You can make it beforehand and stick it in the fridge."

"I'm on it." Deacon stuck up a thumb.

It occurred to Macy that she'd love to lean over and put that thumb in her mouth. But he was wrong for her, and that would be trashy. She was horrified, in a thrilled-horrified way, at the wayward turn her thoughts were taking. "We'll learn so much about how they *feel* about each other by the way they act tomorrow morning," she said. "And the best part is, they will too."

"So you're saying all this silly unpleasantness, experienced together, will bond them." Deacon's thumb was now back to its rightful place, sadly—alongside his fingers and hanging harmlessly at his side.

"Yes." Macy felt a little wistful at the lost fantasy.

"It'll be like a smack upside the head," added George.

"Exactly." Her mind was spinning with too many sexy thoughts to really know what George had said, so she added, "They're in a rut, all right," because it was true.

They were back home, thank God. She needed to get back to her room and calm down.

"Why don't you just come over for breakfast too?" Deacon was nonchalant. "You got us into this, after all."

"Thank you. I'd love to. Although the truth is, I'd already planned to crash the party."

George stuck up his hand, and the three of them high-fived.

"Envision success, gentlemen," Macy said, wishing she'd only high-fived George.

George kissed her on the cheek. "See you tomorrow."

"Bright and early." She grinned as he bounded up the stairs of their house, his cape reminding her now of a superhero's.

"I'll walk you to your house." Deacon's expression was kind. Calm. Maybe a bit reflective.

She felt the opposite: flustered, bold, and sort of bouncy.

"No, thank you," she said firmly. "My doorstep is only a hundred feet from yours."

"I just want to make sure. I'll be good. Honestly."

She sighed. "All right."

They walked those hundred feet so slowly, it was ridiculous. She had no idea what their dragging feet meant.

"Okay then," she said as they walked. "See you in the morning."

"That's right." He was so hot, it killed her.

"Let me know if you need me to do anything else to help."

"I can't think what," he said.

Macy thought of her bed upstairs. Imagined him in it. For the millionth time.

"So." He put his hand on the side of her fake front door.

And he came closer.

No.

No, no, no.

Her mouth was only a few inches from his. "Don't do it," she whispered although everything in her wanted him to kiss her so badly. "Because if you do, we won't stop. And both of us deserve better than a cheap one-night stand."

He froze. Made a sudden motion with his free hand. Caught something in the air and closed his fist. Then he backed down the steps, stood on the sidewalk, opened his fist, and blew on his empty palm.

She refused to blink. "What was that?"

He smiled a wicked, devastating smile. "A little Christmas spirit, is all. I hear there's plenty more where that came from."

"For goodness' sake."

"What?"

"You know what," she said.

"I do?"

"Yes, you do. I'm not stupid. You were about to kiss me. And you need to know you're playing with fire."

"I like fire," he said.

"Not my kind. It'll burn you."

He laughed. "I like when you get sexually frustrated, Frost. Your dime-store villain act is cute."

"I hate cute. And people who think I'm cute can go jump in a lake. I'm so much better than that."

"I know you are. You're amazing."

She wasn't prepared for that. She wasn't prepared for that look on his face either. He wanted something from her, that was clear. Sex. All she had to do was crook a finger, and he'd be in her bed. But she saw something more. He wanted to know what *she* wanted too, and she could tell he craved giving it to her . . . whatever it was. She saw uncertainty and hope and confidence that he could make her happy—if she'd let him.

For some reason, that look of his made her feel like a princess. Everything in her shimmered and shone and stood at attention.

But she was unable to speak.

She wasn't sure what she wanted. She was scared. He was asking too much, without even saying a word. So she retreated to what she could handle, which was a brush-off. "Good night," she told him.

A flash of disappointment crossed his face. "Sleep well," he replied softly, then put his hands in his front pockets, thumbs out, and sauntered down the street toward Fran's house.

"I hope you get coal in your stocking," she called after him quietly, her inner villain turning soft.

He turned back and laughed. "Where'd you get that fruitcake? I've never met anyone who actually eats it."

"I made it." She couldn't help feeling proud. "My dad likes it. It's actually pretty good if you soak it in enough rum."

He shot her a skeptical look. "Are you sure your family's from planet Earth?"

She laughed. "You don't know what you're missing."

"Oh yes I do," he said, his voice getting very sexy. "I know very much what I'm missing. And I hate that I am."

Her entire body tingled with entirely inappropriate sensations. "You need to stop talking." She yanked open her door. "See you tomorrow morning." She paused on her steps, waiting for a reply. Like a fool.

"I can't wait," he said.

Something invisible and dangerous shimmered between them, which she needed to ignore, and the only way to do that was to cross her threshold and push the piazza door shut behind her.

So she did.

Maybe that would keep it out, whatever the danger was. She leaned against the door, closed her eyes, and pretended that she was safe.

CHAPTER TWENTY-FOUR

Yes!

When Deacon woke up at 6:15 the next morning, it was dark and cold, and he remembered that Hell awaited. So why had he thought *Yes*? Maybe because it smelled like Christmas with the pungent evergreen in the living room and the leftover scent of the special holiday bayberry tapers Fran lit every night at dinner. He rolled out of bed with more energy than usual—like a Boy Scout, with a need to help, to be a part of things.

He felt young and hopeful.

It was weird.

He shivered as he pulled on his jeans and donned a T-shirt and sweater, all while half-asleep, that is until George showed up at his bedroom door with a steaming hot cup of coffee.

"I hate to say it because your head's big already, but you rock," Deacon told him.

"I know." George's face looked freshly scrubbed. He already wore cologne—subtly, thank God—and a green silk tunic and black skinny jeans.

They grinned at each other, but the attempts came out more as grimaces.

"I'm obviously ready," George said. "Are you?"

"As I'll ever be," Deacon replied. "Hey. What do you want for Christmas?"

"True love," George said, "and maybe a red Camaro. But I wouldn't know where to keep it in the city."

"Are you always this difficult?"

"You mean splendid?" George huffed. "Yes."

The doorbell rang. The colonel was five minutes early. Figured.

Operation Boot Camp was underway.

Aunt Fran was discombobulated when Deacon knocked on her bedroom door. Rightly so. It was 6:25, and she never got up that early.

"Aunt Fran!" he called to her. There was something scary about waking up other people. You never knew what you'd get.

"Wha—?"

"It sucks to wake you. Sorry. But Colonel Block is here for breakfast." He wished Macy was there, but she hadn't made an appearance yet.

His aunt's head popped up from the pillow. "Is this a joke?"

"No. He just rang the doorbell. You didn't hear it?"

"Of course not, kid!" That was what she used to call him. Still did, sometimes, when she was extra loosey-goosey. She let her head drop back to the pillow. "If this is some kind of joke, tell George it's not funny."

"It's not a joke. We just let the colonel in the front door. He says you invited him, and he wants to thank you for something, I think."

"Hell's bells," she said in a croaky morning voice. "What's he going to thank me for?" She threw her blankets off. *A good sign*, Deacon thought. "I'm going to kill him," she muttered.

Maybe not such a good sign, after all.

"Should I send him home?" First test.

She paused. "No." Her voice was quivery with self-pity.

Deacon pitied her too. It was wrong to wake a diva from her sleep. But she hadn't asked him to send the colonel home.

Macy would be thrilled to hear that.

"I can't believe he would do this." Aunt Fran stood and moved like a robot with dying batteries toward her walnut wardrobe. "It makes no sense."

"It *is* pretty early."

She flung the wardrobe door open and shook her head at her robe, hanging on a hook. He'd never seen her second-guess its frayed hem. "This thing is my favorite. But it's looking pretty crappy."

"Lived in." Deacon helped her put her arms through the armholes, turned her around, and tied the sash for her.

"You weren't awake either, I presume."

"No," he said. "But who's going to stay in bed when the colonel comes over? He might have 'Reveille' on his iPhone. I can just see him delighting in blasting it by my ear."

"He doesn't scare *me*."

It was a not-so-veiled insult directed at Deacon, not the colonel. But he let her get away with it because her morning was about to go downhill even further.

His was too, if Macy didn't get there soon. Where was she? He imagined her walking right past George, Aunt Fran, and the colonel to his bedroom. He'd follow, and they'd fall into bed together. It was a useless daydream. But it passed the yawning seconds between now and the next time he'd see her.

Aunt Fran stalked past him. She'd gathered steam.

Deacon was hopeful. Worried, but hopeful. He followed her into the living room, where the tree lights were already lit.

"Colonel Block," she said in plain, bold terms, as if she were a general on the warfront about to meet with another commander.

"Good morning." Her visitor sounded more good-humored than usual. He still scowled, but there was a certain softness about him Deacon had never seen before.

"I'm not a morning person, Colonel," Fran said. "But you look and sound awfully chipper. What's on your mind?"

"I'm here for breakfast," he said, "and to have a pow-wow."

He indicated the resplendent table in the drawing room, set with sparkling china and demure silver place settings. It was separated from the living room by a wide arch decorated with Christmas greenery. It looked like something from a glossy magazine, except for the Corgis sniffing each other's rears by the chair legs.

Fran looked at George. Said nothing.

He waved his hand dismissively. "I went overboard, but the colonel's a special guest. Enjoy."

When George strode to the kitchen, he left Aunt Fran no choice but to stare at her nephew instead. Deacon graced her with his most enigmatic smile, designed to dissuade questions and disarm the recipient.

"You're looking lovely this morning, Fran," said the colonel.

"Am I?" she said languidly.

Deacon loved her 1940s movie star class. And sass. She was going to take this situation and run with it.

Good for her!

"I like a woman who knows herself so well." The colonel headed to the table. "You don't need folderols."

Folderols! Deacon was amused.

The colonel held out a chair. "Take a seat, madam."

Aunt Fran put her nose in the air but complied.

The doorbell rang again.

"Who is it this time?" the queen of the condo asked sharply.

"Macy," Deacon said. "I can tell by the way she rings the bell. A long press before the release, as if she doesn't trust the mechanism to work properly."

Aunt Fran *tsked*. "She's a control freak, that girl. I suppose you invited her to breakfast, the same way I invited the colonel?" Her tone was dry.

"You got it." Deacon winked and left to get his quarry.

"How's it going?" Macy said inside their little lobby area. She was wearing a Chicago Bears knit cap, a Detroit Red Wings jersey, jeans, and Eskimo boots. In her hands, she held a basket of beautifully decorated sweet rolls that smelled like heaven.

"Are you a Christmas elf?" Deacon inhaled the delicious fragrance of freshly baked rolls mingled with her light flower scent. "Or maybe Mrs. Claus's cousin?"

"Neither." She smirked. "I'm a woman alone who likes to bake."

"And drive people crazy. In more ways than one."

"No more sex talk." She sounded like a schoolteacher but she smiled, so she must not hate him too much. "It's Christmas."

"Christmas is a great time for sex talk." Upsetting schoolteachers was his specialty too. "At least I think so. There are sleigh blankets to cuddle under. Warm fires. Everyone has red cheeks and stays a little tipsy 'til New Year's Day."

"How's your aunt this morning?" She was adept at simply ignoring his stupid banter when she felt like it, which made him feel special, like a real friend—or one of her genuine annoyances in life.

At least she wasn't actively hating on him.

"So far she hasn't thrown the colonel out or cursed at

George and me. I can tell she's aggravated. But she's also intrigued. She loves to be droll. And obstreperous. Especially with people who don't put up with her."

"Perfect." Macy clomped up the stairs next to him.

"I didn't know you were such a sports fan." *Such a sexy, adorable sports fan*, he really wanted to say, but he knew she'd slap him down.

"I told you how much I like the College of Charleston men's basketball team. The Cougars. This hat and jersey belong to my dad. I'm slummin' it today." She sent him a "But what can ya do?" kind of look.

"I think you look fantastic," he said.

"In an alternative universe, maybe," she said with a little snort.

They were at the door. He put his arm around her shoulder and squeezed. "Don't be so hard on yourself. You made rolls with green icing wreaths on top. And some of them have Christmas trees. With sprinkles."

"I sure did." She seemed peppier then. "So what about the colonel and your aunt? Do we hope this works out between them?"

Deacon thought about it for a second. "I don't think that matters as much as just giving them the opportunity to figure it out together. She's barely gotten to live here, and she already loves this condo. If she paired up with the colonel, she'd become part of old Charleston, but she'd probably move to his house, and, honestly? I think she'd rather be unencumbered—at least for a while."

"I can see that."

"Are you a morning person?" He smiled.

"Nope. And you are, obviously."

"Only around Christmastime. But don't tell anyone else." He held the door open for her.

In the dining room, the colonel and Aunt Fran sat across

from each other. Corgis lounged at their feet until they saw Macy and rushed at her.

"Come in, come in." Aunt Fran sat up taller when she saw Macy.

Deacon loved that his aunt looked forward to Macy's neighborly visits.

"Over here, guys." Deacon tried to divert the Corgis by sitting on his haunches near the Christmas tree. They loved when he scratched their ears and pushed them onto their bellies.

But they liked Macy's rolls better. With them sniffing her feet and legs, she slowly navigated her way across the living room to the dining room. Deacon knew better than to relieve her of those sweet confections, so he put Dean Martin on the sound system. It took her at least a quarter of the way through "Baby, It's Cold Outside" before she could get to Fran.

"Join us, hon," Deacon's aunt said mildly, "but don't ask for coffee. It's cold. And now George says the machine's broken and he left his French press carafe in New York."

"What a shame." Macy bent to hug Aunt Fran's neck while Deacon took a seat next to the colonel.

"Mmm," said Aunt Fran. "Look at those rolls! Pure decadence!"

"They smell real good," affirmed the colonel.

Macy's face brightened. "You like them? I made them for the Marines."

"Oh." Aunt Fran wilted just a little.

"They're coming over today to help us set up the Toys for Tots party." Macy made brief eye contact with the colonel. "I'll go put these in the kitchen and join y'all in a minute. Thanks for the invite."

There was a lull at the table when she disappeared.

Deacon knew he could fill it, but he refused.

Aunt Fran glanced at the colonel. He cleared his throat. "So," she said.

"The fruitcake—" the colonel said at the same time.

She let out a short laugh. "You go."

"Thank you for it," Colonel Block said abruptly.

Aunt Fran's smile faded. "For the . . . fruitcake?"

George burst forth from the kitchen, humming along with Dean Martin, Macy trailing behind him.

"Who or what else do you have for me?" Aunt Fran narrowed her eyes at her personal chef.

"This." George put down a bowl of cream of wheat in front of her and another in front of the colonel.

"I'll skip it," said Deacon.

"Me too." Macy was now seated.

"As you wish." George smiled smugly around the table.

"You don't want to know what I wish," muttered Aunt Fran. She lifted her spoon and let the cream of wheat dribble off it.

The colonel took a bite. "Hmmmph." He put his spoon down.

"Not to your liking, Colonel?" Aunt Fran asked rather archly.

He wasn't going to let on for a skinny second that he was disappointed. "It's everything cream of wheat should be," he said with a fake-polite smile. "But I'm full of fruitcake. *Your* fruitcake."

Aunt Fran's brow furrowed, and then she let out a little laugh. "Full of fruitcake. How charmingly you phrase things."

"I already had a slice this morning," he said, "and it was marvelous. Fruitcakes by Fran! You ought to start selling them."

Deacon had no idea if the man was being sarcastic or truly loved fruitcake.

There was a long pause. "I suppose I *should* sell them," Aunt Fran said with a piquant smile.

The colonel cleared his throat. "Truth is, I hate fruitcake. Too fancy for me. But because you made it, I thought I should at least try a piece off the bottom before I regifted it to my brother Gary."

"You've never told me about him." Aunt Fran was the epitome of gracious lady.

"He takes anything—even an Elvis Presley blanket someone gave me as a prank." The colonel chuckled. "But when I tried this fruitcake of yours, Fran, I loved it. So if selling your fruitcake is what you want to discuss, I'm all for helping you develop a business plan."

Deacon had never heard the colonel talk so much before. It was shocking. Even more shocking was how well Aunt Fran held it together. She acted as if she knew what the colonel was talking about.

"Coffee," she said weakly. "I don't care how cold it is. Just load it up with cream and sugar. Macy, darling, would you mind?"

Macy stood. "I'll be right back."

Deacon stood too. He would play the colonel's manservant. "Will you have some, too, Colonel?"

"Of course," he said, "*black*," then looked at Fran as if taking his coffee black was a very big deal, a sign of his manliness.

"We're out of cream, milk, and sugar," George called from the kitchen doorway, "and coffee. Sorry. I'll get some later. Right now I'm obsessed with Channel Five's news anchor. She's holding a piglet. It's Farm Animal week. And it's adorbz."

Aunt Fran stood. "I'm going to McDonald's. Freddie, would you take me there?"

"Absolutely." The colonel didn't bat an eye at the

request or the nickname. "We'll go through drive-thru in my Jeep."

Aunt Fran looked down at her robe. "I *could* change."

"Nah." The colonel waved a hand. "Why mess with perfection?"

Aunt Fran's head came up sharply. "All right then." She smiled. "Shall we walk to your house?"

"That's where my Jeep is," the colonel said. "You'd better bundle up first."

"You drive the kind with no doors? The sort Patton and MacArthur rode in?"

"You mean there's another kind?" The colonel look well-pleased with himself.

Aunt Fran disappeared around the corner to her room.

George and Macy, holding the basket of rolls, came out of the kitchen.

"I'm so glad I got to stop by." Macy exchanged a glance with Deacon.

Operation Boot Camp is working, he attempted to convey to her. But she didn't send a message back. She was too busy playing the dutiful—and innocent—neighbor.

And maybe she still hated him. But he hoped not.

Aunt Fran emerged from the back hall with a navy-blue wool coat and bright-red plaid scarf over her bathrobe. She'd dumped her slippers in favor of George's favorite shabby brown leather cowboy boots.

George's eyes nearly popped out of his head when he saw those. Like Deacon, he was probably wondering what had happened to his glamorous employer. But neither one of them would dare challenge her on that—or her brazen stealing of those boots, which were too big but lent her a certain panache.

"We're off," she said with particular energy.

Whether it was born of defiance, frustration, caffeine

deprivation, or anticipation of spending more time with the colonel, Deacon couldn't say.

But the boots made him think the colonel was definitely on Aunt Fran's mind—and maybe in her heart.

"I'll walk out with you," Macy said.

Deacon's good mood evaporated. He wanted her to stay and celebrate with him and George.

The colonel held open the front door. Aunt Fran went first. Macy went under his arm next.

"Macy." Deacon realized he was saying her name as if she were some kind of lifeline, and he wondered if anyone else could tell.

"Yes?" She looked back.

A flicker of impatience crossed the colonel's face.

Stay, Deacon wished he could say. *Let's celebrate.* "Have a good day."

"Sure." She smiled politely. "You too." And disappeared.

Deacon felt George's amusement, or maybe his pity. It was Christmas, after all, and they needed to be nice to each other. But Deacon remained stoic, his hands in his back pockets. The colonel, dammit all, was still looking at him. Fran and Macy started down the stairs.

"I know Fran doesn't make fruitcake," the colonel said to both him and George, "so thank Macy for me, will you?" then winked and pulled the door firmly shut behind him.

CHAPTER TWENTY-FIVE

Two days after Operation Boot Camp, Macy ran over to Anne's house between client conferences to say hello and ask which pairs of earrings went better with the dress she'd chosen to wear to a party that night at the mayor's house. Deacon would no doubt be there with Fran. Everything in Macy knew she was dressing up for him, but she shrugged it off as a natural compulsion because he was the last guy she'd slept with. She didn't *really* want to impress him, she told herself. Only her ego did.

She also wanted to check out Anne's stash of Christmas presents for the kids. Do some sister bonding.

"You okay?" Anne asked her in her bedroom.

"Fine," Macy said, then sighed.

Anne's forehead puckered. "You're obviously not fine. Are you in love with Deacon?"

Macy threw herself on the bed and stared at the ceiling. "I don't know. I've known him for such a short time."

"I knew with Kyle the second I saw him, and look at us now." Anne pointed to her bureau, where two silver-framed pictures of Lucy and Sam gleamed in the late afternoon sun.

"But Mom and Dad." Macy gulped hard and kept her

eyes on the ceiling. For the first time in a long time, she allowed herself to think of them and their history.

"They're okay now," said Anne in a soothing voice.

Macy covered her eyes with a hand. "But they weren't for such a long time."

Anne sat down next to her and pulled Macy's hand off her face. "That's because Mom pretended not to know what was going on. And Dad let her."

Macy turned to look at her. "*We* knew."

Anne took her hand. "That was tough."

"I always wonder if I should have told her when I found out," Macy whispered.

"No." Anne squeezed her hand. "You did the right thing. You were too young to be involved. Maybe if you'd been older, yes. Maybe. But you were only nine. I was twelve. And even then, I had no idea what to do. We helped each other through it."

A tear trickled down Macy's cheek. "They really are okay now, aren't they?"

"Yes, darling." Anne paused. "For the last twenty years. I'm sad that you're still carrying this burden."

"Me too," said Macy.

They were silent for a moment.

Anne sighed. "At first things were rocky, but don't you remember that they started trying to repair things almost right away?"

Macy caught her sister's earnest, loving gaze. "Yes. I do remember."

"Well, focus on that. Not the rest. Think about the outcome instead."

Macy closed her eyes and tried. "But I still can't believe Dad would have done that to her."

"You're thinking like the child Macy," Anne said firmly. "Try to see it now as an adult. You understand now how people can damage relationships, right? They're such complex things. They require a lot of attention."

Macy opened her eyes again. "Yes, actually. I do get it. I've really messed up with Deacon. It's not hard to screw things up royally."

"Exactly," Anne said. "Try to forgive Dad for being human. Mom did."

"I thought I had."

"Maybe you couldn't. Not until you understood yourself."

Macy let that sink in. "I think maybe you're right," she said eventually. "But I wonder why you were able to come to grips with it before I was?"

"We all learn different things at different times for reasons we may never understand fully. But maybe it's because I was the older sister, and I was used to facing things head-on. Being the firstborn and all."

"You're always so wise." Macy sat up and smiled at her sister.

"No, I'm not!" Anne made a comic face. "I still mess up all the time."

"Even with Kyle?"

"Especially with Kyle!"

They laughed together.

"Do you think Celia knows?" Macy had never had the courage to ask her.

Anne nodded. "I'm sure that's why she hates you so much. Her mother spiraled down when Dad broke it off with her. She's never really recovered."

"But maybe Celia *doesn't* know." Macy was insistent on that.

"How could she not?" Anne shook her head. "They were careless. If you found them once, don't you think she might have? I got the impression that a lot of it took place at Celia's house."

"Poor Celia."

"Her mother was a widow. Maybe Celia welcomed Dad into their lives as a father figure."

"True. So taking him away might have been the difficult part for her."

"We'll never know."

Macy leaned on her sister's shoulder. "I can't believe I'm bringing up ancient history."

Anne hugged her. "It's because you're falling in love. And it scares you. But we're not our parents. Affairs don't have to happen to us. And if, God forbid, one does, at least we know our parents got past theirs. They're very happy."

Macy smiled to herself thinking of the last time she'd seen them, only a few days before. They'd made her a delicious spaghetti dinner, and Dad had kissed Mom in the kitchen while she was stirring the sauce, the same way Deacon had kissed Macy in Fran's kitchen over those shrimp and grits. "They are happy," she said.

"Very," said Anne.

They stayed together on the bed chatting for another fifteen minutes, then sifted through the gifts Anne still had to wrap. They talked about what to make for Christmas dinner and laughed over the old Christmas photo album their mother had put together. It was while she was looking at pictures of her and Anne on all those Christmas mornings growing up that Macy gave into impulse and decided to call into the office. She told them she was going home early because she simply needed a little Christmas. Anne was all for it.

"I want you to be happy," Anne said.

"I am," Macy said, "as much as I can be, considering nothing's settled between Deacon and me."

"You'll figure it out," Anne said. "If there's any time of year that can help love find a way, this is it."

"You're right." Macy hugged her sister good-bye, walked

home with a lighter heart, and lit a new log in the fire-place in the kitchen. She got cozy in an old armchair and listened to holiday music while she wrote Christmas cards.

After her talk with Anne, she almost felt like her world was starting over, and she felt ready for it. And so it was with a great deal of excitement that she prepared for the party that night. Fran called and asked her to attend with her and the colonel. Deacon, Fran said, was going some-where else first for drinks, and would meet them there.

Originally, Macy had been planning to go with Greer, Ella, and Miss Thing, but she said yes to her new neighbor. Fran was going out of her way to be thoughtful, despite the obvious rift between Macy and her nephew.

Fortunately, the mayor and his wife took a liking to Fran at the party. Plus, the colonel hovered nearby—not quite a date, yet obviously escorting the newly arrived New York City maven. Everyone respected the colonel, so Fran wasn't persona non grata in the least. That was a good start for her.

As for Macy, when Penelope headed her way in a perky ivory-and-black-lace number, she felt ready to take on the world in her own emerald-green satin strapless cocktail dress.

"Macy! How are you?" Penelope's expression was hope-ful but concerned.

"Doing well," Macy said. "How about you?"

"Great, thanks." Penelope's smile was genuine. "But I still think you should go after Deacon. He's not interested in me. We're friends—good friends—which is nice. But nothing more."

"Aw, Penelope, you're so kind and smart, and I adore you." Macy hugged her. Even with a half-finished drink in her hand, it was a tight embrace. Because they both knew the heartache of not being The One or finding The One. Of not connecting. Of wishing. Of hating yourself for wishing because they knew they were enough on their own.

They *were*.

They talked about it too, plainly, honestly, reminding each other of their worth. And then they hugged again and promised to look for each other at Macy's Toys for Tots party.

When Penelope left her, a passing server grabbed Macy's empty champagne flute, and some very odd ideas entered her head. *Why am I setting everyone else up? What am I waiting for?*

Ella and Greer walked in—Ella in pale-pink taffeta and Greer in shimmery gold—with Miss Thing in tow in sky-blue silk. They almost immediately got sucked into the social vortex by the Christmas tree. Macy felt almost traitorous looking at them because of the turn her thoughts were taking. She had never felt this way before. She was all about the business that Two Love Lane excelled at—matchmaking other people.

Not herself.

Why not *me?* the rebellious inner voice taunted her.

Because, she answered. *Because* . . .

Because of her parents. Of her shame at discovering her father with Celia's mother. She'd never forget it. She'd never forget how living at her house was like walking on shards of glass for what seemed like forever but was really one school grade—fourth grade, the only year she got *B*s.

She laughed to herself. *B*s. *B*s were the fallout, or so she'd thought.

The truth was, her entire life ever afterward was. She had denied herself her life. She'd denied herself love. Her signet ring twinkled up at her: *Dives in caritate.* "Rich in love." It had been there all along, a message reminding her of her identity. And she'd ignored it.

She needed a drink.

Miraculously, one appeared.

"This has your name all over it." Louisa approached at rapid speed, stopping a few inches in front of her, and handed her a colorful concoction. "A Harvey Wallbanger. Vodka and OJ topped with Galliano and a cherry. Only grandmothers drink them. Mine happens to be here, and she's already had three, so I had to take this one away. Try it. It's damned good."

Macy took a sip, and it was. "Wow. What are you drinking?"

"The usual, Jim Beam and Coke. It's my dad's drink."

"Oh."

"I won't ever drink any other bourbon. You know, the good stuff. It's sad because he wasn't always the greatest father, but I love him." Louisa made a comic face.

"Someday let's talk about it," Macy said.

Louisa's brows shot up. "Really?"

"I love my dad too. But there were some issues."

"I didn't know you ever dealt with that. Your family seems so perfect." Louisa stared at her as if she were a strange lab experiment.

"Far from it." Macy couldn't help laughing.

Louisa poked her in the belly, which was unusual in grownups to do, but somehow not for Louisa. "It's good to see you laugh. You were looking a bit stricken a few minutes ago."

"I was?"

"For sure."

"It has nothing to do with your arrangement with Deacon to get me together with him," Macy told her. "Just some different things happening at work."

Louisa's eyes nearly popped out of her head. "You know about that?"

Macy nodded. "You mean, you haven't talked to him?"

"No." Louisa had the grace to blush. "We were doing it

because we wanted you to have fun. You're always taking care of everyone else."

"Thanks." Macy was touched. She wished Ella, Greer, and Miss Thing would appear at her side. Just seeing them up close would lift her spirits.

"So?" asked Louisa. "Are you and Deacon together?"

Macy shook her head. "Not even close."

"Aw, that's too bad." Louisa jetted a breath. "There he is. He just walked in. Alone."

Macy made a discreet quarter-turn to see him. He was swoon-worthy in a classic black tux. "You really didn't mind giving up a date with him for me?" she asked Louisa.

Louisa laughed. "I'm stuck on someone else. Someone unavailable. But I'm not bitter. Truly. That's life."

"Can you tell me who?"

"Over my dead body."

"Oh, okay."

"It's an impossible situation. So I'm trying to move on."

"You've got a good attitude. Any time you want me to help, come see me at Two Love Lane. Friend to friend."

Louisa winked. "I'll keep that in mind. See you, Macy."

"Bye." She felt vaguely unsettled again. Why was romance so hard? Her job was to take some of the annoyances away from her clients, and hopefully, some of the hurt. But no matter which way she looked at it, it was a difficult road, even for people who fall in love at first sight, like Anne.

There was something beyond technique and logistics, which they talked a lot about at Two Love Lane. There was a leaping over a dark abyss. On one side was absence of trust. On the other was total faith and commitment.

She couldn't help her clients make that leap. No hired person could. Because at its core, love was a mystery for each and every couple. Only they knew where the abyss was in their relationship.

So she was like a tour guide dropping these hopeful people off at a canyon and telling them that somehow they, on their own, had to make their way across. They had to find their own ladders, parachutes, bridges, whatever.

For the first time in Macy's career as a matchmaker, she felt some doubts about the importance of what she was doing. Maybe she should have gotten the message when she'd set up Celia and her almost-fiancé and he'd obviously not been willing to commit to Celia at a deep soul level.

That terrible situation was a clear indicator that Macy couldn't control what happened in her clients' world. Only they could.

So she wasn't doing much, really. Positioning people on a giant chessboard, advising them as to the first couple of moves. But in the end, they'd have to take over. She'd have to retreat.

And watch.

I'm useless.

She knew that was a stupid thought, but at that moment she believed it.

Not only was she having a crisis of confidence about her job—her passion—she'd been walking around with blinders on about her own feelings.

About her feelings and her fate.

And she thought she knew herself pretty damned well.

She needed to get out of there, so she headed as fast as she could to an exit. All around her was noise, flashes of color. But she was separate. Inside, she felt like a swirling snowflake in a blizzard, tossed on the winds.

She was scared, unable to think straight.

She'd go home and text Fran from the comfort of her kitchen that she felt sick and had to depart the party abruptly. It wouldn't be far from the truth. Her stomach had butterflies in it. Her head felt light.

But a solid pillar of tuxedoed man stood in her way.

"Hey, you." It was Trent Gillingham, the star of *Bless Your Heart*, the one Fran had a crush on. His eyes were bloodshot, and his mouth hung open a little. He looked drunk. No surprise there. Almost every time Macy saw him out and about, he was.

"Hi, Trent." She flashed him a plastic smile. "I wish I could stay and chat. But I don't feel well. I've got to go."

He immediately grabbed her elbow. "Lemme help you. I'll get you home."

She shook her head and pulled her arm gently away from his grip. "No, thank you. I'd like to go alone."

"Tha's not right."

"I'm *fine*." She slipped past him. The exit was only a few feet away.

For a drunk guy, he moved pretty fast. He stood directly in the doorway. "Come on now, Macy. Let's party."

Without speaking another word to him, she did a one-eighty and headed to an alternate door. A crowd stood in her way. Inhaling a silent breath, she prepared to move through them somehow without stopping to chat.

That was tough in Charleston. You couldn't walk a few steps without someone asking you how you were doing. Or catching you up on what they were doing.

Her chest constricted. Trent came up to her and took her arm.

Again.

This time, she had no patience. "Please leave me alone." Maybe she said it too loudly, because a few people in front of her stopped talking and stared.

Trent's face got redder, and he held her arm harder. "She doesn't feel well," he explained. "Please excuse us." And he pulled her forward.

"*No*," Macy told him in as firm a voice as she could muster without making a scene. Like a stubborn donkey, she dug in her heels. Luckily, she was standing on a plush carpet.

"You okay, Macy?" a friendly older woman from the mayor's office asked.

Macy sent her a pained smile. "I'd like to go home, is all."

"I'll take you." Deacon appeared to her right, but he wasn't looking at her. He was staring at Trent. "You may think you can steal someone's Christmas tree in a church parking lot," he said in his highly noticeable New York accent, "but you sure as hell aren't going to remove this woman from the mayor's house."

Hearing him come to her defense like that in his sleek, sophisticated tuxedo, and seeing his face like that—scary and hard, on her behalf—plucked at every needy place within her.

"I'm okay," she said. "Really."

But she had to admit, she was feeling a little out of it. The quick rush of champagne, combined with the day's fatigue and the new revelations she'd only just had, served to throw her off her game.

Deacon sensed this. And she knew why. *Because he was her soulmate.*

Tears nearly welled up in Macy's eyes, but she blinked once and pushed them back down. "I am *fine*," she said for the last time.

"Of course you are," Deacon said.

He wasn't talking about that moment. He was saying she mattered in general, that her place in the universe was assured. And she only had to trust herself to believe it, the way he did.

How did she know this?

Because they were soulmates.

Did he know yet?

She still didn't think so. He lived on the surface. Not that that was a bad thing. She'd obviously been doing it herself. Look at how she'd been sleepwalking. Here was her actual soulmate right in front of her eyes.

Maybe the sleeping together part had actually gotten in the way of figuring it out. She might have put up some barriers afterward, the old defense mechanisms. You didn't want to get rejected after baring your entire naked body and—let's face it—at least part of your soul to another human being.

It was a natural reaction.

"Get the hell outta my way," she heard Trent say from a distance.

She heard a crack then—a sharp sound like bone against bone.

Then everything went black.

CHAPTER TWENTY-SIX

Deacon knew Trent was a lame adversary—he hated wasting a punch on him—but sometimes bugs must be squashed. Or taught a lesson. Or both.

This was one of those times.

The reality TV star might learn to become a halfway decent guy, but right now his selfish, boozy exterior dominated. He was vain as hell and couldn't handle his liquor.

Over the years Deacon had learned—with very little mentorship from a father figure—that a gentleman was modest about his superior skills, whether in the bedroom or the boardroom, around the poker table, on a football field or golf course, or when hunting or fishing.

And a gentleman sure as hell knew when to stop drinking. The only exceptions to that rule were when he'd been presented with divorce papers or lost a beloved family member or friend. Apart from that, no excuses for alcohol-fueled bad choices were acceptable, especially when a lady was involved.

A lady was involved.

Not only that, that lady was Macy, whom Deacon had great neighborly fondness for and a serious sexual attraction to, one that he couldn't shake no matter how many alluring women he met in Charleston.

"Why'd you do that?" someone asked him.

"You knocked him out," another person said.

Duh.

The whole party stopped. Even the music. Deacon rubbed his knuckles and was pushed out of the way by an older man.

"I'm the chief of police here in Charleston," the guy said. "I expect the truth ASAP."

Deacon grimaced. "He was harassing Miss Frost, sir. Dragging her toward the door while she was saying no. I saw the whole thing. So did several other witnesses."

The chief looked around. "I don't see any."

Deacon was disappointed but not surprised. Trent was from an A-list family.

Macy finally sat up, surrounded by Miss Thing and her two colleagues at Two Love Lane. She looked groggy but okay. Deacon felt relief, but it wasn't warm and sustaining, like brandy on a polar-arctic day, the way he imagined it was for most people. It weakened him.

He hated being vulnerable.

He hated turning into Gumby.

"Oh boy," Macy whispered, and looked up at him with worried, sad eyes.

"I punched Trent," he said. Like a dork. Like a kid hoping someone would give him a big fat reward. He'd take a kiss, a real one, from the woman who'd just fainted.

But she'd fainted. That wasn't good. Worry descended once more. It made him want to punch Trent again for making Macy so upset. It was a guy thing, but he suppressed the thought and focused on those sad eyes of hers. She was okay. That was all that mattered at this point.

Trent groaned. The loser. Okay, the loser who might be

redeemable if he had decent friends and family, which apparently he had. They just needed to get to work teaching him some lessons. Maybe tonight would give them a little push in the right direction.

And then Macy saw Trent. She audibly gasped. It was such a feminine thing to do. "What happened to him?"

Several accusing stares were leveled Deacon's way, but he wasn't going to apologize to anyone. "He needed a warning from a policeman," he explained to Macy. "Since I had no idea there was one nearby—sorry, Chief—I took it upon myself to provide it before he took you outside."

"I'm sorry you hurt your hand," Macy said. "But glad you—you stopped him. He wouldn't listen to me."

Their eyes locked. Something passed between them. Some kind of awareness that they'd come close to when they'd slept together—it had been a moment when he'd looked in her eyes and she'd smiled back with some kind of affection and . . . tenderness. And he had lost his breath.

Tenderness.

He wasn't used to getting that. To *feeling* that.

Aunt Fran loved him, but she was brisk. The few moments of tenderness they'd shared over his lifetime he completely remembered. The time he'd had appendicitis when he was eleven. She'd gently fed him scrambled eggs and brushed a lock of hair out of his eye. The hug she'd given him the day he'd graduated high school. Her tears, and the way she couldn't speak, when he showed her his diploma right after his college graduation, and she'd laid trembling fingers on his arm, almost as if she needed help to remain standing.

Could Macy see what he was feeling now? That he was proud he'd protected her? That he was worried? That he cared—a lot? He wanted to get on the ground next to her and hug her close.

And be tender with her. The opposite of what Trent had been.

Mrs. Gillingham came running up in silver high heels and a scarlet-red cocktail dress. She looked at Trent, now groaning on the ground, his hand over his right cheekbone.

"Do you want to press charges, Mr. Gillingham?" the police chief asked Trent. "Technically, you can. I wouldn't recommend it, but I need to let you know you can."

"Hell, yes, I'll press charges." Trent stood, his nostrils flared, and stared through slitted eyes at Deacon.

Good. One of those eyes was slitted because it was swelling up and turning yellow. Soon it would be green.

"You will *not* press charges," said Trent's mother. She was a fine-looking woman. Trent got a lot of his good looks from her. "You deserved it, son, I'm sure." She looked at the police chief. "He's a real ass sometimes, and it's gotten worse since that damned reality show took off in the ratings. He needed a comeuppance."

"Mom?" Trent's face reddened. "Are you kidding me? You haven't even heard what happened!"

"I don't need to hear," she said low. "Leave before you make more of a fool of yourself."

"Wait a minute," said the chief. "Miss Frost, would you like to press charges against Mr. Gillingham? I understand he tried to forcibly remove you from the party."

Her face paled. "No, thank you. I hope his black eye will wake him up."

Trent said nothing.

"Say you're sorry," Deacon told him.

"Sorry," Trent said sulkily to Macy. "I like you, okay? You're the only girl in town who doesn't suck up to me to get on the show. And in high school, you never put up with my rude comments. You might have been a wild child with nerdy scholar parents, but you turned out like my mom. Classy. *I* want to be classy. Geez."

"Oh." Macy shot him a tremulous smile. "Thank you, Trent. That means a lot to me."

He shook his head. "I really am sorry. I didn't mean to pull so hard on your arm. I need to lay off the bourbon."

"I know you won't do it again, right?" Macy asked. "With me or anyone else?"

"Right." Trent let out a big sigh. "I'm done with that asinine show too. Someone call the network. I'm pulling out." Everyone moved out of his way as he walked with bowed shoulders to the door, his hand cradling his eye.

It would be on social media within the hour, Deacon knew. Hashtag *bohunkbooboo*. Or something similar.

Macy wiped away a tear. "I need to go," she said, and looked around. "Greer? Ella? Miss Thing?"

"I can take you home," Deacon volunteered.

But Miss Thing was already at Macy's side. "We've got her," she said in comforting tones.

And then Macy was gone, being led toward another door by Miss Thing on one side and Greer on the other.

Deacon wanted to be the one to take her home. He wanted to carry her out of the mayor's house in his arms, walk the couple of blocks to the Battery with her arms around his neck and her legs swinging in time with his stride, put her in his bed, and tuck her in.

But that was another impossible daydream—not when the Two Love Lane ladies were guarding her so assiduously and when he had an aunt watching him like a hawk, as well as a cook/housekeeper doing the same thing. Not to mention Corgis breathing and yapping everywhere.

Damn, he missed his bachelor freedoms.

Ella appeared at his shoulder. "Thanks for taking care of Trent. Maybe he'll get the message now."

"I hope so."

"And don't worry." Ella's gaze was soft and caring, which he appreciated. "Macy's going to be fine. She's been working too hard and drank her champagne too fast. She's a lightweight, you know. She'll never admit it. The most she can tolerate are those wine punches at Fast and French."

He felt a jolt of warm memory thinking of her drinking those wine punches. They needed to go back and get more of those—and that soup, too.

"Your aunt told me to tell you she left," Ella said. "It was before all this happened. She didn't have time to cross the room and let you know. She and the colonel seemed in an awful hurry."

"Really?"

"Uh-huh. But she said not to worry. She's fine. She just had somewhere to be."

"Okay, thanks."

"My pleasure." Ella shot him a parting smile and left the party.

Deacon said his good-byes to the mayor—apologized to him and his wife and again to the chief of police—and left the party too.

He texted George. Because of course Aunt Fran didn't know how to text, even though she carried a sleek smartphone.

Aunt Fran home? he typed.

Nope, George texted back.

Damn.

She's not there? George added.

She left with the colonel 20 min ago, Deacon wrote back.

My, oh, my, texted George. And then he added an emoji of bright red kissy lips.

Oh, no. That thought had never occurred to Deacon. *Come on, now. Maybe they stopped to get a drink somewhere*, he texted.

Operation Boot Camp, George wrote, *and now the old folks are showing us up.*

Deacon couldn't believe the sexy scenario George was implying, but hey—he should be happy for Aunt Fran. This was why he was here in Charleston, to help her get settled, to feel at home. And if that involved her finding a boyfriend faster than anticipated, then Deacon would be okay with that.

Meanwhile, his own love life was going nowhere. Was he getting old? A different girl each night didn't appeal anymore. Neither did a different girl each week. Or each month for that matter. He was tired of having a revolving bed. It was too much work. Not enough payoff.

Fooling around was great, but dare he say it? There was more to life than sex, sports, drinking with his buddies, and making those especially shiny start-up deals that left his competitors in the dust.

What was happening to him? He couldn't let any of his guy friends hear him say any of that out loud. Or his team at work.

"Hey, you!" It was Penelope. "How are the knuckles?"

"Just fine." At the moment, he couldn't work up a grin.

Her smile faded. "I won't waste your time talking about what happened. Only to say that if you punched Trent, I know he deserved it."

"Thanks. He did. But hopefully, it's blue skies from here on out. Hey, you look beautiful." And she did. She was also brainy, kind, and fun to be around. But not for him.

"Thanks." Her cheeks turned pink. "Go after Macy, Deacon. I know she cares."

And before he could answer her, she walked away and disappeared into the crowd.

CHAPTER TWENTY-SEVEN

Knock, knock, knock.

It was the mystery sound from Ella's office.

The day after Macy fainted at the mayor's Christmas party—the day after she finally embraced her feelings for Deacon—she leaned against Ella's door at Two Love Lane. *Knock. Knock.* Long silence. *Knock, knock.* She tapped on the door. "Ella?"

"Yes?"

"May I come in?"

There was a long pause. "Sorry. Not right now."

Macy jetted a breath. "Ella, please tell us what's going on in there."

"Everyone has a right to privacy." *Knock, knock.*

"I know that, but we're a team here. And this is our office. Quite frankly, you're driving us all a little batty. Don't you trust us?" Macy stood and waited.

Ten seconds passed, and Ella opened the door a crack. "I'm wrapping Christmas presents."

"No, you're not." Macy knew she was risking Ella's wrath, which was rare, but when it showed up, it was very Italian, involving lots of hand gestures and many *Mio Dio*s. "Miss Thing said you were doing this last summer too."

Ella sighed. "Okay, I'm not wrapping Christmas presents. But I really don't feel I should tell you. You guys will think I'm strange."

Macy rolled her eyes. "We know you, Ella. You have your quirks. As do we all. We're not going to think you're strange."

"Well, Greer will."

"Not true."

"She doesn't believe in anything but logic."

"It doesn't come naturally to her, but she admitted last night that she knows there's something deeper going on about love and its mysteries, right? I call it listening to your intuition or your inner voice. You call it fate or magic or destiny. Greer thinks an expenditure of time and effort—which we can graph—might make love happen. But we all dabble a little bit in each other's philosophies, don't we?"

"I guess." Ella sounded blue.

"Of course we do. We combine them. So don't underestimate how much Greer respects you."

"Okay." A little hope entered Ella's voice.

"Aren't you tired of keeping this secret?" Macy asked softly.

Ella slowly opened the door. "Yes. I really am."

Macy walked across the threshold into the heretofore forbidden space.

Ella closed the door behind her. "Sit down."

Macy sat. She was so glad her friend was willing to speak to her. A few beats passed. "So?"

Ella pulled up a chair. "When my nonna—the one still in Sicily—came for a visit last summer, she said something about my office."

"Okay." Macy waited while her friend settled into her chair. Ella was so petite, it looked like a throne beneath her.

"First of all," Ella said, "when a Sicilian grandmother speaks, you listen. They don't waste words. What they say *matters*."

"I understand."

"So my nonna came in here, and she said"—Ella inhaled—" 'Ella? There's something precious here. I sense buried treasure.' And then she said it again: 'Buried treasure.' "

Macy drew in her chin. "Really?"

Ella nodded. "Macy, it has to be true. My nonna is never wrong."

"Oh. Okay." Macy would agree with her. Ella knew her grandmother best.

"So anyway, you know how in Revolutionary War times and during the Civil War people hid their family valuables in Charleston and other places in the South? So they wouldn't be found by the British or the Yankees?"

"Yes. I do. Those folks were pretty ingenious too."

"They were. And I found out that even during the 1920s prohibition years, people who ran bootleg liquor were very careful. If you suddenly started appearing richer than you normally were, that aroused the suspicion of the police. So you hid your valuables."

"Makes sense."

"So," Ella said, her cheeks blooming with high color, "I truly believe, with all the Sicilian in me, that some kind of treasure is hidden in this room, and no one ever recovered it. Maybe they died before they could."

"That could have happened, for sure."

Ella gripped her armrests. "You're not excited?"

"No, I *am*." Macy decided to be brave, since Ella had been brave to confide in her. "But you've been doing this off and on since last summer, and you've found nothing. Not to diss your nonna."

Ella's face fell. "I know. It looks pretty hopeless, but I have to keep trying." She was nothing if not loyal to her family.

"By the way," Macy ventured, "why do you stop searching for long stretches?"

"Sometimes I get so frustrated," Ella said. "I give up. I could never tell my nonna that. But I always get back in the saddle and try. She writes Momma letters and asks about it. That helps motivate me, you know? I have to find something before—" She sliced a hand across her throat.

Macy gave a discreet cough. "Before your nonna passes on?"

"Exactly." Ella crossed herself and shuddered. "I have to do this. For my nonna."

"Well, I'll help," Macy said, standing up.

Ella leapt to her feet. "You will?"

"Of course. On one condition—that we all know what this is about."

"All right." Ella's eyes shone with excitement.

Macy hugged her. "It's so great to have the air cleared. No one will make fun of you. I promise."

And no one did. Miss Thing was delighted to help.

Greer showed great restraint when Ella mentioned her nonna's mystical powers and latched onto the historical aspect of the situation. "You know, this old house might very well contain treasure. We've never really looked."

"True," Macy agreed, although inside, she figured that by now, someone in some other decade or century had already found the treasure, if it existed.

Ella went up to her wall on the north side of the house and tapped. "I've been knocking on the walls. And on the floor, hoping to hear a hollow sound."

"So we're looking for a hidey-hole." Miss Thing was into it. She's already Googled "how to find hidden treasure," which had led her to Disney World's website, and "where to conceal your valuables in your home," a blog post written by a former burglar turned police informant.

"Right," Ella said. "Problem is, I've tapped every inch of this floor numerous times. And every bit of the wall, up to about ten feet."

Macy locked gazes with Greer. The ceiling was fourteen feet high. And Ella was five foot two.

"We still have a lot of ground to cover then." Miss Thing clapped her hands.

"How did you get to ten feet?" Macy couldn't wait to find out because the chairs wouldn't get Ella that high.

Ella blushed. "That other noise you heard? The squeaking? That was me unfolding an old ladder I brought from home and stepping on the rungs. I hide it behind my window curtain."

Miss Thing marched up to the curtain of one window and flung a panel back. Sure enough, there was the ladder, looking rickety and rusty.

"How did the cleaning team miss this?" Greer threw up her arms.

"I told them I do my own windows," Ella said in a small voice.

They all laughed.

Macy got back to business. "So we need a better, taller ladder. There's one in the garden shed. The cleaners use it to change light bulbs in the chandeliers."

Ella gave a small sniffle. Her eyes were bright with unshed tears. "You're really going to help me, aren't you?"

"Of course," the rest of them said in unison.

And they got started right away.

An hour and many cries for caution later to whomever was standing on the taller ladder at the time—and maybe a few choice swear words—they still hadn't heard anything suspicious in the wall. But they had half the room to go.

Macy climbed down. "I hate to bail, but I'm meeting

my sister and her family for supper over the bridge in about twenty minutes."

"Let's call it a night," said Ella.

"We'll start in the morning." Miss Thing had snagged her panty hose on the ladder and decided to wear pants the next day.

"I'm totally up for it." Greer folded the taller ladder up herself and moved it behind the curtain. It was a long window, so it fit.

They grabbed their coats and scarves and headed out. Macy felt the house watching them in a friendly manner as they wended their way down the cobblestone street.

She looked back at its proper windows, lit with electric candles on the sill for the holidays. *Give up your secrets*, she silently asked the house, *if you have any left*.

When she stuck her hands into her pockets, she realized she had some too. And secrets didn't sit well with her. She was a natural sharer. But she'd learned the value of secrets. Her network of friends and professional acquaintances was as large as it was because she was trustworthy. You could tell her something, and it would stay in the vault.

Macy wished she could confide in Greer, Ella, and Miss Thing about her feelings for Deacon and how she couldn't deny them any longer. But something in her held back.

A short while later, she was crossing the Ravenel Bridge with Anne, Kyle, and the kids. Anne sounded happy and relaxed in the car. She tuned the radio station to all Christmas music, all the time, and everyone sang along.

This is what Christmas is about, Macy thought from her perch in the middle of the back seat as she held Lucy's hand on one side and Sam's on the other.

At the restaurant, they sat at a plastic table, the kind you see by a pool, with semi-wobbly plastic chairs. The table had paper placemats, and the food arrived on paper plates.

"Fried shrimp is my favorite," Sam said, dipping an entire one in a small paper condiment holder filled with ketchup.

Lucy squeezed lemon over her fried flounder. "I love fish."

Anne looked at Macy and smiled. "A place that serves only fried seafood. You can't beat that."

"Just don't let my boss see me here," Kyle said. "Or my patients."

Sam held up the shrimp dripping with ketchup. "This place is cool." He dropped the shrimp into his mouth and chewed it with gusto. "It's a secret restaurant," he said with his mouth full. "No signs on the door. No pictures in the paper or commercials on TV."

"Sam." Anne said. "Better manners, please. And the people who live in Charleston know it's a secret. That's why we're here eating dinner. It's only visitors who don't know about it. I always tell the nice ones I meet so they can come too."

"Ohhh," he said, then laughed.

"Secrets are bad to keep, usually," Kyle told Sam.

It was typical parent talk, but it made Macy feel a little awkward. After all, she was keeping a secret about how she felt about Deacon from the people she loved.

"So I should tell you what Mommy got you for Christmas?" Lucy asked her father.

"No," he said. "That's a secret you can keep."

Everyone laughed, Sam most of all. "Good thing you told me not to tell, Dad! I was gonna tell Mommy about the—"

"Sssh!" Just as Macy put her finger over his ketchup-covered mouth, she caught something out of the corner of her eye. *What on earth?*

Deacon and Penelope were waiting at the hostess stand!

Anne saw them too, and looked swiftly at Macy. "Who's that guy with Penelope?"

"My neighbor," is all Macy said. She dipped a fried scallop into cocktail sauce.

"Oh. Is that Deacon?" Anne wore a delighted grin.

"Yes." Macy took a sip of her ice tea. Her throat was parched. And she was sorely embarrassed.

"Deacon who?" asked Kyle, a little loudly. "Am I missing something?"

Macy turned her wince into a smile. "He was a client. And he's still my neighbor. At least temporarily. His aunt is Fran Banks."

"Oh, I heard about them." Kyle did his best to be discreet when he made a quarter-turn to check. "Did you set him up with Penelope?"

"No." Macy fumbled with her napkin. "They might be just friends. I don't know." She'd die if they walked into the restaurant holding hands.

Kyle nodded. "She's cute. I've heard good things about her."

"She's great." Macy kept chewing. She was miserable inside. Just miserable. Because she had a feeling that Penelope and Deacon were on a real date. Penelope had brought him to a local place. It wasn't fancy, but it was super special.

No tourists came here, unless they'd been tipped off by a local. And when you drove past it, you had no idea it was anything but an old warehouse. It was a secret restaurant, setting the perfect atmosphere for cozy confidences shared up close.

Macy's imagination was running away from her.

Anne could tell. She put her hand over her sister's. "Are you okay?"

"Sure. It's fine. I mean, they're good friends."

"Maybe." Anne took a long draw on her beer.

But Macy wasn't fooled. Anne was on high alert, which didn't make things easier.

When Deacon and Penelope walked by them to get to their table, of course the two of them acted shocked to see Macy and her family. Everyone laughed. Deacon told a joke. So did Kyle. Penelope chatted briefly with Anne, then bent down and hugged Macy.

It was a polite Hell. Macy hated every minute.

But she endured.

She even wished them a fun night.

That was what good matchmakers did.

And good aunts acted cheerful and fun. She didn't let on to Lucy or Sam, or even to Anne and Kyle, that she pitied herself that night—not until she went home and told Oscar, who ignored her, as usual. So she took a bubble bath, which didn't help.

She was in love. No two ways about it. Deacon didn't know it, and Christmas was coming.

It would be her worst Christmas ever, which was why she let two fat tears roll down her cheeks into the bath, and why she ate an entire pint of Ben & Jerry's Phish Food in bed.

CHAPTER TWENTY-EIGHT

"Have a good time?" George asked Deacon when he got home.

Thank God George loved to read fat novels and play video games with faraway friends, because lately Fran had been out a lot. Deacon too.

"Sure." Deacon tossed his car keys into a bowl by the front door. He'd hardly used the car at all since he'd been in Charleston.

"That doesn't sound too good." George kept his eyes on his book.

"It was fine." Deacon ignored all the Corgis at his feet. He threw himself down on the sofa and then realized for the umpteenth time there was no TV in the living room, only in his bedroom. So he was forced to talk. "Penelope's a great person. We're just friends, and she knows that's all I want. I'm not here for long, and even if I was, it would never get past the friend stage."

"You sure Penelope knows that?"

"Positive."

"Then you've got nothing to worry about." George shrugged and kept reading.

Deacon watched him for another minute. "Except we

saw Macy at the restaurant we went to," he finally said. "And she looked at me like I was the worst person on earth. I could tell she thought Penelope and I were on a date."

George finally looked up. "Uh-oh."

"Yep. It was pretty bad."

"Not really. Not if you and Macy are kaput."

"We never even got started."

"So who cares what she thinks?"

Deacon looked at the clock on the mantel. "Ten thirty."

"Yep." George yawned.

"I can't believe Aunt Fran is still out. And I'm at home."

George squinted at him. "Maybe you like Macy. Maybe you want to go see her. Maybe you're just being a stupid lunkhead." He shrugged and went back to his book.

"Shut up." The foul mood Deacon had felt coming on grew worse.

A few minutes passed in silence, except for the Christmas music George kept on and the sound of the Corgis snorting and whining because nobody was paying attention to them.

George slammed his book shut. "Nothing's stopping you from going over to see her."

"I know that."

"In fact"—George's expression brightened—"I made a particularly delicious banana bread. Two loaves. You could bring her one."

"Take it over yourself."

George *tsked*. "You're such a bear when you ignore the obvious."

Deacon stood. "I'm going to bed."

"Suit yourself."

Deacon paused. "But first—" He didn't wait to finish the sentence. He just walked to the door and grabbed his keys.

"Good plan," said George.

"There *is* no plan."

"Even better." George smiled at him. And there wasn't an ounce of insincerity in it. "Have fun."

"Okay, Dad." Deacon opened the door a crack. Any more and Corgis would get out.

"Dads don't usually advise their sons to woo the girl next door. Not unless your intentions are honorable."

"Come on. I'm only here until New Year's Day."

"You'd better stay with me, then." George stared him right in the eye. "I like Macy too much for her to be considered a mere dalliance by anyone. She deserves better."

"George?"

"Yes?"

"*Finish your book*," Deacon said as he pulled the door shut behind him. Then he texted Macy. *Coming over.*

All right, she texted right back. No hesitation.

He looked at his calendar. December 21. The winter equinox. He'd forgotten.

She had to walk out her front door and down the length of her piazza to open the door to the street. Deacon didn't know what he was going to say. He did know why he was there. He got the feeling she did too.

But maybe she didn't know that he was coming to sweep her off her feet and take her to bed. On the other hand, maybe she did.

But if not, he had no strategy. He felt at the mercy of the tides that pulled and pushed between them.

When she opened the street door, he saw she wore no makeup. Her lips were pale pink. Her eyelids, translucent. She was in gray pajamas with little gold pineapples all over them and a soft pink fuzzy bathrobe. She looked fresh and natural and gorgeous.

"I appreciate you seeing me." Deacon wondered why he sounded so stiff and formal. Not the best voice for seducing someone.

"Come in," she replied. She sounded formal too.

He'd done this a lot—he was single, after all—but he was in new territory somehow.

He'd go with it. He was where he wanted to be.

In fact, just walking in beside her was nice. He got to look at her bare feet padding across the cold wooden floor of the piazza. No toenail polish. And he smelled that flower smell in her hair.

She'd left the front door open, and when they crossed the threshold, she stopped in the foyer. He stopped too. Their eyes met and held.

"My family enjoyed talking to you tonight," she said.

He couldn't help but smile. "I enjoyed it too."

A late-night gull cawed from the Battery wall. And like a stealthy thief, a wall of cold, outdoor air intercepted the heat-baked air inside the house and swiftly moved up the stairs.

"You're not wearing slippers," he said.

"You're not wearing a coat."

He pushed the door shut behind him. And then he wrapped his arms around her fluffy robe, reveling in the weight of her body against his, and kissed her.

Sweet Jesus, did he kiss her!

It was the only thing—the *only* thing—that mattered. It was why he had come to Charleston. Even if he hadn't know it at the time.

This kiss.

With this woman.

She grabbed his hand and pulled. "Come on."

He had to walk slightly behind her up the narrow stairs. And then he was in her bedroom. It was just like he imagined it would be. Very feminine. But practical too, with shelves of books and a desk that looked well used, paper notecards with her monogram engraved up top stacked neatly on the surface, a pen nearby.

And there was Oscar on the bed.

He looked balefully up at Deacon.

"That's right," Macy said. "You've got to go."

Oscar didn't even need a push. He went, his tail slightly puffed up as he raced from the room.

"Sorry," Deacon murmured, and pulled a lock of her hair back from her face.

"Nothing to be sorry about." She smiled. "He had it coming. He's been terribly unsympathetic company."

"You need sympathy?"

"Not anymore."

They started slow. There was some talk. Some laughter. No rummaging for protection. She had some. He came prepared too. And before he knew it, Deacon was above her, both of them stripped naked and ready.

But he made her wait, with her legs wide open, her hands flung on her pillow, her hair swirled about her face. He went low. He took his time. He couldn't believe how lucky he was.

"Wow," she said on a long sigh when the arch of her back flattened again into the mattress.

"Yeah. Wow." She was so beautiful.

"And this is only the beginning." She pulled him on top of her.

It was amazing how they were together. The heat. The passion. The tenderness.

Not that Deacon would ever tell. No. It was between him and Macy. She enchanted him.

Their spent bodies were entwined.

"Do you have any mermaid blood?"

She laughed softly.

"You live on the harbor," he said, "a hundred feet from the water. You're gorgeous. Charming. Sexy. I've got this feeling you're going to slip away at a moment's notice"—he lifted her chin for a kiss—"and I might never see you again."

She rolled away from him and faced her bedside table and lamp.

He stroked her silky-smooth back. Admired the curve of her hip.

"I love the old legends," she murmured, "about the ladies of the sea bewitching sailors." She sounded so relaxed.

He felt relaxed around her, as if a big knot in his chest had untied. He kissed her between the shoulder blades. "Your wish is my command."

She laughed and rolled back to face him.

"You're ticklish," he said.

"Just a little."

She ran a languid hand over his chest, and he almost gave in to the temptation to close his eyes. But he'd rather look at her.

"So all I have to do is text?" she asked him. "And you'll come over?"

So fast he'd burn a trail up the stairs. And be naked by the time he reached the top step.

"You bet," is all he said. Had to be manly. Stoic.

"I like that." She smiled, and her eyes crinkled at the corners.

He wanted to anoint those corners with kisses. Run a fingertip down her nose. Part her lips just so with his own and taste her mouth again. "This is the winter equinox, by the way."

"You're right." She chuckled.

"It's a potent time." He waggled his eyebrows.

"Hopefully, not too potent," she said wryly.

He gazed into her eyes, today the color of the harbor.

"We'd better not waste it. We only have about twenty-three hours to go."

They made love one more time, slowly, tenderly, until the fierceness overcame them and the bedframe creaked and thumped, creaked and thumped, while they each made their own primal sounds that mingled into an erotic song. When it was over, he kissed her with everything he had in him. Well, almost everything. But more than he'd ever shown another woman. So that was saying something.

She pulled back. "This was awesome." Her eyes were warm. "And fun."

"It sure was."

It was her turn to push some hair from his forehead. "I'll see you soon. Okay?"

Ah. He was getting the boot. "Sounds good."

She blinked and sat up, and in a matter of a second, Macy the lover was gone. In her place was Macy the matchmaker.

"Deacon . . ." she started.

He stood, grabbed his boxer briefs and his pants from the floor. "Your timing is really bad."

"I know, but—"

"*Seriously* bad." He was panicked. He knew it, and it wasn't like him. "I already know what you're going to say, that this wasn't a good idea."

"It's not that black and white," she said as she watched him dress. Her rapt attention was flattering. "We were done with each other"—she smiled up at him, and he felt a flash of hope—"for good reason. It was a matter of trust lost. On both sides. I totally get why you were mad at me for ignoring your wishes. And I hope you understand where I was coming from, that I was only trying to do my job."

"I did understand. Yes."

"But this new sexual relationship between us makes things very complicated."

"It doesn't have to. It can be a new start."

"Okay. But if it is, we need to clear some things up. I know it might feel awkward to do that, especially because we just had so much fun—"

"You're stark naked." He ran his gaze over her breasts. "We definitely had fun."

She laughed and wrapped her arms around her knees. "So . . . this thing with Penelope."

"Yes?" The panic kept pushing at him. He wasn't sure what it was about. He didn't like Penelope that way—so it wasn't like he was hiding anything.

"You like her."

"Sure I do." He couldn't read her expression. "But we're just friends."

"I'm glad." She bit her lip.

"What's on your mind?"

"So, what about us then? Is the only thing between us sexual attraction?"

Thunk. So they were there, at the point of no return. He didn't know what to say. When he looked inside himself, everything was quiet, dark, slumbering. "I never said that."

There. That should be enough.

"Then what exactly *is* between us?"

It scared him to see her look so earnestly at him. "We're friends, aren't we? Really good friends." The panic kept pushing.

"Yes," she said. "We *are* good friends."

He relaxed a little more. "And hell, there is the sex."

"True." She shot him a sweet smile.

His panic receded. He was doing well. "And I like you a lot," he added.

"I already know that."

Maybe he wasn't doing so well. "Yeah, but I think about you when you're not there."

"That's nice," she said. *He* thought so. "Is that all?"

The point of no return again. They were back. He made an instantaneous decision. "That's pretty terrific, don't you think?"

She leapt up, picked up the pink fluffy robe from an armchair, and quickly donned it. "Since that's about all that's between us, maybe I should find you some more dates before you leave. I can't be the only woman in town willing to hang out with you until you leave."

"No. Don't be ridiculous."

"Hah." She swept past him and down the stairs. "Sleeping with you was a mistake. But you can bet it won't happen again."

He hated to see her so upset—his heart knocked against his chest wall in a way he hadn't felt since he was a kid—but he followed at a leisurely pace. He sensed an imminent throw-out. It had happened to him plenty times before—because he was a "cad," a term his aunt was fond of. Why shouldn't Macy hate him? She'd asked what she meant to him—and he'd given her nothing.

But it was better to piss off a woman than be a fool and give her his heart on a platter. That was his motto, and he was sticking to it. It had worked for him up until now . . . and he didn't have a replacement plan.

She'd already thrown open the door. "Go hang out with Penelope."

"Don't bring *her* into this."

"Why not?"

"She's an innocent bystander. Are you jealous of her?" He hoped she was jealous. He really did.

"Oh, please." Her eyes filled. "Why are you doing this? You're being plain *mean*."

He paused before he crossed the threshold onto the piazza. "I'm not trying to be. I honestly want to know. Is there something about Penelope that rankles? As your client—"

"Former client."

"Fine, as your *neighbor*—"

"Not really. Fran is my new neighbor." Her face was pale. Something more than anger was going on.

What was it?

"As your friend, then," he said gently, "and your most recent lover, could you please share with me if there's something about Penelope that bothers you?"

She stood still, her face a picture of hurt, and stared unblinking at his upper chest. "Why do you care?"

He took his time, despite the freezing air swirling around them. "I won't see her again if you don't want me to."

He meant it. But he couldn't say more. He simply couldn't. He wasn't sure what that "more" was. It was lodged somewhere in his chest. Deep. And he liked keeping it there, in the place where he didn't have to feel it.

All the fight seemed to go out of her. "No," she said quietly. "Keep seeing Penelope. She's a good person. A *very* good person. You couldn't date a finer woman. That's not only my professional opinion, it's my personal one."

His heart sank. He walked out the door onto the piazza and turned back around. "I'm sorry I let you down again."

"Apology accepted," she said in a thin voice. She even tried to smile, but she couldn't quite manage it.

He put his hands in his pockets. "See you around."

"Okay." She shut the door gently. Polite to the end.

Because it was most certainly the end.

Not that he thought he'd been starting something with her. He lived in the moment. They'd had a short Christmas fling while he was on vacation.

And now it was over.

CHAPTER TWENTY-NINE

Macy wasn't going to think about her feelings for Deacon, their even deeper rift, or the fact that she'd seen him at an oyster roast in the country with Penelope and then again at a big holiday party at Mrs. Beauchamp's house. She'd acknowledged them both with a polite greeting but never lingered long enough to carry on a conversation.

"How are you?" Greer asked her after they'd hung the last streamer from the ceiling of the Green Room. The Toys for Tots party was the following day.

"Fine," Macy said. She was now officially unassigned from Deacon's file, which was labeled inactive. They didn't expect him back at Two Love Lane, but if he decided to ask for any advice at all, Greer was his new point of contact.

Macy and Deacon were beyond done. He'd been a holiday fling, a fun guy with a great personality who was gorgeous and amazing in bed.

What more could a girl ask for in a fling?

She couldn't expect commitment. Nor could she expect the man to guess that they were made for each other. Good sex made one tend to forget everything but the present moment.

But the present moment is everything, a voice in her head said.

What she felt in the present moment with Deacon was all she needed to know that he was The One for her.

Too bad he hadn't seen it too.

"Maybe Penelope's a distraction until Deacon goes back to New York," said Miss Thing.

"Or maybe she's his soulmate." As a matchmaker, Macy should be happy that one of her former clients might be making a romantic connection.

But she wasn't. She was depressed.

"Remember, we tell our clients they have to stand up for love," Ella said.

"They have to claim it," Miss Thing added.

"I remember." Macy gave a feeble shrug. She didn't care how mopey she looked. She *was* mopey. "But I don't know that I want to take that risk. I practically begged him to tell me why he kept pursuing me, and he said we were friends. And he really liked me. And the sex was good. End of story."

All of them exchanged gloomy glances.

"At least the sex—" Miss Thing started to say, but at the looks Ella, Macy, and Greer threw her, she thought better of it.

There was a knock on the Green Room door. It was Louisa.

"Come on in." Macy was always glad to see her.

Louisa burst into the room, completely changing the energy. "Howdy, everyone!"

They returned her greeting just as warmly, although inside Macy knew they were only putting on a good act.

Louisa gazed around at the festive scene. "This looks terrific."

"Thank you." Miss Thing blew her a kiss.

"My, oh, my . . ." Louisa kept looking. And looking. At the same old decorations they used every year.

Macy began to wonder why she was there.

"Can we help you with something, Louisa?" Ella finally asked.

Their visitor swung around to face Macy—a little dramatically, Macy thought. But Louisa was always dramatic. So Macy wasn't particularly worried, although in the back of her mind, she still felt guilty about what she and Deacon had done in Louisa's bedroom.

"I have to ask you something, Macy." Louisa's eyes narrowed the slightest bit.

A smidgeon of alarm arose in Macy's breast. "Go ahead." She adjusted all the Christmas cards on the mantel. Surely, she looked breezy and innocent.

Louisa held up a business card. "Did you leave this in my bedroom? When you went to look at my flatiron that night I skipped out on Yo-Yo Ma? The night I was supposed to be on a date with Deacon Banks?"

Macy instantly recognized the logo as Deacon's company, and her pulse picked up, sounding like a drum in her ears. The card must have fallen out of Deacon's wallet when he'd looked for a condom.

"Macy?"

Macy took the card. "It belongs to Deacon."

"I'm aware of that," Louisa said. "But I sure as hell didn't think *he'd* have any reason to be in my house."

Macy's mind was spinning. What should she say? "It must have fallen out of my purse."

That was lame, and she knew it. But she wasn't good at sneaking around, not to mention lying, except maybe to herself.

Louisa looked at her oddly. "Why, pray tell, would I have found this card under my bureau?"

Macy couldn't help a nervous laugh. "I was nosy. I

peeked in your room and saw those three tricycles. They were so cute."

Louisa smiled. "They are. But you haven't explained why you'd be opening your purse in my room."

"To answer a call." Macy's voice came out as a squeak.

Her colleagues were silent. She could hear people laughing up at Roastbusters. Another Christmas carol played, and it just didn't seem right to hear it, not when there was so much stress in the room.

Louisa's expression was almost sad. "Why do I think you might be lying to me? Aren't we friends?"

"Yes, of course." Macy sat down on a chair and put her head in her hands. "I *am* lying, Louisa." She looked up. "I took Deacon with me. To the house. He knew I was worried about you ditching him with so little explanation, and he probably felt guilty. That's the truth."

Louisa didn't blink. "But he was upstairs, why?"

"Because I saw the tricycles. I thought they were adorable. So I called him upstairs to see them. I'm so sorry we invaded your privacy. I thought you wouldn't mind since we're friends."

Louisa still didn't look happy. "I don't mind. We *are* friends. But it's still . . . weird that his card wound up under my bureau. Did you really have a phone call?"

Macy had to own her feelings. All of them. The bad ones about her family that she'd ignored for so long. The good feelings about Deacon. She had to be *honest*. She'd always felt the most at peace when she stuck with the truth. It had been a long time since she had.

Silently, she told her nerves to take a hike.

"The truth is," she said to Louisa, "everything started off innocently enough. But Deacon and I got into a conversation. A very deep one that those tricycles inspired. And we—"

She couldn't go on.

"Don't tell me y'all had sex on my bed." Louisa drew back as if a tiger were about to pounce on her.

Macy shook her head. "On the floor."

Louisa's face paled beneath her discreet spray tan. "And this happened the night you'd set him up with *me*?"

Macy nodded slowly. "I know. I was extremely unprofessional. I'm really sorry. I don't deserve your trust."

Her colleagues gathered around them both.

Louisa laughed. She laughed until she cried. She had to sit on the floor, she was so weak from it.

No one else said a word. Macy tried. She wracked her brain. But all she could think to say, she already had.

"Oh, Lord." Louisa looked up at them. "If this doesn't beat all. Our plan not only worked—it went way beyond anything I'd ever envisioned. You two got down and dirty in *my* bedroom! You in a long gown and Deacon in a tux!"

Macy fingered her signet ring. "I'm truly sorry, Louisa. I never meant to sleep with Deacon that night, much less fall in love with him." Tears pricked her lids and a sob choked her throat, but she refused to cry. She didn't want Louisa or any of her other friends to think she was making a bid for sympathy. "I deserve your censure, and if you don't want to remain friends, I understand."

Louisa waved a hand at her. "Oh, shush. I'm more annoyed with myself than you."

"You shouldn't be," Macy said. "What about? Surely not the flat iron. Everyone leaves those on by accident— or think they do."

Louisa laughed. "I'm not mad about the flat iron. I'm annoyed because I did something really dumb. And selfish."

What? What had she done? Macy was dying to know. So, apparently, were Ella, Greer, and Miss Thing. Their mouths were frozen halfway open.

"Wh-What did you do, Louisa?" Macy asked.

Her friend released a gusty sigh. "I told you I had a

crush on an unavailable guy. Remember? At the mayor's party."

"Yes." Macy remembered the conversation well.

Louisa exhaled a breath. "I never planned on telling a soul who that guy is. But I think I will today. It's Celia's husband Walter, of all people. I've been in love with him for years."

"Are you kidding me?" cried Miss Thing.

Macy wanted to express a similar sentiment but held back. So did Greer and Ella.

"I'm not kidding." Louisa made one of her comic faces. "It's so ridiculous! He's not even fun. Or great-looking. He's just super smart, and he turns me on like no one else I've ever met."

Miss Thing loved being let in on delicious secrets. "We can't understand how or why Cupid strikes," she soothed Louisa, "so give yourself a break."

"What Miss Thing said." Macy's temple pounding with stress. This was all so strange.

Louisa shook her head. "I set up a stupid plan. I knew Celia was infatuated with Deacon. So when Penelope asked me if I'd be willing to help Deacon win you over and I found out his plans for that night, I was like, I can use this to my advantage! While you two were with Celia at the concert, I'd make a play for Walter. He was in Myrtle Beach at a medical convention. I knew where he was staying and everything. So I went up there. I lied to you when you called to check on me. I didn't meet up with an old friend who'd come to town. I headed to Myrtle Beach."

"You did?"

"Yes. And I didn't feel guilty because I was doing Deacon this really nice favor. Like the bad would be canceled out by the good." She snorted. "That was dumb logic. But I was horny for Walter. Madly in love too. You know how that goes."

"Yes, I do," said Macy. "I'm not gonna lie." She was reeling from Louisa's revelation, but she'd be a hypocrite if she acted too shocked. What people did for love wasn't always right or smart, but often they did it anyway.

"You were so funny on the phone," Louisa said, "how worried you were about me!"

Macy remembered how close Deacon had stood to her on Louisa's front doorstep. "I felt like something wasn't right."

"Your gut was on target," Louisa said.

"I honestly thought Celia had somehow intimidated you into not coming to Yo-Yo Ma, so she could be with Deacon and sabotage my matchmaking plans at the same time."

Louisa laughed. "Really? Poor Celia."

"I know," said Macy. "I'm ashamed of myself."

"Well, if she weren't all over Deacon, then you never would have jumped to that conclusion," said Greer.

"What ever happened with Walter?" Ella asked.

"He was completely uninterested," Louisa said. "I don't think he even understood what I was trying to do—seduce his ass. Meanwhile, I still held out hope that Celia would somehow move in on Deacon eventually. She's Fran Banks' social consultant. She's at her condo a lot."

"She does drop in," Macy said. "But I get the feeling Deacon's not exactly fond of her."

Louisa chuckled. "How many people really are?"

No one said a word. It seemed kinder not to.

"Can you forgive me, Louisa, for my professional and personal lapse—sleeping with a client in your bedroom?" Macy asked.

Louisa looked sheepish. "I felt a little guilty worrying you like that at the concert. But karma's a bitch. Look what happened when I tried to do something sneaky. Two people going at it on my bedroom floor, and I'm not even one of them."

"Oh, Louisa!" Macy laughed and got down on the floor. "You're so funny. Your time will come, I know it."

Louisa threw her arm around her shoulder. "I thought Walter Waterford was destined to be mine if I wanted him enough. But clearly he's not. I think he really does love Celia, even though she doesn't appreciate him."

They gave each other a long hug.

"Let's celebrate what we do have," Macy said. "Good friends are important."

"Cheers to that," said Louisa.

After six bottles of champagne and lots of dancing to their favorite songs in the Green Room, the five of them were feeling pretty good.

"To friendship," Miss Thing said for the umpteenth time, and took a large swallow from her vintage champagne saucer glass. "This is *sho* much better than a flute. You have to pinch your mouth up like a guppy to get anything from one of those. But this saucer glass"—she demonstrated by taking another large swallow—"ish perfect."

They all laughed.

"Good thing no one has to drive home." Ella threw her arm around Miss Thing.

Home.

Now every time Macy walked into her bedroom, she'd think of Deacon being there. She'd remember how whole she felt when they were making love, how happy she'd been.

She started crying. Big buckets of tears. "I'm s-sad," she managed to say, "about Deacon."

"Oh, baby!" all of them said at once. Or words to that effect. And hugged her close.

"I understand why things don't work out sometimes." Macy hiccupped and gulped. "Honestly, I do. But I think I might have ruined everything. I-I've always been scared to fall in love. But I never told you why."

So she did. She told them about walking into her den one day after school, when her father and mother were usually at work and she was usually at piano lessons or tennis, and seeing her father kissing Celia's mother. Both of them were only half-dressed. Neither one of them saw her.

"They were too . . . well, you know, *involved*," said Macy. Miss Thing handed her a tissue, and she wiped her eyes.

Ella patted her back. "How awful for you. And you've been holding it in all these years?"

"I never told anyone but my sister," Macy said, "and she said we should keep it a secret. Somehow Mom figured it out, though, and she and Dad fixed things. But that year . . . I remember I couldn't breathe. Now I know it's because I was so stressed and scared."

Macy was never good with drinking a lot. And her tears had been buried too long. If they were going to come out, along with that long-held secret, she was really glad they did with these women.

Ten minutes later, in the mirror, her face was beet red and her eyes were swollen. "How am I going to be able to act as a hostess at the Toys for Tots party in the morning?"

"The schwelling will go down," said Miss Thing, who got too close to her face to observe it. "Ish bad right now."

"Great." Macy sighed.

"Don't listen to Miss Thing," Ella said. "You can put cucumbers or tea bags on your eyes before the party if you need to. I've got some really awesome herbal tea bags in my office. Let's put a couple on right now."

Everyone followed her. She turned on the light in her office and went rummaging through her desk.

"What's this?" Miss Thing was at one of Ella's bookcases. A beautiful coffee table book of Charleston was displayed, front cover out.

"Oh, I got that from a client for Christmas," Ella said. "It's lovely."

Miss Thing picked it up. And then she promptly dropped it on the floor.

In the rush to pick it up, Greer and Miss Thing bumped heads.

"Ouch," they both said at once.

Miss Thing rubbed her scalp. Greer sat in Ella's chair. The chair rolled gently backward and landed with a thud against the wall. Greer chuckled and spun it around with her feet. Then she pushed against the baseboard to get the chair back to its original position at the desk.

While she was rolling back, the baseboard swung open about two inches.

"You kicked it too hard," said Louisa.

But Macy had a feeling. Her heart started racing. "Ella—"

"Oh my God." Ella put her hand to her heart. "Something precious," she whispered.

Sure enough, her nonna had been right. A treasure, they soon found, was hidden behind that baseboard. There was a fresh round of tears, happy ones. This time even Louisa cried. She was enthralled by the whole story.

"Before we all leave tonight, let's run up the street to Roastbusters to celebrate," said Greer. "Peppermint cocoa for everyone. My treat. Macy, we'll hide you in the corner with your extra puffy eyes and bring you yours."

"You'd better hide me too," said Miss Thing. "I'm shit-faced. But I'm glad I dropped that book."

Everyone laughed. Miss Thing was quite ridiculous, and they loved that about her.

"Andy knows just how to make my cocoa," Macy said.

And he did. He made it perfectly, with the cherry on top. Everyone razzed Macy about it. But not Andy. He only winked. She felt very loved when she walked home that night—very loved and very excited.

The treasure . . . the precious treasure. It had been found!

CHAPTER THIRTY

"Get up!" Aunt Fran pushed on Deacon's shoulder. "Time for the Toys for Tots party."

He groaned. "It's too early."

"It's noon, kid. Rise and shine." Aunt Fran was too perky for her own good now that she and the colonel were an item.

The colonel called her Frannie.

She called him Freddie.

Deacon wanted to gag. Love was a pain in the ass. And he really wanted to get back to New York to forget that fact.

Also, Christmas sucked. Didn't everyone know?

"George? Can you help me, please?" Aunt Fran's voice was more shrill than usual.

"I'll be right there," George called. "Gareth has particularly bad body odor today. He found a dead squirrel and rolled all over it in the park. Let me put him right under Deacon's nose. That'll get him moving."

Deacon groaned. "I hate you all."

"That's fine," Aunt Fran replied mildly. "As long as you get your ass out of bed and you're ready to roll in thirty minutes. Did you buy a present for a deserving child?"

"Yes. I bought a bunch of bikes for teenagers."

"That's a shock," said Aunt Fran. "You've been sulky and uncooperative, I assumed you hadn't done anything, so I used the money I was going to put toward your Christmas suit to buy a few sets of mini Bluetooth speakers."

Deacon's head hurt. That was all he cared about. "I didn't want a new suit anyway."

"Good," Aunt Fran said. "You're acting childish. You've only been given a million blessings and don't seem to appreciate them."

"Stop with the badgering. I'm not on your show." He sat up and winced.

"That's right. You're not." She sat next to him and put her hand on his back. "You're not someone I say hi and bye to. You're my nephew. I love you more than anyone on the planet. And I know you have great things inside you."

He shook his head. "I'm ordinary, Aunt Fran. I'm not like you—someone everyone relates to. You've got a special quality—"

"That *you* have too. And don't you dare squander it." She stood. "You don't have to be on TV to do amazing things. Nor do you have to work yourself to the bone at your job to prove you're a captain of the tech industry. Why don't you try to relax? Like you have this month? And get to know yourself better? Cut your workload in half. You'll still make plenty of money."

"I'll think about it."

"Your father—"

"Don't talk about him." Deacon put his head in his hands.

She threw open the curtains, and a shaft of sunlight pierced him between the eyes. "Your father," she insisted on saying, "valued every second of his life with your mother."

"Please," Deacon said, "don't make me feel guilty."

Aunt Fran stomped her foot. "You think I'm worried about *you*? *I* feel guilty! Here I've brought up my brother's son, and I must have done a piss-poor job because you love a certain woman very dear to me too, and you don't have the balls to tell her so, for reasons I cannot fathom. Son, you're a Banks. And Banks don't run."

Deacon shifted. The bedsprings creaked under his weight. "Did I just hear you tell me I have no balls?"

"I don't know. Did you?"

"Hey." He cast a bleary eye in her direction. "That's not nice."

"Well, you haven't been nice yourself."

"And you're wrong, you know. About Macy. I don't love her. I *like* her. A lot."

"Is that so?" Aunt Fran pierced him with a knowing look. "I'm glad your heart's not involved. Because any day now some brilliant, sensitive man is going to recognize he can't live without her. And he's going to sweep her off her feet while you're flirting with sweet young girls half your age. What a shame."

George was in the room now. He looked upset. Angry. Concerned. All the emotions people feel when someone they love is screwing up their lives without any help from anyone else.

Deacon stood, ignoring the nausea in his belly and his crashing headache, all self-induced from slamming too many beers the night before. As he put his hands on his aunt's shoulders, he could feel those frail bones of hers trembling.

That broke his heart.

"Coming to Charleston," he said, "has made me realize there are things I need to face, and things I'm missing out on. I'm not going to run anymore. I promise. I always felt safer that way. But I'm learning that safe is dull."

"Ain't that the truth." His aunt had some of her perkiness back, but there was still an edge of seriousness in her tone. "I know that sometimes I rush through life too fast too. No one likes to stop and feel the hard parts, you know? But we need to. They're worse when we avoid them. And eventually, they catch up with us." She paused. "I know you've always had a big hole in your life."

He wouldn't deny it.

"And you feel guilty because sometimes you wonder what life would have been like with your parents," she said softly.

Deacon raked a hand through his hair. "I *have* wondered that. And I *do* feel guilty sometimes. But if someone told me I could choose another life—a different path—I'd say no. I love my life exactly the way it is. And I have you to thank for it." He took a deep, cleansing breath. "You've been the greatest aunt in the world. And you've taught me all the right things. I'm sorry for how I've been acting. I love you." He hugged her close.

He looked over at George, who had a tear rolling down his cheek.

"I love you too," Aunt Fran said into Deacon's chest. "I can't breathe, but I do."

He managed a chuckle and let her go. She laughed.

"I need a tissue." George whimpered quite convincingly as he left the room.

Deacon gathered his resolve. "I have a couple of plans I've been thinking about, and I'm done with thinking. I'm ready to *do* something about them."

When he had told his aunt all the details, she patted his cheek. "A little tough love can wreak miracles. It worked on me too, when you forced me out of bed to see the colonel."

"George is next," Deacon said.

They both turned. There he was in the doorway.

"When hell freezes over," George replied serenely. His tears were gone. "Chop-chop!" He clapped his hands together twice. "It's time for a Toys for Tots party. And a lot else, apparently."

CHAPTER THIRTY-ONE

When the three young Marines showed up at Two Love Lane—two men and one woman—to oversee the collection of the toys they would gather that morning, Macy's heart filled with pride. Their community *cared*. And it was made up of awesome individuals like these military heroes and all the people of Charleston who'd brought an unwrapped gift to share with a child or a teen.

The colonel was Santa, and as usual, he did a fantastic job putting kids on his lap and asking them their wildest Christmas desires. Fran was so besotted, she handed out cookies to the children when they finished detailing their Christmas lists to the colonel.

Andy from Roastbusters sang "O Holy Night" in his beautiful tenor voice. And then the children's choir from a local elementary school sang a merry assortment of Christmas carols.

George brought all the Corgis, each one sporting reindeer antlers, and took pictures for anyone who wanted to pose with them. Bubbles snarled at only one person—Celia—because he remembered the night she came over and called him fat.

At least that was George's explanation to Celia, who listened patiently.

Macy realized she owed Celia an apology. A big one.

When the last Christmas carol had been sung and all the toys were piled high, ready to be put in a truck for delivery to the main Toys for Tots station, she took Celia by the elbow. "I need to say I'm sorry. The night of Yo-Yo Ma, I thought you'd sabotaged Louisa's date with Deacon."

Celia made a typical Celia face—half-shocked, half-disgusted. "I wondered why you were being so catty after the performance."

Macy felt terrible. "It was wrong of me. Please forgive me. I should never, ever have assumed you were involved."

Celia shifted uneasily. "That's okay. . . . I guess."

Macy decided to take the plunge. "How are things with Walter?"

"Fine." Celia snorted. "Aren't you being a little nosy?"

"Yes." Macy admitted. "I just hope—"

"You hope what?"

"I wasn't able to help you with one of your relationships," Macy said in a rush, "but I hope by telling you this, I can maybe help you save this one."

"*What?*" Celia's mouth gaped.

Macy blew a piece of hair out of her eye. The Santa hat she was wearing had fallen too low. "That sounded really bad. Let me finish. Please."

Celia crossed one arm over the other. "Go on." Her reluctance meter was obviously on high.

Macy prayed she'd do this right. "I know someone who had a huge crush on your husband. She's extremely attractive and smart. And a great person. She actually made a play for him that night."

"The night we went to see Yo-Yo Ma?"

Macy nodded.

"But Walt was at a medical conference," Celia said defensively.

"I know." Macy felt her anguish. "This woman went there."

Celia's eyes widened. "To Myrtle Beach?"

"Yes." Macy bit her lip. "She said I could tell you her name, because she's no longer crazy about your husband. She sees that he loves you. He totally blew her off in Myrtle Beach."

Celia's face paled. "It went that far?"

"He never even figured it out," Macy said. "If he did, he played dumb to avoid any awkwardness. If you love him, maybe this is a good time to show him."

Celia's eyes narrowed. "Who is she?"

"Louisa."

Celia nearly choked. "No. She—she could have anyone she wants. She's pretty, and funny, and Walt is so serious—" She sniffed. "I'm never going to speak to her again." She said it as if she meant it.

Macy needed to be blunt. "You might as well get over it. We're going to have to see each other for the next fifty years, if we're lucky. And Louisa said she never would have done it if you hadn't acted so besotted with Deacon and uninterested in Walter."

Celia gasped.

"Besides," Macy forged on, "she likes someone else now. So you dodged a bullet."

Tears formed in Celia's eyes.

Macy laid a hand on her arm. "Don't forget—friends and neighbors for the next fifty years. And hate causes wrinkles. The important thing is, do you love Walter?"

"Hell yes, I do!"

"Well, go get him. But leave us your unwrapped gift

first, and stop flirting with Deacon. Okay? I love him, and it pisses me off."

"All right." Celia softened her glare just a tad. "And thank you, Macy. For the apology and for telling me this other story. I know I've been unfair to you."

"Can we start over?" Macy couldn't believe she was asking that question. Was she in an alternative universe? Or had she just become a real adult, perhaps?

"How so?" Celia asked.

"We've both been hurt by what happened when we were kids. You know what I'm talking about, right?"

Celia sighed. "Yes."

"We had nothing to do with it."

"Yeah." Celia looked away.

"I'm sorry if my dad hurt your mom."

Celia looked up at the sky. "I'm sorry my mom interfered with your parents' relationship." She looked back at Macy. "She was lonely. Still is." She hesitated. "But it's her fault. She's a real bitch."

Macy gave a little laugh. "I know I shouldn't laugh, it's sad. But—"

"It's funny," said Celia. "She never learns, and I just keep telling her she needs to lighten up." Her mouth drooped. "I'm no good at that either."

"Keep coming over to Fran's house," Macy said. "And mine. We'll help you lighten up. Your mother too. I'd love to see her."

Celia looked doubtful. "You're a good egg, Macy."

"Thanks." Macy chuckled. "Let's give each other a real hug, not the fake social kind."

So they did. And it was nice, even though Celia told Macy she didn't like the smell of her shampoo and thought she should switch brands. "Good luck with Deacon," she added. "Does he know you love him?"

"No."

"Why isn't he here?"

Macy's heart felt like it was in a million pieces. "I don't know."

Celia shot her a look of actual sympathy. "Well, I'll hope for the best."

"And I'll hope the same for you." Macy smiled at her.

Celia smiled back.

And Macy knew she'd made a new friend. A *real* friend. Her life was so weird. And wonderful!

Except for the romance part.

That was terrible. Worse than waking up on Christmas morning to a piece of coal in your stocking. Far worse.

Half an hour later, it was time to make the surprise announcement, before everyone left. Macy was genuinely happy to see Penelope Gordon show up in time.

"Have you seen Deacon?" Penelope wore a beautiful cashmere blue scarf that matched her eyes.

Macy shook her head. "Sorry." And she was. Sorrier than anyone would ever know, except Oscar. She told Oscar everything.

"Listen." Penelope stalled a second. "Um, maybe I shouldn't bring this up. But you're aware that Deacon and I are only friends."

"Yes."

"But you also know we've been seeing each other a lot lately. And you might have thought we'd ramped things up."

"I did wonder, yes."

"Well, I honestly hoped we would. I'm sorry, Macy. I hope you forgive me—"

"It's okay. I understand completely."

"But it didn't work. I made a play for him, and . . . he's

not interested. He apologized for leading me on, and I said, no, he never did. It was a mess, but we're fine now. Still friends."

"I'm glad." And she was.

Penelope shrugged. "It's so apparent he has you on his mind. He tried very hard not to show that with me. But it was impossible not to see it."

Macy was at a loss for words.

Penelope gave a little laugh. "I just want to assure you—he never even kissed me good night beyond a peck on the cheek." Her expression softened. "The truth is, it's always nice to make a new friend—a true friend—and that's what he is to me now."

"Real friends are hard to come by," Macy said as she took her hand. "You okay?"

Penelope nodded. "Thanks."

"I have to be honest," Macy said. "I was worried. I love Deacon. And I want to be with him. But he doesn't seem to think of me as anything more than a good friend. Falling in love is a real hassle. I thought it would be easy peasy."

"When it comes, you have to go for it," Penelope said with a wistful smile. "I hope it works out for you two, Macy. I really do. Meanwhile, I've got some news about Deacon's ancestry. Is this a good time to share it?"

"Sure." It didn't seem possible that a New Yorker like Deacon would have connections in Charleston, but that was silly. Of course he could.

"There's a report in the old city records that a traveling craftsman stopped here for three months in 1779. His name was Shepard Banks. We don't know what he did, exactly. But he was paid very well for his services by a family on Love Lane."

"Shepard Banks?" Macy actually felt lightheaded at the news. "This is the only house on Love Lane, of course, so he must have worked here. Penelope, I think you've provided the missing detail—an amazing, awesome missing detail. Thank you."

"What? What missing detail?"

"You'll find out in a minute." Macy squeezed her hand. She wanted Ella to speak so badly!

"You look really excited." Penelope's voice was a mere squeak.

"Sorry if I'm making you nervous," Macy said. "You'll be excited, I promise. Just a few more seconds, and you'll see."

"I'll hold out," Penelope agreed. "But when I told Deacon about Shepard Banks, he had no reaction. It dumbfounded me. And so I asked him about it, and he confessed that he was very unhappy."

"He did?" Macy hated hearing that. Suddenly, she didn't care about Penelope's research and Ella's forthcoming speech. All she cared about was Deacon. He was everything. It was probably stupid of her, but he was. She couldn't be happy if he wasn't happy.

Penelope sighed. "He told me it always seems that just when he starts to belong somewhere, he feels the compulsion to move on. He's going back to New York. So Macy, you have to move fast. No time to lose. Get that man to stay. I think he might leave the day after Christmas."

"I need to be honest with him," Macy said, panicking at the idea of him leaving so soon. "I need to tell him how I feel. Even if he does think of me just as a friend."

"Of course you should tell him," Penelope said stoutly. "And I know he has feelings for you. Just remember—matchmakers need to take care of themselves too, not just other people. Cupid's also after you."

"I will." Macy hugged her friend long and hard. "We need to go to lunch. Or have a spend-the-night party at my house, just the two of us. Wait—Celia too."

Penelope raised a brow. "Celia?"

"She could use some fun friends," Macy whispered. "We'll dance, watch a movie, and have a decadent dinner and dessert."

"I'd love that."

They stood shoulder-to-shoulder when Ella took to the small stage the colonel had set up for them. Her petite self was absolutely adorable and sexy. She wore a body-hugging red dress that stopped at the top of her toned thighs, a cropped black leather jacket over it, playful snow-flake tights, and cool black ankle boots. Of course, she wore the requisite Santa hat too.

As usual, when she got on a stage, she sparkled. She was like Fran that way, a born performer. Everyone knew her from the many plays she'd starred in at the Dock Street Theatre, so there were lots of whistles and applause. She smiled broadly and waited for the crowd to settle down.

Finally, she found her moment. "Something special happened yesterday at Two Love Lane," she said loud enough for the people in the back of the crowd to hear, "so let me get right to it. You know how they say truth is stranger than fiction?"

"Yes!" the crowd roared.

Macy blew her a kiss, and Ella winked back.

"Well, guess what," Ella said, a little swagger in her tone. "We found a hidden compartment in my office, and behind it was this sheaf of papers." She held a few yellowed scraps high in the air.

The crowd reacted with stomps and whistles.

"They appear to be part of a journal," Ella said. She was doing a great job getting the crowd excited, and Macy could tell she was having fun. "A journal that belonged to a young woman named Miranda Langford, who used to live here." She paused and her expression grew serious. "You're never gonna guess how old it is."

"How old?" cried the partygoers.

"It dates all the way back to the Revolutionary War," Ella said.

The crowd went even crazier.

"You're right to be excited." Ella beamed and held the papers aloft again. "This document is part of Charleston's history."

Penelope laid her hand on Macy's arm. "Is this for real?"

Macy laughed. "Yes. Listen closely. Your historian's heart will love this. I think it relates to your information about Shepard Banks."

"I'm listening all right." Penelope tightened her grip on Macy's arm.

The clapping and noise eventually subsided.

"Apparently," Ella said, "these pages were ripped out of the journal so no one would ever find them. We're guessing Miranda didn't burn them because they meant a great deal to her. They tell a fascinating love story."

A master craftsman, Ella explained, had come to Two Love Lane to forge its iron gate. In her journal, Miranda never let on who this man was beyond using his initials, SB. But according to her, they were madly in love. Sadly, he wasn't considered a worthy suitor. But he left behind a loving, lasting token of his love for Miranda. His initials were in the design of the gate, entwined with hers.

As one, everyone turned toward the piece of art that served as a gate.

"You can see those initials if you look closely," Ella said. "The most obvious design is the two interlocking hearts, which Miranda's father approved. He meant those to represent his own love for his deceased wife. The craftsman—SB—satisfied that wish but managed to add his own secret romantic message to Miranda as well. It's near the bottom, below the interlocking hearts."

Greer stood at the gate, practically bursting with excitement. Slowly, she ran her finger over the nearly hidden initials SB and ML to point them out to the crowd.

"Wow," said Penelope. "I see it! SB and ML . . . SB *has* to stand for Shepard Banks."

"I think so too." Macy couldn't help but be ebullient at the discovery. "But can we really be sure this Shepard Banks was Deacon's relative?"

"No," said Miranda. "But Deacon can continue the research, especially now that he has a solid name to go on."

"Honestly, I think Shepard Banks *is* Deacon's ancestor," Macy said. "I feel it in my gut. Why else would his grandfather have held onto that family fact—that a Banks had lived in Charleston? This was a Banks to be proud of, a master craftsman. The details might have been lost over the generations, but look at Deacon's family. They're all artistic in one way or another."

"I wouldn't be a bit surprised, now that I know Deacon." Penelope flipped her scarf over her shoulder as if she were an explorer about to embark on a big adventure. "The Historical Society will be anxious to get their hands on Miranda's papers. They're a priceless treasure. What a story to add to our collection."

Macy smiled. *Priceless treasure.* Just like Ella's nonna had said. "It makes Two Love Lane all the more special." Her heart brimmed with pride. And she was so happy for Deacon.

He had roots here. At least a very strong likelihood. That was a wonderful thing. Plus, his family connection might be directly related to Two Love Lane's history. *That* was something extra special, and Macy had goose bumps just thinking about it.

While everyone clapped, Macy looked over to where the colonel had sat with the children to ask them what they wanted for Christmas—and saw Santa sitting there *again*.

It was a different Santa this time. And when their gazes met, he stood with a bag on his shoulder and made his way to the stage. Macy had no idea what was happening. But she knew who this Santa was by his eyes—and his confident gait.

Deacon.

She had a massive flock of butterflies in her middle. And a buzzing in her ears. She felt alive—raw and exposed. But she also felt real and full—and bright.

A crazy thought went through her, that she was like a Christmas star shining in the night. Suspended. Alone. But looking smack dab at love.

Celebrating love.

The colonel made eye contact with her, grinned, and shrugged. Fran smiled broadly and clapped like mad, her eyes glued on her special Santa nephew.

The new Santa made the universal sign to encourage the clapping to continue, raising both his arms repeatedly, and the applause went on as he kissed Ella's cheek and exchanged places with her. Then he put up one hand to still the crowd, and instant silence reigned.

"Ho Ho Ho," he said first, in an awesome New York–style Santa voice that made Macy giggle. "Merry Christmas!"

"Merry Christmas!" the audience shouted back.

His gaze met Macy's. He grinned, and her stomach did another huge flip-flop.

Love, love, love!

She was sick with it. The smile she shot him was wobbly and full of tears and laughter and a need to hold him tight and just *be*.

With him.

But all that was on hold. Deacon cleared his throat

importantly, the way Santa might. "I want to tell you all about a young lady I know," he said, "a modern Miranda Langford, if you will. She belongs to this house. And I love her dearly. Macy Frost, can you come up here, please?"

Everyone clapped madly.

Without hesitation, she went. And as soon as she got up there, she kissed Santa for all she was worth.

That really brought the house down. Santa was forced to ask everyone to be quiet so he could continue. "I have a present for you, Macy."

"Yes, Santa?" Her heart was already full.

He took a small, square box from the bag, got down on one knee, and opened it. A beautiful diamond-and-emerald ring sat nestled in blue velvet. He paused a beat, then said, "Macy, my love, will you marry me?"

A child in the audience yelled for everyone to hear. "Mom! I thought Santa was already married!"

"Mrs. Claus wants me to ask her every year," Deacon ad-libbed. "Isn't she lovely?"

He squeezed Macy's hand tighter.

She laughed.

"Mrs. Claus lives in *Charleston*?" another child asked.

"Santa and I have a second home here," Macy explained.

"Ohhhh," several children exclaimed.

Deacon's eyes were genuinely twinkling up at her. They were digging themselves a deeper and deeper hole. But if that was what commitment meant, she was all in. And so was he.

Ella, Greer, and Miss Thing had their arms around each other's waists, all of them beaming up at her with pride and love. And there were Anne, Kyle, Lucy, and Sam—the children wide-eyed, Anne crying. Anne blew Macy a kiss. Kyle held a special guest—Oscar, in his tote bag. Macy's favorite feline's ears were flat, and he was almost cross-eyed with annoyance because he didn't like all the noise.

And there were the colonel and Fran, and George, pointing his camera her way. She was glad he was filming everything for posterity.

And there were her parents! Her mom was wiping away happy tears. Her father was grinning from ear to ear as he held up a sign written in thick black marker in his familiar scrawl: HE'S BEEN TO DINNER TO ASK PERMISSION. AND WE LOVE HIM!

Her mom had added little red hearts all over the sign. Macy knew she would keep that sign forever.

Tears blurred her vision. "Yes Santa, I'll marry you," she said. She quickly added, "A-Again" for the skeptical children's sake.

Gazing into her beloved's handsome face, she realized that she wouldn't mind marrying him over and over, every day from then on for the rest of their lives. Not only that, they would keep Christmas all year round. They'd never lose the hope of the season. Love would guide them. Love would sustain them.

"Merry Christmas, my love," she whispered, and gave Deacon—whose great-great-great-great-grandfather had stood with a full heart in that exact same spot centuries before—a lingering kiss.

EPILOGUE

Deacon had made huge changes since the colonel's cannon had gone off on New Year's Day and he and Macy had won their cooking contest. He'd reduced his start-up investing by seventy-five percent, and now he was a full-time Charleston resident and CEO of The Sustainability Project, his new nonprofit business.

It was April. And he and Macy were marrying in late May.

"What's The Sustainability Project?" the visitor asked him at the front door of his office, a newly constructed building on Charleston's underutilized East Side.

"It's a nonprofit that works on making our housing greener," Deacon said. "Both new construction and old."

"So if you're building a hotel," the visitor said, "you can hire one of your experts to come in and show you what kind of materials to buy to make it green?"

"Yes. Starting next month. I'm almost done hiring. The grand opening is May first. I hope you can come."

"I'll be here. Mind if I bring a cake? Or three?"

"Be my guest."

"Cool. What else can you tell me?" The visitor was

Macy, of course. His favorite. She took a seat in front of Deacon's desk.

He picked her up and sat down there himself. And then he put her right back on his lap. "A couple great things we'll do," he said, "are energy audits and retrofits. So we might take an old house and try to update the insulation, seal cracks around windows, things like that, to use less energy and lower the resident's monthly bill. And we'll provide air conditioners for people who can't afford them."

"And in the winter," Macy said, "you'll work on heat for people who either don't have it or can't afford their heating bills."

"Right."

Macy smiled. "I met an Uber driver right before Christmas who told me his mother's heating bill was sky-high, and she couldn't afford it. She lives in an older house."

"That guy works for me now. He's in training."

Macy kissed Deacon full on the mouth. "I know," she said, "and I couldn't be more proud of you."

Deacon felt suddenly serious. "When you start asking the universe questions, it answers, you know?"

She nodded. "I know."

They smiled at each other. And then she stood up from his lap. He hated to see her go. But she'd brought lunch for the two of them since he was the only one working that day, and she hated for him to eat lunch alone.

"Whatcha got?" he asked.

"Pimento cheese on toasted bagels." She held up a tub of orange cheese and a paper bag of bagels. "We have to toast them here. Otherwise, this award-winning sandwich is no good."

"Sounds fantastic. What else?"

"I brought the losing dessert in an auspicious contest

that drew a crowd of at least seventeen fans of Freddie and Frannie, Charleston's newest 'it' couple."

"I thought we were Charleston's newest 'it' couple."

"Honey, we're ordinary, remember?"

"And we like it that way," he said. "So where's this dessert? Because I kind of like it."

"Right here." Macy pulled out a plastic wrap–covered plate with two pale white wedges on it. "New York cheesecake on a Carolina Gold rice crust. It should have won the cooking contest, actually."

"I think so too."

"Why didn't it?"

"Because Freddie and Frannie were making out on the piazza," he reminded her. "And they missed the vote."

"Their loss," Macy said with an adorable shrug.

He pulled her close. "You're my one and only. Forever."

"You're mine too, sweetie."

"I love when you talk Southern to me. Can we christen this place?"

"We already have," she reminded him.

"I mean, again?"

"I'm all for it."

Deacon locked the front door, returned, and picked Macy up. They heard a rusty meow from a tote bag sitting on his desk.

"You hold down the fort, Oscar," Deacon told him.

"We'll be back soon," added Macy. She kissed Deacon on the cheek.

"I love you," he said, and carried her down a hall that still smelled of fresh paint.

Her legs bounced in time with his gait. "I love you too."

"I couldn't be any happier." His voice was rough with emotion.

"Me either." She clung hard to his neck. "I made you a coconut cake."

"I'm happier," he said.

The sound of their laughter made Oscar open one eye. But he shut it right back and returned to his nap.

DON'T MISS THE NEXT BOOK BY
KIERAN KRAMER

A Wedding at Two Love Lane

Available in January 2018
from St. Martin's Paperbacks

KRAMER   Kramer, Kieran.

          Christmas at Two Love
            Lane.

$7.99

DATE			